INDUSTRIAL ORGANIZATION

OXFORD IN INDIA READINGS

Readers in Economics
(Themes in Economics Series)

GENERAL EDITORS

- Kaushik Basu
- Prabhat Patnaik

INDUSTRIAL ORGANIZATION

Edited by

ANINDYA SEN

DELHI
OXFORD UNIVERSITY PRESS
CALCUTTA CHENNAI MUMBAI
1998

Oxford University Press, Great Clarendon Street, Oxford OX2 6DP

Oxford New York
Athens Auckland Bangkok Calcutta
Cape Town Chennai Dar es Salaam Delhi
Florence Hong Kong Istanbul Karachi
Kuala Lumpur Madrid Melbourne Mexico City
Mumbai Nairobi Paris Singapore
Taipei Tokyo Toronto

and associates in

Berlin Ibadan

First Published 1996
First Published in Oxford India Paperbacks 1998

ISBN 0 19 564433 6

Typeset by Rastrixi, New Delhi 110070
Printed in India at Pauls Press, New Delhi 110 020
and published by Manzar Khan, Oxford University Press
YMCA Library Building, Jai Singh Road, New Delhi 110 001

Note from the General Editors

Each volume in this series brings together a selection of important contributions on a particular theme, comprising excerpts from books and previously published journal articles. The need for publishing these *Readers* arises from the fact that over the years economic journals have become both numerous and expensive. Most of the journals and a good many of the books have gone beyond the reach of scholars and students in developing countries. It is for them that these volumes are primarily meant. The topics selected for these volumes are also those which are of particular interest to them.

The present series of *Readers* is a companion to the series on *Themes in Economics*, which is already being brought out by Oxford University Press. While the two series have the common objective of providing easy access to research in particular areas to students and teachers in developing countries, their contents are different. The *Themes* volumes carry freshly written survey articles while the *Readers* put together already published work which has stood the test of time.

KAUSHIK BASU
PRABHAT PATNAIK

Acknowledgements

The publishers wish to thank the following for granting permission to reprint the articles included in this volume: American Economic Association for Oliver E. Williamson, 'The Modern Corporation: Origins, Evolutions, Attributes', *Journal of Economic Literature*, 1981, 19: 1537–70, A.K. Dixit and J.E. Stiglitz, 'Monopolistic Competition and Optimum Product Diversity', *American Economic Review*, June 3, 1977, 67: 297–308, and William J. Baumol, 'Contestable Markets: An Uprising in the Theory of Industry Structure', *American Economic Review*, March 1982, 1: 1–15; *International Economic Review* for Avinash K. Dixit, 'Comparative Statics for Oligopoly', 1986, 27: 107–2; University of Chicago Press for Jeremy I. Bulow, 'Durable-Goods Monopolists', *Journal of Political Economy*, 1982, 90: 314–32; *Rand Journal of Economics* for Eric Maskin and John Riley, 'Monopoly with Incomplete Information', 1984, 15: 171–96; and Richard Gilbert and Carl Shapiro, 'Optimal Patent Length and Breadth', 1990, 21: 106–12; Oxford University Press, UK, for G De Fraja and F. Delbono, 'Alternative Strategies of a Public Enterprise in Oligopoly', *Oxford Economic Papers*, 41, 2, April 1989, 302–11 (by permission of Oxford University Press); *International Journal of Industrial Organization* for H. Cremer, M. Marchand and J-.F. Thisse, 'Mixed Oligopoly with Differentiated Products', 1991, 9: 43–53; *Journal of Development Economics* for K. Basu and C. Bell, 'Fragmented Duopoly: Theory and Applications to Backward Agriculture', 1991, 36: 146–66, and S. Levy and S. Nolan, 'Trade and Foreign Investment Policies under Imperfect Competition', 1992, 37: 31–62, Elsevier Science B.V., Amsterdam, The Netherlands (for the three preceding articles); *Econometrica* for C. d'Aspremont, J. Gabszewicz and J.-F. Thisse, 'On Hotellings "Stability in Competition"', 1979, 47: 1145–50, E.J. Green and R.H. Porter, 'Noncooperative Collusion Under Imperfect Price Information', 1984, 52: 87–100, D.P. Baron and R.B. Myerson, 'Regulating a Monopolist With Unknown Costs', 1982, 50: 911–30, and P. Milgrom and J. Roberts, 'Limit Pricing and Entry Under Incomplete Information: An Equilibrium Analysis', 1982, 50: 443–59; Blackwell Publishers for A.K. Dixit, 'The Role of Investment in Entry-Deterrence', *Economic Journal*, 1980, 90: 95–106, P. Dasgupta and J.E. Stiglitz, 'Industrial Structure and the Nature of Innovative Activity', *Economic Journal*, 1980, 90: 266–93, and C. Fershtman, 'The Interdependence Between Ownership Status and Market Structure: The Case of Privatization', *Economica*, 1990, 57: 319–28.

Contributors

ANINDYA SEN
Indira Gandhi Institute of Development Research

OLIVER E. WILLIAMSON
University of California, Berkeley, USA

AVINASH K. DIXIT
Princeton University, USA

ERIC MASKIN
Harvard University, USA

JOHN RILEY
University of California at Los Angeles, USA

JEREMY I. BULOW
Stanford University, USA

C. D'ASPREMONT
Universite Catholique de Louvain, Belgium

J. JASKOLD GABSZEWICZ
Universite Catholique de Louvain, Belgium

JACQUES-FRANÇOIS THISSE
Universite de Paris I — Sorbonne, France

JOSEPH E. STIGLITZ
The Chairman, Council of Economic Advisers, Executive Office of the President, USA

HELMUTH CREMER
Virginia Polytechnic Institute, USA

MAURICE MARCHAND
Universite Catholique de Louvain, Belgium

PAUL MILGROM
Stanford University, USA

JOHN ROBERTS
Stanford University, USA

William J. Baumol
New York University, USA

Edward J. Green
Federal Reserve Bank of Minneapolis, USA

Robert H. Porter
Northwestern University, USA

P. Dasgupta
University of Cambridge, UK

Richard Gilbert
University of California, Berkeley, USA

Carl Shapiro
University of California, Berkeley, USA

Kaushik Basu
Cornell University, USA, and Delhi School of Economics, India

Clive Bell
Vanderbilt University, USA

Santiago Levy
Federal Competition Commission in Mexico

Sean Nolan
Harvard University, USA

Harvey Averch
Florida International University, USA

Leland L. Johnson
The Rand Corporation, USA

David P. Baron
Stanford University, USA

Roger B. Myerson
Northwestern University, USA

Chaim Fershtman
Tel Aviv University, Tel Aviv, Israel

Giovanni De Fraja
The University of York, UK

Flavio Delbono
Universita di Bologna, Italy

Contents

Introduction

ANINDYA SEN

The editor's brief for this volume was to introduce the reader to some of the major issues in industrial organization with a developing-country slant. The term industrial organization (IO) is sometimes very broadly defined and can include sub-categories like theory of the firm, regulation, antitrust policy, contract theory and even parts of organization theory. My selection is therefore defined equally by exclusions and inclusions.

To explain the exclusions: First, if some parts of the material are relatively easily accessible, they have not been included. Thus, even though game theory has become one of the most important tools of IO, I have not included any chapter on game theory because there are now fine surveys and books on game theory available (e.g. Fudenberg and Tirole, 1993; Aumann and Hart, 1992; etc). Similarly, since most of the articles relating to the concept of Cournot-Nash equilibrium are brought together in Daughety's volume (Daughety, 1988), I have refrained from including this material. Secondly, I have strictly avoided the temptation of including empirical work because only a separate volume can do justice to the vast literature on empirical testing of theoretical results. For identical reasons, I have not tried to represent topics in contract theory or organization theory, though a couple of articles touch upon these in passing.

On the other hand, my task was to select readings with applicability to developing countries. There is an extreme view that the tools developed in the context of western countries have very limited applicability to developing-country issues. To some extent, this view has been predicated on the experience of using tools from neoclassical economics to analysing developmental issues. However, I believe that the tools of industrial organization can be applied far more fruitfully to analysing developmental issues than the traditional tools provided by neoclassical economics.

I follow Basu's suggestion (Basu, 1995) that there are primarily two areas in which the tools of industrial organization can be found useful in the treatment of developmental issues: (1) Given the intimate nature of interactions between the bureaucracy and private sector managers in developing countries, the relationship between the 'babu' (the bureaucrat) and the 'boxwallah' (manager in a private sector firm) needs special consideration. Such interactions increase in complexity when public sector enterprises compete in the marketplace with private sector enterprises. While this interaction goes far beyond the confines of the usual set of regulatory issues, this volume restricts itself to articles on regulatory policies and performance of public sector enterprises in the marketplace. Such issues have gained added relevance after the switch to liberalized policy regimes in many of these countries. (2) Secondly, one can use tools from industrial organization to analyse some structural features that are peculiar to developing countries. This is illustrated in a number of selections. Williamson's paper on the transactions-cost theory of the firm provides a rich discussion that seems to be especially relevant to the workings of corporations in developing countries. Basu and Bell's paper show how the phenomenon of fragmented markets can be modelled using the tools developed in location theory and the theory of switching costs. The paper by Levy and Nolan on the adoption of strategic trade policy by developing countries clarifies issues often clouded in heated debates.

The current volume also brings together articles relating to some of the major topics in industrial organization, viz., price discrimination, product differentiation, entry deterrence and collusion and innovations. They have been selected to convey a flavour of the range and depth of the issues involved.

It is impossible to do justice to the entire field of industrial organization in a single article. I therefore confine myself to a discussion primarily of the articles included in this volume, and try to link these up to highlight some of the common themes being explored and the tools being employed. In addition, I comment on some works that are closely related to the ideas contained in the papers in the present volume.

1. THEORY OF THE FIRM

The familiar neoclassical view of the firm is that of an anonymous actor on a par with the anonymous consumer, whose existence seems to be necessary basically to explain the demand for inputs. Many of the questions that readily come to mind in connection with the existence and activities of the modern corporate giants seem to be too large and too complex to fit into the neoclassical frame of reference. For example, since the firm is viewed as a 'black box', the internal organizations of firms are left unexplored. Williamson's survey, which presents a contractual theory of the firm and touches on a number of issues related to contract theory and organization theory, attempts to pose and answer some of these questions.

There are two main contractual theories of the firm, which may be referred to as the Coasian view and the Knightian view.[1] Both views try to explain what takes place within the firm, but in different ways. The Coasian view stresses the *transaction costs* of using markets versus contracting within organizations while the Knightian view is reflected in work that stresses the importance of *information* and *uncertainty*. It is clear that problems stemming from incomplete information can form important components of transaction costs.

In the Coasian theory, the *existence* of firms is explained on the basis of contractual efficiency. 'The firm represents a set of contracts that are more efficient than market-mediated contracts either in terms of contract formation or performance', Spulber (1992). Coase (1937) pointed out that there is a cost of using the price mechanism and this cost includes searching for prices, negotiation of individual transactions, and the cost of specifying contingencies in long-term contracts. The relative costs of markets and of organizations are viewed as the main determinants of the extent of the firm's activities. Thus, for example, a firm trying to decide whether to manufacture a particular component itself or to buy it from the market must consider (a) the production cost of the component in relation to its market price *and* (b) the costs of organizing production in relation to the costs of finding out and bargaining with the suppliers of the component. It is thus obvious that for standardized parts, the cost of going to the market may be much less than the cost of organizing production.

[1] I have drawn on Spulber (1992) for this discussion.

Williamson distinguishes between transaction costs of ex ante and ex post types. The first are the costs of drafting, negotiating and safeguarding an agreement. The ex post costs refer to all the costs that are incurred when unforeseen contingencies arise and efforts are made to resolve these contingencies with reference to the original agreement. He identifies three major sources of these costs—bounded rationality, uncertainty and complexity. *Bounded rationality* refers to human behaviour that is 'intendedly rational but only limitedly so'. That is, human beings try to behave rationally (optimize). However, they are faced with both neurophysiological limits as well as language limits. The former refer to the limits on the power of individuals to receive, sort, retrieve and process information without error. Language limits refer to the inability of individuals to articulate their knowledge or feelings by the use of words, numbers or graphics in a way that permits them to be understood by others. Bounded rationality is important when the limits of rationality have been reached—i.e. under conditions of *uncertainty* and/or *complexity*. The implication of all these is that comprehensive contracting is not a realistic organizational alternative. In other words, the transaction costs of negotiating and enforcing contracts make it prohibitively costly to write long-term contracts which specify all obligations under all contingencies. Williamson also assumes *opportunism*, by which he means self-seeking with guile. Since contracts cannot be complete, agents will try to behave opportunistically when unanticipated events arise. In such situations, there must be institutions to settle disputes. Such institutions may be external (e.g. the legal system) or internal (governance structures). The relative efficiency of the different types of institutions determines which one shall be adopted in any particular context.

When will the conditions of bounded rationality together with opportunism be severe? Williamson identifies the condition of *asset specificity* as a key determinant in the organization of firms. Asset specificity refers to investments that are specific to transactions in the sense that their values in alternative transactions are significantly lower. An example is a rail line built to carry coal from the pithead to the city. If the coal mine were to close down, the rail line might be useless, i.e. there might not be any alternative goods to carry. Asset specific investments often permit significant cost savings to be realized—the cost of transporting coal by trucks would be much higher. But obviously, such investments are risky in that specialized assets cannot be redeployed without sacrifice of value if contracts should be interrupted or prematurely terminated.

Asset specificity creates the possibility of opportunism: once two parties have entered into an agreement and one party (say party A) has made specific investments relying on the initial contract, the other party (say party B) realizes that to some extent A is at its mercy. A is 'locked into' this relationship because of the specific nature of its investment. Hence B will have an incentive to force A to give up more than the originally agreed upon share of gains, threatening otherwise to terminate the relationship. But realizing this possibility ex ante, A might be reluctant to enter into a contract with B. Thus, from society's point of view, some opportunities of welfare-enhancing trade could well be forsaken.

Some of these problems can be solved by building into the contract safeguards against such opportunism, e.g. through price-indexing clauses and arbitration provisions. However, when asset specificity is substantial, contractual governance may become very costly. Internal organization of the exchange may then be the more efficient governance structure. Moreover, the form of internal organization itself might be (at least partly) explained by the need to evolve *more efficient* governance structures. As an example, consider the gradual evolution of the M-form structure (where the firm is organized into semi-autonomous divisions) from the U-form (where firms were organized into functional departments) in large American corporations that was recorded by Chandler. Williamson has argued that this occurred because the M-form organization added (1) a strategic planning and resource allocation capability and (2) monitoring and control apparatus, thus cutting down significantly on governance costs. This analysis of relative governance costs is complemented with relative production costs. A high degree of asset specificity leads to a loss of economies of scale or scope because it becomes more difficult, for example, to make sales to other buyers. Contractual exchange therefore might have an additional production cost advantage for a given degree of asset specificity.

One of the important applications of the transaction-costs approach has been to explain vertical integration by firms. Some of the earlier explanations focussed on the incentive to create market power, avoid government restrictions, assure steady supply of inputs, etc.[2] The

[2] See Perry (1989) for a discussion of these issues.

transaction-costs approach, by posing the problem in terms of 'in-house' versus 'arms length' production and with its emphasis on specific assets, can explain a number of features of vertical integration and vertical restriction as efficiency-enhancing, without having to attribute ulterior motives for monopolization of the market to the firms involved.

Williamson's analysis suffers from an exclusive focus on internal factors for explaining the size and scope of the firm. The choice of governance structure can also be influenced by the nature of strategic interactions in the product and factor markets. While the transaction-costs approach is by no means sufficient to form a complete theory of the firm (a point admitted by Williamson himself), it has performed a signal service by forcing economists to think of the firm as something more than a fleshless, bloodless cost function. It has also succeeded in highlighting the fact that non-standard business practices should not be condemned out of hand but judged on efficiency grounds, particularly in the context of transaction-cost reduction. Williamson's paper, with its detailed analysis of organizational forms (the U-form, the M-form, the conglomerate and the multinational enterprises) should prove to be particularly useful for policy-making in developing countries where all kinds of organizational forms coexist.

2. STATIC OLIGOPOLY MODELS

Even if we ignore the complexity of the internal organizations of firms and treat them merely as production functions, the introduction of imperfect competition by itself forces us to re-examine the methodology of neoclassical analysis. Use of comparative static analysis forms a basic instrument in the toolbox economists employ. The comparative static properties of equilibria in competitive and monopolistic markets have been extensively analysed and the general principles are by now well known. In contrast comparative static analyses of oligopolistic equilibria date only from the early eighties. Dixit tries to derive some general principles for comparative static analysis for oligopolistic markets and finds that while stability conditions can be linked to the second-order conditions, there are important differences from the competitive case. He considers (a) a differentiated products duopoly and (b) a homogeneous product oligopoly, noting that general results for differentiated products oligopoly are difficult to derive.

Consider the duopoly case. Dixit employs a conjectural variations model[3] with quite general demand and cost functions. The conjectural variations model allows for the consideration of a range of competitive outcomes. A natural myopic adjustment process is assumed where each firm increases its output if its *perceived marginal profit* from doing so is positive. Necessary and sufficient conditions for stability can then be derived. Dixit shows that: (i) the stability conditions subsume the second order conditions in the Cournot case, but not otherwise; (ii) the stability conditions are not sufficient to ensure that the reaction functions are downward sloping; and (iii) in the consistent conjectures case, stability conditions imply second-order conditions.

Similarly, one can examine the homogeneous product oligopoly. But for this case, there is no one set of conditions that are both necessary and sufficient, so that necessity and sufficiency have to be considered separately.

Dixit sounds a note of caution in two respects, for economists doing comparative statics for oligopoly situations. Firstly, one has to carefully distinguish between direct and indirect effects. These indirect effects play an important role in many two-stage games; e.g. in the strategic choice of capital stocks in the first period, subgame-perfectness considerations would imply that both direct and indirect effects are taken into account, while simultaneous or non-strategic choice would ignore the indirect effects. Secondly, the widespread practice of using linear demand and/or cost functions bypasses many of the problems in ensuring second-order conditions. Dixit's paper succeeds in emphasizing the need to apply with care results obtained with such special functional forms.

Dixit employs a general parameter of the profit function as the shift parameter when examining comparative static properties. This subsumes both cost and demand shift parameters. Several papers have examined the details of the cost shift case (Katz and Rosen, 1985; Salop and Scheffman, 1983; etc). Quirmbach (1988) examines the

[3] The conjectural variations term is $v_1 = dX/dx_1$, where X is the aggregate output of all firms other than the ith firm. It represents firm i's conjecture about the effect of a change in its own output on the outputs of other firms. For example, $v_1 = 0$ represents Cournot conjecture, i.e. that other firms will not react at all to a change in the *i*th firm's output.

details of the demand shift case and shows that a number of interesting possibilities arise: when demand shifts, an imperfectly competitive industry's quantity, price, consumer surplus and welfare can either rise or fall, although in certain combinations. Further profits can fall when the demand curve rises, but *only* in the middle ground between competition and perfect collusion.

3. PRICE DISCRIMINATION

Price discrimination is one of the most prevalent of market practices and comes in all kinds of guises. It is not the same as having price differentials: different prices to different consumers may simply reflect differences in quality, transportation costs etc., rather than discrimination, while uniform prices like uniform delivered prices may actually be discriminatory (in India, states like West Bengal have long protested against the Central Government's practice of fixing uniform prices for raw materials like steel under the so-called 'freight rationalization policy' for being discriminatory against the states where these raw materials originate). Price discrimination may take place not only with respect to consumers at the same place and same time, but also temporally and spatially.

As Varian (1989) points out, price discrimination can be practised viably only when (a) the firm has some market power and can set prices, (b) it can sort customers into distinct groups and (c) prevent resale between different groups of customers. In certain situations, these conditions are readily fulfilled, e.g. in the pricing of cinema tickets by the time of the day. In other cases, the firm has to adopt innovative measures to achieve the fulfillment of these three conditions.

It is usual to employ the Pigovian distinction between first (perfect), second and third degree price discrimination. Under first degree price discrimination, the seller is able to capture the entire consumer's surplus by charging the maximum prices that consumers are willing to pay for each unit. First degree price discrimination leads to the Pareto-efficient, competitive level of output being produced. However, this presupposes that the seller possesses perfect knowledge about the demand schedules and is allowed to charge different prices to different buyers for different units. A mechanism that might theoretically allow the seller to achieve the same objective is the two-part tariff. Each consumer has to pay a fixed access charge and a per unit cost. Two-part tariffs are in general use, particularly in utility pricing for electricity, telephones etc. where resale is difficult. Oi (1971), in a pioneering treatment of two-part tariffs, derived the optimal two-part tariff and showed that this involves setting price equal to marginal cost for each consumer and then charging an access fee equal to the area under the demand curve at this price. He also examined the case when consumers are not identical and the seller is forced to charge the same access fee and the same per unit price to all consumers. In this case, there emerges the possibility of charging some customers prices below marginal cost, because then these customers would remain in the market and an access fee can be imposed on them. The monopolist therefore has to determine the size of the market by controlling the magnitude of the access fee: too high an access fee would drive some customers out of the market. A more extended treatment of the two-part problem is to be found in Schmalensee (1981).

More generally, the monopolist seller may know only the distribution of buyer-types, not the identity of each individual buyer. The problem of the monopolist is then to select a price schedule that will induce buyers to reveal their types, i.e. self-select. This is a problem in second-degree or non-linear pricing, where different prices are charged for different amounts, though all consumers face the same price schedule. In terminology that has become standard in the literature, the general problem of this type is an adverse selection problem in the principal-agent framework where the seller is the principal and the buyers are agents. The monopolist maximizes profit subject to the individual rationality constraints (i.e. buyers participate in the market) and self-selection constraints (no buyer finds it better to accept the price-quantity pair designed for another type). Maskin and Riley's paper tackles this problem.

The following diagram (taken from Maskin and Riley) illustrates the basic point. There are two types of buyers—'high' demanders and 'low' demanders. The monopolist offers quantity-payment pairs to the buyers. This problem is transformed into an equivalent one where the quantities are paired with the returns to the seller (R): thus the transactions between the buyer and the seller can be viewed as one of giving each buyer the entire social surplus (generated by the sale)

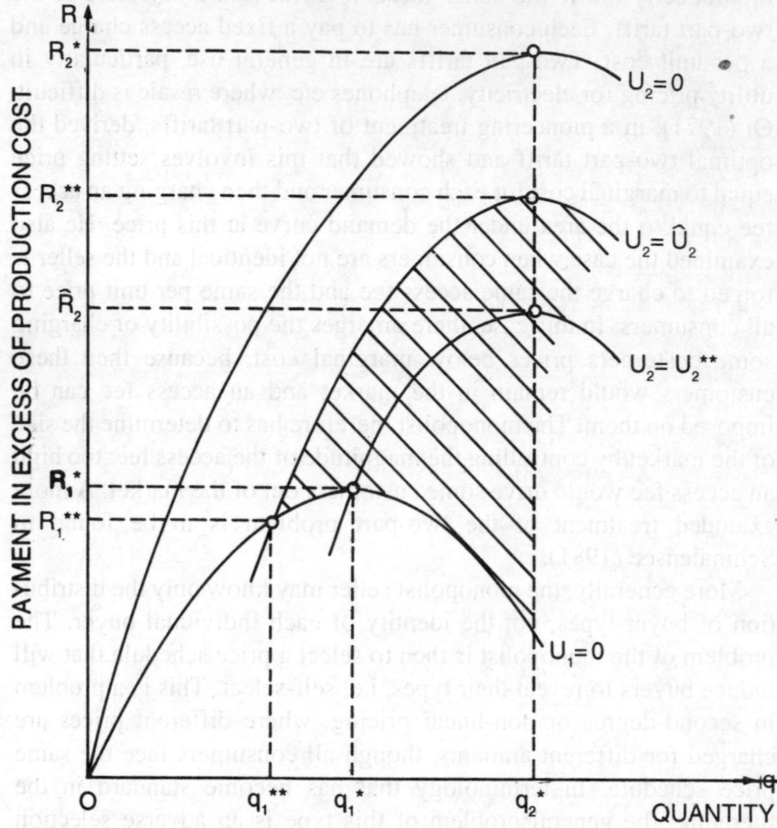

Figure 1 Price Discrimination with Two Types of Buyer

less a 'fee' of R to the seller. The indifference curves are then concave to the quantity axis. If the seller had complete information about buyer-types then the entire consumer surplus could be extracted by offering the schedule $I^* = \{(q_1^*, R_1^*), (q_2^*, R_2^*)\}$. However, if the seller has no direct means of distinguishing buyer-types (the man walking into the store wearing Chaplinesque clothes may well be a millionaire), then high demanders are better off by accepting the quantity-payment pair aimed at low-demanders. To maximize returns, the monopolist in fact has to introduce inefficiency, e.g. offer the low-demanders a pair like (q_1^{**}, R_1^{**}) while high demanders are offered (q_2^*, R_2^{**}). This makes sense because (compared with the efficient pairs) the fall in return from the low demanders is approximately zero, but there is a first order rise in return from the high demanders. Maskin and Riley establish that in general, the high demanders will pay a price equal to the marginal cost while for the low demanders, the price will exceed marginal cost. In other words, the optimal schedule typically involves deviations from the first-best at all save one point.

Maskin and Riley also establish the conditions under which the seller would find it optimal to completely sort out all the buyers, i.e. offer a schedule where each type is offered a different (q, R) pair and conditions under which all or some subset of buyers are offered the same (q, R) pair. The underlying principles of the problem are quite generally applicable. Maskin and Riley consider in detail quantity discounts and pricing of products of differing quality as examples of non-linear pricing. Other applications include the theory of optimal income taxation, the monopoly pricing of insurance, the monopoly pricing of a product line, the regulation of a producer with unknown costs (see Baron and Myerson's paper in this volume), etc.

An interesting type of price discrimination takes place over time. Units of durable goods at different points of time tend to be substitutes: if I buy a TV this year, it is highly unlikely that I would want to buy another TV next year. Suppose that there are two periods and an unchanged number of buyers over the two periods. If the monopolist seller charges the price that maximizes today's profit, then a certain number of people buy TVs today. Tomorrow's residual demand curve then lies below today's demand curve and the monopolist is tempted to charge a lower price tomorrow. But if buyers can correctly anticipate this, then they will postpone their purchases today. The problem then is to work out the equilibrium time path of prices, given the expectations of the buyers about future price changes. Coase (1972) had conjectured that if the time periods are short enough and consumers can rationally anticipate buyer's actions, then price might immediately drop down to the level of marginal cost and the monopolist forfeit all his monopoly power.

This problem is taken up by Bulow who makes a crucial distinction between the options of renting out and selling a product. Renting does not create any problem of the sort just mentioned. However, for a number of reasons, renting may not be a viable option for a firm. So far as selling is concerned, Bulow shows that the seller can devise a production strategy that will make it better off than the competitive firm, though not nearly as well off as the renter. This will involve a declining schedule of prices over time. In the limit, as period length grows small, Stokey (1981) has shown that the Coasian result is achieved. Bulow also shows that selling firms will produce goods that are less durable than those produced by renting firms or a competitive market. He discusses different ways sellers can convince buyers that they will not lower prices in the future. The credibility of a policy of not lowering prices in the future can be established through precommitments, e.g. when an artist who makes lithographs, destroys the plates, or through the production of less durable goods.

The problem posed by Bulow is in the context of a fixed set of buyers. In dynamic situations, the population may be continuously expanding and this may be pushing out the demand curve over time, so that the sellers have less incentive to cut prices in the future.

4. PRODUCT DIFFERENTIATION

The discussion in the previous section leads us naturally to a consideration of Hotelling's model which is an example of both product differentiation and spatial price discrimination. Bertrand's result that price competition will lead to marginal cost pricing when firms sell identical products is well known. Hotelling showed that with product differentiation, this result does not hold. Suppose that there are two firms (stores) in a town located at different points on the main street. Their different locations can be interpreted as product differentiation, in the sense that customers prefer to buy from the nearby store because of lower transportation costs. This confers a degree of monopoly power on the stores and they can charge different prices. Hotelling also considered the case when firms can choose both their prices and locations, and derived the principle of *minimum differentiation*, i.e. the result that firms will tend to locate at the same point.

However, when firms can costlessly change their prices *and* locations, there is a problem of non-existence of equilibrium in Hotelling's model, due to the assumption of linear transport costs. One way of tackling the problem is to use Salop-type circular location model (Salop, 1979). In the paper included in this volume, d'Aspremont, et al.

show that this problem can also be fixed by assuming quadratic transport costs. They show that there will be then be a tendency for sellers to *maximize* their differentiation.

Hotelling's model is an example of the characteristics approach to product differentiation, where each commodity is defined by its attributes or characteristics (e.g. 'sweetness') and consumers have preferences over attributes. The reason is that spatial location can also be interpreted as location in a space of characteristics. An example is ranking chocolates on the basis of their 'sweetness':

Chocolates A

Less sweet ————————> More sweet

By deciding to produce a chocolate with the level of sweetness denoted by, say A, a firm gains an advantageous position vis-à-vis customers who prefer chocolates with degree of sweetness close to A. This confers on it some monopoly power.

The other approach is one where firms produce differentiated products but compete for the same set of customers. Dixit and Stiglitz's paper is in this tradition. They try to answer the question of what is the optimum amount of product diversity from society's point of view. In the presence of increasing returns to scale, society faces a real choice between producing larger quantities of a small variety of goods (witness the limited variety of cars available in pre-liberalization India) or smaller quantities of a larger variety of goods. In the usual graphical representation of Chamberlinian long-run equilibrium, the firm operates to the left of the minimum point of the long-run average cost curve. Does this represent inefficiency, as compared to long-run competitive equilibrium? The question cannot be answered unless preferences for varieties are explicitly taken into account.

Dixit and Stiglitz model the preference for variety simply and directly by assuming convexity of indifference surface for the representative consumer. Then consumers prefer averages to extremes, e.g. they prefer the bundle (.5, .5) to any of the two bundles (0, 1) and (1, 0). When there is product variety, one important question relates to the definition of the industry and interindustry and intraindustry substitutability of goods becomes critical. The general form of the utility function in Dixit and Stiglitz is $u = U(x_0, V(x_1, x_2 \ldots))$. Here x_0 refers to the commodity produced by the 'rest of the economy' and

x_1, x_2 etc. to the commodities produced by the industry in question. This way of characterization of the representative consumer immediately makes it possible to incorporate different types of substitutability through the cross-elasticity measures. Two cases are considered: (a) U is arbitrary but V is given a CES form and (b) U is Cobb-Douglas but V is given a more general additive form. Market equilibrium is of the familiar Chamberlinian type, where each firm maximizes profit and entry drives profits to zero. Each firm sets price on the assumption that other prices will not change and in equilibrium, zero variation is, in fact, the best reply of the other firms. Also, each firm can be shown to produce only one commodity in equilibrium, so that n, the number of firms, measures the variety of goods available. This n is determined endogenously by the zero-profit condition. One can then go on to compare this n with the n for (a) unconstrained social optimum which requires pricing below average cost and (b) constrained social optimum where each firm must have non-negative profits.

Dixit and Stiglitz do not analyse the case where product differentiation is used as a strategic instrument, for example by incumbent firms to prevent entry (Schmalensee, 1983). Moreover, the representative consumer purchases some of every commodity, which is in contrast to real life consumers having different tastes and preferences and buying different sets of goods. A number of authors have derived the demand function from diverse consumer tastes (see Hart, 1985; Perloff and Salop, 1985).[4] The other important issues arise in relation to signalling product quality to consumers, perhaps through advertising.[5] These have been extensively researched (see, e.g. Kihlstrom and Riordan, 1984; Milgrom and Roberts, 1986). Cremer, et al. examine a more neglected issue, that of the impact of a public firm in a differentiated industry. Their policy conclusions differ markedly from those derived where all firms produce a homogeneous good. It turns out that even if the public firm is as efficient as private firms, having a public firm maximizing social surplus is not necessarily socially desirable. Moreover private firms may earn higher profits in the

[4] See Hay and Morris (1991) for a penetrating critique of the Dixit and Stiglitz model.

[5] Dorfman and Steiner (1954) first analysed the optimal advertising decision for a firm and this was further explored by Schmalensee (1973) and Nerlove and Arrow (1962). Needham (1975) points out the similarity of the analysis of the effects of product innovation with the Dorfman and Steiner approach.

presence of a public firm than otherwise. These results can be traced to the fact that in trying to maximize social surplus, the public firm adopts a less aggressive pricing policy than the private firms.

5. ENTRY DETERRENCE AND COLLUSION

It has been seen that Hotelling's model and the paper by Cremer, et al. incorporate strategic decision making by firms, i.e. they analyse situations where firms explicitly take account of actions by rival firms while deciding on their own actions. Both neoclassical theories and industrial organization theories treat the firm as a cost function. However, by assuming imperfect competition and employing the tools of game theory to analyse strategic interactions, industrial organization has succeeded in exploring issues not amenable to neoclassical analysis and developing new insights.

Both normal form and extensive form games have been employed to analyse strategic interactions. The important lessons that have been learnt are that (a) one can gain by making appropriate threats, (b) such threats must be credible to be effective, (c) credibility is ensured through commitments and (d) commitments are often undertaken by limiting one's options. Thus, in strategic contexts, it is not true that leaving one's options open is always desirable. One's lack of freedom can have strategic value.

The literature on entry-deterrence has exemplified all these lessons. Modigliani (1958) and Sylos-Labini (1962) had hypothesized that an incumbent firm could deter entry by engaging in limit pricing, i.e. threatening to produce a large output and therefore forcing prices down to unviable levels in the event of entry. This, as Dixit pointed out, left the question of credibility unanswered: in the event of actual entry the incumbent might find it better to share the market than fight. Realizing this, the new firms would enter. One way of circumventing this criticism was to use the Sylos postulate: that is, assume that incumbents have to choose their level of production before entry occurs and they cannot alter this whether or not entry occurs. Dixit (1979) used the Sylos postulate to provide a neat classification of the various possible cases with potential entry. However, the use of the Sylos postulate to characterize the post-entry situation is rather unsatisfactory. Dixit, in the paper included in this volume, permits the incumbent to change output level in the event of entry and shows that by making appropriate commitments in capacity, the incumbent can make its threat to engage in limit pricing credible.

A simple example of entry deterrence can highlight these issues. First, consider the following game in normal form. Firm 2 is a monopoly and firm 2 is a potential entrant. If firm 1 does enter the market, firm 2 has the option of 'fighting' (e.g. by flooding the market and hence lowering prices) or 'sharing' the market. The hypothetical payoffs are shown below (the first number in each pair is firm 1's payoff):

		Firm 2	
		Fight	Share
Firm 1	Not Enter	(0, 100)	(0, 100)
	Enter	(–50, 30)	(60, 40)

At first sight, it seems that there are two Nash equilibria (in pure strategies)—(Not Enter, Fight), (Enter, Share). However, let us assume that firm 1 gets to move first, i.e. it gets to decide whether to enter or not. Then firm 2 decides whether to fight or share. This sequence of moves can be represented in a extensive form game by means of a game tree (the first number in each pair represents firm 1's payoff):

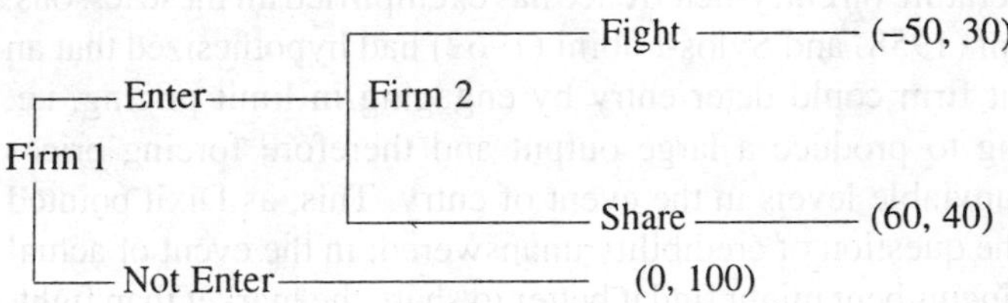

The way to analyse this game is to go to the end and work backward. Suppose firm 1 has already made a choice and firm 2 is on one branch of the game tree. If firm 1 has chosen to stay away, firm 2 will earn 100. If firm 1 decides to enter, then the sensible thing for firm 2 to do is to 'share' and get 40 (rather than the 30 it earns if it 'fights'). Firm 1 will therefore enter and earn 60. Firm 2 can of course threaten to fight if firm 1 enters. If this threat is taken seriously, it will be better for firm 1 not to enter. However, firm 1 realizes that this threat is an empty threat given that firm 2 is a rational player: if it does enter, given the payoffs, firm 2 will find it optimal to share in the event of entry (and get 40 instead of 30). Knowing this, firm 1 will enter and earn 60.

Now suppose that the incumbent can purchase some extra productive capacity that will allow it to produce more at a lower marginal cost. For the sake of concreteness, assume that buying the extra capacity adds 10 to the fixed cost of the firm and lowers variable cost by 20 (if extra output is produced). The payoffs are now given in the figure below:

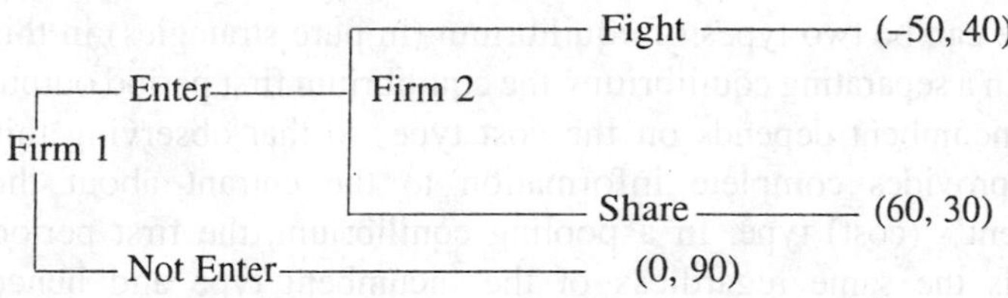

Building the extra capacity dramatically changes the complexion of the game. It is now rational for firm 2 to fight rather than share, and this makes its threat to fight *credible*. Recognizing this, firm 1 will decide not to enter, and firm 2 will continue to earn monopoly profit of 90. Note that firm 2 does not need to actually use the excess capacity. The presence of the excess capacity represents a *commitment* to fight on the part of firm 2, because by incurring the expenditure on this, the incumbent has denied itself the (rational) option of sharing the market.[6]

In a situation where all firms have complete information about all the relevant parameters, post-entry profits are fully independent of pre-entry prices and hence entry decisions will be independent of pre-entry prices. The Dixit–Spence–Spulber approach focuses on the role of commitment to ensure credibility of threats and link up post-entry profits with pre-entry prices. An alternative way to do this

[6] One can also consider a number of incumbents (see Gilbert and Vives, 1986) or a sequence of entry (see Bernheim, 1984) as generalizations of the model of entry deterrence. Further, see Gaskins (1971) as one of the first attempts to characterize optimal pricing over time for an industry faced with a continuous threat of entry.

is to consider a scenario where firms are uncertain about each other's costs. This is specially the case when one firm is not yet in the market, but is contemplating entry. The article by Milgrom and Roberts examines this possibility. Thus suppose that there is an incumbent firm that is a monopoly in the first period and a second firm that is contemplating entry, in the second period. Each firm can be a 'high-cost' or a 'low-cost' firm. If the incumbent is a high-cost type, either type of entrant will enter. The entrant tries to infer the incumbent's type from its output in the first period. A high-cost incumbent can try to signal that it is a low-cost type by selecting a low price in the first period. But a rational entrant can anticipate this (and the incumbent can in turn anticipate that the entrant will anticipate this, and so on).

There can be two types of equilibrium (in pure strategies) in this model. In a separating equilibrium, the equilibrium first period output of the incumbent depends on the cost type, so that observing this output provides complete information to the entrant about the incumbent's (cost) type. In a pooling equilibrium, the first period output is the same regardless of the incumbent type and hence provides no information to the entrant. The entrant will be deterred from entry if its expected profit is negative.

The entry-deterrence literature succeeds in substantially modifying the unidirectional nature of the structure–conduct–performance paradigm, where structure is viewed as determining conduct which in turn determines performance. Entry-deterrence type conduct directly affects the structure of the industry. On the other hand, the research on contestable markets shows that the mere threat of entry, in certain cases, can produce competitive conduct even in markets characterized by monopoly.

The notion of perfect contestability, developed by Baumol and others, is an attempt to generalize the concept of the perfectly competitive market. 'Perfect entry' serves to achieve optimal behaviour in a range of imperfectly competitive markets. It also, to a large extent, eliminates the complexities of strategic behaviour by showing that the conduct of incumbent firms is uniquely determined by the force of *potential* competition. A perfectly contestable market is characterized by the following features (see Dixit, 1982): all producers have access to the same technology, there may be fixed costs *but no sunk costs*, incumbents cannot change price instantly and consumers respond immediately to price differences. In such a market, if the incumbents are not minimizing the cost of production or are making aggregate positive profits or are cross-subsidizing, they lay themselves open to the possibility of 'hit-and-run entry'. New firms enter the market, undercut the existing firms and take away their customers and exit costlessly when price retaliation occurs. This possibility serves to keep the incumbents on their toes and the sustainable prices that prevent entry have desirable social properties.

Like the theory of perfect competition, the notion of perfect contestability is an abstraction. In most markets sunk costs of entry are present, incumbents can often react swiftly and consumers do not immediately respond to price differentials, perhaps because of brand loyalties. But the theory has made a significant contribution by emphasizing the role of potential rather than actual entry. It has forced economists to re-examine the traditional case for regulating natural monopolies: the absence of sunk costs of entry might obviate the need to regulate such industries.

One positive externality of the research on contestable markets has been the rather thorough characterization of multi-product firms that it engendered. This is, of course, again squarely within the neoclassical tradition of defining the firm as a cost function. In the contestable markets literature, potential competition endogenously determines industry structure in accordance with the nature of the cost functions.

Another way the unidirectional link between structure and conduct can be broken is through the formation of cartels. In any market, monopoly profits represent the highest aggregate profits attainable. If more than one firms compete in the market, their output will be higher than monopoly output and their joint profit is bound to fall short of the monopoly profit. It then makes sense for the firms to enter into a collusive agreement and restrict aggregate output to the monopoly level to earn monopoly profits, which can then be shared appropriately amongst themselves (of course, given that the costs of collusion do not outweigh the potential gains from collusion). One would then expect to come across many instances of collusion (cooperative behaviour). However, collusion is usually very difficult to sustain. The classic case of collusion is the OPEC oil price cartel. This cartel had some initial successes in raising oil prices by enforcing production quotas amongst member countries, but in recent years has been relatively ineffective. The issue of sustaining cooperative behaviour is actually a much broader one; in fact, the existence of society itself is predicated upon cooperative behaviour.

A very simple normal form game can be used to throw light on the difficulty of sustaining cooperation. In a duopoly, firms 1 and 2 produce the same commodity and face the (inverse) demand curve $p = 8 - (q_1 + q_2)$. Each has a cost function given by $C_1 = 4q_1$.

(1) In a monopoly, the two firms act as one firm and try to maximize the monopoly profit $\pi_m = pq - cq = (8 - q)q - 4q = 4q - 2q^2$. The monopoly output then should be $q = 2$ and $p =$ Rs 6. Total profit then is 4. Since the firms are duplicates of each other, it makes sense to assume that they will agree to produce half the monopoly output each and earn half the profit, i.e. 2. Each agrees to charge a price of Rs 6 in the market.

(2) Suppose firm 1 charges 6 in the market, as per the agreement. If firm 2 charges 5, it can grab all the customers. Since $q_1 = 0$, $q_2 = 8 - 5$. Firm 1's profit is 0, while firm 2's profit is $5 \times 3 - 4 \times 3 = 3$.

(3) If firm 2 keeps to the agreement and firm 1 cheats, by a similar argument 2 earns 0 while 1 earns 3.

(4) If both firms break the agreement and charge 5, total output has to be 3. Again, assuming that each firm gets half the customers at this price, each produces 1.5 units and earns profit of $5 \times .15 - 4 \times 1.5 = 1.5$.

These payoffs are summarized in the payoff matrix below:

		Firm 2	
		Charge Rs 6 (cooperate)	Charge Rs 5 (cheat)
Firm 1	Charge Rs 6	(2, 2)	(0, 3)
	Charge Rs 5	(3, 0)	(1.5, 1.5)

It is clear that cheating is the dominant strategy for both firms and the proposed cartel breaks down. That is, independently of what the other firm does, each firm's best strategy is to charge Rs 5. Hence each ends up earning a profit of 1.5. Note that this is a happy situation from the point of view of customers who pay a lower price. The market output (3) is also higher than the monopoly outcome (2).

Can cooperation then emerge in a world of egoists?[7] The players who get locked in a prisoners' dilemma type situation will want to escape and achieve the joint-payoff-maximizing outcome. Others may like to see them remain trapped in the dilemma (e.g. the consumers in the duopoly situation). Whatever be the point of view, we want to understand the ways in which prisoners' dilemma can be averted. Then we can try to facilitate or block these ways, depending on our preferences. The central questions are: Can an agreement be reached? How can cheating be detected? What prospect of punishment will deter it?

Reaching an agreement may not be a simple matter. In brief, the more heterogeneous the industry and larger the number of firms, the more difficult is it to reach an agreement. If, for example, cost conditions differ and product differentiation exists to a significant degree, different firms will have different expectations and it will not be easy to reach an agreement. Also, the larger the number of items on which firms have to agree, the greater the hurdles in the way of concluding successful negotiations. If conditions in the market are uncertain, agreements must be reached more often, thereby increasing negotiation costs. In addition, divergence of opinion about future conditions becomes likely.

Detection of cheating can be difficult because of the following reasons: (1) It may be difficult to disentangle random factors from deliberate cheating. For example, a fall in prices may be due either to cheating, i.e. one agent producing more than the agreed upon quota, or simply to a fall in demand. (2) In real life, there are many dimensions of choice. Producers not only select prices, they also have to decide on product quality, services etc. It is often well-nigh impossible to reach an agreement on all these dimensions. Even if agreement can be reached, it adds to the difficulty of detecting cheating because cheating can take place in various ways. In fact, the chances are that collusion will focus on the more transparent dimensions of choice while competition shifts to the less observable ones. (3) Identifying the cheater may be even more difficult than detecting cheating when there are several players. In this case, punishment cannot be selective, but will affect the innocent and guilty alike.

[7] See Hofstadter (1985, Ch. 29) for an interesting discussion of prisoners' dilemma games.

The willingness and ability to punish cheating have to be present. Moreover, the existence of a suitable punishment plan is vital. 'Punishment' in this context does not necessarily refer to physical punishment.[8] More generally, the possibility of punishment arises from the fact of repeated interactions between players. Thus consider the following hypothetical game (where each payoff is in units of a million dollars and the second number in each pair relates to Iran's payoff):

		Iraq's Output (millions of barrels per day)	
		2	4
Iran's Output	2	(52, 56)	(54, 36)
(millions of barrels per day)	4	(32, 62)	(34, 42)

Suppose Iran cheats for a day successfully, while Iraq stays honest. Iran gains $6 million. When Iraq finds out Iran has cheated, the mutual trust breaks down. The two settle down to a regime of high outputs. Relative to cooperation, Iran now loses $14 million a day. Even if it takes Iraq a while to detect the cheating, Iran loses in the long run. For example, if it takes Iraq a month to detect the cheating, Iran's gain is $180 million. Once cheating is detected, it takes only 13 days ($13 \times 14 = 182$) to wipe out Iran's gain from cheating.

What characteristics should punishments have to deter cheating? How severe should they be? To take the second question first, one might think that the punishment should be as severe as possible. Then the mere threat of punishment will deter cheating and the punishment need never be employed at all. The problem with this line of thinking is that it ignores the possibility of mistakes. The detection process may fail, indicating cheating where there is none. If the punishment is too big, such mistakes will be very costly.

An answer to the first question emerged from a computer tournament conducted by Robert Axelrod of University of Michigan, Ann Arbor. In 1979, Axelrod invited a number of professional game theorists to submit strategies to be used in a series of prisoners'

[8] In the Gulf War, Iraq complained that Kuwait had cheated on the agreement to fix oil prices by restricting production and tried to administer direct physical punishment for this alleged cheating.

dilemma games. He asked for strategies to be encoded as computer programmes that could respond to a 'C' (cooperate) or 'D' (defect, cheat) of another player, taking into account the remembered history of previous interactions with that same player. A programme should always reply with a 'C' or 'D', but its choice could be random. Fifteen strategies were entered, and each was made to play with every other programme and itself 200 times. The overall goal was to amass as many points as possible.

The programme that won is called TIT FOR TAT and its strategy is: cooperate on move 1; thereafter, do whatever the other player did on the previous move. A second and larger tournament was held later. Altogether 62 entries were received, including TIT FOR TAT. The result of the tournament surprised everybody: TIT FOR TAT was again the winner.

How did TIT FOR TAT manage to win? One can use a mini-tournament to explore this question. Suppose that there are only two strategies—TIT FOR TAT and ALWAYS DEFECT. They play against themselves and each other 200 times. The payoff matrix is the one already discussed:

		Player B	
		C	D
Player A	C	(2, 2)	(0, 3)
	D	(3, 0)	(1.5, 1.5)

The results of head on collisions are as follows:

ALWAYS DEFECT VS. ALWAYS DEFECT

	Strategies		Payoffs	
Move	A	B	A	B
1–200	D	D	1.5	1.5
Total			300	300

TIT FOR TAT VS. ALWAYS DEFECT

	Strategies		Payoffs	
Move	A	B	A	B
1	C	D	0	3
2–200	D	D	1.5	1.5
Total			298.5	321.5

TIT FOR TAT VS. TIT FOR TAT

	Strategies		Payoffs	
Move	A	B	A	B
1–200	C	C	2	2
Total			400	400

The total payoffs are then:

TIT FOR TAT: Rs 400 + Rs 298.5 = Rs 698.5
ALWAYS DEFECT: Rs 300 + Rs 321.5 = Rs 621.5

Thus TIT FOR TAT wins this mini-tournament, even though it *never wins* in head-to-head competition (it defects only after the other player defects). If there is any prospect that an opposing strategy permits some degree of cooperation, playing TIT FOR TAT will yield a higher payoff than ALWAYS DEFECT.

Axelrod argues that TIT FOR TAT embodies four principles that should be present in any effective strategy: clarity, niceness, provocability and forgiveness. TIT FOR TAT is a clear and simple strategy and easy for other players to understand. It is nice in that it never initiates cheating. It is provocable, that is, it never lets cheating go unpunished. On the other hand, it is forgiving, because it does not hold a grudge and is willing to restore cooperation.

Dixit and Nalebuff (1991), however, argue that TIT FOR TAT is a flawed strategy because it does not allow for the possibility of misperceptions. The moment the player with the TIT FOR TAT strategy thinks that the opponent has cheated, she immediately switches to cheating, making no allowance for the possibility of a mistake being made. Moreover, it lacks a way of saying 'enough is enough', i.e. it never initiates a move towards cooperation. One should be more forgiving when a defection seems to be a mistake rather than the rule. Even if the defection was intentional, after a long-enough period of punishments it may still be time to call it quits and try re-establishing cooperation.

There is now a substantial body of literature on 'repeated games' where cooperation can emerge in equilibrium. A 'repeated game' is one where the agents play the same 'stage game', perhaps the one-shot prisoners' dilemma game, repeatedly. Selten (1978) had shown that in finite numbers of repeated prisoners' dilemma games, the strategy of cheating always emerges in equilibrium. In the last period, knowing that the game would end anyway, players always cheat, independently of what happened earlier. But then they should cheat on the last but one round, and so on. It then became a challenge to show how collusion/cooperation can emerge in equilibrium.

A large and growing literature has shown that the collusive outcome can be supported as a Nash equilibrium under various scenarios in repeated games, for example, by considering infinitely repeated games or by introducing incomplete information (Kreps et al., 1982). In fact, a famous 'folk theorem' asserts that in infinitely repeated games with sufficiently patient players (who do not discount the future too much), 'almost anything' can be an equilibrium outcome. Benoit and Krishna (1985) show that if there is a large enough (finite) number of one-shot games, then any reasonable payoff vector for the one-shot game can be supported as an average payoff over the entire length of the game. Abreu (1986) characterizes the 'worst/harshest' punishments that can be used to sustain cooperation among players.

One type of punishment strategy that has attracted attention involves the employment of 'trigger strategies'. An example of a trigger strategy is found in Friedman (1971). Friedman presents a strategy in which firms respond to a drop in the market price below the price that obtains when all firms produce at agreed-upon levels by producing at Cournot levels thereafter. Then for all firms to adopt the collusive strategy would be a non-cooperative equilibrium. However, Green and Porter point out that this story works too well: the incentives are so perfect that the deterrent mechanism is never observed in equilibrium. In their model, there is imperfect information in that price is determined by industry output and a random variable Θ. Each firm can observe this price and its own output, but not the output of its rivals. An unusually low price may be due either to cheating or to a low demand. Green and Porter show that cheating can be deterred by the threat to produce at Cournot–Nash levels for a period of fixed duration if the market price falls below some trigger price p^*. More interestingly, '. . . collusive conduct may, in a particular industry structure, result in a pattern of industry performance marked by recurrent episodes in which price and profit levels sharply decrease'. Thus firms engage periodically in punishing rivals (and themselves) to maintain the credibility of the threat of punishment, even though the market price might have fallen due to exogenous rather than strategic reasons.

6. INNOVATIONS

At the microlevel, firms compete amongst themselves not only by setting prices and quantities, but also through product differentiation and increasingly, in industries where technological progress is rapid and the risk of economic obsolescence high, by engaging in research and development (R & D). Further, Solow (1957) had shown that only about 10 per cent of per capita growth for the US non-farm sector over the period 1909–49 could be associated with an increase in the ratio of capital to labour. This drew the attention of economists to the significant contribution of technological progress to the improvement of welfare of the population. Therefore, it becomes imperative to examine the incentives of firms to innovate and to adopt new technologies.

It is customary to distinguish between: (i) basic research (relating to the development and testing of new theories, i.e. it is 'new science'); (ii) applied research (that relates to the application of the results from basic research to the marketplace); (iii) development (applying prototypes to actual marketplace and building lines of production around them) and; (iv) diffusion (the spread of the innovation throughout the industry).

Basic research is often carried out in universities and scientific institutes and there is an ongoing debate about how desirable and/or feasible it is to relate basic research to applied research. One can also distinguish between product and process innovation. Finally, one should keep in mind the distinction between static efficiency that relates to pricing and output levels of existing products and dynamic efficiency that relates to the speed and extent of innovations over time.

One immediate question in this context can be placed squarely within the structure–conduct–performance paradigm: what effect will market structure have on the incentives to innovate? Schumpeter had hypothesized that monopoly situations are conducive to innovation and thus there is a tradeoff between static and dynamic efficiency. This is due to the public goods nature of R & D in addition to the fact that the individual firm is probably more risk-averse than society as a whole. In his pioneering article of 1962, Arrow examined the gains from innovation to a firm that is the only one to undertake R & D, given that its innovation is protected by an infinitely lived patent. Arrow reached the conclusion that the gains from innovation were the highest under competition (primarily because the innovating firm becomes a monopoly, whereas an innovating monopoly merely replaces itself). Thus so far as the 'pure' incentive to innovate is concerned, Arrow's result was the polar opposite of the conclusions reached by Schumpeter. Arrow himself admitted that his result might be reversed if the *appropriability* of profits from an invention were greater for a monopolist than for a perfectly competitive industry. Moreover, his analysis abstracted from all strategic considerations.

Dasgupta and Stiglitz point out that it is wrong to pose the question as one of market structure determining the pace and nature of innovative activity. Rather, both market structure and the nature of inventive activity are endogenously determined by more primitive conditions relating to demand, the nature of the capital market etc. To establish this, they consider the choice of a cost-reducing type of expenditure by the firms in an oligopoly. First, one can analyse the socially optimal amount of R & D expenditure. It can be shown that both optimum output and optimum R & D expenditure are greater in industries that face larger markets. Next, compare this with a free-entry oligopoly where firms employ Cournot conjectures. In a symmetric equilibrium, the Nash equilibrium is a pair (Q^*, n^*) such that no firm wants to change its output given the outputs of other firms and the number of firms n^*, and no firm makes positive profit. Therefore both market structure (n, the number of firms) and R & D expenditure (reflected via Q) are jointly determined by more fundamental factors. Dasgupta and Stiglitz employ special functional forms for the utility and demand functions to compare the free-entry oligopoly equilibrium with the social optimum and find that the market equilibrium output is less than the socially optimal output. There is also sub-optimal expenditure on R & D (x^*) in the market equilibrium for each firm. But what about industry-wide expenditure (i.e. n^*x^*) ? It can be shown that the market economy may be characterized by excessive expenditure on R & D if demand is highly inelastic.

Conspicuously lacking from this analysis is the externality effect of R & D expenditure by one firm on the cost functions of other firms—each firm's cost depends only on the level of its own R & D expenditure. Moreover, the static analysis of R & D decisions fails to capture any of the dynamic features associated with R & D. Hay & Morris (1991, p. 478) summarize these dynamic features as follows

'. . . in a more satisfactory model, innovative activity would take the form of a race over time, and the winner of the race would have a substantial excess payoff compared with the 'also-rans', but the size of this payoff to the winner would not be the same for all contestants'. The excess payoff referred to here may arise not only from the patents, but also from the ability to keep new processes secret or occupy a market niche, making it difficult for new firms to enter. The size of the payoff to the winner is not expected to be the same for all contestants because of fundamental asymmetries between firms. Some of these issues are explored in Dasgupta and Stiglitz (1980), Lee and Wilde (1980) and Reinganum (1981).

The discussion so far has centered around process innovations rather than product innovations.[9] One way of thinking about product innovations is as product selection. There are two opposing forces here. Firms may have too little incentive to innovate because the private surplus from doing so will be less than the social surplus. On the other hand, the 'business-stealing' effect, according to which the firm does not internalize the loss suffered by its rivals, suggests too much innovation (perhaps this is outweighed by the gain to consumers). Therefore, on balance, one cannot say a priori whether there will be less-than optimal or greater-than optimal amount of innovation. Product innovation is intimately linked to questions of product differentiation and advertising: if the new, superior product is costlier than the existing products, then one has to investigate what firms can do to 'create' a demand for it. This in turn indicates that the 'primitives' economists talk about are not so primitive after all, but can be modified by appropriate strategies undertaken by the firms.

Patents are probably the most commonly used instruments for granting temporary monopoly to provide inducements to innovate. Since the monopoly power leads to a deadweight loss, patents in most countries are of finite duration. Gilbert and Shapiro note that in rewarding innovators, there is a tradeoff between patent *length* and *breadth*. Patent 'breadth' refers to the power to earn profit under the patent. Gilbert and Shapiro's analysis clarifies the point that patent policy refers not only to the patent length, but also to the policies that restrict the patentholder's ability to earn profits. For example, the government may work through policies that restrict the

[9] See Needham (1975).

patentholder's ability to charge high prices. The scope of the patent laws in allowing other firms to 'invent around' the original patent is one such instrument.

7. GOVERNMENT INTERVENTION

Patent policy is merely one instrument whereby the government can seek to intervene in the marketplace. Traditionally government intervention has been subsumed under the heads of antitrust action and regulation. However, in many countries, the government also directly participates in the production process, and in many instances government-owned firms compete with private firms in the marketplace.

In developing countries, big business has often been viewed 'inhospitably in the tradition of antitrust law', at least in the pronouncements of leading politicians. The MRTP Act in India, though never applied seriously, was an example of this. In addition, a set of very detailed controls was imposed on industries to achieve 'socialistic' goals. It is only recently that attention has turned to the problem of regulating industries with a view to achieving the goal of economic efficiency.

Regulation, broadly speaking, is the study of government intervention in markets. Its central focus is on the *characteristics* and *consequences* of the rules and institutions governing markets. It includes as subcases studies (i) of specific industries and (ii) of administrative procedure. The important problem here relates to the appropriate choice of policy instruments to achieve regulatory goals. Policy instruments may refer to detailed orders issued on a case by case basis or broad restrictions on market transactions. Objectives may range from simple rules of thumb through politically motivated actions to various welfare objectives. One has to keep in mind that regulation works within the broader context of rules which include administrative institutions, legal rules, and patterns established by custom and tradition.[10]

A primary requisite of regulation is to define areas of *market failures*. We can distinguish between three broad categories of market failure: (i) Entry and exit barriers—For example, regulation of prices,

[10] See Spulbar (1989) for a more complete discussion of regulation.

entry and quality of service in the utility industries, such as electricity, attempts to address imperfections in competition associated with barriers to entry; (ii) Externalities—Environmental regulations directed at water or air pollution are aimed at externalities, where transactions create costs for third parties; (iii) Internalities—Regulation of product quality, workplace safety, or contract terms is directed at internalities, i.e. costs or benefits accruing to parties to a transaction that are not fully accounted for by the terms of the transaction.

The paper by Averch and Johnson was a pioneering attempt to show that regulation, despite the best of intentions, might produce undesirable side-effects. They consider rate of return regulation, i.e. a situation where the regulator selects the maximum allowable rate of return, s, which is assumed to strictly exceed the cost of capital, r. The firm maximizes profits subject to the rate of return constraint. The first order necessary conditions imply

$$R'(Q)\,f_k(K, L) = r - (\lambda/(1-\lambda))\,(s-r)$$

where R is the total revenue function and lambda is the shadow price on the rate of return constraint. It can be shown to be positive and less than one. It then immediately follows that the capital-labour ratio exceeds the cost-minimizing capital-labour ratio. Averch and Johnson also pointed out that such rate of return regulation provides an incentive to the firm to enter other regulated markets if the fair rate of return criterion is based on the firm's overall value of plants and equipment: 'expanding into other markets enables the firm to inflate its rate base to satisfy the constraint and permit it to earn a greater total constrained profit than would have been possible in the absence of second markets'.

In general, regulators do not possess full information about the regulated firms' cost functions. In other words, a firm has better information regarding its costs than would a regulator. The firm therefore has an incentive to misrepresent its cost and this must be taken into account while framing the regulatory policy. Baron and Myerson consider a regulator who is aware of the distribution of a monopolist's costs, but not of the exact cost function. The optimal policy must be incentive-compatible so that the firm has no incentive to misrepresent its cost. In other words, given any regulatory policy, the firm's profit should be maximized when it represents its cost truthfully. The task of the regulator is then to maximize a weighted sum of expected gains to consumers and the expected profit for the firm subject to the constraint that the firm finds it optimal to tell the truth. The optimal policy is essentially a pair of schedules—the price schedule and the subsidy schedule (each depending on the cost declaration of the firm). The optimal regulated price is in general strictly higher than the firm's marginal cost. Firms with a low cost parameter are allowed to earn greater profits than the ones with high cost parameter in order to provide a reward for reporting lower costs. Thus more efficient firms earn an information rent due to the presence of asymmetric information. The discerning reader must have realized by now that the Baron and Myerson paper can be treated as a special case of the model considered in Maskin and Riley.

One shortcoming of both the Averch–Johnson and Baron–Myerson papers is that they assume a benevolent regulator who uses the instruments at her disposal to maximize some measure of social welfare. It is increasingly being realized that the regulator's goal may be endogenously determined. Spulber (1989), e.g. models this goal as the result of bargaining between consumers and producers, an extreme possibility being the 'capture theory of regulation', when the regulator only considers the firm's goal.

A second way in which governments can interfere in the marketplace is by participating in the production process. In two related papers, De Fraja and Delbono and Fershtman examine some of the questions raised in this context. De Fraja and Delbono consider an oligopoly where there are *n* private firms and one public firm, and these differ only in their objective functions. The private firms try to maximize their profits while the public firm tries to maximize social welfare, given by the sum of producers' and consumers' surplus. They have the same technology and there is no principal-agent problem in that managers share the goals of the owners (or the government, as the case may be). The demand function is linear and the cost function is quadratic. The Cournot–Nash equilibrium is considered. The main result can be summarized as follows:

$$W_M > W_S > \max\{W_N, W_E\}$$

Here W_M refers to the welfare when the public firm is a monopoly, W_S when the public firm acts as a Stackelberg leader, W_N when the

Nash equilibrium is considered and W_E when all firms are privately owned. What is interesting is that the welfare with a public firm (W_N) can actually be lower than the welfare in a situation in which all firms are privately owned (W_E). If the market is competitive enough, it is better for the public firm to try to maximize profit rather than welfare. Otherwise, it drives down private profits to a level that cannot be compensated by the gain to consumers' surplus. The policy implications are obvious.

There was a time when, motivated by socialistic considerations, governments went in for 'nationalization' on a large scale, i.e. converting to government-owned enterprises firms that were earlier privately owned. The argument was that the privately-owned firm would be trying to maximize profits rather than achieve other social goals like employment generation, fair prices etc. The government therefore needed to have control over the 'commanding heights' of the economy to steer the economy in the required direction. The subsequent poor performance of nationalized firms produced a backlash and in the 1980s, the reverse process of 'privatization' became the mantra of the economies trying to liberalize. However, privatization can be of various degrees and types, as the wide range of experience of third world and the East European countries shows.

Fershtman employs a simple yet interesting model to highlight the interdependence between the ownership status of firms and the market structure in which they operate. Consider a duopolistic industry in which one firm is privately owned and the other firm is 'partly nationalized'. The reaction function of the latter firm is of the form $\theta q_1 (q_2) + (1 - \theta)\theta_1 (q_2)$, where $q_1(q_2)$ is the reaction function of a privately owned firm maximizing profit while $\theta_1(q_2)$ is the reaction function of a firm maximizing social welfare. Thus the objective of the 'partly nationalized' firm is a mixture of the goals of privately owned and fully nationalized firms, with $1 - \theta$ indicating the extent of nationalization ($\theta = 0$ indicates that the firm is fully nationalized).[11] Fershtman shows that when $\theta < 0.6$, the profits of

[11] Such a reaction function can also be generated by considering a weighed social function of the form $CS + mPS$, $m > 1$ where CS and PS are consumer and producer surplus, respectively (see Sen, 1990). The argument then is that the government puts greater weight on producers' surplus as a source of investible funds for developmental purposes.

the partly nationalized firm are above the regular Cournot equilibrium profits, and that so long as $0 < \theta < 1$, the partly nationalized firm earns higher profits than its private competitor. If one of the firms in the industry has higher costs than its rival, nationalization of this firm may reduce social welfare. Moreover, even partial nationalization may deter entry.

In analysing the performance of public enterprises, it is necessary to take account of a number of factors. Fershtman highlights one of these—the question of formulation of the objectives of the firm. The question of incentives is equally important. There has been much penetrating discussion of the lack of incentives in public enterprises and Laffont and Tirole have modelled this as an information problem in natural monopolies. Other reasons may include the multiplicity of principals who are in a position to affect the operations of the enterprise, the de facto job security (performance of any individual cannot be observed and/or monitored, or even if it can be, penalty can be imposed on only a small fraction of the income) enjoyed by workers, etc.

8. INDUSTRIAL ORGANIZATION AND DEVELOPING ECONOMIES

In a slight modification of T.N. Srinivasan's observation (Srinivasan, 1992), we can say that there is a golden opportunity to engage in intellectual arbitrage by applying industrial organization theories to development economics. According to Basu, 'there are two broad ways in which industrial organization and development economics relate to each other'. First, industrial organization provides a ready-made box of tools for application to the analysis of issues relating to such economies. Secondly, it can raise issues and concerns that are peculiar to developing economies and 'distinct from those raised in industrialized nations'. The two readings I now take up for discussion illustrate these two approaches.

Levy and Nolan's article deal with the application of industrial organization to international trade theory. Once upon a time, the conventional wisdom in trade theory was that interventionist trade policies were almost always unsuitable, and could only be supported by 'third-best' or 'fourth-best' arguments and adoption of such policies only reflected stupidity or rent-seeking. The 1980s saw the emergence of a body of theories built around the idea that most markets are characterized by imperfect competition that produced conclusions sharply at variance with the conventional wisdom. The normative message from these theories seems to be that when domestic firms compete with foreign firms, the government can use appropriate trade policy measures to shift the competitive outcome in favour of the domestic firms and thereby increase aggregate welfare. Levy and Nolan provide a unified survey of this literature, using a differentiated goods duopoly model, in which the foreign and the domestic firms can have different costs. Some of the striking policy lessons they draw are that: (1) Competition from foreign firms need not always be beneficial; (2) Imports can be excessive under laissez-faire; (3) Foreign investment can be harmful, even under free trade; (4) Policies that discriminate in favour of domestically-owned firms can be beneficial.

These conclusions can, and have been, challenged on various grounds. Given that the foreign government does not retaliate, the home government finds it optimal (a dominant strategy) to pursue interventionist policies. A prisoners' dilemma type situation can then develop, with both countries pursuing interventionist policies and therefore ending up in sub-optimal positions. This also highlights that the static model Levy and Nolan employ ignores the possibility of repeated interactions and retaliatory actions where 'punishment strategies' may be employed to ensure cooperative outcomes. However, the hard reality is that almost every country employs interventionist trade policies in one guise or the other, and until and unless there is a credible mechanism for ensuring that other countries pursue non-interventionist policies, no individual country will find it in its self-interest to do so.

The final article in this volume demonstrates how the tools of industrial organization can be used to analyse problems that appear to be peculiar to developing countries. It is generally held that integration of markets and the free mobility of goods and services are necessary for the efficient functioning of markets. However, for various reasons, markets in developing countries are 'fragmented': each firm/seller may have a 'captive' set of clientale, reflecting its local monopoly power, but there is also a floating set of customers who are free to deal with any of the sellers in the market. This idea consisting of a contested as well as a captive segment generalizes the usual practice of treating markets as consisting of a set of local monopolies at any period of time, with no overlap of customers. While Basu and Bell obtain a number of results from their model, what is important is the technique of analysis that can be applied to a wide range of problems.

Industrial Organization is a dynamic and exciting field of research. It provides the opportunity to raise and answer interesting questions about the economy at the microlevel, both theoretical and empirical. The editor hopes that this volume of readings will give the reader a flavour of this dynamism and excitement and convince her/him of the usefulness of the tools of Industrial Organization in analyzing issues in developing economies.

REFERENCES

ABREU, D. (1986), 'Extreme Equilibrium of Oligopolistic Supergames, *Journal of Economic Theory*, 39, 191–225.

ARROW, KENNETH J. (1962), 'Economic Welfare and the Allocation of Resources for Invention', in NBER Conference No. 13, 'The Rate and Direction of Inventive Activity: Economic and Social Factors', Princeton N.J.: Princeton University Press.

AUMANN, R.J. and S. HART (1992), *Handbook of Game Theory*, Vols I and II, Amsterdam: North-Holland.

AXELROD, R. (1984), *The Evolution of Cooperation*, New York: Basic Books.

BERNHEIM, B.D. (1984) 'Strategic Deterrence of Sequential Entry into an Industry', *Rand Journal of Economics*, 15, 1–11.

BASU, K. (1995) 'Industrial Organization Theory and Development Economics', in D. Mookherjee (ed.), *Indian Industry—Policies and Performance*, Delhi: Oxford University Press.

BAUMOL, W., J. PANZAR and R. WILLIG (1982), *Contestable Markets and the Theory of Industry Structure*, Harcourt Brace Jovanovitch.

BENOIT, J.P. and V. KRISHNA (1985), 'Finitely Repeated Games', *Econometrica*, 53, 905–22.

COASE, R. (1937), 'The Nature of the Firm', *Economica*, 4, 386–405.

—— (1972), 'Durability and monopoly', *Journal of Law and Economics*, 15, 142–9.

DASGUPTA, P. and J. STIGLITZ (1980), 'Uncertainty, Market Structure and the Speed of R and D', *Bell Journal of Economics*, 11, 1–28.

DAUGHETY, A.F. (ed.)(1988), *Cournot Oligopoly*, Cambridge: Cambridge University Press.

DIXIT, A.K. (1979), 'A Model of Duopoly Suggesting a Theory of Entry Barriers', *Bell Journal of Economics*, 10, 20–32.

—— (1982), 'Recent Developments in Oligopoly Theory', *American Economic Review*, 72, 12–17.

DIXIT, A.K. and B.J. NALEBUFF (1991), *Thinking Strategically*, New York: W.W. Norton.

FERGUSON (1983), 'On the Theory of Demand for Differentiated Goods', mimeo, University of Victoria.

FUDENBERG, D. and JEAN TIROLE (1993), *Game Theory*, Cambridge, MA.: MIT Press.

GASKINS, D. (1971), 'Dynamic Limit Pricing: Optimal Pricing Under Threat of Entry', *Journal of Economic Theory*, 2, 306–22.

GILBERT, R. and X. VIVES (1986), 'Entry Deterrence and the Free Rider Problem', *Review of Economic Studies*, 53, 71–84.

HART, O.D. (1985), 'Monopolistic Competition in the Spirit of Chamberlin: Special Results', *Economic Journal*, 95, 889–908.

HAY, D.A. and D.J. MORRIS (1991), *Industrial Economics and Organization*, Oxford: Oxford University Press.

HOFSTADTER, D.R. (1985), *Metamagical Themes*, New York: Basic Books.

HOTELLING, H. (1929), 'Stability in Competition', *Economic Journal*, 39, 41–57.

KATZ, M.L. and H.S. ROSEN (1985), 'Tax Analysis in an Oligopoly Model', *Public Finance Quarterly*, 13, 3–19.

KIHLSTROM, R. and M. RIORDAN (1984), 'Advertising as a Signal', *Journal of Political Economy*, 92, 427–50.

KREPS, D.M., P. MILGROM, J. ROBERTS and R. WILSON (1982), 'Rational Cooperation in the Finitely-repeated Prisoners' Dilemma', *Journal of Economic Theory*, 27, 245–52.

LEE, T. and L. WILDE (1980), 'Market Structure and Innovation: A Reformulation', *Quarterly Journal of Economics*, 94, 429–36.

MILGROM, P. and J. ROBERTS (1986), 'Price and Advertising Signals of Product Quality', *Journal of Political Economy*, 94, 796–821.

MODIGLIANI, F. (1958), 'New Developments on the Oligopoly Front', *Journal of Political Economy*, 66, 215–32.

NEEDHAM, D.C. (1975), 'Market Structure and Firms' R and D Behaviour', *Journal of Industrial Economics*, 23, 241–55.

NERLOVE, M. and K.J. ARROW (1962), 'Optimal Advertising Policy Under Dynamic Conditions', *Economica*, 29, 129–42.

OI, W. (1971), 'A Disneyland Dilemma: Two-part Tariffs for a Mickey Mouse Monopoly', *Quarterly Journal of Economics*, 85, 77–96.

PERLOFF, J.M. and S.C. SALOP (1985), 'Equilibrium with Product Differentiation'; *Review of Economic Studies*, 52, 107–20.

PERRY, M.K. (1989), 'Vertical Integration: Determinants and Effects', in R. Schmalensee and R. Willig (eds), *Handbook of Industrial Organization*, New York: North-Holland.

QUIRMBACH, H.C. (1988), 'Comparative Statics for Oligopoly: Demand Shift Effects', *International Economic Review*, 29, 451–9.

REINGANUM, J. (1981), 'Dynamic Games of Innovation', *Journal of Economic Theory*, 25, 21–41.

SALOP, S.C. (1979), 'Monopolistic Competition with Outside Goods, *Bell Journal of Economics*, 10, 141–56.

—— (1986), 'Practices that (Credibly) Facilitate Oligopoly Coordination', in J. Stiglitz and F. Mathewson (eds), *New Developments in the Analysis of Market Structure*, 265–90, Cambridge, MA.: MIT Press.

SALOP, S.C. and D.T. SCHEFFMAN (1983), 'Raising Rivals' Costs', *American Economic Review*, 73, 267–71.

SCHERER, F.M. and D. ROSS (1990), *Industrial Market Structure and Economic Performance*, Boston: Houghton Mifflin Company.

SCHMALENSEE, R. (1973), *The Economics of Advertising*, New York: Humanities Press.

—— (1983), 'Advertising and Entry Deterrence', *Journal of Political Economy*, 90, 636–53.

SELTEN, R. (1978), 'The Chain Store Paradox', *Theory and Decision*, 9, 127–59.

SEN, A. (1990), 'Privatisation and Social Welfare', IGIDR Discussion Paper No. 32.

SPENCE, A.M. (1977), 'Entry, Investment and Oligopolistic Pricing', *Bell Journal of Economics*, 8, 534–44.

SPULBER, D.F. (1981), 'Capacity, Output and Sequential Entry', *American Economic Review*, 75, 897–9.

—— (1989), *Regulation and Markets*, Cambridge, MA.: MIT Press.

—— (1992), 'Economic Analysis and Management Strategy: A Survey', *Journal of Economics and Management Strategy*, 1, 535–74.

—— (1994), 'Economic Analysis and Management Strategy: A Survey

Continued', *Journal of Economics and Management Strategy*, 3, 355–406.

Solow, R.M. (1957), 'Technical Change and the Aggregate Production Function', *Review of Economics and Statistics*, 39, 312–20.

Srinivasan, T.N. (1992), Recent Theories of Imperfect Competition and International Trade: Any Implications for Development Strategy?' in D. Lal (ed.) *Development Economics*, Vol. III, Edward Elgar.

Stokey, N.L. (1981), 'Rational Expectations and Durable-goods Pricing', *The Bell Journal of Economics*, 12, 112–28.

Sylos-Labini, P. (1962), *Oligopoly and Technical Progress*, Cambridge, MA.: Harvard University Press.

Varian H.R. (1989), 'Price Discrimination', in R. Schmalensee and R. Willig (eds), *Handbook of Industrial Organization*, Vol. I, Amsterdam: North-Holland.

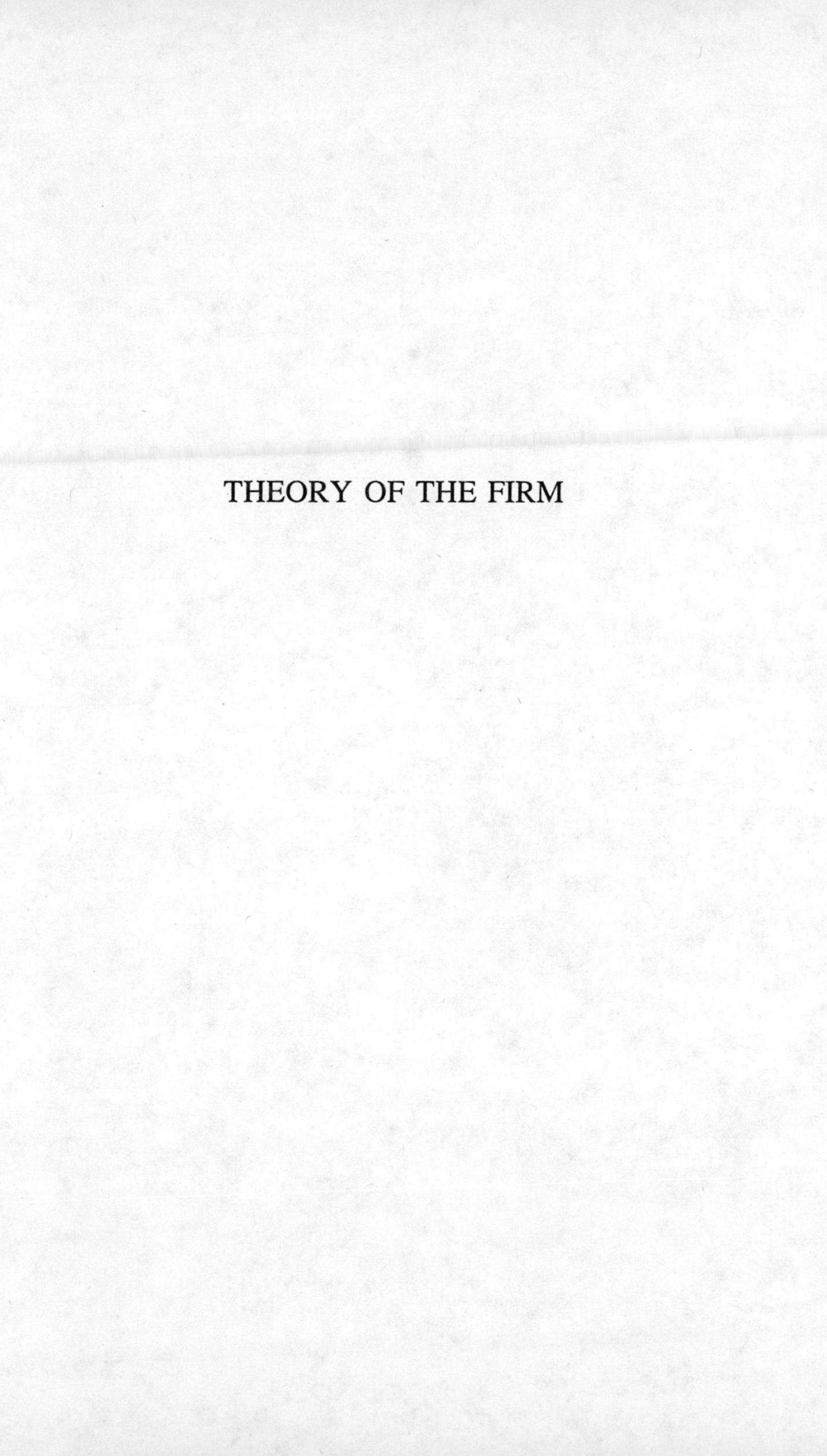

THEORY OF THE FIRM

The Modern Corporation: Origins, Evolution, Attributes*

Oliver E. Williamson

There is virtual unanimity with the proposition that the modern corporation is a complex and important economic institution. There is much less agreement on what its attributes are and on how and why it has successively evolved to take on its current configuration. While I recognize that there have been numerous contributing factors, I submit that the modern corporation is mainly to be understood as the product of a series of organizational innovations that have had the purpose and effect of economizing on transaction costs.

Note that I do not argue that the modern corporation is to be understood exclusively in these terms. Other important factors include the quest for monopoly gains and the imperatives of technology. These mainly have a bearing on market shares and on the absolute size of specific technological units; but decisions to make or buy, which determine the distribution of economic activity, as between firms and markets, and the internal organization (including both the shape and the aggregate size) of the firm are not explained, except perhaps in trivial ways, in these terms. Inasmuch as these are core issues, a theory of the modern corporation that does not address them is, at best, seriously incomplete.

* This paper has benefited from the very helpful comments of Moses Abramovitz, Alfred Chandler, Sanford Grossman, Paul Joskow, Scott Masten, Richard Nelson, and Douglass North. Parts of it were given at Rice University as a 1981 Peterkin Lecture, and comments of the faculty and students in attendance were also helpful. For related recent assessments of the modern corporation which, however, emphasize somewhat difference aspects, see Richard Caves (1980), Robin Marris and Dennis Mueller (1980), and Richard Cyert and Charles Hedrick (1972).

Specifically, the study of the modern corporation should actively concern itself with and provide consistent explanations for the following features of the organization of economic activity: What are the factors that determine the degree to which firms integrate—in backward, forward, and lateral respects? What economic purposes are served by the widespread adoption of divisionalization? What ramifications, if any, does internal organization have for the long-standing dilemma posed by the separation of ownership from control? Can the 'puzzle' of the conglomerate be unravelled? Do similar considerations apply in assessing multinational enterprise? Can an underlying rationale be provided for the reported association between innovation and direct foreign investment?

It is my contention that transaction-cost economizing figures prominently in explaining these (as well as related) major features of the business environment. Since transaction-cost economizing is socially valued, it follows that the modern corporation serves affirmative economic purposes. But complex institutions often serve a variety of purposes—and the corporation can and sometimes is used to pursue antisocial objectives. I submit, however, that (1) objectionable purposes can normally be recognized and dealt with separately and (2) failure to understand the main purposes of the corporation has been the source of much confusion and ill-conceived public policy.[1] Specifically, antisocial purposes have often been attributed where none existed.

Inasmuch as a sensitivity to transactions and transaction-cost economizing can be traced to the 1930s (John Commons, 1934; Ronald Coase, 1937), it is somewhat surprising that the importance of the modern corporation as a means of reducing transaction costs has been so long neglected. The main reason is that the origins of transaction costs must often be sought in influences and motives that lie outside the normal domain of economics. Accordingly, a large gap separated an identification of transaction costs, as the main factor to which the study of the organization of economic activity must repair, and efforts to give operational content to that insight.

This paper is organized in two parts. Sections 1 and 2 sketch the

[1] This argument is elaborated in Williamson (1981). It is briefly discussed below in conjunction with what is referred to as the 'inhospitality tradition' within anti-trust. See Sec. 1.

background and set forth the arguments that are subsequently employed to interpret a series of organizational innovations that have successively yielded the modern corporation. Sections 3 and 4 deal with these changes. My discussion of organizational innovation begins with the latter half of the nineteenth century. In this regard, I follow Alfred Chandler who traces the origins of complex hierarchical forms of business organization to this period (1977). To be sure, others have identified interesting organizational developments in both Japanese[2] and English[3] business history that predate, if not prefigure, those in the USA. But these earlier developments were not widely adopted by other firms—and in any event represent very primitive forms of divisionalization.[4] As a consequence, these earlier developments were of isolated economic importance and are properly distinguished from the general transformation of American industry that began in the nineteenth century and has continued since.

Key legal features of the corporation—limited liability and the transferability of ownership—are taken as given. Failure to discuss these does not reflect a judgment that these are either irrelevant or uninteresting. The main focus of this essay, however, is on the internal organization of the corporation. Since any of a number of internal structures is consistent with these legal features, an explanation for the specific organizational innovations that were actually adopted evidently resides elsewhere. Among the more significant of these innovations, and the ones addressed here, are: the development of line-and-staff organization by the railroads; selective forward integration by manufacturers into distribution; the development of the multidivisional corporate form; the evolution of the conglomerate; and the appearance of the multinational enterprise. The first three of these changes have been studied by business historians, the contributions of Chandler (1962, 1977) being the most ambitious and notable.

2 Sadao Takatera and Nobaru Nishikawa, in an unpublished manuscript (undated), discuss the 'Genesis of Divisional Management and Accounting Systems in the House of Mitsui, 1710–30'.

3 Gary Anderson, Robert E. McCormick, and Robert D. Tollison, in an unpublished manuscript (May, 1981), describe the 'East India Company as a Multidivisional Enterprise' early in the eighteenth century.

4 Primitive divisionalization is often confused with but needs to be distinguished from multidivisionalization. See Alfred Sloan (1965) and Chandler (1962) a discussion of the origins of the M-form structure in the twentieth century.

1. SOME BACKGROUND

1.1 General

Assessing the organization of economic activity in an advanced society requires that a bewildering variety of market, hierarchical, and mixed modes be evaluated. Economists, organization theorists, public policy specialists, and historians all have an interest and each have offered interpretations of successive organizational innovations. A coherent view, however, has not emerged.

Partly this is because the principal hierarchical structure to be assessed—the modern corporation—is formidably complex in its great size, diversity, and internal organization. The natural difficulties which thereby resulted would have been overcome sooner, however, had it not been for a number of conceptual barriers to an understanding of this institution. Chief among these are the following: (1) the neoclassical theory of the firm, which is the main referrent to which economists appeal, is devoid of interesting hierarchical features; (2) organization theorists, who are specialists in the study of internal organization and unencumbered by an intellectual commitment to neoclassical economic models, have been preoccupied with hierarchy to the neglect of market modes of organization and the healthy tension that exists between markets and hierarchies; (3) public policy analysts have maintained a deeply suspicious attitude toward nonstandard or unfamiliar forms of economic organization; and (4) organizational innovation has been relatively neglected by business and economic historians.

To be sure, this indictment sweeps too broadly. As discussed in 1.2 below, there have been important exceptions. The main features, however, are as I have described. Thus neoclassical theory treats the firm as a production function to which a profit maximization objective has been ascribed. Albeit useful for many purposes, such a construction is unhelpful in attempting to assess the purposes served by hierarchical modes of organization. The firm as production function needs to make way for the view of the *firm as governance structure* if the ramifications of internal organization are to be accurately assessed. Only recently has this latter orientation begun to make headway—and is still in a primitive state of development.

The pre-occupation of organization theory specialists with internal organization is a potentially useful corrective. An understanding of the purpose served by internal organization has remained elusive, however, for at least two reasons. First, efficiency analysis plays a relatively minor role in the studies of most organization theory specialists—many of whom are more inclined to emphasize power. The economizing factors that are crucial to an understanding of the modern corporation are thus effectively suppressed. Second, and related, firms and markets are treated separately rather than in active juxtaposition with one another. The propositions that (1) firms and markets are properly regarded as alternative governance structures to which (2) transactions are to be assigned in discriminating (mainly transaction-cost economizing) ways are unfamiliar to most organization theory specialists and alien to some.

Public policy analysts with an interest in the modern corporation might also have been expected to entertain a broader view. In fact, however, many of these likewise adopted a production function orientation—whereby markets were regarded as the 'natural, hence efficient' way by which to mediate transactions between technologically separable entities. This was joined by a pervasive sense that the purposes of competition are invariably served by maintaining many autonomous traders. Even sensitive observers were trapped by this combined technological/atomistic logic. Thus Donald Turner, at a time when he headed the Antitrust Division, expressed skepticism over nonstandard business practices by observing that 'I approach territorial and customer restrictions not hospitably in the common law tradition, but inhospitably in the tradition of antitrust law'.[5] The possibility that efficiency might be served by imposing restraints on autonomous market trading was evidently thought to be slight. This inhospitality tradition also explains ingrained public policy animosity towards vertical integration and conglomerate organization; more generally, industrial organization specialists were encouraged to discover what were often fanciful 'distortions' at the expense of a more basic understanding of the modern corporation in economizing terms.

The neglect of organizational innovations by business and economic historians has been general but by no means complete and

[5] The quotation is attributed to Turner by Stanley Robinson, 1968, N.Y. State Bar Association, Anti-trust Symposium, p. 29.

shows recent signs of being corrected.[6] Mainly, however, interpretation has played a secondary role to description in most historical studies of organizational change—which, while understandable, contributes to the continuing confusion over the purposes served by the changing organizational features of the corporation.

This essay attempts to provide a coherent view of the modern corporation by (1) augmenting the model of the firm as production function to include the concept of the firm as governance structure, (2) studying firms and markets as alternative governance structures in a comparative institutional way, (3) supplanting the presumption that organizational innovations have anticompetitive purposes by the rebuttable presumption that organizational innovations are designed to economize on transaction costs, and (4) interpreting business history from a transactions cost perspective. Such an approach to the study of the modern corporation (and more generally, to the study of organizational innovation) owes its origins to antecedent contributions of four kinds.

1.2 Antecedents

Theory of Firms and Markets

The unsatisfactory state of the theory of the firm was recognized by Ronald Coase in his classic 1937 article on 'The Nature of the Firm'. As he observed:

> Outside the firm, price movements direct production, which is co-ordinated through a series of exchange transactions on the market. Within a firm, these market transactions are eliminated and in place of the complicated market structure with exchange transactions is substituted the entrepreneur–co-ordinator, who directs production. It is clear that these are *alternative means of co-ordinating production* (1952, p. 333; emphasis added).

Coase went on to observe that firms arose because there were costs of using the price system (1952, pp. 336–8). But internal organization was no cost panacea, since it experienced distinctive costs of its own (1952, pp. 340–2). A balance is struck when the firm has expanded to the point where 'the costs of organizing an extra transaction within

[6] For an interesting commentary and contribution, see Douglass North (1978). The earlier Lance Davis and North book, however, gave relatively little attention to institutional changes that occurred within firms (1971, p. 143).

the firm become equal to the costs of carrying out the same transaction by means of an exchange in the open market or the costs of organizing in another firm' (1952, p. 341).

Related insight on the study of firms and markets was offered by Friedrich A. Hayek, who dismissed equilibrium economics with the observation that 'the economic problem of society is mainly one of adaptation to changes in particular circumstances of time and place' (1945, p. 524), and who held that the 'marvel' of the price system was that it could accomplish this without 'conscious direction'. Setting aside that possibility that Hayek did not make adequate allowance for the limitations of the price system, three things are notable about these observations. First is his emphasis on change and the need to devise adaptive institutional forms. Second, his reference to particular circumstances, as distinguished from statistical aggregates, reflects a sense that economic institutions must be sensitive to dispersed knowledge of a microanalytic kind. And third was his assistance that attention to the details of social processes and economic institutions was made necessary by the 'unavoidable imperfection of man's knowledge' (1945, p. 530).

The organization of firms and markets has been a subject to which Kenneth Arrow has made repeated contributions. He has addressed himself not only to the economics of the internal organization but also to an assessment of the powers and limits of markets (Arrow, 1969). Like Coase, he expressly recognizes that firms and markets are alternative modes of organizing economic activity (Arrow, 1974). Moreover, whereas the limits of markets were glossed over by Hayek, Arrow specifically traces these to transaction cost origins: 'market failure is not absolute; it is better to consider a broader category, that of transaction costs, which in general impede and in particular cases block the formation of markets' (1969, p. 48)—where by transaction costs Arrow has reference to the 'costs of running the economic system' (1969, p. 48).

Organization Theory

Although organization theorists have not in general regarded efficiency as their central concern, there have been notable exceptions. The early works of Chester Barnard (1938) and Herbert Simon (1947) both qualify.

Barnard was a businessman rather than a social scientist and he addressed internal organizational issues that many would regard as outside the scope of economics. Economizing was nevertheless strongly featured in his approach to the study of organizations. Understanding the employment relation was among the issues that intrigued him. Matters that concerned him in this connection included: the need to align incentives, including noneconomic inducements, to achieve enterprise viability; the importance of assent to authority; a description of the authority relation within which hierarchical organizations operate; and the role of 'informal organization' in supporting the working rules upon which formal organization relies. The rationality of internal organization, making due allowance for the attributes of human actors, was a matter of continuous concern to Barnard.

Simon expressly relies on Barnard and carries rationality analysis forward. A more precise vocabulary than Barnard's is developed in the process. Simon traces the problem of organization to the joining of rational purposes with the cognitive limits of human actors: 'it is precisely in the realm where human behaviour is *intendedly* rational, but only *limitedly* so, that there is room for a genuine theory of organization and administration' (1957, p. xxiv). Intended rationality supplies purpose, but meaningful economic and organizational choices arise only in a limited (or bounded) rationality context.

Simon makes repeated reference to the criterion of efficiency (1957, pp. 14, 39–41, 172–97), but he also cautions that organizational design should be informed by 'a knowledge of those aspects of the social sciences which are relevant to the broader purposes of the organization' (1957, p. 246). A sensitivity to subgoal pursuit, wherein individuals identify with and pursue local goals at the possible expense of global goals[7] (Simon, 1957, p. 13), and the 'outguessing' or gaming aspects of human behaviour (Simon, 1957, p. 252) are among these.

[7] The term 'local goals' subsumes both the functional goals of a subunit of the enterprise and the individual goals of the functional managers. In a perfectly harmonized system, private goals are consonant with functional goals, the realization of which in turn promotes global goals. Frequently, however, managers become advocates for parochial interests that conflict with global goal attainment. If, for example, R&D claims a disproportionate share of resources—because of effective but distorted partisan representations from the management and staff of this group—profits (global goals) will suffer. Aggressive sub-goal (or local goal) pursuit of this kind is a manifestation of opportunism (see 2.2, below).

Although Simon examines the merits of centralized versus decentralized modes of organization (1947, pp. 234–40), it is not until his later writing that he expressly addresses the matter of factoring problems according to rational hierarchical principles (Simon, 1962). The issues here are developed more fully in Sec. 2.

Non-strategic Purposes

The 'inhospitality tradition' referred to above maintained a presumption of illegality when nonstandard or unfamiliar business practices were brought under review. These same practices, when viewed 'through the lens of price theory'[8] by Aaron Director (and his students and colleagues at Chicago), were regarded rather differently. Whereas Turner and others held that anticompetitive purposes were being served, Director and his associates reported instead that tie-ins, resale price maintenance, and the like were promoting more efficient resource allocation.

In fact, nonstandard business practice (such as tie-ins) are anomalies when regarded in the full information terms associated with static price theory. Implicitly however, Chicago was also relying on the existence of transaction costs—which, after all, were the reason why comprehensive price discrimination could not be effected through simple contracts unsupported by restrictive practices from the outset.[9] Be that as it may, Chicago's insistence that economic behaviour be assessed with respect to its economizing properties was a healthily antidote and encouraged further scrutiny of these same matters—with the eventual result that an economizing orientation is now much more widely held. Indirectly, these view have spilled over and influenced thinking about the modern corporation as an economizing, rather than mainly a monopolizing, entity.[10]

Business History

The study of organizational innovation has been relatively neglected by business and economic historians. Aside from the Research Center

[8] The phrase is Richard Posner's (1979, p. 928).

[9] For a discussion of this point, see Williamson (1975, pp. 11–3, 109–10).

[10] Although the nonstrategic tradition inspired by Aaron Director makes insufficient allowance for anti-competitive behaviour, it was a useful counterweight to the inhospitality tradition to which it was paired. For a critique of the more extreme versions of this non strategic—or, as Posner (1979, p. 932) put it, the 'diehard Chicago'—tradition, see Williamson (1981).

in Entrepreneurial History at Harvard, which was established in 1948 and closed its doors a decade later there has not been a concerted effort to work through and establish the importance of organizational innovation. Probably the most important reason for this neglect is that business history has not had the support of an established system of 'theory' (Henrietta Larson, 1948, p. 135).

Despite this general neglect, notable contributions have nevertheless been made. The works of Lance Davis and Douglass North (1971) and of Alfred Chandler (1962; 1977) have been especially important. The first of these takes a sweeping view of institutional change and employs a market failure theory for assessing successive changes. It pays only limited attention, however, to the corporation is a unit. Whose attributes need to be assessed.[11]

Chandler, by contrast, is expressly and deeply concerned with the organization from changes which, over the past 150 years, have brought us the modern corporation as we know it. The story is told in two parts, the first being the evolution of the large, multifunctional enterprise, the second being the subsequent divisionalization of these firms. Both of these transformations are described and interpreted in Secs 3 and 4 below. Suffice it to observe here that: (1) Chandler's is the first treatment of business history that describes organizational changes in sufficient detail to permit a transaction cost interpretation to be applied, (2) Chandler's 1962 book was significant not only for its business history contributions but because it clearly established that organization form had an important impact on business performance—which neither economics nor organization theory had done (nor, for the most part, even attempted) previously, and (3) although

[11] Davis and North make repeated reference to the limited liability and unlimited life features of the corporate form and explicitly discuss the importance of organizational changes made by the rail-roads. Their treatment of organization form changes in manufacturing, however, emphasizes economies of scale, monopolization (cartelization), protection against foreign competition, and resistance to regulation (pp. 167–90). A sense that the corporation is progressively refining features that economize on transaction costs—in labour, capital, and intermediate product markets—is nowhere suggested.

Although this is partly rectified in North's recent survey paper, where he observes that recent organizational changes have had transaction cost origins, he defines transaction costs narrowly in terms of the 'measurement of the separable dimensions of a good or services'. As developed below, measurement is only one aspect—and not, in my judgment, the most important one—for understanding the modern corporation.

Chandler is more concerned with the description than with the interpretation of organizational change, his careful descriptions are nevertheless suggestive of the economic factors that are responsible for the changes observed.

2. TRANSACTION COST ECONOMICS

Each of the antecedent literatures just described has a bearing on the transaction-cost approach to the study of economic institutions in general and the modern corporation in particular. Following Commons (1934), the transaction is made the basic unit of analysis. Specifically, attention is focused on the transaction costs of running the economic system (Coase, 1937; Arrow, 1969), with emphasis on adaptation to unforeseen, and often unforeseeable, circumstances (Hayek, 1945). The issues of special interest are connected with the changing structure of the corporation over the past 150 years (Chandler, 1962; 1977). Rather than regard these inhospitably, the new approach maintains the rebuttable presumption that the evolving corporate structure has the purpose and effect of economizing on transaction costs. These transaction cost and business history literatures are linked by appeal to selective parts of the (mainly older) organization theory literature.

As Barnard (1938) emphasized, differences in internal organization often had significant performance consequences and could and should be assessed from a rationality viewpoint. Simon (1947) extended and refined the argument that internal organization mattered and that the study of internal organization needed to make appropriate allowance for the attributes of human actors—for what Frank Knight has felicitously referred to as 'human nature as we know it' (1965, p. 270). Then, and only then, does the comparative institutional assessment of alternative organizational forms take on its full economic significance.

2.1 Comparative Institutional Analysis

The costs of running the economic system to which Arrow refers can be usefully thought of in contractual terms. Each feasible mode of conducting relations between technologically separable entities can be examined with respect to the ex ante costs of negotiating and writing, as well as the ex post costs of executing, policing, and, when disputes arise, remedying the (explicit or implicit) contract that joins them.

A transaction may thus be said to occur when a good or service is transferred across a technologically separable interface. One stage of processing or assembly activity terminates and another begins. A mechanical analogy, while imperfect, may nevertheless be useful. A well-working interface, like a well-working machine, can be thought of as one where these transfers occur smoothly.

In neither case, however, is smoothness desired for its own sake: the benefits must be judged in relation to the cost. Both investment and operating features require attention. Thus extensive prior investment in finely tuned equipment and repeated lubrication and adjustment during operation are both ways of attenuating friction, slippage, or other loss of mechanical energy. Similarly, extensive pre-contract negotiation that covers all relevant contingencies may avoid the need for periodic intervention to realign the interface during execution so that a contract may be brought successfully to completion. Simultaneous attention to both investment (pre-contract costs) and operating expenses (harmonizing costs) is needed if mechanical (contractual) systems are to be designed effectively. The usual study of economizing in a production function framework is thus extended to include an examination of the *comparative costs of planning, adapting, and monitoring task completion under alternative governance structures*—where by governance structure I have reference to the explicit or implicit contractual framework with which a transaction is located (markets, firms, and mixed modes—e.g. franchising—included).

The study of transaction-cost economizing is thus a comparative institutional undertaking which recognizes that there are a variety of distinguishably different transactions on the one hand and a variety of alternative governance structures on the other. The object is to match governance structures to the attributes of transactions in a discriminating way. Microanalytic attention to differences among governance structures and microanalytic definition of transactions are both needed in order for this to be accomplished.

Although more descriptive detail thus is associated with neoclassical analysis is needed for this purpose, a relatively crude assessment will often suffice. As Simon has observed, comparative institutional analysis commonly involves an examination of discrete structural alternatives for which marginal analysis is not required: 'In general, much cruder and simpler arguments will suffice to demonstrate an inequality between two quantities than are required to show the conditions under which these quantities are equated at the margin' (1978, p. 6).

2.2 Behavioural Assumptions

Human nature as we know it is marvellously rich and needs to be reduced to manageable proportions. The two behavioural assumptions on which transaction cost analysis relies—and without which the study of economic organization is pointless—are bounded rationality and opportunism. As a consequence of these two assumptions, the human agents that populate the firms and markets with which I am concerned differ from economic man (or at least the common caricature thereof) in that they are less competent in calculation and less trustworthy and reliable in action. A condition of bounded rationality is responsible for the computational limits of organization man. A proclivity for (at least some) economic agents to behave opportunistically is responsible for their unreliability.

The term bounded rationality was coined by Simon to reflect the fact that economic actors, who may be presumed to be 'intendedly rational', are not hyper-rational.. Rather, they experience limits in formulating and solving complex problems and in processing (receiving, storing, retrieving, transmitting) information (Simon, 1957, p. 198). Opportunism is related to but is a somewhat more general term that the condition of 'moral hazard' to which Knight referred in his classic statement of economic organization (1965, pp. 251–6).[12] Opportunism effectively extends the usual assumption of self-interest seeking to make allowance for self-interest seeking with guile.

[12] Moral hazard is a technical term with a well defined meaning in the insurance literature. It refers to an ex post insurance condition and is clearly distinguished from adverse selection, which is responsible for a troublesome ex ante insurance screening problem. Opportunism is a less technical but more general term that applies to a wide set of economic behaviour—of which adverse selection and moral hazard are specific kinds. Unless, therefore, moral hazard is given a broader meaning, the substitution of moral hazard for opportunism focuses attention on a subset of the full range of human and economic conditions of concern.

But for the *simultaneous* existence of both bounded rationality and opportunism,[13] all economic contracting problems are trivial and the study of economic institutions is unimportant. Thus, but for bounded rationality, all economic exchange could be effectively organized by contract. Indeed, the economic theory of comprehensive contracting has been fully worked out.[14] Given bounded rationality, however, it is impossible to deal with complexity in all contractually relevant respects (Radner, 1968). As a consequence, incomplete contracting is the best that can be achieved.

Ubiquitous, albeit incomplete, contracting would nevertheless be feasible if economic agents were completely trustworthy. Principals would simply extract promises from agents that they will behave in a stewardship fashion, while agents would reciprocally ask principals to behave in good faith. Such devices will not work, however, if some economic actors (either principals or agents) are dishonest (or, more generally, disguise attributes or preferences, distort data, obfuscate issues, and otherwise confuse transactions) and it is very costly to distinguish opportunistic from nonopportunistic types ex ante.

Although the dual assumptions of bounded rationality and opportunism complicate the study of economic behaviour and may be unessential for some purposes, the study of alternative modes of organization does not qualify as an exception. To the contrary, failure to recognize and make allowance for both is virtually to invite mistaken assessments of alternative modes.[15] Taking these two

[13] The coexistence of cunning and bounded rationality is troublesome to some. How can economic agents simultaneously be more clever and less competent than the hyperrational man that populates neoclassical models? Is he a maximizer or is he not? This is not a useful dichotomy. Maximizing is an analytical convenience the use of which is often justified by the fact that human agents are '*intendedly* rational' (Simon, 1957b, p. xxiv). As discussed in the text, however, comprehensive contracting, which is an ambitious form of maximizing, is infeasible. Opportunism has important economic ramifications for this reason.

[14] I have reference, of course, to the Arrow–Debreu contracting model.

[15] The argument that effective ex ante competition for the right to supply service (franchise bidding) vitiates the need to regulate decreasing cost industries sometimes goes through but not always. Incomplete contracting (bounded rationality) coupled with the hazards of ex post opportunism place great strain on the franchise bidding mode if assets are durable and specific. For a critique of what I believe was a mistaken assessment of the feasibility of using franchise bidding for CATV, see Williamson (1976).

behavioural assumptions into account, the following compact statement of the problem of economic organization is suggested: assess alternative governance structures in terms of their capacities to economize on bounded rationality while simultaneously safeguarding transactions against opportunism. This is not inconsistent with the imperative 'maximize profits!', but it focuses attention somewhat differently.

2.3 Dimensionalizing

As Coase observed in 1972, his 1937 paper was 'much cited but little used' (1972, p. 63). The reasons for this are many, including a preoccupation by economists with other matters during the intervening thirty-five years. The main reason, however, is that transaction costs had not been operationalized and it was not obvious how this could be accomplished.

The postwar market failure literature, especially Arrow's insight (1969) that market failures had transaction costs origins, served to focus attention on the troublesome issues. A recognition that market (and internal) failures of all kinds could be ultimately traced to the human factors described above was a second step. The remaining step was to identify the critical dimensions with respect to which transactions differ.

The attributes of transactions that are of special interest to the economics of organization are: (1) the frequency with which transactions recur, (2) the uncertainty to which transactions are subject, and (3) the degree to which transactions are supported by durable, transaction specific investments.[16] A considerable amount of explanatory power turns on the last.[17]

Asset specificity can arise in any of three ways: site specificity, as when successive stations are located in cheek-by-jowl relation to each other so as to economize on inventory and transportation expenses;

[16] As Knight observes: 'With uncertainty entirely absent, every individual being in possession of perfect knowledge of the situation, there would be no occasion for anything of the nature of responsible management or control of productive activity' (1965, p. 267).

[17] Williamson (1979). Also see Benjamin Klein Robert Crawford, and Armen Alchian (1978) for illuminating discussion of transaction specific investment in the context of what they refer to as 'appropriable quasi-rents'.

physical asset specificity, as where specialized dies are required to produce a component; and human asset specificity that arises in a learning-by-doing fashion. The reason why asset specificity is critical is that, once the investment has been made buyer and seller are effectively operating in a bilateral (or at least quasi-bilateral) exchange relation for a considerable period thereafter. Inasmuch as the value of highly specific capital in other uses is, by definition, much smaller than the specialized use for which it has been intended the supplier is effectively 'locked into' the transaction to a significant degree. This is symmetrical, moreover, in that the buyer cannot turn to alternative sources of supply and obtain the item on favourable terms, since the cost of supply from unspecialized capital is presumably great. The buyer is thus committed to the transaction as well. Accordingly, where asset specificity is great, buyer and seller will make special efforts to design an exchange relation that has good continuity properties. Autonomous contracting gives way to more complex forms of market contracting and sometimes to internal organization for this reason.

2.4 Three Principles of Organizational Design

The criterion for organizing commercial transactions is assumed to be the strictly instrumental one of cost economizing. Essentially this takes two parts: economizing on production expense and economizing of transaction costs. In fact, these are not independent and need to be addressed simultaneously. The study of the latter, however, is much less well developed and is emphasized here.

The three principles of organizational design employed here are neither exhaustive nor refined. They nevertheless offer considerable explanatory power in dealing with the main changes in corporate organization reported by Chandler and addressed here. Transaction cost reasoning supports all three, although only the first, the asset-specificity principle, is tightly linked to dimensionalizing. Bounded rationality and opportunism, however, operate with respect to all three.

The asset-specificity principle turns on the above described transformation of an exchange relation from a large-numbers to a small-numbers condition during the course of contract execution. The second, the externality principle, is often discussed under the heading of 'free rider' effects. The more general phenomenon, however, is that of subgoal pursuit, that is, in the course of executing contracts, agents also pursue private goals which may be in some degree inconsistent with the contract's intended purpose. These two principles influence the choice of contracting form (mainly firm or market). In fact, however, the efficacy of internal organization depends on whether sound principles of internal organizational design are respected, which is to say that the details of internal organization matter. The hierarchical decomposition principle deals with this last.

It will be convenient to assume that transactions will be organized by markets unless market exchange gives rise to serious transaction costs. In the beginning, so to speak, there were markets. Both bureaucratic and production cost considerations favour this presumption. The bureaucratic argument is simply this: market exchange serves to attenuate the bureaucratic distortions to which internal exchange is subject. (Although the reasons for this have been set out elsewhere—James Thompson, 1967, pp. 152–4; Williamson, 1975, Chapter 7—the study of firm and market organization is greatly in need of a more adequate theory of bureaucracy). The production cost advantages of market procurement are three: static scale economies can be more fully exhausted by buying rather than making if the firm's needs are small in relation to the market; markets can aggregate un-correlated demands, to thereby realize risk pooling benefits; and markets may enjoy economies of scope[18] in supplying a related set of activities of which the firm's requirements are only one. Accordingly, transactions will be organized in markets *unless* transaction cost disabilities appear.[19]

[18] Whereas scale economies refer to declining average costs associated with increasing output of a single line of commerce, scope economies are realized 'where it is less costly to combine two or more product lines in one firm rather than to produce them separately' (John Panzar and Robert Willig, 1981, p. 268). Retail outlets that carry many products and brands (drug stores, department stores) presumably enjoy significant economies of scope in the retailing function.

[19] Bureaucratic disabilities aside, any given firm could realize all of these production benefits for itself by an appropriate increase in the scale and scope of its activities. Pursuit of this logic, however, leads to the following anomaly: all firms, of which there will be few, will be comprehensively integrated and diversified in sufficient degree to obviate the need for market exchange. The fact that we do not observe comprehensive integration—as Coase puts it, 'Why is not all production carried on by one big firm?'(1952, p. 340)—suggests that the bureaucratic disabilities of internal

Asset Specificity Principle (All Transactions)

Recall that transactions are described in terms of three attributes: frequency, uncertainty, and asset specificity. Although interesting organizational issues are posed when transactions are of only an occasional kind (Williamson, 1979, pp. 245–54), this paper deals entirely with the governance of recurring transactions. Also, it will facilitate the analysis to hold uncertainty constant in intermediate degree—which is to say that we are dealing neither with steady state nor highly uncertain events. Accordingly, asset specificity is the transactional dimension of special interest. The first principle of efficient organizational design is this: *the normal presumption that recurring transactions for technologically separable goods and services will be efficiently mediated by autonomous market contracting is progressively weakened as asset specificity increases.*

The production cost advantages of markets decrease and the (comparative) governance costs of markets increase as assets become progressively more specific. Thus as assets become more fully specialized to a single use or user, hence are less transferable to other uses and users, economies of scale can be as fully realized when a firm operates the asset under its own internal direction as when its services are obtained externally by contract. And the market's advantage in pooling risks likewise shrinks. Simultaneously, the transactions in question take on a stronger bilateral character, and the governance costs of markets increase relatively.

The distinction between ex ante and ex post competition is essential to an understanding of this condition. What may have been (and commonly is) an effective large numbers-bidding situation at the outset is sometimes *transformed* into a bilateral trading relation thereafter. This obtains if, despite the fact that large numbers of qualified bidders were prepared to enter competitive bids for the initial contract, the winning bidder realizes advantages over nonwinners at contract renewal intervals because nontrivial investments in durable specific assets are put in place or otherwise accrue, say in a learning-by-doing fashion) during contract execution. As set out elsewhere

organization are very serious. But since we do observe that some transactions are organized within firms, this poses the question of which and why. The answer resides in the transaction cost disabilities of markets that arise when asset specificity and demand externalities appear.

(Williamson, 1979), the efficient governance of recurring transactions will vary as follows: classical market contracting will be efficacious wherever assets are nonspecific to the trading parties; bilateral or obligational market contracting will appear as assets become semi-specific; and internal organization will replace markets as assets take on a high specific character.[20]

Internal organization enjoys advantages over market contracting for transactions that are supported by highly specific assets at both contract-writing and contract execution stages. Since highly specific assets cannot be redeployed without sacrificing productivity, both suppliers and purchasers will insist upon contractual safeguards before undertaking such projects. Writing and negotiating such contracts is costly. Additionally, implementation problems need to be faced. The internal direction of firms confers execution advantages over bilateral trading in three respects. First, common ownership reduces the incentives of the trading units to pursue local goals. Second, and related, internal organization is able to invoke fiat to resolve differences whereas costly adjudication is needed when an impasse develops between autonomous traders. Third, internal organization has easier and more complete access to the relevant information when disputes must be settled. The incentive to shift bilateral transactions from markets to firms also increases as uncertainty increases, since the costs of harmonizing a relation among parties vary directly with the need to adjust to changing circumstances.

Externality Principle (Forward Integration)

Whereas the asset specificity principle refers to transactions that are transformed from large- to small-numbers bidding situations—as buyers, who initially obtained assets or their services in a competitive market, subsequently face suppliers with some degree of monopoly

[20] Note that the nature of the asset specificity matters. If the assets in question are mobile and the specificity is due to physical but not human asset features, market procurement may still be feasible. This can be accomplished by having the buyer own the specific assets (e.g. dies). He puts the business up for bid and awards it to the low bidder, to whom he ships the dies. Should contractual difficulties arise, however, he is not locked into a bilateral exchange. He reclaims the dies and reopens the bidding. This option is not available if the specific asserts are of a human asset kind or if they are nonmobile. See David J. Teece (1980) for a related discussion.

power—the externality principle involves no such market transformation. Also, the asset-specificity principle applies to backward, forward, and lateral integration; by contrast, the externality principle mainly applied to distribution stages.

The externalities of concern are those that arise in conjunction with the unintended debasement of quality for a branded good or service. As discussed below, such debasement is explained by costly metering. The externality is thus a manifestation of the measurement problems to which North refers in his discussion of transaction costs (1978, p. 972). It appears mainly at the interface between production and distribution. The differential ease of inspecting, and thereby controlling, the quality of components and materials that are purchased from earlier-stage and lateral suppliers as compared with the cost of exercising quality controls over distributors is responsible for this condition.[21]

End-games and fly-by-night distributors aside, the unintended debasement of quality by distributors poses a problem only where the activities of individual distributors affect one another, as when one retailer's poor service in installation or repair injures a product's reputation for performance and limits the sales of other retailers. More generally, if the quality enhancement (debasement) efforts of distributors give rise to positive (negative) externalities, the benefits (costs) of which can be incompletely appropriated by (assigned to) the originators, failure to extend quality controls over distribution will result in suboptimization. Autonomous contracting thus gives way to obligational market contracting (e.g. franchising) if not forward integration into distribution[22] as demand interaction effects become more important. More generally, the second principle of efficient organizational design is this: *the normal presumption that exchange between producers of differentiated goods and distribution stages will be efficiently mediated by autonomous contracting is progressively weakened as demand externalities increase.*

Product differentiation is a necessary but not a sufficient condition for troublesome demand externalities to appear. Manufacturers can

[21] Manufacturers may, of course, decide to integrate into components if work-in-process inspections are much cheaper than final inspections.

[22] Franchising will be more prevalent if aggregation economies are present at the distribution stage. It will be inefficient in these circumstances for a single product firm to integrate forward into distribution.

sometimes insulate a product against deterioration by special packaging (say by selling the item in hermetic containers with an inert atmosphere and providing replacement guarantees). If, however, such safeguards are very costly, and if follow-on checks and penalties to discourage distributors from debasing the quality image of a product are likewise expensive, autonomous trading will give way to forms of distribution that have superior quality control properties.

Hierarchical Decomposition Principle (Internal Organization)[23]

Merely to transfer a transaction out of the market into the firm does not, by itself, assure that the activity will be effectively organized thereafter. Not only are bounded rationality and opportunism ubiquitous, but the problems presented by both vary with changes in internal organization. Accordingly, a complete theory of value will recognize that firm structure as well as market structure matters.

Simon makes provision for bounded rationality effects in arguing that the organizational division of decision making labour is quite as important as the neoclassical division of production labour, where, from 'the information processing point of view, division of labour means factoring the total system of decisions that need to be made into relatively independent subsystems, each one of which can be designed with only minimal concern for its interactions with the others' (Simon, 1973, p. 270). This applies to both vertical and horizontal aspects of the organization. In both respects the object is to recognize and give effect to conditions of near decomposability. The vertical slice entails grouping the operating parts into separable entities, the interactions within which are strong and between which are weak. The horizontal slice has temporal ramifications of a strategic versus operating kind. Problems are thus factored in such a way that the higher frequency (or short run dynamics) are associated with the operating parts which the lower frequency (or long run dynamics) are associated with the strategic system (Simon, 1962, p. 477). These operating and strategic distinctions correspond with the lower and

[23] The hierarchical decomposition principle is due to Simon (1962; 1973). As he observes, the anatomy of an organization can be viewed either in terms of the groupings of human beings or the flows and transformations of symbols (1973, p. 270). He emphasizes the latter, which is in the spirit of transaction cost analysis.

higher levels in the organizational hierarchy, respectively. Internal incentives and information flows need, of course, to be aligned, lest distortions be deliberately or inadvertently introduced into the internal information summary and transmittal processes.

The hierarchical decomposition principle can thus be stated as follows: *internal organization should be designed in such a way as to effect quasi-independence between the parts, the high frequency dynamics (operating activities) and low frequency dynamics (strategic planning) should be clearly distinguished, and incentives should be aligned within and between components* so as to promote both local and global effectiveness.

Each of these three principles of organizational design is responsive to considerations of both bounded rationality and opportunism. Thus asset specificity would pose no problems if comprehensive contracting were feasible (which is tantamount to unbounded rationality) or if winning bidders could be relied upon to behave in an utterly reliable and trustworthy fashion (absence of opportunism). The externality principle is mainly a reflection of opportunism (autonomous distributors permit their suppliers' reputations to be degraded because they bear only part of the costs), but, of course, quality control checks would be unneeded if all relevant information could be costlessly displayed and assessed. The hierarchical decomposition principle recognizes the need to be divide problems into manageable units and at the same time prevent agents from engaging in dysfunctional pursuit of local goals, which reflect bounded rationality and opportunism concerns, respectively.

A more comprehensive analysis would embed these principles of organization within a larger optimizing framework where demand as well as cost consequences are recognized and where production versus transaction costs tradeoffs are made explicit.[24] For the purposes at

[24] Thus, whereas I argue that the object is to minimize the sum of production and transaction costs, treating output and design as given, the more general problem is to maximize profits, treating output and design as decision variables. A rudimentary statement of the optimizing problem, for a given organization form *(f)*, is to choose output *(Q)* and design *(D)* so as to maximize:

$$\pi(Q, D; f) = P(Q, D) \cdot Q - C_f(Q, D; S) - G_f(Q, D),$$

where π denotes profit, $P(Q, D)$ is the demand curve, S denotes combinatorial economies of scope, and C_f and G_f are the production costs and governance (transaction)

hand, however, which take product design as given and focus on distinguishably different rather than close cases, such refinements do not appear to be necessary.

3. THE NINETEENTH CENTURY CORPORATION

The 1840s mark the beginning of a great wave of organizational change that has evolved into the modern corporation (Chandler, 1977). According to Stuart Bruchey, the fifteenth century merchant of Venice would have understood the term of organization and methods of managing men, records, and investment used by Baltimore merchants in 1790 (1956, pp. 370–1). These practices evidently remained quite serviceable until after the 1840s. The two most significant developments were the appearance of the railroads and, in response to this, forward integration by manufacturers into distribution.

3.1 The Railroads

Although a number of technological developments—including the telegraph (Chandler, 1977, p. 189), the development of continuous process machinery (Chandler, pp. 252–3), the refinement of interchangeable parts manufacture (Chandler, 1977, pp. 75–7), and related mass manufacturing techniques (Chandler, Ch. 8)—contributed to organizational changes in the second half of the nineteenth century, none was more important than the railroads (Glenn Porter and Harold Livesay, 1971, p. 55). Not only did the railroads pose distinctive organizational problems of their own, but the incentive to integrate forward from manufacturing into distribution would have been much

costs of mode *f*. Transaction costs become relatively more important to this calculus as the assets needed to support specialized designs become progressively more specific —which they normally will as designs become more idiosyncratic.

Plainly the tradeoffs that run through this optimizing relation are more extensive than my earlier discussion discloses, but a detailed assessment of these is not needed for the types of purposes to which the asset specificity principle is herein applied. Both the externality and hierarchical decomposition principles should likewise be qualified to recognize tradeoffs. Again, however, second order refinements are not needed for the comparative institutional purposes to which these are applied below.

less without the low cost, reliable, all-weather transportation afforded by the railroads. Forward integration is discussed in 3.2 below; the railroads are treated here.

The appearance and purported importance of the railroads have been matters of great interest to economic historians. But with very few exceptions, the organizational—as opposed to the technological—significance of the railroads has been neglected. Thus Robert Fogel (1964) and Albert Fishlow (1965)

> investigated the railroad as a construction activity and as a means of transport, but not as an organizational form. As with most economists, the internal workings of the railroad organizations were ignored. This appears to be the result of an implicit assumption that the organization form used to accomplish an objective does not matter (Peter Temin, 1980, p. 3).

The economic success of the railroads entailed more, however, than the substitution of one technology (rails) for another (canals). Rather, organizational aspects also required attention. As Chandler puts it:

> (the) safe, regular, reliable movement of goods and passengers, as well as the continuing maintenance and repair of locomotives, rolling stock, and track, roadbed, stations, roundhouses, and other equipment, required the creation of a sizeable administrative organization. It meant the employment of a set of managers to supervise these functional activities over an extensive geographical area; and the appointment of an administrative command of middle and top executives to monitor, evaluate, and coordinate the work of managers responsible for the day-to-day operations. It meant, too, the formulation of brand new types of internal administrative procedures and accounting and statistical controls. Hence, the operational requirements of the railroads demanded the creation of the first administrative hierarchies in American business (1977, p. 87).

The 'natural' railroad units, as these first evolved, were lines of about fifty miles in length. These roads employed about fifty workers and were administered by a superintendent and several managers of functional activities (Chandler, 1977, p. 96). This was adequate as long as traffic flows were uncomplicated and short hauls prevailed. The full promise of the railroads could be realized, however, only if traffic densities were increased and longer hauls introduced. How was this to be effected?

In principle, successive end-to-end systems could be joined by contract. The resulting contracts would be tightly bilateral in negotiation, interpretation and execution, however, since investments in site-specific assets by each party were considerable. Severe contractual difficulties would, therefore, predictably arise.[25] Unless supporting governance structure were simultaneously created,[26] the potential of the railroads for long-haul and high-density traffic would evidently go unrealized. One possibility was for heavily traveled end-to-end links to be joined under common ownership.

But while the consolidation of ownership reduced the restraints on long-hand operations, it did not guarantee that the end-to-end systems would work smoothly. Indeed, early operation of the Western and Albany road, which was just over 150 miles in length and was built in three sections each operated as a separate division with its own set of functional managers, quickly proved otherwise (Chandler, 1977, pp. 96–7). As a consequence, a new organizational structure was fashioned whereby the first 'formal administrative structure manned by full-time salaried managers' in the USA appeared (Chandler, 1977, pp. 97–8).

This structure was progressively perfected, and the organizational innovations that the railroads eventually evolved is characterized by Chandler as the 'decentralized line-and-staff concept of organization'. This provided that 'the managers on the line of authority were responsible for ordering men involved with the basic function of the enterprise, and other functional managers (the staff executives) were responsible for setting standards' (Chandler, 1977, p. 106). Geographic divisions were defined and the superintendents in charge were held responsible for the 'day-to-day movement of trains and traffic by an express delegation of authority' (Chandler, 1977, p. 102). These division superintendents were on the 'direct line of authority from the president through the general superintendent' (Chandler, 1977, p. 106), and the functional managers within the geographic

25 Problems of two kinds would need to be faced. Not only would the railroads need to reach agreement on how to deal with a series of complex operating matters—equipment utilization, costing, and maintenance; adapting cooperatively to unanticipated disturbances; assigning responsibility for customer complaints, breakdown, etc.—but problems of customers contracting with a set of autonomous end-to-end suppliers would need to be worked out. Plainly, complex contracting issues proliferate.

26 Railroad regulation can be interpreted, in part, as an effort to deal with these contractual difficulties by inventing specialized governance structures. Pursuit of these matters is beyond the scope of this paper. Aspects of the general problem are dealt with in Williamson (1976) and Victor Goldberg (1976).

divisions—who dealt with transportation, motive power, maintenance of way, passenger, freight, and accounting—reported to them rather than to their functional superiors at the central office (Chandler, 1977, pp. 106–7).

Confronted, as they were, by the contractual dilemmas that arise when highly specific assets are in place and by complexities that exceeded, perhaps by several orders of magnitude, those that had been faced by earlier business enterprise, the managements of the railroads supplanted markets by hierarchies of a carefully crafted kind. Although military organizations had earlier devised similar structures, the railroad innovators brought engineering rather than military backgrounds to the task (Chandler, 1977, Ch. 3). The hierarchical structure that they evolved was consistent, at least broadly, with the hierarchical principles stated by Simon. Thus support activities (lower frequency dynamics) were split off from operations (higher frequency dynamics), and the linkages within each of these classes of activity were stronger than the linkages between. This organizational innovation, in Chandler's judgment, paved the way for modern business enterprise. As with most significant organizational developments, it evolved in a piecemeal rather than a full-blown way (Richard Nelson and Sidney Winter, 1981). Failure to recognize the opportunities for decomposition of functions and to perfect the hierarchical governance structures by which these could be realized would have arrested the development of the modern corporation at a very primitive stage.

3.2 Forward Integration

Forward integration by manufacturers into distribution was one of the significant consequences of the appearance of the railroads. Low cost transportation combined with telegraph and telephone communication permitted manufacturers efficiently to service a larger market and, as a consequence, realize greater economies of scale in production. The points of connection between manufacturing, wholesaling, and retailing, however, also required attention. Forward integration was a common but by no means uniform response. To the contrary, it was highly selective rather than comprehensive, and it is this selectivity that is the matter of special interest to this paper.

At least four degrees of forward integration can be recognized. From least to most, these are:

A. None—in which event traditional wholesale and retail distribution was continued (many grocery, drug, hardware, jewelry, liquor, and dry goods items were of this kind) [Porter and Livesay, 1971, p. 214].

B. Minor—efforts to presell product and to monitor wholesale inventories, but not to include the ownership and operation of wholesale plants, are examples. Certain branded nondurables (soups, soaps), especially those for which staling was a problem (cigarettes, cereals), are included.

C. Wholesale—this was undertaken for perishable, branded items that required special handling;[27] often specialized investments in refrigeration were involved (meat and beer are examples) [Chandler, 1977, p. 299].

D. Retail—integration into retail was rare and was reserved for 'new, complex, high priced machines that required specialized marketing services—demonstration, installation, consumer credit, after-sales service and repair' (Chandler, 1977, p. 288). Certain consumer durables (sewing machines, automobiles) and producer durables (some electrical machinery and office machines) were of this kind.

Actually, there is a variant of this fourth category that I will designate 'mistaken' retail integration. Such integration involved none of the transaction specific investments in sales and service referred to above but had the purpose of foreclosing rivals. The ill-fated efforts of American Tobacco to integrate forward into the wholesaling and retailing of cigars and of American Sugar Refining to 'drive its competitor John Arbuckle out of business by buying into wholesale and retail houses' (Porter and Livesay, 1971, pp. 52, 211) are examples.[28]

[27] The Whitman candy case involved the use of two different merchandising methods. Wholesalers were bypassed in the sale of high-grade, packaged candies. Small, inexpensive, bar and packaged candies, by contrast, were sold through the usual jobber and wholesale grocer network. Control of the wholesaling function for the former was arguably more important for quality control purposes. These high-grade items were 'sold directly to retailers so that the company could regulate the flow of the perishable items and avoid alienating customers' (Porter and Livesay, 1971, p. 220)—who were presumably prepared to pay a premium to avoid stale candy.

[28] This is not to say that foreclosure will never be successful unless accompanied by transaction specific investments. But it should not entail sacrifice of scale

The question is how to interpret these developments. Although the data that would be needed for a quantitative analysis have yet to be worked up, a systematic qualitative interpretation along the lines of the discussion in Secs 2.2 and 2.3 above is nevertheless feasible. The attributes of the five integration classes are set out in Table 1, where ++ denotes considerable, + denotes some, ~ is uncertain, and 0 is negligible.

Table 1

Integration Class	*Economies of Scope*	*Externalities*	*Asset Specificity*
A: none	++	0	0
B: minor	+	+	0
C: wholesale	~	+	+
D_1: retail/viable	0	+	++
D_2: retail/mistaken	+	0	0

Markets remain the main mode for effecting distribution for classes A and B. Markets enjoy substantial economies of scope for these products while asset specificity is negligible and externalities are dealt with by monitoring inventory. Integration into wholesale occurs for products that involve some asset specificity (refrigeration) and the reputation of branded products needs protection. Integration into retail does not occur, however, until asset specificity at the retail level is great (and these are products for which separate sales and service entails negligible loss of scope economies).[29] Finally, mistaken retail integration involves the sacrifice of scope economies without offsetting governance cost benefits (externalities and asset specificity are negligible). This pattern of integration is broadly consistent with

economies. Forward integration by the motion picture producers into theatres may have been a viable means of foreclosing entry into the production stage because theatre ownership by major producers entailed little or no sacrifice of scale economies.

[29] Concessions in department stores are devised for effecting retail sales for products that are efficiently marketed in conjunction with others but which nevertheless require transaction specific investments. Chandler does not discuss such product but a more comprehensive microanalytic analyse would, I conjecture, disclose the existence of somewhere mixed modes arise because aggregation economies and asset specificity are simultaneously present.

transaction cost reasoning and explains why forward integration occurred selectively rather than comprehensively in response to the transportation and communication infrastructure.[30]

4. THE TWENTIETH CENTURY CORPORATION

Three developments are particularly noteworthy in the evolution of the modern corporation in the twentieth century. The first of these was the appearance of the multi-divisional (or M-form) organization. Later developments are the conglomerate and the multinational corporation.

4.1 The Multi-divisional Structure

The most significant organizational innovation of the twentieth century was the development in the 1920s of the multidivisional structure. Surprisingly, this development was little noted or widely appreciated as late as 1960. Leading management texts extolled the virtues of 'basic departmentation' and 'line and staff authority relationships', but the special importance of multidivisionalization went unremarked.[31]

Chandler's pathbreaking study of business history, *Strategy and Structure*, simply bypassed this management literature. He advanced the thesis that 'changing developments in business organization presented a challenging area for comparative analysis' and observed that 'the study of (organizational) innovation seemed to furnish the proper focus for such an investigation' (1966, p. 2). Having identified the multidivisional structure as one of the more important of such innovations, he proceeded to trace its origins, identify the factors that gave rise to its appearance, and describe the subsequent diffusion of this organizational form. It was uninformed and untenable to argue that organization form was of no account after the appearance of Chandler's book.

The leading figures in the creation of the multidivisional (or M-form) structure were Pierre S. du Pont and Alfred P. Sloan; the period was the early 1920s; the firms were Du Pont and General

[30] For a more complete assessment, on which the above is based, see Williamson (1980).

[31] The treatment of these matters by Harold Koontz and Cyril O'Donnell (1955) is representative.

Motors; and the organizational strain of trying to cope with economic adversity under the old structure was the occasion to innovate in both. The structures of the two companies, however, were different.

Du Pont was operating under the centralized, functionally departmentalized or unitary (U-form) structure. General Motors, by contrast, had been operated more like a holding company by William Durant—whose genius in perceiving market opportunities in the automobile industry (Livesay, 1979, pp. 232–4) evidently did not extend to organization. Chandler summarizes the defects of the large U-form enterprise in the following way:

> The inherent weakness in the centralized, functionally departmentalized operating company . . . became critical only when the administrative load on the senior executives increased to such an extent that they were unable to handle their entrepreneurial responsibilities efficiently. This situation arose when the operations of the enterprise became too complex and the problems of coordination, appraisal, and policy formulation too intricate for a small number of top officers to handle both long-run, entrepreneurial, and short-run, operational administrative activities (1966, pp. 382–3).

The ability of the management to handle the volume and complexity of the demands placed upon it became strained and even collapsed. Unable meaningfully to identify with or contribute to the realization of global goals, managers in each of the functional parts attended to what they perceived to be operational subgoals instead (Chandler, 1966, p. 156). In the language of transaction cost economics, bounds on rationality were reached as the U-form structure laboured under a communication overload while the pursuit of subgoals by the functional parts (sales, engineering, production) was partly a manifestation of opportunism.

The M-form structure fashioned by du Pont and Sloan involved the creation of semi-autonomous operating divisions (mainly profit centers) organized along product, brand, or geographic lines. The operating affairs of each were managed separately. More than a change in decomposition rules were needed, however, for the M-form to be fully effective. Du Pont and Sloan also created a general office 'consisting of a number of powerful general executives and large advisory and financial staffs' (Chandler, 1977, p. 460) to monitor divisional performance, allocate resources among divisions, and engage in strategic planning. The reasons for the success of the M-form innovation are summarized by Chandler as follows:

The basic reason for its success was simply that it clearly removed the executives responsible for the destiny of the entire enterprise from the more routine operational activities, and so gave them the time, information, and even psychological commitment for long-term planning and appraisal.

(The) new structure left the broad strategic decisions as to the allocation of existing resources and the acquisition of new ones in the hands of a top team of generalists. Relieved of operating duties and tactical decisions, a general executive was less likely to reflect the position of just one part of the whole (1966, pp. 382–3).

In contrast with the holding company—which is also a divisionalized form but has little general office capability and hence is little more than a corporate shell—the M-form organization adds (1) a strategic planning and resource allocation capability and (2) monitoring and control apparatus. As a consequence, cash flows are reallocated among divisions to favour high yield uses, and internal incentive and control instruments are exercised in a discriminating way. In short, the M-form corporation takes on many of the properties of (and is usefully regarded as) a miniature capital market,[32] which is a much more ambitious concept of the corporation than the term holding company contemplates.

Although the structure was imitated very slowly at first, adoption by American firms proceeded rapidly during the period 1945 to 1960. Acceptance of this structure by European firms came later. Lawrence Franko (1972) reports that most large European companies administered their domestic operations through U-form or holding company structures until late in the 1960s, but that rapid reorganization along M-form lines has occurred since. The advent of zero tariffs within the European Economic Community and the post-war penetration of European markets by American multinationals were, in his judgment, important contributing factors.

As W. Ross Ashby has observed, it is not sufficient to determine the behaviour of a whole machine to know the behaviour of its parts: 'only when the details of coupling are added does the whole's behaviour become determinate' (1956, p. 53). The M-form structure represented a different solution to the coupling problem than the earlier unitary form structure. It effected decomposability along

[32] Others who reported that the modern corporation was assuming capital market resource allocation and control functions include Richard Heflebower (1960) and Armen Alchian (1969).

product or brand lines to which profit center standing could be assigned and it more clearly separated operation from strategic decision making. It carried Simon's hierarchical decomposition principles to a higher degree of refinement.[33]

As compared with the U-form organization of the same activities, the M-form organization of the large, complex corporation served both to economize on bounded rationality and attenuate opportunism. Specifically:

> Operating decisions were no longer forced to the top but were resolved at the divisional level, which relieved the communication load. Strategic decisions were reserved for the general office, which reduced partisan political input into the resource allocation process. And the internal auditing and control techniques which the general office had access to served to overcome information impactedness conditions and permit fine timing controls to be exercised over the operating parts (Williamson, 1975, pp. 137–8).

4.2 The Conglomerate

Chandler's studies of organizational innovation do not include the conglomerate and multinational form of corporate enterprise. These are more recent developments, the appearance of which would not have been feasible but for the prior development of the M-form structure. Inasmuch as transaction cost economizing is socially valued and has been relatively neglected by prior treatments, my discussion of both of these emphasizes affirmative aspects. But this is intended to redress an imbalance and should not be construed to suggest either that a transaction cost interpretation is fully adequate or that conglomerates and multinationals pose no troublesome public policy issues.[34] Unrelieved hostility to these two forms of organization, however, is clearly inappropriate. Specifically, conglomerates that have the capacity to allocate resources to high valued uses and multinationals that use the M-form to facilitate technology transfer warrant more sympathetic assessments.

[33] Moreover, whereas the line-and-staff structure that the railroads adopted in the 1850s could be said to have been prefigured by the military, there is no such military precedent for the M-form. Rather the reorganization of the military after World War II has certain M-form attributes.

[34] For a discussion of the public policy issues posed by conglomerates, see Williamson (1975, pp. 163–4).

Although diversification as a corporate strategy certainly predates the 1960s, when general awareness of the conglomerate began to appear, the conglomerate is essentially a post World War II phenomenon. To be sure, General Electric's profit centers number in the hundreds and GE has been referred to as the world's most diversified firm. Until recently, however, General Electric's emphasis has been the manufacture and distribution of electrical appliances and machinery. Similarly, although General Motors was more than an automobile company, it took care to limit is portfolio. Thus Sloan remarked that 'tetraethyl lead was clearly a misfit for GM. It was a chemical product, rather than a mechanical one. And it had to go to market as part of the gasoline and thus required a gasoline distribution system' (Burton and Kuhn, 1979, p. 6). Accordingly, although GM retained an investment position, the Ethyl Corporation became a free-standing entity rather than an operating division (Sloan, 1965, p. 224). Similarly, although Durant had acquired Frigidaire, and Frigidaire's market share of refrigerators exceeded 50 per cent in the 1920s, the position was allowed to deteriorate as rivals developed market positions in other major appliances (radios, ranges, washers, etc.) while Frigidaire concentrated on refrigerators. The suggestion that GM get into air conditioners 'did not register on us, and the proposal was not . . . adopted' (Sloan, 1965, p. 361). As Richard Burton and Arthur Kuhn conclude, GM's 'deep and myopic involvement in the automobile sector of the economy, (prevented) product diversification opportunities in other market areas—even in product lines where GM had already achieved substantial penetration—(from being) recognized' (1979, pp. 10–11).

The conglomerate form of organization, whereby the corporation consciously took on a diversified character and nurtured its various parts, evidently required a conceptual break in the mind-set of Sloan and other prewar business leaders. This occurred gradually, more by evolution than by grand design (Robert Sobel, 1974, p. 377); and it involved a new group of organizational innovators—of which Royal Little was one (Sobel, 1974). The natural growth of conglomerates, which would occur as the techniques for managing diverse assets were refined, was accelerated as antitrust enforcement against horizontal and vertical mergers became progressively more severe. Conglomerate acquisitions—in terms of numbers, assets acquired, and as a proportion of total acquisitions—grew rapidly with the result that 'pure' conglomerate mergers, which in the period 1948–53 constituted only 3 per cent of the assets acquired by merger, had grown to 49 per cent by 1973–77 (Frederic Scherer, 1980, p. 124).

Morris Adelman's (1961) explanation for the conglomerate is that this form of organization has attractive portfolio diversification properties. But why should the conglomerate appear in the 1960s rather than much earlier? After all, holding companies, which long predated the conglomerate, can accomplish portfolio diversification. And individual stockholders, through mutual funds and otherwise, are able to diversify their own portfolios. At best the portfolio diversification thesis is a very incomplete explanation for the postwar wave of conglomerate mergers.[35]

The Federal Trade Commission also ventured an early assessment of the conglomerate in which organization form features were ignored. The conglomerate was a natural target for the inhospitality tradition. Thus the FTC Staff held that the conglomerate had the following properties:

> With the economic power which it secures through its operations in many diverse fields, the giant conglomerate corporation may attain an almost impregnable economic position. Threatened with competition in any one of its various activities, it may sell below cost in that field, offsetting its losses through profits made in its other lines—a practice which is frequently explained as one of meeting competition. The conglomerate corporation is thus in a position to strike out with great force against smaller business in a variety of different industries (1948, p. 59).

I submit that some phenomena, of which changing internal organization is one, need to be addressed on their own terms. Adopting this view, the conglomerate is best understood as a logical outgrowth of the M-form mode for organizing complex economic affairs. Thus once the merits of the M-form structure for managing separable, albeit related, line of business (e.g. a series of automobile or a series of chemical divisions) were recognized and digested, its extension to manage less closely related activities was natural. This is not to say that the management of product variety is without problems of its

[35] The diversification of personal portfolios is not a perfect substitute for conglomerate diversification because bankruptcy has real costs that the firm, but not individuals, can reduce by portfolio diversification. Bankruptcy costs have not sharply increased in the past thirty years, however, hence these differences do not explain the appearance of the conglomerate during this interval.

own. But the basic M-form logic whereby strategic and operating decisions are distinguished and responsibilities are separated, carried over. The conglomerates in which M-form principles of organization are respected are usefully thought of as internal capital markets where cash flows from diverse sources are concentrated and directed to high yield uses.

The conglomerate is noteworthy, however, not merely because it permitted to M-form structure to take this diversification step. Equally interesting are the unanticipated systems consequences which developed as a byproduct. Thus once it was clear that the corporation could manage diverse assets in an effective way, the possibility of takeover by tender offer suggested itself. In principle, incumbent managements could always be displaced by waging a proxy contest. In fact, it is a very expensive and relatively ineffective way to achieve management change (Williamson, 1970, Ch. 6). Moreover even if the dissident shareholders should succeed, there was still a problem of finding a successor management.

Viewed in contractual terms, the M-form conglomerate can be thought of substituting an administrative interface between an operating division and stockholders where a market interface had existed previously. Subject to the condition that the conglomerate does not diversify to excess, in the sense that it cannot competently evaluate and allocate funds among the diverse activities in which it is engaged, the substitution of internal organization can have beneficial effects in goal pursuit, monitoring, staffing, and resource allocation respects. The goal-pursuit advantage is that which accrues to M-form organizations in general: since the general management of an M-form conglomerate is disengaged from operating matters, a presumption that the general office favours profits over functional goals are warranted. Relatedly, the general office can be regarded as an agent of the stockholders whose purpose is to monitor the operations of the constituent parts. Monitoring benefits are realized in the degree to which internal monitors enjoy advantages over external monitors in access to information—which they arguably do (Williamson, 1975, pp. 145–8). The differential ease with which the general office can change managers and reassign duties where performance failures or distortions are detected is responsible for the staffing advantage. Resource-allocation benefits are realized because cash flows no longer return automatically to their origins but instead revert to the center, thereafter to be allocated among competing uses in accordance with prospective yields.[36]

This has a bearing on the problem of separation of ownership from control, noted by Adolph Berle and Gardiner C. Means in 1932. Thus they inquired, 'have we any justification for assuming that those in control of a modern corporation will also choose to operate it in the interests of the stockholders' (1932, p. 121). The answer, then as now, is almost certainly no. Indeed, the evident disparity of interest between managers and stockholders gave rise in the 1960s to what has become known as the managerial discretion literature (William Baumol, 1959; Robin Marris, 1964; Williamson, 1964).

There are important differences, however, between the U-form structure, which was the prevailing organization form at the time Berle and Means were writing, and the M-form structure, which in the US was substantially in place by the 1960s. For one thing, as argued above, U-form managers identified more strongly with functional interests and hence were more given to subgoal pursuit. Secondly, and related, there was a confusion between strategic and operating goals in the U-form structure which the M-form served to rectify—with the result that the general office was more fully concerned with enterprise goals, of which profits is the leading element. Third, the market for corporate control, which remained ineffectual so long as the proxy contest was the only way to challenge incumbent managements, was activated as conglomerates recognized that tender offers could be used to effect corporate takeovers. As a consequence, managements that were otherwise secure and would have permitted managerial preferences to prevail were brought under scrutiny and induced to self-correct against egregious managerial distortions.

To be sure, managerial preferences (for salary and perquisites) and stockholder preferences for profits do not become perfectly consonant as a result of conglomerate organization and the associated activation

[36] To be sure, this substitution of internal organization for the capital market is subject to tradeoffs and diminishing returns. Breadth—that is, access to the widest range of alternatives—is traded off for depth—that is, more intimate knowledge of a narrower range of possible investment outlets—(Alchian and Harold Demsetz, 1972, p. 29), where the general office may be presumed to have the advantage in the latter respect. The diminishing returns feature suggests that the net benefits of increased diversity eventually become negative. Were further diversification thereafter to be attempted, effective control would pass back into the hands of the operating divisions with problematic performance consequences.

of the capital market. The continuing tension between management and stockholder interests is evident in the numerous efforts that incumbent managements have taken to protect target firms against takeover (William Cary, 1969; Williamson, 1979; George Benston, 1980). Changes in internal organization have nevertheless relieved these concerns. A study of capitalist enterprises which makes no allowance for organization form changes and their capital market ramifications will naturally overlook the possibility that the corporate control dilemma posed by Berle and Means has since been alleviated more by *internal* than it has by regulatory or external organizational reforms.

Not all conglomerates respected M-form principles when they were first organized. The above argument applies only to those where rational decomposition principles were observed and leads to the following testable proposition: conglomerates that were organized along holding company rather than M-form lines (as many were initially) would be less able to cope when adversity appeared, at which time they would be reorganized as M-form firms. Voluntary divestiture is also an interesting conglomerate phenomenon. Such a rationalization of assets is commonly accompanied by internal organizational reforms. Growth maximization theories are mainly at a loss to explain such behaviour.

4.3 Multinational Enterprise

The discussion of the multinational enterprise (MNE) that follows deals mainly with recent developments and, among these, emphasizes organizational aspects—particularly those associated with technology transfer in manufacturing industries. As Mira Wilkins has reported, direct foreign investment by American firms has a long history: the book value of cumulative American direct foreign investment, expressed as a percentage of GNP, was in the range of 7 to 8 per cent in 1914, 1929, and 1970 (Wilkins, 1974, p. 437). Both the character of this investment and relatedly, the organization structure within which this investment takes place have been changing, however. It is not accidental that the term MNE was coined neither in 1914 or 1929 but is of much more recent origin.

Thus whereas the ratio of the book value of US foreign investments in manufacturing as compared with all other (petroleum; trade;

mining; public utilities) was 0.47 in 1950, this had increased to 0.71 in 1970 (Wilkins, 1974, p. 329). Also, 'what impressed Europeans about American plants in Europe and the United States [in 1929, was mass production, standardization, and scientific management; in the 1960s, Europeans were remarking that American superiority was based on technological and managerial advantage . . . (and) that this expertise was being exported via direct investment' (Wilkins, 1974, p. 436).

The spread of the multinational corporation in the post World War II period has given rise to considerable scrutiny, some puzzlement, and even some alarm (Yoshihiro Tsurumi, 1977, p. 74). One of the reasons for this unsettled state of affairs is that transaction-cost economizing and organization form issues have been relatively neglected in efforts to assess MNE activity. An important exception is the work of Peter Buckley and Mark Casson (1976).

Organization form is relevant in two related respects. First is the matter of US-based as compared with foreign-based investment rates. Tsurumi reports in the connection that the rate of foreign direct investments by American firms increased rapidly after 1953, peaked in the mid-1960s and has leveled off and declined since (Tsurumi, 1977, p. 97). The pattern of foreign direct investments by foreign firm by contrast, has lagged that of the US by about a decade (Tsurumi, 1977, pp. 90–2).

Recall that the conglomerate uses the M-form structure to extend asset management from specialized to diversified lines of commerce. The MNE counterpart is the use of the M-form structure to extend asset management from a domestic base to include foreign operations. Thus the domestic M-form strategy for decomposing complex business structures into semi-autonomous operating units was subsequently applied to the management of foreign subsidiaries. As noted in 4.1 above, the transformation of the corporation along M-form lines came earlier in the US than in Europe and elsewhere. US corporations were for this reason better qualified to engage in foreign direct investments at an earlier date than were foreign-based firms. Only as the latter took on the M-form structure did this multinational management capability appear. The pattern of foreign direct investments recorded by Tsurumi and reported above is consistent with the temporal differences of American and foreign firms in adopting the M-form structure.

That American corporations possessed an M-form capability earlier than their foreign counterparts does not, however, establish that they used it to organize foreign investment. John Stopford and Louis Wells have studied this issue. They report that while initial foreign investments were usually organized as autonomous subsidiaries, divisional status within an M-form structure invariably appeared as the size and complexity of foreign operations increased (Stopford and Wells, 1972, p. 21). This transformation usually followed the organization of domestic operations along M-form lines (Stopford and Wells, 1972, p. 24). The adoption of a 'global' strategy or 'worldwide perspective'—whereby 'strategic planning and major policy decisions' are made in the central office of the enterprise—could only be accomplished within a multidivisional framework (Stopford and Wells, 1972, p. 25).

Even more interesting than these organization form issues is the fact that foreign direct investments by US firms have been concentrated in a few industries. Manufacturing industries that have made substantial foreign direct investments include chemicals, drugs, automobiles, food processing, electronics, electrical and non-electrical machinery, nonferrous metals, and rubber. Tobacco, textiles and apparel, furniture, printing, glass, steel, and aircraft have, by comparison, done little foreign direct investment (Tsurumi, 1977, p. 87).

Stephen Hymer's 'dual' explanation for the multinational enterprise is of interest in this connection. Thus Hymer observes that direct foreign investment 'allows business firms to transfer capital, technology, and organizational skill from one country to another. It is also an instrument for restraining competition between firms of different nations' (1970, p. 443).

Hymer is surely correct that the MNE can service both of these purposes and examples of both kinds can doubtlessly be found. If is nevertheless useful to ask whether the overall character of MNE investment, in terms of its distribution among industries, is more consistent with the efficiency purposes to which Hymer refers (transfer of capital, technology, and organizational skill) or with the oligopolistic restraint hypothesis. Adopting a transaction cost orientation discloses that the observed pattern of investment is more-consistent with the efficiency part of Hymer's dual explanation.

For one thing, oligopolistic purposes can presumably be realized by portfolio investment coupled with a limited degree of management involvement to segregate markets. Put differently, direct foreign investment and the organization of foreign subsidiaries within an M-form structure are not needed to effect competitive restraints. Furthermore, if competitive restraints were mainly responsible for these investments, then presumably all concentrated industries—which would include tobacco, glass, and steel—rather than those associated with rapid technical progress would be active in MNE creation. Finally, although many of the leading US firms that engaged in foreign direct investment enjoyed 'market power', this was by no means true for all.

By contrast, the pattern of foreign direct investments reported by Tsurumi appears to be consistent with a transaction cost economizing interpretation. Raymond Vernon's 1970 study of the *Fortune* 500 corporations disclosed that 187 of these firms had a substantial multinational presence. R&D expenditures as a percentage of sales were higher among these 187 than among the remaining firms in the *Fortune* 500 group. Furthermore, according to Vernon, firms that went multinational tended to be technological innovators at the time of making their initial foreign direct investments.

This raises the question of the attributes of firms and markets for accomplishing technology transfer. The difficulties with transferring technology across market interface are of three kinds: recognition, disclosure, and team organization (Arrow, 1962; Williamson, 1975, pp. 31–3, 203–7; Teece, 1977).[37] Of these three, recognition is probably the least severe. To be sure, foreign firms may sometimes fail to perceive the opportunities to apply technological developments originated elsewhere. But enterprising domestic firms that have made the advance can be expected to identify at least some of the potential applications abroad.

Suppose, therefore, that recognition problems are set aside and consider disclosure. Technology transfer by contract can break down if convincing disclosure to buyers effectively destroys the basis for exchange. A very severe information asymmetry problem exists, on which account the less informed partly (in this instance the buyer) must be wary of opportunistic representations by the seller.[38] Although

[37] The material that follows is based on Williamson and Teece (1979). Our argument is similar to that advanced by Buckley and Casson (1976).

[38] Markets for information are apt to be especially costly and/or hazardous when

sometimes this asymmetry can be overcome by sufficient ex ante disclosure (and veracity checks thereon), this may shift rather than solve the difficulty. The 'fundamental paradox' of information is that 'its value for the purchase is not known until he has the information, but then he has in effect acquired it without costs' (Arrow, 1971, p. 152).

Suppose, *arguendo*, that buyers concede value and are prepared to pay for information in the seller's possession. The incentive to trade is then clear and for some items this will suffice. The formula for a chemical compound or the blueprints for a special device may be all that is needed to effect the transfer. Frequently, however, and probably often, new knowledge is diffusely distributed and is poorly defined (Nelson, 1981). Where the requisite information is distributed among a number of individuals all of whom understand their speciality in only a tacit, intuitive way, a simple contract to transfer the technology cannot be devised (Michael Polanyi, 1962).

Transfer need not cease, however, because simple contracts are not feasible. If the benefits of technology transfer are sufficiently great, exchange may be accomplished either by devising a complex trade or through direct foreign investment. Which will be employed depends on the circumstances. If only a one-time (or very occasional) transfer of technology is contemplated, direct foreign investment is a somewhat extreme response.[39] The complex contractual alternative is to negotiate a tie-in sale whereby the technology and associated know-how are transferred as a package. Since the know-how is concentrated in the human assets who are already familiar with the technology, this entails the creation of a 'consulting team' by the seller to accompany the physical technology transfer—the object being to overcome start up difficulties and to familiarize the

transmission across a national boundary is attempted. Language differences naturally complicate the communication problem, and differences in the technological base compound these difficulties. If, moreover, as is commonly the case, cultural differences foster suspicion, the trust that is needed to support informational exchange may be lacking. Not only will contract negotiations be more complex and costly on this account but execution will be subject to more formal and costly procedures than would obtain under a region of greater trust.

[39] This is an implication of transaction cost reasoning in which the frequency dimension has explanatory power (Williamson, 1979, pp. 245–54).

employees of the foreign firm, through teaching and demonstration, with the idiosyncrasies of the operation.[40]

Inasmuch as many of the contingencies that arise in the execution of such contracts will be unforeseen and as it will be too costly to work out appropriate ex ante responses for others, such consulting contracts are subject to considerable strain. Where a succession of transfers is contemplated, which is to say, when the frequency shifts from occasional to recurring, complex contracting is apt to give way to direct foreign investment. A more harmonious and efficient exchange relation—better disclosure, easier reconciliation of differences, more complete cross-cultural adaptation, more effective team organization and reconfiguration—all predictably result from the substitution of an internal governance relation for bilateral trading under these recurrent trading circumstances for assets, of which complex technology transfer is an example, that have a highly specific character.[41]

The upshot is that while puzzlement with and concerns over MNEs will surely continue, a transaction cost interpretation of this phenomenon sheds insight on the following conspicuous features of multinational investment: (1) the reported concentration of foreign direct investment in manufacturing industries where technology transfer is of special importance; (2) the organization of these investments within M-form structures; and (3) the differential timing of foreign direct investment between US and foreign manufacturing enterprises (which difference also has organization form origins). I furthermore conjecture that the application of transaction cost reasoning will lead to a deeper understanding of other specific features of MNE activity as these are discovered and/or become subject to public policy scrutiny.

[40] On the importance of on-site observation and of teaching-by-doing, see Polanyi (1962), Peter Doeringer and Michael Piore (1971, pp. 15–16), and Williamson, Michael Wachter, and Jeffrey Harris (1975).

[41] The argument can be extended to deal with such observations as those of Edwin Mansfield, Anthony Romeo and Samuel Wagner (1979), who report that firms use subsidiaries to transfer their newest technology overseas but rely on licensing or joint ventures for older technology. The transaction cost argument is that the latter are more well defined, hence are more easily reduced to contract, and require less firm specific know-how to effect successful transfer.

5. CONCLUDING REMARKS

There is widespread agreement, among economists and noneconomists alike, with the proposition that the modern corporation is an important and complex economic institution. Such agreement is mainly explained by the obtrusive size of the largest firms—running to tens of billions of dollars of assets and sales, with employment numbering in the hundreds of thousands. The economic factors that lie behind the size, shape, and performance of the modern corporation, however, are poorly understood.

This puzzlement is not of recent origin. Edward Mason complained over twenty years ago that

> 'the functioning of the corporate system has not to date been adequately explained. . . . The man of action may be content with a system that works. But one who reflects on the properties or characteristics of this system cannot help asking why it works and whether it will continue to work'.

The predicament to which Mason refers is, I submit, largely the product of two different (but not unrelated) intellectual traditions. The first of these holds that the structural features of the corporation are irrelevant. This is the neoclassical theory of the firm that populates intermediate theory textbooks. Structural differences are suppressed as the firm is described as a production function to which a profit maximization objective has been assigned. The second has public policy roots; this is the inhospitality tradition that I referred to earlier. In this tradition, distinctive structural features of the corporation are believed to be the result of unwanted (anti-competitive) intrusions into market processes.

The transaction-cost approach differs from both. Unlike neoclassical analysis, internal organization is specifically held to be important. Unlike the inhospitality tradition, structural differences are assumed to arise primarily in order to promote economy in transaction costs. The assignment of transactions between firms and markets and the economic ramifications of internal structure both come under scrutiny in these terms. The application of these ideas to the study of transactions in general and of the modern corporation in particular requires that (1) the transaction be made the principal unit of analysis, (2) an elementary appreciation for 'human nature as we know it' supplant the fiction of economic man, (3) transactions be dimensionalized, (4) rudimentary principles of market and hierarchical organization be recognized, and (5) a guiding principle of comparative institutional study be the hypothesis that transactions are assigned to and organized within governance structures in a discriminating (transaction cost economizing) way.

The view that the corporation is first and foremost an efficiency instrument does not deny that firms also seek to monopolize markets, sometimes by engaging in strategic behaviour, or that managers sometimes pursue their own goals to the detriment of system goals. But specific structural preconditions need to be satisfied if strategic behaviour is to be feasible[42]—and most firms do not qualify, which is to say that strategic behaviour is the exception rather than the rule. Furthermore, most firms will be penalized if efficiency norms are seriously violated for extended periods of time—which serves to curb managerial discretion. The strongest argument favouring transaction cost economizing, however, is that this is the only hypothesis that is able to provide a discriminating rationale for the succession of organizational innovations that have occurred over the past 150 years and out of which the modern corporation has emerged.

To recapitulate, although railroad mergers between parallel roads can have monopolizing purposes, the joining of end-to-end systems under common management is explained by transaction cost economics. The hierarchical structures evolved by the railroads were the outcome of internal efforts to effect coordination across interfaces to which common operating responsibilities had been assigned. Older and simpler structures were unable to manage such complex networks, while coordination by end-to-end contracts between successive stations was prohibitively costly.

Forward integration out of manufacturing into distribution was widespread at the turn of the century. More interesting however, than this general movement is the fact that forward integration was selective—being extensive in some industries (e.g. sewing machines), negligible in others (e.g. dry goods), and mistaken in still others (e.g. sugar). This selective pattern is predicted by and consistent with transaction-cost reasoning—whereas no other hypothesis makes comparably detailed predictions.

[42] For a discussion of these preconditions—mainly high concentration coupled with high barriers to entry—see Joskow and Klevorick (1979) and Williamson (1981).

The efficiency incentive to shift from the earlier U-form to the M-form structure is partly explained in managerial discretion terms: the older structure was more subject to distortions of a managerial discretion kind—which is to say that opportunism had become a serious problem in the large U-form firm. Equally and probably more important, however, is that the managerial hierarchy is the U-form enterprise was simply overburdened as the firm became large and complex. The M-form structure represented a more rational decomposition of the affairs of the firm and thereby served to economize on bounded rationality.[43] The subsequent diffusion of this structure was hastened by a combination of product market (pressure on rivals) and capital market (takeover) competition.

The M-form structure, which was originally adopted by firms in relatively specialized lines of commerce was subsequently extended to manage diversified assets (the conglomerate) and foreign direct investments (MNE). A breadth-for-depth tradeoff is involved in the former case, as the firm selectively internalizes functions ordinarily associated with the capital market. MNE activity has also been selective—being concentrated in the more technologically progressive industries where higher rates of R&D are reported and technology transfer arguably poses greater difficulties than is true of technologically less progressive industries. This pattern of foreign direct investment cannot be explained as the pursuit of monopoly but is consistent with transaction-cost reasoning.

The upshot is that a transaction-cost approach to the study of the modern corporation permits a wide variety of significant organizational events to be interpreted in a coherent way.[44] It links up

[43] Had 'normal' managerial preferences prevailed, the U-form, which favoured the exercise of those preferences, would presumably have been retained.

[44] Recent contributions to the theory of the firm that are held to have a bearing on the study of the modern corporation are Alchian and Demsetz (1972) and Michael Jensen and William Meckling (1976). Both, however, deal with a microcosm much smaller than the modern corporation. Thus Alchian and Demsetz focus on the reasons why technological nonseparabilities give rise to team organization. Although small groups may be explained in this way (manual freight loading, whereby two men are required to lift coordinately, is the standard example), the existence of complex hierarchies cannot be explained in terms of the imperatives of such nonseparabilities. (The largest work group which, to my knowledge, qualifies is the symphony orchestra.)

Similarly, while the Jensen and Meckling paper is an important contribution to the principal-agent literature, it does not generalize to the modern corporation—as they

comfortably with the type of business history studies that have been pioneered by Chandler. It has ramifications for the study of regulation (Williamson, 1976; Goldberg, 1976) and for antitrust enforcement. Applications to aspects of labour economics and comparative systems have been made, and others would appear to be fruitful. More generally, while there is room for and need for refinement, a comparative approach to the study of economic institutions in which the economy of transaction costs is the focus of analysis, appears to have considerable promise.

REFERENCES

ADELMAN, M.A. (1961), 'The Antimerger Act, 1950–60', *American Economic Review*, 51, 236–44.

ALCHIAN, A.A. (1969), 'Corporate Management and Property Rights', in H.G. Manne (ed.), *Economic Policy and Regulation of Corporate Securities*, Washington: American Enterprise Institute for Public Policy Research, 337–60.

—— and H. DEMSETZ (1972), 'Production, Information Costs, and Economic Organization', *American Economic Review*, 62(5), 777–95.

ARROW, KENNETH J. (1962), 'Economic Welfare and the Allocation of Resources of Invention', in *The Rate and Direction of Inventive Activity: Economic and Social Factors* (ed.), NBER, Princeton: Princeton University Press, 609–25.

—— (1964), 'Control in Large Organizations', *Management Science*, 10(3), 397–408.

—— (1969), 'The Organization of Economic Activity: Issues Pertinent to the Choice of Market Versus Nonmarket Allocation', in *The Analysis and Evaluation of Public Expenditure: The PPB System*, Vol. 1, U.S. Joint Economic Committee, 91st Congress, 1st Session: U.S. Government Printing Office, 59–73.

—— (1971), *Essay in the Theory of Risk-Bearing*, Chicago: Markham Pub. Co.

—— (1974), *The Limits of Organization*, First edition, New York: W.W. Norton & Co.

---

expressly acknowledge (1976, p. 356). Although they conjecture that their analysis can be applied to the large, diffusely owned corporation whose managers own little or no equity (1976, p. 356), I have serious doubts.

ASHBY, W.R. (1956), *An Introduction to Cybernetics*, New York: John Wiley and Sons.

BARNARD, C.I. (1938), *The Functions of the Executive*, Cambridge, Mass.: Harvard University Press.

BAUMOL, W.J. (1967), *Business Behavior, Value and Growth*, New York: Macmillan: Harcourt, Brace and World.

BENSTON, GEORGE J. (1980), *Conglomerate Mergers: Causes, Consequences and Remedies*, Washington, DC: American Enterprise Institute for Public Policy Research.

BERLE, A.A. and G.C. MEANS (1932), *The Modern Corporation and Private Property*, New York: Macmillan.

BRUCHEY, STUART W. (1956), *Robert Oliver, Merchant of Baltimore, 1783–1819*, Baltimore: Johns Hopkins University Press.

BUCKLEY, P.J. and M. CASSON (1976), *The Future of Multinational Enterprise*, New York: Holmes and Meier.

BURTON, R.H. and A.J. KUHN (1979), 'Strategy Follows Structure: The Missing Link of their Intertwined Relation', Working Paper No. 260, Fuqua School of Business, Duke University.

CARY, W. (1969–70), 'Corporate Devices Used to Insulate Management from Attack', *Antitrust Law Journal*, 39(1), 318–24.

CAVES, R.E. (1980), 'Corporate Strategy and Structure', *Journal of Economic Literature*, 18(1), 64–92.

CHANDLER, A.D., JR. (1962; 1966), *Strategy and Structure: Chapters in the History of the Industrial Enterprise*, Cambridge, Mass.: MIT Press; Garden City, N.J.: Doubleday & Co.

—— (1977), *The Visible Hand: The Managerial Evolution in American Business*, Cambridge, Mass.: Belknap Press.

COASE, R.H. (1937), 'The Nature of the Firm', *Economica N.S.*, 4, 386–405; and in G.J. STIGLER and K.E. BOULDING (eds) (1952) *Readings in Price Theory*, Chicago: Richard D. Irwin for the American Economic Association.

—— (1972), 'Industrial Organization: A Proposal for Research', in VICTOR R. FUCHS (ed.), *Policy Issues and Research Opportunities in Industrial Organization: Economic Research Retrospect and Prospect*, New York: NBER; distributed by Columbia University Press, New York and London, 59–73.

COMMONS, JOHN R. (1934; 1951), *Institutional Economics: Its Place in Political Economy*, New York: Macmillan.

CYERT, RICHARD M. and CHARLES HEDRICK (1972), 'Theory of the Firm:

Past, Present, and Future: An Interpretation', *Journal of Economic Literature*, 10(2), 398–412.

DAVIS, LANCE E. and DOUGLASS C. NORTH (1971), *Institutional Change and American Economic Growth*, Cambridge: Cambridge University Press.

DOERINGER, P. and M. PIORE (1971), *Internal Labour Markets and Manpower Analysis*, Boston: D.C. Heath and Co.

DRUCKER, P. (1974), *Management: Tasks, Responsibilities, Practices*, New York: Harper & Row.

FISHLOW, ALBERT (1965), *American Railroads and the Transformation of the Antebellum Economy*, Cambridge, Mass.: Harvard University Press.

FOGEL, WILLIAM R. (1964), *Railroads and American Economic Growth: Essays in Econometric History*, Baltimore: Johns Hopkins University Press.

FRANKO, LAWRANCE G. (1972), 'The Growth, Organizational Efficiency of European Multinational Firms: Some Emerging Hypotheses', *Colloques International aux C.N.R.S.*, 335–66.

GOLDBERG, V.P. (1976), 'Regulation and Administered Contracts', *Bell Journal of Economics*, 7(2), 426–52.

HAYEK, F. (1945), 'The Use of Knowledge in Society', *American Economic Review*, 35, 519–30.

HEFLEBOWER, R.B. (1960), 'Observation on Decentralization in Large Enterprises', *Journal of Industrial Economics*, 9, 7–22.

HYMER, S. (1970), 'The Efficiency (Contradictions) of Multinational Corporations', *American Economic Review*, 60(2), 441–8.

JENSEN, M.C. and W.H. MECKLING (1976), 'Theory of the Firm: Managerial Behavior, Agency Costs and Ownership Structure', *Journal of Financial Economics*, 3(4), 305–60.

JOSKOW, PAUL L. and ALVIN K. KLEVORICK (1979), 'The Framework for Analyzing Predatory Pricing Policy', *Yale Law Journal*, 89, 213–70.

KLEIN, B., CRAWFORD, R.A. and A. ALCHIAN (1978), 'Vertical Integration, Appropriable Rents, and the Competitive Contracting Process', *Journal of Law and Economics*, 21(2), 297–326.

KNIGHT, FRANK H. (1921; 1965), *Risk, Uncertainty and Progress*, New York: Harper & Row.

KOONTZ, H. and C. O'DONNELL (1955), *Principles of Management: An Analysis of Managerial Function*, New York: McGraw-Hill.

LARSON, HENRIETTA M. (1948), *Guide to Business History: Materials for the Study of American Business History and Suggestions for their Use*, Cambridge, Mass.: Harvard University Press.

LIVESAY, H.C. (1979), *American Made: Men Who Shaped the American Economy*, First edition, Boston: Little, Brown.

MANSFIELD, E.; ROMEO, A. and S. WAGNER (1979), 'Foreign Trade and U.S. Research and Development', *Review of Economic and Statistics*, 61(1), 49–57.

MARRIS, R. (1964), *The Economic Theory of Managerial Capitalism*, New York: Free Press.

—— and MUELLER, D.C. (1980), 'The Corporation, Competition, and the Invisible Hand', *Journal of Economic Literature*, 18(1), 32–63.

MARSCHAK, J. and R. RADNER (1972), *Economic Theory of Teams*, New Haven: Yale University Press.

MASON, E.S. 'Introduction', in E.S. MASON (ed.) (1960), *The Corporation in Modern Society*, Cambridge, Mass.: Harvard University Press, 1–24.

NELSON, R.R. (1981), 'Assessing Private Enterprise: An Exegesis of Tangled Doctrine', *Bell Journal of Economics*, 12(1), 93–111.

—— and WINTER, S.G. (1981), *An Evolutionary Theory of Economic Behavior and Capabilities*, Cambridge, Mass.: Harvard University Press.

NORTH, D.C. (1978), 'Structure and Performance: The Task of Economic History', *Journal of Economic Literature*, 16(3), 963–78.

PANZAR, JOHN C. and ROBERT D. WILLIG (1981), 'Economies of Scope', *American Economic Review, Papers and Proceedings*, 71(2), 268–72.

POLANYI, M. (1962), *Personal Knowledge: Towards a Post-critical Philosophy*, New York: Harper & Row.

PORTER, G. and H.C. LIVESAY (1971), *Merchants and Manufacturers: Studies in the Changing Structure of Nineteenth Century Marketing*, Baltimore: Johns Hopkins University Press.

POSNER, R.A. (1979), 'The Chicago School of Antitrust Analysis', *University of Pennsylvania Law Review*, 127(4), 925–48.

RADNER, ROY (1968), 'Competitive Equilibrium Under Uncertainty', *Econometrica*, 36(1), 31–58.

SCHERER, F.M. (1980), *Industrial Market Structure and Economic Performance*, Second edition, Chicago: Rand McNally College Pub. Co.

SIMON, H.A. (1957a), *Models of Man: Social and Rational Mathematical Essays on Rational Human Behavior in a Social Setting*, New York: John Wiley and Sons.

SIMON, H.A. (1947; 1957b), *Administrative Behavior: A Study of Decision-making Processes in Administrative Organization*, Second edition, New York: Macmillan.

—— (1962), 'The Architecture of Complexity', *Proceedings of the American Philosophical Society*, 106(6), 467–82.

—— (1973), 'Applying Information Technology to Organization Design', *Public Administration Review*, 33(3), 268–78.

—— (1978), 'Rationality as Process and as Product of Thought', *American Economic Review*, 68(2), 1–16.

SLOAN, A.P., JR. (1963; 1965), *My Years with General Motors*, New York: MacFadden-Bartell.

SOBEL, R. (1974), *The Entrepreneurs: Explorations Within the American Business Tradition*, New York: Weybright and Talley.

STOPFORD, JOHN M. and LOUIS T. WELLS JR. (1972), *Managing the Multinational Enterprise: Organization of the Firm and Ownership of the Subsidiaries*, New York: Basic Books.

TEECE, D.J. (1977), 'Technology Transfer by Multinational Firms', *Economic Journal*, 87, 242–61.

—— (1980), 'Economies of Scope and the Scope of the Enterprise', *Journal of Economic Behavior and Organization*, 1(3), 223–45.

TEMIN, P. (1981), 'The Future of the New Economic History', *Journal of Interdisciplinary History*, 12(2), 179–97.

THOMPSON, JAMES D. (1967), *Organizations in Action: Social Science Bases of Administrative Theory*, New York: McGraw-Hill.

TSURUMI, Y. (1977), *Multinational Management: Business Strategy and Government Policy*, Cambridge, Mass.: Ballinger.

U.S. FEDERAL TRADE COMMISSION (1948), *Report of the Federal Trade Commission on the Merger Movement: A Summary Report*, Washington, DC: U.S. Government Printing Office.

VERNON, R. (1971), *Sovereignty at Bay: The Multinational Spread of U.S. Enterprises*, New York: Basic Books.

WILKINS, MIRA (1974), *The Maturing of Multinational Enterprise: American Business Abroad from 1914 to 1970*, Cambridge, Mass.: Harvard University Press.

WILLIAMSON, O.E. (1964), *The Economics of Discretionary Behavior: Managerial Objectives in a Theory of the Firm*, Englewood Cliffs, N.J.: Prentice-Hall.

—— (1970), *Corporate Control and Business Behavior*, Englewood Cliffs, N.J.: Prentice-Hall.

Williamson, O.E (1975), *Markets and Hierarchies: Analysis and Antitrust Implications: A Study in the Economics of Internal Organization*, New York: Free Press.

—— (1976), 'Franchise Bidding for Natural Monopolies—in General and with Respect to CATV', *Bell Journal of Economics*, 7(1), 73–104.

—— (1979), 'Transaction-Cost Economics: The Governance of Contractual Relations', *Journal of Law and Economics*, 22(2), 233–61.

—— (1979), 'On the Governance of the Modern Corporation', *Hofstra Law Review*, 8(1), 63–78.

—— (1980), 'Organizational Innovation: The Transaction-cost Approach', Discussion Paper No. 82, Center for the Study of Organizational Innovation, University of Pennsylvania.

—— (1981), 'Antitrust Enforcement: Where It's Been: Where It's Going', Discussion Paper No. 102, Center for the Study of Organizational Innovation, University of Pennsylvania.

Williamson, O.E. and D.J. Teece, 'European Economic and Political Integration: The Markets and Hierarchies Approach', in P. Salmon (ed.), *New Approaches to European Integration*.

Williamson, O.E., Michael L. Wachter and Jeffrey E. Harris (1975), 'Understanding the Employment Relation: The Analysis of Idiosyncratic Exchange', *Bell Journal of Economics*, Spring 1975, 6(1), 50–280.

STATIC OLIGOPOLY MODELS

Comparative Statics for Oligopoly*

Avinash K. Dixit

1. INTRODUCTION

Theories of oligopoly have a long and distinguished tradition. Comparative static analyses of oligopolistic equilibria, directed at specific applications, are a more recent undertaking, but a rapidly growing one. In public finance we have the tax incidence analysis of Seade (1983), Stern (1982), and Katz and Rosen (1983). In international trade, Brander and Spencer (1984), Dixit (1984), Eaton and Grossman (1983), Krugman (1984) and others have examined trade policies. In industrial organization, the effect of a committed capacity choice on a subsequent game in outputs or prices has been examined by Dixit (1980), Brander and Spencer (1983), Bulow, Geanakoplos and Klemperer (1983), Fudenberg and Tirole (1984), Eaton and Grossman (1984), and others.

Each of these papers starts from first principles, and derives conditions that determine the signs of various comparative static effects. From the totality of the work some general principles have emerged. Like the comparative statics of competitive agents and markets, second order conditions and stability conditions have important roles. But the analogy is not exact.

This paper aims for a consolidation of this work. It brings together the different strands, and highlights the general principles in a general model. This is a quantity-setting, conjectural variations oligopoly. It must be admitted at the outset that it is subject to some well-merited criticism. It depicts a static, simultaneous-move game, and concepts

* Research support from the National Science Foundation under grant SES-8308536 is gratefully acknowledged. I am also grateful to Gene Grossman for valuable discussions and comments, and a referee for suggesting useful improvements.

like reactions, conjectures, and their consistency have no real meaning. Stability conditions, which help us fix many signs in comparative statics, are equally without foundation. However, genuinely dynamic models that are equally versatile, and usable in applications, seem far off. In the meantime, the static conjectural variations model will go on being used, and it seems worthwhile to provide a unified treatment of it.

There are two points of particular merit about it. First, by specifying the conjectures appropriately, we can include many different and familiar models in the same formal framework. These include Cournot, Bertrand, and the case with consistent or rational conjectures. Second, the conjectural variations, treated as parameters, allow us to capture the idea of varying degrees of competition.

As for stability conditions, it might be claimed that the myopic adjustment process assumed is no worse than the tatonnement of competitive models. Be that as it may, I shall proceed to construct and use the model with no further apologies.

I shall consider two classes of models: duopoly with quite general demand functions, and homogeneous-product oligopoly. These include all the applications mentioned above. Oligopoly with general forms of product heterogeneity and conjectural variations does not yield useful general results, and each special case (e.g. the Hotelling and Losch models) is best left to be treated *sui generis*.

2. DUOPOLY

The two firms are labelled $i = 1$ and 2. Their inverse demand functions are $p^i\,(x_1, x_2)$. These satisfy the usual properties in partial equilibrium or industry analysis (with subscripts denoting partial derivatives):

$$\text{downward slopes } p^1_1 < 0, p^2_2 < 0, \tag{1}$$

$$\text{substitute products } p^1_2 < 0, p^2_1 < 0. \tag{2}$$

If the demands come from utility maximization, i.e. $p^i \equiv \partial U/\partial x_i$ where U is concave in (x_1, x_2), then we have two additional properties:

$$\text{Slutsky symmetry } p^1_2 = p^2_1, \tag{3}$$

$$\text{definiteness, } p^1_1\, p^2_2 - p^1_2\, p^2_1 \geq 0, \tag{4}$$

with equality in (4) if the products are perfect substitutes. The cost functions are $c^i(x_i)$, and the marginal costs are denoted by $c^i_x(x_i)$.

The profit of firm i is given by

$$\pi^i = p^i(x_1, x_2)\, x_i - c^i(x_i). \tag{5}$$

The partial derivative with respect to x_i is π^i_x. But this is not the marginal profit that is perceived by the firm. This is because firm i is assumed to believe that the other firm's output is linked to its own by the 'conjectural variation' relation

$$dx_j/dx_i = \upsilon^i(x_1, x_2), \qquad (j \neq i). \tag{6}$$

Using this when differentiating π^i, the perceived marginal profit is

$$\begin{aligned}\mu^i(x_1, x_2) = p^i(x_1, x_2) + x_i\, \{p^i_i(x_1, x_2) \\ + p^i_j(x_1, x_2)\, \upsilon^i(x_1, x_2)\} - c^i_x(x_i), \qquad (j \neq i).\end{aligned} \tag{7}$$

The concept of conjectural variations allows us to capture different kinds of equilibria in a unified model. Some examples, in order of increasing implied collusion in the outcome, are as follows.

Competitive: Here firm i conjectures that its own price p^i will remain unchanged as it changes x_i, i.e.

$$\upsilon^i(x_1, x_2) = -\, p^i_i/p^i_j \qquad (j \neq i) \tag{8}$$

using the implicit function theorem on $p^j(x_i, x_2) =$ constant.

Bertrand: Here firm i conjectures that the other firm's price p^j will remain unchanged as it changes x_i, i.e.

$$\upsilon^i(x_1, x_2) = -\, p^j_i/p^i_j \qquad (j \neq i)$$

using the implicit function theorem on $p^j(x_1, x_2) =$ constant.

Cournot: Here $\upsilon^i(x_1, x_2) = 0$.

Market-share: Here firm j conjectures that its change in x_i will encounter an equiproportionate response of x_j, i.e.

$$\upsilon^i(x_1, x_2) = x_j/x_i \qquad (j \neq i). \tag{9}$$

It can be verified that if Slutsky symmetry holds, then the equilibrium is collusive in that $(\pi^1 + \pi^2)$ is maximized; see Bramness (1979). Of course there may be further problems of agreeing and implementing side payments if the firms are not identical.

The case of consistent conjectures will be dealt with after 'reaction functions' have been defined. Given the firms' conjectural variations, the first-order conditions for profit maximization are obtained by setting the perceived marginal profits equal to zero, i.e.

$$\mu^i (x_1, x_2) = 0. \tag{10}$$

The second-order condition for firm 1 is

$$2p_1^1 + 2p_2^1\upsilon^1 + x_1 [p_{11}^1 + 2p_{12}^1\upsilon^1 + p_{22}^1 (\upsilon^1)^2] + x_1 p_2^1 (\upsilon_1^1 + \upsilon_2^1\upsilon^1) - c_{xx}^1 < 0.$$

where the arguments are omitted for brevity. It will be convenient to define

$$a_1 \equiv \mu_1^1 = 2p_1^1 + p_2^1\upsilon^1 + x_1 (p_{11}^1 + p_{12}^1\upsilon^1) + x_1 p_2^1\upsilon_1^1 - c_{xx}^1 \tag{11}$$

and

$$b_1 \equiv \mu_2^1 = p_2^1 + x_1 (p_{12}^1 + p_{22}^1\upsilon^1) + x_1 p_2^1\upsilon_2^1, \tag{12}$$

so that the second-order condition becomes $a_1 + \upsilon^1 b_1 < 0$. Similarly, for firm 2, let $a_2 \equiv \mu_2^2$ and $b_2 \equiv \mu_1^2$. Then the second-order conditions are

$$a_i + \upsilon^i b_i < 0. \tag{13}$$

The duopoly equilibrium is defined by the pair of first-order conditions in (10) for $i = 1$ and 2. Before introducing shift parameters in these and doing comparative statics, let us examine some useful properties of the equilibrium.

(i) *Stability:* The natural myopic adjustment process is one where each firm increases its output starting at a given point (x_1, x_2) if it perceives positive marginal profit from doing so. Thus

$$\dot{x}_i = s_i \mu^i (x_1, x_2), \tag{14}$$

where $s_i > 0$ are the adjustment speeds. Taking linear approximations around the equilibrium (x_1^*, x_2^*), we find

$$\begin{bmatrix} \dot{x}_1 \\ \dot{x}_2 \end{bmatrix} = \begin{bmatrix} s_1 a_1 & s_1 b_1 \\ s_2 b_2 & s_2 a_2 \end{bmatrix} \begin{bmatrix} x_1 - x_1^* \\ x_2 - x_2^* \end{bmatrix}.$$

For stability, the coefficient matrix should have eigenvalues with negative real parts. This is so if and only if its trace is negative and determinant positive, i.e.

$$s_1 a_1 + s_2 a_2 < 0, \quad s_1 s_2 (a_1 a_2 - b_1 b_2) > 0. \tag{15}$$

If this is to hold independently of adjustment speeds, we need

$$a_1 < 0, \quad a_2 < 0, \quad \Delta \equiv a_1 a_2 - b_1 b_2 > 0. \tag{16}$$

These will, henceforth, be referred to as the stability conditions. Note that in the Cournot case the second-order conditions become $a_i < 0$ and can be subsumed in the stability conditions. In other cases, the two differ.

Seade (1980, Appendix) sets up a somewhat different adjustment process (each $\dot{x}_i$ is proportional to the distance in the i direction between the current position and firm i's reaction function). He obtains stability conditions $|b_i/a_i| < 1$. These, together with $a_i < 0$, imply $\Delta > 0$, and so are closely related to the ones I shall use.

(ii) *'Reaction function'*: The first-order condition for firm 1, $\mu^1(x_1, x_2) = 0$, implicitly defines x_1 as a function of x_2, and is called firm 1's reaction function; similarly for firm 2. This is an inappropriate phrase in a simultaneous-move game. 'Firm 1 (resp. 2) equilibrium locus' would be better, but the tradition is too firmly set, and the advantage of brevity favours 'reaction function'.

The slope of firm 1's reaction function is given by

$$r_1 = -\mu^1_2/\mu^1_1 = -b_1/a_1, \tag{17}$$

and similarly for r_2.

Given the stability condition $a_i < 0$, the reaction function of firm i is downward sloping if and only if $b_i < 0$. From (12) we see that the products being substitutes ($p^i_j < 0$) is conducive to this property. But the other terms cannot be signed and there can be no general presumption in this regard.

If demand curves are linear, the second order derivatives of p^i vanish, and if conjectures are constant, the derivatives of υ^i vanish. Then $b_i = p^i_j < 0$. Both assumptions are often made, but are quite special.

In the Cournot model, $\upsilon^i = 0$ and $b_i = p^i_j + x_i p^i_{ij}$. The second term can still pose problems, but now there is a natural interpretation for

$b_i < 0$: an increase in x_j should lower firm i's true marginal revenue $p^i + x_i p^i_i$. This condition was assumed by Hahn (1962). Downward-sloping reaction functions are usually thought to be the 'normal' case in Cournot oligopoly.[1] Note that Seade's stability conditions can be written as $|r_i| < 1$.[2]

We are now in a position to define 'consistent conjectures'. The idea is that the slope of each firm's reaction function at the equilibrium point equals the conjectural variation entertained by the other firm. Since this is consistency to the first order, it is natural to assume that the conjectured reactions are linear. Thus one starts with constants υ^1 and υ^2, and checks for

$$r_1 = \upsilon^2 \quad \text{and} \quad r_2 = \upsilon^1. \tag{18}$$

If such is the case, the equilibrium has 'consistent conjectures'. This is a fixed point problem in (υ^1, υ^2), i.e. the υ^i are endogenous magnitudes to be determined as part of the equilibrium. Even if one does not take the story of verification of conjectures seriously, it turns out that the case where (18) is satisfied proves an important dividing line for many comparative static results.

In the consistent-conjectures case, the second-order condition for firm 1 becomes

$$\begin{aligned} 0 > a_1 + \upsilon^1 b_1 &= a_1 + r_2 b_1 \\ &= a_1 - (b_2/a_2) b_1 \\ &= (a_1 a_2 - b_1 b_2)/a_2 \end{aligned}$$

and similarly for firm 2. In this case, therefore, stability conditions imply second-order conditions. The case $\upsilon^2 = 0$ and $\upsilon^1 = r_2$ represents Stackelberg leadership by firm 1, and similarly the other way round. I shall leave the details of these to the readers.

At last we are ready for comparative statics. Let θ_i be a parameter in the expression (5) for firm i's profit. This can be a demand or cost shift, a tax or other policy instrument, or a prior-stage decision variable like capacity or advertising that affects this period's costs or demand. Each firm is given its own parameter to allow the

[1] See Bulow et al. (1983) for a counter argument.

[2] Seade has a homogeneous-product model. Otherwise, the units of measurement of different products can be chosen independently, and a unit-free bound like 1 cannot be obtained.

greatest width of interpretation: results for cases where a common parameter affects both firms are readily obtained from the general formulas.

Totally differentiating the first-order conditions (10), we have

$$\begin{bmatrix} a_1 & b_1 \\ b_2 & a_2 \end{bmatrix}\begin{bmatrix} dx_1 \\ dx_2 \end{bmatrix} = -\begin{bmatrix} \mu_\theta^1 & d\theta_1 \\ \mu_\theta^2 & d\theta_2 \end{bmatrix} \tag{19}$$

where μ_θ^i are the shifts in perceived marginal profits at given (x_1, x_2). These will have obvious forms and interpretations in specific applications; for example, a per unit tax θ_1 on the output of firm 1 will give $\mu_\theta^1 = -1$.

The solution to (19) is readily seen to be

$$\begin{bmatrix} dx_1 \\ dx_2 \end{bmatrix} = \frac{1}{\Delta}\begin{bmatrix} -a_2 & b_1 \\ b_2 & -a_1 \end{bmatrix}\begin{bmatrix} \mu_\theta^1 & d\theta_1 \\ \mu_\theta^2 & d\theta_2 \end{bmatrix}$$

$$= \frac{-1}{\Delta}\begin{bmatrix} a_2 & a_1 r_1 \\ a_2 r_2 & a_1 \end{bmatrix}\begin{bmatrix} \mu_\theta^1 & d\theta_1 \\ \mu_\theta^2 & d\theta_2 \end{bmatrix} \tag{20}$$

using the reaction function formulas (17). Once we have the effects on (x_1, x_2), we can easily compute those on prices and profits.

To examine these results more closely, consider the case where only firm 1's parameter shifts ($d\theta_2 = 0$), and the shift is *prime facie* favourable to firm 1 at the margin in that it shifts up its marginal profit ($\mu_\theta^1 d\theta_1 > 0$). Then

$$dx_1 = -a_2(\mu_\theta^1 d\theta_1)/\Delta,$$

i.e. stability conditions ensure that firm 1's output increases. Also

$$dx_2 = -a_2 r_2 (\mu_\theta^1 d\theta_1)/\Delta,$$

i.e. firm 2's output falls (resp. rises) if its reaction function is downward (resp. upward) sloping. In fact $dx_2 = r_2 dx_1$: there is no shift in firm 2's reaction function, and the equilibrium point must slide along it.

Turning to prices, we have

$$\begin{aligned} dp^1 &= p_1^1 dx_1 + p_2^1 dx_2 + p_\theta^1 d\theta_1 \\ &= -(p_1^1 + r_2 p_2^1)\, a_2 (\mu_\theta^1 d\theta_1)/\Delta + p_\theta^1 d\theta_1 \end{aligned}$$

and similarly

$$dp^2 = -(p_1^2 + r_2 p_2^2)\, a_2\, (\mu_\theta^1 d\theta_1)/\Delta.$$

Not much can be said about these. Since x_1 rises, and x_2 falls in many examples, there might be a presumption that p_1 falls (or more accurately, rises by less than any direct effect $p_\theta^1 d\theta_1$) and p_2 rises. A much weaker statement is true: we can rule out the joint occurance of $dp^1 > p_\theta^1 d\theta_1$ and $dp^2 < 0$. These would imply $(p_1^1 + r_2 p_2^1) > 0$ and $(p_1^2 + r_2 p_2^2) < 0$; then simple manipulations yield a contradiction of (4).

Finally, consider profits. Differentiating (5),

$$d\pi^1 = [p^1 + x_1 p_1^1 - c_x^1]\, dx_1 + x_1 p_2^1 dx_2 + \pi_\theta^1 d\theta_1.$$

Using (7) and (10), this becomes

$$d\pi^1 = -x_1 p_2^1 \upsilon^1 dx_1 + x_1 p_2^1 dx_2 + \pi_\theta^1 d\theta_1.$$

Substituting from (20), we obtain

$$d\pi^1 = x_1 p_2^1 a_2\, (\upsilon^1 - r_2)\, (\mu_\theta^1 d\theta_1)/\Delta + \pi_\theta^1 d\theta_1. \tag{21}$$

Similarly,

$$d\pi^2 = -x_2 p_1^2 a_2\, (1 - r_2 \upsilon^2)\, (\mu_\theta^1 d\theta_1)/\Delta. \tag{22}$$

The cross-effect is easy to determine. We have

$$1 - r_2 \upsilon^2 = 1 + (b_2/a_2)\upsilon^2 = (a_2 + b_2 \upsilon^2)/a_2$$

which is positive, since the numerator is negative by the second-order condition (13), and so is the denominator, by the stability condition (16). Then, with $p_1^2 < 0$, $a_2 < 0$, $\Delta > 0$ and $\mu_\theta^1 d\theta_1 > 0$, we have $d\pi^2 < 0$. Thus a shift favourable to one firm reduces the other's profit.

Next consider the effect of a change in θ_1 on the own profits π_1. This can be split into two parts: (i) the direct effect of the shift in the profit function itself, $\pi_\theta^1 d\theta_1$, and (ii) the indirect effect of the shift in the marginal profit, $\mu_\theta^1 d\theta_1$, which in turn changes the duopoly equilibrium. Many parametric shifts $d\theta_1$ will shift the total and the marginal profit functions in the same directions: taxes are the simplest example. But some parameters can shift the two in opposite directions. For example, if θ_1 represents sunk capital, then an increase in it always lowers marginal cost, but can raise total cost if there is already too much capital relative to the long-run cost minimizing level.

More interesting is the question of whether the first term in (21), which is indirect effect acting via output changes, augments or counteracts the direct effect. There is an obvious case where it does neither, namely when $\upsilon^1 = r_2$, i.e. firm 1's conjecture is consistent. In other prominent cases, we have to compute it explicitly. The sign of the indirect effect is the same as that of $(\upsilon^1 - r_2)$.

The Cournot model corresponds to $\upsilon^1 = 0$. In the 'normal' case of a downward-sloping reaction function ($r_2 < 0$), therefore, the indirect effect adds to firm 1's profit.

The calculation for the Bertrand model is messy, and I shall omit it to save space. But the result has a natural interpretation: if the reaction function of firm 2 plotted in the price space is upward-sloping (the presumed normal case), then the indirect effect subtracts from firm 1's profit. For details see Eaton and Grossman (1983). The competitive case yields clearer results. Using the relevant definition (8) in the expressions for a_2 and b_2 and simplifying, we find

$$a_2 = p_2^2 - c_{xx}^2, \; b_2 = p_1^2$$

and

$$a_2 + \upsilon^2 b_2 = -c_{xx}^2.$$

Therefore, firm 2's second-order condition is $c_{xx}^2 > 0$, which in turn ensures the part $a_2 < 0$ of the stability condition. Then $r_2 < 0$, and

$$\upsilon^1 - r_2 = -p_1^1/p_2^1 + p_1^2/(p_2^2 - c_{xx}^2)$$
$$= \frac{-(p_1^1 p_2^2 - p_2^1 p_1^2) + p_1^1 c_{xx}^2}{p_2^1 (p_2^2 - c_{xx}^2)}$$

which is negative given the various conditions on demand (1)–(4), and the second-order condition. Thus in the competitive case the indirect effect of a *prima facie* favourable shift lowers the firm's profit.

Finally, consider the case of market-share maintenance conjectures (9). Substituting and simplifying, we find

$$a_2 = 2p_2^2 + x_2 p_{22}^2 + x_1 p_{21}^2 - c_{xx}^2$$

and

$$b_2 = 2p^2_1 + x_2 p^2_{12} + x_1 p^2_{11}.$$

As with Cournot, the 'normal' case is $b_2 < 0$ and hence $r_2 < 0$. Then $\upsilon^1 - r_2 > 0$ since $\upsilon^1 = x_2/x_1 > 0$. But the second-order derivatives p^2_{11} and p^2_{12} can upset this result. A more precise result can be found in the homogeneous-product case, where

$$p^1(x_1, x_2) = p^2(x_1, x_2) = \phi(x_1 + x_2)$$

for some decreasing function ϕ. Then, writing $X = x_1 + x_2$, we find

$$\begin{aligned} b_2 &= 2\phi'(X) + X\phi''(X) \\ &= \phi'(X)\{2 + X\phi''(X)/\phi'(X)\}, \end{aligned}$$

and $b_2 < 0$ if and only if the industry marginal revenue is declining. The condition can be written as $E \equiv -X\phi''/\phi' < 2$. This elasticity appears in different contexts in Seade (1983), and Perry (1982).

These indirect effects play an important role in many two-stage duopoly games. As an example, let the parameters θ_1 and θ_2 represent the capital stocks of the two firms. Their values are to be chosen (irrevocably) first, and the output game is to be played later. The capital stocks will be chosen at levels where their perceived marginal contribution to profits equals the cost of capital. The usual assumption of subgame perfectness says that in making this calculation the firms look ahead rationally to be outcome of the output game, i.e. include both indirect and direct effects. If the firms were not so strategic, or if capital and output decisions were made simultaneously, only the direct effect would count. Thus the indirect effect constitutes the difference between strategic and non-strategic capital choice. If the indirect effect is positive, each firm will have the incentive to push its capital stock to a larger level in the strategic context than in the non-strategic one. Thus we see that the comparison depends crucially on the kind of equilibrium we specify for the output game. In the 'normal' case of downward-sloping reaction functions in Cournot or market-share games, there is overinvestment in the strategic context; with Bertrand there is underinvestment: with consistent conjectures there is no difference. For details see Bulow et al. (1983) and Fudenberg and Tirole (1984). The same insight was developed independently in the context of trade policy by Eaton and Grossman (1983), and they discovered the role of the term $(\upsilon^1 - r_2)$.

The indirect effects also raise the possibility that a prima facie unfavourable change proves to be profitable in the final analysis. As an illustrative example, consider the case of a vertical upward shift in the marginal costs of both firms, e.g. a per unit tax or selling expense. Here $d\theta_1 = d\theta_2 = d\theta$, $\mu^1_\theta = \mu^2_\theta = -1$, and $\pi^i_\theta = -x_i$. The formulas (21) and (22) must be modified by bringing in the $d\theta_2$ effects, but this is readily done. For algebraic simplicity consider the consistent conjectures case. Then

$$d\pi^1 = -x_1 d\theta + x_1 p^1_2 a_1 (1 - r_1 \upsilon^2) d\theta/\Delta$$

and

$$1 - r_1\upsilon^2 = 1 - r_1 r_2 = (a_1 a_2 - b_1 b_2)/(a_1 a_2).$$

Therefore,

$$d\pi^1 = (p^1_2/a_2 - 1)x_1 d\theta$$

and $d\pi^1 > 0$ if $p^1_2/a_2 > 1$, i.e. $p^1_2 > a_2$. This is compatible with the second-order and stability conditions. We can even have $d\pi^2 > 0$ at the same time.

Thus a tax, or an increase in costs, can benefit one or both of the firms. The conditions are examined in greater detail by Seade (1983). The possibility now arises that one firm, or both, may strive to raise costs; the implications for industrial organization are examined by Salop and Scheffman (1983) in the case of leadership by a dominant firm. The intuition is that the cost increase leads to a new equilibrium in which the firms produce less and charge higher prices, i.e. the outcome is more collusive. The benefit from this can outweigh the direct effect of the higher cost.

I hope these examples adequately illustrate the general formulas like (20) (22), and the role of second-order and stability conditions in fixing many comparative static signs. There are two important magnitudes whose signs depend on the curvature of demand and on the precise specification of conduct: (i) the actual slopes of the reaction functions, and (ii) the differences between conjectured and actual slopes.

3. OLIGOPOLY

Here we have n firms, indexed $i = 1, 2 \ldots n$. Their outputs are denoted by x_i, with

$$X = \sum_{i=1}^{n} x_i, \quad y_i = X - x_i = \sum_{j \neq i} x_j. \tag{23}$$

There is no product heterogeneity, and the industry inverse demand function is

$$p = \phi(X), \quad \phi' < 0. \tag{24}$$

The cost functions are $c^i(x_i)$, and the marginal costs are written as c^i_x.

The profit of firm i is given by

$$\pi^i = \phi(X)x_i - c^i(x_i). \tag{25}$$

Each firm is assumed to have a conjectural variation relating the output y_i of the rest of the industry to its own x_i. This variation can in principle be a function of the whole vector $x = (x_1, x_2, \ldots, x_n)$ of the firms' outputs, but I shall assume that it depends only on the pair of numbers (x_i, y_i). This is sufficient to handle all the usual equilibrium concepts. Thus the conjectural variations can be written

$$dy_i / dx_i = \upsilon^i(x_i, y_i) \tag{26}$$

with partial derivatives υ^i_x and υ^i_y. With this notation, the perceived marginal profit of firm i is

$$\begin{aligned} \mu^i(x_i, y_i) = {} & \phi(x_i + y_i) \\ & + x_i\phi'(x_i + y_i)\,\{1 + \upsilon^i(x_i, y_i)\} - c^i_x(x_i), \end{aligned} \tag{27}$$

with partial derivatives μ^i_x and μ^i_y.

Once again we can show some commonly used models as special cases. Cournot is of course the case $\upsilon^i = 0$, Bertrand as well as competitive conjectures become

$$\upsilon^i = -1, \tag{28}$$

while the case of market-share collusion is

$$\upsilon^i(x_i, y_i) = y_i/x_i. \tag{29}$$

The equilibrium values of the x_i are defined by the n first-order conditions

$$\mu^i(x_i, y_i) = 0. \tag{30}$$

The second-order conditions are[3]

$$2\phi'(1+\upsilon^i) + x_i\phi''(1+\upsilon^i)^2 + x_i\phi'(\upsilon^i_x + \upsilon^i\upsilon^i_y) < 0,$$

again omitting the arguments for brevity. Defining

$$a_i \equiv \mu^i_x = \phi'(2+\upsilon^i) + x_i\phi''(1+\upsilon^i) + x_i\phi'\upsilon^i_x - c^i_{xx}, \tag{31}$$

and

$$b_i \equiv \mu^i_y = \phi' + x_i\phi''(1+\upsilon^i) + x_i\phi'\upsilon^i_y, \tag{32}$$

they can be written as

$$a_i + \upsilon^i b_i < 0. \tag{33}$$

As in the case of duopoly, let us consider stability and reaction functions before embarking on comparative statics.

(i) *Stability:* The myopic adjustment process, where each firm increases its output if it perceives positive marginal profit from this action, is defined by the differential equations

$$\dot{x}_1 = s_i\,\mu^i(x_i, y_i), \tag{34}$$

where $s_i > 0$ are the adjustment speeds. Linearizing around the equilibrium point $x^* = (x_1^*, x_2^*, \ldots, x_n^*)$, we have

$$\begin{bmatrix} \dot{x}_1 \\ \dot{x}_2 \\ \dot{x}_n \end{bmatrix} = \begin{bmatrix} s_1a_1 & s_1b_1 \ldots s_1b_1 \\ s_2b_2 & s_2a_2 \ldots s_2b_2 \\ s_nb_n & s_nb_n \ldots s_na_n \end{bmatrix} \begin{bmatrix} x_1 - x_1^* \\ x_2 - x_2^* \\ x_n - x_n^* \end{bmatrix}. \tag{35}$$

For stability, all eigenvalues of the coefficient matrix should have

[3] These are sufficient conditions; the corresponding necessary conditions have weak inequalities. This distinction will become important at a later point.

negative real parts. Unlike the duopoly case, necessary *and* sufficient conditions for this property are hard to find or interpret. Therefore we have to consider necessary conditions and sufficient conditions separately.

One necessary condition is that the sum of the eigenvalues be negative. This is the trace of the coefficient matrix, so

$$s_1 a_1 + s_2 a_2 + \ldots + s_n a_n < 0.$$

If this is to be true for all adjustment speeds, we have a necessary condition

$$a_i < 0 \tag{36–i}$$

for all i. Another necessary condition is that the product of the roots should have the same sign as $(-1)^n$. This product is just the determinant of the coefficient matrix. The special structure of the matrix allows us to compute the determinant as

$$\left\{ \prod_{i=1}^{n} [s_i(a_i - b_i)] \right\} \left\{ 1 + \sum_{i=1}^{n} b_i/(a_i - b_i) \right\};$$

see Seade (1983). Therefore our necessary condition is

$$(-1)^n \left\{ \prod_{i=1}^{n} (a_i - b_i) \right\} \left\{ 1 + \sum_{i=1}^{n} b_i/(a_i - b_i) \right\} > 0. \tag{36–ii}$$

The simplest set of sufficient conditions is obtained by requiring diagonal dominance in the coefficient matrix, i.e.

$$|a_i| > (n-1)\,|b_i|$$

for all i. In conjunction with the necessary condition (36–i), this can be written

$$a_i \pm (n-1) b_i < 0 \tag{36–iii}$$

for all i. In turn, (36–iii) implies

$$a_i - b_i < 0 \tag{36–iv}$$

for all i. To see this, consider cases of positive and negative b_i separately. If $b_i > 0$, we have

$$a_i - b_i < -nb_i < 0,$$

while if $b_i < 0$, then

$$(n-1)(a_i - b_i) < (n-1)a_i - a_i = (n-2)a_i \leq 0.$$

Given (36–iv), we can write (36–ii) as

$$\Gamma = 1 + \sum_{i=1}^{n} b_i/(a_i - b_i) > 0. \qquad (36\text{–v})$$

I shall refer to (36–i, ii, iii, iv, v) collectively as stability conditions, but shall state in each instance which part is being invoked.

Incidentally, $b_i < 0$ means that the perceived marginal revenue of firm i falls as the output of any of the other firms increases. This might be called a generalized Hahn condition.

(ii) *Reaction functions:* The first-order conditions for all firms other than i, namely $\mu^j(x_j, y_j) = 0$ for all $j \neq i$, implicitly define their outputs x_j as functions of x_i. Call these the reaction functions facing firm i.[4] Finding their slopes amounts to solving a comparative statics problem for these firms, treating x_i as a parameter. Total differentiation gives

$$a_j dx_j + b_j dy_j = 0,$$

or

$$(a_j - b_j)dx_j + b_j dX = 0.$$

Dividing by $(a_j - b_j)$ and adding over $j \neq i$,

$$dy_i + \left\{\sum_{j \neq i} b_j/(a_j - b_j)\right\} dX = 0.$$

This gives us the slope of the aggregate reaction function from the rest of the industry facing firm i:

$$R_i \equiv dy_i/dx_i = -B_i/(1 + B_i) \qquad (37)$$

where

$$B_i = \sum_{j \neq i} b_j/(a_j - b_j).$$

[4] This is Perry's (1982) definition, and it 'rationalizes the full equilibrium response of the rest of the industry'.

Now observe that

$$1+B_i=\frac{1}{n}+\sum_{j\neq i}\left\{\frac{1}{n}+\frac{b_j}{a_j-b_j}\right\}$$

$$=\frac{1}{n}+\sum_{j\neq i}\frac{a_j+(n-1)b_j}{a_j-b_j}$$

$$>1/n>0$$

given the stability conditions (36–iii). But $1+R_i=1/(1+B_i)$, so we have $n>(1+R_i)>0$, i.e. $-1<R_i<(n-1)$.

The sign of R_i depends on that of B_i. If the generalized Hahn condition is assumed to hold for all firms $j\neq i$, and the stability condition (36–iv) is invoked, we get $B_i>0$, i.e. $R_i<0$.

A consistent-conjectures equilibrium is characterized by constants υ^i such that

$$R_i=\upsilon^i \tag{38}$$

for all i. Perry (1982) examines the properties of such an equilibrium in the symmetric case where all firms have identical cost functions and conjectures. He finds that if marginal costs are constant, then Bertrand conjectures are consistent. This can be verified in the above framework if some care is exercised. With $\upsilon^i=-1$, (31) and (32) become $a_i=b_i=\phi'$. Then the second-order conditions (33) and the stability conditions (36–iv) only hold as weak inequalities. Also, division by (a_i-b_i) is not permissible. But we can take a more direct approach. Treating x_i as a parameter and differentiating the first-order condition for any firm $j\neq i$, we get $a_jdx_j+b_jdy_j=0$, i.e. $dX=dx_j+dy_j=0$. Then $dx_i+dy_i=0$, i.e. $R_i=dy_i/dx_i=-1$.

Turning to comparative statics, let us introduce parameters θ_i in the first-order conditions, and differentiate totally. We have

$$a_idx_i+b_idy_i=-\mu_\theta^1 d\theta_i \tag{39–i}$$

for all i, or in matrix form

$$\begin{bmatrix} a_1 & b_1 & \ldots & b_1 \\ b_2 & a_2 & \ldots & b_2 \\ b_n & b_n & \ldots & a_n \end{bmatrix}\begin{bmatrix} dx_1 \\ dx_2 \\ dx_n \end{bmatrix}=-\begin{bmatrix} \mu_\theta^1 \; d\theta_1 \\ \mu_\theta^2 \; d\theta_2 \\ \mu_\theta^n \; d\theta_n \end{bmatrix} \tag{39–ii}$$

The matrix can be inverted in closed form; see Maddala (1977, p. 446) and Seade (1983). In fact the special structure enables us to work directly from (39–i), in a way similar to that used above in deriving the reaction function slopes R_i.

However, the matrix form is useful in clarifying why I did not think it worth-while to examine oligopoly with a general form of product heterogeneity. Had I done so, the μ^i would have to be functions of the whole vector x. In each row the off-diagonal elements would all be different, and the matrix would be just the general n-by-n matrix. No structure could be imposed on its inverse, and no meaningful results could emerge. Progress can only be made by looking at particular forms of product heterogeneity, and using the resulting special structures of the coefficient matrix.

If product heterogeneity is symmetric in the sense that we can write $p^i = p^i(x_i, y_i)$, then the above formalism goes through with slight reinterpretations of a_i and b_i. To solve the homogeneous-product case write (39–i) as

$$(a_i - b_i)dx_i + b_i dX = -\mu^i_\theta d\theta_i,$$

or

$$dx_i + b_i dX/(a_i - b_i) = -\mu^i_\theta d\theta_i/(a_i - b_i).$$

Summing over i,

$$dX + \left\{\sum_{i=j}^{n} b_i/(a_i - b_i)\right\} dX = -\sum_{i=1}^{n} \mu^i_\theta d\theta_i/(a_i - b_i)$$

or

$$dX = -(1/\Gamma)\sum_{i=1}^{n} \mu^i_\theta d\theta_i/(a_i - b_i). \tag{40}$$

Substituting back

$$dx_i = -\frac{\mu^i_\theta d\theta_i}{a_i - b_i} + \frac{b_i}{\Gamma(a_i - b_i)}\sum_{j=1}^{n}\frac{\mu^j_\theta d\theta_j}{a_j - b_j}. \tag{41}$$

In terms of partial derivatives,

$$\frac{\partial X}{\partial \theta_i} = -\frac{1}{\Gamma}\frac{\mu^i_\theta d\theta_i}{a_i - b_i}, \tag{41–i}$$

$$\frac{\partial x_i}{\partial \theta_i} = -\frac{\mu^i_\theta d\theta_i}{a_i - b_i}\left\{1 - \frac{b_i/(a_i - b_i)}{\Gamma}\right\}, \tag{41–ii}$$

and for $j \neq i$,

$$\frac{\partial x_i}{\partial \theta_j} = \frac{b_i}{\Gamma(a_i - b_i)} \frac{\mu^j_\theta d\theta_j}{a_j - b_j}. \tag{41–iii}$$

To interpret these, consider a shift that is prima facie favourable to firm i, i.e. $\mu^i_\theta d\theta_i > 0$, with $d\theta_j = 0$ for all $j \neq i$. If the stability conditions (36–iii) and (36–v) are assumed, such a shift will (a) raise x_i, (b) raise X, (c) lower or raise x_j for $j \neq i$ according as b_j is negative or positive. Only (a) needs proof. Note that

$$\Gamma - b_i/(a_i - b_i) = 1 + \sum_{j \neq i} b_j/(a_j - b_j)$$
$$> 1/n > 0$$

using the earlier argument in connection with reaction functions. Then (41–ii) gives the result.

Effects on prices are immediate, since $dp = \phi' dX + \phi_\theta d\theta_i$. Turning to profits, we have

$$\begin{aligned} d\pi_i &= (p - x_i\phi' - c^i_x)dx_i + x_i\phi' dy_i + \pi^i_\theta d\theta_i \\ &= -x_i\phi'\upsilon^i dx_i + x_i\phi' dy_i + \pi^i_\theta d\theta_i. \end{aligned}$$

If $d\theta_j = 0$ for $j \neq i$, the first-order conditions for the other firms do not shift. The equilibrium moves along their reaction functions, and $dy_i = R_i dx_i$. Thus

$$\partial\pi_i/\partial\theta_i = x_i\phi'(R_i - \upsilon^i)\partial x_i/\partial\theta_i + \pi^i_\theta. \tag{42}$$

As in the duopoly case, we have a direct effect and an indirect effect. Taking $\partial x_i/\partial\theta_i > 0$, the sign of the indirect effect is the same as that of $(\upsilon^i - R_i)$. Proceeding as before, there are various cases to consider, for example

Bertrand or competitive: $\upsilon^i = -1$, $R_i > -1$, so $\upsilon^i - R_i < 0$
Consistent conjectures: $\upsilon^i - R_i = 0$
Cournot: $\upsilon^i = 0$, and in the 'normal' case (with the Hahn condition)

$$R_i < 0, \text{ so } \upsilon^i - R_i > 0.$$

If $d\theta_j > 0$ for some $j \neq i$, while all the other firms' parameters do not change, then

$$d\pi_i = x_i\phi' \{-\upsilon_i dx_i + dy_i\}$$
$$= x_i\phi' \{-(1+\upsilon_i)dx_i + dX\}.$$

Substituting and simplifying, we have

$$d\pi_i = -\frac{x_i\phi'}{\Gamma}\frac{a_i + \upsilon^i b_i}{a_i - b_i}\frac{\mu^i_\theta d\theta_j}{a_j - b_j}. \tag{43}$$

Given the second-order condition (33), and the stability conditions (36–iii, v), we have the result that a shift that is prima facie favourable to firm j ($\mu^j_\theta\, d\theta_j > 0$) lowers the profits of all firms $i \neq j$.

Once again, a cost increase common to all firms can, by making the equilibrium more collusive, raise the profits of all firms. In the case with constant marginal costs and constant υ_i, and with full symmetry across firms, the condition is simply $E > 2$; see Seade (1983) for details.

4. CONCLUDING COMMENT

Comparative statics of oligopoly is seen to be governed by the same general principles and techniques as the more familiar competitive model. I hope the readers will be encouraged to apply these methods to particular problems, and develop interesting cases of product heterogeneity along similar systematic lines.

REFERENCES

Bramness, G. (1979), 'The General Conjectural Model of Duopoly—Some Classical Points Revisited', Warwick Economic Research Paper No. 142.

Brander, J.A. and B.J. Spencer (1983), 'Strategic Commitment with R & D: The Symmetric Case', *Bell Journal of Economics*, 14, 225–35.

—— (1984), 'Tariff Protection and Imperfect Competition', 194–206, in H. Kierzkowski (ed.), *Monopolistic Competition in International Trade*, Oxford: Oxford University Press.

BULOW, J.I., J.D. GEANAKOPLOS and P.D. KLEMPERER (1983), 'Multimarket Oligopoly: Strategic Substitutes and Complements', Working Paper, Stanford Graduate School of Business.

DIXIT, A.K. (1980), 'The Role of Investment in Entry Deterrence', *Economic Journal*, 90, 95–106.

—— (1984), 'International Trade Policy for Oligopolistic Industries', *Economic Journal*, 94, Supplement, 1–16.

EATON, J. and G.M. GROSSMAN (1983), 'Optimal Trade and Industrial Policy under Oligopoly', Discussion Paper No. 59, Woodrow Wilson School, University of Princeton.

—— (1984), 'Strategic Capacity Investment and Product Market Competition', Discussion Paper No. 80, Woodrow Wilson School, University of Princeton.

FUDENBERG, D. and J. TIROLE (1984), 'The Fat-Cat Effect, the Puppy Dog Ploy, and the Lean and Hungry Look', *American Economic Review, Papers and Proceedings*, 74, 361–6.

HAHN, F.H. (1962), 'The Stability of the Cournot Oligopoly Solution', *Review of Economic Studies*, 29, 329–31.

KATZ, M.L. and H.S. ROSEN (1983), 'Tax Analysis in an Oligopoly Model', NBER Working Paper No. 1088.

KRUGMAN, P.R. (1984), 'Import Protection as Export Promotion', 180–93, in H. Kierzkowski (ed.), *Monopolistic Competition in International Trade*, Oxford: Oxford University Press.

MADDALA, G.S. (1977), *Econometrics*, McGraw-Hill, New York.

PERRY, M.K. (1982), 'Oligopoly and Consistent Conjectural Variations', *Bell Journal of Economics*, 13, 197–205.

SALOP, S.C. and D.T. SCHEFFMAN (1983), 'Raising Rivals' Costs', *American Economic Review, Papers and Proceedings*, 73, 267–71.

SEADE, J.K. (1980), 'The Stability of Cournot Revisited', *Journal of Economic Theory*, 15, 15–27.

—— (1983), 'Price, Profits and Taxes in Oligopoly', Working Paper, University of Warwick.

STERN, N.H. (1982), 'Market Structure, Dual Pricing, and Taxes', DERC Discussion Paper No. 13, University of Warwick.

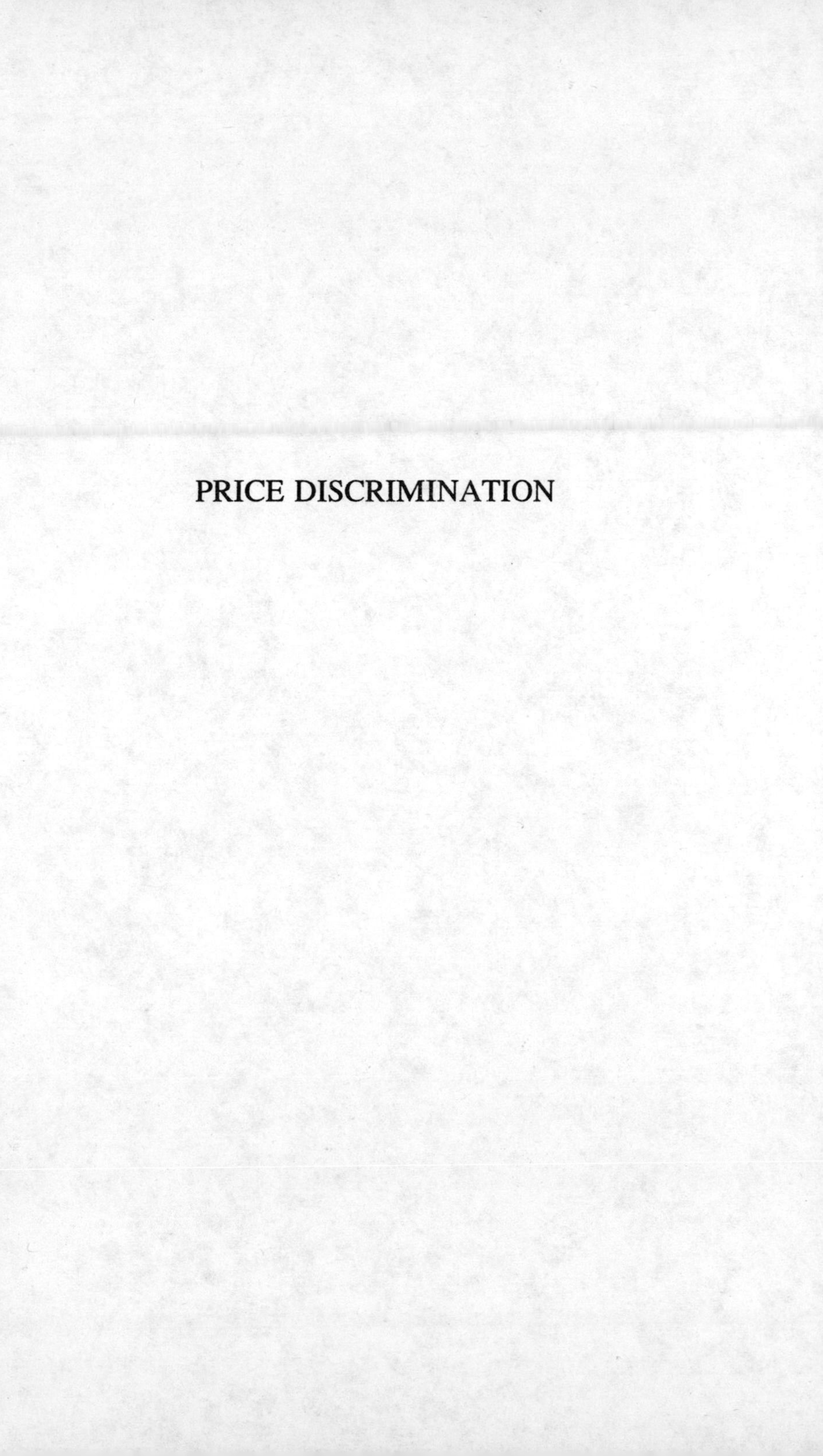

PRICE DISCRIMINATION

Monopoly with Incomplete Information*

ERIC MASKIN AND JOHN RILEY

1. INTRODUCTION

In the last few years much theoretical work has considered incentive schemes (or 'principal-agent' relationships) where the parties involved are constrained either by asymmetric information or by their inability to monitor each other's actions. In this article we concentrate on the former constraint, known in the literature as 'adverse selection', rather than on the latter, often called 'moral hazard'.

We show that a variety of issues can be viewed formally as members of a single family of principal-agent problems. In this article we consider in detail: (i) price discrimination via quantity discounts (Goldman, Leland, and Sibley, 1980; Oi, 1971; Roberts, 1979; Spence, 1977)[1] and (ii) monopoly pricing of products of differing quality (Mussa and Rosen, 1978). In a companion piece, Maskin and Riley (1983a), we study (iii) the choice of an auction for selling a fixed number of identical items. (See Harris and Raviv (1981), Maskin and Riley (1980, 1984), Milgrom and Weber (1982), Myerson (1981), and Riley and Samuelson (1981), as well as the seminal paper by Vickrey (1961).)

* The helpful comments of the participants in numerous workshops and, in particular, of David Kreps, David Levine, Paul Milgrom, and Roger Myerson are gratefully acknowledged. This research was supported by the National Science Foundation, the U.K. Social Science Research Council, and the Sloan Foundation.

[1] There is also a much earlier literature which recognizes the potential gains to differential unit pricing for different sized purchases. Pigou (1930), for example, discusses 'block pricing'. He does not, however, consider its role as a screening mechanism in the absence of complete information. Instead he views it as an approximation to perfect ('first-degree') price discrimination.

For each of these problems, the central issue is how to construct a sorting mechanism to extract the greatest possible private gain. Our main contribution is to show that, under a separability assumption, we can draw strong conclusions about the nature of optimal incentive schemes. Our results also shed new light on a wide range of closely related topics. These include the theory of optimal income taxation (Mirrlees, 1971), the monopoly pricing of insurance (Stiglitz, 1977), the monopoly provision of excludable public goods (Brito and Oakland, 1980), multiproduct monopoly pricing (Mirman and Sibley, 1980), the regulation of a producer with unknown costs (Baron and Myerson, 1982), and monopoly pricing of a product line (Oren, Smith, and Wilson, 1984).

In the following section, we begin with a heuristic discussion of the issues involved for the simplest application: nonlinear pricing. Then, in Sec. 3 we examine the self-selection constraints that the monopolist faces and show that the choice of an optimal selling procedure reduces to a tractable variational problem. In Sec. 4 we present the fundamental characterization theorem for the optimal selling strategy of the monopolist. Using this result, we are able to show that, in a broad class of cases, the optimal selling strategy involves pricing larger quantities at successively lower unit prices; that is, using quantity discounts. We also provide a strong result on the effect of a change in the distribution of preferences on the profit-maximizing quantity discount scheme.

Finally, in Sec. 5, we extend the Mussa and Rosen (1978) analysis of the pricing of quality to preferences that are defined over both quality and quantity. In this case a seller's optimal strategy is to sell multiple units in bundles. Higher quality units are sold in packages of a different size from those of lower quality units. For a simple parameterization of preferences, we provide a complete characterization of the optimal bundling strategy. We conclude in Sect. 6 with a discussion of further applications of the theory and with some comments on the central assumptions.

2. DESCRIPTION OF THE PROBLEM

To introduce the general principles involved we focus on the simplest application—the use of a nonlinear price schedule to discriminate among customers. A monopolist produces a single product at constant marginal cost, c. A buyer of type i has preferences represented by the utility function[2]

$$U_i\,(q, -T) = \int_0^q p\,(x; \upsilon_i)dx - T, \tag{1}$$

where q is the number of units purchased from the monopolist and T is total spending on these units. That is, we take the standard consumer surplus approach and assume that differences in tastes are captured by the single parameter υ. The seller does not observe υ, but knows $F(\upsilon)$, the distribution of buyers' preferences.[3] Throughout we shall assume that higher levels of υ are associated with a higher demand. We also assume that the demand price $p\,(q; \upsilon)$ is decreasing in q and that there is some maximum quantity $q^e\,(\upsilon)$ for which demand price exceeds marginal cost. For each υ, $q^e\,(\upsilon)$ is thus the efficient consumption level.

To be precise we impose the following restrictions.

Assumption 1. (i) For all feasible υ the demand price function $p\,(q; \upsilon)$ is nonincreasing in q and nonnegative, and there exists $q^e(\upsilon) \geq 0$ such that $p\,(q; \upsilon)$ is decreasing in q for $q \leq q^e\,(\upsilon)$, and $p\,(q; \upsilon) \geq c$ if and only if $q \leq q^e\,(\upsilon)$. (ii) $p\,(q; \upsilon)$ is twice continuously differentiable for $q \leq q^e\,(\upsilon)$. (iii) $p\,(q; \upsilon)$ is strictly increasing in υ whenever $p\,(q; \upsilon)$ is positive.

A selling procedure is then a schedule of pairs $\langle \hat{q}_s, \hat{T}_s \rangle_{s \in S}$, which

[2] Thus we exclude income effects. Notice that we do not rule out the possibility that differences in income *across* consumers may account for differences in demand; such effects can be embodied in the parameter υ_i. What we are assuming, in effect, is that the proportion of any *single* consumer's income spent on the good in question is so small that variations in p have a negligible effect on income.

[3] Throughout this section, we shall interpret $F\,(\upsilon)$ to be the underlying probability distribution from which the parameters of a population of buyers are drawn independently. Therefore, in considering expected seller profit, we are assuming risk neutrality on the part of the seller. Alternatively we could think of $F\,(\upsilon)$ as the actual—i.e. the realized—distribution of the υ's. The analysis would remain unchanged except that profit-maximization would replace expected-profit-maximization. Actually, there is a slight difficulty with the latter (traditional) interpretation of $F\,(\upsilon)$. If all buyers but one revealed their υ's through their purchasing behaviour, the seller could infer the parameter value of the remaining buyer without observing it directly. This problem arises, however, only if the seller knows the actual distribution *exactly*, which seems improbable in practice.

the seller offers to the buyers. If a buyer chooses s, he receives $\hat{q}_s$ and pays a total of $\hat{T}_s$. The profit or 'return' to the seller is then

$$\hat{R}_s = \hat{T}_s - c\hat{q}_s. \qquad (2)$$

Throughout we shall assume that any selling procedure includes the pair $\langle 0, 0 \rangle$, that is, the buyer always has the option of buying (and paying) nothing.

Combining (1) and (2), we can rewrite the utility of a buyer of type i as

$$U(q, R; \upsilon_i) = \int_0^q p(x; \upsilon_i)\,dx - cq - R \equiv N(q; \upsilon_i) - R, \qquad (3)$$

where $N(q; \upsilon_i)$ is the social surplus generated by the sale. Thus, we can think of the trades between the seller (the 'principal') and buyers ('agents') as giving each buyer the entire surplus less a fee R. The selling procedure is then a schedule of pairs $\langle q_s, R_s \rangle_{s \in S}$ offered to each of the buyers. This latter formulation proves more convenient.[4]

Before considering the choice of a selling procedure, we note that our formulation can be reinterpreted, without modification, as the choice of an optimal piece-rate schedule. Let $C(q; \upsilon_i)$ be the opportunity cost to a worker of type υ_i of producing q units for a potential employer with some monopsony power. Suppose that the employer (the principal) knows the distribution of υ_i but cannot observe υ_i directly. If m is the value of each unit of output to the employer and the worker is offered a payment Ω for q units, the net gain to the worker is

$$U(q, \Omega; \upsilon_i) = \Omega - C(q; \upsilon_i), \qquad (4)$$

whereas the employer's return is

$$R = mq - \Omega. \qquad (5)$$

As before, we define $N(q; \upsilon)$ to be the social surplus, that is,

[4] Our formulation embraces a vast array of selling procedures that the notation perhaps conceals. We allow, for example, for selling procedures involving multiple rounds of moves by buyer and seller, as long as the only things that ultimately matter to the buyer and seller are the quantity sold and the payment. Two possibilities that our formulation *does* exclude are (i) allowing one buyer's quantity-payment pair to depend on the choices of other buyers and (ii) permitting $q(s)$ and $T(s)$ to be random functions of s. As we argue below, however, neither possibility is advantageous for the seller, given our assumptions (see, however, the minor qualification in footnote 3).

$$N = mq - C(q; \upsilon_i). \qquad (6)$$

Substituting (5) and (6) in (4), we find that the net gain to an agent (worker) of type i is given once again by (3).[5]

Returning to the original interpretation, we begin with a diagrammatic derivation of the seller's optimal price schedule. A buyer's utility from any pair $\langle q, R \rangle$ is, from (3), just the social surplus $N(q; \upsilon_i)$ less the seller's profit R. Given our definition of $q^e(\upsilon)$ as the efficient level of consumption by a buyer with parameter υ_i, it follows that, for any R, $U(q, R; \upsilon_i)$ increases with q until it reaches a maximum at $q = q^e(\upsilon_i)$.

Thus, indifference curves must be as depicted in Fig. 1. Note that at $\langle q, R \rangle$ the slope of the corresponding indifference curve is

$$\left.\frac{dR}{dq}\right|_{dU=0} = -\left.\frac{\partial U}{\partial q}\right| \frac{\partial U}{\partial R} = p(q; \upsilon) - c.$$

Therefore, at any point $\langle q, R \rangle$ the indifference curve for a buyer with a higher parameter value has a greater slope. Sorting is feasible precisely because different individuals have different marginal rates of substitution between the commodity and income. Our assumption that one individual's marginal rate of substitution is everywhere higher than another's is an important analytical simplification.

For the simplest case of two buyer types we can illustrate the profit-maximizing selling strategy with the help of Fig. 1. If the seller had complete information about buyer types, he could extract all buyer surplus by introducing the schedule $I^* = \{\langle q_1^*, R_1^* \rangle, \langle q_2^*, R_2^* \rangle\}$. But since

[5] To make the problem exactly equivalent, we also introduce the constraint that the worker will participate only if his utility exceeds some reservation level $\bar{u}$. This description suggests that the relationship between an employer and worker begins only after the worker has observed his υ_i (an ex post relationship), but we can equally well suppose that the two parties sign a contingent contract before υ_i is realized. By making the payment and output contingent on υ_i, such a contract serves to share risk. If we assume that the employer is risk neutral and the worker infinitely risk averse and maintain the hypothesis that only the worker can observe the realization of υ_i, then this ex ante contract generates the same contingent payments and outputs as the ex post relationship. This results because, given the worker's extreme risk aversion, the constraint on his utility in the contract is simply that net gain should exceed some minimum, $\bar{u}$, which is the same as in the *ex post* relationship. Hence, the literature on labour contracts with asymmetric information (Hart, 1983) can also be fit into our framework.

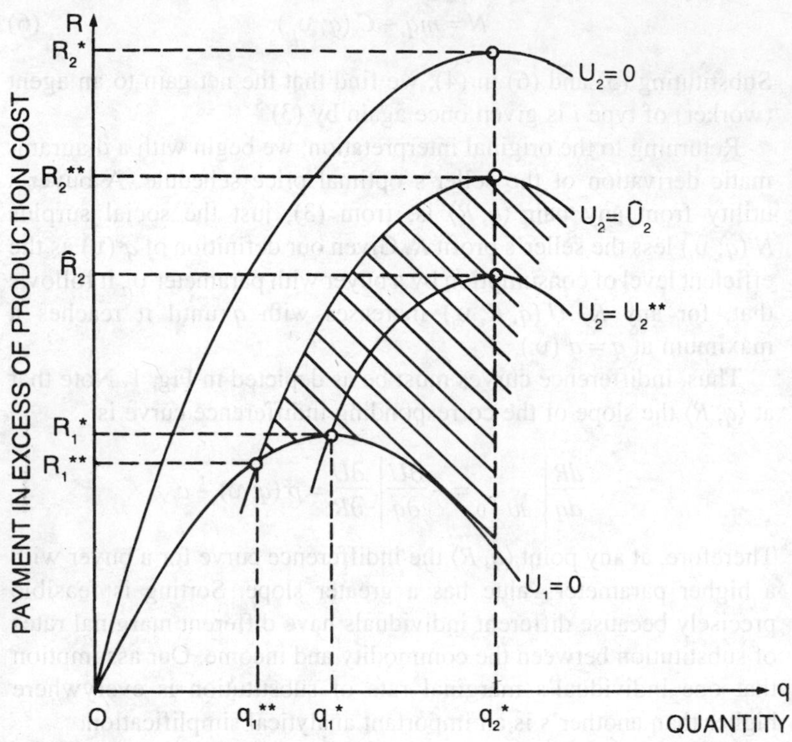

Figure 1 Price Discrimination with Two Types of Buyer

we assume that he has no direct means of distinguishing buyer types, this selling procedure will not extract all surplus. Indeed, high demanders ($\upsilon = \upsilon_2 > \upsilon_1$) are strictly better off buying q_1^* units at a total cost of $R_1^* + cq_1^*$.

From the figure it is easy to see, moreover, that the seller can do strictly better than I^*. Consider the indifference curve for a high demander through $\langle q_1^*, R_1^* \rangle$. Any such buyer cannot be dissuaded from choosing $\langle q_1^*, R_1^* \rangle$ if available, unless also offered an alternative on or below this curve. Thus, assuming he also offers $\langle q_1^*, R_1^* \rangle$, we find that the seller maximizes his return by offering the alternative pair $\langle q_2^*, \hat{R}_2 \rangle$. Note that at the points chosen by each type, the associated indifference curves have zero slope. That is, the pairs $\langle q_1^*, R_1^* \rangle$ and $\langle q_2^*, \hat{R}_2 \rangle$ are efficient.

We next establish, however, that the monopolist can do better than

$\hat{I} = \{\langle q_1^*, R_1^* \rangle; \langle q_2^*, \hat{R}_2 \rangle\}$ by introducing inefficiency. Consider the alternative $\langle q_1^{**}, R_1^{**} \rangle$, depicted in Fig. 1, which also extracts all the surplus from low demanders. Much as before, the monopolist maximizes his return from high demanders, given that he offers $\langle q_1^{**}, R_1^{**} \rangle$, by also offering $\langle q_2^*, R_2^{**} \rangle$. By presenting buyers with $I^0 = \{\langle q_1^{**}, R_1^{**} \rangle, \langle q_2^*, R_2^{**} \rangle\}$ rather than $\hat{I}$, the monopolist gains relatively from high demanders ($R_2^{**} > \hat{R}_2$) and loses from low demanders ($R_1^{**} < R_1^*$). But observe that at least for small moves to the left of q_1^*, the slope of the indifference curve for type 1 buyers is approximately zero. Therefore, the fall in the return from type 1 buyers is approximately zero. To be precise, there is a first-order rise in the return from high demanders and only a second-order decline from low demanders.

As the ratio of high to low demanders increases, the offer $\langle q_1^{**}, R_1^{**} \rangle$ moves further to the left until eventually $\langle q_1^{**}, R_1^{**} \rangle = \langle 0, 0 \rangle$. Then, if the ratio of high to low demanders is sufficiently great, I^0 in effect becomes simply $\{\langle q_2^*, R_2^* \rangle\}$. Regardless of whether I^0 or $\{\langle q_2^*, R_2^* \rangle\}$ is optimal, however, only high demanders purchase the efficient quantity $q_2^* = q^e(\upsilon_2)$, and the low demanders' demand price for the last unit purchased exceeds marginal cost.

A straightforward generalization of this argument establishes that, with more than two types of buyer, demand price will exceed marginal cost for all except the highest demanders. To summarize, we have:

Proposition 1: Inefficiency of monopoly price discrimination.[6] Under Assumption 1, if $V = \{\upsilon_1, \ldots, \upsilon_n \mid \upsilon_i < \upsilon_{i+1}\}$ is the set of possible parameter values, then the profit-maximizing selling procedure of the form $\langle q_s^*, R(q_s^*) \rangle_{s \in S}$ will result in purchases $q(\upsilon_i)$ by a type i buyer such that $p(q(\upsilon_i); \upsilon_i) \geq c$ for all i, and the inequality is strict for $i < n$.

This proposition is an instance of a very general principle that has emerged from the rapidly growing literature on incentive schemes (e.g. income taxation and piece-rate schemes); viz. the optimal incentive schedule typically involves distortions (that is, deviations from the first-best) at all but one point.

The primary goal of this article is to show that by introducing only mild restrictions, we can provide a *complete* characterization of the expected profit-maximizing nonlinear price schedule for any smooth

6 The graphical derivation of this proposition is easily formalized.

distribution of demand curves. In so doing we lay a broad foundation for future empirical investigations of monopolistic pricing practices.

To preview the issues involved and the results to follow, consider a selling procedure $\langle q(s), R(s)\rangle = \langle q(s), \bar{R}(q(s))\rangle$, where $\{q(s)\}_{s \in S}$ consists of all nonnegative quantities, and the return function $\bar{R}(q)$ is continuously differentiable, as depicted in Fig. 2a. Because indifference curves are steeper for larger υ, the response $q^*(\upsilon)$ (that is, the purchase by a type υ buyer) will be a strictly increasing function for all υ above some minimum α^1 where purchases are zero. Thus, the buyer types who actually make purchases are completely 'sorted out'.

Figure 2a is somewhat misleading, however, since it is not generally optimal for the seller to sort completely. One alternative possibility is illustrated in Fig. 2b. Instead of being continuously differentiable, the return function, $\bar{R}^*(q)$, has an upward kink at A. As depicted, any buyer with $\upsilon > \alpha^3$ chooses $q^*(\upsilon) > q_A$. Those with $\upsilon \in [\alpha^2, \alpha^3]$ all choose $q^*(\upsilon) = q_A$. By using the function $\bar{R}^*(q)$ rather than $\bar{R}(q)$, a seller obtains a lower return from those buyers for whom $\upsilon \in [\alpha^2, \alpha^3]$. But the kinked schedule generates a greater return from high values of υ. It is therefore intuitively plausible that if the proportion of the buyer population with intermediate values of υ is sufficiently low relative to the proportions with high or low υ's, seller profit is increased by the introduction of such a kink. As we shall see, kinked nonlinear pricing schemes are optimal under weaker conditions as well.

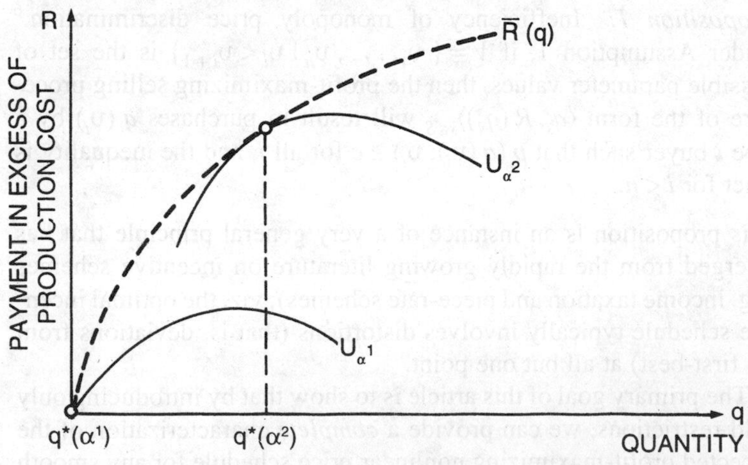

Figure 2a Complete Sorting of All Buyers Making Purchases

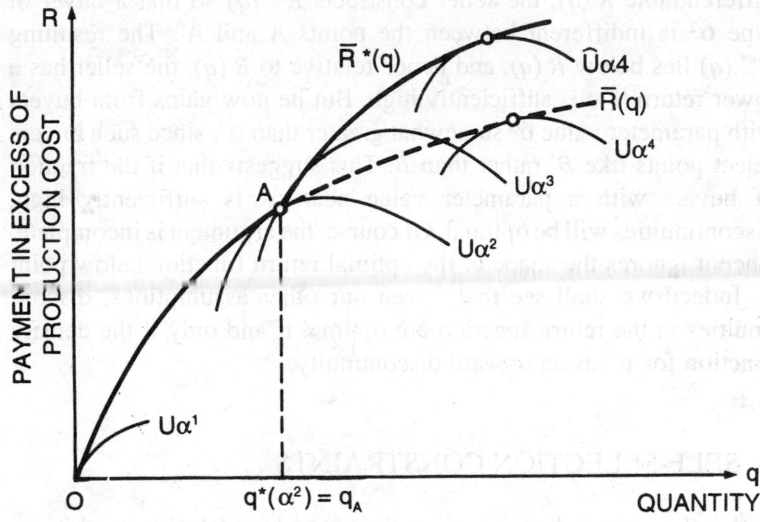

Figure 2b Kinked Price Function

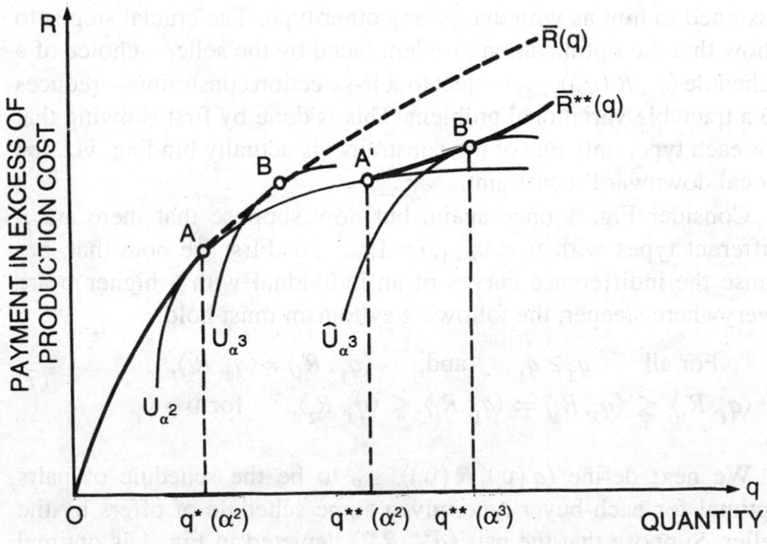

Figure 2c Discontinuous Price Function

A third possibility is depicted in Fig. 2c. Instead of the continuously differentiable $\bar{R}(q)$, the seller constructs $\bar{R}^{**}(q)$ so that a buyer of type α^2 is indifferent between the points A and A'. The resulting $\bar{R}^{**}(q)$ lies below $\bar{R}(q)$, and hence relative to $\bar{R}(q)$, the seller has a lower return if υ is sufficiently high. But he now gains from buyers with parameter value α^3 somewhat greater than α^2, since such buyers select points like B' rather than B. This suggests that if the fraction of buyers with a parameter value near α^3 is sufficiently high, discontinuities will be optimal. Of course, the argument is incomplete, since it ignores the shape of the optimal return function below point A. Indeed we shall see that, given our other assumptions, discontinuities in the return function are optimal if and only if the density function for υ has an upward discontinuity.

3. SELF-SELECTION CONSTRAINTS

Rather than proceeding directly to the general model with an arbitrary continuous cumulative distribution function $F(\upsilon)$, we first examine the 'self-selection' constraints for the discrete case. These constraints require that each consumer type be as happy with the $\langle q, R\rangle$ pair assigned to him as with that of any other type. The crucial step is to show that the optimization problem faced by the seller—choice of a schedule $\langle q_s, R(q_s)\rangle_{s \in S}$, subject to self-selection constraints—reduces to a tractable variational problem. This is done by first showing that for each type, only *one* of the constraints is actually binding, viz. the 'local downward' constraint.

Consider Fig. 1 once again, but now suppose that there are n different types with $\upsilon_1 < \upsilon_{i+1}$, $i = 1, \ldots, n$. First we note that, because the indifference curves of an individual with a higher υ are everywhere steeper, the following syllogism must hold:

$$\begin{gathered}\text{For all} \quad q_2 \geq q_1 \quad \text{and} \quad \langle q_1, R_1\rangle \neq \langle q_2, R_2\rangle, \\ \langle q_1, R_1\rangle \underset{\upsilon_i}{\lesssim} \langle q_2, R_2\rangle \Rightarrow \langle q_1, R_1\rangle \underset{\upsilon}{\lesssim} \langle q_2, R_2\rangle, \quad \text{for } \upsilon > \upsilon_i.\end{gathered} \tag{7}$$

We next define $\langle q(\upsilon_i), R(\upsilon_i)\rangle_{\upsilon_i \in V}$ to be the schedule of pairs optimal for each buyer type, given some schedule of offers by the seller. Suppose that the pair $\langle q_1^{**}, R_1^{**}\rangle$ depicted in Fig. 1 is optimal for type 1. Then all other offers $\langle q_s, R_s\rangle$ must lie on or above the indifference curve for type 1 through $\langle q_1^{**}, R_1^{**}\rangle$. Given Assumption 1, we know that the indifference curve for type 2 through this same point is steeper at any level of q. Then either $q(\upsilon_2) = q(\upsilon_1)$ or a buyer of type 2 chooses a pair $\langle q_s, R_s\rangle$ on or below this steeper indifference curve. But we have already argued that all the alternatives must lie above the flatter indifference curve for type 1. Then either $q(\upsilon_2) = q(\upsilon_1)$ or $\langle q(\upsilon_2), R(\upsilon_2)\rangle$ must lie in the shaded region, that is,

$$q(\upsilon_2) \geq q(\upsilon_1).$$

Since exactly the same logic applies for any two neighbouring types, we can conclude that the response function

$$q(\upsilon) \text{ is a non-decreasing function.} \tag{8}$$

A further important implication of Assumption 1 is that, for each type, the 'local downward' constraint is strictly binding. That is, there is no type υ_i such that

$$\langle q(\upsilon_i), R(\upsilon_i)\rangle \underset{\upsilon_i}{\succ} \langle q(\upsilon_{i-1}), R(\upsilon_{i-1})\rangle. \tag{9}$$

To confirm this, suppose (9) holds for some i. Since $\langle q(\upsilon_{i-1}), R(\upsilon_{i-1})\rangle$ is optimal for type υ_{i-1}, we also have

$$\langle q(\upsilon_{i-1}), R(\upsilon_{i-1})\rangle \underset{\upsilon_{i-1}}{\succsim} \langle q(\upsilon_k), R(\upsilon_k)\rangle, \qquad k = 1, \ldots, i-1.$$

Then appealing to (7) and (8)

$$\langle q(\upsilon_{i-1}), R(\upsilon_{i-1})\rangle \underset{\upsilon_i}{\succ} \langle q(\upsilon_k), R(\upsilon_k)\rangle, \qquad k = 1, \ldots, i-1. \tag{10}$$

Now consider the alternative scheme

$$\hat{q}_k = q(\upsilon_k)$$

$$\hat{R}_k = \begin{cases} \tilde{R}(y_k), & k < i \\ R(\upsilon_k) + \delta, & k \geq i. \end{cases}$$

For sufficiently small δ, (9) continues to hold. Then (10) holds also. That is, type υ_i will not switch to a lower level of q. An almost identical argument establishes that no type υ_j, $j > i$, will do so either. Finally we note that, since indifference curves are vertically parallel, rankings over $\langle \hat{q}(\upsilon_j), \hat{R}(\upsilon_j)\rangle_{j \geq i}$ are identical to the rankings over $\langle q(\upsilon_j), R(\upsilon_j)\rangle$ for all types $\upsilon_j, j \geq i$.

Thus, the new scheme results in the same choices of q by each type and a strictly greater return to the monopolist. But this is impossible since, by assumption, $\langle q(\upsilon_i), R(\upsilon_i)\rangle_{i=1,\ldots,n}$ is the monopolist's optimal scheme. Therefore, (9) is false, and the local downward constraint is binding; that is,

$$\langle q(\upsilon_i), R(\upsilon_i)\rangle \underset{\upsilon_i}{\sim} \langle q(\upsilon_{i-1}), R(\upsilon_{i-1})\rangle, \quad i = 2, \ldots, n. \tag{11}$$

This argument implies that a buyer with the lowest υ obtains no surplus, that is,

$$\langle q(\upsilon_1), R(\upsilon_1)\rangle \underset{\upsilon_1}{\sim} \langle 0, 0\rangle. \tag{12}$$

Figure 3 depicts a possible optimal selling procedure with three different types. All the pairs $\langle q(\upsilon_i), R(\upsilon_i)\rangle$ lie along the dashed curve, where each segment corresponds to an indifference curve for a different demander. From this figure, it should be clear that the indifference curve for each type υ_i through $\langle q(\upsilon_i), R(\upsilon_i)\rangle$ never lies

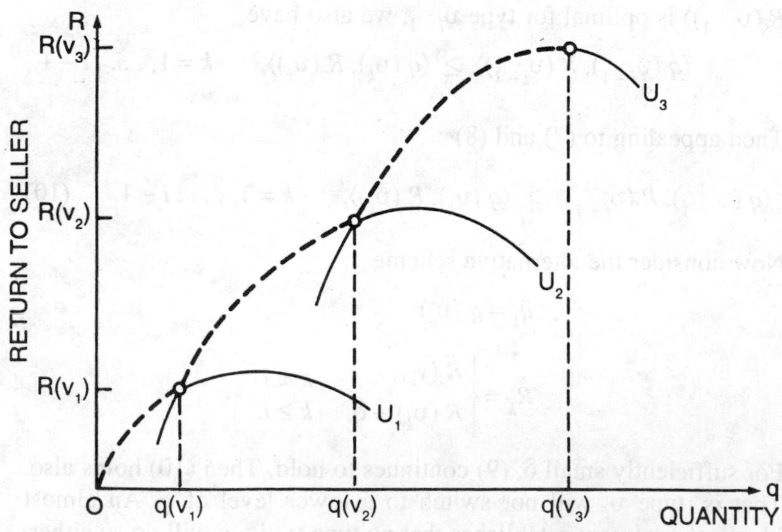

Figure 3 Complete Sorting with Three Different Buyer Types

above the dashed curve. Thus, if conditions (8) and (11) are satisfied, $\langle q(\upsilon_1), R(\upsilon_i)\rangle$ is indeed the global optimum for type υ_i. That is, we assert that besides being necessary properties of a monopolist's optimum, (8) and (11) are also conditions sufficient for *all* self-selection constraints to be satisfied.

From this analysis of the finite case we can now move easily to the limit with the buyer's demands continuously distributed. In what follows we shall make use of the next assumption.

Assumption 2. The cumulative distribution function for υ, $F(\upsilon)$, is a strictly increasing, continuously differentiable function on the interval $[0, \bar{\upsilon}]$ with $F(0) = 1 - F(\bar{\upsilon}) = 0$.

With $\langle q(\upsilon_i), R(\upsilon_i)\rangle$ optimal for a buyer with parameter υ_i, we can write maximized utility as

$$U^*(\upsilon_i) \equiv N(q(\upsilon_i); \upsilon_i) - R(\upsilon_i). \tag{13}$$

From (11)

$$U^*(\upsilon_{i+1}) \equiv N(q(\upsilon_{i+1}); \upsilon_{i+1}) - R(\upsilon_{i+1}) = N(q(\upsilon_i); \upsilon_{i+1}) - R(\upsilon_i)$$

Therefore,

$$\begin{aligned} U^*(\upsilon_{i+1}) - U^*(\upsilon_i) &= N(q(\upsilon_i); \upsilon_{i+1}) - N(q(\upsilon_i); \upsilon_i) \\ &= \int_{\upsilon_i}^{\upsilon_{i+1}} \frac{\partial N}{\partial \upsilon}(q(\upsilon_i); x)dx. \end{aligned} \tag{14}$$

From (12), we know that the utility of the lowest demanders must equal the utility of not participating, that is,

$$U^*(0) = 0.\text{[7]} \tag{15}$$

Combining (14) and (15), we obtain

$$U^*(\upsilon_i) = \sum_{j=0}^{i-1} \int_{\upsilon_j}^{\upsilon_{j+1}} \frac{\partial N}{\partial \upsilon}(q(\upsilon_j); x)dx, \qquad \text{where} \qquad \upsilon_0 = 0.$$

Substituting this expression in (13), we can write the expected seller revenue from a buyer of type υ_i in terms of $q(\cdot)$:

[7] Oren, Smith, and Wilson (1984) consider a case in which there is an additional fixed cost, k, of supplying each customer. Then (15) becomes $U^*(0) = k$. Their analysis is easily generalized by using our methods.

$$R(\upsilon_i) = N(q(\upsilon_i); \upsilon_i) - \sum_{j=0}^{i-1} \int_{\upsilon_j}^{\upsilon_{j+1}} \frac{\partial N}{\partial \upsilon}(q(\upsilon_j); x)dx.$$

Taking the limiting case of a continuous distribution of types, we have

$$R(\upsilon) = N(q(\upsilon); \upsilon) - \int_0^{\upsilon} \frac{\partial N}{\partial \upsilon}(q(x); x)dx. \tag{16}$$

From the monopolist's viewpoint, υ and, hence, $R(\upsilon)$ are random variables. He, therefore, chooses $q(\upsilon)$ to maximize the expectation of $R(\upsilon)$ subject to the constraint (8) that $q(\upsilon)$ is non-decreasing. The expectation of $R(\upsilon)$ is

$$\int_0^{\bar{\upsilon}} \left[N(q(\upsilon); \upsilon) - \int_0^{\upsilon} \frac{\partial N}{\partial \upsilon}(q(x); x)dx \right] dF(\upsilon),$$

or, after integration by parts,

$$\int_0^{\bar{\upsilon}} \left[N(q(\upsilon); \upsilon) - \frac{\partial N}{\partial \upsilon}(q(\upsilon); \upsilon)/\rho(\upsilon) \right] dF(\upsilon),$$

where $\rho(\upsilon) \equiv F'(\upsilon)/(1 - F(\upsilon))$ is the hazard rate of F. Summarizing, we can state the following proposition.

Proposition 2: Expected profit from second-degree price discrimination. If Assumptions 1 and 2 are satisfied, the expected profit obtainable from a selling procedure $\langle q(\upsilon), R(\upsilon) \rangle$, where $q(\upsilon)$ is non-decreasing, can be expressed as

$$\int_0^{\bar{\upsilon}} I(q(\upsilon); \upsilon)dF(\upsilon),$$

where

$$I(q; \upsilon) = N(q; \upsilon) - \frac{\partial N}{\partial \upsilon}(q; \upsilon)/\rho(\upsilon), \tag{17}$$

$$N(q, \upsilon) \equiv \int_0^q \rho(x, \upsilon)dx - cq \text{ is the net social benefit,}$$

and

$$\rho(\upsilon) \equiv F'(\upsilon)/(1 - F(\upsilon))\,.$$[8]

To maximize expected revenue, the seller thus chooses $q^*(\upsilon)$ to solve

$$\max_{q(\upsilon)} \left\{ \int_0^{\bar{\upsilon}} I(q(\upsilon); \upsilon) dF(\upsilon) \mid q(\upsilon) \text{ is non-decreasing} \right\}. \tag{18}$$

Assume that $q^*(\cdot)$ is piecewise differentiable. (We shall see below that this assumption is justified.) Then, from (16), the return to the seller from a buyer of type υ is

$$R^*(\upsilon) = N(q^*(\upsilon); \upsilon) - \int_0^{\upsilon} \frac{\partial N}{\partial \upsilon}(q^*(x); x)dx$$

$$= \int_0^{\upsilon} \frac{\partial N}{\partial q}(q^*(x); x) \frac{dq^*(x)}{dx} dx.$$

Let $\phi(q) = \min\{\upsilon \mid q^*(\upsilon) = q\}$. Because $q^*(\upsilon)$ is non-decreasing, we can write $\upsilon = \phi(q)$. We can, therefore, write

$$R^*(\phi(q)) = \int_0^q \frac{\partial N}{\partial q}(z; \phi(z))dz$$

$$= \int_0^q p(z; \phi(z))dz - cq.$$

Hence we have following proposition.

Proposition 3: Optimal non-linear pricing. Under Assumptions 1 and 2 expected monopoly profit is maximized by introducing the non-linear total payment schedule

$$\bar{T}(q) = \int_0^q p(z; \phi(z))dz, \tag{19}$$

where $\phi(z)$ is defined by $\phi(z) = \min\{\upsilon \mid q^*(\upsilon) = z\}$ and $q^*(\upsilon)$ is the solution to (18).

We have derived Propositions 1–3 somewhat informally to emphasize the ideas behind the proofs. In fact, we have left certain gaps

[8] In deriving the formula for expected profit in the case of only finitely many values of υ, we invoked the assumption that $\langle q(\upsilon), R(\upsilon)\rangle$ is optimal for the monopolist. In particular, we used this assumption to show that the local downward incentive constraint is binding. One can show, however, (see the lemma following Proposition 3) that formula (17) is valid even for nonoptimal selling schemes.

in the analysis. First of all, our derivation of (16) by taking limits was rather loose. In Maskin and Riley (1983b) we provide a formal proof. In fact, we establish the following lemma.

Lemma. For any $q(\upsilon)$, a non-decreasing function on $[0, \bar{\upsilon}]$, there exists a unique return function, $R(\cdot)$, given by (16), such that $\langle q(\cdot), R(\cdot)\rangle$ satisfies all the self-selection constraints and (15).

We should note that the uniqueness of $R(\cdot)$ in this lemma depends crucially on the continuity of $F(\cdot)$. If $F(\cdot)$ is, by contrast, a discrete distribution, then corresponding to each $q(\cdot)$ there will be a continuum of $R(\cdot)$'s such that the self-selection constraints and (15) are satisfied (although only one that is profit-maximizing).

Another point we ignored is the possibility that the seller might offer a schedule $\langle \tilde{q}_s, \tilde{R}\rangle_{s \in S}$, where $\tilde{q}_s$ and $\tilde{R}_s$ are random rather than deterministic functions. We consider this possibility in Maskin and Riley (1983a), wherein it is established that gains from randomization are ruled out if the following assumption is satisfied.

Assumption 3: Non-decreasing price elasticity. Demand elasticity is non-decreasing in the demand price. That is,

$$\frac{\partial}{\partial \upsilon}\left(\frac{-q}{p}\frac{\partial p}{\partial q}\right) \leq 0. \tag{20}$$

For a buyer of type υ, utility is

$$U(q, T\text{: } \upsilon) = \int_0^q p(x, \upsilon)dx - T.$$

Hence, for such a buyer,

$$\frac{\partial}{\partial \upsilon}\left(\frac{-\dfrac{\partial^2 U}{\partial q^2}}{\dfrac{\partial U}{\partial q}}\right) = \frac{1}{q}\frac{\partial}{\partial \upsilon}\left(\frac{-q}{p}\frac{\partial p}{\partial q}\right) \tag{21}$$

Assumption 3 implies, therefore, that absolute risk aversion is non-increasing in υ, if we interpret U as a von Neumann–Morgenstern utility function.

We should note that we have a great deal of flexibility in our choice of a parameterization. In particular, if $p(q; \upsilon)$ represents a family of inverse demand curves satisfying Assumptions 1, 2 and 3, then

$p(q, \omega(\upsilon))$ represents the same family and also satisfies these three assumptions if $\omega(\cdot)$ is strictly increasing. For convenience, we shall choose, without loss of generality, a parameterization for which the increases in demand price are diminishing as υ rises.

Assumption 4. $p_{22}(q; \upsilon) \leq 0$.

Since we shall appeal to Assumptions 1, 2, 3 and 4 in much of what follows, we observe that they are satisfied for large classes of preferences. For example, they are satisfied if

$$p(q; \upsilon) = \alpha(\upsilon)a(q) - \beta(\upsilon)h(q), \tag{22}$$

where $a(q)$ is positive and non-increasing, $h(q)$, $\alpha(\upsilon)$, and $\alpha(\upsilon)/\beta(\upsilon)$ are all nonnegative and non-decreasing, $\alpha''(\upsilon) \leq 0$, $\beta''(\upsilon) \geq 0$, $\alpha(\upsilon)a(0) - \beta(\upsilon)h(0) \geq 0$, and $\alpha(\upsilon)a'(0) - \beta(\upsilon)h'(0) < 0$.

One special case of (22) is the family of linear demand curves. Without loss of generality, we can set $\alpha(\upsilon) = \upsilon$, $a(q) = 1$, and $h(q) = q$ so that

$$p(q; \upsilon) = \upsilon - \beta(\upsilon)q.$$

A second important case is the family of constant elasticity demand functions $p(q; \upsilon) = \alpha(\upsilon)q^{-1/\eta}$. As we shall see, the seller's optimization problem is especially straightforward for this family.

4. CHARACTERIZATION OF THE OPTIMAL SELLING PROCEDURE

We now turn to the solution of the seller's optimization problem, (18). First, we provide conditions under which there is complete sorting of all those buyers actually making purchases.

Proposition 4: Complete sorting optimum. Suppose Assumptions 1, 2, 3 and 4 hold. Then the $\bar{q}(\upsilon)$ that solves $\max_q I(q; \upsilon)$ is non-decreasing and, whenever $\bar{q}$ is positive, strictly increasing if either

$$J(\upsilon) \equiv \upsilon - \frac{1 - F(\upsilon)}{F'(\upsilon)} \text{ is increasing} \tag{23}$$

or

$$\frac{1}{p_2(\bar{q}(\upsilon); \upsilon)} \frac{\partial}{\partial \upsilon}\left(\frac{p_2(\bar{q}(\upsilon); \upsilon)}{\rho(\upsilon)}\right) < 1. \tag{24}$$

Proof. We first establish that Assumptions 1, 2 and 3 together imply that $I(q; \upsilon)$ is a strictly quasi-concave function of q. From (17)

$$\frac{\partial I}{\partial q} = p(q; \upsilon) - p_2(q; \upsilon)/\rho(\upsilon) - c.$$

Hence

$$\frac{\partial I}{\partial q} \geq 0 \Longrightarrow 1/\rho < p/p_2. \tag{25}$$

Also

$$\frac{\partial^2 I}{\partial q^2} = p_1 - p_{12}/\rho. \tag{26}$$

If p_{12} is non-negative, $\partial^2 I/\partial q^2$ is negative since, by Assumption 1, $p_1 < 0$ for $q > 0$. If p_{12} is negative, then by (25)

$$\frac{\partial I}{\partial q} \geq 0 \Longrightarrow \frac{\partial^2 I}{\partial q^2} < p_1 - \frac{p_{12}\,p}{p_2} = \frac{p^2}{qp_2}\frac{\partial}{\partial \upsilon}\left(\frac{-qp_1}{p}\right).$$

By Assumption 3 the final term is non-positive. Thus $I(q, \upsilon)$ is indeed strictly quasi-concave.

Furthermore,

$$\frac{\partial^2 I}{\partial q \partial \upsilon} = p_2\left(1 - \frac{1}{p_2}\frac{\partial}{\partial \upsilon}\left(\frac{p_2}{p}\right)\right) = \frac{p_2}{p}\left(\rho + \frac{\rho'}{\rho} - \frac{p_{22}}{p_2}\right). \tag{27}$$

Since $\bar{q}(\upsilon)$ maximizes $I(q, \upsilon)$, either $\bar{q}(\upsilon) = 0$ or $\bar{q}(\upsilon)$ satisfies the first-order condition $\partial I/\partial q = 0$. Totally differentiating the latter equation, we obtain

$$\frac{d\bar{q}}{d\upsilon} = -\left.\frac{\partial^2 I}{\partial q \partial \upsilon}\right| \frac{\partial^2 I}{\partial q^2}.$$

We have just argued that the denominator is negative, hence the derivative exists. Also, if (24) holds, then, from (27), $\partial^2 I/\partial q \partial \upsilon$ is positive. Alternatively, since

$$J'(\upsilon) = \frac{1}{\rho}\left(\rho + \frac{\rho'}{\rho}\right),$$

and by hypothesis $p_{22} \leq 0$, it follows from (27) that if (23) is satisfied, $\partial^2 I/\partial q \partial \upsilon$ is again positive.

Hence $\bar{q}(\upsilon)$ is either zero or strictly increasing. Thus $\bar{q}(\upsilon)$ solves the monopolist's optimization problem (18). *Q.E.D.*

Although condition (24) has the advantage of being invariant to parameterization, the somewhat stronger condition (23) is easier to interpret. It requires that the hazard rate $\rho(\upsilon)$ not decline too rapidly with υ, a requirement that accords well with our heuristic discussion of complete sorting in Sec. 2. Certainly, this condition is satisfied for a large subclass of distribution functions. It is not difficult, however, to produce instances in which it is violated. For example, if, holding the support of υ fixed, the variance of υ is made sufficiently small, $J(\upsilon)$ is non-monotonic.[9] We shall see below that whenever there exists a υ such that $J(\upsilon)$ is positive and decreasing, complete sorting is no longer optimal.

Example 1: Vertically parallel demand:

$$p(q;\upsilon) = \upsilon - h(q),\ h'(\cdot) > 0.$$

For this simple case

$$\frac{\partial I}{\partial q}(q;\upsilon) = J(\upsilon) - h(q) - c,$$

where

$$J(\upsilon) = \upsilon - \frac{1 - F(\upsilon)}{F'(\upsilon)}.$$

Then if $J(\upsilon)$ is increasing.

$$\bar{q}(\upsilon) = h^{-1}(\max\{0, J(\upsilon) - c\}) \text{ is non-decreasing, and}$$

by Proposition 3 the optimal non-linear price function is

$$\bar{T}(q) = \int_0^q [J^{-1}(h(z) + c) - h(z)]dz.$$

Example 2: Constant price elasticity of demand:

$$p(q;\upsilon) = \upsilon q^{-1/\eta}, \quad \eta > 1$$

[9] It is easy to give other examples for which $J(\upsilon)$ is not monotonic. For instance, if

$$F(\upsilon) = \upsilon(7 - 9\upsilon + 4\upsilon^2)/2$$

so that $\bar{\upsilon} = 1$, it may be confirmed that $J(1/2) = J(5/8) = J(3/4) > 0$.

$$\frac{\partial I}{\partial q}(q; \upsilon) \equiv J(\upsilon) q^{-1/\eta} - c.$$

Then, once again, $\bar{q}(\upsilon)$ is monotonic if $J(\upsilon)$ is increasing. Substituting into (19), we obtain

$$\bar{T}(q) = \int_0^q J^{-1}(cz^{1/\eta}) z^{-1/\eta} dz.$$

Under the hypothesis of Proposition 4, it is in principle possible to compute the optimal non-linear pricing scheme for any family of demand curves. One important qualitative issue is how a change in the underlying distribution affects the optimal price function. Suppose that there is a rightward shift in the distribution, so that the new distribution $G(\upsilon)$ is strictly less than $F(\upsilon)$ for all $\upsilon < (0, \bar{\upsilon})$. Since higher values of υ are associated with higher demanders, keeping the same pricing scheme will make the seller better off. Less obvious, however, is the effect on the optimal payment function $\bar{T}(q)$.

One condition sufficient to ensure that $G(\upsilon) < F(\upsilon)$ is that the hazard rate for F exceeds the hazard rate for G. We now show that this condition ensures that the optimal payment function $\bar{T}_G(q)$ is strictly steeper for all q than the corresponding function for F.

Proposition 5. If for all $\upsilon \in (0, \bar{\upsilon})$ the distribution $G(\upsilon)$ has a lower hazard rate than $F(\upsilon)$ and Assumptions 1, 2 and 3 are satisfied, then

$$\frac{d}{dq}\bar{T}_G(q) > \frac{d}{dq}\bar{T}_F(q).$$

Proof. We consider only the case in which the optimal response function, $\bar{q}(\upsilon)$, is the solution to $\max_q I(q; \upsilon)$. That the proof generalizes follows directly from the Characterization Theorem (Proposition 7).

From the proof of Proposition 4, $I(q; \upsilon)$ is strictly quasi-concave. Also, from (17), if $\rho_F > \rho_G$, then

$$\frac{\partial I_F}{\partial q} > \frac{\partial I_G}{\partial q}.$$

But if $\bar{q}_G(\upsilon) > 0$, $(\partial I_G/\partial q)(\bar{q}_G(\upsilon); \upsilon) = 0$. Thus, $\bar{q}_G(\upsilon) > 0$ implies that $\bar{q}_F(\upsilon) > \bar{q}_G(\upsilon)$, so that the two inverse functions satisfy $\phi_F(q) < \phi_G(q)$. Since $p_2 > 0$, the result then follows directly from (19), the definition of $\bar{T}(q)$. *Q.E.D.*

Intuitively, by making the payment function steeper, the monopolist is able to extract more revenue from the highest demanders. Thus, as the number of high relative to low demanders rises, a steeper price function becomes more desirable. This intuition, however, is incomplete, since it suggests that any rightward shift in the distribution will raise the entire payment schedule. A counter-example, in which there are just three types, is illustrated in Fig. 4. Suppose that, for the initial probability weights, the optimal selling procedure is to offer the three pairs, A_1, A_2, A_3. Next suppose that the distribution is shifted to the right via a reduction in the probability weight for the lowest demanders and an increase in the weight on type 2, with intermediate demand. This raises the marginal benefit to increasing the payment by type 2. The new optimum is then A_1, B_2, B_3 with a lower profit from the type 3 demanders. Since the highest demanders are allocated the same output, $\bar{T}(q\ (\upsilon_3)) = \bar{R}(q\ (\upsilon_3)) + cq\ (\upsilon_3)$ is also lower.

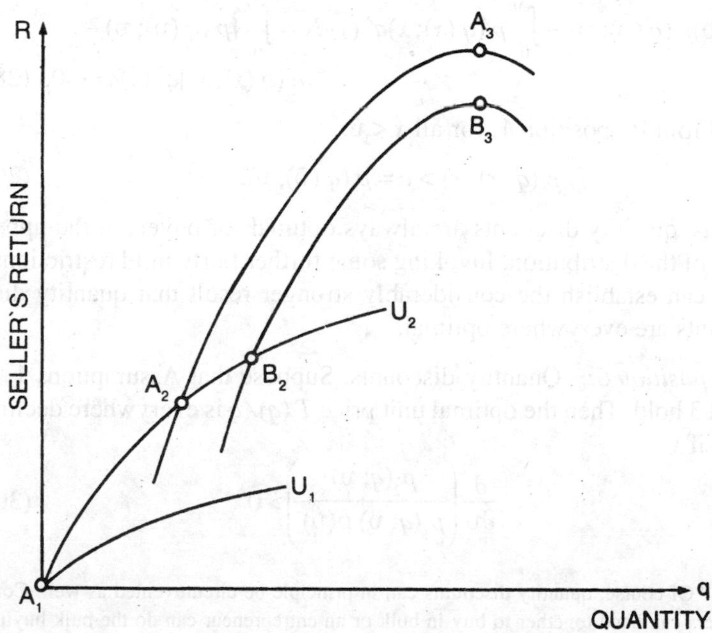

Figure 4 Impact of a Shift to a More Favourable Distribution

One feature common to non-linear pricing schemes in practice is the use of quantity discounts. We often see offers such as 'one for a dollar, three for two dollars', and the more complicated multipart tariffs of utility companies almost invariably involve offers of lower unit prices for greater consumption. A reason why quantity premiums ('one for a dollar, two for three dollars') may not be used is that they may be difficult to enforce; a customer might be able to circumvent a premium by successively buying small quantities under different guises.[10] There are many commodities, however, (e.g. utilities) for which enforcement is possible. We, therefore, consider whether or not premiums are desirable in the absence of enforcement costs. For a broad class of cases, we shall see, they are not.

The payment per unit purchased is, under the hypotheses of Proposition 3,

$$\frac{T(q(\upsilon))}{q(\upsilon)} = \int_0^{\upsilon} \frac{p(q(x); x)q'(x)dx}{q(\upsilon)}$$

This is decreasing in υ, and hence in q, if and only if

$$q(\upsilon)p(q(\upsilon); \upsilon) - \int_0^{\upsilon} p(q(x); x)q'(x)dx = \int_0^{\upsilon} [p(q(\upsilon); \upsilon) - p(q(x); x)]q'(x)dx < 0. \quad (28)$$

From Proposition 1, for all $x < \bar{\upsilon}$.

$$p(q(x); x) > c = p(q(\bar{\upsilon}), \bar{\upsilon}). \quad (29)$$

Thus, quantity discounts are always optimal for buyers at the upper tail of the distribution. Invoking some further fairly mild restrictions, we can establish the considerably stronger result that quantity discounts are everywhere optimal.

Proposition 6: Quantity discounts. Suppose that Assumptions 1, 2 and 3 hold. Then the optimal unit price $T(q)/q$ is everywhere declining if

$$\frac{\partial}{\partial \upsilon}\left(\frac{p_2(q; \upsilon)}{p_1(q; \upsilon)\,\rho(\upsilon)}\right) > 0 \quad (30)$$

[10] Of course, quantity discounts can in principle be circumvented as well. Consumers can band together to buy in bulk or an entrepreneur can do the bulk buying for them. But such evasive actions, unlike those for quantity premiums, require the coordination of more than one agent.

for $q = q^*(\upsilon)$, where $q^*(\upsilon)$ is the optimal response function.

Proof. We consider only the case where the optimal response function $q^*(\upsilon)$ solves max $I(q, \upsilon)$. That the proposition holds in general, however, follows directly from the Characterization Theorem (Proposition 7).

From (28), quantity discounting is optimal for all q if $p^*(q(\upsilon); \upsilon)$ is a decreasing function of υ for all $q^*(\upsilon) > 0$. From the proof of Proposition 4, $q^*(\upsilon) > 0$ implies that

$$\frac{dq^*}{d\upsilon} = \frac{-\dfrac{\partial^2 I}{\partial q \partial \upsilon}}{\dfrac{\partial^2 I}{\partial q^2}} = \frac{-p_2 + \dfrac{\partial}{\partial \upsilon}\left(\dfrac{p_2}{\rho}\right)}{p_1 - \dfrac{p_{12}}{\rho}} \tag{31}$$

Furthermore, the denominator $\partial^2 I/\partial q^2$ is negative. Differentiating $p(q(\upsilon); \upsilon)$ and substituting from (31), we obtain

$$\begin{aligned} \frac{d}{d\upsilon} p(q^*(\upsilon); \upsilon) &= p_1 \frac{dq}{d\upsilon} + p_2 \\ &= p_1^2 \frac{\partial}{\partial \upsilon}\left(\frac{p_2}{p_1 \rho}\right) \Big/ \frac{\partial^2 I}{\partial q^2}, \end{aligned}$$

which, given (30), is negative. *Q.E.D.*

Sufficient conditions for condition (30) to be satisfied are that Assumption 3 hold ($p_{22} \le 0$), that the hazard rate $\rho(\upsilon)$ be nondecreasing, and that $p_{12} \le 0$.[11]

Finally, we turn to the general characterization of the optimal selling procedure when $\bar{q}(\upsilon)$ is not monotonic. Proposition 7 reveals that the optimal response function $q^*(\upsilon)$ is continuous. There are subintervals over which $q^*(\upsilon)$ is constant, whereas on all other subintervals $q^*(\upsilon) = \bar{q}(\upsilon)$. As depicted in Fig. 2b, a transition from the former to the latter corresponds to an upward kink in the payment schedule, $\bar{T}(q) = cq + \bar{R}(q)$. Given Assumptions 1, 2 and 3, Proposition 7 also

[11] It is easy to see that $p_{12} \le 0$ is not necessary to establish the desirability of quantity discounts globally. For example, if $p(q; \upsilon) = 1 - (q/1 + \upsilon)$ and $F(\upsilon) = \upsilon$, then (30) is satisfied while $p_{12} > 0$.

shows that the intuitively plausible alternative depicted in Fig. 2c is never optimal.[12]

In the proof of Proposition 7, which appears in the Appendix, we require the following two restrictions.

Assumption 5. $I(q; \upsilon)$ is strictly quasi-concave.

Assumption 6.

$$\int_{\upsilon}^{y} \frac{\partial I}{\partial q}(q; z)dF(z) \geq 0 \rightarrow \int_{\upsilon}^{y} \frac{\partial^2 I}{\partial q^2}(q; z)dF(z) < 0, \quad \upsilon < y.$$

Both assumptions are fairly weak. For example, Assumption 6 holds if

$$p(q; \upsilon) = \phi(\upsilon)a(q) - h(q),$$

and we have already seen that Assumption 3 is a sufficient condition for Assumption 5.

Proposition 7: General characterization of the optimal response function.

(A) Suppose Assumptions 1, 2 and 5 are satisfied. Assume that there exists an optimal response function, $q^*(\upsilon)$. Then there exists a set of subintervals

$$\{[x^i, y^i] \subseteq [0, \bar{\upsilon}] \mid x^{i-1} > y^i\}_{i \in 1},$$

possibly empty, such that for all i

(i) $\quad \bar{q}(x^i) = \bar{q}(y^i),$

and

(ii) $$\int_{\upsilon}^{y} \frac{\partial I}{\partial q}(\bar{q}(y); z)\, dF(z) \leq 0, \quad \upsilon < y, \quad y \notin \bigcup_{i \in 1} (x^i, y^i)$$

with equality if $y = y^i$ and $\upsilon = x^i (x^i > 0)$. Moreover,

(iii) $$q^*(\upsilon) = \begin{cases} \bar{q}(y^i) & \text{if } \upsilon \in [x^i, y^i] \text{ for some } i \\ \bar{q}(\upsilon) & \text{otherwise.} \end{cases}$$

(B) Given Assumptions 1, 2 and 5, a collection of subintervals

[12] Proposition 7 continues to hold if $F(\upsilon)$ is a strictly increasing continuous piecewise differentiable function. It then follows immediately that if the density rises discontinuously at some υ', $q^*(\upsilon)$ will have an upward discontinuity at υ'.

satisfying (i) and (ii) exists. If, in addition, Assumption 6 holds, then $q^*(\upsilon)$ defined by (iii) is an optimal response function.

Proof. See the Appendix.

Notice that in part (A) of Proposition 7, the existence of an optimal response function is *assumed*, whereas in part (B), existence is *asserted*. To understand this result consider Fig. 5, which illustrates a simple case where $\bar{q}(\upsilon)$ is decreasing over one subinterval. Since $\bar{q}(\upsilon)$ solves $\max_q I(q; \upsilon)$ and since $I(q; \upsilon)$ is, by assumption, strictly quasi-concave, we have

$$\frac{\partial I}{\partial q}(q; \upsilon)\begin{cases} >0, & q < \bar{q}(\upsilon) \\ <0, & q > \bar{q}(\upsilon). \end{cases}$$

The seller seeks to solve

$$\max_{q(\upsilon)}\left\{\int_0^{\bar{\upsilon}} I(q; \upsilon)dF(\upsilon) \mid q(\upsilon) \text{ non-decreasing}\right\}$$

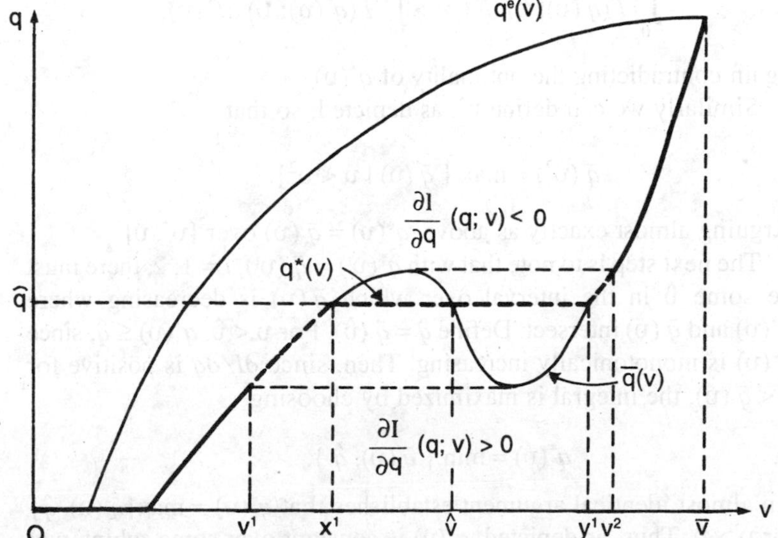

Figure 5 Solving for the Expected Profit-Maximizing Response Function

To derive the optimal response function, $q^*(\upsilon)$, we begin by defining υ^1 as depicted, so that

$$\upsilon^1 = \min \{\upsilon \mid \exists\, \hat{\upsilon} > \upsilon \text{ with } \bar{q}(\hat{\upsilon}) \leq \bar{q}(\upsilon)\}.$$

We next establish that $q^*(\upsilon) = \bar{q}(\upsilon)$ for $\upsilon \leq \upsilon^1$.

Since $\partial I(q; \upsilon)/\partial q$ is positive for $q^*(\upsilon) < \bar{q}(\upsilon)$ and negative for $q^*(\upsilon) > \bar{q}(\upsilon)$, it follows immediately that

$$\int_0^{\upsilon^1} I(\bar{q}(\upsilon); \upsilon)dF(\upsilon) \geq \int_0^{\upsilon^1} I(q^*(\upsilon); \upsilon)dF(\upsilon).$$

Thus, $q^*(\upsilon^1) > \bar{q}(\upsilon^1)$ cannot be optimal, at least if q^* is continuous, since, without violating the constraint that q^* be non-decreasing, and without altering q^* for $\upsilon > \upsilon^1$, we can set $q^* = \bar{q}$ over $[0, \upsilon^1]$. If $q^*(\upsilon^1) < \bar{q}(\upsilon^1)$, define

$$\hat{q}(\upsilon) = \begin{cases} \bar{q}(\upsilon), & \upsilon \leq \upsilon^1 \\ \max\{ q^*(\upsilon), \bar{q}(\upsilon^1) \}, & \upsilon > \upsilon^1 \end{cases}$$

For $\upsilon > \upsilon^1$ and $q \in (q^*(\upsilon^1), \bar{q}(\upsilon^1))$, $\partial I/\partial q\,(q; \upsilon) > 0$. Then

$$\int_0^{\bar{\upsilon}} I(\hat{q}(\upsilon); \upsilon)dF(\upsilon) > \int_0^{\bar{\upsilon}} I(q^*(\upsilon); \upsilon)\, dF(\upsilon),$$

again contradicting the optimality of $q^*(\upsilon)$.

Similarly we can define υ^2, as depicted, so that

$$\bar{q}(\upsilon^2) = \max\{ \bar{q}(\upsilon) \mid \upsilon < \upsilon^2\}.$$

Arguing almost exactly as above, $q^*(\upsilon) = \bar{q}(\upsilon)$ over $[\upsilon^2, \bar{\upsilon}]$

The next step is to note that with $q^*(\upsilon^i) = \bar{q}(\upsilon^i)$, $i = 1, 2$, there must be some $\hat{\upsilon}$ in the interval over which $\bar{q}(\upsilon)$ is decreasing where $q^*(\upsilon)$ and $\bar{q}(\upsilon)$ intersect. Define $\hat{q} = \bar{q}(\hat{\upsilon})$. For $\upsilon < \hat{\upsilon}$, $q^*(\upsilon) \leq \hat{q}$, since $q^*(\upsilon)$ is monotonically increasing. Then, since $\partial I/\partial q$ is positive for $q < \bar{q}(\upsilon)$, the integral is maximized by choosing

$$q^*(\upsilon) = \min\{ \bar{q}(\upsilon), \hat{q} \}.$$

An almost identical argument establishes that $q^*(\upsilon) = \max\{\bar{q}(\upsilon), \hat{q}\}$ for $\upsilon > \hat{\upsilon}$. Thus, as depicted, $q^*(\upsilon)$ is constant over some subinterval $[x^1, y^1]$ and equal to $\bar{q}(\upsilon)$ otherwise, establishing (iii) in Proposition 7.

Notice that $\bar{q}(x^1) = \bar{q}(y^1) = q^*(\upsilon)$ for all $\upsilon \in (x^1, y^1)$, establishing (i). To determine the location of x^1 and y^1, consider the monopolist's total profit

$$\int_0^{x^1} I(\bar{q}(\upsilon); \upsilon)dF(\upsilon) + \int_{x^1}^{y^1(x^1)} I(\bar{q}(x^1); \upsilon)dF(\upsilon) + \int_{y^1(x^1)}^{\bar{\upsilon}} I(\bar{q}(\upsilon); \upsilon)dF(\upsilon),$$

where $y^1 = y^1(x^1)$ satisfies $\bar{q}\,(y^1(x^1)) = \bar{q}\,(x^1)$. Differentiating this expression with respect to x^1, we obtain the further necessary condition

$$\int_{x^1}^{y^1} \frac{\partial I}{\partial q}(\bar{q}\,(x^1); \upsilon)dF\,(\upsilon) = 0.$$

Given our assumptions, this uniquely defines the interval $[x^1, y^1]$.

5. MONOPOLY PRICING OF PRODUCT QUALITY AND OPTIMAL BUNDLING

Our analysis of optimal pricing tactics in Secs 2–4 can be readily adapted to determine the optimal selling strategy of a monopolist selling products of differing quality levels. Indeed, in the simplest case we need only reinterpret the basic model. We assume that each consumer wishes to purchase only one quality level. Furthermore, following Mussa and Rosen (1978), we begin by assuming that consumers either do not buy the good or purchase just one unit (in this case, of course, the one quality level assumption is satisfied automatically).

Consider the Marshallian utility function

$$\hat{u}\,(y, q, z; \upsilon) = y + zB\,(q; \upsilon), \tag{32}$$

where y is spending on other goods, q is the quality level of the single unit purchased, υ represents the strength of preference for quality, and z is a dichotomous variable equal to unity with purchase and zero otherwise. If a consumer with income level I pays T for a unit of quality level q, we can rewrite his indirect utility as

$$u\,(q, T, z; \upsilon) = z\,(B\,(q; \upsilon) - T) + I. \tag{33}$$

Assumption 1 then requires that the marginal utility of higher quality is, *ceteris paribus*, at least as high for consumers with higher levels of υ.

With little loss of generality, we can define units of quality in such a way that the marginal cost of a unit of quality level q is cq.[13] Then the monopolist's problem is identical to the problem considered in Secs 2–4, expect that q is now to be interpreted as quality rather than quantity.

The natural generalization of this problem is to incorporate the choice of both quality q and the number of units purchased, z. Then, instead of (33), we have the indirect utility function

$$u\,(q, T, z; \upsilon) = B\,(q, z; \upsilon) - T + I, \tag{34}$$

where T is the total payment by the consumer for z units of quality level q. Adopting only slightly the derivations of Propositions 2 and 3, we can state the following proposition.

Proposition 8: Optimal bundling. Let consumer surplus for an individual of type υ, purchasing z units of quality level q at a cost of T, be

$$B\,(q, z; \upsilon) - T,$$

where υ is an independent draw from the distribution $F\,(\cdot)$. Let the cost of producing each unit of quality level q be cp. Suppose, for simplicity, that unit cost is independent of quantity. If both $\partial B/\partial q$ and $\partial B/\partial z$ are increasing functions of υ, and if $z^*(\upsilon)$, $q^*(\upsilon)$ which solve

$$\max_{z,\,q} \{\, B\,(q, z; \upsilon) - B_3(q, z; \upsilon)/\rho\,(\upsilon) - cq \,\}$$

are each either zero or strictly increasing in υ, then the expected profit-maximizing selling strategy consists of the schedule $\langle q^*(x), z^*(x), T^*(x)\rangle_{x \in [0,1]}$, where

$$T^*(x) = B\,(q^*(x), z^*(x); x) - \int_0^x B_3(q^*(s), z^*(s); s)ds. \tag{35}$$

[13] Mussa and Rosen consider the special case in which preferences are given by

$$u = z\,(\upsilon r - T) + I$$

and $C\,(r)$, the cost of producing a unit of quality level r, is an increasing convex function. Defining $q \equiv C\,(r)$, we can rewrite preferences as

$$u = z\,(\upsilon A\,(q) - T) + I,$$

where $A\,(q) = C^{-1}(q)$ is an increasing concave function. In the new quality units, marginal cost is constant and equal to unity.

As an immediate corollary, note that with $q^*(x)$ strictly increasing whenever q^* is greater than zero, we can define the inverse function $x = \phi(q)$ and hence the number of units and total payments as functions of q,

$$z^{**}(q) \equiv z^*(\phi(q)), T^{**}(q) = T^*(\phi(q)).$$

Then the optimal selling strategy can be reinterpreted as a schedule of offers of the form $\langle q, z^{**}(q), T^{**}(q)\rangle$. That is, the monopolist announces that quality level q will be sold in bundles of $z^{**}(q)$ units for a total cost of $T^{**}(q)$.

It is perhaps surprising that the monopolist does not gain by announcing a different quantity discount schedule for each quality level. But with only a single unobservable characteristic, υ, the optimal schedule of bundles, $\langle q^*(\upsilon), z^*(\upsilon)\rangle$, traces out a curve in quality-quantity space. Given the hypotheses of Proposition 8, quantity increases with quality along this curve. Thus, both the unit price and the number of units in the bundle can be expressed as a function of product quality.

Space constraints preclude the derivation of conditions that ensure the monotonicity of $q^*(\cdot)$ and $z^*(\cdot)$ defined in Proposition 8 (that is, the counterpart of Proposition 4). Instead, we conclude with a simple example.

Example 3:

$$B(q, z; \upsilon) = 2\upsilon q z^{1/2} - q^3/3; \quad F(\upsilon) = \upsilon.$$

Applying Proposition 8, we solve for $q^*(x)$ and $z^*(x)$ and obtain

$$q^*(x) = \begin{cases} 0, & x < ½ \\ (2x-1)/c^{½}, & x \geq ½. \end{cases} \tag{36}$$

$$z^*(x) = \begin{cases} 0, & x < ½ \\ (q^*(x)^2/c, & x \geq ½. \end{cases} \tag{37}$$

Since both $q^*(x)$ and $z^*(x)$ satisfy the hypotheses of the proposition, we can substitute them into (35), the expression for $T^*(x)$, to obtain

$$T^*(x) = q^*(x)^3/3 + q^*(x)^2/c^{½}. \tag{38}$$

Combining (36)–(38), we therefore obtain

$$\langle q, z^{**}(q), T^{**}(q)\rangle = \langle q, q^2/c, q^3/3 + q^2/c^{1/2}\rangle,$$

the optimal bundling strategy.

6. CONCLUDING REMARKS

In this article we have suggested a method for solving the choice problem of a principal (seller) who selects the rules of a game that is then played non-cooperatively by a set of agents (buyers). We should repeat the two assumptions that are crucial to the success of this method.

First, buyers are assumed to exhibit no income effects and to be neutral toward income risk (although not necessarily neutral toward risk associated with the good being sold). With risk aversion, the analysis is much more complicated. For the relatively simple case where a single item is up for auction, several papers have compared specific auction rules such as the high bid and English auctions. See, for example, Holt (1980), Riley and Samuelson (1981), and Milgrom and Weber (1982). More recently; Matthews (1983) and Maskin and Riley (1984) have characterized the *optimal* auction, given risk aversion.

Second, we suppose that the underlying family of demand curves can be described by the variation of a single parameter. This is an assumption common to virtually all work to date on adverse selection. Unfortunately, work by Laffont, Maskin, and Rochet (1982) suggests that extensions to even two-parameter families will not be easy.

One restrictive feature of the models of Secs 2–5 is that the seller simply offers buyers a price schedule; there is no negotiation between the parties. That is, the seller effectively has all the monopoly power. In many cases, however, we might expect points on the Pareto frontier other than the seller's favourite to emerge as the outcome of contracting.

For example, consider the problem facing a manager (the 'principal') who must engage an expert (the 'agent') to perform some service. The principal's payoff is an increasing function of the quality, q, of the service provided and a decreasing function of the payment, Ω, to the agent. In fact, suppose that the principal is neutral toward income risk, with payoff function

$$R = B(q) - \Omega.$$

Quality is an increasing function of the agent's effort, e, and a random exogenous parameter $\tilde{\upsilon}$:

$$q = D(e; \tilde{\upsilon}).$$

The principal observes neither υ, the realization of $\tilde{\upsilon}$, nor the agent's effort. He does, however, know the distribution, $F(\cdot)$, of $\tilde{\upsilon}$. A contract, negotiated before the realization of $\tilde{\upsilon}$, specifies a payment by the principal to the agent contingent on the quality, q, that is observed by both parties. The agent can observe υ and choose an effort level after making this observation. We suppose further that, after observing υ, the agent has the option of terminating the contract.[14] In that event, both the principal and agent obtain a zero payoff. Finally, we suppose that the agent is also neutral towards income risk, with payoff function

$$U = \Omega - A(e).$$

Because the principal can observe neither the random shock nor effort, it may appear as though this model, unlike those of the previous sections, exemplifies moral hazard as well as adverse selection (see the Introduction). But because we suppose that the agent chooses an effort level only *after* he observes υ, the problem reduces, in effect, to one of pure adverse selection. This results because, assuming a monotonic production function, the principal could deduce the agent's effort if he knew the realization of $\tilde{\upsilon}$. Thus, only the asymmetric information about the value of $\tilde{\upsilon}$ prevents an efficient allocation. Indeed, we can 'eliminate' effort from the model by defining the net social benefit function

$$N(q; \upsilon) = \max_{e} \{ B(q) - A(e) \mid q \leq D(e; \upsilon) \}$$

and reexpressing the agent's payoff function as

$$U = N(q; \upsilon) - R.$$

[14] If an agreement between the principal and agent prohibiting the agent from later terminating can be costlessly enforced, the incentive problem is readily solved. Since both parties are assumed to be neutral towards income risk, the principal simply offers to pay the total benefit $B(q)$ less some fixed sum P. The agent thus receives the full marginal benefit of his action.

Thus, the problem has exactly the same structure as that of monopoly pricing. Assuming that there are no other individuals in the economy with the same skills as the expert, both parties have monopoly power. Thus, the outcome of efficient contracting will be some point on the Pareto frontier.

Under the assumptions of Secs 2–4, it is possible to say quite a bit about the shape of this frontier (for the details, consult Maskin and Riley (1983b)). For example, under Assumptions 1, 2 and 3, a movement along the Pareto frontier in favour of the agent lowers the return function $\bar{R}(q)$ for each value of q. Furthermore, such a movement reduces q for each value of υ, unless q equals zero. Under this same set of assumptions, we can also conclude that the Pareto frontier is concave, i.e. bowed outwards.

APPENDIX

Proposition 7 and its proof follow.

Proposition 7: General characterization of the optimal response function.

(A) Suppose Assumptions 1, 2, and 5 are satisfied. Then if there exists an optimal response function, $q^*(\upsilon)$, there exists a set of subintervals $\{ [x^i, y^i] \subseteq [0, \bar{\upsilon}] \mid x^{i-1} > y^i \}_{i \in 1}$, possibly empty, such that for all i

(i) $\bar{q}(x^i) = \bar{q}(y^i)$

(ii) $\displaystyle\int_{\upsilon}^{y} \frac{\partial I}{\partial q}(\bar{q}(y), z)dF(z) \leq 0, \quad \upsilon < y \quad y \notin \bigcup_{i \in I} (x^i, y^i)$

with equality if $y = y^i$ and $\upsilon = x^i (x^i > 0)$. Moreover,

$$\text{(iii)} \quad q^*(\upsilon) = \begin{cases} \bar{q}(y^i) & \text{if } \upsilon \in [x^i, y^i] \text{ for some } i \\ \bar{q}(\upsilon) & \text{otherwise.} \end{cases}$$

(B) Given Assumptions 1, 2, and 5, a collection of subsets satisfying (i) and (ii) exists. If, in addition, Assumption (6) holds, then $q^*(\upsilon)$, defined by (iii), is an optimal response function.

Proof of (A). Assume that Assumptions 1, 2, and 5 hold and suppose that $q^*(\upsilon)$ is an optimal response function. That is, $q^*(\upsilon)$ solves

$$\max_{q(\upsilon)} \left\{ R_0 = \int_0^{\bar{\upsilon}} I(q(\upsilon); \upsilon) dF(\upsilon) \mid q(\upsilon) \right.$$
$$\left. \text{non-negative and non-decreasing} \right\}. \quad \text{(A1)}$$

We note first that for υ such that $\bar{q}(\upsilon) > 0$, $(\partial I/\partial q)(\bar{q}(\upsilon); \upsilon) = 0$. Therefore, for such υ, Assumption 5 implies that $(\partial^2 I/\partial q^2)(\bar{q}(\upsilon); \upsilon) < 0$. Hence,

$$\frac{d\bar{q}}{d\upsilon} = -\frac{\partial^2 I}{\partial q \partial \upsilon} \Bigg| \frac{\partial^2 I}{\partial q^2},$$

and we conclude that $\bar{q}(\upsilon)$ is differentiable.

We next establish that, for any $\hat{\upsilon}$,

if $q^*(\hat{\upsilon}) \neq \bar{q}(\hat{\upsilon})$, there exists a non-empty interval $[z_1, z_2]$ such that $\hat{\upsilon} \in [z_1, z_2]$ $\upsilon \in [z_1, z_2]$ and $q^*(\upsilon) = q^*(\hat{\upsilon})$ for all $\upsilon \in [z_1, z_2]$. (A2)

Suppose that this is false and there exists $\hat{\upsilon}$ such that $q^*(\hat{\upsilon}) \neq \bar{q}(\hat{\upsilon})$, but q^* is strictly increasing at $\hat{\upsilon}$ both from the left and to the right. If $\bar{q}^*(\hat{\upsilon}) < \bar{q}(\hat{\upsilon})$, then, because $\bar{q}(\upsilon)$ is continuous, there exists $\upsilon_* < \hat{\upsilon}$ such that

$$q^*(\upsilon) < q^*(\hat{\upsilon}) < \bar{q}(\upsilon) \quad \text{for all } \upsilon \in (\upsilon_*, \hat{\upsilon}).$$

Define

$$\hat{q}(\upsilon) = \begin{cases} q^*(\hat{\upsilon}), & \upsilon \in (\upsilon_*, \hat{\upsilon}) \\ q^*(\upsilon), & \text{otherwise.} \end{cases}$$

Then from assumption 5, $\int_0^{\bar{\upsilon}} I(\hat{q}(\upsilon); \upsilon) dF(\upsilon) > \int_0^{\hat{\upsilon}} I(q^*(\upsilon); \upsilon)\, dF(\upsilon)$, a contradiction of the optimality of q^*. A similar contradiction results if $q^*(\hat{\upsilon}) > \bar{q}(\hat{\upsilon})$. Hence, (A2) holds.

We next show that

$$q^*(\upsilon) \text{ is a continuous function.} \quad \text{(A3)}$$

Let $\{ (x^i, y^i) \mid y^{i-1} > x^i \}_{i \in I}$ be the set of 'maximal' intervals on which $q^*(\upsilon)$ is constant: That is,

$$\forall\, \upsilon < x^i, \quad q^*(\upsilon) < q^*(x^i), \qquad \text{and} \quad \forall\, \upsilon > y^i, \quad q^*(\upsilon) > q^*(y^i).$$

From (A2) and the continuity of $\bar{q}(\upsilon)$, $q^*(\upsilon) = \bar{q}(\upsilon)$ for $\upsilon \notin \bigcup_{i \in I} [x^i, y^i]$, and it remains to show that $q^*(\upsilon)$ is continuous at x^i, if $x > 0$, and at y^i. Suppose there is an upward discontinuity at y^i. Since $\bar{q}(\upsilon)$ is continuous, there exists $z < y^i$ such that

$$\bar{q}(\upsilon) > \lim_{\upsilon \uparrow y^i} q^*(\upsilon), \quad \upsilon \in [z, y^i].$$

Suppose that over $[z, y^i]$, $\bar{q}(\upsilon)$ takes on its minimum at $\hat{\upsilon}$. Then

$$q^*(\upsilon) = \lim_{\upsilon \uparrow y^i} q^*(\upsilon) < \bar{q}(\hat{\upsilon}), \quad \upsilon \in [z, y^i].$$

Define

$$\hat{q}(\upsilon) = \begin{cases} q^*(\hat{\upsilon}), & \upsilon \in (z, y^i) \\ q^*(\upsilon), & \text{otherwise.} \end{cases}$$

Arguing exactly as before, one can show that expected seller revenue is greater under $\hat{q}$ than q^*, thereby contradicting the hypothesis that q^* is an optimal response function. Then $q^*(\upsilon)$ is continuous at y^i. Similarly, $q^*(\upsilon)$ is continuous at x^i as well, if $x^i > 0$.

Given (A2) and (A3), we can readily establish that the following conditions are also necessary:

$$\int_{\hat{\upsilon}}^{\bar{\upsilon}} \frac{\partial I}{\partial q}(q^*(\upsilon); \upsilon)dF(\upsilon) \leq 0, \quad \hat{\upsilon} < \bar{\upsilon} \tag{A4}$$

and

$$\int_{x^i}^{y^i} \frac{\partial I}{\partial q}(q^*(\upsilon); \upsilon)dF(\upsilon) = 0, \quad i \in I, \quad x^i > 0. \tag{A5}$$

For any $\upsilon \in [0, \hat{\upsilon}]$, define the non-decreasing function

$$q^+(\upsilon, s) = \begin{cases} q^*(\upsilon); & \upsilon < \hat{\upsilon} \\ q^*(\upsilon) + s; & \upsilon \geq \upsilon \end{cases} \tag{A6}$$

for $s \geq 0$. Replacing $q^*(\upsilon)$ by $q^+(\upsilon, s)$, we can write expected seller revenue $\bar{R}_o(s)$ as a function of s:

$$\bar{R}_o(s) = \int_0^{\bar{\upsilon}} I(q^+(\upsilon, s); \upsilon)dF(\upsilon).$$

At $s = 0$, the right derivative of $\bar{R}_o(s)$ is

$$\frac{d\bar{R}_0^+}{ds}(0) = \int_{\hat{\upsilon}}^{\bar{\upsilon}} \frac{\partial I}{\partial q}(q^*(\upsilon); \upsilon)dF(\upsilon).$$

Since $q^*(\upsilon)$ is optimal, $(d\bar{R}_0^+/ds)$ (0) must be non-positive; hence, we obtain (A4).

Because $\frac{\partial I}{\partial q}(q^*(\upsilon); \upsilon) = \frac{\partial I}{\partial q}(\bar{q}(\upsilon); \upsilon) = 0$ on $[y^1, \bar{\upsilon}]$,

$$\int_{x^1}^{y^1} \frac{\partial I}{\partial q}(q^*(\upsilon); \upsilon)dF(\upsilon) = \int_{x^1}^{\bar{\upsilon}} \frac{\partial I}{\partial q}(q^*(\upsilon); \upsilon)dF(\upsilon). \quad \text{(A7)}$$

Define the non-decreasing function

$$\bar{q}(\upsilon, s) = \begin{cases} \min\{q^*(\upsilon), q^*(x^1) - s\}, & \upsilon < x^1 \\ q^*(\upsilon) - s & \upsilon \geq x^1. \end{cases}$$

Because $q^*(\upsilon)$ is strictly increasing in a left neighbourhood of x^1, there exists a function $\upsilon(s)$ such that for small non-negative s,

$$\bar{q}(\upsilon, s) = \begin{cases} q^*(\upsilon), & \upsilon < \upsilon(s) \\ q^*(x^1) - s, & \upsilon(s) \leq \upsilon \leq x^1, \end{cases}$$

and $\upsilon(s)$ is differentiable, and tends to x^1 as s tends to zero. Replacing $q^*(\upsilon)$ by $\bar{q}(\upsilon, s)$, we obtain expected seller revenue

$$\bar{\bar{R}}_o(s) = \int_0^{\bar{\upsilon}} I(\bar{q}(\upsilon, s); \upsilon)dF(\upsilon).$$

At $s = 0$, the right derivative of $\bar{\bar{R}}(s)$ is

$$\frac{d\bar{\bar{R}}(0)^+}{ds} = -\int_{x^1}^{\bar{\upsilon}} \frac{\partial I}{\partial q}(q^*(\upsilon); \upsilon)dF(\upsilon). \quad \text{(A8)}$$

The optimality of $q^*(\upsilon)$ implies that $(d\bar{\bar{R}}^+/ds)$ (0) must be non-positive. Thus (A8) implies

$$\int_{x^1}^{\bar{\upsilon}} \frac{\partial I}{\partial q}(q(\upsilon); \upsilon)dF(\upsilon) \geq 0. \quad \text{(A9)}$$

Formula (A9), together with (A4) and (A7), establishes that (A5) must hold for $i = 1$. Virtually the same argument establishes that (A5) holds for $i > 1$ as well.

By assumption, $q^*(\upsilon) = \bar{q}\,(\upsilon)$ for $\upsilon \notin \bigcup_{i \in 1} (x^i, y^i)$. By the continuity of q^* and from (A2), $q^*(\upsilon) = q^*(y^i)$ for all $\upsilon \in [x^i, y^i]$. Hence, (i) and (iii) of the statement of the Proposition hold. Conditions (A4) and (A5) imply that (ii) holds. *Q.E.D.*(A)

Proof of (B). An alternative way of deriving (A2) to (A5) is to formulate the seller's optimization as an exercise in optimal control, with the associated Lagrangian

$$\dot{L} = \int_0^{\bar{\upsilon}} [I\,(q\,(\upsilon);\,\upsilon)F'\,(\upsilon) + \lambda(\upsilon)q'(\upsilon)]dv.$$

If we take

$$\lambda(\upsilon) \equiv -\int_{\upsilon}^{\bar{\upsilon}} I\,(q\,(z);\,z)dF\,(z), \tag{A10}$$

then it is straightforward to show that, given subintervals satisfying (i) and (ii), (A2)–(A5), together with the requirements that $q\,(\upsilon)$ be non-negative and non-decreasing, are equivalent to the first-order conditions for a maximum corresponding to this Lagrangian. Hence, $q^*(\upsilon)$ defined by (iii) satisfies the first-order conditions.

As for the second-order conditions, sufficient conditions for a critical point (one satisfying the first-order conditions) to be a local maximum are that

$$\frac{\partial^2 I}{\partial q^2}\,(q\,(\upsilon);\,\upsilon) < 0 \quad \text{if} \quad \lambda(\upsilon) = 0, \tag{A11}$$

$$\int_{\alpha}^{\beta} \frac{\partial^2 I}{\partial q^2}\,(q\,(\upsilon);\,\upsilon)dF\,(\upsilon) < 0 \;\; \text{if} \;\; \lambda(\alpha) = \lambda(\beta) = 0 \;\; \text{and} \;\; \lambda(\upsilon) > 0 \;\; \text{for all} \;\; \upsilon \in (\alpha,\,\beta), \tag{A12}$$

and

$$\int_0^{\beta} \frac{\partial I}{\partial q}\,(q\,(z);\,z)dF\,(z) \le 0 \;\; \text{if} \;\; \lambda(\beta) = 0 \;\; \text{and} \;\; \lambda(\upsilon) > 0 \;\; \text{for all} \;\; \upsilon \in (0,\,\beta). \tag{A13}$$

Now given (A10), $\lambda(\upsilon) = 0$ implies that

$$\int_{\upsilon}^{\bar{\upsilon}} \frac{\partial I}{\partial q}\,(q\,(z);\,z)dF\,(z) = 0. \tag{A14}$$

If $q(\upsilon) \neq \bar{q}(\upsilon)$, then $\upsilon \in (x^i, y^i)$ for some i. Furthermore, Assumption 5 implies that $(\partial I/\partial q)(q(\upsilon); \upsilon) \neq 0$. Therefore, in view of (A14), there exists $\bar{\upsilon}$ in a neighbourhood of υ such that

$$\int_{\upsilon}^{\bar{\upsilon}} \frac{\partial I}{\partial q}(q(z); z) dF(z) > 0, \tag{A15}$$

a contradiction of (A4). Hence $\lambda(\upsilon) = 0$ implies that $(\partial I/\partial q)(q(\upsilon); \upsilon) = 0$. Thus, if Assumption 5 is satisfied, (A11) holds.

If $\lambda(\alpha) = \lambda(\beta) = 0$ and $\lambda(\upsilon) > 0$ for all $\upsilon \in (\alpha, \beta)$, then $(\alpha, \beta) = (x^i, y^i)$ for some i. Hence $q(\upsilon) = \bar{q}(\beta)$ for all $\upsilon \in (x^i, y^i)$, and $\int_\alpha^\beta (\partial I/d\upsilon)(\bar{q}(\beta); \upsilon) dF(\upsilon) = 0$. Therefore, Assumption 6 implies that (A12) holds. Similarly, it also implies (A13). Hence, under Assumptions 1, 2, 5 and 6, any $q(\upsilon)$ satisfying (A2)–(A5) is a global maximum.

It remains to show that there exists a collection of subintervals satisfying (i) and (ii) (since, from the above argument, $q^*(\upsilon)$ defined by (iii) will then be an optimal response function). Let

$$Y^1 = \left\{ \upsilon \mid \int_x^y \frac{\partial I}{\partial q}(\bar{q}(y); z) dF(z) \leq 0, \forall\, x \leq y\ \forall\, y \geq \upsilon \right\} \tag{A16}$$

For $\bar{q}(\upsilon) > 0$, we have

$$0 = \frac{\partial I}{\partial q}(\bar{q}(\upsilon); \upsilon) = p(\bar{q}(\upsilon); \upsilon) - c - \frac{p_2(\bar{q}(\upsilon), \upsilon)}{\rho(\upsilon)}$$

By Assumption 1 and from the definition of $\rho(\upsilon)$, the last term is negative for $\upsilon < \bar{\upsilon}$ and zero at $\bar{\upsilon}$. Thus by Assumption 5,

$$\begin{aligned} \bar{q}(\upsilon) &< q^e(\upsilon), & \upsilon &< \bar{\upsilon} \\ &= q^e(\upsilon), & \upsilon &= \bar{\upsilon}, \end{aligned}$$

where $q^e(\upsilon)$ is the efficient quantity level. Therefore, from Assumption 5, $(\partial I/\partial q)(\bar{q}(\bar{\upsilon}); \upsilon) < 0$ for all $\upsilon < \bar{\upsilon}$, and so, for all υ sufficiently close to $\bar{\upsilon}$, $\upsilon \in y^1$.

Let $y^1 = \inf Y^1$. Then $y^1 < \bar{\upsilon}$. If $y^1 = 0$, we are done; the sequence is of zero length. Therefore, assume that $y^1 > 0$. By continuity

$$\int_x^{y^1} \frac{\partial I}{\partial q}(\bar{q}(y^1); z) dF(z) \leq 0 \qquad \text{for all} \qquad x \leq y^1. \tag{A17}$$

We first argue that there exists $\varepsilon > 0$ such that $\bar{q}$ is non-decreasing on $[y^1 - \varepsilon, y^1]$. If not, then because $\bar{q}$ is piecewise differentiable, $\bar{q}$ must be decreasing in some interval $[y^1 - \varepsilon, y^1]$. But then, from Assumption 5, $\int_{y^1-\varepsilon}^{y^1} (\partial I/\partial q)\,(\bar{q}\,(y^1); z)dF\,(z) > 0$, thereby contradicting (A17).

By definition of y^1, there exists an increasing sequence $\{\upsilon_n\} \subseteq [y^1 - \varepsilon, y^1]$ such that for each n there exists $w_n < \upsilon_n$ with

$$\int_{w_n}^{\upsilon_n} \frac{\partial I}{\partial q}\,(\bar{q}\,(\upsilon_n); z)dF\,(z) > 0. \tag{A18}$$

Because $\bar{q}$ is non-decreasing on $[y^1 - \varepsilon, y^1]$, $w_n < y^1 - \varepsilon$ for all n. Let $w = \lim_{n\to\infty} w_n$ (if $\{w_n\}$ does not converge, let w be the limit of a subsequence that does). Then $w < y^1$ and in view of (A17) and (A18),

$$\int_{w}^{y^1} \frac{\partial I}{\partial q}\,(\bar{q}\,(y^1); z)dF\,(z) = 0.$$

Thus, the set $X^1 = \left\{x \mid \int_x^{y^1} (\partial I/\partial q)\,(\bar{q}\,(y^1); z)dF\,(z) = 0, x < y^1\right\}$ is nonempty. Let $x^1 = \inf X^1$. Then

$$\int_{x^1}^{y^1} \frac{\partial I}{\partial q}\,(\bar{q}\,(y^1); z)dF\,(z) = 0. \tag{A19}$$

If $x^1 = 0$, we are done. Therefore, assume that $x^1 > 0$.
We claim that $\bar{q}\,(x^1) = \bar{q}\,(y^1)$. First, suppose that $\bar{q}\,(x^1) < \bar{q}\,(y^1)$. From Assumption 5, $(\partial I/\partial q)\,(q; x^1) < 0$ for all $q > \bar{q}\,(x^1)$. Thus, $(\partial I/\partial q)$ $(\bar{q}\,(y^1); x^1) < 0$, and so, from (A19), for small $\varepsilon > 0$,

$$\int_{x^1+\varepsilon}^{y^1} \frac{\partial I}{\partial q}\,(\bar{q}\,(y^1); z)dF\,(z) > 0,$$

a contradiction of (A17). If, on the other hand, $\bar{q}\,(x^1) > \bar{q}\,(y^1)$, then from Assumption 5, $(\partial I/\partial q)\,(\bar{q}\,(y^1); x^1) > 0$, in which case $\int_{x^1-\varepsilon}^{y^1} (\partial I/\partial q)\,\bar{q}\,(y^1); z)dF\,(z) > 0$ for $\varepsilon > 0$ sufficiently small, again a contradiction. Thus,

$$\bar{q}\,(x^1) = \bar{q}\,(y^1).$$

Let

$$Y^2 = \left\{ \upsilon \leq x^1 \mid \int_x^y \frac{\partial I}{\partial q} (\bar{q}\,(y); z) dF\,(z) \leq 0, \forall x \leq y \,\forall y \in [\upsilon, x^1] \right\}.$$

For all $\upsilon \leq x^1$, $\int_\upsilon^{x^1} (\partial I/\partial q)(\bar{q}(x^1), z) dF(z) = \int_\upsilon^{y^1} (\partial I/\partial q) \bar{q}(y^1); z) dF(z) \leq 0$, from (A17) and (A19) and from the fact that $\bar{q}\,(x^1) = \bar{q}\,(y^1)$. Therefore, $x^1 \in Y^2$. If $x^1 = \inf Y^2$, then from the above argument, there exists $x < x^1$ such that $\int_x^{x^1} (\partial I/\partial q)\,(\bar{q}\,(x^1); z) dF\,(z) = 0$. But then $\int_x^{y^1} (\partial I/\partial q)$ $(\bar{q}\,(y^1); z) dF\,(z) = 0$, thereby contradicting the fact that $x^1 = \inf X^1$. Thus, $\inf Y^2 < x^1$. If we take $y^2 = \inf Y^2$, we can continue, iteratively, to generate $x^2, y^3, \ldots$. The process terminates because q is piecewise differentiable. *Q.E.D.*(B)

REFERENCES

BARON, D. and R.B. MYERSON (1982), 'Regulating a Monopolist with Unknown Costs', *Econometrica*, 50, 911–30.

BRITO, D.L. and W.H. OAKLAND (1980), 'On the Monopolistic Provision of Excludable Public Goods', *American Economic Review*, 70(4), 674–91.

GOLDMAN, M.B., H.E. LELAND and D.S. SIBLEY (1980), 'Optimal Nonuniform Prices' (mimeo).

HARRIS, M. and A. RAVIV (1981), 'Theory of Monopoly Pricing with Uncertain Demand', *American Economic Review*, 71, 347–65.

HART, O.D. (1983), 'Optimal Labour Contracts under Asymmetric Information: An Introduction', *Review of Economic Studies*, 50, 3–36.

HOLT, C. (1980), 'Competitive Bidding for Contracts under Alternative Auction Procedures', *Journal of Political Economy*, 88, 433–45.

LAFFONT, J.J., E.S. MASKIN and J.C. ROCHET (1982), 'Optimal Nonlinear Pricing with Two-Dimensional Characteristics' (mimeo).

MASKIN, E.S. and J.G. RILEY (1980), 'Auctioning an Indivisible Object', Kennedy School of Government Working Paper No. 87D, Harvard University.

—— (1983a), 'Optimal Multiunit Auctions', UCLA Discussion Paper.

—— (1983b), 'Monopoly with Incomplete Information', UCLA Discussion Paper.

—— (1984), 'Optimal Auctions with Risk Averse Buyers', *Econometrica*, 52.

Matthews, S. (1983), 'Selling to Risk Averse Buyers with Unobservable Tastes', *Journal of Economic Theory*, 30, 370–400.

Milgrom, P.R. and R.J. Weber (1982), 'A Theory of Auctions and Competitive Bidding', *Econometrica*, 50, 1089–1122.

Mirman, L.J. and D. Sibley (1980), 'Optimal Nonlinear Prices for Multiproduct Monopolies', *Bell Journal of Economics*, 11(2), 659–70.

Mirrlees, J. (1971), 'An Exploration in the Theory of Optimum Income Taxation', *Review of Economic Studies*, 38, 175–208.

Mussa, M. and S. Rosen (1978), 'Monopoly and Product Quality', *Journal of Economic Theory*, 18, 301–17.

Myerson, R.B. (1981), 'Optimal Auction Design', *Mathematics of Operations Research*, 6, 58–73.

Oi, W. (1971), 'A Disneyland Dilemma: Two-Part Tariffs for a Mickey Mouse Monopoly', *Quarterly Journal of Economics*, 85, 77–96.

Oren, S.S., S.A. Smith and R.B. Wilson (1984), 'Pricing a Product Line', *Journal of Business*, 57(1), part 2, S73–S100.

Pigou, A.C. (1930), *The Economics of Welfare*, London: Macmillan.

Riley, J.G. and W.F. Samuelson (1981) 'Optimal Auctions', *American Economic Review*, 71, 381–92.

Roberts, K.W.S. (1979), 'Welfare Implications of Nonlinear Prices', *Economic Journal*, 89, 66–83.

Spence, A.M. (1977), 'Nonlinear Prices and Welfare', *Journal of Public Economics*, 8, 1–18.

Stiglitz, J.E. (1977), 'Monopoly, Nonlinear Pricing, and Imperfect Information: The Insurance Market', *Review of Economic Studies*, 44, 407–30.

Vickrey, W. (1961), 'Counterspeculation, Auctions, and Competitive Sealed Tenders', *Journal of Finance*, 16, 8–37.

Durable-Goods Monopolists*

Jeremy I. Bulow

1. INTRODUCTION

This paper explains the special type of monopoly power held by a firm that is a monopolist in the production and sale of a durable good. This power can be substantial but is notably less than the power held by a monopolist who produces a durable good which is rented rather than sold.

The distinction of the renter and the seller is what makes durable-goods monopolists interesting. When such a monopolist can rent, he can achieve all the standard results of the non-durable monopolist.[1] Selling is a much more difficult problem, involving an important incompleteness of contracts and an expectational problem.

Coase (1972) brought the durable-goods monopoly problem to attention in an interesting paper.[2] Assume the seller cannot sign contracts limiting his future production. Then, upon his sale of a unit, the best thing for him to do seems to be to try to sell another unit at as high a price as he can get. Seemingly, this should go on until price equals

* The author would like to thank Ben Bernanke, Ralph Braid, Stanley Fischer, David Garvin, Jay Helms, Eric Maskin, John Shoven, Robert Solow, and members of the Sloan Finance Seminar for reading earlier drafts of this paper and providing valuable comments. Also John Geanakoplos, David Kreps, Robert Wilson, and an anonymous referee for more recent help. The support of the Alfred P. Sloan Foundation is gratefully acknowledged.

1 Those results have been best developed in Swan (1970a; 1970b; 1971; 1972, and 1977) and Sieper and Swan (1973).

2 Another very good paper which discussed similar issues is Gaskins (1974), recently criticized by Swan (1980). Douglas and Goldman (1969) made an even earlier effort in this area, but their consumers were consistently fooled. For a comprehensive survey of the literature on durable-goods monopolists, see Schmalensee (1979).

marginal cost. Now suppose that very little time is needed to transact. Then intelligent consumers, assuming the price will soon fall to the competitive level, will be unwilling to pay more than the competitive price for the early units. It is possible that the monopolist can lose complete control of the situation and forfeit all his monopoly power.

For some products there may be a very simple way to convince buyers that future production will be limited. The simplest case is the artist who makes a lithograph and destroys the plates. In other markets, the seller may be able to create contracts that make his position mathematically equivalent to that of a renter. (That is, the producer remains responsible for any changes in the good's asset value.) However, there are many markets where renting or its mathematical equivalent is not feasible.

For example, durable intermediate products must be sold and not rented. When steel was first produced and began replacing iron for railroad tracks, it would have been impractical for the steel companies to rent the steel bars. What would have happened if, in year two, a rental price could not be agreed upon? It would have been possible to sign a long-term rental agreement, but for the purposes of this model such a contract is similar to an outright sale. Only a complicated, 'floating-rate' rental contract, with rental price tied by formula to market prices, could replace the outright sale. Such contracts may be very costly to write. Repurchase agreements may also not be feasible for, say, designer clothing. Along the same lines, a consumer of diamonds may wish to cut and mount a stone. Since such a change is irreversible, a sale may be the only kind of arrangement which will allow for alteration of the stone.

A more compelling example involves products such as automobiles. While a rental market exists, few people will rent on a month-to-month basis rather than buy. A significant factor is that people who rent cars may not find it in their interests to be as careful with them as owners are. This is because it may be extremely costly to measure the damage caused by an individual renter. Thus, we will argue because the producer controls the supply side of the market he determines the general price level of the product. However, in many markets the user's behaviour may have the more significant impact on the market value of a given individual unit. In such a market it may make more sense for the purchaser to be responsible for changes in unit value than for the producer to maintain ownership.

Finally, it must be noted that for the purposes of this paper 'durable good' can be broadly defined. Of course, all products that yield a flow of services to the owner over a significant period of time may be included. However, other products whose current demand depends on previous consumption may also qualify. A ticket to a first-run movie has the durable quality that once someone has seen the film that person is unlikely to buy a second ticket. Thus, the movie company will find the demand for tickets on any re-release of the film to be negatively related (*ceteris paribus*) to the number of viewers who saw the film when it first came out. Similarly, the expectation that a viewing will be available at a cheaper price on a second run affects demand for the first-run film. (The market for hardcovers and paperbacks works this way also.) It is quite clearly impractical for firms to sell first-run movie tickets and give viewers a right to get some money back if the film is ever re-released with lower ticket sales prices.

This paper will show that often the seller can devise a production strategy that will make it better off than the competitive firm, though not nearly as well off as the renter. The crucial difference between the seller and the renter is that if a renter 'overproduces' he suffers the capital loss on old units; thus, the costs of production are internalized. If a seller overproduces, the losses are suffered by old purchasers in whose welfare the seller has no direct interest. The loss is not internalized, and the firm will end up overproducing relative to the renter. Naturally, the intelligent buyers will foresee any incentives for overproduction and will factor those incentives into determining the price they will pay for a unit at any given time. Thus, it is the monopolist rather than his customers who must pay for this lack of complete contracts, for this inability to internalize the effects of overproduction.

In minimizing the effect of this incompleteness, the seller finds it in his interest to behave in a substantially different manner than either a renter or a competitive firm. The seller must find ways to make precommitments about production. Discrete-time models, of course, embody a certain amount of precommitment: You decide how much to produce and then produce no more until one period later. Sometimes a form of precommitment can be purchased by the firm at the price of producing a less durable product, running a high marginal-cost operation, or restricting capacity. Such induced behaviour on the part of the seller produces the following results:

1. An almost perfect analogy can be drawn between the renter and the conventional non-durable-goods monopolist.
2. Sellers may choose to produce using an 'inefficient' production technology. That is, the firm may select a technology and an output path such that the identical output would have been produced with a lower present value of total costs by using a different technology. In general, the seller will choose to produce by paying too little for fixed costs and too much for marginal costs—a reverse Averch–Johnson result.
3. Selling firms will prefer to produce goods that are less durable than those produced by competitive firms. However, a renter firm would produce goods just as durable as those produced by the competitive industry.
4. Society may suffer greater deadweight loss when a monopolist seller exists than when a renter exists. This is true even though the renter must necessarily make greater profits than the seller.

It is important to emphasize that this paper argues that the results of virtually all the literature on durable-goods monopolists yield correct results only for the case where the product can be rented or the firm can make some costless commitment to guarantee it will do the same thing as a renter. But such earlier results have limited value because a renter is a monopolist in a non-durable good (rental services).[3]

2. THE MODEL

In the market studied here, the product produced never depreciates. There is no technological obsolescence. Demand for the services yielded by the good is constant, following the demand curve

[3] An exception is the useful paper by Swan (1980). Swan makes the important point that, even if the producer can precommit on production, buyers may find recycling an attractive activity even if their costs exceed the cost of new production by the monopolist. These higher costs will come out of the monopolist's profit. The reason is that the present value of the monopolist's profit is equal to the present value of industry rents minus the present value of industry costs (competitive recyclers make nothing). The existence of recyclers who operate at cost levels greater than what the monopolist would find profitable if it also controlled the recycling market ends up thus reducing the monopolist's profits. The monopolist's effective marginal cost becomes that of the recycler.

$$p = \alpha - \beta q, \tag{1}$$

where p is one-period rental price, q is cumulative quantity produced to date, and α and β are constants. That is, if the firm produced α/β units and sold them, it could literally only give its production away thereafter. There are no worries about another firm entering the market, perhaps due to a patent. The interest rate is assumed to be a constant. All available production technologies involve constant marginal costs.

The commodity produced is assumed to be perfectly divisible. All purchases are competitive—no individual purchaser believes he has any effect on the output of the firm. Perfect information about the demand curve, production costs, and production is available.

A perfect second-hand market exists. One way to think of the effect of the second-hand market in the case of the seller is to imagine that all output is sold to competitive leasing firms. These leasing firms charge a high enough rental so that the short-run leasing market always clears, implying that the consumers who are willing to pay the most for the output are always the ones who have it. The second-hand market serves two roles: (1) It eliminates price discrimination and (2) it makes allowance for the fact that even with a static demand curve different individuals may do the demanding each period. To elaborate on the second point, consider the demand for baby carriages. In 1954 my parents had a high demand for one unit. In the current period their demand is zero, while someone else is doing the demanding. With no second-hand market, even though the baby carriage has a long physical life, its economic life is very short because the demanders of one period have no demand in the next. The product is the equivalent of a non-durable good. If the demanders remained the same each period there would be no need for second-hand transactions. Thus, either correlation in demanders from one point in time to the next or a second-hand market is needed to make durability a significant characteristic. Aesthetically, perfect second-hand markets are preferable here so that it will be clear that all results derive strictly from the lone imperfection that firms must sell instead of rent.

Three types of markets are studied. Competitive firms may either sell or rent their output. A renter could sell if he wished but always makes more money by renting, given perfect foresight. A monopolist seller cannot rent, although he may be able to sell to competitive leasing firms which can rent to consumers. Renting generally may be ruled out for selling firms for legal or practical reasons. For example, United Shoe Company, IBM, and Xerox all began by only renting their products but are now required to also make sales. DeBeers, the diamond monopolists, are in a business where renting would simply not be practical. In other markets (such as the market for automobiles), renting may be uneconomic because renters may abuse products. For a product such as aluminum, renting is clearly an impossibility. For the purposes of this paper, it will be assumed that manufacturer renting does not occur for legal reasons, and future contracts between selling firms and customers are also not allowed.

3. EXPECTATIONS

There are no expectational difficulties in the competitive case or in the case of the monopolist renter. Given the technologies available, this simple model yields deterministic competitive results directly from minimum average cost and zero-profit conditions.

The monopolist renter also poses no expectational problems. Firms need only examine the current rental price to determine whether a machine is worth renting this period. The monopolist's profits are the difference between the present value of rents and the present value of costs, and he simply adopts the strategy which maximizes this difference. The profit-maximization and cost-minimization problems are somewhat separable, in that for any given production stream the monopolist would clearly choose the technology which produced the lowest total costs. The renter's problem is as easy to solve as the competitive problem, being very similar to the problem of a monopolist in a non-durable-good industry. This is an intuitive result, since by renting his product rather than selling it the renter is effectively making his monopoly one in providing the (non-durable) services of his output.

The monopolist seller does provide severe expectational difficulties. Once he sells a machine he is no longer interested in what happens to the value of that machine. However, his customers presumably realize this and take this factor into account in determining how much they are willing to pay for a machine.

In a two-period model (or, in principle, in an n-period model) the expectational problem of the seller can be solved recursively: One can see what the trivial optimal strategy will be in period 2 given any strategy in period 1, and then the best strategy in period 1 can be calculated. I will develop the two-period model in the next section of the paper because it brings out most of the paper's important results and then will comment on its weaknesses in the following section.

4. THE TWO-PERIOD MODEL

Assume for simplicity that there are no costs of production. The interest rate is ρ. The demand curve for rental services of the product is of the form $p = \alpha - \beta q$, as described in equation (1). (These assumptions are stronger than necessary, but generalization adds nothing to intuition.)

Next, make two artificial and crucial assumptions: (1) There are discrete periods of time, production occurs at the beginning of a period, and no further production occurs until the beginning of the next period; (2) there are two periods (the crucial element here is that there are a finite number of periods so that the problem can be solved recursively).

Let q_{iC} = quantity produced by the competitive industry in the ith period, q_{iR} = quantity produced by the monopolist renter in the ith period, and q_{iS} = quantity produced by the monopolist seller in the ith period.

In the competitive case, all production will occur immediately:

$$q_{1C} = \alpha/\beta;\ q_{2C} = 0. \tag{2}$$

Profits are zero and price = marginal cost of zero. Rental price is zero in both periods. The renter will also produce some units in period 1 and none in period 2 and then rent the same units in both periods. The renter's problem is

$$\max_{q_{2R},\, q_{1R}} q_{1R}\,(\alpha - \beta q_{1R}) + \frac{(q_{1R} + q_{2R})\,[\alpha - \beta(q_{1R} + q_{2R})]}{(1 + \rho)} \tag{3}$$

which solves to $q_{1R} = \alpha/2\beta;\ q_{2R} = 0$.

Rental price in each period is $\alpha/2$. The number of units rented each period is $\alpha/2\beta$. Profits each period are $(\alpha/2\beta)\,(\alpha/2) = \alpha^2/4\beta$. The present value of all profits is $[(2+\rho)/(1+\rho)]\,(\alpha^2/4\beta)$.

Now consider the case of the monopolist seller. Assume that the firm chooses to produce $\bar{q}_{1S}$ in period 1. Then in period 2 the firm faces an effective demand curve for rental services of $(\alpha - \beta\bar{q}_{1S}) - \beta q_{2S}$. Since this is also the last period, the demand curve for purchases equals the demand curve for rentals. To maximize profits in that situation the firm will choose to produce $q_{2S} = (\alpha - \beta\bar{q}_{1S})/2\beta$ (see Fig. 1).

The firm maximizes the revenue obtained from second-period sales by placing $[\,(\alpha/\beta) - \bar{q}_{1S})\,]/2$ units. That is the point where marginal revenue equals zero. At such a point marginal production reduces the value of previous sold units; however, this is not something for the firm to consider directly. Those units are already sold, and once they are sold the monopolist has no interest in maintaining their price. In the first period, then, upon observing the choice of q_{1S} consumers can reasonably be expected to form expectations that period 2 production will be $(\alpha - \beta q_{1S})/2\beta$. With this expectation about production it is easy to calculate the present value of rentals from period 1 sales (i.e.

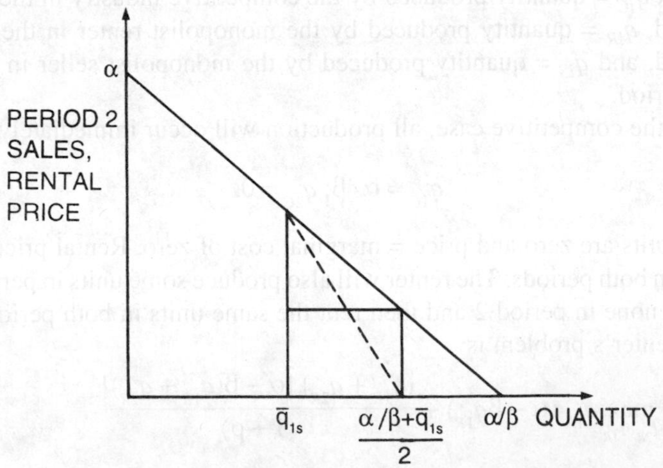

Figure 1

the period 1 sales demand curve). The sales price in period 1, p_1, can be written as

$$p_1 = (\alpha - \beta q_{1S}) + [(\alpha - \beta q_{1S})/2(1+\rho)]. \tag{4}$$

The problem of the monopolist seller can now be written as

$$\max_{q_{1S},\, q_{2S}} q_{1S}\, p_1\,(q_{1S}) + \frac{1}{1+\rho}\,(\alpha - \beta q_{1S} - \beta q_{2S})q_{2S}\,, \tag{5}$$

which solves to

$$q_{1S} = \frac{\alpha/\beta}{2 + \{1/[2(1+\rho)]\}}\; q_{2S} = \frac{\alpha}{2\beta}\left(\frac{1 + \{1/[2(1+\rho)]\}}{2 + \{1/[2(1+\rho)]\}}\right) \tag{6}$$

Substituting (6) into (5) makes it possible to calculate firm profits, which are unambiguously lower than in the renter's case.

This two-period model can be extended to achieve results 2 and 3 in the Introduction:

2. The selling firm will choose to spend 'too little' on fixed costs. Unlike the results of previous models (see, e.g. Swan, 1972; 1977), the cost-minimization and revenue-maximization problems cannot be separated. Firms will choose to invest little in plant so as to keep their marginal costs high. High marginal costs are a signal of lower future output and thus high future prices; the prospect of high future prices raises current prices and thus firm revenues. The firm is therefore willing to sacrifice efficiency to achieve this result.

Assume that the firm can invest in a continuum of technologies which have constant marginal cost c and one-time fixed sunk cost $F\,(c)$.

Then proceeding as above, the problem of the monopolist seller can be written as

$$\max_{q_{1S},\, q_{2S},\, c} q_{1S}\,[p_1(q_{1S}, c) - c] + \frac{1}{1+\rho}\, q_{2S}(\alpha - \beta q_{1S} - \beta q_{2S} - c) - F(c) \tag{7}$$

$$q_{1s}, q_{2s} \geq 0$$

The greater the value of c, the lower the optimal value of q_{2S}. The lower the projected q_{2S}, the greater the price p_1 given any level of q_{1S}.

To simplify further, consider the case where $\rho = 0$. Then (7) can be solved to find

$$\begin{aligned}
&(a) && q_{1S}=\frac{2}{5}\frac{\alpha}{\beta},\ q_{2S}=\frac{3}{10}\frac{\alpha}{\beta}-\frac{c}{2\beta} && \text{for} && 0\le c\le\frac{3\alpha}{5};\\
&(b) && q_{1S}=\frac{\alpha}{\beta}-\frac{c}{\beta},\ q_{2S}=0 && \text{for} && \frac{3\alpha}{5}\le c\le\frac{2\alpha}{3};\\
&(c) && q_{1S}=\frac{1}{2}\left(\frac{\alpha}{\beta}-\frac{c}{2\beta}\right),\ q_{2S}=0 && \text{for} && \frac{2\alpha}{3}\le c\le 2\alpha;\\
&(d) && q_{1S}=0,\ q_{2S}=0 && \text{for} && c\ge 2\alpha.
\end{aligned} \tag{8}$$

In region a, as marginal costs rise firms do not cut first-period production: Rising costs convince customers that second-period output will be lower, thus raising prices and maintaining the attractiveness of first-period production.

In region b, the seller produces more than the renter with the same marginal cost curve. If the seller produced the renter's quantity ($\frac{1}{2}[(\alpha/\beta)-(c/2\beta)]$ throughout cases *a*, *b*, and *c*), customers would realize that it will make sense for the seller to produce a little more in the second-period. It makes more sense for the seller to produce extra output now and at least get the benefit of reducing customers' expectations of second-period output.

In region c, the seller can do exactly the same thing as the renter: Profits can be maximized assuming period 2 production will be zero and, in fact, period 2 production will optimally be zero.

In region d, costs are so high that the firm closes up shop.

Examining region a more carefully, we find the present value of profits to be

$$\pi=\frac{.20\alpha^2}{\beta}+\frac{.25(\alpha-c)^2}{\beta}-F. \tag{9}$$

A profit-maximizing firm would, by (8), be willing (in this region) to spend an extra dollar on fixed costs only up to the point where $\partial c/\partial F=\beta/[-.5(\alpha-c)]$ (assuming $\partial^2 c/\partial F^2>0$). However, production over the two periods is $(.7\alpha/\beta)-(.5c/\beta)$ from (8a). Thus an extra dollar spent on fixed costs would reduce the total marginal costs of producing the same output by $[(.7\alpha/\beta)-(.5c/\beta)]/[(.5\alpha/\beta)-(.5c/\beta)]=(1.4\alpha-c)/(\alpha-c)$, or between \$1.40 and \$2.00 for $0\le c\le 3/5\alpha$, at the point where the firm would stop making its fixed investment. In region b, the seller will also invest less in fixed investment than the renter because his benefit from reducing costs is lower—even though his output is higher.

As a numerical example, consider the firm that is choosing between two technologies. One technology involves zero marginal costs ($c = 0$) and fixed costs $F(0) = .22\alpha^2/\beta$. Assume that the interest rate $\rho = 0$. The second technology involves constant marginal costs $c = .6\alpha$ but zero fixed costs.

Then the firm with zero marginal costs will, by (6), produce $.4\alpha/\beta$ in period 1 and $.3\alpha/\beta$ in period 2. Its total revenues (which need not be discounted because $\rho = 0$) will be $.45\alpha^2/\beta$. In period 1 the sales price will be $.9\alpha$, while in period 2 the sales price drops to $.3\alpha$. Imputed rental prices are $.6\alpha$ in period 1 and $.3\alpha$ in period 2. After subtracting off fixed costs of $.22\alpha^2/\beta$ the firm is left with net profits of $.23\alpha^2/\beta$.

The firm with marginal costs equal to $.6\alpha$ will also produce $.4\alpha/\beta$ in period 1. However, it will produce zero units in period 2. Its total revenues will be $.48\alpha^2/\beta$. In period 1 the sales price will be 1.2α, while in period 2 the resale price drops to $.6\alpha$. Customers know that the firm cannot produce any more cheaply than for $.6\alpha$; thus any positive second-period production would be a money-losing venture. The total costs for this firm are $.24\alpha^2/\beta$—all incurred in the first period. Net profits are $.24\alpha^2/\beta$.

The result here is as follows. By adopting the low (no) fixed-cost strategy, the firm's optimal production path has been altered so that in each period it produces less than or equal to the number of units it would have produced with low marginal costs. The present value of total costs associated with producing this reduced output is higher than the present value of costs associated with the higher production. Nevertheless, the high-cost strategy is still more profitable because a commitment to hold down future output is effectively developed.

3. Selling firms will produce goods that are less durable than those produced by renting firms, or a competitive market. Again, this is in contrast to the results of Swan (1972), who implicitly treats renters and sellers identically and concludes that durable-goods monopolists will produce output as durable as competitive firms.

The reason for this 'planned obsolescence' result is quite simple: We have shown that renters can make more money than sellers. By producing a less durable product the monopoly seller becomes more like a renter. A renter provides services for his market one period at a time. A monopolist seller can achieve the same result by producing goods that only last one period at a time.

Again, consider a numerical example derived from the two-period model. Setting the interest rate $\rho = 0$, the profits for a monopolist seller with no fixed or marginal costs is $.45\alpha^2/\beta$. However, assume that the life of the product is shortened to one period. Then first-period production will be $[.5(\alpha - c)]/\beta$ and first-period profits will be $[.25(\alpha - c)^2]/\beta$. In the second period profits will be either $[.25(\alpha - c)^2]/\beta$ or $.25\alpha^2/\beta$, depending upon whether the firm can switch back to producing the cheaper (and more durable) output in the second period. In any event, cumulative profits will be at least $[.5(\alpha - c)^2]/\beta$. If $c < (1 - .9^{1/2})\ \alpha \approx .0513\alpha$, then the firm does better by producing the less durable good.

Thus, the result in this example is that the firm produces a version of its product that is costly to build rather than a more durable version that can be constructed at zero cost. This result is achieved even though firms and consumers face the same discount rate (in contrast to Barro, 1972), and consumers have full knowledge of the product's durability—and thus pay less for the product that has a shorter life.

In general, the seller will not produce as durable a product as the competitive market, or the renter. Roughly speaking, if production costs are very low relative to rental price (as in the example above), the firm could conceivably be willing to pay more to produce a less durable product. More usually, as the cost becomes a larger fraction of price, durability will be a virtue—but not as much of a virtue to a seller as a renter.

It is possible to speculate that this relationship between the value of durability and the cost/price ratio of the product may also provide insights into research and development by a monopolist. If R & D serves the role of making an old product obsolete, monopolists in fields with low cost/price ratios may be willing to spend a good deal on new product development so that they can sell new products to their customers. Firms with high costs will have less incentive to make old products obsolete—it is important for such firms that customers be willing to pay a significant purchase price, representing the value of several years' worth of services, in order to make production profitable. A company with low per unit costs will do better to make profits by creating obsolescence and selling new units.

5. DIFFICULTIES WITH THE TWO-PERIOD MODEL

The crucial difference between the Coase model and the two-period model is the ability of the firm to precommit to limiting its production. With Coase, once one unit is sold the second unit is then quickly sold as well. With a two-period model, once today's output is sold no more is marketed for an entire period. If periods have significant length, this is important. (In a one-period model the sellers' and renters' problems are trivially identical.) Stokey (1980), in a paper which criticizes an earlier version of this paper, rigorously shows that in the limit, as period length becomes small, the Coase result is achieved. The Coase result is most intuitive when output is not infinitely divisible. Then following Coase's logic it is clear that in each period it will make sense to sell at least one unit. Delay for a period will not alter the firm's situation (except that in a finite-time model there will be a period less until the end), but a period's worth of interest is lost. As time periods grow smaller, sales of one unit each period will produce the competitive quantity in less and less real time.

The Coase result is also analogous to results by Calvo (1978) and others in the time-consistency literature in monetary theory.[4] Calvo asks how the government can maximize the seignorage it will receive from printing money. If the government can, it will do something like the monopolist renter does. In a stagnant economy the government may print an arbitrary quantity of money in the first period, and by promising not to print any more it will hold the level of real balances at a constant level. All seignorage is earned at the outset. In a growing economy there may be some optimal positive money growth.

However, suppose the government cannot precommit. If there are t periods left the firm will choose a path of money production independent of past money growth. (Optimal growth rates can be solved optimally from the last period back.) This implies that real balances held with $t-1$ periods to go are independent of money growth at period t. Seignorage in period t is the real balance held at $t-1$ times the percentage of the nominal money supply printed in period t. Obviously, the higher the period-t inflation rate is, the higher is seignorage in that period. Future seignorage is unhurt by printing

[4] Important papers in this literature include Pollak (1968), Friedman (1969), and Kydland and Prescott (1977).

a great deal of money, because $t-1$ real balances are unaffected by the current money growth rate. Thus the firm produces money at the maximum possible rate in each period. Because it is assumed that holding down the current rate of money growth does not provide any information about what will be done in the future, there is no incentive to hold down the current growth rate. Similarly, in the durable-goods monopolist case Coase (and Stokey) does not permit the firm to reduce customer expectations about production over the next few periods by simply lowering current production.

Three questions arise out of this discussion. First, can firms successfully lengthen periods, and if so how? Second, can firms actually influence expectations of future production via their current production behaviour? Third, what alternative methods are available for restricting production?

All three questions are clearly related: They all amount to questions about the firm making commitments about future production either through explicit action (such as building a less durable product or a high marginal cost plant) or through implicit action (creating beliefs about future behaviour by following a consistent strategy different from the Nash equilibrium in this model or developing a reputation in other markets that convinces people you will restrict production).

There may be some 'natural' constraints on the firm that effectively make periods last a long time. For example, it may be quite costly to alter production levels. Thus there is an inertia which causes current production rates to be maintained. Costs of changing prices work in the same direction.

Periods may also be limited implicitly. Virtually all major commercial banks will only sell certificates of deposit once a day—so dealers know that at least for that day (the typical trader's longest possible time horizon) there will be no more of that specific product flooding the market.

Implicit restrictions on production—without the firm incurring the cost of producing inefficiently—may be possible via establishing a reputation. For example, people may be willing to believe that a monetary authority which has printed little money in the last 10 years will not start to print great amounts tomorrow, despite the theoretical arguments made above. Kreps and Wilson (1980) have done rigorous work in the area of reputation. They argue that a conglomerate, operating in many markets, may be able to maintain its monopoly positions by responding in a very tough manner to anyone who tries to enter an individual market—even if profits in the individual market are hurt by following a tough strategy.

In the extreme form, a firm which had monopolies in many markets at different times might even be able to convince customers that it would operate like a renter. A more likely outcome is that the producer will be able to establish a less than perfect reputation. For example, an author may be able to establish that he will not put out a low-cost edition (paperback) for at least a year after the hardcover comes out. However, it may be difficult to convince anyone that a paperback will never come out.

If the firm must decide its production a long time in advance (for technological reasons, say) it will benefit from being able to precommit itself. Another promising way to gain some monopoly power is to be in a situation where the firm has some maximum productive capacity. Even if the firm has the ability to construct additional capacity, it might be against its interest to do so. Consider, for example, the optimal seignorage problem. Calvo (1978) shows that the government will print money as fast as it can. However, its seignorage will be highest if the maximum printing rate possible is relatively low. The durable-goods monopolist with a capacity constraint can commit to only gradually pushing the price down and thus do better than the unconstrained seller.

6. A MODEL WITH CAPACITY CONSTRAINTS

As a numerical example, consider a firm which faces a demand curve for the rental services of its product of $p_T = \alpha e^{-\beta Q_T}$, where p is the rental price and $Q_T = \int_0^T q_t$ or the cumulative production at time t. Assume marginal costs of production are zero.

Furthermore, assume that capacity can be constructed costlessly, but once it is constructed it cannot be destroyed. (Allowing the capacity to also be destroyed costlessly would mean that the problem is in no way different from the case of not having a capacity constraint.) For the time being, make the important assumption that there is an infinite horizon.

The exponential demand curve is chosen because no matter how many units have been sold in the past the firm is still facing an exponential demand curve with the same relative slope. That is, a change in the monetary unit will make the demand curve the firm faces after producing a large number of units identical with the one it faced at the outset. This means that if at any time in the future the firm were to again choose its optimal capacity it would opt for the same amount—given that capacity is costless. If capacity is costly, obviously it will become less attractive to build as the market winds down. This factor will be important when we discuss relaxing the infinite time horizon assumption.

Given that whatever capacity q the firm chooses everyone accurately assumes will be the production level from here on (an assumption to be justified soon), the firm's problem can be written as

$$\max_{q} \pi = \int_{0}^{\infty} qt\alpha e^{(-\beta q + \rho)t} dt. \tag{10}$$

The explanation of (10) is that the firm's profits will equal the present value of the rental value of all output to be on the market at each point in time. After t periods qt units will be outstanding, each receiving a rent of $\alpha e^{-\beta qt}$, which must be discounted by $e^{-\rho t}$.

Solving (10) yields $q = \rho/\beta$, $\pi = \alpha/4\rho\beta$.

It can now be easily seen that the firm will produce up to capacity at each moment: At time t the sales price of a unit of output will be $\alpha e^{-\rho t}/2\rho$ while the present value of future profits will be $\alpha e^{-\rho t}/4\beta p$. Producing an extra unit today with future output unchanged would increase current revenues by $\alpha e^{-\rho t}/2\rho$, while the present value of future profits would be decreased by $\alpha e^{-\rho t}/4\rho$. Thus, the firm would find an increase in current output to be profitable, if only adding capacity did not increase customers' expectations about future output. For this level of capacity, then, it is true that the firm would produce up to capacity at each moment regardless of what consumers think (if consumers expect lower future production, current sales are made even more attractive), and consumers will rationally expect the firm to always produce at capacity.

No additions to capacity will be expected. The reason is that if capacity is raised customers will realize that at each individual moment it would pay the firm to produce at the higher level. This would lead customers to pay lower sales prices and reduce profits. Thus, if the extra capacity is built the firm will use it at each moment and profits will be lower. There is therefore no incentive to ever build more capacity.

In this example, a renter would have produced $1/\beta$ units immediately and never any future output. Comparing the seller and the renter, the seller's franchise would be 32 per cent less valuable. Discounting the deadweight loss caused by the renter and seller at the interest rate ρ yields the result that deadweight loss is 36 per cent greater with a seller than a renter. Even though the renter eventually reaches the point of producing almost the competitive quantity, it takes a long time to get there. Early on the seller has fewer units on the market than the renter and so causes a larger deadweight loss. The effects of these early periods dominate. The present value of consumers' surplus is 5 per cent lower with a seller than with a renter. All these results are independent of α, β, and ρ. Furthermore, the deadweight loss result is fairly insensitive to the exact level of production chosen by the seller. Even if a constant output 70 per cent greater than profit maximizing is chosen, deadweight loss is still greater with a seller than with a renter.

Thus, the effect of forcing a renter monopolist to sell is that the present value of profits falls by almost a third. However, this loss of monopoly power does not make consumers any better off. In fact, they end up slightly worse off, and deadweight loss increases dramatically.

A problem with the capacity model above is that it does depend on the infinite horizon. A finite horizon would cause the problem to unravel from the end, much like a repeated game of Prisoner's Dilemma: It is clear that the firm would decide to add capacity in any final period. This would make adding capacity in the next-to-last period more attractive, and so on. The problem would solve out in exactly the same way as the no-capacity-limitation problem.

There are suggestions for saving the capacity solution. The first is to make capacity costly. Then even in a finite-time version of the model the problem will not reduce to the competitive problem. The reason is that at the end of the game there will be no incentive to build new capacity because the costs could not be recaptured through higher output in the brief remaining time. Now adding capacity in an earlier period has two costs—the cost of building and the cost that customers will rationally expect higher output (than without the new capacity) in the remaining periods. If capacity is costless, neither of these costs appears. The firm can effectively constrain itself and earn some monopoly profits. A finite-horizon model with costly capacity has not yet been developed.

Moorthy (1980) has developed a solution for the finite-capacity problem when there is asymmetrical information about the firm's capacity. In Moorthy's model, capacity is exogenously given, as might be true with a diamond mine where there is a maximum rate at which the diamonds can be extracted before the costs of increasing output become prohibitive. The firm knows its capacity, but customers only have a probability distribution as to whether capacity is high or low.

If the firm ever produces a large amount it will be obvious that capacity is high, and customers will assume high output in the remaining periods. It may pay the firm in the early periods to produce at a low level even if it has high capacity to keep customers from altering their probabilistic estimates of capacity and lowering the prices they will pay. Finally, when only a few periods remain it will pay to produce at the high level.

7. EXTENSIONS OF THE RESULTS

This section is meant to indicate further types of activity which may be observed due to the durable monopolist's special problem.

1. *Price guarantees*

A firm which could only sell rather than rent might wish to write various types of contracts to give its customers the same kind of protection that a renter would have. In the models in this paper, if the firm were able to give its customers an American put (money-back guarantee exercisable at any time), it could achieve the renter's profits. However, that is because we did not consider products where user abuse can affect the value (like automobiles) and products that cannot be easily transferred (such as installed railroad tracks). Such realistic problems do not render price guarantees worthless but do prevent sellers from being able to reproduce renters' results.

2. *Service contracts*

If the monopolist also has a monopoly in servicing his product he may be able to come closer to achieving the renter's result. Services are non-durables, so to the extent that the firm can transfer its monopoly power to the service area it can take greater advantage of its position. (Polaroid may choose to take its profits in film rather than cameras; Gillette, in blades rather than razors—even independent of the usual price-discrimination reasons for these two particular results.) Another type of service contract may tend to reduce the liquidity of the second-hand market. A firm may agree to guarantee performance so long as the original owner holds the product. Naturally, this discourages second-hand sales. If demand among different customers fluctuates substantially (as opposed to aggregate demand varying), then normally an active second-hand market would ensue. If production costs are low relative to price, the monopolist is more likely to want a poor second-hand market and write such a contract.

3. *Implicit contracts*

If a firm cannot write explicit contracts to control its future production and be like a renter, it may take implicit contracts. For example, DeBeers, the South African diamond monopolist, has a policy of never reducing the nominal price of its diamonds. This is an implicit contract that DeBeers will hold down sales sufficiently to keep the market price of its product up. In 1978 there was a tremendous surge in the speculative demand for diamonds, and DeBeers's fixed price was below the market level. This placed the firm in a dilemma. If it raised its prices substantially and the speculative bubble burst, then it would either have to violate its implicit contract or have very low sales for a long time. (That is, increased uncertainty about future equilibrium prices reduced the desirability of a permanent commitment to a high price.) On the other hand, if sales prices were not raised, DeBeers would be rationing its output at below market prices and not capturing the maximum potential profits. The firm's solution to the problem was to impose a *price surcharge* rather than a price increase. Using the surcharge was a way to signal that the current price increase was revocable and not in the nature of the more usual increases. This way, price could be first raised and then lowered without violating the implicit contract. What actually occurred was that the surcharge was reduced and then replaced by a permanent price increase.

8. SUMMARY OF RESULTS AND APPLICATIONS

On some occasions firms have been required by law to sell rather than rent their products. In some durable-goods markets renting is simply impractical. This paper discusses the contrasting problems of the durable-goods monopolists who can rent their products and those who must sell.

Firms that can rent resemble monopolists producing non-durable goods. The direct analogy between monopolists renting a durable and those producing a non-durable good is always transparent. As with the non-durable-goods monopolists, the renter will always choose the cost-minimizing production strategy for any chosen stream of rental services to be produced.

Monopolist sellers do not do as well as renters. This is a perfectly general result unless it is assumed that consumers can be fooled as to future production. The seller makes less money because he has the ability to reduce the capital value of the outstanding stock of durables (via new production) and no way of guaranteeing that this power will not be used. As a matter of policy, however, it is unclear that the government should force durable-goods monopolists to sell. There may be a welfare cost in forcing firms to sell their products. Of course, a policy of forcing monopolists to sell will also discourage the development of monopolies, which may be good or bad.

The monopolist seller cannot choose his production technology independent of the demand for his products. Thus, if one is told what the production strategy of the seller will be, one cannot assume that the production will be produced in the most efficient way possible. A 'reverse Averch–Johnson' result—that the seller will choose to spend too little on fixed costs and too much on marginal costs—is derived.

A similar, curious application of this work involves DeBeers. Diamonds must be sold rather than rented for various institutional reasons. However, suppose DeBeers was able to guarantee that it would close its mines ten or fifteen years from now and in the interim their production was limited by some capacity constraints. Then DeBeers's position would be more like that of the monopoly renter. Prices of currently sold diamonds would rise enough so that the value of the firm would rise despite profits from the mines going to zero once they close.

Of course, DeBeers cannot make such a promise. However, suppose political turmoil in South Africa increases so that people think the government will eventually go under, and it is believed that after the government falls DeBeers's production will be sharply curtailed for a long time. The company's stock could easily rise because of this predicted future trouble. On the other hand, if the trouble increases the chance of the mine being closed very soon, the firm is obviously going to be worth less. Presumably, the best thing for DeBeers then is news which decreases the chance of a short-term problem and increases the chance that they will be forced to shut down at the some date in the medium-distant future.

REFERENCES

BARRO, ROBERT J. (1972), 'Monopoly and Contrived Depreciation', *Journal of Political Economy*, 80, 3, Part 1, 598–602.

CALVO, GUILLERMO A. (1978), 'Optimal Seigniorage from Money Creation: An Analysis in Terms of the Optimum Balance of Payments Deficit Problem', *Journal of Monetary Economics*, 4, 503–17.

COASE, RONALD H. (1972), 'Durability and Monopoly', *Journal of Law and Economics*, 15, 143–9.

DOUGLAS, A.J. and STEVEN M. GOLDMAN (1969), 'Monopolistic Behaviour in a Market for Durable Goods', *Journal of Political Economy*, 77, 1, 49–59.

FRIEDMAN, MILTON (1969), 'The Optimum Quantity of Money', in *The Optimum Quantity of Money and Other Essays*, Aldine, Chicago.

GASKINS, DARIUS W., Jr. (1974), 'ALCOA Revisited: The Welfare Implications of a Secondhand Market', *Journal of Economic Theory*, 7, 254–71.

KREPS, DAVID M. and ROBERT WILSON (1980), 'On the Chain-Store Paradox and Prediction: Reputation for Toughness', Research Paper No. 551, Stanford University, Graduate School of Business.

KYDLAND, FINN E. and EDWARD C. PRESCOTT (1977), 'Rules Rather than Discretion: The Inconsistency of Optimal Plans', *Journal of Political Economy*, 85, 3, 473–91.

MOORTHY, SRIDHUR (1980), 'Notes on Durable Goods Monopolists and Rational Expectations Equilibria', Unpublished notes, Stanford University, Graduate School of Business.

POLLAK, ROBERT A. (1968), 'Consistent Planning', *Review of Economic Studies*, 35, 201–8.

SCHMALENSEE, RICHARD (1979), 'Market Structure, Durability, and Quality: A Selective Survey', *Economic Inquiry*, 17, 177–96.

SIEPER, E. and PETER L. SWAN (1973), 'Monopoly and Competition in the Market for Durable Goods', *Review of Economic Studies*, 40, 333–51.

STOKEY, N.L. (1980), 'Rational Expectations and Durable Goods Pricing, Discussion Paper 408R, Northwestern University, Department of Managerial Economics and Decision Science.

SWAN, PEPTER L. (1970a), 'Durability of Consumption Goods', *American Economic Review*, 60, 884–94.

—— (1970b), 'Market Structure and Technological Progress: The Influence of Monopoly on Product Innovation', *Quarterly Journal of Economics*, 84, 627–38.

—— (1971), 'The Durability of Goods and Regulation of Monopoly', *Bell Journal of Economics and Management Science*, 2, 347–57.

—— (1972), 'Optimum Durability, Second-Hand Markets, and Planned Obsolescence', *Journal of Political Economy*, 80, 3, Part 1, 575–85.

—— (1977), 'Product Durability under Monopoly and Competition: Comment', *Econometrica*, 45, 229–35.

—— (1980), 'ALCOA: The Influence of Recycling on Monopoly Power', *Journal of Political Economy*, 88, 1, 76–99.

PRODUCT DIFFERENTIATION

On Hotelling's 'Stability in Competition'

C. D'ASPREMONT, J. JASKOLD GABSZEWICZ
AND JACQUES-FRANÇOIS THISSE

The purpose of this note is to show that the so-called *Principle of Minimum Differentiation*, as based on Hotelling's 1929 celebrated paper, is invalid. Firstly, we assert that, contrary to the statement formulated by Hotelling in his model, nothing can be said about the tendency of both sellers to agglomerate at the centre of the market. The reason is that no equilibrium price solution will exist when both sellers are not far enough from each other. Secondly, we consider a slightly modified version of Hotelling's example, for which there exists a price equilibrium solution everywhere. We show however that, for this version, there is a tendency for both sellers to maximize their differentiation. This example thus constitutes a counter-example to Hotelling's conclusions.

We shall first recall Hotelling's model and notations. On a line of length l, two sellers A and B of a homogeneous product, with zero production cost, are located at respective distances a and b from the ends of this line ($a + b \leq l$; $a \geq 0$, $b \geq 0$). Customers are evenly distributed along the line, and each customer consumes exactly a single unit of this commodity per unit of time, irrespective of its price. Since the product is homogeneous, a customer will buy from the seller who quotes the least delivered price, namely the mill price plus transportation cost, which is assumed linear with respect to the distance. Let p_1 and p_2 denote, respectively, the mill price of A and B and let c denote the transportation rate.

The situation described above gives rise to a two-person game with *players A* and *B*, *strategies* $p_1 \in S_1 \underset{\text{def}}{=} [0, \infty]$, and $p_2 \in S_2 = S_1$, and *payoff functions* given by the profit functions:

$$\pi_1(p_1, p_2) = ap_1 + \frac{1}{2}(l-a-b)p_1 + \frac{1}{2c}p_1p_2 - \frac{1}{2c}p_1^2, \quad \text{if } |p_1 - p_2| \le c(l-a-b);$$

$$= lp_1, \quad \text{if } p_1 < p_2 - c(l-a-b);$$

$$= 0, \quad \text{if } p_1 > p_2 + c(l-a-b);$$

$$\pi_2(p_1, p_2) = bp_2 + \frac{1}{2}(l-a-b)p_2 + \frac{1}{2c}p_1p_2 - \frac{1}{2c}p_2^2, \quad \text{if } |p_1 - p_2| \le c(l-a-b);$$

$$= lp_2, \quad \text{if } p_2 < p_1 - c(l-a-b);$$

$$= 0, \quad \text{if } p_2 > p_1 + c(l-a-b).$$

The profit function of seller *A* is illustrated in Fig. 1 for a fixed value $\bar{p}_2$.

Clearly a particular feature of these profit functions is the presence of two discontinuities which appear at the price where a whole group of buyers is indifferent between the two sellers.

A strategy p_1 of player *A* is a *best reply against* a strategy p_2 of player *B* when it maximizes $\pi_1(\cdot, p_2)$ on the whole S_1 for the given p_2. Similarly for player *B*. A *Nash–Cournot equilibrium point* is a pair (p_1^*, p_2^*) such that p_1^* is a best reply against p_2^* and vice-versa.

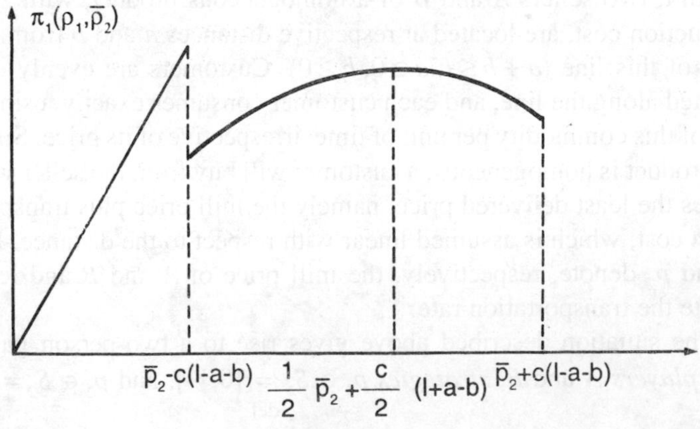

Figure 1

In the following proposition we shall treat the problem of existence of such an equilibrium for every location a and b. More specifically, we shall derive necessary and sufficient conditions on a and b for such an equilibrium to exist, and compute all equilibrium points.

Proposition: For $a + b = l$, the unique equilibrium point is given by $p_1^* = p_2^* = 0$. For $a + b < l$, there is an equilibrium point if, and only if

$$\left(l + \frac{a-b}{3}\right)^2 \geq \frac{4}{3} l\,(a + 2b), \tag{1}$$

$$\left(l + \frac{b-a}{3}\right)^2 \geq \frac{4}{3} l\,(b + 2a), \tag{2}$$

and, whenever it exists, an equilibrium point is uniquely determined by

$$p_1^* = c\left(l + \frac{a-b}{3}\right), \tag{3}$$

$$p_2^* = c\left(l - \frac{a-b}{3}\right) \tag{4}$$

Proof: The case $a + b = l$ is immediate. Then both sellers arc located at the same place and, as in Bertrand (1883), there always exists an equilibrium uniquely determined by $p_1^* = p_2^* = 0$. So let $a + b < l$. We shall begin by showing that any equilibrium must satisfy the condition $|p_1^* - p_2^*| < c(l - a - b)$.

Suppose first on the contrary that (p_1^*, p_2^*) is an equilibrium but $|p_1^* - p_2^*| > c(l - a - b)$. Then, one of the two sellers—the one who charges the strictly larger (and hence positive) price—gets a null profit and so may gain by charging a positive price equal to the delivered price of the other. But this contradicts the fact that (p_1^*, p_2^*) is an equilibrium. Suppose now that $|p_1^* - p_2^*| = c(l - a - b)$, say, for instance, $p_2^* - p_1^* = c(l - a - b)$. If $p_1^* = 0$, then the profit of A is zero and so he would profit by charging a positive price less than $p_2^* + c\,(l - a - b)$. If $p_1^* > 0$, two cases may arise. Either A gets the whole market and so B, who charges a positive price, can increase his profit by decreasing his price. Or A gets only a fraction of the market, i.e. $q_1 < l$, and it is then sufficient for A to charges a slightly lower price to capture the whole market and make a larger profit: indeed for

$0 < \varepsilon < (l - q_1)p_1^*/l$ we have $\pi_1(p_1^* - \varepsilon, p_2^*) = l(p_1^* - \varepsilon) > q_1 p_1^* = \pi_1(p_1^*, p_2^*)$. In any case we always get a contradiction. Accordingly any equilibrium (p_1^*, p_2^*) must satisfy the condition $|p_1^* - p_2^*| < c(l - a - b)$.

A consequence of this condition is that, for any equilibrium (p_1^*, p_2^*), p_1^* must maximize $ap_1 + \frac{1}{2}(l - a - b)p_1 + (1/2c)p_2^* p_1 - (1/2c)p_1^2$ in the open interval $]p_2^* - c(l - a - b), p_2^* + c(l - a - b)[$, and similarly for p_2^*. Taking first order conditions we get (3) and (4). Hence, we shall now verify that the pair of prices given by (3) and (4) is indeed an equilibrium. Recall that to be an equilibrium strategy p_1^* must maximize $\pi_1(p_1, p_2^*)$ not only in the above interval but on the whole domain S_1, and similarly for p_2^*. Let us see that this is true only on a restricted set of possible locations. Indeed, given a and b, for p_1^* to be an equilibrium strategy against p_2^*, we must have in particular that, for any $\varepsilon > 0$,

$$\pi_1(p_1^*, p_2^*) = \frac{c}{2}\left[l + \frac{a-b}{3}\right]^2 \geq l\,[p_2^* - c(l - a - b) - \varepsilon]. \qquad (*)$$

The right hand side of the inequality is the profit of A, should he quote a delivered price slightly smaller than p_2^*. But condition (*) can be rewritten as (1). By symmetry we get condition (2).

To show that conditions (1) and (2) are also sufficient for (p_1^*, p_2^*) to be an equilibrium it remains only to check that they imply $|p_1^* - p_2^*| < c(l - a - b)$. This completes the proof of our proposition.

Note in passing that if we consider only symmetric locations around the centre ($a = b$), then the necessary and sufficient conditions (1) and (2) reduce to $a = b \leq 1/4$. In other words, both the duopolists must be located outside the quartiles to get a Cournot equilibrium in prices.

If conditions (1) and (2) are strictly verified, then, as noted by Hotelling, both $\partial\pi_1(p_1^*, p_2^*)/\partial a$ and $\partial\pi_2(p_1^*, p_2^*)/\partial b$ are strictly positive, which implies a tendency of both sellers towards the centre. But a major consequence of the preceding proposition is that, as far as the Cournot equilibrium is taken as the market solution, nothing can be said on this solution when conditions (1) and (2) are violated. Hotelling seems to be unaware of this difficulty while deriving the implications of his model, and in particular the tendency of both sellers is agglomerate at the centre of the market.[1] Indeed should conditions (1) and (2) be violated, i.e. should the firms be located relatively close to each other, the Cournot equilibrium could no longer serve as a reference point since it no longer exists![2]

Having reached this negative outcome, it seems natural to work out an example, which is as close as possible to Hotelling's one, but avoiding the difficulty exhibited above.[3] If, for this alternative example, the principle of minimal differentiation could be retrieved, the defect in Hotelling's argumentation would be immaterial. Unfortunately, this principle is invalidated by the following re-examination.

A slightly modified version of Hotelling's example for which there exists a price equilibrium solution for *any* pair of locations (a, b) obtains if, in place of considering linear transportation costs we assume that these costs are quadratic with respect to the distance, i.e. for any distance x, transportation costs are given by cx^2. Under this assumption, an easy computation leads to the following expressions for the demand and profit functions:

$$q_1(p_1, p_2) = a + \frac{p_2 - p_1}{2c(l-a-b)} + \frac{l-a-b}{2},$$

$$\text{if } 0 \le a + \frac{p_2 - p_1}{2c(l-a-b)} + \frac{l-a-b}{2} \le l;$$

$$= l, \qquad \text{if } a + \frac{p_2 - p_1}{2c(l-a-b)} + \frac{l-a-b}{2} > l;$$

$$= 0, \qquad \text{if } a + \frac{p_2 - p_1}{2c(l-a-b)} + \frac{l-a-b}{2} < 0;$$

[1] In footnote (8) of his paper, Hotelling (1929) remarks however that, for some values of a and b, the pair of prices defined by (3) and (4) cannot be an equilibrium, but proposes then another pair of prices as an equilibrium. By our proposition, we know that they are not. It seems that Hotelling has neglected to consider strategies through which a merchant undercuts the delivered price of the other, and attracts to him the whole market. These strategies are particularly advantageous when both merchants are close to each other.

[2] Here we only consider equilibrium with price strategies. However, it is easily verified that if each seller's strategy is a price location pair, which has to be chosen simultaneously, then again no Nash equilibrium exists.

[3] This example is particularly illustrative in regard to footnote (9) of Hotelling's paper.

$$q_2(p_1, p_2) = b + \frac{p_1 - p_2}{2c(l-a-b)} + \frac{l-a-b}{2},$$
$$\text{if } 0 \le b + \frac{p_1 - p_2}{2c(l-a-b)} + \frac{l-a-b}{2} \le l;$$

$$= l, \quad \text{if } b + \frac{p_1 - p_2}{2c(l-a-b)} + \frac{l-a-b}{2} > l;$$

$$= 0, \quad \text{if } b + \frac{p_1 - p_2}{2c(l-a-b)} + \frac{l-a-b}{2} < 0;$$

$\pi_1(p_1, p_2) = p_1 \cdot q_1(p_1, p_2)$ and $\pi_2(p_1, p_2) = p_2 \cdot q_2(p_1, p_2)$. These profit functions ensure the existence of a price equilibrium, *whatever the locations a and b may be*. It is indeed easily checked that the pair of prices (p_1^*, p_2^*) defined by

$$p_1^* = c(l-a-b)\left(l + \frac{a-b}{3}\right) \tag{5}$$

$$p_2^* = c(l-a-b)\left(l + \frac{b-a}{3}\right), \tag{6}$$

is the unique Nash–Cournot equilibrium point for fixed a and b, and that this is true without any condition on these location parameters. We verify however that, if we substitute these equilibrium prices in the profit functions of both players, both $\partial\pi_1(p_1^*, p_2^*)/\partial a$ and $\partial\pi_2(p_1^*, p_2^*)/\partial b$ are negative! Consequently, at any given pair of locations, each merchant gains an advantage from moving away as far as possible from the other.[4]

[4] In other terms, for the game where the strategies are the locations and the payoff functions the profits $\pi_1(p_1^*(a, b), p_2^*(a, b))$ and $\pi_2(p_1^*(a, b), p_2^*(a, b))$—which can be viewed as a sequential game where first locations, and then prices, are chosen—the equilibrium locations are the two extremes. As a referee pointed out to us, Hay (1976) and Prescott and Visscher (1977) use a similar sequential approach. In particular, Prescott and Visscher analyse the existence problem by numerical methods in a revised Hotelling problem and find equilibrium locations 'far apart'. We should stress however that the existence is not restored simply because the discontinuities of the demand functions are eliminated as, for example, by introducing the assumption of strictly convex transportation costs. We have indeed worked out an example which verifies the latter assumption and does not possess any equilibrium prices.

The preceding example, far from confirming the minimal differentiation principle, suggests that this principle cannot be based on spatial competition. Certainly many comments derived from Hotelling's contribution should be carefully re-examined before taking them as granted. The outcome of this note should not however be considered as too negative. Indeed, although Hotelling's example suggested the contrary, one should expect intuitively that product differentiation must be an important component of oligopolistic competition. It seems to be clear that oligopolists should gain an advantage by dividing the market into submarkets in each of which some degree of monopoly would reappear.[5] But this important subject would need more imagination.

REFERENCES

BERTRAND, J. (1883), 'Théorie mathématique de la richesse sociale', *Journal des Savants*, 48, 499–508.

HAY, D.A. (1976), 'Sequential Entry and Entry-Deterring Strategies, *Oxford Economic Papers*, 28, 240–57.

HOTELLING, H. (1929), 'Stability in Competition', *Economic Journal*, 39, 41–57.

JASKOLD GABSZEWICZ, J. and J.-F. THISSE (1979), 'Price Competition, Quality, and Income Disparities', *Journal of Economic Theory*, 20, 340–59.

PRESCOTT, E.C. and M. VISSCHER (1977), 'Sequential Location among Firms with Foresight', *The Bell Journal of Economics*, 8, 378–93.

SALOP, S. (1977), 'Monopolistic Competition Reconstituted or—Circular Fashions in Economic Thought' (mimeo), Federal Reserve Board, Washington, D.C.

[5] An example of this advantage is studied in Jaskold Gabszewicz and Thisse (1979) and Salop (1977).

Monopolistic Competition and Optimum Product Diversity*

AVINASH K. DIXIT AND JOSEPH E. STIGLITZ

The basic issue concerning production in welfare economics is whether a market solution will yield the socially optimum kinds and quantities of commodities. It is well known that problems can arise for three broad reasons: distributive justice; external effects; and scale economies. This paper is concerned with the last of these.

The basic principle is easily stated.[1] A commodity should be produced if the costs can be covered by the sum of revenues and a properly defined measure of consumer's surplus. The optimum amount is then found by equating the demand price and the marginal cost. Such an optimum can be realized in a market if perfectly discriminatory pricing is possible. Otherwise we face conflicting problems. A competitive market fulfilling the marginal condition would be unsustainable because total profits would be negative. An element of monopoly would allow positive profits, but would violate the marginal condition.[2] Thus we expect a market solution to be suboptimal. However, a much more precise structure must be put on the problem if we are to understand the nature of the bias involved.

It is useful to think of the question as one of quantity versus diversity. With scale economies, resources can be saved by producing fewer goods and larger quantities of each. However, this leaves less variety, which entails some welfare loss. It is easy and probably not

* Stiglitz's research was supported in part by NSF Grant SOC 74–22182 at the Institute of Mathematical Studies in the Social Sciences, Stanford. We are indebted to Michael Spence, to a referee, and the managing editor for comments and suggestions on earlier drafts.

[1] See also the exposition by Michael Spence.

[2] A simple exposition is given by Peter Diamond and Daniel McFadden (1974).

too unrealistic to model scale economies by supposing that each potential commodity involves some fixed set-up cost and has a constant marginal cost. Modelling the desirability of variety has been thought to be difficult, and several indirect approaches have been adopted. The Hotelling spatial model, Lancaster's product characteristics approach, and the mean-variance portfolio selection model have all been put to use.[3] These lead to results involving transport costs or correlations among commodities or securities, and are hard to interpret in general terms. We therefore take a direct route, noting that the convexity of indifference surfaces of a conventional utility function defined over the quantities of all potential commodities already embodies the desirability of variety. Thus, a consumer who is indifferent between the quantities (1, 0) and (0, 1) of two commodities prefers the mix (1/2, 1/2) to either extreme. The advantage of this view is that the results involve the familiar own- and cross-elasticities of demand functions, and are therefore easier to comprehend.

There is one case of particular interest on which we concentrate. This is where potential commodities in a group or sector or industry are good substitutes among themselves, but poor substitutes for the other commodities in the economy. Then we are led to examining the market solution in relation to an optimum, both as regards biases within the group, and between the group and the rest of the economy. We expect the answer to depend on the intra- and intersector elasticities of substitution. To demonstrate the point as simply as possible, we shall aggregate the rest of the economy into one good labeled 0, chosen as the numeraire. The economy's endowment of it is normalized at unity; it can be thought of as the time at the disposal of the consumers.

The potential range of related products is labeled 1, 2, 3, . . . Writing the amounts of the various commodities as x_0 and $x = (x_1, x_2, x_3 \ldots$, we assume a separable utility function with convex indifference surfaces:

$$u = U(x_o, V(x_1, x_2, x_3 \ldots)) \tag{1}$$

In Secs 1 and 2 we simplify further by assuming that V is a symmetric function, and that all commodities in the group have equal

[3] See the articles by Harold Hotelling (1929), Nicholas Stern (1972), Kelvin Lancaster (1975), and Stiglitz (1975).

fixed and marginal costs. Then the actual labels given to commodities are immaterial, even though the total number n being produced is relevant. We can thus label these commodities 1, 2, . . . , n, where the potential products $(n+1)$, $(n+2)$, . . . are not being produced. This is a restrictive assumption, for in such problems we often have a natural asymmetry owing to graduated physical differences in commodities, with a pair close together being better mutual substitutes than a pair farther apart. However, even the symmetric case yields some interesting results. In Sec. 3, we consider some aspects of asymmetry.

We also assume that all commodities have unit income elasticities. This differs from a similar recent formulation by Michael Spence, who assumes U linear in x_0, so that the industry is amenable to partial equilibrium analysis. Our approach allows a better treatment of the intersectoral substitution, but the other results are very similar to those of Spence.

We consider two special cases of (1). In Sec. 1, V is given a *CES* form, but U is allowed to be arbitrary. In Sec. 2, U is taken to be Cobb-Douglas, but V has a more general additive form. Thus the former allows more general intersector relations, and the latter more general intrasector substitution, highlighting different results.

Income distribution problems are neglected. Thus U can be regarded as representing Samuelsonian social indifference curves, or (assuming the appropriate aggregation conditions to be fulfilled) as a multiple of a representative consumer's utility. Product diversity can then be interpreted either as different consumers using different varieties, or as diversification on the part of each consumer.

1. CONSTANT-ELASTICITY CASE

1.1 Demand Functions

The utility function in this section is

$$u = U\left(x_0, \left\{\sum_i x_i^\rho\right\}^{1/\rho}\right) \tag{2}$$

For concavity, we need $\rho < 1$. Further since we want to allow a situation where several of the x_i are zero, we need $\rho > 0$. We also assume U homothetic in its arguments.

The budget constraint is

$$x_0 + \sum_{i=1}^{n} p_i x_i = I \tag{3}$$

where p_i are prices of the goods being produced, and I is income in terms of the numeraire, i.e. the endowment which has been set at 1 plus the profits of the firms distributed to the consumers, or minus the lump sum deductions to cover the losses, as the case may be.

In this case, a two-stage budgeting procedure is valid.[4] Thus we define dual quantity and price indices

$$y = \left\{ \sum_{i=1}^{n} x_i^{\rho} \right\}^{1/\rho} \qquad q = \left\{ \sum_{i=1}^{n} p_i^{-1/\beta} \right\}^{-\beta} \tag{4}$$

where $\beta = (1-\rho)/\rho$, which is positive since $0 < \rho < 1$. Then it can be shown[5] that in the first stage,

$$y = I\frac{s(q)}{q} \qquad x_0 = I\,(1 - s(q)) \tag{5}$$

for a function s which depends on the form of U. Writing $\sigma(q)$ for the elasticity of substitution between x_0 and y, we define $\theta(q)$ as the elasticity of the function s, i.e. $qs'(q)/s(q)$. Then we find

$$\theta(q) = \{1 - \sigma(q)\}\,\{1 - s(q)\} < 1 \tag{6}$$

but $\theta(q)$ can be negative as $\sigma(q)$ can exceed 1.

Turning to the second stage of the problem, it is easy to show that for each i,

$$x_i = y\left[\frac{q}{p_i}\right]^{1/(1-\rho)} \tag{7}$$

where y is defined by (4). Consider the effect of a change in p_i alone. This affects x_i directly, and also through q; thence through y as well. Now from (4) we have the elasticity

[4] Green (1964, p. 21).

[5] These details and several others are omitted to save space, but can be found in the working paper by the authors, cited in the references.

$$\frac{\partial \log q}{\partial \log p_i} = \left(\frac{q}{p_i}\right)^{1/\beta} \tag{8}$$

So long as the prices of the products in the group are not of different orders of magnitude, this is of the order $(1/n)$. We shall assume that n is reasonably large, and accordingly neglect the effect of each p_i on q; thus the indirect effects on x_i. This leaves us with the elasticity

$$\frac{\partial \log x_i}{\partial \log p_i} = \frac{-1}{(1-\rho)} = \frac{-(1+\beta)}{\beta}. \tag{9}$$

In the Chamberlinian terminology, this is the elasticity of the *dd* curve, i.e. the curve relating the demand for each product type to its own price with all other prices held constant.

In our large group case, we also see that for $i \neq j$, the cross elasticity $\partial \log x_i / \partial \log p_j$ is negligible. However, if all prices in the group move together, the individually small effects add to a significant amount. This corresponds to the Chamberlinian *DD* curve. Consider a symmetric situation where $x_i = x$ and $p_i = p$ for all i from 1 to n. We have

$$\begin{aligned} y &= xn^{1/\rho} = xn^{1+\beta} \\ q &= pn^{-\beta} = pn^{-(1-\rho)/\rho}, \end{aligned} \tag{10}$$

and then from (5) and (7),

$$x = \frac{Is(q)}{pn}. \tag{11}$$

The elasticity of this is easy to calculate; we find

$$\frac{\partial \log x}{\partial \log p} = -[1 - \theta(q)]. \tag{12}$$

Then (6) shows that the *DD* curve slopes downward. The conventional condition that the *dd* curve be more elastic is seen from (9) and (12) to be

$$\frac{1}{\beta} + \theta(q) > 0. \tag{13}$$

Finally, we observe that for $i \neq j$,

$$\frac{x_i}{x_j} = \left[\frac{p_j}{p_i}\right]^{1/(1-\rho)} \tag{14}$$

Thus $1/(1-\rho)$ is the elasticity of substitution between any two products within the group.

1.2 Market Equilibrium

It can be shown that each commodity is produced by one firm. Each firm attempts to maximize its profit, and entry occurs until the marginal firm can only just break even. Thus our market equilibrium is the familiar case of Chamberlinian monopolistic competition, where the question of quantity versus diversity has often been raised.[6] Previous analyses have failed to consider the desirability of variety in an explicit form, and have neglected various intra- and intersector interactions in demand. As a result, much vague presumption that such an equilibrium involves excessive diversity has built up at the back of the minds of many economists. Our analysis will challenge several of these ideas.

The profit-maximization condition for each firm acting on its own is the familiar equality of marginal revenue and marginal cost. Writing c for the common marginal cost, and noting that the elasticity of demand for each firm is $(1+\beta)/\beta$, we have for each active firm,

$$p_i\left(1-\frac{\beta}{1+\beta}\right)=c.$$

Writing p_e for the common equilibrium price for each variety being produced, we have

$$p_e = c(1+\beta) = \frac{c}{\rho}. \tag{15}$$

The second condition for equilibrium is that firms enter until the next potential entrant would make a loss. If n is large enough so that 1 is a small increment, we can assume that the marginal firm is exactly breaking even, i.e. $(p_n - c)x_n = a$, where x_n is obtained from the demand function and a is the fixed cost. With symmetry, this implies zero profit for all intramarginal firms as well. Then $I = 1$, and using (11) and (15) we can write the condition so as to yield the number n_e of active firms,

[6] See Chamberlin (1950), Kaldor (1934) and Bishop (1967).

$$\frac{s(p_e n_e^{-\beta})}{p_e n_e} = \frac{a}{\beta c}. \tag{16}$$

Equilibrium is unique provided $s(p_e n^{-\beta})/p_e n$ is a monotonic function of n. This relates to our earlier discussion about the two demand curves. From (11) we see that the behaviour of $s(pn^{-\beta})/pn$ as n increases tells us how the demand curve *DD* for each firm shifts as the number of firms increases. It is natural to assume that it shifts to the left, i.e. the function above decreases as n increases for each fixed p. The condition for this in elasticity form is easily seen to be

$$1 + \beta\theta(q) > 0. \tag{17}$$

This is exactly the same as (13), the condition for the *dd* curve to be more elastic than the *DD* curve, and we shall assume that it holds.

The condition can be violated if $\sigma(q)$ is sufficiently higher than one. In this case, an increase in n lowers q, and shifts demand towards the monopolistic sector to such an extent that the demand curve for each firm shifts to the right. However, this is rather implausible.

Conventional Chamberlinian analysis assumes a fixed demand curve for the group as a whole. This amounts to assuming that $n \cdot x$ is independent of n, i.e., that $s(pn^{-\beta})$ is independent of n. This will be so if $\beta = 0$, or if $\sigma(q) = 1$ for all q. The former is equivalent to assuming that $\rho = 1$, when all products in the group are perfect substitutes, i.e. diversity is not valued at all. That would be contrary to the intent of the whole analysis. Thus, implicitly, conventional analysis assumes $\sigma(q) = 1$. This gives a constant budget share for the monopolistically competitive sector. Note that in our parametric formulation, this implies a unit-elastic *DD* curve, (17) holds, and so equilibrium is unique.

Finally, using (7), (11), and (16), we can calculate the equilibrium output for each active firm:

$$x_e = \frac{a}{\beta c}. \tag{18}$$

We can also write an expression for the budget share of the group as a whole,

$$s_e = s(q_e) \tag{19}$$

where

$$q_e = p_e n_e^{-\beta}.$$

These will be useful for subsequent comparisons.

1.3 Constrained Optimum

The next task is to compare the equilibrium with a social optimum. With economies of scale, the first best or unconstrained (really constrained only by technology and resource availability) optimum requires pricing below average cost, and therefore lump sum transfers to firms to cover losses. The conceptual and practical difficulties of doing so are clearly formidable. It would therefore appear that a more appropriate notion of optimality is a constrained one, where each firm must have non-negative profits. This may be achieved by regulation, or by excise or franchise taxes or subsidies. The important restriction is that lump sum subsidies are not available.

We begin with such a constrained optimum. The aim is to choose n, p_i, and x_i so as to maximize utility, satisfying the demand functions and keeping the profit for each firm non-negative. The problem is somewhat simplified by the result that all active firms should have the same output levels and prices, and should make exactly zero profit. We omit the proof. Then we can set $I = 1$, and use (5) to express utility as a function of q alone. This is of course a decreasing function. Thus the problem of maximizing u becomes that of minimizing q, i.e.

$$\min_{n,\,p} pn^{-\beta}$$

subject to

$$(p - c)\,\frac{s(pn^{-\beta})}{pn} = a. \tag{20}$$

To solve this, we calculate the logarithmic marginal rate of substitution along a level curve of the objective, the similar rate of transformation along the constraint, and equate the two. This yields the condition

$$\frac{\dfrac{c}{p-c} + \theta(q)}{1 + \beta\theta(q)} = \frac{1}{\beta}. \tag{21}$$

The second-order condition can be shown to hold, and (21) simplifies to yield the price for each commodity produced in the constrained optimum, p_c, as

$$p_c = c(1 + \beta). \tag{22}$$

Comparing (15) and (22), we see that the two solutions have the same price. Since they face the same break-even constraint, they have the same number of firms as well, and the values for all other variables can be calculated from these two. Thus we have a rather surprising case where the monopolistic competition equilibrium is identical with the optimum constrained by the lack of lump sum subsidies. Chamberlin once suggested that such an equilibrium was 'a sort of ideal'; our analysis shows when and in what sense this can be true.

1.4 Unconstrained Optimum

These solutions can in turn be compared to the unconstrained or first best optimum. Considerations of convexity again establish that all active firms should produce the same output. Thus we are to choose n firms each producing output x in order to maximize

$$u = U(1 - n(a + cx), xn^{1+\beta}), \tag{23}$$

where we have used the economy's resource balance condition and (10). The first-order conditions are

$$-ncU_0 + n^{1+\beta}U_y = 0 \tag{24}$$

$$-(a + cx)U_0 + (1 + \beta)xn^{\beta}U_y = 0. \tag{25}$$

From the first stage of the budgeting problem, we know that $q = U_y/U_0$. Using (24) and (10), we find the price charged by each active firm in the unconstrained optimum, p_u, equal to marginal cost

$$p_u = c. \tag{26}$$

This, of course, is no surprise. Also from the first-order conditions, we have

$$x_u = \frac{a}{c\beta}. \tag{27}$$

Finally, with (26), each active firm covers its variable cost exactly. The lump sum transfers to firms then equal an, and therefore $I = 1 - an$, and

$$x = (1 - an)\,\frac{s(pn^{-\beta})}{pn}$$

The number of firms n_u is then defined by

$$\frac{s(cn_u^{-\beta})}{n_u} = \frac{a/\beta}{1 - an_u}. \tag{28}$$

We can now compare these magnitudes with the corresponding ones in the equilibrium or the constrained optimum. The most remarkable result is that the output of each active firm is the same in the two situations. The fact that in a Chamberlinian equilibrium each firm operates to the left of the point of minimum average cost has been conventionally described by saying that there is excess capacity. However, when variety is desirable, i.e. when the different products are not perfect substitutes, it is not in general optimum to push the output of each firm to the point where all economies of scale are exhausted.[7] We have shown in one case that is not an extreme one, that the first best optimum does not exploit economies of scale beyond the extent achieved in the equilibrium. We can then easily conceive of cases where the equilibrium exploits economies of scale too far from the point of view of social optimality. Thus our results undermine the validity of the folklore of excess capacity, from the point of view of the unconstrained optimum as well as the constrained one.

A direct comparison of the numbers of firms from (16) and (28) would be difficult, but an indirect argument turns out to be simple. It is clear that the unconstrained optimum has higher utility than the constrained optimum. Also, the level of lump sum income in it is less than that in the latter. It must therefore be the case that

$$q_u < q_c = q_e. \tag{29}$$

Further, the difference must be large enough that the budget constraint for x_0 and the quantity index y in the unconstrained case must lie outside that in the constrained case in the relevant region, as shown in Fig. 1. Let C be the constrained optimum, A the unconstrained optimum, and let B be the point where the line joining the origin to C meets the indifference curve in the unconstrained case. By homotheticity the indifference curve at B is parallel to that at C, so each of the moves from C to B and from B to A increases the value of y. Since the value of x is the same in the two optima, we must have

[7] See Starrett (1974).

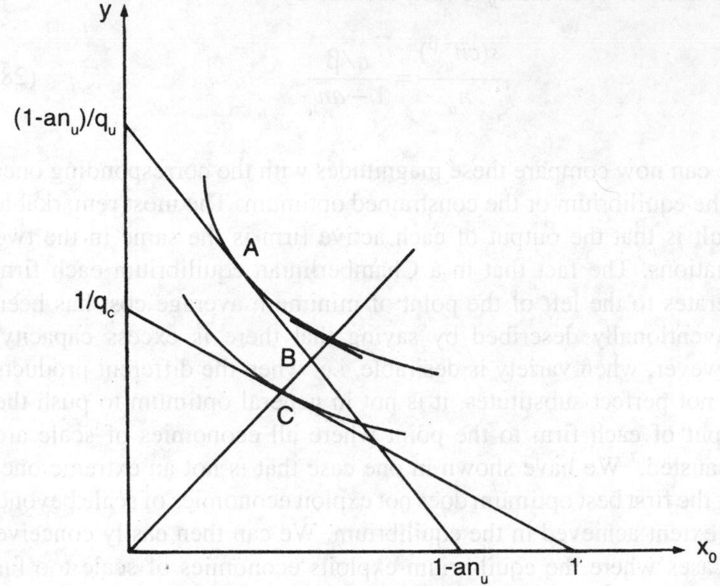

Figure 1

$$n_u > n_c = n_e. \tag{30}$$

Thus the unconstrained optimum actually allows more variety than the constrained optimum and the equilibrium; this is another point contradicting the folklore on excessive diversity.

Using (29) we can easily compare the budget shares. In the notation we have been using, we find $s_u \gtrless s_c$ as $\theta(q) \gtrless 0$, i.e. as $\sigma(q) \gtrless 1$ providing these hold over the entire relevant range of q.

It is not possible to have a general result concerning the relative magnitudes of x_0 in the two situations; an inspection of Fig. 1 shows this. However, we have a sufficient condition:

$$\begin{aligned} x_{0u} &= (1 - an_u)(1 - s_u) < 1 - s_u \leq 1 - s_c \\ &= x_{0c} \ \text{ if } \sigma(q) \geq 1. \end{aligned}$$

In this case the equilibrium or the constrained optimum use more of the numeraire resource than the unconstrained optimum. On the other hand, if $\sigma(q) = 0$ we have L-shaped isoquants, and in Fig. 1, points A and B coincide giving the opposite conclusion.

In this section we have seen that with a constant intrasector elasticity of substitution, the market equilibrium coincides with the constrained optimum. We have also shown that the unconstrained optimum has a greater number of firms, each of the same size. Finally, the resource allocation between the sectors is shown to depend on the intersector elasticity of substitution. This elasticity also governs conditions for uniqueness of equilibrium and the second-order conditions for an optimum.

Henceforth we will achieve some analytic simplicity by making a particular assumption about intersector substitution. In return, we will allow a more general form of intrasector substitution.

2. VARIABLE ELASTICITY CASE

The utility function is now

$$u = x_0^{1-\nu}\left\{\sum_i \nu(x_i)\right\}^{\nu} \tag{31}$$

with ν increasing and concave, $0 < \gamma < 1$. This is somewhat like assuming a unit intersector elasticity of substitution. However, this is not rigorous since the group utility $V(\underset{\sim}{x}) = \Sigma_i \nu(x_i)$ is not homothetic and therefore two-stage budgeting is not applicable.

It can be shown that the elasticity of the *dd* curve in the large group case is

$$-\frac{\partial \log x_i}{\partial \log p_i} = -\frac{\nu'(x_i)}{x_i \nu''(x_i)} \quad \text{for any } i. \tag{32}$$

This differs from the case of Sec. 1 in being a function of x_i. To highlight the similarities and the differences, we define $\beta(x)$ by

$$\frac{1+\beta(x)}{\beta(x)} = -\frac{\nu'(x)}{x\nu''(x)}. \tag{33}$$

Next, setting $x_i = x$ and $p_i = p$ for $i = 1, 2, \ldots, n$, we can write the *DD* curve and the demand for the numeraire as

$$x = \frac{I}{np}\,\omega(x), \quad x_0 = I\,[1 - \omega(x)] \tag{34}$$

where

$$\omega(x) = \frac{\gamma\rho(x)}{[\gamma\rho(x) + (1-\gamma)]} \tag{35}$$

$$\rho(x) = \frac{x v'(x)}{v(x)}$$

We assume that $0 < \rho(x) < 1$, and therefore have $0 < \omega(x) < 1$.

Now consider the Chamberlinian equilibrium. The profit-maximization condition for each active firm yields the common equilibrium price p_e in terms of the common equilibrium output x_e as

$$p_e = c[1 + \beta(x_e)]. \tag{36}$$

Note the analogy with (15). Substituting (36) in the zero pure profit condition, we have x_e defined by

$$\frac{cx_e}{a + cx_e} = \frac{1}{1 + \beta(x_e)}. \tag{37}$$

Finally, the number of firms can be calculated using the *DD* curve and the break-even condition, as

$$n_e = \frac{\omega(x_e)}{a + cx_e}. \tag{38}$$

For uniqueness of equilibrium we once again use the conditions that the *dd* curve is more elastic than the *DD* curve, and that entry shifts the *DD* curve to the left. However, these conditions are rather involved and opaque, so we omit them.

Let us turn to the constrained optimum. We wish to choose n and x to maximize u, subject to (34) and the break-even condition $px = a + cx$. Substituting, we can express u as a function of x alone:

$$u = \gamma^{\gamma}(1-\gamma)^{(1-\gamma)} \frac{\left[\dfrac{\rho(x)v(x)}{a + cx}\right]^{\gamma}}{\gamma\,\rho(x) + (1-\gamma)}. \tag{39}$$

The first-order condition defines x_c:

$$\frac{cx_c}{a + cx_c} = \frac{1}{1 + \beta(x_c)} - \frac{\omega(x_c)x_c\rho'(x_c)}{\gamma\,\rho(x_c)}. \tag{40}$$

Comparing this with (37) and using the second-order condition, it can be shown that provided $\rho'(x)$ is one-signed for all x,

$$x_c \gtrless x_e \text{ according as } \rho'(x) \lessgtr 0. \tag{41}$$

With zero pure profit in each case, the points (x_e, p_e) and (x_c, p_c) lie on the same declining average cost curve, and therefore

$$p_c \lessgtr p_e \text{ according as } x_c \gtrless x_e. \tag{42}$$

Next we note that the *dd* curve is tangent to the average cost curve at (x_e, p_e) and the *DD* curve is steeper. Consider the case $x_c > x_e$. Now the point (x_c, p_c) must lie on a *DD* curve further to the right than (x_e, p_e), and therefore must correspond to a smaller number of firms. The opposite happens if $x_c < x_e$. Thus,

$$n_c \lessgtr n_e \text{ according as } x_c \gtrless x_e. \tag{43}$$

Finally, (41) shows that in both cases that arise there, $\rho(x_c) < \rho(x_e)$. Then $\omega(x_c) < \omega(x_e)$, and from (34),

$$x_{0c} > x_{0e}. \tag{44}$$

A smaller degree of intersectoral substitution could have reversed the result, as in Sec. 1.

An intuitive reason for these results can be given as follows. With our large group assumptions, the revenue of each firm is proportional to $xv'(x)$. However, the contribution of its output to group utility is $v(x)$. The ratio of the two is $\rho(x)$. Therefore, if $\rho'(x) > 0$, then at the margin each firm finds it more profitable to expand than what would be socially desirable, so $x_e > x_c$. Given the break-even constraint, this leads to there being fewer firms.

Note that the relevant magnitude is the elasticity of utility, and not the elasticity of demand. The two are related, since

$$x\frac{\rho'(x)}{\rho(x)} = \frac{1}{1+\beta(x)} - \rho(x). \tag{45}$$

Thus, if $\rho(x)$ is constant over an interval, so is $\beta(x)$ and we have $1/(1+\beta) = \rho$, which is the case of Sec. 1. However, if $\rho(x)$ varies, we cannot infer a relation between the signs of $\rho'(x)$ and $\beta'(x)$. Thus the variation in the elasticity of demand is not in general the relevant consideration. However, for important families of utility functions there is a relationship. For example, for $v(x) = (k + mx)^j$, with $m > 0$

and $0 < j < 1$, we find that $-xv''/v'$ and xv'/v are positively related. Now we would normally expect that as the number of commodities produced increases, the elasticity of substitution between any pair of them should increase. In the symmetric equilibrium, this is just the inverse of the elasticity of marginal utility. Then a higher x would correspond to a lower n, and therefore a lower elasticity of substitution, higher $-xv''/v'$ and higher xv'/v. Thus we are led to expect that $\rho'(x) > 0$, i.e. that the equilibrium involves fewer and bigger firms than the constrained optimum. Once again the common view concerning excess capacity and excessive diversity in monopolistic competition is called into question.

The unconstrained optimum problem is to choose n and x to maximize

$$u = [nv(x)]^{\gamma}[1 - n(a + cx)]^{1-\gamma}. \tag{46}$$

It is easy to show that the solution has

$$p_u = c \tag{47}$$

$$\frac{cx_u}{a + cx_u} = \rho(x_u) \tag{48}$$

$$n_u = \frac{\gamma}{a + cx_u}. \tag{49}$$

Then we can use the second-order condition to show that

$$x_u \lesseqgtr x_c \text{ according as } \rho'(x) \gtreqless 0. \tag{50}$$

This is in each case transitive with (41), and therefore yields similar output comparisons between the equilibrium and the unconstrained optimum.

The price in the unconstrained optimum is of course the lowest of the three. As to the number of firms, we note

$$n_c = \frac{\omega(x_c)}{a + cx_c} < \frac{\gamma}{a + cx_c}$$

and therefore we have a one-way comparison:

$$\text{If } x_u < x_c, \text{ then } n_u > n_c. \tag{51}$$

Similarly for the equilibrium. These leave open the possibility that the unconstrained optimum has both bigger and more firms. That is not unreasonable; after all the unconstrained optimum uses resources more efficiently.

3. ASYMMETRIC CASES

The discussion so far imposed symmetry within the group. Thus the number of varieties being produced was relevant, but any group of n was just as good as any other group of n. The next important modification is to remove this restriction. It is easy to see how interrelations within the group of commodities can lead to biases. Thus, if no sugar is being produced, the demand for coffee may be so low as to make its production unprofitable when there are set-up costs. However, this is open to the objection that with complementary commodities, there is an incentive for one entrant to produce both. However, problems exist even when all the commodities are substitutes. We illustrate this by considering an industry which will produce commodities from one of two groups, and examine whether the choice of the wrong group is possible.[8]

Suppose there are two sets of commodities beside the numeraire, the two being perfect substitutes for each other and each having a constant elasticity subutility function. Further, we assume a constant budget share for the numeraire. Thus the utility function is

$$u = x_0^{1-s}\left\{\left[\sum_{i_1=1}^{n} x_{i_1}^{\rho_1}\right]^{1/\rho_1} + \left[\sum_{i_2=1}^{n_2} x_{i}^{\rho_2}\right]^{1/\rho_2}\right\}^{s}. \tag{52}$$

We assume that each firm in group i has a fixed cost a_i and a constant marginal cost c_i.

Consider two types of equilibria, only one commodity group being produced in each. These are given by

$$\bar{x}_1 = \frac{a_1}{c_1\,\beta_1}, \bar{x}_2 = 0 \tag{53a}$$

[8] For an alternative approach using partial equilibrium methods, see Spence (1976).

$$\bar{p}_1 = c_1(1+\beta_1)$$
$$\bar{n}_1 = \frac{s\,\beta_1}{a_1(1+\beta_1)}$$
$$\bar{q}_1 = \bar{p}_1 \bar{n}_1^{-\beta_1} = c_1(1+\beta_1)^{1+\beta_1}\left(\frac{a_1}{s}\right)^{\beta_1}$$
$$\bar{u}_1 = s^s(1-s)^{1-s}\,\bar{q}_1^{\,-s}$$
$$\bar{x}_2 = \frac{a_2}{c_2\,\beta_2},\ \bar{x}_1 = 0 \tag{53b}$$
$$\bar{p}_2 = c_2(1+\beta_2)$$
$$\bar{n}_2 = \frac{s\,\beta_2}{a_2(1+\beta_2)}$$
$$\bar{q}_2 = \bar{p}_2 \bar{n}_2^{-\beta_2} = c_2(1+\beta_2)^{1+\beta_2}\left(\frac{a_2}{s}\right)^{\beta_2}$$
$$\bar{u}_2 = s^s(1-s)^{1-s}\,\bar{q}_2^{\,-s}.$$

Equation (53a) is a Nash equilibrium if and only if it does not pay a firm to produce a commodity of the second group. The demand for such a commodity is

$$x_2 = \begin{cases} 0 & \text{for} \quad p_2 \geq \bar{q}_1 \\ s/p_2 & \text{for} \quad p_2 < \bar{q}_1 \end{cases}$$

Hence we require

$$\max_{p_2}\,(p_2 - c_2)x_2 = s\left(1 - \frac{c_2}{\bar{q}_1}\right) < a_2$$

or

$$\bar{q}_1 < \frac{sc_2}{s - a_2}. \tag{54}$$

Similarly, (53b) is a Nash equilibrium if and only if

$$\bar{q}_2 < \frac{sc_1}{s - a_1}. \tag{55}$$

Now consider the optimum. Both the objective and the constraint are such as to lead the optimum to the production of commodities from only one group. Thus, suppose n_i commodities from group i are being produced at levels x_i each, and offered at prices p_i. The utility level is given by

$$u = x_0^{1-s}\{x_1 n_1^{1+\beta_1} + x_2^{1+\beta_2}\}^s \tag{56}$$

and the resource availability constraint is

$$x_0 + n_1(a_1 + c_1 x_1) + n_2(a_2 + c_2 x_2) = 1. \tag{57}$$

Given the values of the other variables, the level curves of u in (n_1, n_2) space are concave to the origin, while the constraint is linear. We must therefore have a corner optimum. (As for the break-even constraint, unless the two $q_i = p_i n_i^{-\beta_i}$ are equal, the demand for commodities in one group is zero, and there is no possibility of avoiding a loss there.)

Note that we have structured our example so that if the correct group is chosen, the equilibrium will not introduce any further biases

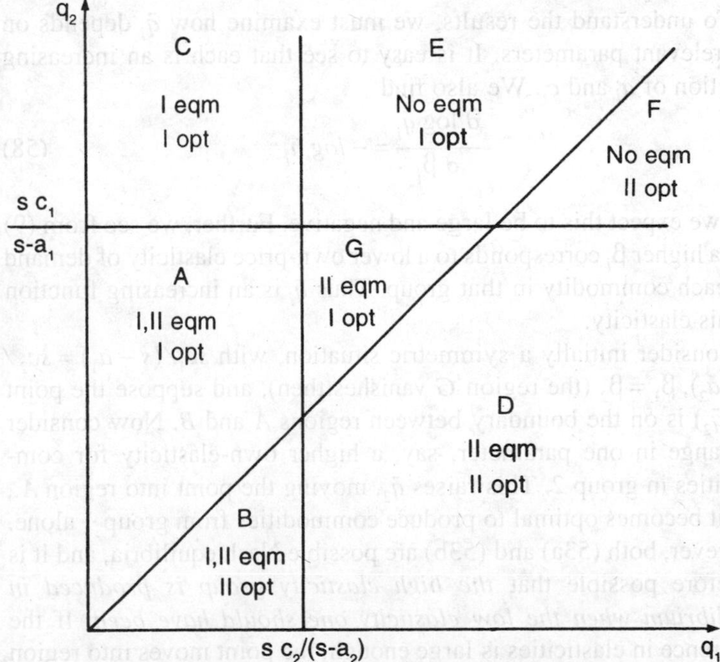

Figure 2 Solutions Labelled I Refer to Equation (53a); Solutions Labelled II Refer to Equation (53b)

in relation to the constrained optimum. Therefore, to find the constrained optimum, we only have to look at the values of $\bar{u}_i$ in (53a) and (53b) and see which is the greater. In other words, we have to see which $\bar{q}_i$ is the smaller, and choose the situation (which may or may not be a Nash equilibrium) defined in (53a) and (53b) corresponding to it.

Figure 2 is drawn to depict the possible equilibria and optima. Given all the relevant parameters, we calculate $(\bar{q}_1, \bar{q}_2)$ from (53a) and (53b). Then (54) and (55) tell us whether either or both of the situations are possible equilibria, while a simple comparison of the magnitudes of $\bar{q}_1$ and $\bar{q}_2$ tells us which is the constrained optimum. In the figure, the non-negative quadrant is split into regions in each of which we have one combination of equilibria and optima. We only have to locate the point $(\bar{q}_1, \bar{q}_2)$ in this space to know the result for the given parameter values. Moreover, we can compare the location of the points corresponding to different parameter values and thus do some comparative statics.

To understand the results, we must examine how $\bar{q}_i$ depends on the relevant parameters. It is easy to see that each is an increasing function of a_i and c_i. We also find

$$\frac{\partial \log \bar{q}_i}{\partial \beta_i} = -\log \bar{n}_i \tag{58}$$

and we expect this to be large and negative. Further, we see from (9) that a higher β_i corresponds to a lower own-price elasticity of demand for each commodity in that group. Thus $\bar{q}_i$ is an increasing function of this elasticity.

Consider initially a symmetric situation, with $sc_1/(s-a_1) = sc_2/(s-a_2)$, $\beta_1 = \beta_2$ (the region G vanishes then), and suppose the point $(\bar{q}_1, \bar{q}_2)$ is on the boundary between regions A and B. Now consider a change in one parameter, say, a higher own-elasticity for commodities in group 2. This raises $\bar{q}_2$, moving the point into region A., and it becomes optimal to produce commodities from group 1 alone. However, both (53a) and (53b) are possible Nash equilibria, and it is therefore possible that *the high elasticity group is produced in equilibrium when the low elasticity one should have been.* If the difference in elasticities is large enough, the point moves into region C, where (53b) is no longer a Nash equilibrium. But, owing to the existence of a fixed cost, a significant difference in elasticities is necessary before entry from group 1 commodities threatens to destroy the 'wrong' equilibrium. Similar remarks apply to regions *B* and *D*.

Next, begin with symmetry once again, and consider a higher c_1 or a_1. This increases $\bar{q}_1$ and moves the point into region *B*, making it optimal to produce the low-cost group alone while leaving both (53a) and (53b) as possible equilibria, until the difference in costs is large enough to take the point to region *D*. The change also moves the boundary between *A* and *C* upward, opening up a larger region *G*, but that is not of significance here.

If both q_1 and q_2 are large, each group is threatened by profitable entry from the other, and no Nash equilibrium exists, as in regions *E* and *F*. However, the criterion of constrained optimality remains as before. Thus we have a case where it may be necessary to prohibit entry in order to sustain the constrained optimum.

If we combine a case where $c_1 > c_2$ (or $a_1 > a_2$) and $\beta_1 > \beta_2$, i.e. where commodities in group 2 are more elastic and have lower costs, we face a still worse possibility. For the point $(\bar{q}_1, \bar{q}_2)$ may then lie in region *G*, where only (53b) is a possible equilibrium and only (53a) is constrained optimum, i.e. the market can produce only a low cost, high demand elasticity group of commodities when a high cost, low demand elasticity group should have been produced.

Very roughly, the point is that although commodities in inelastic demand have the potential for earning revenues in excess of variable costs, they also have significant consumers' surpluses associated with them. Thus it is not immediately obvious whether the market will be biased in favour of them or against them as compared with an optimum. Here we find the latter, and independent findings of Michael Spence in other contexts confirm this. Similar remarks apply to differences in marginal costs.

In the interpretation of the model with heterogeneous consumers and social indifference curves, inelastically demanded commodities will be the ones which are intensively desired by a few consumers. Thus we have an 'economic' reason why the market will lead to a bias against opera relative to football matches, and a justification for subsidization of the former and a tax on the latter, provided the distribution of income is optimum.

Even when cross elasticities are zero, there may be an incorrect choice of commodities to be produced (relative either to an unconstrained or constrained optimum) as Fig. 3 illustrates. Figure 3

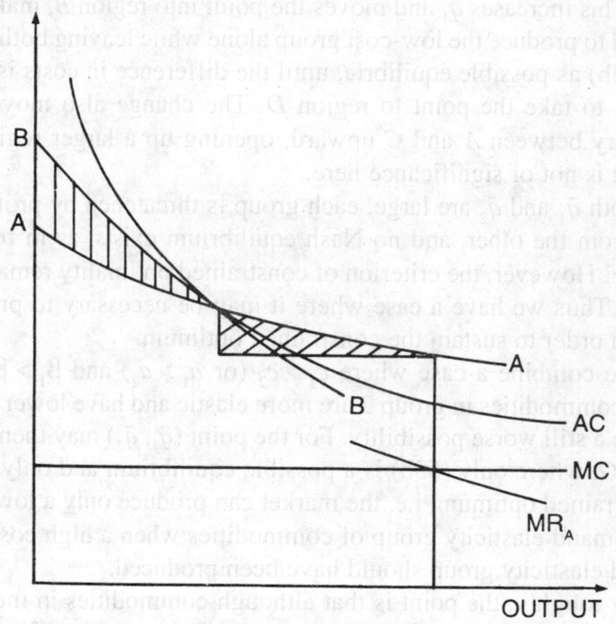

Figure 3

illustrates a case where commodity *A* has a more elastic demand curve than commodity *B*; *A* is produced in monopolistically competitive equilibrium, while *B* is not. But clearly, it is socially desirable to produce *B*, since ignoring consumer's surplus it is just marginal. Thus, the commodities that are not produced but ought to be are those with inelastic demands. Indeed, if, as in the usual analysis of monopolistic competition, eliminating one firm shifts the demand curve for the other firms to the right (i.e. increases the demand for other firms), if the consumer surplus from *A* (at its equilibrium level of output) is less than that from *B* (i.e. the cross hatched area exceeds the striped area), then constrained Pareto optimality entails restricting the production of the commodity with the more elastic demand.

A similar analysis applies to commodities with the same demand curves but different cost structures. Commodity *A* is assumed to have

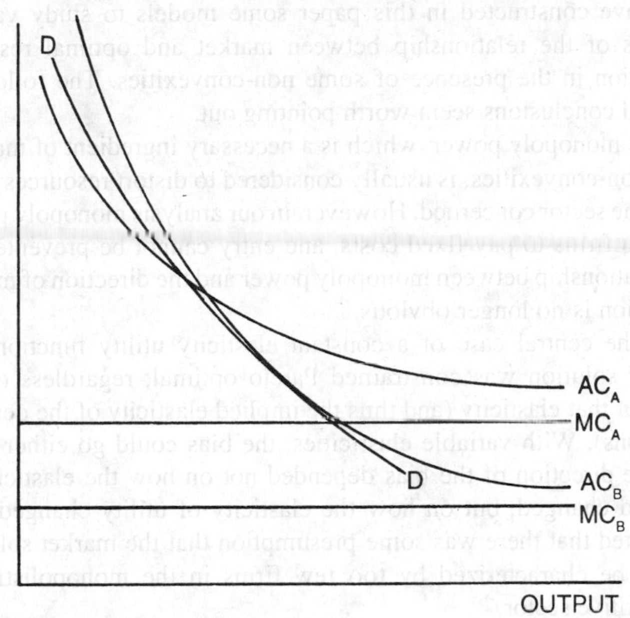

Figure 4

the lower fixed cost but the higher marginal cost. Thus, the average cost curves cross but once, as in Fig. 4. Commodity *A* is produced in monopolistically competitive equilibrium, commodity *B* is not (although it is just at the margin of being produced). But again, observe that *B* should be produced, since there is a large consumer's surplus; indeed, since were it to be produced, *B* would produce at a much higher level than *A*, there is a much larger consumer's surplus. Thus if the government were to forbid the production of *A*, *B* would be viable, and social welfare would increase.

In the comparison between constrained Pareto optimality and the monopolistically competitive equilibrium, we have observed that in the former, we replace some low fixed cost-high marginal cost commodities with high fixed cost-low marginal cost commodities, and we replace some commodities with elastic demands with commodities with inelastic demands.

4. CONCLUDING REMARKS

We have constructed in this paper some models to study various aspects of the relationship between market and optimal resource allocation in the presence of some non-convexities. The following general conclusions seem worth pointing out.

The monopoly power, which is a necessary ingredient of markets with non-convexities, is usually considered to distort resources away from the sector concerned. However, in our analysis monopoly power enables firms to pay fixed costs, and entry cannot be prevented, so the relationship between monopoly power and the direction of market distortion is no longer obvious.

In the central case of a constant elasticity utility function, the market solution was constrained Pareto optimal, regardless of the value of that elasticity (and thus the implied elasticity of the demand functions). With variable elasticities, the bias could go either way, and the direction of the bias depended not on how the elasticity of demand changed, but on how the elasticity of utility changed. We suggested that there was some presumption that the market solution would be characterized by too few firms in the monopolistically competitive sector.

With asymmetric demand and cost conditions we also observed a bias against commodities with inelastic demands and high costs.

The general principle behind these results is that a market solution considers profit at the appropriate margin, while a social optimum takes into account the consumer's surplus. However, applications of this principle come to depend on details of cost and demand functions. We hope that the cases presented here, in conjunction with other studies cited, offer some useful and new insights.

REFERENCES

BISHOP, R.L. (1967), 'Monopolistic Competition and Welfare Economics', in Robert Kuenne (ed.), *Monopolistic Competition Theory*, New York.

CHAMBERLIN, E. (1950), 'Product Heterogeneity and Public Policy, *American Economic Review, Proceedings*, 40, 85–92.

DIAMOND, P.A. and D.L. MCFADDEN (1974), 'Some Uses of the Expenditure Function in Public Finance', *Journal of Public Economics*, 82, 1–23.

DIXIT, A.K. and J.E. STIGLITZ (1975), 'Monopolistic Competition and Optimum Product Diversity', Economic Research Paper No. 64, University of Warwick, England.

JOHN GREEN, H.A. (1964), *Aggregation in Economic Analysis*, Princeton.

HOTELLING, H. (1929), 'Stability in Competition', *Economic Journal*, 39, 41–57.

KALDOR, N. (1934), 'Market Imperfection and Excess Capacity', *Economica*, 2, 33–50.

LANCASTER, K. (1975), 'Socially Optimal Product Differentiation', *American Economic Review, 65, 567–85.*

SPENCE, A.M. (1976), 'Product Selection, Fixed Costs, and Monopolistic Competition', *Review of Economic Studies*, 43, 217–35.

STARRETT, D.A. (1974), 'Principles of Optimal Location in a Large Homogeneous Area', *Journal of Economic Theory*, 9, 418–48.

STERN, N.H. (1972), 'The Optimal Size of Market Areas', *Journal of Economic Theory*, 4, 159–73.

STIGLITZ, J.E. (1975), 'Monopolistic Competition in the Capital Market', Tech. Rep. No. 161, IMSS, Stanford University.

Mixed Oligopoly with Differentiated Products*

HELMUTH CREMER, MAURICE MARCHAND AND JACQUES-FRANÇOIS THISSE

1. INTRODUCTION

The purpose of this paper is to study the impact of a public firm in a differentiated industry. Whereas it is common to observe public and private firms competing within the same industry, such 'mixed oligopolies' have received little attention in the literature. The issue has become even more important because of the recent debates concerning the privatization of public firms. Economic theory has very little to say when the firm to be privatized operates in the context of a differentiated industry. It is thus no surprise that most of the arguments used to favour or against privatization are guided by ideological considerations rather than based on sound economic justifications.

The few existing contributions (see, e.g. Beato and Mas-Colell, 1984; Bös, 1986, Ch. 11; Cremer et al., 1989 and De Fraja and Delbono, 1989) all assume an industry formed by firms selling a homogeneous product. Though product homogeneity is convenient as a first approximation, it can hardly be denied that most real world markets are characterized by product differentiation. Hence, we believe that introducing heterogeneous products is a significant step towards achieving a better understanding of actual mixed oligopolies.

Several approaches have been taken for modelling product differentiation in industries with private firms (see the recent survey by Eaton and Lipsey, 1989). One of the most—if not the most—popular

* We thank J. Cremer, A. Kats and one referee for their comments. The second and third authors are grateful to the FRFC and CIM (Belgium) for financial support.

approaches is the spatial competition model à la Hotelling (see Gabszewicz and Thisse, 1986 for a detailed overview). The major advantage of this approach is that it allows one for an explicit analysis of price competition and product selection.

It is this model that we use for studying the market equilibrium which emerges when a public firm operates in a differentiated oligopoly. This analysis appears to be interesting for at least two reasons. First, our results suggest that policy recommendations differ markedly from those derived in the case of a homogeneous product. It turns out, indeed, that having a public firm maximizing social surplus is not necessarily socially desirable, even when this firm is as performant as its private competitors in terms of costs (we assume constant and identical marginal production costs). It also appears that private firms may benefit from the presence of a public firm in the sense that they earn higher profits than in the private oligopoly case. The second reason for our study is that we can deal explicitly with the important issue of product selection by the public firm vis-à-vis the private firms.

One major problem with the introduction of differentiated products is that it complicates the analysis substantially. Accordingly, we have been forced to use quite a restrictive setting. The results and, therefore, the policy recommendations must be considered with the necessary qualifications. However, one of the few principles that emerge from this paper is that the optimal policy of the government is very sensitive to the particular market structure considered, that is, the number of firms (even when we stay within the same framework). Also, our results on product selection by the public firm show that intuition can be very misleading indeed, thus pointing out the need for systematic analyses.

The remainder of the paper is organized as follows. The model is presented in Sec. 2. Our solution-concept is a subgame perfect Nash equilibrium. Some properties of the price subgame equilibria are given. In Sec. 3, the choice of a product location by the public firm and its impact on the outcome of the game are analysed. In particular, the relative position of the public firm in the product configuration is discussed. This enables us to determine how the presence of one or several public firms (as well as their relative positions) affects social welfare and how the results depend on the total number of firms. Our conclusions are given in Sec. 4.

2. THE MODEL AND SOME PRELIMINARY RESULTS

Consider the following spatial competition model. There are n (private or public) firms producing a homogeneous product at zero marginal cost; they are indexed by $1 \ldots n$. In the first stage of the game, firms choose simultaneously their location in the unit interval [0, 1]; let $x = (x_1 \ldots x_i \ldots x_n)$ be the location vector[1] with firms indexed such that $x_{i+1} > x_i$ for $i = 1 \ldots n-1$. In the second stage, given some x, firms choose simultaneously their (mill) price; denote by $p = (p_1 \ldots p_i \ldots p_n)$ the price vector.

Consumers are uniformly distributed over the interval [0, 1] with a unit density. They consume a single unit of the product irrespective of its price. Each consumer patronizes the firm with the lowest full price (i.e. mill price plus transportation costs). Transportation costs are quadratic in distance.[2] Hence, the full price paid by a consumer located at $y \in [0, 1]$ and purchasing from firm i is equal to $p_i + (y - x_i)^2$.

For any given x, it is readily verified that firms always select prices so as to have positive demands. Denote by $\alpha_{i,\,i+1}$ $(i = 1 \ldots n-1)$ the location of the consumer indifferent between buying from firms i and $i+1$, that is, $\alpha_{i,\,i+1}$ is the solution of the equation

$$p_i + (\alpha_{i,\,i+1} - x_i)^2 = p_{i,\,i+1} + (\alpha_{i,\,i+1} - x_{i+1})^2 \tag{1}$$

which is given by

$$\alpha_{i,\,i+1} = \frac{p_{i+1} - p_i}{2(x_{i+1} - x_i)} + \frac{x_{i+1} + x_i}{2} \tag{2}$$

Clearly, in equilibrium we have

$$0 \le \alpha_{i,\,i+1} \le \alpha_{i+1,\,i+2} \le 1, \quad i = 1 \ldots n-2. \tag{3}$$

For notational convenience, we set $\alpha_{0,\,1} = 0$ and $\alpha_{n,\,n+1} = 1$. Accordingly, in the relevant price domain, firm i's demand is defined by

[1] For simplicity, we assume that all firms have different locations. It can be shown that any two firms never locate coincidentally in equilibrium.

[2] Notice that we have normalized the marginal production costs to zero, the length of the interval to one and the coefficient of the transportation costs to one. This implies no loss of generality.

$$D_i(p; x) = \alpha_{i,i+1} - \alpha_{i-1,i}. \tag{4}$$

There are two types of firms: private and public. Private firms aim at maximizing their profits

$$\Pi_i(p; x) = p_i(\alpha_{i,t+1} - \alpha_{i-1,i}) \tag{5}$$

(where fixed costs are disregarded). As to public firms, their objective is to reach the highest social surplus. Individual demands being perfectly inelastic, this amounts to minimizing total transportation costs. This is so because prices above marginal cost do not create here distortions in the allocation of resources. In other words, the social surplus can be written as

$$S(p; x) = -\sum_{i=1}^{n} \int_{\alpha_{i-1,i}}^{\alpha_{i,i+1}} (y - x_i)^2 dy. \tag{6}$$

For notational simplicity, we denote by $P_i(p; x)$ firm i's payoff function.

Our solution-concept is a subgame perfect Nash equilibrium in which firms choose locations, looking ahead to the resulting equilibrium prices. Given x, in the second stage each firm i maximizes $P_i(p; x)$ with respect to $p_i \in \mathbb{R}_+$. The outcome of the corresponding subgame is a Nash price equilibrium p^*:

$$P_i(p_i^*, p_{-i}^*; x) \geq P_i(p_i, p_{-i}^*; x) \qquad \text{for all } p_i \geq 0 \text{ and } i = 1 \ldots n.$$

For each subgame, standard arguments show that there exists a single Nash price equilibrium (see, e.g. Neven, 1985 for an analysis of the private firm case), it is denoted $p^*(x)$. Let $P_i^*(x) = P_i[p^*(x); x]$ be the equilibrium payoff function of firm i. In the first stage, each firm i maximizes $P_i^*(x)$ with respect to $x_i \in [0, 1]$. The outcome of this game is a Nash location equilibrium x^*, i.e.

$$P_i^*(x_i^*, x_{-i}^*) \geq P_i^*(x_i, x_{-i}^*) \quad \text{for all } x_i \in [0, 1] \text{ and } i = 1 \ldots n.$$

In the remainder of this section, we show how to determine the Nash equilibrium prices for any given location vector x. We know that these prices are solutions of the system of best reply functions that we denote by $\tilde{p}_1 \ldots \tilde{p}_n$. For private firms, these functions are given by Neven (1985):

Firm 1: $\tilde{p}_1 = \dfrac{p_2}{2} + \dfrac{x_2^2 - x_1^2}{2},$ (7a)

Firms 2 . . . $n-1$: $\tilde{p}_i = \dfrac{p_{i+1}}{2} \cdot \dfrac{x_i - x_{i-1}}{x_{i+1} - x_{i-1}} + \dfrac{p_{i-1}}{2} \cdot \dfrac{x_{i+1} - x_i}{x_{i+1} - x_{i-1}}$

$$+ \frac{(x_{i+1} - x_i)(x_i - x_{i-1})}{2}, \tag{7b}$$

Firm n: $\tilde{p}_n = \dfrac{p_{n-1}}{2} + (x_n - x_{n-1}) - \dfrac{x_n^2 - x_{n-1}^2}{2}$ (7c)

For public firms, we proceed as follows. For firm 1, the maximization of $S(p; x)$ with respect to p_1 is equivalent to the minimization of $\int_0^{\alpha_{1,2}} (y - x_1)^2\, dy + \int_{\alpha_{1,2}}^{\alpha_{2,3}} (y - x_2)^2 dy$ since p_1 affects only $\alpha_{1,2}$. Using (1), the first-order condition yields

$$(p_2 - p_1) \frac{\partial \alpha_{1,2}}{\partial p_1} = 0.$$

As $\partial \alpha_{1,2} / \partial p_1 \neq 0$ by (2), public firm 1 sets its price at the same level as firm 2, i.e.

$$\tilde{p}_1 = p_2. \tag{8a}$$

Intuitively, the reason for this result is as follows. By equating p_1 to p_2, (2) implies that $\alpha_{1,2} = (x_1 + x_2)/2$ so that firm 1 minimizes the total transportation costs on the interval $[0, x_2]$. This is achieved by firm 1 supplying consumers located in $[0, (x_1 + x_2)/2]$ and firm 2 serving those in $[(x_1 + x_2)/2, x_2]$. The same argument applies, *mutatis mutandis*, to firm n so that

$$\tilde{p}_n = p_{n-1}. \tag{8b}$$

Let us now turn to the case of internal firms ($i = 2 \ldots n-1$). Maximizing $S(p; x)$ with respect to p_i and using (1) leads to

$$\tilde{p}_i = \frac{x_{i+1} - x_i}{x_{i+1} - x_{i-1}} p_{i-1} + \frac{x_i - x_{i-1}}{x_{i+1} - x_{i-1}} p_{i+1}. \tag{8c}$$

If $p_{i+1} = p_{i-1}$, then public firm i chooses $p_i = p_{i-1} = p_{i+1}$ in order to minimize transportation costs on $[x_{i-1}, x_{i+1}]$: consumers located in $[x_{i-1}, x_i]$ are equally divided between firms $i-1$ and i, and likewise for those located in $[x_i, x_{i+1}]$. Such divisions are no more possible when $p_{i-1} \neq p_{i+1}$. Firm i faces a tradeoff between transportation costs over $[x_{i-1}, x_i]$ (minimized if $p_i = p_{i-1}$) and those over $[x_i, x_{i+1}]$ (minimized if $p_i = p_{i+1}$). Accordingly, it chooses p_i as a weighted average of p_{i-1} and p_{i+1}, the weights being the inverse of the relative distances to the neighbouring firms.

Suppose now that there are m public firms ($0 \leq m \leq n$) and $n - m$ private firms, with given locations.[3] The Nash equilibrium prices are obtained by picking the appropriate best reply functions from (7) and (8) and by solving the corresponding system of linear equations.

3. THE OPTIMAL NUMBER AND LOCATION OF PUBLIC FIRMS

The purpose of this section is to determine, for any given number of firms n, the corresponding subgame perfect Nash equilibrium as a function of the number m of public firms and of their relative position. Comparing the levels of social surplus obtained at those equilibria will enable us to find how many of the n competitors should be public and where they should be established in the locational configuration in order to maximize social welfare.

As we shall see, the answer depends critically on the number of firms. For $n > 5$, the results appear stable in the sense that the same qualitative conclusions hold whatever the value of n. On the other hand, for $2 \leq n \leq 5$, conclusions vary with the corresponding value of n. When $n = 2$, the subgame perfect Nash equilibrium can be found analytically. Given that analytical derivations become very quickly unmanageable when $n > 2$, we have resorted to a numerical solution, for up to 30 firms.[4]

[3] When several public firms are on the market, they can either act independently or coordinate their decisions. It can be shown that the choice of locations and prices by the public firms is identical under the two assumptions. In our model, public firms are supposed to behave independently of each other.

[4] As all parameters have been normalized, a numerical solution is formally identical to an analytical solution.

$n = 2$

Assume, first, that there is no public firm ($m = 0$). Then, it is well known that the two firms choose to relax price competition by locating as far as possible from each other, i.e. $x_1^* = 0$ and $x_2^* = 1$; they set prices given by $p_1^* = p_2^* = 1$ and earn identical profits equal to 0.5 (see d'Aspremont et al., 1979). The corresponding social surplus is –0.08333.

Suppose now that there is one public firm ($m = 1$) which is taken to be firm 1 without loss of generality. For given locations (x_1, x_2), the Nash equilibrium prices are easily shown to be

$$p_1^*(x_1, x_2) = p_2^*(x_1, x_2) = 2(x_2 - x_1) - (x_2^2 - x_1^2), \tag{9}$$

the market boundary being situated at $\alpha_{1,2}^* = (x_1 + x_2)/2$. The profits of the private firm are then

$$\Pi_2^*(x_1, x_2) = p_2^*(x_1, x_2)\,[1 - \alpha_{1,2}^*(x_1, x_2)].$$

For $x_1 \leq \frac{1}{2}$, firm 2's best reply is

$$\tilde{x}_2 = \frac{2}{3} + \frac{x_1}{3}. \tag{10}$$

(If $x_1 > \frac{1}{2}$, the best reply is $\tilde{x}_2 = 1 - ((2/3) + (x_1/3)) < x_1$. This case can be dealt with as the first one.) As to public firm, it chooses its location by maximizing

$$S^*(x_1, x_2) = -\int_0^{\alpha_{1,2}^*} (y - x_1)^2\, dy - \int_{\alpha_{1,2}^*}^{1} (y - x_2)^2 dy$$

which yields the best reply function

$$\tilde{x}_1 = \frac{x_2}{3}. \tag{11}$$

Hence, firm 1 selects its location in $[0, x_2]$ such that the two intervals $[0, x_1]$ and $[x_1, x_2]$ have the same length. In this way, firm 1 minimizes transportation costs over $[0, x_2]$ (recall that by convention $x_1 \leq x_2$). Solving (10) and (11), one gets

$$x_1^* = \frac{1}{4} \quad \text{and} \quad x_2^* = \frac{3}{4}$$

with $p_1^* = p_2^* = \frac{1}{2}$, $\Pi_2^* = \frac{1}{4}$ and $S^* = -0.02083$.

Hence, *when $n = 2$, having one public firm allows one to obtain the first best locational configuration.* In other words, there is here a strong argument in favour of a public firm: one switches from a very inefficient locational configuration ($x_1 = 0$ and $x_2 = 1$) to the efficient one ($x_1 = 1/4$ and $x_2 = 3/4$).

•$n = 3$

As mentioned above, we resort to numerical analysis to determine the equilibria for $n > 2$. The price and location equilibria along with other magnitudes (prices, profits and social surplus) are presented in Table 1 for $m = 0$, 1 and 2 public firms and for different relative positions in the locational configuration.

The private triopoly equilibrium ($m = 0$) is inefficient on two accounts: (i) the firm's locations (1/8, 1/2, 7/8) are different from the optimal ones (1/6, 1/2, 5/6) as is the case in a duopoly; (ii) firms charge different prices ($p_2^* < p_1^* = p_3^*$) so that the allocation of consumers among firms is inefficient. This inequality in prices results from the fact that peripheral firms compete with the central firm only, whereas this one faces two competitors.

Table 1
Outcomes of the game with three firms where *i* is the index of the public firm(s)

	$m = 0$	$m = 1$ ($i = 1$)	$m = 1$ ($i = 2$)	$m = 2$ ($i = 1, 2$)	$m = 2$ ($i = 1, 3$)
x_1	0.125	0	0.25	0.1666	0.1666
x_2	0.5	0.264	0.5	0.5	0.5
x_3	0.875	0.788	0.75	0.8333	0.8333
p_1	0.203	0.1	0.1875	0.222	0.111
p_2	0.172	0.1898	0.1875	0.222	0.111
p_3	0.203	0.3433	0.1875	0.222	0.111
Π_1	0.055	–	0.073	–	–
Π_2	0.079	0.103	–	–	0.037
Π_3	0.055	0.124	0.073	0.074	–
S	−0.0113932	−0.027939	−0.0130208	−0.009259	−0.009259

If there is one public firm ($m = 1$), this can be either a peripheral firm ($i = 1$ or 3) or the central one ($i = 2$). Intuitively, one would expect the public firm being centrally located to be the best social configuration. This is indeed true. However, the other results are rather surprising. First, no matter its location, *having a single public firm in the market leads to an outcome which is less efficient than the private triopoly*. Second, *the profits of the remaining private firms increase with one public firm in the market*, and they do so more when the public firm selects a peripheral location.

The larger inefficiency of the mixed triopoly (when compared with the private triopoly) is similar to results obtained in a completely different setting by De Fraja and Delbono (1989). In the present context, this paradoxical result can be understood as follows. We have seen that the optimal configuration with one public firm implies this one to be located at the centre. If the locations of peripheral (private) firms were unaffected by the central firm being public, the mixed triopoly would be more efficient because prices would be equal and, consequently, total transportation costs would be lower. But peripheral firms adjust their locations: they move closer to the central firm because the latter adopts a less aggressive pricing policy than its counterpart in the private triopoly.

Finally, with two public firms ($m = 2$), the socially optimal configuration is reached independently of the relative position of the public firms. However, prices and profits are higher when the unique private firm is located peripherally rather than centrally. This is so because the private firm competes only upon one side of the market instead of two.

Table 2
Outcomes of the game with six firms

	$m=0$	$m=1$ ($i=1$)	$m=1$ ($i=2$)	$m=1$ ($i=3$)	$m=4$ ($i=1, 3, 4, 6$)
Π_1	0.0069	–	0.0035	0.0075	–
Π_2	0.0063	0.0044	–	0.0057	0.0046
Π_3	0.0043	0.0053	0.0046	–	–
Π_4	0.0043	0.0060	0.0068	0.0047	–
Π_5	0.0063	0.0085	0.0106	0.0088	0.0046
Π_6	0.0069	0.0092	0.0115	0.0105	–
S	−0.003518	−0.003383	−0.003909	−0.005199	−0.002314

•$n = 4$ and $n = 5$

The results obtained with four firms resemble those holding for five firms. As in the case of three firms, the allocation achieved with one public firm is less efficient than that associated with the private oligopoly. Unlike the case $n = 3$, however, the social surplus rises monotonically when the public firm moves from the central position to a peripheral one. Nevertheless, the profits of the $n - 1$ private firms are in general higher with one public firm (this may not be true in some configurations for the neighbouring firms).

Increasing the number of public firms raises social welfare and the first-best configuration is obtained when $m = n - 1$, wherever the public firms are placed. However, when $n = 5$, three public firms are already enough to reach the optimal configuration if their relative positions are $i = 1$, 3 and 5.

Notice that this result can be generalized to any odd value of n: having $(n + 1)/2$ public firms suffices to reach the first best solution provided that the locations of public and private firms alternate and firm 1 is public. When n is an even number, the first best solution is obtained with $(n/2) + 1$ public firms which are appropriately located.

•$n > 5$

As mentioned above, results remain qualitatively the same for any n between six and thirty (no computation was undertaken beyond 30). Unlike the cases where $n = 3$, 4, and 5, *the existence of a public firm always leads to an increase in social welfare*, provided that this firm is located appropriately. Specifically, the closer the public firm is to a peripheral position, the larger is the social surplus. (Up to $n = 14$, a peripheral position is the only position for the public firm to be associated with a rise in social welfare.) Finally, when there is one public firm, except for its neighbours the profits of the private firms are always higher than in the private oligopoly. These results are illustrated in Table 2 for $n = 6$.

4. CONCLUSIONS

Two of our results do not seem to be in accord with intuition. First, it is only for $n = 2$ or n sufficiently large $n \geq 6$) that a mixed oligopoly with one public firm is socially preferable to the preferable to the private oligopoly. Instead, one would have expected the benefit generated by a public firm to be larger in the case of a small number of firms. Second, for $n \geq 4$, the best position for the public firm is a peripheral one, and not a central position as expected.

Concerning the second result, one can think of the following argument. In terms of its pricing behaviour, a public firm can operate more effectively if it is established near one of the market extremities. In such a case, the public firm can always set its price so as to share consumers equally with its neighbouring competitors. This turns out not to be possible if it occupies an intermediate position in the configuration of firms.

It is more difficult to understand why having a public firm enhances social welfare only if the number of firms is large enough. (The result for $n = 2$ is a special case of the efficiency property obtained when $m = n - 1$.) It should be noted, however, that a public firm maximizing social surplus leads to asymmetries in the players' behaviour which, in turn, gives rise to specific inefficiencies. For example, as seen above in the case of three firms, a public firm adopts a pricing policy which is not aggressive enough. This causes the two peripheral firms to get too close to the public firm. Such inefficiencies are reduced when the number of firms increases. At some point, they are dominated by the benefit generated by the choice of a peripheral location.

What policy recommendations emerge from the above analysis? The answer depends crucially upon the number of firms operating in the market (which results, for example, from the level of fixed costs). If the firms are private and if, for whatever reason, only one firm can be nationalized, our analysis suggests that such a decision should be taken if $n = 2$ or if n is sufficiently large. It is interesting to observe that the remaining private firms would favour such a decision because it allows them to earn higher profits. Conversely, if there is a single public firm in the industry, it would be socially beneficial to privatize this firm only when n is different from 2 and is not too large. Somewhat surprisingly, the existing private firms would lobby against such a move.

As a final remark, notice that it would be interesting to study the mixed oligopoly problem within the context of alternative approaches to modelling product differentiation (see Eaton and Lipsey, 1989 for further details) and to evaluate the robustness of our main results.

REFERENCES

BEATO, P. and A. MAS-COLELL (1984), 'The Marginal Cost Pricing as a Regulation Mechanism in Mixed Markets', 81–100, in M. Marchand, P. Pestieau and H. Tulkens (eds), *The Performance of Public Enterprises*, Amsterdam: North-Holland.

BÖS, D. (1986), *Public Enterprise Economics*, Amsterdam: North-Holland.

CREMER, H., M. MARCHAND and J.-F. THISSE (1989), 'The Public Firm as an Instrument for Regulating an Oligopolistic Market', *Oxford Economic Papers*, 41, 283–301.

D'ASPREMONT, C., J.J. GABSZEWICZ and J.-F. THISSE (1979), 'On Hotelling's "Stability in Competition" ', *Econometrica*, 47, 1045–50.

DE FRAJA, G. and F. DELBONO (1989), 'Alternative Strategies of a Public Enterprise in Oligopoly', *Oxford Economic Papers*, 41, 302–11.

EATON, B.C. and R.G. LIPSEY (1989), 'Product Differentiation, 723–68, in R.E. Schmalensee and R.D. Willig (eds), *Handbook of Industrial Organization*, Amsterdam: North-Holland.

GABSZEWICZ, J.J. and J.-F. THISSE (1986), 'Spatial Competition and the Location of Firms', *Fundamentals of Pure and Applied Economics*, 5, 1–71.

NEVEN, D. (1985), 'On the Pricing and Selection of Differentiated Products in Oligopoly', unpublished Ph. D. Dissertation, Oxford University.

ENTRY DETERRENCE AND COLLUSION

The Role of Investment in Entry-Deterrence*

AVINASH K. DIXIT

The theory of large-scale entry into an industry is made complicated by its game-theoretic aspects. Even in the simplest case of one established firm facing one prospective entrant, there are some subtle strategic interactions. The established firm's pre-entry decisions can influence the prospective entrant's view of what will happen if he enters, and the established firm will try to exploit this possibility to its own advantage.

The earliest treatments met these problems by adopting the Bain–Sylos postulate, where the prospective entrant was assumed to believe that the established firm would maintain the same output after entry as its actual pre-entry output. Then the established firm naturally acquired a Stackelberg leadership role. However, the assumption is dubious on two opposing counts. First, faced with an irrevocable fact of entry, the established firm will usually find it best to make an accommodating output reduction. On the other hand, it would like to threaten to respond to entry with a predatory increase in output. Its problem is to make the latter threat credible given the prospective entrant's knowledge of the former fact. (A detailed exposition of the Bain–Sylos model and its critique can be found in Scherer (1970, Ch. 8).

In a seminal treatment of games involving such conflicts, Schelling (1960, Ch. 2) suggested that a threat which is costly to carry out can be made credible by entering into an advance commitment which makes its fulfilment optimal or even necessary. This was applied to

* I am grateful to Gunnar Bramness and Michael Waterson for useful comments on an earlier version.

the question of entry by Spence (1977), who recognized that the established firm's prior and irrevocable investment decisions could be a commitment of this kind. He assumed that the prospective entrant would believe that the established firm's post-entry output would equal its pre-entry capacity. In the interests of entry-deterrence, the established firm may set capacity at such a high level that in the pre-entry phase it would not want to utilize it all, i.e. excess capacity would be observed.

The Bain–Sylos and Spence analyses were extended in Dixit (1979) by considering whether the established firm will find it best to prevent entry or to allow it to occur. However, the basic assumptions concerning the post-entry developments were maintained.

Since it is at best unclear whether such assumptions will be valid, it seems useful to study the consequences of some alternatives. In reality, there may be no agreement about the rules of the post-entry game, and there may be periods of disequilibrium before any order is established. Financial positions of the firms may then acquire an important role. However, even when the two have a common understanding of the rules of the post-entry duopoly, there are several possibilities. An obvious case is where a Nash equilibrium will be established after entry, either in quantities as in Cournot (see also Wenders, 1971) or in prices as in Bertrand. Yet another case is where the entrant is destined to take over Stackelberg leadership in setting quantities (see Salop, 1978).

In this paper I examine some of these possibilities. The basic point is that although the *rules* of the post-entry game are taken to be exogenous, the established firm can alter the *outcome* to its advantage by changing the initial conditions. In particular, an irrevocable choice of investment allows it to alter its post-entry marginal cost curve, and thereby the post-entry equilibrium under any specified rule. It will be seen that it can use this privilege to exercise limited leadership.

1. THE MODEL

The basic point is most easily seen in a simplified model. I shall reduce the dynamic aspects to the barest essentials by ignoring all lags. Either entry does not occur at all, in which case the established firm continues in a stationary state, or else it occurs at once, and the post-entry equilibrium is also established at once, so that the resulting duopoly continues in its stationary state. It is as if the two players see through the whole problem and implement the solution immediately.[1] The result is that we can confine attention to the constant streams of profits, avoiding the complication of reducing a varying pair of profit flows to discounted present values. However, once the underlying principle is understood, an added complication in this respect is not difficult to admit in principle.

The second simplification made in the main body of the analysis is with regard to the costs of production. Let the subscript 1 denote the established firm and 2 the prospective entrant. Each firm will be supposed to have a constant average variable cost of output, and a constant unit cost of capacity expansion, and a set-up cost. If firm i has capacity k_i and is producing output x_i (with $x_i \leq k_i$), its cost per period will be

$$C_i = f_i + w_i x_i + r_i k_i, \tag{1}$$

where f_i is the fixed set-up cost, r_i the constant cost per unit of capacity (both expressed in per period or flow terms), and w_i the constant average variable cost for output. The possibility that the two firms have the same cost functions ($f_1 = f_2$, etc.) is not excluded. The special form (1) has some analytical and empirical merit; I examine a more general cost function in Sec. 3.

The revenues per period for the two firms will be functions $R^i(x_1, x_2)$. Each will be increasing and concave in that firm's output. Also, each firm's total and marginal revenue will be decreasing in the other's output.

The rules of the game are as follows. The established firm chooses a pre-entry capacity level $\bar{k}_1$. This may subsequently be increased, but cannot be reduced. If the other firm decides to enter, the two will achieve a duopoly Cournot–Nash equilibrium with quantity-setting. Otherwise the established firm will prevail as a monopoly.

First suppose that firm 1 has installed capacity $\bar{k}_1$. If it is producing output within this limit, i.e. if $x_1 \leq \bar{k}_1$, its total costs are

$$C_1 = f_1 + r_1 \bar{k}_1 + w_1 x_1.$$

[1] Compare the exchange between Moriarty and Holmes in *The Final Problem*: 'All that I have to say has already crossed your mind', said he. 'Then possibly my answer has crossed yours', I replied.

However, if it wishes to produce greater output, it must acquire additional capacity. If $x_1 > \bar{k}_1$, therefore,

$$C_1 = f_1 + (w_1 + r_1)\, x_1.$$

Correspondingly, firm 1's marginal cost is w_1 so long as its output does not exceed $\bar{k}_1$, and $(w_1 + r_1)$ thereafter. Firm 2 has no prior commitment in capacity. For all positive levels of output x_2, it acquires capacity k_2 to match, yielding

$$C_2 = f_2 + (w_2 + r_2)\, x_2$$

and a marginal cost of $(w_2 + r_2)$. The choice of $\bar{k}_1$ thus affects the shape of the marginal cost curve of firm 1, which in turn affects its reaction curve. When the two firms interact, the resulting duopoly equilibrium depends on $\bar{k}_1$, and therefore so do the profits of the two firms in it. If the profits for the second firm are positive, it will enter; otherwise it will not. Bearing this in mind, firm 1 will choose that $\bar{k}_1$ which maximizes its profit. Whether this is done by preventing entry or by allowing it to occur remains to be seen. However, I shall assume for simplicity of exposition that the established firm's maximum profit is positive, i.e. exit is not its best policy.

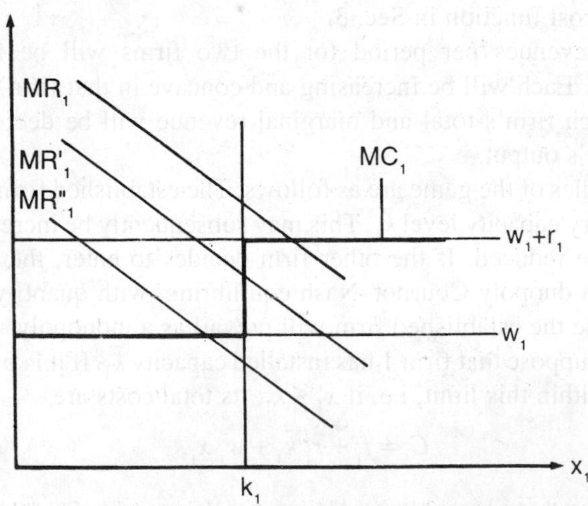

Figure 1

The analysis follows the scheme just outlined. For a given $\bar{k}_1$, Fig. 1 shows the marginal cost curve for the established firm, MC_1, as the heavy kinked line. It equals w_1, the marginal cost when there is spare capacity, up to the output level $\bar{k}_1$ and $(w_1 + r_1)$, the marginal cost including capacity expansion cost, thereafter. On this we superimpose the marginal revenue curve, the position of which depends on the assumed output level x_2 of the other firm. For a sufficiently low value of x_2, the curve is in a position like the one labelled MR_1, and the first firm's profit-maximizing choice of x_1 lies to the right of its previously fixed capacity level. For successively higher levels of x_2, the marginal revenue curve shifts downwards to occupy positions like MR_1' and MR_1'', yielding choices of x_1 at, or below, the capacity level. This response of x_1 to x_2 is just the established firm's reaction function to the entrant's output.

This function can be shown in a more familiar direct manner in the space of two quantities, and this is done in Fig. 2. I have shown two 'reference' curves *MM'* and *NN'*. The first becomes the reaction function if capacity expansion costs matter, and the second if there is spare capacity. Therefore the first is relevant for outputs above $\bar{k}_1$

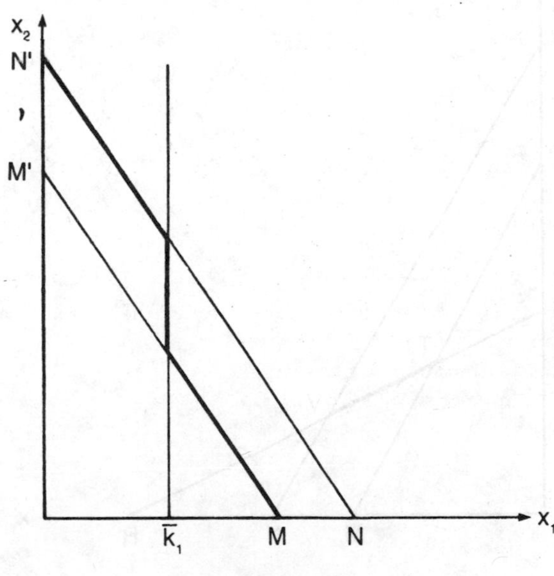

Figure 2

and the second for outputs below this level. For fixed $\bar{k}_1$, then, the reaction function is the kinked curve shown in heavy lines.

Let the points M and N have respective coordinates $(M_1, 0)$ and $(N_1, 0)$. The quantities M_1 and N_1 can be interpreted as follows. Both are profit-maximizing quantity choices of firm 1 when the output level of firm 2 is held fixed at zero, i.e. when the possibility of entry is ignored. However, M_1 is the choice when capacity expansion costs matter, and N_1 is relevant when there is sufficient capacity already installed and only variable costs matter.

Since firm 2 has no prior commitment in capacity, its reaction function RR' is straightforward. I assume that it intersects both MM' and NN' in a way that corresponds to the usual 'stable' Cournot solution, in order to minimize complications other than those of immediate interest (see Fig. 3).

For given $\bar{k}_1$, we have a duopoly Nash equilibrium at the intersection of the two reaction functions. However, the established firm has the privilege of choosing $\bar{k}_1$ in advance, and thus determining which reaction function it will present in the post-entry duopoly. Suppose firm 2's reaction function meets MM' at $T = (T_1, T_2)$ and NN' at

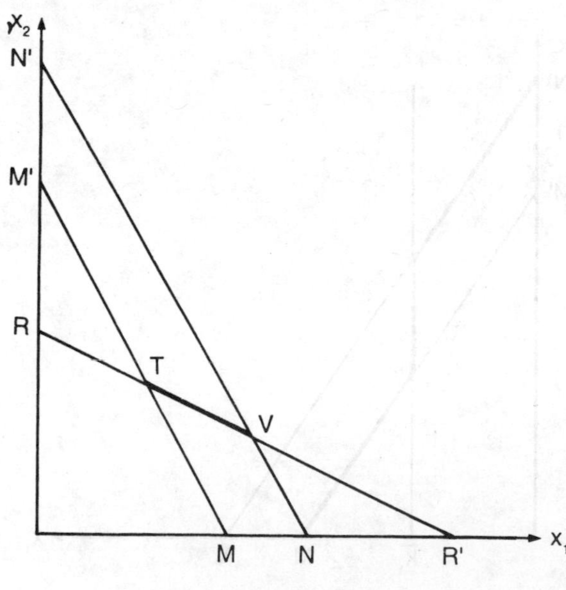

Figure 3

$V = (V_1, V_2)$ as shown in Fig. 3. Clearly T and V can be interpreted as Nash equilibria under alternative extréme circumstances, T when capacity expansion costs matter for firm 1, and V when they do not. It is then evident on comparing Fig. 2 and 3 that for a choice of $\bar{k}_1 \leq T_1$, the post-entry equilibrium will be at T, while for $\bar{k}_1 \geq V_1$, it will occur at V. Most importantly, for $T_1 \leq \bar{k}_1 \leq V_1$, it will occur at the appropriate point on the heavy line segment of the entrant's reaction function lying between T and V. Here the established firm will produce output $x_1 = \bar{k}_1$, and the entrant will produce the same output as would a Stackelberg follower faced with this x_1. It is in this sense that even when the post-entry game is accepted as leading to a Nash equilibrium, the established firm can exercise leadership over a limited range by using its capacity choice to manipulate the initial conditions of that game.

However, the qualification of the limited range is important. In particular, it means that capacity levels above V_1 are not credible threats of entry-deterrence. When a prospective entrant is confident of its ability to sustain a Nash equilibrium in the post-entry game, it does not fear such levels. And when the established firm knows this, it does not try out the costly and empty threats.

Since $N_1 > V_1$, we see a fortiori the futility of maintaining capacity levels above N_1 as threats to deter entry. Nor are such capacity levels justified by considerations of pre-entry production; in fact a monopolist saddled with capacity above N_1 will choose to leave the excess idle. Under the rules of the game assumed here, therefore, we will not observe the established firm installing capacity above N_1. The Spence excess capacity strategy will not be employed.

Nor will we ever see the established firm installing pre-entry capacity of less than T_1: if entry is to occur it will want more capacity, and if entry is not to occur it will want capacity of at least $M_1 > T_1$.

In the model used by Spence, it is simply assumed that a prospective entrant expects the established firm will respond to entry by producing an output level equal to its pre-entry capacity, no matter how high that may be. It is then possible that constrained monopoly profits made by keeping capacity at the entry-deterring level and producing at N exceed what is possible with a lower capacity leading to a Stackelberg duopoly equilibrium. This is the excess-capacity strategy of entry prevention. When the credibility of the threat is questioned, matters can be different, and the above argument shows that they are indeed different under the particular modification of the rules of the game.

2. CLASSIFICATION OF OUTCOMES

The discussion so far was confined to the post-entry duopoly, i.e. both firms were assumed to have incurred the set-up costs. When we come to the ex ante decision about whether to enter, set-up costs matter, and the choice is governed by the sign of the profits net of them. (Dixit, 1979 uses an alternative geometric approach involving discontinuous reaction functions.)

We have seen above that at all points that are ever going to be observed without or with entry, the established firm will be producing an output equal to its chosen pre-entry capacity. Therefore we may write the profits of the two firms as functions of their outputs alone, i.e.

$$\pi_i(x_1, x_2) = R^i(x_1, x_2) - f_i - (w_i + r_i)\, x_i.$$

It will often be convenient to indicate the point of evaluation (x_1, x_2) by a letter label such as that used in the corresponding figure. I have assumed that the maximum value of π_1 is always positive. Depending on the sign of π_2, various cases arise. Note that along firm 2's reaction function, its profit decreases monotonically from T to V. Therefore we can classify the possibilities as follows.

Case 1. $\pi_2(T) < 0$. Now the prospective entrant cannot make a profit in any post-entry equilibrium. So it will not try to enter the industry at all. Entry being irrelevant, the established firm will enjoy a pure monopoly by setting its capacity and output at M_1.

Case 2. $\pi_2(V) > 0$. Here the prospective entrant will make a positive profit in any post-entry equilibrium, so the established firm cannot hope to prevent entry. It can only seek the best available duopoly position. To this end, it will compute its profit along the segment TV. Since all these choices involve output equal to capacity, we can simply use the conventional iso-π_1 contours in (x_1, x_2) space and find the highest contour along the segment TV. If there is a Stackelberg tangency to the left of V, that is firm 1's best choice. However, if the conventional tangency occurs to the right of V, we now have a corner solution at V, which can then be thought of as a sort of generalized Stackelberg leadership point.

Case 3. $\pi_2(T) > 0 > \pi_2(V)$. This presents the richest set of possibilities. Now there is a point $B = (B_1, B_2)$ along such TV that $\pi_2(B) = 0$. If the established firm sets its capacity above B_1, the prospective entrant will reckon on making a negative profit in the post-entry Nash equilibrium, and therefore will not enter. Thus the capacity level B_1 is the entry-barring level. Knowing this, firm 1 wants to know whether it is worth its while to prevent entry.

Subcase i. If $B_1 < M_1$, then the established firm's monopoly choice is automatically sufficient to deter entry. In Bain's terminology, entry can be said to be blockaded.

If $B_1 > M_1$, the established firm can only bar entry by maintaining capacity (and output) at a level greater than it would want to as a monopolist; thus it is faced with a calculation of the costs and benefits of entry-prevention. To prevent entry, it needs a capacity of just greater than B_1. Since $B_1 < V_1 < N_1$, we know that it will want to use all this capacity in its monopoly choice of output, so its profit will be $\pi_1(B_1, 0)$. The alternative is to allow entry and settle for the best duopoly point, which may be a tangency in the segment TV, or a corner solution at V. Whichever it is, call it the generalized Stackelberg point S, with coordinates (S_1, S_2). Then we have:

Subcase ii. $\pi_1(S) < \pi_1(B_1, 0)$, when it is better to prevent entry by choosing a limit-capacity or limit-output at B_1. There is a corresponding limit-price. In Bain's usage, entry is effectively impeded. Incidentally, for this subcase to arise, it is sufficient to have $S_1 \geq B_1$. For, with $B_1 > M_1$, we have $\pi_1(S_1, S_2) < \pi_1(S_1, 0) \leq \pi_1(B_1, 0)$.

Subcase iii. $\pi_1(S) > \pi_1(B_1, 0)$, when it is better to allow entry, i.e. entry is ineffectively impeded, and a duopoly solution is observed at S. Remember that S is the post-entry Nash equilibrium.

An alternative way of distinguishing between the sub-cases *ii* and *iii* is to draw the iso-π_1 contour through S and see if it intersects the x_1-axis to the right or the left of B_1. This would follow Dixit (1979), except for one new feature: the Stackelberg point S can be at the corner solution V.

For particular demand functions, we can evaluate all these profit expressions explicitly, and thereby express the classification of outcomes in terms of the underlying parameters.

3. EXTENSIONS AND MODIFICATIONS

Of the numerous extensions conceivable, I consider three. The first involves an alternative and rather extreme post-entry equilibrium, where the rules of the game are that the entrant acquires the role of quantity leadership (see Salop, 1978). Thus firm 2 chooses a point on firm 1's post-entry reaction function to maximize its own profit. However, firm 1, by its initial commitment to capacity, can decide which reaction function to present to the entrant, and can manipulate this choice to its own advantage.

Figure 4 shows the possibilities. The notation is the same as in Fig. 3, with some additions. Let $F = (F_1, F_2)$ be the ordinary Stackelberg point where firm 2 is the leader and firm 1 the follower, taking into account capacity expansion costs, i.e. using the reference curve MM'. If firm 1 sets its capacity $\bar{k}_1$ at a level less than F_1, then its reaction function as drawn in Fig. 2 will drop from NN' to MM' at $\bar{k}_1$ to the left of F. Firm 2's profit will then be maximized on this reaction function at the tangency point F. For $\bar{k}_1$ between F_1 and T_1,

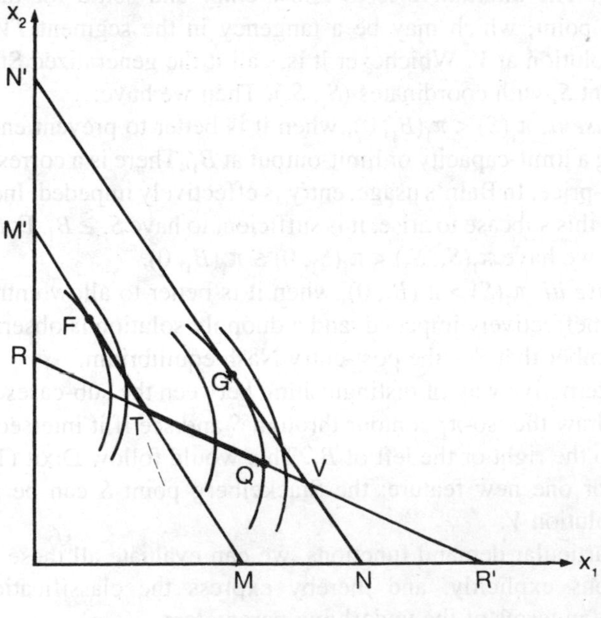

Figure 4

there will be a maximum at the kink in firm 1's reaction function where it meets MM', yielding an equilibrium at the appropriate point along the segment FT. For a while to the right of T, we will have a tangency solution along TV, an iso-π_2 contour being tangential to the vertical portion of firm 1's reaction function. Let G be the point where an iso-π_2 contour is tangential to NN', and let this contour meet RR' at $Q = (Q_1, Q_2)$. Then the vertical tangency will be the best choice for firm 2 so long as $\bar{k}_1 \leq Q_1$. For $\bar{k}_1 > Q_1$, however, it will prefer the tangency at G.

By its choice of $\bar{k}_1$, the established firm can therefore secure as the post-entry equilibrium any point along the kinked line segment FTQ, shown in heavy ink in the figure, and the isolated point G. In other words, even though the rules of the game require it to surrender post-entry quantity leadership, the established firm can use its commitment to capacity to seize a limited initiative back from the entrant. It remains to choose the best available point. Now G is clearly inferior from the point of view of firm 1 to the point directly below it on the segment TQ. Similarly, all points along FT are worse than T. However, there is a genuine choice to be made, i.e. leadership exercised, along the segment TQ. This is smaller than the segment TV which was available when the post-entry rules led to a Nash equilibrium. But the qualitative features are unchanged, and all of my earlier analysis applies on replacing V by Q throughout.

The second extension I consider allows a more general cost function. The form (1), up to the given capacity level, has marginal cost constant at the level w_1, and since capacity cannot be exceeded, the marginal cost of output can be said to jump to infinity where output hits capacity. An increase in capacity then lowers marginal cost from infinity to w_1 over the added range. Now I replace this by a form which has a more flexible notion of capacity. Let

$$C_1 = C^1(x_1, \bar{k}_1). \tag{2}$$

This will be increasing in x_1, and convex at least beyond a certain point. For each x_1 there will be a cost-minimizing choice of $\bar{k}_1$, so C^1 will be decreasing in $\bar{k}_1$ up to this level and increasing thereafter. Finally, a higher level of $\bar{k}_1$ will lower marginal cost of output, i.e.

$$C^1_{x_1 \bar{k}_1} < 0, \tag{3}$$

with subscripts denoting partial derivatives in the usual way. All this follows the theory of the familiar textbook short-run cost functions. This is similar to the more general model in Spence (1977) except that price discipline does not break down completely after entry.

Begin with the post-entry Nash equilibrium given that firm 1 has set its capacity variable at the level $\bar{k}_1$. Firm 2's reaction function is again straightforward. That for firm 1 is found by choosing x_1 to maximize

$$R^1(x_1, x_2) - C^1(x_1, \bar{k}_1)$$

for given x_2 and $\bar{k}_1$. This has the first-order condition

$$R^1_{x_1}(x_1, x_2) - C^1_{x_1}(x_1, \bar{k}_1) = 0 \tag{4}$$

and the second-order condition

$$R^1_{x_1 x_1}(x_1, x_2) - C^1_{x_1 x_1}(x_1, \bar{k}_1) < 0. \tag{5}$$

Equation (4) defines firm 1's post-entry reaction function, and also tells us how it shifts as $\bar{k}_1$ changes. Total differentiation gives

$$dx_1 = [-R^1_{x_1 x_2}/(R^1_{x_1 x_1} - C^1_{x_1 x_1})]\, dx_2 + [C^1_{x_1 \bar{k}_1}/(R^1_{x_1 x_1} - C^1_{x_1 x_1})]\, d\bar{k}_1.$$

Given our assumption that the commodities are substitutes in the sense that an increased quantity of the second lowers the marginal revenue for the first, and using (5), we see that the reaction function slopes downward. Also, using (3) and (5), we see that it shifts to the right as $\bar{k}_1$ increases.

Figure 5 shows a collection of firm 1's reaction functions for different choices of $\bar{k}_1$, as a set of dashed lines. Where each meets firm 2's reaction function RR', there is a post-entry Nash equilibrium for the appropriate choice of $\bar{k}_1$. Thus, once again, firm 1 by its choice of capacity can achieve any one of a range of points along firm 2's reaction function. This is almost as if it acquired the privilege of quantity leadership. There are two limitations. First, the possible reaction functions found by varying $\bar{k}_1$ may trace out only a limited part of firm 2's reaction function, as happened in the case of Sec. 1. Secondly, in any post-entry Nash equilibrium, the $\bar{k}_1$ which achieves it is not the ideal choice for producing the x_1 that prevails there; so the policy involves a cost that does not appear in straightforward

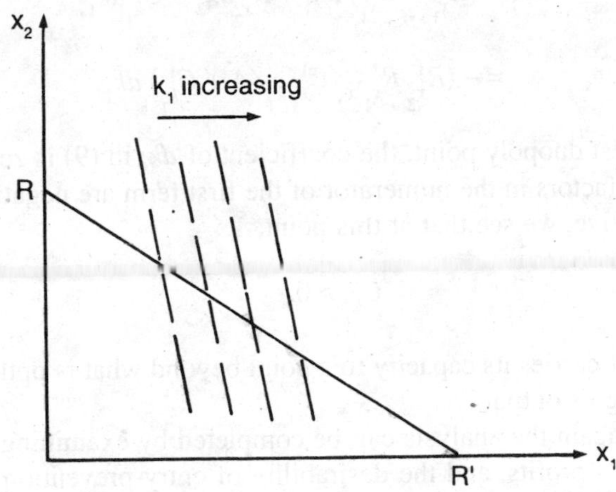

Figure 5

quantity leadership. To see this, we must examine the equilibrium in more detail. Firm 2 maximizes $R^2(x_1, x_2) - C^2(x_2)$ in obvious notation, so its reaction function is given by

$$R^2_{x_2}(x_1, x_2) - C^2_{x_2}(x_2) = 0. \qquad (6)$$

Then (4) and (6) define the duopoly equilibrium as a function of $\bar{k}_1$. Differentiating the equations totally, we have

$$\begin{bmatrix} R^1_{x_1 x_1} - C^1_{x_1 x_1} & R^1_{x_1 x_2} \\ R^2_{x_1 x_2} & R^2_{x_2 x_2} - C^2_{x_2 x_2} \end{bmatrix} \begin{bmatrix} dx_1 \\ dx_2 \end{bmatrix} = \begin{bmatrix} C^1_{x_1 \bar{k}_1} \; d\bar{k}_1 \\ 0 \end{bmatrix} \qquad (7)$$

Write Δ for the determinant of the coefficient matrix; it is positive by the stability condition for the equilibrium. Then we have the solution

$$\begin{bmatrix} dx_1 \\ dx_2 \end{bmatrix} = \frac{1}{\Delta} \begin{bmatrix} R^2_{x_2 x_2} - C^2_{x_2 x_2} \\ - R^1_{x_1 x_2} \end{bmatrix} C^1_{x_1 \bar{k}_1} \; d\bar{k}_1. \qquad (8)$$

Firm 1 uses this in its choice to $\bar{k}_1$ to maximize its profit, therefore

$$d\pi_1 = (R^1_{x_1} - C^1_{x_1})\, dx_1 + R^1_{x_2}\, dx_2 - C^1_{\bar{k}_1}\, d\bar{k}_1$$

$$= -\,(R^1_{x_2}\, R^2_{x_1 x_2}\, C^1_{x_1 k_1} / \Delta + C^1_{\bar{k}_1})\, d\bar{k}_1 . \qquad (9)$$

At the best duopoly point, the coefficient of $d\bar{k}_1$ in (9) is zero. Since all three factors in the numerator of the first term are negative while Δ is positive, we see that at this point,

$$C^1_{\bar{k}_1} > 0,$$

i.e. firm 1 carries its capacity to a point beyond what is optimum for producing its output.

Once again the analysis can be completed by examining the sign of firm 2's profits, and the desirability of entry-prevention for firm 1. This more flexible notion of capacity can be interpreted in terms of other types of investment such as dealer networks and advertising, and this provides a basis for arguments that such expenditures can be used by an established firm in its efforts to deter entry. This counters recent expressions of pessimism (e.g. Needham, 1978, pp. 177–9) concerning the effectiveness of such tactics.

For the last modification, I revert to a rigid concept of capacity, but consider price-setting in the post-entry duopoly, the solution rule being the Bertrand–Nash equilibrium. Some added complications can arise due to possible non-convexities even with reasonable demand and cost functions, but I ignore these and show the simplest possible case. This is done in Fig. 6, with notation analogous to the corresponding quantity-setting case of Fig. 3. The prospective entrant's reaction function is RR'. For the established firm, we have two reference curves MM' and NN', the former when capacity expansion costs matter and the latter when they do not. Their relative positions are naturally reversed as compared to the quantity-setting case. The former is relevant for $x_1 \geq \bar{k}_1$ and the latter for $x_1 \leq \bar{k}_1$, where x_1 is found from the demand function $D^1(p_1, p_2)$. The boundary curve $x_1 = \bar{k}_1$ is shown for a particular $\bar{k}_1$, and the corresponding reaction function for the established firm is shown by the heavy lines. It is then clear that by varying $\bar{k}_1$, the established firm can secure any point along the segment TV of the prospective entrant's reaction function as the post-entry

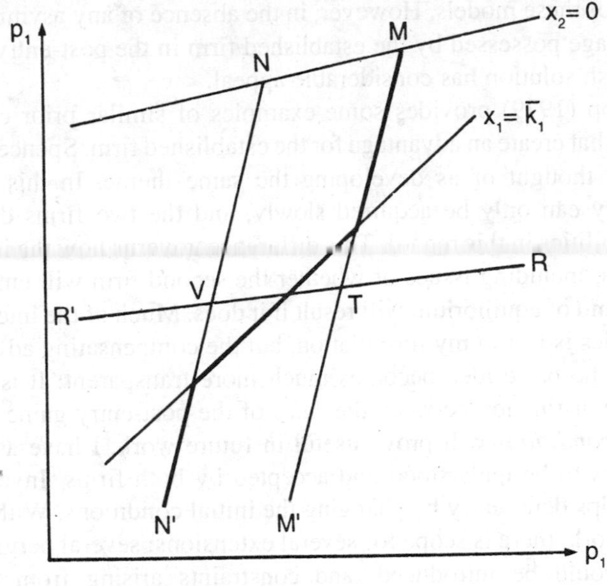

Figure 6

Nash equilibrium. Once again, we observe a limited leadership possibility arise by virtue of the established firm's advantage in being the first to make a commitment to capacity.

4. CONCLUDING COMMENTS

The theme of the paper is that the role of an irrevocable commitment of investment in entry-deterrence is to alter the initial conditions of the post-entry game to the advantage of the established firm, for any fixed rule under which that game is to be played. This was illustrated in several simple models. Prominent among the conclusions was the observation that if the post-entry game is agreed to be played according to Nash rules, the established firm will not wish to install capacity that would be left idle in the pre-entry phase. This contrasts with the results of Spence (1977), where the post-entry game involves leadership by the established firm, and its threat of producing at a level equal to its pre-entry capacity is assumed to be believed by the prospective entrant. It is not possible to claim universal validity for either of these models. However, in the absence of any asymmetrical advantage possessed by the established firm in the post-entry phase, the Nash solution has considerable appeal.

Salop (1979) provides some examples of similar prior commitments that create an advantage for the established firm. Spence (1979) can be thought of as developing the same theme. In this model, capacity can only be acquired slowly, and the two firms differ in their abilities in this regard. This difference governs how the industry evolves, including issues of whether the second firm will enter, and what kind of equilibrium will result if it does. Much of the interesting dynamics is lost in my formulation, but the compensating advantage is that the basic idea becomes much more transparent. It is hoped that the distinction between the *rules* of the post-entry game and its *initial conditions* will prove useful in future work. I have assumed the rules to be understood and accepted by both firms. Investment then helps deter entry by changing the initial conditions. Within this framework, there is scope for several extensions: several periods and firms could be introduced, and constraints arising from capital markets could be imposed. The question of whether one firm can change the rules in its own favour is more interesting, but much more difficult.

REFERENCES

DIXIT, A. (1979), 'A Model of Duopoly Suggesting a Theory of Entry Barriers', *Bell Journal of Economics*, 10, 20–32.

NEEDHAM, D. (1978), *The Economics of Industrial Structure, Conduct and Performance*, London: Holt, Rinehart and Winston.

SALOP, S. (1978), 'A Note on Self-enforcing Threats and Entry Deterrence', Discussion Paper No. 14, University of Pennsylvania.

—— (1979), 'Strategic Entry Deterrence', *American Economic Review*, Papers and Proceedings.

SCHELLING, T.C. (1960), *The Strategy of Conflict*, Cambridge, Mass.: Harvard University Press.

SCHERER, F.M. (1970,) *Industrial Market Structure and Economic Performance*, Chicago: Rand-McNally.

SPENCE, M. (1977), 'Entry, Investment and Oligopolistic Pricing', *Bell Journal of Economics*, 8, 534–44.

—— (1979), 'Investment, Strategy and Growth in a New Market', *Bell Journal of Economics*, 10, 1–19.

WENDERS, T. (1971), 'Collusion and Entry', *Journal of Political Economy*, 79, 1258–77.

Limit Pricing and Entry Under Incomplete Information: An Equilibrium Analysis*

PAUL MILGROM AND JOHN ROBERTS

1. INTRODUCTION

The basic idea of limit pricing is that an established firm may be able to influence, through its current pricing policy alone,[1] other firms' perceptions of the profitability of entering the firm's markets, and that the firm may thus set its prices below their short run maximizing levels in order to deter entry. As such, limit pricing has constituted a major theme in the industrial organization literature for at least the last thirty years, and during the past decade in particular it has been the subject of a number of papers employing formal models of maximizing behaviour.[2] For the most part, these latter analyses have

* Much of the work reported here first appeared in Milgrom and Roberts (1980). This work has been presented at a large number of conferences, meetings, and seminars, and we would like to thank our audiences at each of these events for their comments. We are particularly indebted to Eric Maskin, Roger Myerson, Steve Salop, Robert Wilson, and two referees for their helpful suggestions, to David Besanko for his excellent research assistance, and to Armando Ortega-Reichert, whose work on repeated competitive bidding (Ortega-Reichert, 1962) has influenced our thinking on the present subject. Finally, we gratefully acknowledge the financial support of the Graduate School of Business at Stanford, the J.L. Kellogg Graduate School of Management at Northwestern, and the National Science Foundation (Grants SOC 77–06000 to the IMSSS at Stanford and SOC 79–07542 and SES 80–01932 to Northwestern).

[1] Although some recent treatments of entry deterrence incorporate other strategic variables, the standard, traditional approach is to treat the choice of the pre-entry price as the firm's only decision and to assume no dependence of post-entry profits on this choice.

[2] The idea behind limit pricing can be traced back through the work of J. Bain (1949) and J.M. Clark (1940) at least to a paper by N. Kaldor (1935). The recent

concentrated on the decision problem of the established firm, taking as given the limit-pricing assumption that a lower pre-entry price will deter or restrict entry. In this context, the typical conclusion is that an optimal price–output policy in the face of threatened entry will involve prices which are below the short-run monopoly level, but still above the level that would prevail after entry. This conclusion had led to some debate as to the appropriate public policy regarding such limit pricing, since there appears to be a tradeoff between the benefits to society of lower pre-entry prices and the costs arising from entry being limited or deterred.

In this paper we present a re-examination of the limit pricing problem. Our model differs from most of the existing literature in that we treat both the established firm and potential entrant as rational, maximizing economic agents. This naturally leads to a game-theoretic, equilibrium formulation. However, once one adopts this approach, it is not immediately obvious why limit pricing should emerge at all.

This point has been made explicitly by J. Friedman (1979) in one of the few existing game-theoretic treatments of pricing in the face of potential entry of which we are aware. Friedman notes that, under the usual sort of assumptions on demand, the profits which would accrue should entry occur are completely independent of the pre-entry price. Since in Friedman's model both the established firm and the entrant are completely informed as to demand and cost conditions, these post-entry profits are fully known when the entry decision is made. Then the inescapable logic of (perfect) equilibrium (Selten, 1975) requires that the entry decision be independent of the pre-entry price. This means that any attempt at limit pricing would serve only to squander pre-entry profits and so there would be no limit pricing.

Friedman's argument will be generally valid in any complete-information, game-theoretic model in which the established firm's pre-entry actions do not influence post-entry costs and demand. In such a model, then, the intuitive idea underlying the traditional concept of limit pricing—that potential entrants would read the pre-entry price as a signal concerning the price and market shares they can expect to prevail after entry—finds no formal justification.

---

formal investigations begin with D. Gaskins (1971), M.I. Kamien and N.L. Schwartz (1971) and G. Pyatt (1971). See F.M. Scherer (1979) and S. Salop (1979) for further references.

In contrast, a formalization of this intuition is the very heart of our model.

Specifically, we consider situations in which neither the established firm nor the potential entrant is perfectly informed as to some characteristic of the other which is relevant to the post-entry profits of both. The central example of such a characteristic, and the one on which we initially concentrate, is the other firm's unit costs. In such a situation, the pre-entry price may become a signal regarding the established firm's costs, which in turn are a determinant of the post-entry price and profits for the entrant. Thus the relationship assumed in the earlier literature emerges endogenously in equilibrium in our model: a lower price (by signalling lower costs) tends to discourage entry. Thus, too, limit-pricing behaviour arises in equilibrium, with the established firm attempting to influence the entry decision by charging a pre-entry price which is below the simple monopoly level.

The entrant, meanwhile, will seek to infer the established firm's costs (and thus the profitability of entry) from observation of the pre-entry price. In making this inference, of course, it will have to employ some conjecture regarding the established firm's pricing policy, i.e. the relationship between the established firm's cost and the price it charges. In Nash equilibrium, this conjecture must be correct. Indeed the very definition of equilibrium in this context involves rational expectations by each firm about the other's behaviour. Thus, the entrant will allow for limit pricing in making its inferences and its entry decision.

Thus, in equilibrium, the established firm practises limit pricing, but the entrant is not fooled by this strategy. Consequently, the probability that entry actually occurs in equilibrium need not be any lower than it would be in a world of full information, where limit pricing would not arise. Indeed, the probability of entry in the limit pricing equilibrium may even be higher than with complete information, even though the pre-entry price is lower. In particular, this means that the alleged tradeoff for society between lower prices and delayed or deterred entry may never arise.

In the next section, we illustrate these claims in the context of a simple model with linear demand and constant unit costs. In this model we compute equilibria for two specific examples. One of these involves only two possible levels of costs for the entrants and for the established firm; the other involves a continuum of possibilities on each side. In Sec. 3 we consider a more general model. The final section contains our conclusions.

2. TWO EXAMPLES

Consider the market for a homogeneous good in which there is an established firm, denoted firm 1, and a potential entrant, firm 2. Initially, each firm knows its own unit cost, c_i, $i = 1, 2$, but it does not know the other firm's cost level. Firm 1 is a monopolist, and it must pick a quantity Q to produce (or a price to charge) as a monopolist, given its knowledge of c_1 and its beliefs about c_2. Firm 2 will observe this choice and then (knowing c_2 but not c_1) must either enter the market or decide to stay out. If it enters, it incurs an entry cost of K, each firm learns the other's cost, and then the two firms operate as Cournot duopolists. If it does not enter, firm 1 will henceforth enjoy its monopoly profits without further fear of entry.

Table 1

Present value to i of \$1 accruing after entry	δ_i
Unit production cost of firm i	c_i
Fixed cost of entry for firm 2	K
Inverse demand	$P = a - bQ$
Simple monopoly output	$m(c_1) = (a - c_1)/2b$
First period profit for firm 1	$\Pi_1^0(Q, c_1) = (a - bQ - c_1)Q$
Monopoly profit for firm 1	$\Pi_1^M(c_1) = (a - c_1)^2/4b$
Cournot profit for firm i	$\Pi_i^C(c_1, c_2) = (a - 2c_i + c_j)^2/9b$
Reward to firm 1 from deterring entry	$R(c_1, c_2) = \Pi_1^M(c_1) - \Pi_1^C(c_1, c_2)$
Payoff to 1 if entry occurs	$\Pi_1^0(Q, c_1)$
Payoff to 1 if no entry	$\Pi_1^0(Q, c_1) + \delta_1 R(c_1, c_2)$
Payoff to 2 if entry	$\delta_2 \Pi_2^C(c_1, c_2) - K$
Payoff to 2 if no entry	0
Range of possible c_i values	$[\underline{c}_i, \bar{c}_i]$
Probability distribution function for c_i (j's beliefs about c_i)	H_i

We summarize the notation and profit formulae with linear demand and constant unit costs in Table 1. To simplify the payoff formulae, we normalize the post-entry profits of the established firm to be zero if entry occurs, so it receives only its first period profit as its payoff in this event. If entry does not occur, its payoff is its first period profit plus the discounted value of a reward to deterring entry. This reward is equal to the excess of its monopoly profit over its profit as a Cournot duopolist.

The extensive form game corresponding to this set-up is one of incomplete information, since the players do not know the numerical values of the payoffs corresponding to any pair of decisions they make. Attempting to analyse such a game directly would easily lead one into a morass of infinite regress. The approach we adopt instead is that proposed by Harsanyi [6], which involves replacing this *incomplete* information game by a game of *complete* but *imperfect* information.[3] One then treats the Nash equilibria of this second game as the equilibria of the original game.

The imperfect information game involves another player, 'Nature', which is indifferent over all possible outcomes. Nature moves first and selects c_1 and c_2 according to the probability distributions, H_i, giving the players' beliefs. Then player i is informed about c_i but not about c_j, and for each realization of c_1 and c_2 the game tree unfolds as above.

In any extensive form game, a player's strategy is a specification of the action it will take in any information set, i.e. the player's actions at any point can depend only on what it knows at that point. Here, the information sets for firm 1 are defined by the realized values of c_1 (given by 'Nature's move') and those for firm 2 by a realization of c_2 and a choice of Q by firm 1. Thus, a (pure) strategy for 1 is a map s from its possible cost levels into the possible choices of Q and a (pure) strategy for 2 is a map t from $\mathbb{R}^2$ into $\{0, 1\}$ giving its decision for each possible pair (c_2, Q), where we interpret 1 as 'enter' and 0 as 'stay out'.

A pair of strategies constitutes an equilibrium if each maximizes the expected payoff of the player using it, given that the other is using its specified strategy. This is the standard Nash equilibrium notion.

[3] An extensive form game has imperfect information if some player at some point must make a move without having been fully informed about all the previous moves made by the other players.

However, to accentuate the rational expectations character of Nash equilibrium, it is helpful to use the following, equivalent definition. An equilibrium consists of a pair of strategies (s^*, t^*) and a pair of conjectures $(\bar{s}, \bar{t})$ such that (i) firm 1's pricing policy s^* is a best response to its conjecture $\bar{t}$ about firm 2's entry rule, (ii) the strategy t^* is a best response for firm 2 to its conjecture $\bar{s}$, and (iii) the actual and conjectured strategies coincide. We formalize these conditions as follows: (i) for any $c_1 \in [\underline{c}_1, \bar{c}_1]$ and any $s : [\underline{c}_1, \bar{c}_1] \to \mathbb{R}_+$,

$$\Pi_1^0(s^*(c_1), c_1) + \delta_1 \int_{\underline{c}_2}^{\bar{c}_2} R(c_1, c_2)\left[1 - \bar{t}(c_2, s^*(c_1))\right] dH_2(c_2)$$

$$\geq \Pi_1^0(s(c_1), c_1) + \delta_1 \int_{\underline{c}_2}^{\bar{c}_2} R(c_1, c_2)\left[1 - \bar{t}(c_2, s(c_1))\right] dH_2(c_2),$$

(ii) for any $c_2 \in [\underline{c}_2, \bar{c}_2]$ and any $t : [\underline{c}_2, \bar{c}_2] \times \mathbb{R}_+ \to \{0, 1\}$,

$$\int_{\underline{c}_1}^{\bar{c}_1} \left[\delta_2 \Pi_2^C(c_1, c_2) - K\right] t^*(c_2, \bar{s}(c_1))\, dH_1(c_1)$$

$$\geq \int_{\underline{c}_1}^{\bar{c}_1} \left[\delta_2 \Pi_2^C(c_1, c_2) - K\right] t(c_2, \bar{s}(c_1))\, dH_1(c_1), \text{ and}$$

(iii) $(s^*, t^*) = (\bar{s}, \bar{t})$.

Given this framework, we first study a parameterized family of examples where the H_i are two-point distributions and, for specific values of the parameters, compute equilibria. Later in this section we will allow for a continuum of possible cost levels ('types') for the two firms.

Thus, suppose that the demand curve is $P = 10 - Q$, that $K = 7$, that $\underline{c}_1 = 0.5$, $\underline{c}_2 = 1.5$, $\bar{c}_1 = \bar{c}_2 = 2.0$, that $\delta_1 = \delta_2 = 1$, and that the costs are independently distributed with $H_2(c_2 = \bar{c}_2) = p = 1 - H_2(c_2 = \underline{c}_2)$ and $H_1(c_1 = \bar{c}_1) = q = 1 - H_1(c_1 = \underline{c}_1)$.

With these specifications, the payoffs are as follows:

$R(\underline{c}_1, \underline{c}_2) = 10.31,$ $\quad \Pi_2^C(\underline{c}_1, \underline{c}_2) - K = -0.75,$

$R(\underline{c}_1, \bar{c}_2) = 9.12,$ $\quad \Pi_2^C(\underline{c}_1, \bar{c}_2) - K = -2.31,$

$R(\bar{c}_1, \underline{c}_2) = 9.75,$ $\quad \Pi_2^C(\bar{c}_1, \underline{c}_2) - K = 2.00,$

$$R(\bar{c}_1, \bar{c}_2) = 8.89, \qquad \Pi_2^C(\bar{c}_1, \bar{c}_2) - K = 0.11,$$
$$m(\underline{c}_1) = 4.75, \qquad \Pi_1^M(\underline{c}_1) = 22.56,$$
$$m(\bar{c}_1) = 4.00, \qquad \Pi_1^M(\bar{c}_1) = 16.00.$$

Note that if 1's costs were known to be $\underline{c}_1$, neither type of potential entrant would want to enter, while if c_1 were known to be $\bar{c}_1$, both would want to enter. Thus, the probability of entry, if the entrant were to be directly informed of the realized value of c_1, is simply q, the probability that $c_1 = \bar{c}_1$. Of course, if firm 2 were so informed, there would be no point to limit pricing and Q would simply be set at the short-run profit-maximizing level of $m(c_1)$.

Note, too, that if firm 2 were unable to observe Q and were uninformed about c_1, then it would want to enter if its expected profits were positive, i.e. if $q\Pi_2^C(\bar{c}_1, c_2) + (1-q)\Pi_2^C(\underline{c}_1, c_2) - K \geq 0$. If $0.954 > q > 0.273$, then this inequality holds for $\underline{c}_2$ and not for $\bar{c}_2$, so the low cost entrant would come in and the high cost entrant would not. (For $q < 0.273$, neither would want to enter, and for $q > 0.954$, both would want to enter.)

In fact, if 2 is not directly informed about c_1 but can observe Q, it will attempt to make inferences about the actual value of c_1 from its observation of Q, using its conjectures about 1's behaviour. Note that in equilibrium, the only values of Q which could be observed are $s^*(\underline{c}_1)$ and $s^*(\bar{c}_1)$. Now in this set-up there are only two possibilities: either $s^*(\underline{c}_1) = s^*(\bar{c}_1)$, or else the two values differ. An equilibrium with the first of these properties is called *pooling*, while in the other situation the equilibrium is *separating*. Thus, in pooling equilibrium, observing Q gives no information, while the observation of Q in a separating equilibrium allows the value of c_1 to be inferred exactly.

Thus, in a separating equilibrium (s^*, t^*), entry will occur if $s^*(\bar{c}_1)$ is observed and will not if $s^*(\underline{c}_1)$ is observed: *entry takes place in exactly the same circumstances as if the entrant had been informed about the value of* c_1, i.e. with prior probability q. Moreover, this will be true in any separating equilibrium of any model of this type: in any separating equilibrium, observing the equilibrium choice of the established firm allows a precise and accurate inference to be made about the firm's characteristic. Thus, in such an equilibrium, *limit pricing will not limit entry* relative to the complete information case (in which there would be no limit pricing because the possibility of influencing the entrant's decision does not arise).

In a pooling equilibrium, the entrant can infer nothing from observing Q and so enters if its expected profit is positive. Thus, as noted above, if $q \in (0.273, 0.954)$, only the low cost entrant will come in. Thus, in a pooling equilibrium, the probability of entry is $(1-p)$, while in a separating equilibrium the probability of entry is q.

We now will show that, in this example, so long as p is not too small, there are both pooling and separating equilibria, that all equilibria involve limit pricing, and that the probability of entry in a pooling equilibrium may equal, exceed or fall short of that in a separating equilibrium (or, equivalently, under complete information).

First, we show that the following strategies constitute a separating equilibrium:

$$s^*(\underline{c}_1) = 7.2,\ s^*(\bar{c}_1) = m(\bar{c}_1) = 4.0,$$

$$t^*(c_2, Q) = \begin{cases} 1 & \text{if} Q < 7.2, \\ 0 & \text{otherwise.} \end{cases}$$

Note that since $s^*(\underline{c}_1) > m(\underline{c}_1)$, s^* is a limit pricing strategy. Notice too that from our earlier discussion, t^* is clearly a best response to s^*. Thus, we need to check that s^* is optimal, given t^*. First, note that unless the high cost established firm produces at least 7.2, it cannot deter any entry. But, this level is high enough that it is not worthwhile for $\bar{c}_1$ to produce it, even though in so doing it would eliminate all entry. To see this, note that producing $Q = s^*(\underline{c}_1)$ yields the payoff

$$\Pi_1^0(\bar{c}_1, s^*(\underline{c}_1)) + pR(\bar{c}_1, \bar{c}_2) + (1-p)R(\bar{c}_1, \underline{c}_2) = 15.51 - 0.86p$$

while producing $m(\bar{c}_1)$ yields $\Pi_1^0(\bar{c}_1, m(\bar{c}_1)) = 16$, which exceeds $15.51 - 0.86p$ for all $p \geq 0$. Finally, note that the low cost firm has no reason to produce more than $s^*(\underline{c}_1)$. If it produces less, it is sure to face entry, and thus its best choice in this range would be $m(\underline{c}_1)$. But $s^*(\underline{c}_1)$ yields an expected payoff of $26.87 - 1.19p$, which for all $p \leq 1$ strictly exceeds the payoff $\Pi_1^M(\underline{c}_1) = 22.56$ from producing $m(\underline{c}_1)$. Thus, $s^*(\underline{c}_1)$ is also optimal.

We now demonstrate the existence of a pooling equilibrium given by

$$s^*(\underline{c}_1) = s^*(\bar{c}_1) = m(\underline{c}_1) = 4.75,$$

$$t^*(\underline{c}_2, Q) = 1,$$

$$t^*(\bar{c}_2, Q) = \begin{cases} 0 & \text{if } Q \geq 4.75, \\ 1 & \text{otherwise.} \end{cases}$$

Note again that our earlier discussion indicates that t^* is a best response to s^*, given $q \in (0.273, 0.954)$. Further, it is evident that s^* is optimal if $c_1 = \underline{c}_1$, since any increase in Q would not deter entry, and any decrease in output would both increase entry and reduce first period profits. Finally, if the established firm has $c_1 = \bar{c}_1$, it similarly has no incentive to increase output, while cutting output could at best yield the monopoly first period return, but would induce certain entry. This gives a payoff of 16.00, which is, for $p > 0.063$, less than its current return of $\Pi_1^0(\bar{c}_1, 4.75) + pR(\bar{c}_1, \bar{c}_2) = 15.44 + 8.89p$. Thus, if $p > 0.063$, this is also an equilibrium, and since $s^*(\bar{c}_1) > m(\bar{c}_1)$, it, too, involves limit pricing.

To summarize, our pooling equilibrium required that the probability p of the entrant having high costs exceed 0.063 and that q lie in (0.273, 0.954), while our separating equilibrium existed for all p and q. In a separating equilibrium, the probability of entry is q, which is just the probability that the established firm is of the high cost type, while in our pooling equilibrium, the probability of entry is $1 - p$, the probability of the entrant having low costs.[4] Clearly, we may have $1 - p$ greater than, less than, or equal to q and still meet the requirements for existence of both equilibria. *Limit pricing equilibria may involve less, the same, or more entry than occurs in the full information (no limit pricing) case.*

It is, of course, true in either type of equilibrium that if the limit-pricing firm were to charge a higher price than is called for by the equilibrium strategy, then it would face a greater threat of entry. This is because the entrant would interpret this high price as meaning that the firm's costs were higher than they in fact are, and thus entry would appear more attractive. (Note that the entrant's inferences will be correct only if firm 1 adheres to its equilibrium strategy.) Indeed, it is this balancing of foregone first period profits against the reward to deterring entry which characterizes the equilibrium and it is this

[4] If $q < 0.273$, then there is a pooling equilibrium against which the probability of entry is zero. If $q > 0.954$, then entry would be certain if a pooling equilibrium were established. But then each type of established firm would find that its monopoly output represents a profitable deviation. Thus, there could be no such equilibrium.

threat of increased entry which leads the established firm to maintain its expanded output. Thus, in this sense, limit pricing does limit entry.

A useful way to think about these results is to consider limit pricing as the outcome of competition between the types of the established firm, with high cost types attempting to mimic low cost ones and low cost firms attempting to distinguish themselves from the high cost ones. Then whether a pooling or a separating equilibrium is established is a matter of whether it is the high or low cost type which is successful. This competition could, of course, be purely a conjectural one in the mind of the entrant, but it might also be more concrete. Specifically, one can imagine that there are a number of currently monopolized markets, all of which are identical except that a percentage p have high cost incumbents and the rest have low cost incumbents. There is also a limited supply of venture capital, which is available to an entrant whose costs are unknown a priori. Then the competition between types of established firms becomes real, with each established firm attempting to make entry into its market appear unattractive.[5]

The active role assigned to the entrant in this model and the corresponding significance of the beliefs and conjectures embodied in the entrant's strategy lead to the existence of a multiplicity of equilibria, both in this example and more generally. Our example actually has a continuum of both separating and pooling equilibria, where each class of equilibria is parameterized by the critical level of Q such that observation of a lower output than this level induces increased entry. In general, there is a large class of entrant's strategies t such that t and the best response to it constitute an equilibrium: many possible conjectures by the entrant as to the outcome of the competition among established firms are consistent with rational expectations. Thus, there is no unique limit price in these models.[6]

[5] See E. Gal-or (1980) for a more explicit model along these lines. Also see D. Kreps and R. Wilson (1980) and P. Milgrom and J. Roberts (1980) for multi-market models of entry deterrence through predation.

[6] There is a second source of non-uniqueness which involves the specification of $t^*(c_2, Q)$ for values of Q outside the range of s^*. Since such values of Q are observed with probability zero, the maximization of expected return places no constraint on t^* at these points. Then, even within the constraint that s^* be a best response to the entrant's strategy, there are typically many strategies t^* which constitute equilibria with s^*. However, all such t^* for a given s^* give the same evolution of the play of the

One way to attempt to narrow the set of equilibria is to place restrictions on the possible strategies for the entrant. For example, one could require that, conditional on observing *any* Q, the entrant assign probabilities to Q having been the choice of each type of established firm. Then one would require that, for each Q, $t^*(c_2, Q)$ be a best response, given these conjectures. This is the essence of the concept of sequential equilibrium due to David Kreps and Robert Wilson (1980), and it is clearly in the spirit of the perfectness criterion for equilibria (Selten, 1975).[7] However, as is easily verified, our equilibria already satisfy this condition, and still we have the unwanted multiplicity. Thus one might consider further restrictions on the entrant's conjectures. In particular, one might hypothesize that the entrant will not conjecture that the competition between types of established firm will be unnecessarily wasteful. This results in considering only those equilibria (s^*, t^*) for which there is no other equilibrium where the payoffs to the various types of established firms weakly dominate those under (s^*, t^*). The two particular equilibria we have identified here meet this condition. Other separating equilibria all involve $s^*(\bar{c}_1) = m(\bar{c}_1)$ and $s^*(\underline{c}_1) > 7.2$,[8] other pooling equilibria must involve lower payoffs for the low cost established firm,[9] and neither equilibrium dominates the other.

Although there are no equilibria in this example where $s^* \equiv m$, the monopoly output, this strategy could arise in equilibrium with other specifications of the parameters. This would happen if the profit to a high cost firm in producing its monopoly output and then facing certain entry exceeded its profits from producing the monopoly output of the low cost firm and then avoiding all entry. However, if there

game (the same Q values being chosen and the same entry decisions being made). Thus, this non-uniqueness is less crucial.

[7] This correspondence is not coincidence, as Kreps and Wilson (1980) have shown every perfect equilibrium is sequential.

[8] Note, in particular, that $s^* = m$ is not an equilibrium strategy, since the $\bar{c}_1$ firm would be willing to produce $m(\underline{c}_1)$ to eliminate all entry.

[9] While it might seem that any other pooling equilibrium would have $s^*(c_1) > m(\underline{c}_1)$, this need not be the case. However, if the entrant's conjectures regarding the value of c_1, given Q, are continuous in Q, pooling equilibria with higher than monopoly prices disappear. If, in addition, the probability assigned to $c_1 = \underline{c}_1$ rises sufficiently rapidly in Q, then only separating equilibria can exist. These continuity and monotonicity conditions are similar in spirit to Myerson's properness criterion (1978).

are a continuum of types (cost levels) possible for the established firm and the H_i are atomless, this cannot happen: at most only a set of firms of measure zero could produce their monopoly outputs in equilibrium.

Both to establish this claim and to explore more completely the nature of the limit pricing problem in a framework with less discontinuity, we now examine a specification of the model with a continuum of possible cost levels. Thus, suppose that the distribution of c_j is given by a continuous density function $h_j(c_j)$ which is positive on $[\underline{c}_i, \bar{c}_i]$. We will initially concentrate on separating equilibria

Assume that 2 conjectures that 1 will play some strategy $\bar{s}$. Then, for any Q in the range of $\bar{s}$, the entrant's best response is to act as if $c_1 \in \bar{s}^{-1}(Q)$, and to enter if and only if the expected value of $\delta_2\Pi_2^C(c_1, c_2) - K$, conditional on $c_1 \in \bar{s}^{-1}(Q)$, is positive. If $\bar{s}$ is monotone decreasing, then $\bar{s}^{-1}(Q)$ is a singleton and so 2 should enter if and only if $c_2 \leq \gamma(\bar{s}^{-1}(Q))$, where $\gamma(c_1) \equiv (a + c_1 - 3\sqrt{bK})/2$ is the highest level of c_2 permitting successful entry against a firm with costs c_1. Thus, for $Q \in$ range $\bar{s}$, 2's best response satisfies

$$t(c_2, Q) = \begin{cases} 1 & \text{if } c_2 \leq \bar{g}(Q), \\ 0 & \text{otherwise,} \end{cases}$$

where $\bar{g} = \gamma \circ \bar{s}^{-1}$.

Now, suppose that 1's conjecture is that t is of this general form, so that 2 will be deterred from entering if c_2 exceeds some value $g(Q)$. Then 1's expected payoff is

$$G(c_1, Q) = \Pi_1^0(c_1, Q) + \delta_1 \int_{g(Q)}^{\bar{c}_2} R(c_1, c_2)\, h_2(c_2) dc_2.$$

Maximizing with respect to Q yields

$$0 = \frac{\partial \Pi_1^0}{\partial Q} - \delta_1 R(c_1, g(Q))\, h_2(g(Q))\, g'(Q).$$

But, in equilibrium, the conjectures must be correct (i.e. $\bar{s} = s^*$, $g = \gamma \circ s^{*-1}$), so we have that $s^*(c_1)$ must satisfy

$$0 = \frac{\partial \Pi_1^0(c_1, s^*(c_1))}{\partial Q} - \frac{\delta_1 R(c_1, \gamma(c_1))\, h_2(\gamma(c_1))\gamma'(c_1)}{ds^*(c_1)/dc_1} \tag{1}$$

Note that, so long as $R(c_1, \gamma(c_1))$, $h_2(\gamma(c_1))$, and $\gamma'(c_1)$ are positive and $ds^*/dc_1 < \infty$ (i.e. s^* is differentiable at c_1), then this first order condition implies that $\partial\Pi_1^0/\partial Q < 0$. Thus, the simple monopoly solution $m(c_1)$, which is defined by $\partial\Pi_1^0/\partial Q = 0$, cannot arise in equilibrium. If the entrant were to conjecture $\bar{s} = m$ and respond optimally, then by increasing output slightly from $m(c_1)$ to, say, $m(c_1) + \varepsilon = \bar{s}(c_1')$, the established firm can eliminate the threat of entry from firms in the interval $[\gamma(c_1'), \gamma(c_1)]$. This increase in output has a first-order effect on Π_1^0 of zero, since $\partial\Pi_1^0/\partial Q = 0$ at $m(c_1)$, but a non-negligible first-order effect on the expected value of the reward to deterring entry. Thus, in any model of this type, so long as: (i) it is more profitable to be a monopolist than to share the market, (ii) beliefs are given by a positive density, and (iii) higher costs for the established firm encourage entry, essentially all established firms must be limit pricing in a separating equilibrium.

Of course, in such an equilibrium, s^* is invertible and so there is the same entry as if c_1 were known directly.

Now, to obtain an explicit solution for a particular specification, suppose that $\underline{c}_i = 0$ and that h_2 has, for $c_2 \geq \gamma(0)$, the particular form

$$h_2(c_2) = 8b\rho \Big/ \left[4(a - c_2)\sqrt{bK} - 7bK\right],$$

where the parameter ρ reflects the probability of there being a viable potential competitor. Also, assume that $\bar{c}_i < a/2$, which insures that the usual first-order conditions define a Cournot equilibrium after entry. As well, assume that $a \geq 7\sqrt{bK}/2$, which both insures that h_2 is a density for any choice of $\bar{c}_2 < a/2$ and also implies that $\gamma(0) > 0$, so that even low cost established firms are threatened by entry. Finally, assume that $\gamma(\bar{c}_1) < \bar{c}_2$, so that $h_2(\gamma(\bar{c}_1)) \neq 0$.

Then, substituting for $R(c_1, \gamma(c_1)) = [2(a - c_1)\sqrt{bK} - bK]/4b$ and h_1 and rearranging terms yields

$$\frac{ds^*}{dc} = \frac{\delta_1 \rho}{[a - c_1 - 2bs^*(c_1)\,]}.$$

This differential equation was derived on the assumption that s^* was monotone decreasing on $[\underline{c}_1, \bar{c}_1)$. The solutions meeting this condition and satisfying the non-negativity condition for expected profits form a non-intersecting family parameterized by a boundary condition, which we may take to be the value of $s^*(\bar{c}_1)$. Since each member of this family with the appropriate specification of t^* can constitute an equilibrium,[10] the multiplicity of equilibria in the earlier example carries over.

As suggested earlier, it seems reasonable to concentrate on solutions which are Pareto efficient. There is a unique such solution among the separating equilibria. In it, the highest cost firm, which will stand revealed as a weakling in any case, does not limit price. Alternatively, we can also eliminate the multiplicity by imposing the condition that an entrant whose costs exceed $\gamma(\bar{c}_1)$ will never enter, no matter what value of Q is observed, since such an entrant could never expect to recoup the entry cost K. Under either of these specifications, the boundary condition becomes $s^*(\bar{c}_1) = m(\bar{c}_1) = (a - \bar{c}_1)/2b$. The corresponding solution of the differential equation is then given implicitly by

$$0 = m(c_1) - s^*(c_1) + \delta_1\rho - \delta_1\rho \exp\left[\frac{m(\bar{c}_1) - s^*(c_1)}{\delta_1\rho}\right]$$

Now, let t^* be specified by $t(c_2, Q) = 1$ iff $c_2 \leq \gamma(s^{*-1}(Q))$ for Q in the range of s^* and, say, by $t(c_2, Q) = t(c_2, s^*(\underline{c}_1))$ for $Q > s^*(\underline{c}_1)$ and $t(c_2, Q) = t(c_2, s^*(\bar{c}_1))$ for $Q < m(\bar{c}_1)$. For s^* and t^* to be an equilibrium it is clearly sufficient that $G(c_1, Q)$ be pseudo-concave in Q for each c_1, so that the first order condition (1) guarantees an optimum. For this, it is in turn sufficient (see Milgrom and Roberts, 1980a) that

$$\frac{ds^*(z)}{dz} \leq \inf_{c \in [0, c_1]} \frac{\delta_1 \gamma'(z)\,[R(c_1, \gamma(z)) - R(z, \gamma(z))]h_1(\gamma(z))}{(z - c)}$$

$$= \inf_{c_1} \frac{\delta_1(1/2)\left[(z - c_1)(24\sqrt{bK} - 6a - z + 7c_1)/36b\right]}{(z - c_1)}$$

$$\times \left(\frac{8b\rho}{2(a - z)\sqrt{bK} - bK}\right) = \frac{\delta_1\rho[24\sqrt{bK} - 6a - z]}{9[2(a - z)\sqrt{bK} - bK]}.$$

Since $ds^*/dz = -1/[2b(1 - \exp[(m(\bar{c}_1) - s(z))/\delta_1\rho])]$ is strictly decreasing and bounded above by $-1/(2b)$, if the right hand side of the inequality were always positive, i.e. $6a + \sup z < 24\sqrt{bK}$, we would

[10] So long as the first-order condition (1) actually gives a maximum.

then be assured that (s^*, t^*) is an equilibrium. Thus, since $\bar{c}_1 = \sup z < a/2$, $a < 48\sqrt{bK}/13$ provides a sufficient condition.

It is straightforward to obtain comparative statics results for this example. Let $A \equiv [m(\bar{c}_1) - s(c_1)]/(\delta_1 \rho) \leq 0$. Then

$$\partial s^*/\partial \rho = \delta_1 \frac{[1 + (A - 1)\exp A]}{1 - \exp A} > 0,$$

$$\partial s^*/\partial \delta_1 = \rho \frac{[1 + (A - 1)\exp A]}{1 - \exp A} > 0,$$

and

$$\partial s^*/\partial \bar{c}_1 = \frac{\exp A}{2b(1 - \exp A)} > 0.$$

The intuition behind the first two results is clear. Regarding the third, the idea is that the possibility of there being higher cost firms leads the current $\bar{c}_1$ firm to limit price in order to distinguish itself, and then all lower cost firms must further increase their outputs.

Since the particular h function that we chose to permit computation resulted in $R(c_1, \gamma(c_1))h(\gamma(c_1))$ being constant, comparative statics with respect to a and b reveal the effects of changes in first period demand only. Note too that changes in these parameters affect both m and s^*, so interest centers on the effects on $s^* - m$. These are obtained by $\partial s^*/\partial a = 1/2b = \partial m/\partial a$, and $\partial s^*/\partial b < -(a - c_1)/2b^2 - \partial m/\partial b$: increases in a do not affect the amount of limit pricing, while increases in b reduce the amount of limit pricing by increasing the marginal cost of this activity (as measured by c_1 less the marginal revenue at $s^*(c_1)$) while leaving the marginal return (in the second period) unaffected.

Since the density function we used depends on K, comparative statics with respect to K cannot legitimately be interpreted in the natural way as indicating the effect of changing entry barriers.[11] To allow such an analysis, suppose instead that the established firm's beliefs are given by a density function which is independent of K. In this case, if $K = 0$, then $R(c_1, \gamma(c_1))h(\gamma(c_1)) \equiv 0$, and no limit pricing will occur. It is only the fact of positive K that causes the marginal

[11] The possibility of normalizing 2's payoff means that lowering δ_2 corresponds to raising K.

entrant to enter with a strictly positive level of output. With no cost of entry, a marginal entrant comes in with an output which is essentially zero, and there is no return to deterring such entry. Similarly, if K is very large (Bain's blockaded entry case), no possible level of $\underline{c}_2$ will permit positive profits, the threat of entry disappears, and again no limit pricing will occur. In the particular example we calculated, K was such that $\gamma(\underline{c}_1) > \underline{c}_2$, so even low cost established firms were threatened and practised limit pricing. A fourth possibility comes when K is high enough that $\gamma(\underline{c}_1) < \underline{c}_2$, so that there is a set $[\underline{c}_1, c_1^*]$ of firms against which no potential entrant would want to enter. An interesting aspect of our model is that even firms in this range may practice limit pricing. The essential cause of this is that, if $m(c_1') \leq s(c_1'')$ for some $c_1' < c_1^* < c_1''$, then by producing $m(c_1')$, the low cost firm becomes identified with higher cost firms which are subject to entry. These latter firms may be expected to be limit pricing, so $s^*(c_1'') > m(c_1'')$, and thus $m(c_1') = s^*(c_1'')$ is possible. By increasing output to (slightly more than) $s^*(c_1^*)$, which, to a first approximation, does not reduce the value of Π^0, the low cost firm can eliminate the threat of entry and thus increase second period expected returns.

Finally, we should mention that although we have concentrated on separating equilibria, other equilibria are possible in the continuum of types framework. A result of Milgrom and Weber (1980) indicates that we need not concern ourselves with mixed strategy equilibria in games of this type. However, pure pooling equilibria are conceptually possible, as are equilibria where s^* is a decreasing step function.[12] In any pooling equilibrium, all types of the established firm are better off producing the equilibrium output Q^* than they are changing their output and facing the different probability of entry this different value of Q implies. For example, if entry is relatively unlikely when $Q = Q^*$ (perhaps because low values of c_1 are very likely a priori), and any deviation from Q^* brings certain entry, then if the $\bar{c}_1$ type is willing to produce Q^*, a pooling equilibrium will be maintained. In general, the form of the entrant's conjectures (as embodied in its strategy) which is necessary to support a pooling equilibria is typically discontinuous in Q, and the same sort of discontinuities underlie step-function equilibria.

It is clear that the extended example we have been discussing

[12] The possible equilibria are characterized in Milgrom and Roberts (1980a).

involves a number of special features, such as the linearity of demand and cost, and the assumption that post-entry competition yields the full information Cournot outcome. However, these assumptions serve mainly to simplify arguments and facilitate computation; they do not drive the results. Indeed, so long as the entrant's post-entry profits decrease in c_2 and increase in c_1 while the established firm strictly prefers to be a monopolist than to share the market ($R(c_1, c_2) > 0$), our principal conclusions remain: if pre-entry price can be a signal for post-entry profits, even if it does not directly influence profitability, then limit pricing will emerge in equilibrium, but entry need not be deterred relative to the complete information case. Moreover, as we shall argue in the next section, even if we allow for much more general uncertainty and for post-entry profits being dependent on pre-entry actions, a similar conclusion is valid.

3. ENTRY DETERRENCE AND RATIONAL EXPECTATIONS

In this section we consider a fairly general two-period model of entry deterrence and entry under incomplete information. While we do not provide a complete analysis of this model, we do indicate some of the implications of equilibrium for the firms' behaviour.

Rather than setting up a general formal model from scratch, let us reinterpret the model in Sec. 2 with some modifications. In particular, we now view c_1 and c_2 as belonging to some arbitrary measurable spaces, and we will view Q as an action belonging to some other arbitrary space. Suppose further that 2 observes only some variable q which is correlated with Q, and suppose, too, that the payoffs depend not only on c_1, c_2 and the action y taken by the entrant (which may also now belong to some arbitrary space), but also on Q and possibly on a random variable θ, the realization of which is not revealed until the firms make their choices. Finally, let all the random variables have some arbitrary joint distribution.

This framework is obviously very general. In particular, it allows for capital investment which affects marginal costs, advertising and other means of achieving brand loyalty, general forms of demand and cost functions, varying scales and forms of entry, imperfect observability of actions, uncertainty as to how the post-entry game will be played, and arbitrary dependencies among all the random elements of the model.

As before, it is useful to analyse equilibrium via strategies, s^* and t^*, and conjectures, $\bar{s}$ and $\bar{t}$. (These may be taken to be either pure or mixed strategies.) Thus, firm 1 conjectures that 2's strategy is $\bar{t}$, for each value of c_1 it will select an action $Q = s(c_1)$ to maximize the expected value of its perceived payoff, conditional on c_1. Unless expected second-period payoffs are insensitive to Q, both through any direct effect on second period profits and also through the effect on 2's conjectured action, the solution for the established firm's maximization problem will not be the same as the solution to the problem of maximizing the expected value of first period profits. Thus, we would generally expect that the threat of entry will alter behaviour: some generalized form of limit pricing will be a characteristic of equilibrium.

In making its decision, the entrant will seek to maximize its expected payoff conditional on its private information c_2 and its (imperfect) observation of Q, given its conjecture $\bar{s}$. Should it happen that the observation of the signal q in equilibrium permits a precise inference via $\bar{s}$ about c_1, then entry will of course occur in precisely the same circumstances as if c_1 had been directly announced. In this case, the only effect of the generalized limit pricing on entry will be through the direct effect of Q on 2's post-entry profits (as, for example, when the choice of Q affects demand or cost). If this effect is zero, then, as in the example in Sec. 2, limit pricing will still occur, but it need not deter entry relative to the complete information case.

However, the unrestricted dimensionalities allowed for c_1 and Q suggest that an invertible strategy s^* is unlikely. Moreover, so long as the random noise term relating q and Q is neither perfectly correlated with c_1 nor degenerate, then even if s^* is an invertible function of Q one would not expect a noisy observation of Q via q to permit a precise inference of the value of c_1. Thus one must expect that such exact inferences will be impossible in equilibrium, and that residual uncertainty will remain concerning c_1 when the entry decision is made. In this case, the entrant must base its entry decision y on the expected value of its profits, as a function of Q, y and the exogenous uncertainty θ, conditional on the values of c_2 and q, and given its conjecture $\bar{s}$ about 1's behaviour. With some abuse of notation, let us write this as

$$E(\Pi_2(c_1, c_2, \bar{s}(c_1), y, \theta) \mid q(\bar{s}(c_1), \theta), c_2). \quad (2)$$

Then the question is that of whether the established firm can, through its choice of Q, cause the entrant in equilibrium to lower its estimate of the profitability of entry.

Consider what 2's estimate of its prospects are a priori, knowing c_2 but before observing q. This is just the expectation of expression (2), conditional on c_2. Then, in equilibrium, where $\bar{s} = s^*$, so that 2's conjecture is correct, this a priori estimate is

$$E(E\left[\Pi_2(c_1, c_2, s^*(c_1), y, \theta) \mid q(s^*(c_1), \theta), c_2\right] \mid c_2). \quad (3)$$

But, by a standard result in probability theory, expression (3) is equal to $E(\Pi_2(c_1,c_2,s^*(c_1), y, \theta) \mid c_2)$. But this, in turn, is simply what firm 2 would estimate its profits to be if it were to receive no information.

In this sense, then, the observation of the established firm's actions cannot, in equilibrium, systematically bias the entrant's expectations. If without any information it would have estimated its expected profits at $\bar{\Pi}$ then the fact that it will receive the signal cannot lead it to expect to receive less than $\bar{\Pi}$. Put a different way, if there are some values of c_1 and c_2 such that observing $s^*(c_1)$ (directly or indirectly) causes an entrant with characteristics c_2 to underestimate the profitability of entry, then there is an offsetting set of values for c_1 and c_2 where observing $s^*(c_1)$ causes the entrant to overestimate its prospects.

4. SUMMARY AND CONCLUSIONS

In his original analysis of limit pricing, Bain (1949, p. 453) argued that although 'current price . . . need play no direct role [in the entry decision], since the anticipated industry price *after entry* and the entrant's anticipated market share are the strategic considerations,' the potential entrant may 'regard this price as an indicator' of post-entry profitability. Given this, Bain developed his theory of limit pricing, from which a large literature has emerged. A weakness of this literature has been the failure to model both the established firm and the entrant as strategic agents. However, if one models the situation described by Bain as a game of complete information, no limit pricing can emerge in equilibrium [Friedman, 1979].

In this paper we model the problem considered by Bain of entry deterrence and entry as a game of incomplete information. In this game, Bain's arguments are valid: although pre-entry actions by the established firm may not influence post-entry profitability, they may become signals for some unobservable determinants of profits. Limit pricing, or, more generally, deviations from short run maximizing behaviour, then emerge in equilibrium, just as earlier analyses had found. However, an unsuspected feature also emerges. Since the entrant will, in equilibrium, recognize the incentives for limit pricing, its expectations of the profitability of entry will not be consistently biased by the established firm's behaviour. Then, depending on the particular equilibrium that is established and the parameters of the model, the probability of entry may fall short of, equal, or even exceed what it would be if there were complete information and thus no limit pricing.

One conclusion of this analysis is for the appropriate public policy towards limit pricing. If pre-entry price does not influence post-entry demand and if the two-period modelling used here is appropriate, then limit pricing should not be discouraged, since it means lower prices and cannot, overall, limit entry. More generally, the admittedly incomplete analysis in Sec. 3 might suggest a stronger statement regarding strategic moves taken by established firms to deter entry. To the extent that these actions are not objectionable per se, but rather are of potential concern only because of signalling effects which it is feared may deter entry, then they are in fact benign. The question is whether either of these suggestions would stand up under a full examination of a richer model. In particular, it would seem that embedding the opportunity for limit pricing in a multi-period model where predation is possible and where reputations are a factor would be an important extension of the present analysis. This is a problem we hope to address in future work.

REFERENCES

Bain, J. (1949), 'A Note on Pricing in Monopoly and Oligopoly', *American Economic Review*, 39, 448–64.

Clark, J.M. (1940), 'Toward a Concept of Workable Competition', *American Economic Review*, 30, 241–56.

FRIEDMAN, J. (1979), 'On Entry Preventing Behaviour', 236–53, in S.J. Brams, A. Schotter and G. Schwodiauer (eds), *Applied Game Theory*, Wurzburg, Vienna: Physica-Verlag.

GAL-OR, E. (1980), 'Limit Price Entry Prevention and its Impact on Potential Investors—A Game-Theoretic Approach', Ph.D. Dissertation, Northwestern University.

GASKINS, D. (1971), 'Dynamic Limit Pricing: Optimal Pricing Under Threat of Entry', *Journal of Economic Theory*, 2, 306–22.

HARSANYI, J.C. (1967; 1968), 'Games with Incomplete Information Played by "Bayesian" Players', Parts I, II and III, *Management Science*, 14, 159–82, 320–4, and 486–502.

KALDOR, N. (1935), 'Market Imperfection and Excess Capacity', *Economica*, 2, 33–50.

KAMIEN, M.I. and N. SCHWARTZ (1971), 'Limit Pricing and Uncertain Entry', *Econometrica*, 39, 441–54.

KREPS, D. and R. WILSON (1980a), 'On the Chain-Store Paradox and Predation: Reputation for Toughness', Discussion Paper 551, Graduate School of Business, Stanford University.

—— (1980b), 'Sequential Equilibria', Discussion Paper 584, Graduate School of Business, Stanford University.

MILGROM, P. and J. ROBERTS (1980), 'Equilibrium Limit Pricing Doesn't Limit Entry', Discussion Paper 399R, Center for Mathematical Studies in Economics and Management Science, Northwestern University.

—— (1980a), 'Predation, Reputation, and Entry Deterrence', Discussion Paper 427, Center for Mathematical Studies in Economics and Management Science, Northwestern University.

MILGROM, P. and R. WEBER (1980a), 'Distributional Strategies for Games with Incomplete Information', Discussion Paper 428, Center for Mathematical Studies in Economics and Management Science, Northwestern University.

MYERSON, R. (1978), 'Refinements of the Nash Equilibrium Concept', *International Journal of Game Theory*, 7, 73–80.

ORTEGA-REICHERT, A. (1968), 'Models for Competitive Bidding Under Uncertainty', Ph.D. Dissertation, Stanford University.

PYATT, G. (1971), 'Profit Maximization and the Threat of New Entry', *Economic Journal*, 81, 242–55.

SALOP, S.C. (1979), 'Strategic Entry Deterrence', *American Economic Review*, 69, 335–8.

SCHERER, F.M. (1979), *Industrial Market Structure and Economic Performance*, Second Edition, Rand McNally and Company, Chicago.

SELTEN, R. (1975), 'Reexamination of the Perfectness Concept for Equilibrium Points in Extensive Games', *International Journal of Game Theory*, 4, 25–55.

Contestable Markets: An Uprising in the Theory of Industry Structure[*]

WILLIAM J. BAUMOL

The address of the departing president is no place for modesty. Nevertheless, I must resist the temptation to describe the analysis I will report here as anything like a revolution. Perhaps terms such as ‘rebellion’ or ‘uprising’ are rather more apt. But, nevertheless, I shall seek to convince you that the work my colleagues, John Panzar and Robert Willig, and I have carried out and encapsulated in our new book enables us to look at industry structure and behaviour in a way that is novel in a number of respects, that it provides a unifying analytical structure to the subject area, and that it offers useful insights for empirical work and for the formulation of policy.

Before getting into the substance of the analysis I admit that this presidential address is most unorthodox in at least one significant respect—that it is not the work of a single author. Here it is not even sufficient to refer to Panzar and Willig, the coauthors of both the substance and the exposition of the book in which the analysis is described in full. For others have made crucial contributions to the formulation of the theory—most notably Elizabeth Bailey. Dietrich Fischer, Herman Quirmbach, and Thijs ten Raa.

But there are many more than these. No uprising by a tiny band of rebels can hope to change an established order, and when the time

* Presidential address delivered at the ninety-fourth meeting of the American Economic Association, December 29, 1981. I should like to express my deep appreciation to the many colleagues who have contributed to the formulation of the ideas reported here, and to the Economics Programme of the Division of Social Sciences of the National Science Foundation, the Division of Information Science and Technology of the National Science Foundation, and the Sloan Foundation for their very generous support of the research that underlies it.

for rebellion is ripe it seems to break out simultaneously and independently in a variety of disconnected centres each offering its own programme for the future. Events here have been no different. I have recently received a proposal for a conference on new developments in the theory of industry structure formulated by my colleague, Joseph Stiglitz, which lists some forty participants, most of them widely known. Among those working on the subject are persons as well known as Caves, Dasgupta, Dixit, Friedlaender, Grossman, Hart, Levin, Ordover, Rosse, Salop, Schmalensee, Sonnenschein, Spence, Varian, von Weiszäcker, and Zeckhauser, among *many* others.[1] It is, of course, tempting to me to take the view that our book is the true gospel of the rebellion and that the doctrines promulgated by others must be combated as heresy. But that could at best be excused as a manifestation of the excessive zeal one comes to expect on such occasions. In truth, the immediate authors of the work may perhaps be able to justify a claim to have offered some systematization and order to the new doctrines—to have built upon them a more comprehensive statement of the issues and the analysis, and to have made a number of particular contributions. But, in the last analysis, we must look enthusiastically upon our fellow rebels as comrades in arms, each of whom has made a crucial contribution to the common cause.

Turning now to the substance of the theory, let me begin by contrasting our results with those of the standard theory. In offering this contrast, let me emphasize that much of the analysis rests on work that appeared considerably earlier in a variety of forms. We, no less than other writers, owe a heavy debt to predecessors from Bertrand to Bain, from Cournot to Demsetz. Nevertheless, it must surely be acknowledged that the following characterization of the general tenor of the literature as it appeared until fairly recently is essentially accurate.

First, in the received analysis perfect competition serves as the one standard of welfare-maximizing structure and behaviour. There is no similar form corresponding to industries in which efficiency calls for

[1] Such a list must inevitably have embarassing omissions—perhaps some of the author's closest friends. I can only say that it is intended just to be suggestive. The fact that it is so far being complete also indicates how widespread an uprising I am discussing.

a very limited number of firms (though the earlier writings on workable competition did move in that direction in a manner less formal than ours).

Our analysis, in contrast, provides a generalization of the concept of the perfectly competitive market, one which we call a 'perfectly contestable market'. It is, generally, characterized by optimal behaviour and yet applies to the full range of industry structures including even monopoly and oligopoly. In saying this, it must be made clear that perfectly contestable markets do not populate the world of reality any more than perfectly competitive markets do, though there are a number of industries which undoubtedly approximate contestability even if they are far from perfectly competitive. In our analysis, perfect contestability, then, serves not primarily as a description of reality, but as a benchmark for desirable industrial organization which is far more flexible and is applicable far more widely than the one that was available to us before.

Second, in the standard analysis (including that of many of our fellow rebels), the properties of oligopoly models are heavily dependent on the assumed expectations and reaction patterns characterizing the firms that are involved. When there is a change in the assumed nature of these expectations or reactions, the implied behaviour of the oligopolistic industry may change drastically.

In our analysis, in the limiting case of perfect contestability, oligopolistic structure and behaviour are freed entirely from their previous dependence on the conjectural variations of *incumbents* and, instead, these are generally determined uniquely and, in a manner that is tractable analytically, by the pressures of *potential* competition to which Bain directed our attention so tellingly.

Third, the standard analysis leaves us with the impression that there is a rough continuum, in terms of desirability of industry performance, ranging from unregulated pure monopoly as the pessimal arrangement to perfect competition as the ideal, with relative efficiency in resource allocation increasing monotonically as the number of firms expands.

I will show that, in contrast, in perfectly contestable markets behaviour is sharply discontinuous in its welfare attributes. A contestable monopoly offers us some presumption, but no guarantee, of behaviour consistent with a second best optimum, subject to the constraint that the firm be viable financially despite the presence of scale economies which render marginal cost pricing infeasible. That is, a contestable monopoly has some reason to adopt the Ramsey optimal price-output vector, but it may have other choices open to it. (For the analysis of contestable monopoly see Baumol, Bailey and Willig, 1977; Panzar and Willig, 1977; and Baumol, Panzar and Willig, 1982, Chs 7, 8.)

But once each product obtains a second producer, that is, once we enter the domain of duopoly or oligopoly for each and every good, such choice disappears. The contestable oligopoly which achieves an equilibrium that immunizes it from the incursions of entrants has only one pricing option—it must set its price exactly *equal* to marginal cost and do *all* of the things required for a first best optimum! In short, once we leave the world of pure or partial monopoly, any contestable market must behave ideally in every respect. Optimality is *not* approached gradually as the number of firms supplying a commodity grows. As has long been suggested in Chicago, two firms can be enough to guarantee optimality (see, for example, Fama and Laffer, 1972).

Thus, the analysis extends enormously the domain in which the invisible hand holds sway. In a perfectly contestable world, it seems to rule almost everywhere. Lest this seem to be too Panglossian a view of reality, let me offer two observations which make it clear that we emphatically do not believe that all need be for the best in this best of all possible worlds.

First, let me recall the observation that real markets are rarely, if ever, perfectly contestable. Contestability is merely a broader ideal, a benchmark of wider applicability than is perfect competition. To say that contestable oligopolies behave ideally and that contestable monopolies have some incentives for doing so is not to imply that this is even nearly true of all oligopolies or of unregulated monopolies in reality.

Second, while the theory extends the domain of the invisible hand in some directions, it unexpectedly restricts it in others. This brings me to the penultimate contrast I wish to offer here between the earlier views and those that emerge from our analysis.

The older theoretical analysis seems to have considered the invisible hand to be a rather weak intratemporal allocator of resources, as we have seen. The mere presence of unregulated monopoly or oligopoly was taken to be sufficient *per se* to imply that resources are likely to be misallocated *within* a given time period. But *where the market structure is such as to yield a satisfactory allocation of resources within the period*, it may have seemed that it can, at least in theory, do a good job of intertemporal resource allocation. In the absence of any externalities, persistent and asymmetric information gaps, and of interference with the workings of capital markets, the amounts that will be invested for the future may appear to be consistent with Pareto optimality and efficiency in the supply of outputs to current and future generations.

However, our analysis shows that where there are economies of scale in the production of durable capital, intertemporal contestable monopoly, which may perform relatively well in the single period, cannot be depended upon to perform ideally as time passes. In particular, we will see that the least costly producer is in the long run vulnerable to entry or replacement by rivals whose appearance is inefficient because it wastes valuable social resources.

There is one last contrast between the newer analyses and the older theory which I am most anxious to emphasize. In the older theory, the nature of the industry structure was *not* normally explained by the analysis. It was, in effect, taken to be given exogenously, with the fates determining, apparently capriciously, that one industry will be organized as an oligopoly, another as a monopoly and a third as a set of monopolistic competitors. Assuming that this destiny had somehow been revealed, the older analyses proceeded to investigate the consequences of the exogenously given industry structure for pricing, outputs, and other decisions.[2]

The new analyses are radically different in this respect. In our analysis, among others, an industry's structure is determined explicitly, endogenously, and simultaneously with the pricing, output, advertising, and other decisions of the firms of which it is constituted. This, perhaps, is one of the prime contributions of the new theoretical analyses.

[2] Of course, any analysis which considered the role of entry, whether it dealt with perfect competition or monopolistic competition, must implicitly have considered the determination of industry structure by the market. But in writings before the 1970s, such analyses usually did not consider how this process determined whether the industry would or would not turn out to be, for example, an oligopoly. The entry conditions were studied only to show how the *assumed* market structure could constitute an equilibrium state. Many recent writings have gone more explicitly into the determination of industry structure, though their approaches generally differ from ours.

1. CHARACTERISTICS OF CONTESTABLE MARKETS

Perhaps a misplaced instinct for melodrama has led me to say so much about contestable markets without even hinting what makes a market contestable. But I can postpone the definition no longer. A contestable market is one into which entry is absolutely free, *and exit is absolutely costless*. We use 'freedom of entry' in Stigler's sense, not to mean that it is costless or easy, but that the entrant suffers no disadvantage in terms of production technique or perceived product quality relative to the incumbent, and that potential entrants find it appropriate to evaluate the profitability of entry in terms of the incumbent firms' pre-entry prices. In short, it is a requirement of contestability that there be no cost discrimination against entrants. Absolute freedom of exit, to us, is one way to guarantee freedom of entry. By this we mean that any firm can leave without impediment, and in the process of departure can recoup any costs incurred in the entry process. If all capital is saleable or reusable without loss other than that corresponding to normal user cost and depreciation, then any risk of entry is eliminated.

Thus, contestable markets may share at most one attribute with perfect competition. Their firms need not be small or numerous or independent in their decision making or produce homogeneous products. In short, a perfectly competitive market is necessarily perfectly contestable, but not *vice versa*.

The crucial feature of a contestable market is its vulnerability to hit-and-run entry. Even a very transient profit opportunity need not be neglected by a potential entrant, for he can go in, and, before prices change, collect his gains and then depart without cost, should the climate grow hostile.

I will deal rather briefly with two of the most important properties of contestable markets—their welfare attributes and the way in which they determine industry structure. I deal with these briefly because an intuitive view of the logic of these parts of the analysis is not difficult to provide. Then I can deal more with some details of the oligopoly and the intertemporal models.

1.1 Perfect Contestability and Welfare

The welfare properties of contestable markets follow almost directly from their definition and their vulnerability to hit-and-run incursions. Let me list some of these properties and discuss them succinctly.

First, a contestable market never offers more than a normal rate of profit—its economic profits must be zero or negative, even if it is oligopolistic or monopolistic. The reason is simple. Any positive profit means that a transient entrant can set up business, replicate a profit-making incumbent's output at the same cost as his, undercut the incumbent's prices slightly and still earn a profit. That is, continuity and the opportunity for costless entry and exit guarantee that an entrant who is content to accept a slightly lower economic profit can do so by selecting prices a bit lower than the incumbent's.

In sum, in a perfectly contestable market any economic profit earned by an incumbent automatically constitutes an earnings opportunity for an entrant who will hit and, if necessary, run (counting his temporary but supernormal profits on the way to the bank). Consequently, in contestable markets, zero profits must characterize any equilibrium, even under monopoly and oligopoly.

The second welfare characteristic of a contestable market follows from the same argument as the first. This second attribute of any contestable market is the absence of any sort of inefficiency in production in industry equilibrium. This is true alike of inefficiency of allocation of inputs, *X*-inefficiency, inefficient operation of the firm, or inefficient organization of the industry. For any unnecessary cost, like any abnormal profit, constitutes an invitation to entry. Of course, in the short run, as is true under perfect competition, both profits and waste may be present. But in the long run, these simply cannot withstand the threat brandished by potential entrants who have nothing to lose by grabbing at any opportunity for profit, however transient it may be.

A third welfare attribute of any long-run equilibrium in a contestable market is that no product can be sold at a price, p, that is less than its marginal cost. For if some firm sells y units of output at such a price and makes a profit in the process, then it is possible for an entrant to offer to sell a slightly smaller quantity, $y - \varepsilon$, at a price a shade lower than the incumbent's, and still make a profit. That is, if the price p is less than MC, then the sale of $y - \varepsilon$ units at price p must yield a total profit $\pi + \Delta\pi$ which is greater than the profit, π, that can be earned by selling only y units of output at that price. Therefore, there must exist a price just slightly lower than p which enables the entrant to undercut the incumbent and yet to earn at least as much as the incumbent, by eliminating the unprofitable marginal unit.

This last attribute of contestable equilibria—the fact that price must always at least equal marginal cost—is important for the economics of antitrust and regulation. For it means that in a perfectly contestable market, no cross subsidy is possible, that is, no predatory pricing can be used as a weapon of unfair competition. But we will see it also has implications which are most profound theoretically and which are more germane to our purposes. For it constitutes half of the argument which shows that when there are two or more suppliers of any product, its price must, in equilibrium, be exactly equal to marginal cost, and so resource allocation must satisfy all the requirements of first best optimality.

Indeed, the argument here is similar to the one which has just been described. But there is a complication which is what introduces the two-firm requirement into this proposition. $p < MC$ constitutes an opportunity for profit to an entrant who drops the unprofitable marginal unit of output, as we have just seen. It would seem, symmetrically, that $p > MC$ also automatically constitutes an opportunity for profitable entry. Instead of selling the y-unit output of a profitable incumbent, the entrant can now offer to sell the slightly larger output, $y + \varepsilon$, using the profits generated by the marginal unit at a price greater than marginal cost to permit a reduction in price below the incumbent's. But on this side of the incumbent's output, there is a catch in the argument. Suppose the incumbent is a monopolist. Then output and price are constrained by the elasticity of demand. An attempt by an entrant to sell $y + \varepsilon$ rather than y may conceivably cause a sharp reduction in price which eliminates the apparent profits of entry. In the extreme case where demand is perfectly inelastic, there will be no positive price at which the market will absorb the quantity $y + \varepsilon$. This means that the profit opportunity represented by $p > MC$ can crumble into dust as soon as anyone seeks to take advantage of it.

But all this changes when the market contains two or more sellers. Now $p > MC$ does always constitute a real opportunity for profitable entry. The entrant who wishes to sell a bit more than some one of the profitable incumbents, call him incumbent A, need not press against the industry's total demand curve for the product. Rather, he can undercut A, steal away all of his customers, at least temporarily, and, in addition, steal away ε units of demand from any other incumbent, B. Thus, if A and B together sell $y_a + y_b > y_a$, then an entrant can lure away $y_a + \varepsilon > y_a$ customers, for ε sufficiently small, and earn on this the incremental profit $\varepsilon(p - MC) > 0$. This means that the entrant who sells $y_a + \varepsilon$ can afford to undercut the prevailing prices somewhat and still make more profit than an incumbent who sells y_a at price p.

In sum, where a product is sold by two or more firms, any $p > MC$ constitutes an irresistible entry opportunity for hit-and-run entry in a perfectly contestable market, for it promises the entrant supernormal profits even if they accrue for a very short period of time.

Consequently, when a perfectly contestable market contains two or more sellers, neither $p < MC$ nor $p > MC$ is compatible with equilibrium. Thus we have our third and perhaps most crucial welfare attribute of such perfectly contestable markets—their prices, in equilibrium, must be equal to marginal costs, as is required for Pareto optimality of the 'first best' variety. This, along with the conclusion that such markets permit no economic profits and no inefficiency in long-run equilibrium, constitutes their critical properties from the viewpoint of economic welfare. Certainly, since they do enjoy those three properties, the optimality of perfectly contestable equilibria (with the reservations already expressed about the case of pure monopoly) fully justifies our conclusion that perfect contestability constitutes a proper generalization of the concept of perfect competition so far as welfare implications are concerned.

1.2 On the Determination of Industry Structure

I shall be briefer and even less rigorous in describing how industry structure is determined endogenously by contestability analysis. Though this area encompasses one of its most crucial accomplishments, there is no way I can do justice to the details of the analysis in an oral presentation and within my allotted span of time. However, an intuitive view of the matter is not difficult.

The key to the analysis lies in the second welfare property of contestable equilibria—their incompatibility with inefficiency of any sort. I particular, they are incompatible with inefficiency in the *organization* of an industry. That is, suppose we consider whether a particular output quantity of an industry will be produced by two firms or a thousand. Suppose it turns out that the two-firm arrangement can produce the given output at a cost 20 per cent lower than it can be done by the thousand firms. Then one implication of our analysis is that the industry cannot be in long-run equilibrium if it encompasses thousand producers. Thus we already have some hint about the equilibrium industry structure of a contestable market.

We can go further with this example. Suppose that, with the given output vector for the industry, it turns out that *no* number of firms other than two can produce at as low a total cost as is possible under a two-firm arrangement. That is, suppose two firms can produce the output vector at a total cost lower than it can be done by one firm or three firms or sixty or 6000. Then we say that for the given output vector the industry is a *natural duopoly.*

This now tells us how the industry's structure can be determined. We proceed, conceptually, in two steps. First we determine what structure happens to be most efficient for the production of a given output vector by a given industry. Next, we investigate when market pressures will lead the industry toward such an efficient structure in equilibrium.

Now, the first step, though it has many intriguing analytic attributes, is essentially a pure matter of computation. Given the cost function for a typical firm, it is ultimately a matter of calculation to determine how many firms will produce a given output most efficiently. For example, if economies of scale hold throughout the relevant range and there are sufficient complementarities in the production of the different commodities supplied by the firm, then it is an old and well-known conclusion that single firm production will be most economical—that we are dealing with a natural monopoly.

Similarly, in the single product case suppose the average cost curve is U-shaped and attains its minimum point at an output of 10,000 units per year. Then it is obvious that if the industry happens to sell 50,000 units per year, this output can be produced most cheaply if it is composed of exactly five firms, each producing 10,000 units at its point of minimum average cost.

Things become far more complex and more interesting when the firm and the industry produce a multiplicity of commodities, as they always do in reality. But the logic is always the same. When the industry output vector is small compared to the output vectors the firm can produce at relatively low cost, then the efficient industry structure will be characterized by very few firms. The opposite will be true when the industry's output vector is relatively far from the origin. In the multiproduct case, since average cost cannot be defined, two complications beset the characterization of the output vectors which the firm can produce relatively efficiently. First, since here average cost cannot be defined, we cannot simply look for the point of minimum average costs. But we overcome this problem by dealing with output bundles having fixed proportions among commodity quantities—by moving along a ray in output space. Along any such ray the behaviour of average cost *is* definable, and the point of minimum ray average cost (*RAC*) is our criterion of relatively efficient scale for the firm. Thus, in Fig. 1 we have a ray average cost curve for the production of boots and shoes when they are produced in the proportion given by ray *OR*. We see that for such bundles y^m is the point of minimum *RAC*. A second problem affecting the determination of the output vectors the firm can produce efficiently is the choice of output proportions—the location of the ray along which the firm

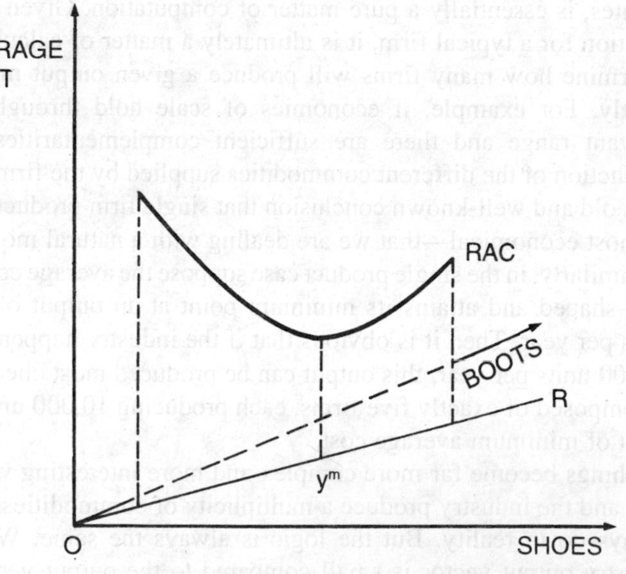

Figure 1

will operate. This depends on the degree of complementarity in production of the goods, and it also lends itself to formal analysis.

We note also that the most efficient number of firms will vary with the location of the industry's output vector. The industry may be a natural monopoly with one output vector, a natural duopoly with another, and efficiency may require seventy-three firms when some third output vector is provided by the industry.

This, then, completes the first of the two basic steps in the endogenous determination of industry structure. Here we have examined what industry structure is least costly for each given output vector of a given industry, and have found how the result depends on the magnitudes of the elements of that output vector and the shape of the cost function of the typical firm. So far the discussion may perhaps be considered normative rather than behavioural. It tells us what structure is most efficient under the circumstances, not which industry structure will emerge under the pressures of the market mechanism.

The transition toward the second, behavioural, stage of the analysis is provided by the observation that the optimal structure of an industry depends on its output vector, while that output vector in turn depends on the prices charged by its firms. But, since pricing depends on industry structure, we are brought full circle to the conclusion that pricing behaviour and industry structure must, ultimately, be determined simultaneously and endogenously.

We are in no position to go much further than this for a market whose properties are unspecified. But, for a perfectly contestable market, we can go much further. Indeed, the properties of perfect contestability cut through every difficulty and tell us the equilibrium prices, outputs, and industry structure, all at once.

Where more than one firm supplies a product, we have already characterized these prices precisely. For we have concluded that each equilibrium price will equal the associated marginal cost. Then, given the industry's cost and demand relationships, this yields the industry's output quantities simultaneously with its prices, in the usual manner. Here there is absolutely nothing new in the analysis.

But what is new is the format of the analysis of the determination of industry structure. As I have already pointed out structure is determined by the efficiency requirement of equilibrium in any contestable market. Since no such equilibrium is compatible with failure to minimize industry costs, it follows that the market forces under perfect contestability will bring us results consistent with those of our normative analysis. Whatever industry structures minimize total costs for the equilibrium output vector must turn out to be the only structures consistent with industry equilibrium in the long run.

Thus, for contestable markets, but for contestable markets *only*, the second stage of the analysis of industry structure turns out to be a sham. Whatever industry structure was shown by the first, normative, portion of the analysis to be least costly must also emerge as the industry structure selected by market behaviour. No additional calculations are required by the behavioural analysis. It will all have been done in the normative cost-minimization analysis and the behavioural analysis is pure bonus.

Thus, as I promised, I have indicated how contestability theory departs from the older theory which implicitly took industry structure to be determined exogenously in a manner totally unspecified and, instead, along with other recent writings, embraces the determination of industry structure as an integral part of the theory to be dealt with simultaneously with the determination of prices and outputs.

At this point I can only conjecture about the determination of industry structure once we leave the limiting case of perfect contestability. But my guess is that there are no sharp discontinuities here, and that while the industry structures which emerge in reality are not always those which minimize costs, they will constitute reasonable approximations to the efficient structures. If this is not so it is difficult to account for the similarities in the patterns of industry structure that one observes in different countries. Why else do we not see agriculture organized as an oligopoly in any free market economy, or automobiles produced by 10,000 firms? Market pressures must surely make any very inefficient market structure vulnerable to entry, to displacement of incumbents by foreign competition, or to undermining in other ways. If that is so, the market structure that is called for by contestability theory may not prove to be too bad an approximation to what we encounter in reality.

2. ON OLIGOPOLY EQUILIBRIUM

I should like now to examine oligopoly equilibrium somewhat more extensively. We have seen that, except where a multiproduct oligopoly firm happens to sell some of its products in markets in which it has no competitors, an important partial monopoly case which I will ignore in what follows, all prices must equal the corresponding marginal costs in long-run equilibrium. But in an oligopoly market, this is a troublesome concept. Unless the industry output vector happens to fall at a point where the cost function is characterized by locally constant returns to scale, we know that zero profits are incompatible with marginal cost pricing. Particularly if there are scale economies at that point, so that marginal cost pricing precludes financial viability, we can hardly expect such a solution to constitute an equilibrium. Besides, we have seen that long-run equilibrium requires profit to be precisely zero. We would thus appear to have run into a major snag by concluding that perfect contestability always leads to marginal cost pricing under oligopoly.

This is particularly so if the (ray) average curve is U-shaped, with its minimum occurring at a single point, y^m. For in this case that minimum point is the only output of the firm consistent with constant returns to scale and with zero profits under marginal cost pricing. Thus, dealing with the single product case to make the point, it would appear, say, that if the *AC*-minimizing output is 1000, in a contestable market, equilibrium is possible if quantity demanded from the industry happens to be exactly 2000 units (so two firms can produce 1000 units each) or exactly 3000 units or exactly 4000 units, etc. But suppose the demand curve happens to intersect the industry *AC* curve, say, at 4030 units. That is, then, the only industry output satisfying the equilibrium requirement that price equals zero profit. But then, at least one of the four or five firms in the industry must produce either more or less than 1000 units of output, and so the slope of its *AC* curve will not be zero at that point, precluding either *MC* pricing or zero profits and, consequently, violating one or the other of the requirements of equilibrium in a perfectly contestable market.

It would appear that equilibrium will be impossible in this perfectly contestable market unless by a great piece of luck the industry demand curve happens to intersect its *AC* curve at 2000 or 3000 units or some other integer multiple of 1000 units of output.

There are a variety of ways in which one can grapple with this difficulty. In his dissertation at New York University, Thijs ten Raa has explored the issue with some care and has shown that the presence of entry costs of sufficient magnitude, that is, irreversible costs which

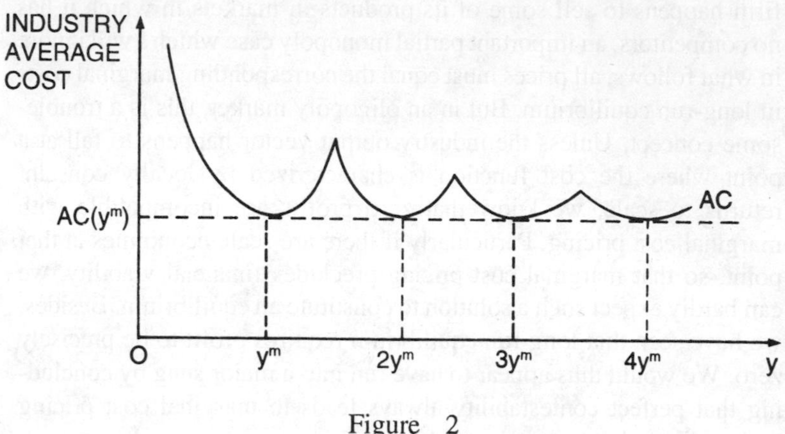

Figure 2

must be borne by an entrant but not by an incumbent, can eliminate the existence problem. The minimum size of the entry cost required to permit an equilibrium will depend on the size of the deviation from zero profits under marginal cost pricing and ten Raa has given us rules for its determination. He has shown also that the existence problem, as measured by the required minimum size of entry cost, decreases rapidly as the equilibrium number of firms of the industry increases, typically attaining negligible proportions as that number reaches, say, ten enterprises. For, as is well known, when the firm's average cost curve is U-shaped the industry's average cost curve will approach a horizontal line as the size of industry output increases. This is shown in Fig. 2 which is a standard diagram giving the firm's and the industry's *AC* curves when the former is U-shaped. As a result, the deviations between average cost and marginal cost will decline as industry output increases and so the minimum size of the entry cost required to preserve equilibrium declines correspondingly.

However, here I want to describe another approach offered in our book to the problem of existence which I have just described—the difficulty of satisfying simultaneously the zero-profit requirement and the requirement of marginal cost pricing. This second avenue relies on the apparently unanimous conclusion of empirical investigators of the cost function of the firm, that *AC* curves are not, in fact, characterized by a unique minimum point as they would be if they had a smooth U-shape. Rather, these investigators tell us, the *AC*

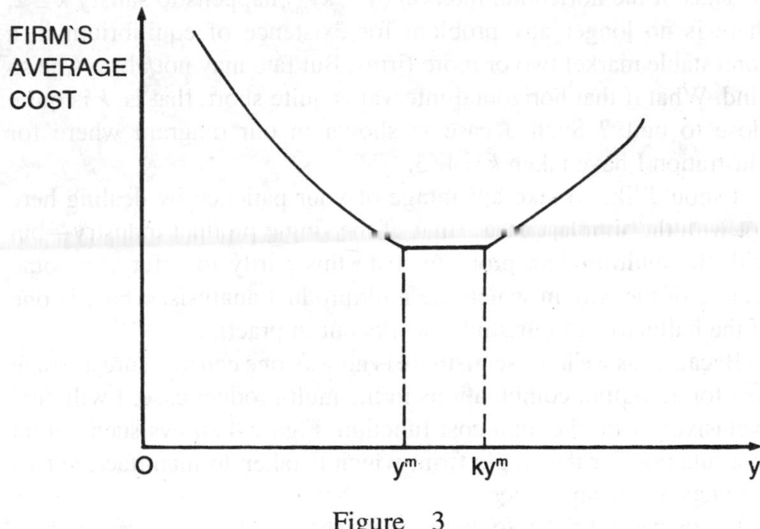

Figure 3

curve of reality has a flat bottom—an interval along which it is horizontal. That is, average costs do tend to fall at first with size of output, then they reach a minimum and continue at that level for some range of outputs, after which they may begin to rise once more. An *AC* curve of this variety is shown in Fig. 3. Obviously, such a flat segment of the *AC* curves *does* help matters because there is now a *range* of outputs over which *MC* pricing yields zero profits. Moreover, the longer the flat-bottomed segment the better matters are for existence of equilibrium. Indeed, it is easy to show that if the left-hand end of the flat segment occurs at output y^m and the right-hand end occurs at ky_m, then if k is greater than or equal to 2 the existence problem disappears altogether, because the industry's *AC* curves will be horizontal for any output greater than y_m. That is, in any contestable market in which two or more firms operate the industry *AC* curve will be horizontal and *MC* pricing will always yield zero profits. To confirm that this is so, note that if, for example, the flat segment for the firm extends from $y = 1000$ to $y = 2000$, then any industry output of, say, $9000 + \Delta y$ where $0 \leq \Delta y \leq 9000$ can be produced by nine firms, each of them turning out more than 1000 but less than 2000 units. Hence, each of them will operate along the horizontal portion of its *AC* curve, as equilibrium requires.

Thus, if the horizontal interval (y^m, ky_m) happens to satisfy $k \geq 2$, there is no longer any problem for existence of equilibrium in a contestable market two or more firms. But fate may not always be so kind. What if that horizontal interval is quite short, that is, k is quite close to unity? Such a case is shown in our diagram where for illustration I have taken $k = 4/3$.

I should like to take advantage of your patience by dealing here not with the simplest case—that of the single product industry—but with the multiproduct problem. I do this partly to offer you some feeling of the way in which the multiproduct analysis, which is one of the hallmarks of our study, works out in practice.

Because, as we have seen, there is no way one can measure average cost for all output combinations in the multiproduct case, I will deal exclusively with the total cost function. Figure 4 shows such a total cost function for the single firm, which is taken to manufacture two products, boots and shoes.

Let us pause briefly to examine its shape. Along any ray such as *OR*, which keeps output proportions constant, we have an ordinary total cost curve, *OST*. With one exception, which I will note soon, I have drawn it to have the usual sort of shape, with marginal costs

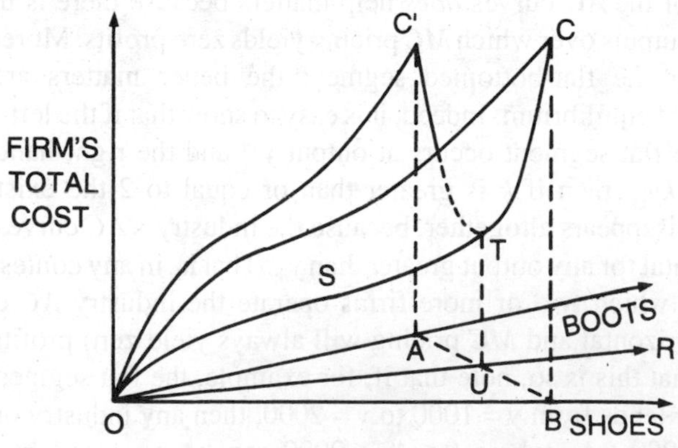

Figure 4

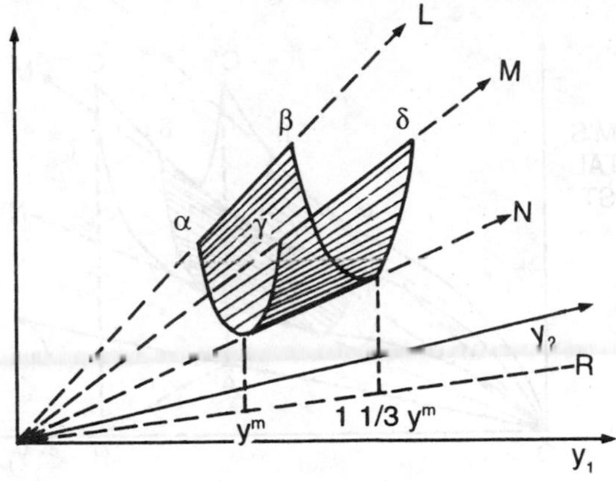

Figure 5

falling near the origin and rising at points much further from the origin. On the other hand, the trans ray cut above *AB* yields a cross section *C′TC* which is more or less U-shaped. This means that it is relatively cheaper to produce boots and shoes together (point *U*) than to produce them in isolation (point *A* or point *B*). That is, this convex trans ray shape is enough to offer us the complementarity which leads firms and industries to turn out a multiplicity of products rather than specializing in the production of a single good.

Now what, in such a case, corresponds to the flat bottom of an *AC* curve in a single product case? The answer is that the cost function in the neighbourhood of the corresponding output must be linearly homogeneous. In Fig. 5 such a region, αβγδ, is depicted. It is linearly homogeneous because it is generated by a set of rays such as *L, M,* and *N*. For simplicity in the discussion that follows, I have given this region a very regular shape—it is, approximately, a rectangle which has been moved into three-dimensional space and given a U-shaped cross section.

Now Fig. 6 combines the two preceding diagrams and we see that they have been drawn to mesh together, so that the linearly homogeneous region constitutes a portion of the firm's total cost surface. We see then that the firm's total cost does have a region in which constant returns to scale occur, and which corresponds to the flat-bottomed segment of the *AC* curve.

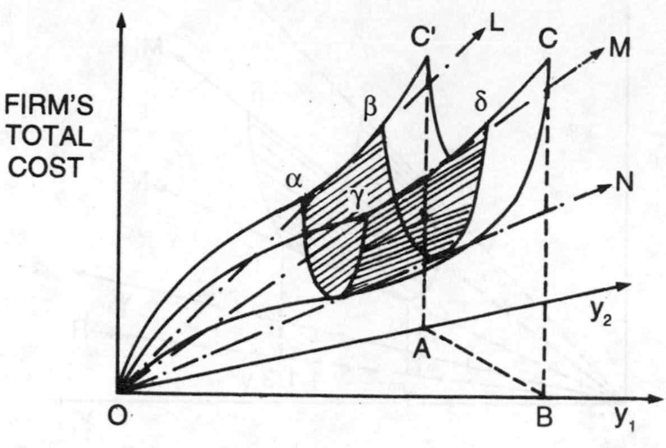

Figure 6

Moreover, as before, I have deliberately kept this segment quite narrow. Indeed, I have repeated the previous proportions, letting the segment extend from a distance y^m from the origin to the distance $1\frac{1}{3}y^m$ along any ray on the floor of the diagram.

Let us now see what happens in these circumstances when we turn to the total cost surface for the *industry.* This is depicted in Fig. 7 which shows a relationship that may at first seem surprising. In Fig. 7 I depict only the linearly homogeneous portions of the industry's cost surface. There we see that while for the firm linear homogeneity prevailed only in the interval from y^m to $1\frac{1}{3}y^m$, in the case of industry output linear homogeneity also holds in that same interval but, in addition, it holds for the interval $2y^m$ to $2\frac{2}{3}y^m$ and in the region extending from $3y^m$ to infinity. That is, everywhere beyond $3y^m$ the industry's total cost function is linearly homogeneous. In this case, then, we have three regions of local linear homogeneity in the industry's cost function, αβγδ, which is identical with that of the individual firm, the larger region *abcd*, and the infinite region *aleph beth* . . . .

Before showing why this is so we must pause to note the implications of the exercise. For it means that even a relatively small region of flatness in the $A\bar{C}$ curve of the individual firm, that is, of linear homogeneity in its total cost function, eliminates the bulk of the existence problem for oligopoly equilibrium in a

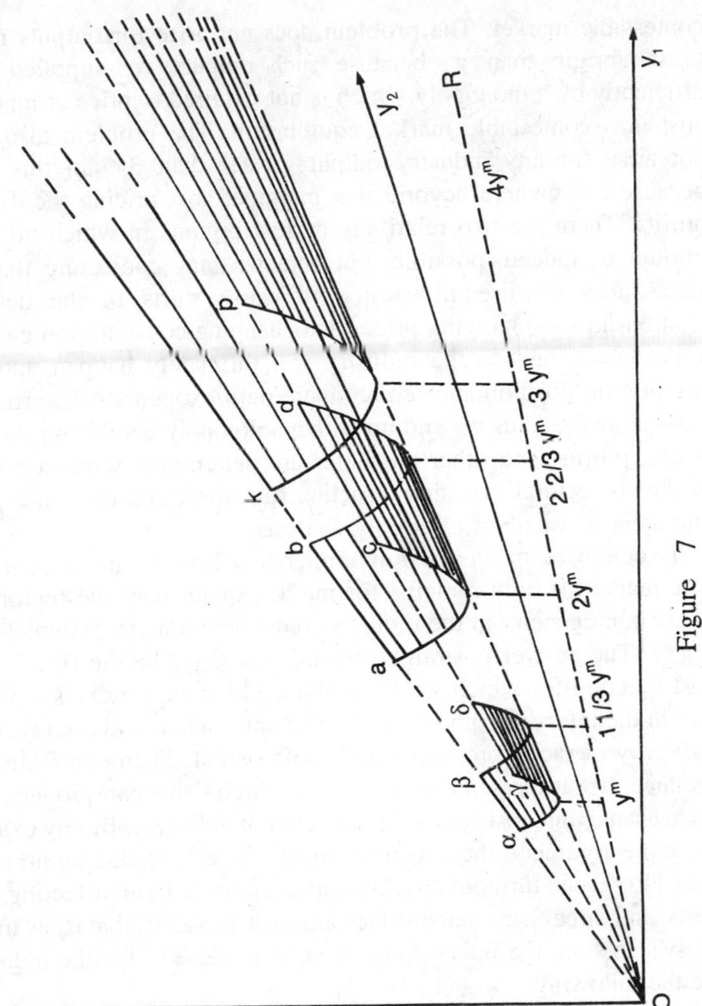
INDUSTRY TOTAL COST
O
y₁
y₂
R
yᵐ
1 1/3 yᵐ
2yᵐ
2 2/3 yᵐ
3 yᵐ
4yᵐ
α
β
γ
δ
a
b
c
d
k
p

Figure 7

contestable market. The problem does not arise for outputs nearer to the origin than y_m because such outputs are supplied most efficiently by a monopoly which is not required to price at marginal cost in a contestable market equilibrium. The problem also does not arise for any industry output greater than $3y^m$ in this case, because everywhere beyond that marginal cost pricing yields zero profits. There are two relatively narrow regions in which no equilibrium is, indeed, possible, but here we may conjecture that the vicissitudes of disequilibrium will cause shifts in the demand relationships as changing prices and changing consumption patterns affect tastes, and so the industry will ultimately happen upon an equilibrium position and remain there until exogenous disturbances move it away. Thus we end up with an oligopoly equilibrium whose prices, profits, and other attributes are determined without benefit of the conjectural variation, reaction functions, and the other paraphernalia of standard oligopoly analysis.

To complete this discussion of oligopoly equilibrium in a contestable market, it only remains for me to explain why the regions of linear homogeneity in the industry's cost function are as depicted in Fig. 7. The answer is straightforward. Let $C(y)$ be the firm's total cost function for which we have assumed for expository simplicity that in the interval from y^m to $1\frac{1}{3}y^m$ along each and every ray, total cost grows exactly proportionately with output. Then two firms can produce $2y^m$ at the same unit cost, and three firms can produce $3y^m$ at that same unit cost for the given output bundle, etc. But by exactly the same argument, the two firms together, each producing no more than $1\frac{1}{3}y^m$, can turn out anything up to $2\frac{2}{3}y^m$ without affecting unit costs, and three firms can produce as much as $3\frac{3}{3}y^m$, that is, as much as $4y^m$. In sum, the intervals of linear homogeneity for the industry are the following:

Interval 1: from y^m to $1\frac{1}{3}y^m$

Interval 2: from $2y^m$ to $2\frac{2}{3}y^m$

Interval 3: from $3y^m$ to $4y^m$

Interval 4: from $4y^m$ to $5\frac{1}{3}y^m$

Interval 5: from $5y^m$ to $6\frac{2}{3}y^m$

That is, each interval begins at an integer multiple of y^m and $1/3\ y^m$ further than its predecessor. Thus, beyond $3y^m$ successive intervals begin to touch or overlap and that is why linear homogeneity extends everywhere beyond $3y^m$ as I claimed.[3]

There is one complication in the multiproduct case which I have deliberately slid over, feeling the discussion was already complicated enough. The preceding argument assumes implicitly that the firms producing the industry output all employ the same output proportions as those in the industry output vector. For otherwise, it is not legitimate to move outward along a single ray as the number of firms is increased. But suppose increased industry output were to permit savings through increased specialization. Might there not be constant returns with fixed output proportions and yet economies of scale for the industry overall? This problem is avoided by our complementarity assumption used to account for the industry's multiproduct operation—our U-shaped transray cross section. This, in effect, rules out such savings from specialization in the regions where linear homogeneity also rules out savings from increased scale.

This, then, completes my discussion of oligopoly equilibrium in perfectly contestable markets, which we have seen, yields a determinate set of prices and outputs that is not dependent upon assumptions about the nature of incumbent firm's expectations relating to entrants' behaviour and offers us a concrete and favourable conclusion on the welfare implications of contestable oligopoly.

3. INTERTEMPORAL VULNERABILITY TO INEFFICIENT ENTRY

Having so far directed attention to areas in which the invisible hand manifests unexpected strength, I should like to end my story by dealing with an issue in relation to which it is weaker than some of us might have expected. As I indicated before, this is the issue of intertemporal production involving durable capital goods.

The analysis is far more general than the following story suggests, but even the case I describe is sufficiently general to make the point. We deal with an industry in which a product is offered by a single

3 The reader can readily generalize this result. If the flat-bottomed segment for the firm extends from y^m to $y^m(1 + 1/w)$, where w is an integer, then there will be w regions of linear homogeneity in the industry cost function and it will be linearly homogeneous for any output $y \geq wy^m$.

firm that provides it period after period. The equilibrium quantity of the commodity that is demanded grows steadily with the passage of time in a manner that is foreseen without uncertainty. Because of economies of scale in the production of capacity the firm deliberately builds some excess capacity to take care of anticipated growth in sales volume. But there is some point, let us say, z = forty-five years in the future, such that it would be uneconomic to take further growth in sales volume into account in the initial choice of capacity. This is so because the opportunity (interest) cost of the capacity that remains idle for forty-five or more years exceeds the savings made possible by the economies of scale of construction. Thus, after forty-five years it will pay the firm to undertake a second construction project to build the added capacity needed to produce the goods demanded of it.

Suppose that in every particular period our producer is a natural monopolist, that is, he produces the industry's supply of its one commodity at a cost lower than it can be done by any two or more enterprises. Then considering that same product in different periods to be formally equivalent to different goods we may take our supplier to be an intertemporal natural monopolist in a multiproduct industry. That is, no combination of two or more firms can produce the industry's intertemporal output vector as cheaply as he. I will prove now under a set of remarkably unrestrictive assumptions that despite its cost advantages, there exists no intertemporal price vector consistent with equilibrium for this firm. That is, whatever his price vector, his market will at some time be vulnerable to partial or complete takeover by an entrant who has neither superior skills nor technological superiority and whose entrance increases the quantities of resources used up in production. In other words, here the invisible hand proves incapable of protecting the most efficient producing arrangement and leaves the incumbent producer vulnerable to displacement by an aggressive entrant. I leave to your imaginations what, if anything, this says about the successive displacements on the world market of the Dutch by the English, the English by the Germans and the Americans, and the Americans, perhaps, by the Japanese.

The proof of our proposition on the intertemporal vulnerability of incumbents to entry that is premature from the viewpoint of cost minimization does require just a little bit of algebra. To keep our analysis simple, I will divide time into two periods, each lasting z = forty-five years so that capacity in the first period is, optimally, just sufficient to satisfy all demand, but in the second, it requires the construction of added capacity to meet demand growth because, by assumption, anticipatory construction to meet growth more than z years in the future simply is too costly. Also for simplicity, I will assume that there are no costs other than cost of construction. Of course, neither this nor the use of only two periods really affects the argument in any way. My only three substantive assumptions are that demand is growing with time, that there are economies of scale, that is, declining average costs in construction, and that there exists some length of time, z, so great that it does not pay in the initial construction to build capacity sufficient for the growth in quantity demanded that will occur beyond that date.

The argument, like the notation, is now straightforward. Let y_t be output in period t, p_t be price in period t, and $K(y)$ be the cost of construction of capacity sufficient to produce (a maximum of) y units, per period. Here, both p_t and $K(y)$ are expressed in discounted present value.[4]

Then, by assumption, our firm will construct at the beginning of the first period capacity just sufficient to produce output y_1 at cost $K(y_1)$ and at the beginning of the second period it will produce the rest of the capacity it needs, $y_2 - y_1 > 0$, at the cost $K(y_2 - y_1)$.

The first requirement for the prices in question to be consistent with equilibrium is that they permit the incumbent to cover his costs, that is, that

$$p_1 y_1 + p_2 y_2 \geq K(y_1) + K(y_2 - y_1). \quad (1)$$

Second, for these prices to constitute an equilibrium they must protect the incumbent against any and all possible incursions by entrants. That is, suppose an entrant were to consider the possibility of constructing capacity y_1 and not expanding in the future, and, by undercutting the incumbent, selling the same output, y_1, in each period. Entry on these terms will in fact be profitable unless the prices are such that the sale of y_1 in each period does not bring in revenues sufficient to cover the cost, $K(y_1)$, of the entrant's once-and-for-all construction. That is, entry will be profitable unless

[4] That is, if p_1^*, p_2^*, represent the undiscounted prices, $p_1 = p_1^*$, $p_2 = p_2^*/(1+r)$, where r is the rate of interest, etc.

$$p_1 y_1 + p_2 y_1 \le K(y_1). \tag{2}$$

Thus, the prices in question cannot constitute an equilibrium unless (2) as well as (1) are satisfied.

Now, subtracting (2) from (1) we obtain immediately

$$p_2(y_2 - y_1) \ge K(y_2 - y_1)$$

or

$$p_2 \ge K(y_2 - y_1)/(y_2 - y_1), \tag{3}$$

but, by the assumption that average construction cost is declining, since $y_1 > 0$,

$$K(y_2 - y_1)/(y_2 - y_1) > K(y_2)/y_2. \tag{4}$$

Substituting this into (3) we have at once

$$p_2 > K(y_2)/y_2$$

or

$$p_2 y_2 > K(y_2). \tag{5}$$

Inequality (5) is our result. For it proves that any prices which satisfy equilibrium requirements (1) and (2) permit a second-period entrant using the same techniques to build capacity y_2 from the ground up, at cost $K(y_2)$, to price slightly below anything the incumbent can charge and yet recover his costs; and that in doing so, the entrant can earn a profit.

Thus, our intertemporal natural monopolist cannot quote, *at time zero*, any prices capable of preventing the takeover of some or all of his market. Moreover, this is so despite the waste, in the form of replication of the incumbent's plant, that this entails. That, then, is the end of the formal argument, the proof that here the invisible hand manifests weakness that is, perhaps, unexpected.

You will all undoubtedly recognize that the story as told here in its barest outlines omits all sorts of nuances, such as entrants' fear of responsive pricing, the role of bankruptcy, depreciation of capital, and the like. This is not the place to go into these matters for it is neither possible nor appropriate here for me to go beyond illustration of the logic of the new analysis.

4. CONCLUDING COMMENTS

Before closing let me add a word on policy implications, whose details must also be left to another place. In spirit, the policy conclusions are consistent with many of those economists have long been espousing. At least in the intratemporal analysis, the heroes are the (unidentified) potential entrants who exercise discipline over the incumbent, and who do so most effectively when entry is free. In the limit, when entry and exit are completely free, efficient incumbent monopolists and oligopolists may in fact be able to prevent entry. But they can do so only by behaving virtuously, that is, by offering to consumers the benefits which competition would otherwise bring. For every deviation from good behaviour instantly makes them vulnerable to hit-and-run entry.

This immediately offers what may be a new insight on antitrust policy. It tells us that a history of absence of entry in an industry and a high concentration index may be signs of virtue, not of vice. This will be true when entry costs in our sense are negligible. And, then, efforts to change market structure must be regarded as mischievous and antisocial in their effects.

A second and more obvious conclusion is the questionable desirability of artificial impediments to entry, such as regulators were long inclined to impose. The new analysis merely reinforces the view that any proposed regulatory barrier to entry must start off with a heavy presumption against its adoption. Perhaps a bit newer is the emphasis on the importance of freedom of exit which is as crucial a requirement of contestability as is freedom of entry. Thus we must reject as perverse the propensity of regulators to resist the closing down of unprofitable lines of activity. This has even gone so far as a Congressional proposal (apparently supported by Ralph Nader) to require any plant with yearly sales exceeding $250,000 to provide fifty-two weeks of severance pay and to pay three years of taxes, before it will be permitted to close, and that only after giving two years notice!

There is much more to the policy implications of the new theory, but I will stop here, also leaving its results relating to empirical research for discussion elsewhere.

Let me only say in closing that I hope I have adequately justified my characterization of the new theory as a rebellion or an uprising.

I believe it offers a host of new analytical methods, new tasks for empirical research, and new results. It permits re-examination of the domain of the invisible hand, yields contributions to the theory of oligopoly, provides a standard for policy that is far broader and more widely applicable than that of perfect competition, and leads to a theory that analyses the determination of industry structure endogenously and simultaneously with the analysis of the other variables more traditionally treated in the theory of the firm and the industry. It aspires to provide no less than a unifying theory as a foundation for the analysis of industrial organization. I will perhaps be excused for feeling that this was an ambitious undertaking.

REFERENCES

BAIN, JOE S. (1956), *Barriers to New Competition*, Cambridge: Harvard University Press.

BAUMOL, WILLIAM J., ELIZABETH E. BAILEY and ROBERT D. WILLIG (1977), 'Weak Invisible Hand Theorems on the Sustainability of Multi-product Natural Monopoly', *American Economic Review*, 67, 350–65.

BAUMOL, WILLIAM J., JOHN C. PANZAR and ROBERT D. WILLIG (1982), *Contestable Markets and the Theory of Industry Structure*, San Diego: Harcourt Brace Jovanovich.

BERTRAND, JULES (1883), Review of *Théorie Mathematique de la Richesse* and *Récherches sur les Principes Mathématiques de la théorie de Richesses, Journal des Savants*, 499–508.

COURNOT, A.A. (1938; 1960), *Researches into the Mathematical Principles of the Theory of Wealth*, New York: A.M. Kelley.

DEMSETZ, HAROLD (1968), 'Why Regulate Utilities?', *Journal of Law and Economics*, 11, 55–65.

FAMA, EUGENE F. and ARTHUR B. LAFFER (1972), 'The Number of Firms and Competition', *American Economic Review*, 62, 670–4.

PANZAR, JOHN C. and ROBERT D. WILLIG (1977), 'Free Entry and the Sustainability of Natural Monopoly', *Bell Journal of Economics*, 8, 1–22.

TEN RAA, THIJS (1980), 'A Theory of Value and Industry Structure', unpublished Ph. D. Dissertation, New York University.

Non-cooperative Collusion Under Imperfect Price Information*

EDWARD J. GREEN AND ROBERT H. PORTER

1. INTRODUCTION

Long-standing questions about how widespread is the occurrence of collusion in industries having several firms, and about the extent to which the performance of industries experiencing such collusion dearts from the competitive norm, continue to provoke spirited debate. In this paper we offer a theory of collusive industry equilibrium which will provide a means of clarifying these questions.

In his classic paper 'A Theory of Oligopoly', George Stigler (1964) appealed to dynamic considerations to explain how apparently cooperative industry performance might result from non-cooperative motives. According to this theory, the firms of an industry form a cartel, which is designed to enforce monopolistic conduct in a self-policing way. 'Self-policing' means precisely that the agreed-upon conduct is non-cooperatively viable and that it remains so over time.

Stigler's theory differs markedly from traditional oligopoly theories based on static equilibrium concepts (e.g. Cournot and Stackelberg). This difference is particularly striking in the case of an industry structure which is essentially immune from entry. The traditional theories would suggest that the performance of such an

* We have accepted the generous help of many colleagues in the course of this research. We would particularly like to thank C. Berry, T. Bresnahan, J. Friedman, J. Mirrlees, S. Salop, H. Sonnenschein, and R. Willig. Robert Porter's research received support from a Sloan Foundation grant to the University of Minnesota Economics Department.

industry should be largely determined by its degree of concentration—the number of firms in the industry and their relative sizes—and by the extent to which substitute goods are available. In contrast, Stigler suggested that the greatest obstacle to collusion in the absence of entry would be what he characterized as 'secret price cutting'. By informally relating concentration and various other features of industry structure to the immunity of a cartel from entry and to its ability to deter inimical firm behaviour, and by assuming that industry profitability reflects successful operation of a cartel, he justified the use of cross-industry regressions to test his theory.

The obvious interpretation of Stigler is that he made explicit a theory of oligopoly which implicitly conceived of a cartel as a 'policeman' which with some frequency is required to punish destabilizing 'offences' of individual cartel members. The somewhat different interpretation of this paper is that Stigler had a view of cartel organization as an instance of an optimization problem: to design an institution which achieves an efficient equilibrium outcome subject to the constraint that agents in the institution behave non-cooperatively. On this interpretation, the optimal cartel structure may be one which provides member firms with strong positive incentives which make collusive behaviour attractive, rather than one which provides insufficient incentives and which severely punishes defecting firms after the fact.

In fact, two formulations of the cartel problem exist already which treat non-cooperative collusion in a rigorous way. Osborne (1976) proposes a reaction function equilibrium in which firms respond to changes in output by other firms in order to maintain their proportionate share of industry output. (See also the extensions of Spence, 1978a, 1978b.) Knowing that other firms will respond in this manner, each firm will realize that it does not pay to deviate from the collusive output level.

Friedman (1971), on the other hand, outlines a strategy in which firms respond to suspected cheating, which they infer from a drop in the market price below the price that obtains when all firms produce at agreed-upon levels, by producing at Cournot levels thereafter. If future profit streams are discounted sufficiently slowly, then a firm would reduce the discounted value of its returns by failing to collude. Therefore, for all firms to adopt the collusive strategy would be a non-cooperative equilibrium.

The trouble with these formulations, from an applied industrial organization viewpoint, is that incentives in these equilibria are so perfect that the deterrent mechanisms are never observed. Then it may be difficult to infer from econometric time-series evidence whether the observed market data is the outcome of a quasicompetitive or collusive equilibrium (T. Bresnahan, 1982). The substance of the present contribution is that this perfection is an artefact of the certainty world, in which these models are formulated. When the considerations of imperfect information, which played a decisive role in Stigler's theory, are reintroduced, optimal incentive structures may involve episodic recourse to the kind of short-run unprofitable conduct which would have been characterized as 'price wars' or 'punishment' previously.

Our argument has three parts. First, we frame a precise definition of collusion in terms of industry conduct. Second, we show that collusive conduct may, in a particular industry structure, result in a pattern of industry performance marked by recurrent episodes in which price and profit levels sharply decrease. Thus we reject the received view that performance of this type necessarily indicates an industry where firms are engaging in a sequence of abortive attempts to form a cartel. Since this opinion is often used as a basis to deny the need for intervention to promote competition in such industries (because the market purportedly is already withstanding the collusive assaults), our argument suggests the need to re-examine a widely-held assumption about policy.

Third, we point out that the distinctive character of the phenomenon just discussed and the necessary appearance of this phenomenon if collusion is to take place (given the particular industry structure in question) make it possible to draw clear-cut conclusions about the presence or absence of collusion in some specific industries on the basis of market data. This is a singular opportunity to learn about whether collusion does indeed exist in situations where it might plausibly occur, without having to face the many problems of interpretation surrounding the usual cross-industry tests of its extent.[1]

[1] These problems, involving both the nature of the cross-industry data and also the logical difficulties of using it as a basis for inference are described in the essays by J. McGee, H. Demsetz, and L. Weiss (1974).

2. COLLUSION UNDER UNCERTAINTY

Collusive equilibria exhibiting stable performance may possibly characterize some industries. For instance, a market might be segmented geographically because firms have divided it. As long as this agreement was adhered to, each firm would be a monopolist within its area. Moreover, poaching by one firm in another's territory would be quickly and surely detected, and would invite retaliation. In that situation, no one would poach. All that would ever be 'observed' is monopolistic conduct.[2]

Similarly, in an industry in which contracts are awarded by competitive bidding, a scheme to rotate winning bids might be perfectly enforceable. Each firm would act as a monopolist when its turn came, and would clearly see that bidding low out of turn would jeopardize a profitable arrangement. Again, only monopolistic conduct would ever be 'observed'.[3]

We will study a model in which demand fluctuations not directly observed by firms lead to unstable industry performance. Intuitively firms will act monopolistically while prices remain high, but they will revert for a while to Cournot behaviour when prices fall. Specifically, it will be assumed that firms agree on a 'trigger price' to which they compare the market price when they set their production.[4] Whenever the market price dips below the trigger price while they have been acting monopolistically, they will revert to Cournot behaviour for some fixed amount of time before resuming monopolistic conduct.

Suppose that, at a given time, firms are supposed to be colluding (i.e. they expect one another to collude). If a firm produces more than its share of the monopoly output, its net return at that time will increase. However, by increasing the probability that the market price will fall below the trigger price, the firm incurs a greater risk that the industry will enter a reversionary episode during which profits will

[2] A referee has suggested that the US steel industry employed such an enforcement device in the first half of this century.

[3] For example, a 'phases of the moon' system has been used to allocate low-bidding privileges in the high voltage switchgear industry. See Scherer (1980, Ch. 6).

[4] It is logically possible for this agreement to be a tacit one which arises spontaneously. Nevertheless, in view of the relative complexity of the conduct to be specified by this particular equilibrium and of the need for close coordination among its participants, it seems natural to assume here that the equilibrium arises from an explicit agreement.

be low for everyone. For producing its monopolistic share to be the firms' non-cooperatively optimal action, the marginal expected loss in future profits from possibly triggering a Cournot reversion must exactly balance (in terms of present discounted value) the marginal gain from overproducing. For appropriate distributions of the demand disturbance, reversionary episodes will sometimes occur without any firm defecting, simply because of low demand. Thus, over a long period, both Cournot behaviour and collusive behaviour will be observed at various times. In this respect, collusion under uncertainty differs markedly from the collusive equilibria under certainty discussed earlier. The fact that both monopolistic and Cournot performance are observed will make it possible to identify statistically the collusive equilibrium under uncertainty.

We now address the question of exactly what sort of industry our model might appropriately describe. Such an industry would have a structure possessing four features.

First, the industry is presumed to be stable over time. Temporal stability is required if the assumption that firms have rational expectations—an assumption which underlies the use of Nash equilibrium—is to be credible. On a more technical level, it justifies the use of stationary dynamic programming to characterize equilibrium.[5]

Second, output quantity is assumed to be the only decision variable which firms can manipulate. In particular, firms should not be able to engage in product differentiation or have ability to divide their market regionally. With firm decisions so restricted, asymmetric cartel incentive schemes are ruled out. In particular, even if one firm were suspected of violating a cartel agreement, other firms would have no way of isolating it and punishing it differentially.

Third, except for each firm's private knowledge about its present and past production, information about the industry and its environment is public. The Nash equilibrium assumption presupposes that firms have an accurate idea of their competitor's cost functions, for example. Also, for firms to coordinate effectively in keeping track of whether the industry is in a collusive or a reversionary state, they must all observe the realization of a common variable.

[5] Radner (1980) considers the case of time-average utilities. His work relies essentially on the measurability of utility in the tail sigma-field of payoffs, which asymptotic-average utility satisfies. In contrast, discounted utility is not measurable with respect to the tail sigma-field, so that our work is not directly comparable to his.

Fourth, the information which firms use to monitor whether the cartel is in a collusive or reversionary state must be imperfectly correlated with firms' conduct. Otherwise, if compliance were optimal for firms in collusive periods, reversion would never occur. Price is not the only information variable which could be used for monitoring—price data with correction for a systematic demand component, or market share information, would also be subject to error. However, this assumption of imperfect information is incompatible with transactions in the industry being few and publicly announced (e.g. with individual contracts being awarded on the basis of sealed-bid auctions) or with completely accurate and current market-share information being available to firms.

In our model, firms monitor market price which imperfectly reflects the output levels of other firms. We assume that the products of the firms are of homogeneous quality, and so they face a common market price. This structure is adopted for expositional ease. An environment in which firms monitored their own market share, which imperfectly reflected the price choices of other firms, would be more in the spirit of Stigler's paradigm.

We now give a formal description of collusion under uncertainty as a Nash equilibrium in contingent strategies. Consider an oligopoly of n firms which produce an undifferentiated product in a stationary and time separable environment. This environment is like that described in Friedman (1971), except that demand is subject to multiplicative uncertainty. Specifically, i, j range over *firms* $1, \ldots, n$. $\pi_i : R_+^2 \to R$ is the *return function* of i. $\pi_i(x_i, p)$ is i's net return from producing x_i units and selling at price p. β is the discount rate. Firms are risk neutral and maximize $E\,[\Sigma_{t=0}^{\infty} \beta^t \pi_i(x_{it}, p_t)\,]$. Observed price $p_t = \theta_t\, p\,(\Sigma_{i=1}^{n} x_{it})$, where $p : R_+ \to R_+$. The random variables θ_t are i.i.d. with c.d.f. F having continuous density f. $E(\theta) = 1$. Each θ_t is a demand shock which firms cannot observe directly.[6]

A *contingent strategy* for firm i is an infinite sequence $s_i = (s_{i0}, s_{i1}, \ldots)$, where s_{i0} is a determinate initial output level x_{i0}, and $s_{it+1} : R_+^{t+1} \to R_+$ determines i's output level at the time $t+1$ as a

[6] James Friedman has suggested to us that the variables θ_t might alternatively be specified to be a martingale, so that the prices p_t would also be a martingale. This property ought to be satisfied if the good is a durable, or if consumption is perfectly substitutable across times. We retain the i.i.d. specification which makes the analysis simpler, but acknowledge that it is restrictive.

function of past prices by $s_{it+1}(p_0, \ldots, p_t) = x_{it+1}$. The choice of domain reflects the assumption that firms do not observe rivals' production levels directly.

A strategy profile $(s_1, \ldots, s_n)$ determines recursively a stochastic process of prices, which in turn induces a probability distribution on the space of infinite sequences of prices. Expectation with respect to this distribution will be denoted by $E_{s_1 \ldots s_n}$.

A Nash equilibrium is a strategy profile $(s_1^*, \ldots, s_n^*)$ which satisfies

$$E_{s_1^* \ldots s_i \ldots s_n^*}\left[\sum_{t=0}^{\infty} \beta^t \pi_i(s_{it}(p_0, \ldots, p_{t-1}), p_t)\right] \tag{1}$$

$$\leq E_{s_1^* \ldots s_i^* \ldots s_n^*}\left[\sum_{t=0}^{\infty} \beta^t \pi_i(s_{it}^*(p_0, \ldots, p_{t-1}), p_t)\right]$$

for all firms i and feasible strategies s_i.

Now consider how the industry might produce at a monopolistic level most of the time (i.e. except during reversionary episodes) in a Nash equilibrium in trigger price strategies. Firms will initially produce their respective shares of this restricted industry output, and will continue to do so until the market price falls below a trigger price $\bar{p}$. Then they will produce Cournot outputs for the duration (we will specify this to be $T - 1$ periods) of a reversionary episode, regardless of what happens to prices during this time. At the conclusion of the episode, T periods after the price drop, they will resume monopolistic production. This will continue until the next time that $p_t < \bar{p}$, and so forth.[7]

Formally, let $y = (y_1, \ldots, y_n)$ be a profile of restricted outputs, and let $z = (z_1, \ldots, z_n)$ be a Cournot output profile. Choose a price level $\bar{p}$ and a length of time T. Define time t to be *normal* if (a) $t = 0$, or (b) $t - 1$ was normal and $\bar{p} \leq p_{t-1}$, or (c) $t - T$ was normal and

[7] For simplicity, we are considering only the simplest variant of a trigger price strategy. For example, firms might condition T on the amount by which $\bar{p}$ exceeds the observed market price.

$p_{t-T} < \bar{p}$. Define t to be *reversionary* otherwise. Define strategies for firms by

$$x_{it} = \begin{cases} y_i & \text{if } t \text{ is normal,} \\ z_i & \text{if } t \text{ is reversionary.} \end{cases}$$

These are well-defined policy strategies.

Each firm faces a stationary two-state (normal and reversionary) T-stage Markov dynamic programming problem. Its optimal policy is to produce z_i in reversionary periods, and to produce some fixed quantity r in normal periods. Let $V_i\,(r)$ be the expected discounted present value of firm i if it sets $x_{it} = r$ in normal periods. Define

$$w_i = \sum_{j \neq i} y_j,\ \gamma_i(r) = E_\theta\,\pi_i(r, \theta p(r + w_i)), \quad \delta_i = E_\theta\,\pi_i\left[z_i, \theta p\left[\sum_{j \leq n} z_j\right]\right].$$

In normal periods, i anticipates that the aggregate output of the other firms will be w_i, and so $\gamma_i(r)$ is the expected profit of then producing r. The expected profit in reversionary periods is δ_i. Let $Pr(\cdot)$ denote probability with respect to the distribution of θ. We assume that $\gamma_i\,(y_i) > \delta_i$ for each firm i. The V_i satisfies the functional equation

$$V_i\,(r) = \gamma_i\,(r) + \beta Pr\,(\bar{p} \leq \theta p(r + w_i))V_i\,(r) \tag{2}$$
$$+ Pr\,(\theta p(r + w_i) < \bar{p}) \left[\sum_{t=1}^{T-1} \beta^t \delta_i + \beta^T V_i(r)\right]$$

$Pr(\theta p(r + w_i) < \bar{p}) = F\,(\bar{p}/p\,(r + w_i))$, so (2) is equivalent to

$$V_i(r) = \frac{\gamma_i(r) + F\,(\bar{p}/p\,(r + w_i))\,((\beta - \beta^T)/(1 - \beta))\,\delta_i}{1 - \beta + (\beta - \beta^T)\,F\,(\bar{p}/p\,(r + w_i))} \tag{3}$$

$$= \frac{\gamma_i(r) - \delta_i}{1 - \beta + (\beta - \beta^T)\,F\,(\bar{p}/p\,(r + w_i))} + \frac{\delta_i}{1 - \beta}.$$

Thus the expected discounted present value of firm i equals what it would be in a Cournot environment, plus the single-period gain in returns to colluding, appropriately discounted. Inequality (1), the defining condition for Nash equilibrium, can now be rewritten

$$V_i(r) \leq V_i(y_i) \text{ for all } r \text{ and } i. \tag{4}$$

The first-order condition for (4) is

$$V_i'(y_i) = 0 \text{ for all } i. \tag{5}$$

Using the fact that $(f/g)' = 0$ if and only if $f'g - fg' = 0$, (5) is equivalent to

$$0 = \left[1 - \beta + (\beta - \beta^T)\, F\left[\bar{p}/p\left(\sum_{j \leq n} y_j\right)\right]\right] \gamma_i'(y_i) \tag{6}$$

$$+ (\beta - \beta^T)\, f\left(\bar{p}/p\left(\sum_{j \leq n} y_j\right)\right)\left[\bar{p}p'\left(\sum_{j \leq n} y_j\right)\Big/\left(p\left(\sum_{j \leq n} y_j\right)\right)^2\right]$$

$$\times (\gamma_i(y_i) - \delta_i)$$

for all i.

Equation (6) states that the marginal return to a firm from increasing its production in normal periods ($\gamma_i'(y_i)$) must be offset exactly by the marginal increase in risk of suffering a loss in returns ($\gamma_i(y_i) - \delta_i$) by triggering a reversionary episode. When this condition holds for all firms, n differential constraints are placed on the n-dimensional vector y of restricted outputs in equilibrium. Thus, the assertion that an equilibrium which satisfies an additional constraint exists will require careful justification. In particular, the output profile which maximizes total returns to the industry may not be supportable in equilibrium.[8]

There are two related final observations about the formal model of collusion under uncertainty. First, no firm ever defects from the cartel. More precisely, no firm i has any private information that would lead it to assess its return function π_i more accurately than its

[8] In Porter (1983) it is shown that, for symmetric firms under imperfect price information, the output profile for normal periods which will maximize discounted industry profits in a non-cooperative equilibrium in trigger price strategies is different from the profile which would be chosen if the industry were a monopoly, i.e. firms forego some profits in normal periods in order to reduce the frequency and duration of reversion needed to provide appropriate incentives, if $\bar{p}$ and T are chosen to maximize expected discounted profits subject to the incentive compatibility constraint (5).

competitors do. Thus, every competitor is able to figure out what i will do to maximize profits. The market price reveals information about demand only, and never leads i's competitors to revise their beliefs about how much i has produced. In equilibrium, the frequency of reversion from normal states will be given by $F(\bar{p}/p(\Sigma y_j))$.

Second, despite the fact that firms know that low prices reflect demand conditions rather than overproduction by competitors, it is rational for them to participate in reversionary episodes.[9] Basically, a reversionary episode is just a temporary switch to a Nash equilibrium in non-contingent strategies. It does not pay any firm to deviate unilaterally from its Nash strategy in this temporary situation, any more than it would if the industry were permanently a Cournot industry. It might be asked why Cournot equilibrium is appropriate at all. If firms know at a particular time that a low price has been observed in the past, and that the cartel has had a perfect record of monopolistic conduct, why do firms not disregard the price and continue to act monopolistically? The answer is that everyone understands the incentive properties of equilibrium. If firms did not revert to Cournot behaviour in response to low prices, equation (5) would not hold the rest of the time, so monopolistic behaviour would cease to be individually optimal for firms.

We realize that the assumptions about industry structure are quite restrictive. We emphasize that the particular Nash equilibrium we are studying is not the only sort of Nash equilibrium which would be collusive according to the definition offered in this section, and that evidence that this particular Nash equilibrium occurs in a specific industry is not the only evidence relevant to forming an opinion about the extent of collusion in various sectors of the economy. However, even though the direct applicability of our model is severely limited, it would be valuable to examine an industry for which it would be appropriate. We believe that the American rail freight industry in the 1880s was one example of an industry which satisfies our structural conditions quite well. Studies of that industry by Paul MacAvoy (1965) and Thomas Ulen (1978; 1980) have produced qualitative conclusions which are consistent with our model. Recent econometric work by Porter (1983) (based on the extensive time series data collected by Ulen) strengthens these conclusions.

[9] To be precise, we argue here that the equilibrium is perfect or sequentially rational. A formal statement and proof of this assertion are given in Green (1980).

3. PRICE PROCESSES GENERATED BY COLLUSION

The equilibrium discussed in the preceding section is noteworthy because it reverses the traditional interpretations of a certain kind of industry price pattern. According to these traditional interpretations, an episode in which price drops sharply, remains low for some time, and then sharply rises again without there being an apparent cost or demand shock would indicate one of two possible events. The episode might be a symptom of the predatory reaction of incumbent firms to a threatened entry. Alternatively, it might signal (as in Stigler's theory) a breakdown of a cartel agreement followed by the re-establishment of the agreement. In either case, such evidence would indicate the fragility of collusion among the incumbents. Thus, in the formulation of policy, it has sometimes been argued that intervention to promote competition would likely be redundant in markets where there episodes are already occurring.

In marked contrast, such episodes play an essential role in the maintenance of an ongoing scheme of collusive incentives in the model presented here. While the traditional views would predict the transience of collusion in a market marked by these episodes of price depression, and with the demise of collusion also the cessation of the price instability which it engendered, our model suggests that industries having certain structural characteristics (i.e. the four characteristics enumerated in the previous section) will exhibit price instability as a feature of a stable, time-stationary pattern of prices if its member firms are colluding. This observation raises the question of whether it is possible to estimate consistently, from the stochastic process of prices generated by a collusive equilibrium of the form described in Sec. 2, the trigger price $\bar{p}$ and the reversionary length T which determine that equilibrium. The answer to this question is affirmative. Moreover, there also exists an estimator which is computationally attractive and which has only a small asymptotic bias if the interval between price observations is short relative to both the length of reversionary episodes and the expected length of normal episodes—the situation which one would expect to encounter in an industry where collusion actually did confer significant market power on firms.

While a discussion of estimation *per se* lies beyond the scope of this paper, we characterize in the Appendix the stochastic process of prices which arises in the equilibrium of the model presented in Sec. 2. It can be shown that any data series of prices may be treated as a sample path of a stationary ergodic process. This result provides a foundation for the study of asymptotic properties of estimation of the model, because it justifies the use of the ergodic theorem (Breiman, 1968; Theorem 6.28) to generalize the role which the law of large numbers plays in the estimation theory of independent processes.[10] (In particular, the existence of consistent estimators of $\bar{p}$ and T is a consequence of the ergodic theorem.) In the Appendix, the price process will be compared to an alternative process which is a Markov version of the well-known Bernoulli switching process (Kiefer, 1980). It can be shown that a data series of prices may be regarded as a 'contaminated sample path' of the alternative process, and the degree of contamination will be computed as a function of the true parameters of the equilibrium.

APPENDIX

To begin, consider a very general definition of the class of stochastic processes which will be under consideration. The observed price process $\{X_t\}_{t \in N}$ will be determined by two processes $\{Y_t\}_{t \in N}$, the price process which would ensue if all periods were normal (i.e. if the industry were to produce the restricted output vector y at all times), and $\{Z_t\}_{t \in N}$, the price process which would ensue if all periods were reversionary (i.e. if the industry were to operate in Cournot equilibrium at all times, producing the output vector z). Whether the observed price is drawn from the normal or the reversionary distribution is determined by a process $\{W_t\}_{t \in N}$, which specifies whether the industry is in a normal or a reversionary state. Note that $\{X_t\}_{t \in N}$ is the only component of the joint process $\{(W_t, X_t, Y_t, Z_t)\}_{t \in N}$ which is observed.

Formally, define a *switching process* to be determined by a probability space (Ω, β, m), a state space S, a subset $N \subseteq S$, and four sequences of random variables $\{W\} = \{W_t : \Omega \to S\}_{t \in N}$,

[10] A stochastic process is ergodic if every event definable in terms of the tails of sample paths (e.g. the set of sample points having convergent paths) has probability zero or one. The ergodic theorem extends the strong law of large numbers to such processes.

$\{X\} = \{X_t : \Omega \to \boldsymbol{R}\}_{t \in N}$, $\{Y\} = \{Y_t : \Omega \to \boldsymbol{R}\}_{t \in N}$, and $\{Z\} = \{Z_t : \Omega \to \boldsymbol{R}\}_{t \in N}$ which satisfy

$$\{Y\} \cup \{Z\} \text{ is a set of independent r.v.'s,} \tag{A1}$$

$$\{Y\} \text{ is identically distributed with c.d.f. } G, \tag{A2}$$

$$\{Z\} \text{ is identically distributed with c.d.f. } H, \tag{A3}$$

$$\{W\} \text{ is a Markov process with stationary transition probabilities,} \tag{A4}$$

$$\forall_t \; S_t \in N \Rightarrow X_t = Y_t \text{ w.p.1,} \tag{A5}$$

$$\forall_t \; S_t \notin N \Rightarrow X_t = Z_t \text{ w.p.1.} \tag{A6}$$

Note that the special case of a switching process usually studied occurs when $S = \{0, 1\}$, $N = \{0\}$, and $\{W\}$ is a Bernoulli process which is independent of $\{Y\} \cup \{Z\}$.

In the case of a collusive price process, G and H are the c.d.f.'s of the normal and reversionary price distributions, respectively. $S = \{0, \ldots, T-1\}$ and $N = \{0\}$. (i.e. $W_t = 0$ signifies that the industry is in a normal period at time t.) The Markov process $\{W\}$ is defined recursively by starting with an arbitrary $W_0 : \Omega \to S$, and then imposing

$$\text{if } W_t(\omega) = 0 \text{ and } Y_t(\omega) \geq \bar{p}, \text{ then } W_{t+1}(\omega) = 0, \tag{A7}$$

$$\text{if } W_t(\omega) = 0 \text{ and } y_t(\omega) < \bar{p}, \text{ then } W_{t+1}(\omega) = 1, \tag{A8}$$

$$\text{if } W_t(\omega) = k,\ 1 \leq k < T-1, \text{ then } W_{t+1}(\omega) = k+1, \tag{A9}$$

$$\text{if } W_t(\omega) = T-1, \text{ then } W_{t+1}(\omega) = 0, \tag{A10}$$

The process $\{W\}$ defined by (A7)–(A10) is Markov with stationary transition probabilities because, by (A1) and (A2), $\{Y\}$ is i.i.d. The transition graph of $\{W\}$ is shown in Fig. 1, in which each arrow is labeled with its transition probability.

The aim is to show that W_0 can be chosen in such a way that $\{X\}$ will be a stationary ergodic process. Conditions (A5) and (A6) show that $X_t(\omega)$ is a function of $(W_t(\omega), Y_t(\omega), Z_t(\omega))$, so by Breiman (1968, Proposition 6.32) it is sufficient to show that the joint process $\{W, Y, Z\}$ is ergodic. By Breiman (1968, Theorem 7.16), this process

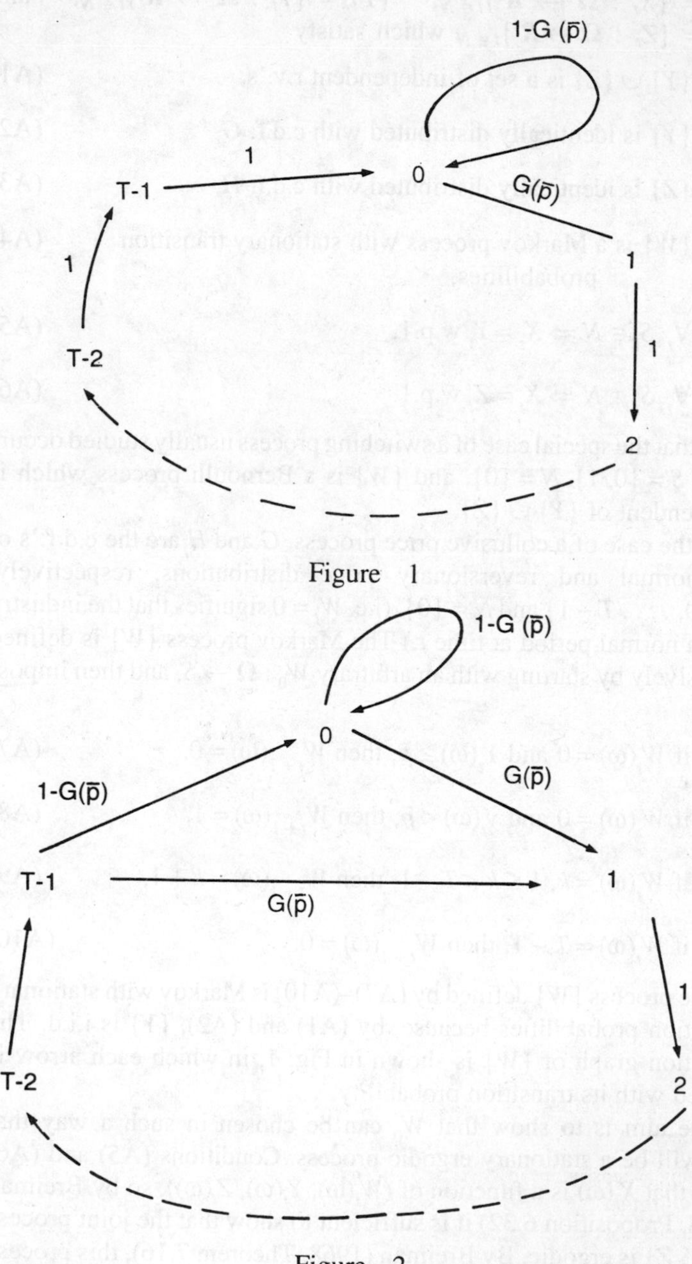

Figure 1

Figure 2

is ergodic if it is a stationary Markov process having a unique invariant distribution (i.e. a unique distribution such that, if W_1 is defined by (A7)–(A10), then $\{W_0, Y_0, Z_0\}$ and $\{W_1, Y_1, Z_1\}$ have identical joint distributions). This follows from Breiman (1968, Theorem 7.18), completing the proof that $\{X\}$ is ergodic.

In Porter (1983a) a maximum likelihood estimator for a switching process somewhat different from (A1)–(A10) is used to study the pre-ICC rail freight cartel in the US That process is obtained by replacing (A1), (A2), and (A7)–(A10) with

$$\{Y\} \text{ is identically distributed with c.d.f.,} \qquad \text{(A11)}$$

$$J(p) = \max\,[(1 - G(\bar{p}))^{-1}\,(G(p) - G(\bar{p})), 0].$$

(I.e. J is the distribution of p according to G, conditional on $p \geq \bar{p}$.)

$$\{W\} \cup \{Y\} \cup \{Z\} \text{ is a set of independent random variables,} \qquad \text{(A12)}$$

and

$\{W\}$ is a stationary Markov process having the transition probabilities specified by Figure 2.[11] (A13)

That is, this process is defined by relaxing the usual assumption that the switching process is Bernoulli, while retaining the assumption that it is independent of the underlying variables which determine the observed prices. Call the process defined by (A1)–(A10) the *price process*, and that defined by (A3)–(A5), (A11)–(A13) the *approximating process*.

The advantage of the approximating process over the price process is that it permits adaptation of much of the work which has been done on maximum-likelihood estimation of the Bernoulli switching process. In particular, it is possible both to compute the ML estimator economically and to appeal to theoretical results asserting its consistency and asymptotic normality. The crucial question raised by use of the approximating process is of how seriously misspecified it is as a model for data actually generated by the price process. We now address this question.

[11] Using extensive information including industry prices, macroeconomic variables, and firm-specific quantity data. Porter estimates the structural equations of a detailed industry model. His method may be viewed as an imposition of prior constraints on the reduced-form estimation described here.

The basis for comparing the two processes is that, given a stationary price process $\{W, X, Y, Z\}$ with parameters $(\bar{p}, T, G, H)$, a stationary approximating process $\{W', X', Y', Z'\}$ with the same parameters can be obtained by a kind of censoring. Looking at the matter from the opposite perspective, the sample paths of Z can be viewed as a contaminated (by reinsertion of the censored observations) version of the approximating process. The extent of the contamination is easily computable from the parameters of the process. If it is slight, and if the ML estimator is regarded as robust, then the ML estimator of the approximating process should also be considered to have small asymptotic bias as an estimator of the price process.

The approximating process $\{W', X', Y', Z'\}$ is defined from $\{W, X, Y, Z\}$ simply by censoring the triggering events (i.e. the events in which $W_t = 0$ and $Y_t < \bar{p}$). Formally, this is done by means of a sequence of stopping times $\{\tau_t : \Omega \to N\}_{t \in N}$. Define

$$\tau_0(\omega) = \begin{cases} 1 & \text{if } W_0(\omega) = 0 \text{ and } Y_0(\omega) < \bar{p}, \\ 0 & \text{otherwise,} \end{cases} \tag{A14}$$

and

$$\tau_{t+1}(\omega) = \begin{cases} \tau_t(\omega) + 2 & \text{if } W_{\tau_t(\omega)+1}(\omega) = 0 \text{ and } Y_{\tau_t(\omega)+1}(\omega) < \bar{p}, \\ \tau_t(\omega) + 1 & \text{otherwise.} \end{cases} \tag{A15}$$

Then define

$$W_t'(\omega) = W_{\tau_t(\omega)}(\omega),\ X_t'(\omega) = X_{\tau_t(\omega)}(\omega), \text{ and } Z_t'(\omega) = Z_{\tau_t(\omega)}(\omega). \tag{A16}$$

Finally, take a set $\{Y_t''\}_{t \in N}$ which are identically distributed with c.d.f. J and such that $\{Y\} \cup \{Z\} \cup \{Y''\}$ is independent, and define

$$Y_t'(\omega) = \begin{cases} Y_{\tau_t(\omega)}(\omega) & \text{if } W_t'(\omega) = 0, \\ Y_t''(\omega) & \text{if } W_t'(\omega) > 0. \end{cases} \tag{A17}$$

(N.B. The definition of the observed component $\{X'\}$ of the approximating process is the same whether $\{Y'\}$ is defined by (A17) or by $Y_t'(\omega) = Y_{\tau_t(\omega)}(\omega)$ for all ω. The reason for using (A17) is both to satisfy (A11) and to keep $\{W'\}$ and $\{Y'\}$ independent so that (A12) is satisfied. Under the simpler definition, (A15) would have introduced dependency between them.)

The effect of (A15) and (A16) is to continue to let a low realization of Y_t be the event which causes the state to change from zero to one, but to censor this event if it occurs. Thus the dependence of W_{t+1} on $\{W_t, Y_t\}$ in the price process is removed, and (A12) holds. By the strong Markov property [(Breiman, 1968) Proposition 7.8], the censored process is a stationary Markov process, so (A13) holds, i.e. $\{W', X', Y', Z'\}$ is an approximating process with parameters $(\bar{p}, T, J, H)$.

It remains to calculate how much censoring of the price series $X(\omega)$ is required to construct the approximating series $X'(\omega)$. (Alternatively, how much contamination of $X'(\omega)$ is required to reconstruct $X(\omega)$?) Formally, what is $\lim_{t\to\infty}(\tau_t(\omega)-t)/\tau_t(\omega)$? If this quotient is close to zero for almost every ω, then the asymptotic bias of the approximating-process ML estimator applied to data generated by the price process should be small.

To calculate the quotient, first define $\sigma(W, Y) = 1$ if $W = 0$ and $Y < \bar{p}$, and $\sigma(W, Y) = 0$ otherwise. By (A14) and (A15), $\tau_t(\omega) = t + \Sigma_{u=0}^{\tau_t(\omega)} \sigma(W_u(\omega), Y_u(\omega))$, or

$$\frac{\tau_t(\omega)-t}{\tau_t(\omega)} = \frac{1}{\tau_t(\omega)}\sum_{u=0}^{\tau_t(\omega)} \sigma(W_u(\omega), Y_u(\omega)) \qquad \text{(A18)}$$

By the ergodic theorem,

$$\lim_{t\to\infty} \frac{1}{\tau_t(\omega)}\sum_{u=0}^{\tau_t(\omega)} \sigma(W_u(\omega), Y_u(\omega)) = m(\{W_0 = 0, Y_0 < \bar{p}\})G(\bar{p}) \text{ a.s.} \qquad \text{(A19)}$$

(Recall that m is the stationary measure on Ω.) Combining (A18) and (A19), and appealing to the fact that the stationarity of the price process forces W_0 and Y_0 to be independent, yields

$$\lim_{t\to\infty} \frac{\tau_t(\omega)-t}{\tau_t(\omega)} = m(\{W_0 = 0\})G(\bar{p}) \text{ a.s.} \qquad \text{(A20)}$$

The calculation of $m(\{W_0 = 0\})$ is an easy matter. For $1 \le k < T-1$, by (A9) and stationarity, we have

$$m(\{W_0 = k\}) = m(\{W_1 = k+1\}) = m(\{W_0 = k+1\}). \qquad \text{(A21)}$$

Also, by (A7) and stationarity, we have

$$m(\{W_0 = 1\}) = m(\{W_1 = 1\}) = m(\{W_0 = 0\})G(\bar{p}). \tag{A22}$$

Since the probabilities of the states sum to unity, (A21) and (A22) yield

$$m(\{W_0 = 0\}) = [1 + (T-1)G(\bar{p})]^{-1}. \tag{A23}$$

Thus, by (A22) and (A23),

$$\lim_{t\to\infty} \frac{\tau_t(\omega) - t}{\tau_t(\omega)} = G(\bar{p})\,[1 + (T-1)G(\bar{p})]^{-1}. \tag{A24}$$

For example, consider a hypothetical industry in which a trade association disseminates weekly price data to its members, i.e. the appropriate interpretation of a period in the discrete-time model is one week. Suppose that the parameters of this industry were estimated using the ML estimator for the approximating process, with the results that $\hat{G}(\hat{p}) = .025$ and $\hat{T} = 11$. Since the expected duration of an episode of normal conduct is $(G(\bar{p}))^{-1}$, these estimates indicate that a reversionary episode occurs once a year on average, and lasts ten weeks. Thus there is (on average) one price observation a year (that being the observation of the price which triggers the reversionary episode), which would not be included if the approximating process were really generating the data. This is a contamination ratio of one in fifty, or $(.025)[1 + .25]^{-1}$ which is the expression which is obtained from (A24).

The ML estimator is computed by dividing the data into two subsamples, one of which is presumed to have been drawn from distribution G and the other from H, and then estimating these distributions from the respective sub-samples. If the 'contaminating' observations were to comprise equal proportions of the two subsamples, then each subsample is being estimated with 2 per cent contamination, and one might reasonably suppose the discrepancy between the price process and the approximating process to be rather small. If all of the 'contaminating' observations were assigned to the subsample presumed to be generated by normal conduct, then this subsample would have 2.5 per cent contamination, which still might reasonably be ignored. However, if the 'contaminating' observations were all included in the subsample presumed to reflect reversionary conduct, then that subsample would have a 10 per cent contamination level. In this worst case, it is easy to imagine that the observations actually drawn from the lower tail of G would seriously bias the estimation of H.

The parameter estimates for the example just given are approximately the same as those reported by Porter (1983b) for the rail freight industry. Thus, while the foregoing analysis is insufficiently precise to rule out the worst-case assumption concerning bias of his estimator relative to the price process, it has shown that under more optimistic assumptions the bias would plausibly be slight. While we acknowledge that there is an inevitable element of subjective judgment in a situation such as this, we suggest that Porter's study provides presumptive evidence that the rail freight industry may have exemplified the kind of equilibrium which has been studied here.

REFERENCES

BREIMAN, L. (1968), *Probability*, Reading: Addison-Wesley.

BRESNAHAN, T. (1982), 'The Oligopoly Solution Concept is Identified', *Economics Letters*, 10, 87–92.

FRIEDMAN, J.W. (1971), 'A Non-cooperative Equilibrium for Supergames', *Review of Economic Studies*, 28, 1–12.

GOLDSCHMID, H.J., H.M. MANN and J.F. WESTON (eds) (1974), *Industrial Concentration: The New Learning*, Boston: Little, Brown and Co.

GREEN, E.J. (1980), 'Non-cooperative Price Taking in Large Dynamic Markets', *Journal of Economic Theory*, 22, 155–82.

KIEFER, N.M. (1980), 'A Note on Switching Regressions and Logistic Discrimination', *Econometrica*, 48, 1065–9.

MACAVOY, P.W. (1965), *The Economic Effects of Regulation*, Cambridge: MIT Press.

OSBORNE, D.K. (1976), 'Cartel Problems', *American Economic Review*, 66, 835–44.

PORTER, R.H. (1983a), 'Optimal Cartel Trigger-Price Strategies', *Journal of Economic Theory*, 29, 313–38.

—— (1983b), 'A Study of Cartel Stability: The Joint Executive Committee 1880–6', *Bell Journal of Economics*.

RADNER, R. (1980), 'Collusive Behavior in Noncooperative Epsilon-Equilibria with Long but Finite Lives', *Journal of Economic Theory*, 22, 136–54.

SCHERER, F.M. (1980), *Industrial Market Structure and Economic Performance*, Second Edition, Chicago: Rand McNally.

SPENCE, M. (1978a), 'Tacit Coordination and Imperfect Information', *Canadian Journal of Economics*, 11, 490–505.

—— (1978b), 'Efficient Collusion and Reaction Functions', *Canadian Journal of Economics*, 11, 527–33.

STIGLER, G.J. (1964), 'A Theory of Oligopoly', *Journal of Political Economy*, 72, 44–61.

ULEN, T.S. (1978), 'Cartels and Regulation', unpublished Ph.D. Dissertation, Stanford University.

—— (1980), 'The Market for Regulation: The ICC from 1887 to 1920', *American Economic Review, Papers and Proceedings*, 70, 306–10.

INNOVATIONS

Industrial Structure and the Nature of Innovative Activity*

P. DASGUPTA AND J.E. STIGLITZ

A substantial portion of the increase in the output of advanced industrial nations is widely judged to have been attributable to technical progress. There is also overwhelming evidence that this progress has not occurred merely in a random manner (see, e.g. Schmookler, 1962). Yet there is not much in the way of economic theory to explain either its rate or its direction, and particularly little that has a reasonably precise micro-economic foundation.[1] This lacuna is important, because a recognition of the importance of technical progress raises serious doubts about the adequacy with which traditional microeconomic models allow one to understand the functioning of modern market economies, and to develop policy prescriptions (e.g. with respect to antitrust policy). The lacuna is also surprising, for it has

* This is a revised and expanded version of the first part of an invited paper (Dasgupta and Stiglitz, 1977) presented at the World Congress of the *International Economic Association on Economic Growth and Resources*, held in Tokyo during 27 August–3 September 1977. This version was prepared whilst Dasgupta was a Visiting Professor at the School of International Studies, Jawaharlal Nehru University, and the Delhi School of Economics, Delhi, and Stiglitz was Oskar Morgenstern Distinguished Fellow at Mathematica, and Visiting Professor at the Institute of Advanced Studies, Princeton, during the Autumn of 1978. We have gained much from discussions with Hans Biswinger, Sukhamoy Chakravarty, A.K. Dasgupta, Paul David, Richard Gilbert, Sanford Grossman, Glen Loury, Edwin Mansfield, and most especially, from the comments of Ashok Guha.

[1] For this last, see, for example Arrow (1962), Barzel (1968), Stiglitz (1970), Kamien and Schwartz (1972), Evenson and Kieslev (1975), Nelson, Winter and Schuette (1976), Dasgupta and Stiglitz (1977), Loury (1977), Nelson and Winter (1977), Dasgupta and Stiglitz (1978), Levin (1978) and, of course, the pioneering work of Schumpeter (1947).

become a commonplace, at least since the work of Schumpeter (1977), that the pace of inventive and innovative activity is related to market structure. Moreover, there must be many who share the Schumpeterian belief that perfect competition is inimical to inventive activity, and that the gains from such activity more than offset the welfare loss arising from production inefficiency associated with market power.[2]

However, a substantial part of the recent industrial organization literature would appear to have interpreted tests of the Schumpeterian thesis in a somewhat different manner.[3] It is often argued now that industrial concentration and large size *spur* inventive activity. It is as though concentration is a *cause* of innovations.[4]

In this paper we attempt to provide an analytical framework relating market structure to the nature of inventive activity. In doing so we have come to modify this neo-Schumpeterian view in a fundamental way. We shall argue that except in the short run *both* market structure and the nature of inventive activity are endogenous; that the degree of concentration in an industry ought not to be treated as given, as it recently has been in the industrial organization literature; that they both depend on more basic ingredients, such as the technology of research, demand conditions, the nature of the capital market (i.e. market rates of interest, and the ability of firms to borrow to finance research and development (R & D)), and the legal structure (e.g. patent rights). We shall, to be sure, explore the relationship between the degree of concentration and the nature of

[2] 'A system . . . that at *every* given point of time fully utilises its possibilities to the best advantage may yet in the long run be inferior to a system that does so at *no* given point of time, because the latter's failure to do so may be a condition for the level or speed of long run performance' (Schumpeter, 1947, p. 83). It should be noted that Schumpeter is here comparing industrial capitalism with perfect competition.

[3] The empirical findings suggest that whilst up to a point industrial concentration is positively correlated with innovative activity, it is negatively correlated when an industry is too concentrated. See Scherer (1970), and Kamien and Schwartz (1975) for a survey of the empirical literature.

[4] Thus, for example, after noting in a sentence that technological change has effects on market structure, the body of the chapter devoted to R & D in Scherer (1970), is ' . . . concerned with a possible causal flow in the opposite direction; from market structure to technological innovation' and, among others, with the question: 'Is monopoly power, e.g. as manifested in high market concentration, a favourable climate for innovation and technical progress?' Scherer (1970), p. 347.

innovative activity. But as they are both endogenous, their relationship, unlike the neo-Schumpeterian thesis, ought not to be regarded as a *causal* one.

A major objective of our study is to formulate models within which the efficiency of a market economy can be assessed and where the tradeoff between atemporal production efficiency and dynamic gains can be meaningfully discussed. Not surprisingly these questions, once properly posed, turn out to be far more complicated than they appear at first sight. It is not a case of a single firm making a single decision (e.g. the total volume of R & D expenditure), but rather a case in which several firms make a complex of decisions; and it is the consequences of these with which we are concerned. For example, each firm needs to decide both on how much to spend on R & D and also on which research strategies to pursue. Moreover, research strategies can differ not only with respect to the probability distribution of the dates at which success occurs, but also as regards how much is learnt even if the principal objectives of the research project fail, and to how similar, both in process and in objectives, they are to those being pursued by other firms. Each of these decisions has important consequences not only for the aggregate rate of technological progress, but also for industrial structure and the performance of a market economy. If firms tend to imitate each other's research strategies then much of R & D expenditure may be essentially duplicative, and consequently socially wasteful. If firms engage in excessively risky projects it may lead to too fast a rate of technical progress and high degrees of industrial concentration. This last in turn may imply large losses in production efficiency. What makes the analysis all the more difficult is that each decision on the part of a firm has to be made within an industrial structure which is itself endogenous.

Questions regarding the *consequences* of market structure on R & D are, of course, not new. That there is *underinvestment* in R & D both under competition and monopoly is probably a general presumption. This presumption is based partly on the fact that knowledge—the output of R & D—has the attributes of a public good; but partly also on an argument, due to Arrow (1962), that relies solely on a comparison of the magnitudes of the payoff to the successful firm under alternative market structures.

In Sec. 1, we shall review this argument and see where it is in error. This review will also help set the stage for the formal analysis that follows. In fact a central conclusion of this paper is that on balance there is no reason for supposing that a market economy sustains too low a level of investment in R & D. There may well be overinvestment.

Sections 2, 3 and 4 contain analyses of various aspects of R & D activity and their relationship to market structure. The discussions are based on models that are natural extensions of a simple model of process innovation presented in Sec. 1. In Sec. 2, we explore the relationship between market structure and expenditure in R & D. The model we shall present, whilst very simple, is at once rich enough to illustrate some points that we have raised above and several that will be raised subsequently. However, it is as well to mention at the outset that a central feature that the model of Sec. 2 is designed to display is that while R & D expenditures on the part of firms are rather like fixed-costs in production, the levels of such 'fixed costs' are themselves choice variables for firms (firms can engage in less or more R & D expenditure). This results in a key difference between the analysis of competition in R & D and the more conventional analysis of product competition, as our subsequent discussion will display. Moreover, we shall note formally that there are some basic non-convexities that may be present in the production and use of knowledge, and since knowledge is the output of R & D effort, any analysis of R & D must take into account such possible non-convexities. To illustrate the matter simply, it should be noted that the indirect social benefit function of a commodity is a decreasing but *convex* function of the unit cost of production (see Fig. 4). An immediate implication of this is that as between two research strategies that yield the same mean reduction in production cost, a risk-averse society will prefer the *riskier* one if the expenditure on the two are more or less the same. Another implication of this, as we shall note in Sec. 2, is that net social benefit of R & D expenditure is not necessarily a concave function even if one postulates diminishing returns in cost reduction due to increased R & D effort. The point is that the same piece of knowledge can in principle be applied at any scale of operation. Thus, the cost of information per unit of scale decreases as the scale increases; but the value of information per unit scale need not. Earlier writings, in the main, have concentrated on the failure of the price system to sustain an efficient production and utilization of knowledge, not only because knowledge has the attributes of a public good, but also because of the impossibility of establishing a complete set of perfectly competitive contingent markets in the face of, say, the phenomenon of moral hazard. A part of our analysis will be directed at noting the natural non-convexities that arise in the production and use of knowledge. Our aim in general is to see how each of these features affects the structure of an industry and the scale and direction of innovative activity.

The example of Sec. 2, being timeless and devoid of uncertainty, suffers from several drawbacks, two crucial ones being that one is unable to study the *degree of risk-taking* in research activity, and that one cannot identify the *speed of research* (the pace of inventive activity). Consequently, it is not possible to analyse how each of these characteristics is related to market structure. It is clear enough in advance, of course, that each is in turn related not only to the structure of the product market but also to the degree of competition in R & D activity.[5] The models that follow will capture this feature sharply. The example discussed in Sec. 3 is similar to that of Sec. 2, but it is now supposed that research activities have uncertain payoffs. In this paper we are concerned with *process* innovation (i.e. R & D designed to reduce cost of production). This means that attention is drawn to the distribution of extreme values. This in turn implies, as was noted by Evenson and Kieslev (1975), that even risk-averse firms might wish to engage in randomization. The example to be discussed in Sec. 3 will bear this out. But the desire for randomization will, in our model, be reinforced by the feature which we have noted earlier.

In Sec. 4 time is introduced into the analysis. It will be supposed that the first firm to invent captures all benefits that are to be had among firms (i.e. we suppose that the winner takes all). No doubt this is a simplification. But it should be transparent in which direction the model needs to be modified, were one to recognize the fact that firms usually are able to invent around patents and that as a result the first firm to make a breakthrough is not necessarily the most advantaged.

A critical assumption of the construction in Sec. 4 is that all firms

[5] Among other things it is this last that distinguishes the analyses undertaken in this paper from those undertaken by Arrow (1962), in that Arrow concentrated exclusively on differing structures of the product market and supposed no competition in R & D activity when analysing the incentives to innovate under different market structures. We shall comment on this at a greater length in Sec. 1.

are obliged to follow the *same* research strategy; i.e. they all face the same decision tree. This has important consequences. In a sequel to this paper we explore the opposite extreme and suppose that firms face uncertainties about the date of success that are independent of one another.

In Sec. 5, we gather together what we regard as the basic morals emerging from our analysis. The Appendices explore the constructions in Secs 2 and 3 in detail, verifying some of the claims made in the text. In particular, Appendix 1 contains a theorem regarding the existence of an equilibrium with free entry which may be of wider interest.

1. MARKET BIAS IN PROCESS INNOVATION

In what follows we suppose an absence of income effects. Let Q denote the quantity of a given commodity. The gross social benefit of consuming Q is $u(Q)$ with $u'(Q) > 0$ and $u''(Q) < 0$. Market demand is given by

$$p = p(Q) = u'(Q). \tag{1}$$

Write $R(Q) = p(Q)Q$ as gross revenue to a monopolist. Assume for the moment that marginal revenue is decreasing in output.

Suppose that the current best-practice technique for producing the commodity involves c as the unit cost of production. Suppose also that a particular process innovation reduces the unit cost of production to c^*. In a pioneering paper Arrow (1962) explored the gain to the innovator under three forms of the product market. The first, the socially managed market, is one where the market price is the cost of production. For this the per period pay-off due to the innovation is the gain in net social surplus, which is represented by the area *ABCD* in Fig. 1. Let π_s denote this gain. The second is the case of the pure monopolist (i.e. where there are barriers to entry). Let π_m represent the increase in per period monopoly profit if the monopolist undertakes the innovation. In Fig. 2, π_m is given by the difference between the areas *IJKL* and *EFGH*. The third is the competitive economy. Assume then that the c-technology is competitively exploited and that the innovator acquires a patent on the c^*-technology. Let π_c denote the per-period monopoly profit accruing to the innovator

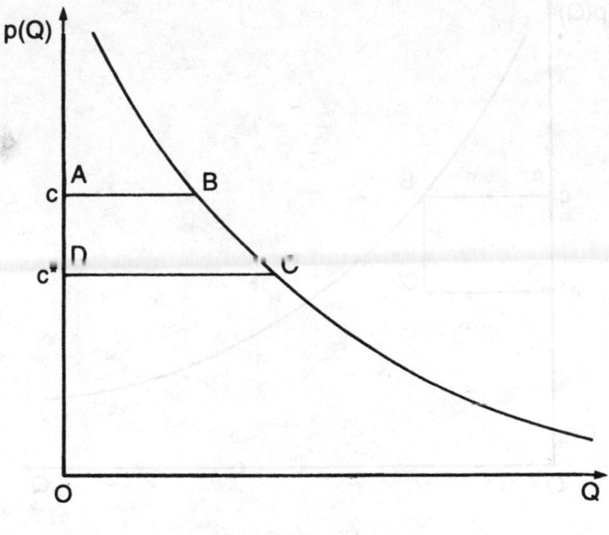

Figure 1

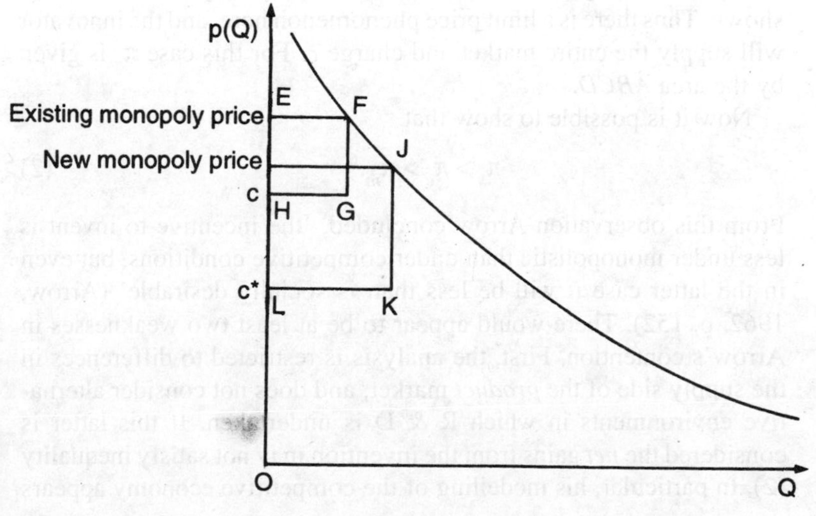

Figure 2

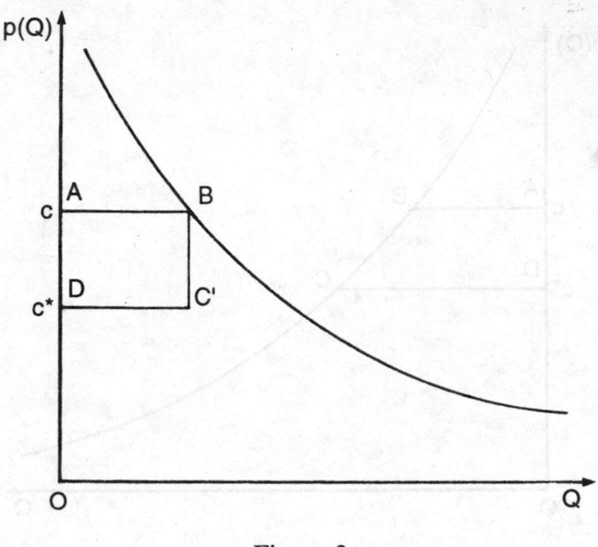

Figure 3

during the life of the patent. There are clearly two cases to be considered. In Fig. 3 the case where the monopoly price exceeds c is shown. Thus there is a limit price phenomenon here, and the innovator will supply the entire market and charge c. For this case π_c is given by the area $ABCD$.

Now it is possible to show that

$$\pi_s > \pi_c > \pi_m.^6 \tag{2}$$

From this observation Arrow concluded, 'the incentive to invent is less under monopolistic than under competitive conditions, but even in the latter case it will be less than is socially desirable' (Arrow, 1962, p. 152). There would appear to be at least two weaknesses in Arrow's contention. First, the analysis is restricted to differences in the supply side of the *product* market, and does not consider alternative environments in which R & D is undertaken. If this latter is considered the *net* gains from the invention may not satisfy inequality (2). In particular, his modelling of the competitive economy appears

6 For a demonstration, see Arrow (1962).

to suppose that there is no competition in R & D activity and that there is a single firm engaged in it (see footnote 5, p. 319 above). Secondly, the model hypothesizes the feasibility of discrete choices only. More generally, one would like to hypothesize the existence of margins of choice: research strategies aimed at a slight lowering of costs, a slight increase in risk, and a slight increase in speed. In the following three sections we explore these three features of process innovation in turn.

2. MARKET STRUCTURE AND THE VOLUME OF R & D EXPENDITURE

(1) The Socially Managed Industry

Imagine first that the market for the commodity in question is socially managed. If c is the (constant) unit cost of production then the net social benefit of consuming Q is $u(Q) - cQ$. Define

$$V(c) = \max_{Q}\, [u(Q) - cQ] \tag{3}$$

as the indirect utility function. It is well known that $V(c)$ is a declining convex function of c (see Fig. 4). We suppose that R & D expenditure is designed to reduce the cost of production. Thus if x is expenditure on R & D then $c(x)$ is the unit cost of production. It is then natural to suppose that $c'(x) < 0$.[7]

Assume for the moment that the government can raise the funds for R & D expenditure from general taxation. Its problem then is to

$$\max_{x \geq 0}\, \{V[c(x)] - x\}. \tag{4}$$

Suppose that a solution to (4) exists. The first point to note is that unless further structure is imposed on $c(x)$ we cannot guarantee that $V[c(x)]$ is a concave function of x. This is so even if we were to assume in addition that $c''(x) > 0$ (i.e. decreasing returns in the

[7] It is as though Mother Nature has a patent on all techniques of production with unit cost $c(x)$, $(x > 0)$ and that society has to pay x to purchase the right to use the technique of production with unit cost $c(x)$.

technology of research). The problems that the possible non-concavity of V raises are the usual ones. Suppose that the solution to (4) dictates that $x > 0$, then optimal R & D expenditure must satisfy the condition

$$\frac{dV}{dc}\,c'(x) = 1,$$

but

$$\frac{dV}{dc} = -\,Q,$$

hence

$$-\,c'(x)\,Q = 1. \tag{5}$$

The interpretation of equation (5) is clear enough. The LHS is the marginal social benefit of increasing R & D expenditure, which in fact is the reduction in production cost when output is optimal. The RHS is, of course, the marginal cost of increasing R & D expenditure. If V is concave in x there is no need for the government to calculate consumer surplus in locating the optimum. But if V is not concave in x the government needs in general to conduct global cost-benefit analysis to locate the optimum. The need for computing consumer surplus in such circumstances is obvious.

In order to bring these points out more clearly it will prove helpful to specify the functions somewhat. Suppose that

$$u(Q) = \frac{\sigma Q^{\,1-\varepsilon}}{(1-\varepsilon)}\quad(\sigma, \varepsilon > 0). \tag{6}$$

Thus if we write by $p(Q)$ the market demand curve,

$$p(Q) = \sigma Q^{-\varepsilon}, \tag{7}$$

where ε^{-1} is the elasticity of demand. Therefore, (7) supposes that market demand is iso-elastic.

It is then simple to confirm that

$$V\,[c(x)] = \left(\frac{\varepsilon}{1-\varepsilon}\right)(\sigma)^{1/\varepsilon}/[c(x)]^{(1-\varepsilon)/\varepsilon}. \tag{8}$$

Suppose in addition that it is a new product which is under consideration. In particular assume

$$c(x) = \beta x^{-\alpha} \quad (\alpha, \beta > 0). \tag{9}$$

In this case

$$V[c(x)] = \left(\frac{\varepsilon}{1-\varepsilon}\right)\frac{\sigma^{1/\varepsilon}}{\beta^{(1-\varepsilon)/\varepsilon}}\, x^{\alpha(1-\varepsilon)/\varepsilon}.$$

We may now note that $V[c(x)]$ is strictly concave in x if $\varepsilon > \alpha(1-\varepsilon)$. If the reverse inequality were to hold, $V[c(x)]$ would be strictly convex in x, and in particular, (4) will not possess a finite solution. Social benefits will continually increase with increasing R & D expenditure.[8]

The foregoing condition for ensuring that $V[c(x)]$ is strictly concave is really rather transparent. It says that $1 + 1/\alpha > 1/\varepsilon$. Since $1/\varepsilon$ is the elasticity of demand, and since $1/\alpha$ is the production cost elasticity of R & D investment, the condition says that this latter elasticity must be sufficiently large to entertain continual diminishing (utility) returns on R & D expenditure. It should be noted that the condition is readily satisfied if demand is inelastic (i.e. $\varepsilon > 1$). It is satisfied even if demand is elastic (i.e. $\varepsilon < 1$) so long, of course, it is not too elastic. The condition makes precise the range on ε that yields a well defined planning problem on the assumption that income effects are nil.[9]

Suppose then that $\varepsilon > \alpha(1-\varepsilon)$. Let x_s and Q_s denote the socially optimal levels of R & D expenditure and total output, respectively. If we now use (7) and (9) in the optimality conditions it is simple to verify that

$$x_s = (\alpha^{\varepsilon}\sigma\,\beta^{\varepsilon-1})^{1/[\varepsilon-\alpha(1-\varepsilon)]} \tag{10}$$

[8] This is, of course, absurd since we would not be justified in supposing the marginal utility of income to remain constant.

[9] Our purpose so far has been solely to draw attention to the *existence* of non-concavities in the payoff function in the context of process innovation under certain circumstances; nothing more. As we noted in footnote 1 it is rather silly to explore non-concavities while assuming away income effects. The obvious question to ask is how to reformulate the model if in fact $\varepsilon < \alpha(1-\varepsilon)$. One obviously needs to assume that the marginal utility of income is not constant. Suppose, for example, that in the obvious notation $u(Q, x) = \sigma[Q^{(1-\varepsilon)}/(1-\varepsilon)]\,[M - x - c(x)\,Q]^{\delta}$, where $1 > \varepsilon, \delta > 0$, and M is total income. Let $W(x) = \max_{Q} u(Q, x)$. It is simple to verify that if $c(x)$ satisfies (9) then $W(x)$ is strictly convex for small x if $1 < \alpha(1-\varepsilon)$. Nevertheless, $W(x)$ has a unique maximum.

and

$$Q_s = (\alpha\,\beta)^{-1}\,(\sigma\alpha^{\varepsilon}\,\beta^{\varepsilon-1})^{(1+\alpha)/[\varepsilon-\alpha(1-\varepsilon)]} \tag{11}$$

It follows immediately from equations (10) and (11) that both optimum output and optimum R & D expenditure are greater in industries that face larger markets (i.e. larger value of σ). Thus the larger is the size of the market the greater ought (unit) cost reduction to be. It is also worth noting that total output ought to be less in industries characterized by more costly R & D technology (i.e. a larger value of β). One expects these features of the optimum. However, equation (10) implies that optimum R & D expenditure is *less* in industries characterized by more costly R & D technology if demand is *elastic* ($\varepsilon < 1$), and is *greater* if demand is *inelastic* ($\varepsilon > 1$). On reflection, this too is possibly in line with intuition.

(2) Oligopoly with Price-Entry

It remains to explore a market economy. Suppose now that R & D activity is undertaken exclusively in the private sector. For simplicity of exposition we consider a market for a new product and suppose, also for simplicity, that all firms face the same R & D technology, $c(x)$. Thus if $x_i(\geq 0)$ is the R & D expenditure of firm i, $c(x_i)$ is the unit cost of production that it faces for the product. In pursuing this formulation we are supposing that knowledge is monopolised by a firm when it pays for it.[10] Firms are profit maximizing, behave non-cooperatively, and our task is to describe an equilibrium for this market. Towards this we assume that firms behave in a Cournot fashion (i.e. each firm chooses its own R & D expenditure level and its own output level) and that they all entertain Cournot conjectures (i.e. each firm supposes that none of the remaining firms will deviate from its course of action if the given firm deviates).

Begin by supposing that there is free entry into the industry; i.e. assume that market structure is endogenous. Let n be the number of

[10] Since the product is new, $c_i(0) = \infty$, by assumption. We leave it to the reader to analyse the case where the existing competitive product price is c and firms spend resources to cut costs (i.e. $c_i(0) = c$). An alternative interpretation of this model would be to suppose that preferences are defined over the *characteristics* of commodities, and that firms in the industry compete to produce *different* commodities but which possess the *same* characteristic. Hence the commodities are perfect substitutes in consumption.

firms in the industry and let $Q_i(\geq 0)$ denote the output of the ith firm $(i = 1, \ldots, n)$. It follows from our assumptions that

$$[n^*, (Q_1^*, x_1^*), (Q_2^*, x_2^*), \ldots, (Q_i^*, x_i^*), \ldots, (Q_{n*}^*, x_{n*}^*)]$$

is an equilibrium with free entry if, for $i = 1, 2, \ldots, n^*$,

$$\left[p\left(\sum_{j \neq i} Q_j^* + Q_i^*\right) - c(x_i^*)\right] Q_i^* - x_i^* \geq \left[p\left(\sum_{j \neq i} Q_j^* + Q_i\right) - c(x_i)\right] Q_i - x_i, \quad \text{for all } x_i, Q_i \geq 0, \tag{12}$$

and

$$\left[p\left(\sum_{i=1}^{n^*} Q_i^* + Q\right) - c(x)\right] Q - x \leq 0 \qquad \text{for all } x, Q \geq 0. \tag{13}$$

Condition (12) is clear enough. It says that (Q_i^*, x_i^*) is profit maximizing for firm i $(i = 1, \ldots, n^*)$ if it assumes that each of the remaining firms in the industry, j $(j \neq i)$, chooses output level Q_j^*, and that those firms outside the industry remain outside. Condition (13) must be satisfied if these are no barriers to entry. It says that there is no way for a firm not in the industry to enter and make positive profits if the ith firm in the industry $(i = 1, \ldots, n^*)$ chooses to produce at the level Q_i^*. We have supposed, therefore, that each firm, whether in the industry or not, entertains Cournot conjectures regarding all other firms.

We are here concerned not only with the question of whether a free-entry market equilibrium exists but also with the characteristics of such equilibria in those circumstances where they do exist. This latter task is greatly simplified if we restrict our attention to *symmetric* equilibria; i.e. equilibria in which firms in the industry behave identically. In Appendix 1, we shall locate circumstances in which symmetric equilibria can be shown to exist. For the moment we suppose that such equilibria exist and we proceed to characterize them.

Let n^* be the equilibrium number of firms in the industry (to be determined, of course). Let $\hat{Q}_i$ denote the total output of all firms other than the ith. Thus $Q = Q_i + \hat{Q}_i$. Firm i chooses x_i and Q_i with a view to

$$\text{maximizing } \{[p(Q_i + \hat{Q}_i) - c(x_i)]\, Q_i - x_i\}. \tag{14}$$

On the assumption that profit maximizing Q_i and x_i are both positive, the first-order conditions are

$$p(Q)\,[1 - \varepsilon\,(Q)\,Q_i/Q\,] = c(x_i) \tag{15}$$

and

$$-\,Q_i\,c'(x_i) = 1, \tag{16}$$

where $\varepsilon(Q) \equiv -\,Qp'(Q)/p(Q)$, is the inverse of the elasticity of demand. Since we are exploring symmetric equilibria, Q_i and x_i must be independent of i for $i = 1, \ldots, n^*$. Therefore, if n^*, Q^*, x^* characterize a symmetric equilibrium with free entry they must satisfy conditions (15) and (16), which reduce to

$$p(Q^*)\,[1 - \varepsilon(Q^*)/n^*] = c(x^*) \tag{17}$$

and

$$-\,c'(x^*)\,Q^*/n^* = 1. \tag{18}$$

(Note that Q^* denotes total output in equilibrium and therefore Q^*/n^* is output per firm in the industry.)

Moreover, the free entry condition (13) reduces to

$$[p(Q^* + Q) - c(x)]\,Q - x \leq 0 \text{ for all } x,\, Q \geq 0. \tag{19}$$

Finally, note that since $(x^*, Q^*/n^*)$ is the profit maximizing pair of choices for the representative firm in the industry in equilibrium, it must yield non-negative profits. Thus

$$[p(Q^*) - c(x^*)]\,Q^* \geq n^*x^*. \tag{20}$$

It is clear that the analysis would be greatly eased if free-entry were to result in firms earning negligible profits. Suppose then that $\{[p(Q^*) - c(x^*)]\,Q^* - n^*x^*\}/n^*x^*$ is small enough to be neglected. We can then, instead of (20), work with the zero-profit condition.

$$[p(Q^*) - c(x^*)]\,Q^* = n^*x^*. \tag{21}$$

If (21) is satisfied, condition (19) is most certainly satisfied. But one can locate conditions in which (19) is satisfied even though (20) is a strict inequality. We shall explore these issues in detail in Appendix 1, where we shall also enquire into the circumstances in which (21) is a good approximation. In fact one expects that (21) is a reasonable approximation in those circumstances where n^* is 'large' and that one can identify parametric conditions for which the number of firms in equilibrium *is* 'large'. In Appendix 1 we shall note by way of an important class of cases that this is so, but that n^* need not *necessarily* be large in those circumstances in which the use of (21) as an equilibrium condition is justifiable. For the moment we assume that it is a good approximation. It follows that n^*, Q^*, x^* are obtained from equations (17), (18) and (21).

A glance at these conditions shows that a market equilibrium is not characterized by an optimal allocation of resources. For one thing producers exercise a degree of monopoly power at a market equilibrium which sustains the level of R & D expenditure they incur. For another the private firm's marginal benefit of its R & D expenditure is calculated on the basis of its contribution to *its* scale of output (condition (18)) and not for the entire market (condition (5)).

We now proceed to analyse the market equilibrium conditions in detail. On using equations (17) and (21) we note that

$$1/n^* = Z^*/\varepsilon(Q^*) \quad (\text{where } Z^* = n^* x^* / p(Q^*)\, Q^*), \tag{22}$$

(22) is the fundamental equation of this section. As we are analysing symmetric equilibria we cannot compare the degrees of concentration in different markets by indices such as the concentration ratio. For our model it would seem natural to regard $1/n^*$ as the index of the *degree of concentration*. Z^*, being the fraction of industry sales that is spent on R & D, is an obvious index for research intensity in the industry. Equation (22) says that if ε is constant they are proportional to each other. Thus, in a cross-section study of different industries with the same demand elasticity in equilibrium, but varying by way of the size of the market and R & D technologies they face, one would observe a linear relationship between research intensity and concentration. *But there is no causality to be imputed to this relationship: industrial concentration and research intensity are simultaneously determined.*[11]

[11] The relationship between the degree of concentration and R & D expenditure established here is not inconsistent with the empirical findings mentioned in footnote 3, p. 316 above, for note that equation (22) has been obtained on the assumption that (21) is a good approximation. In Appendix 1 we shall note that (21) is indeed a good approximation for certain ranges of the parameters underlying the model and, in particular, for those ranges for which n^* is large (i.e. the degree of concentration is

It will have been noted that in arriving at equation (22) no use was made of equation (18). Thus (22) obtains under more general circumstances than we have allowed, in that it does not depend on firms choosing their R & D strategies with a view to profit maximization. We therefore proceed to obtain a somewhat sharper characterization. Let $\alpha(x) \equiv -xc'(x)/c(x)$ denote the elasticity of unit cost of production with respect to R & D expenditure. It then follows from equations (18) and (22) that

$$Z^* \equiv n^* x^* / p(Q^*) Q^* = \alpha(x^*)/[1 + \alpha(x^*)]. \tag{23}$$

Therefore, in a cross-section study of industries facing different demand conditions but the same elasticity of the unit cost function (α) in equilibrium, one would observe that the index of research intensity, Z^*, is the same. But these industries would be characterized by different degrees of concentration; for on using (23) in (22) one obtains the equilibrium number of firms as

$$n^* = \varepsilon(Q^*)[1 + \alpha(x^*)]/\alpha(x^*). \tag{24}$$

Therefore, the greater is the elasticity of demand ($1/\varepsilon(Q^*)$) the smaller is the number of firms that one will observe in such a cross-section study.

Notice, however, that equations (22) and (24) tell us that industries with smaller demand elasticities will, with any given number of firms, be characterized by a higher value of the index of research intensity. The lower demand elasticity leads, with a given degree of concentration, to higher markups; equilibrium is maintained not by entry, but by firms spending enough on R & D to forestall entry (essentially by spending all of their profits on R & D).

These foregoing propositions have an unmistakable Schumpeterian flavour to them. Since R & D involves fixed costs we cannot expect an industry that engages in it to be characterized by perfect competition. Nevertheless, *effective* competition is maintained by firms entering the market. Restrictive practices in our model, such as market price exceeding the unit cost of production (equation (17)), must be understood in the context of what Schumpeter called a 'perennial gale

small). To get a feel for orders of magnitude it may be noted that for firms in the United States in 1961 employing more than 5000 persons, Z was on average 5.2 per cent, for those employing 1000–5000 persons it was 2.2 per cent and for those employing less than 1000 persons it was 2 per cent (see Nelson et al., 1967, p. 67).

of creative destruction'. Our analysis has shown that the number of firms in an industry is no measure of the extent of this effective competition. Nor does the size of the market directly influence the number of firms in an industry for, as equation (24) makes clear, the equilibrium number of firms depends solely on the elasticities of the demand and innovation functions. If these elasticities are constant, as in (7) and (9), the equilibrium number of firms can be calculated directly, and is independent of the size of the market. However, the size of the market does influence the extent to which process innovation occurs in a market economy. To see this sharply suppose that market demand and innovation functions satisfy (7) and (9). If we now use these functional forms in the equilibrium conditions (17), (18) and (21), routine calculations yield their solution as:

$$n^* = \varepsilon(1+\alpha)/\alpha, \tag{25}$$

$$Q^* = \frac{\varepsilon(1+\alpha)}{\alpha^2\beta}[\sigma\alpha^{2\varepsilon}\beta^{\varepsilon-1}\varepsilon^{-\varepsilon}(1+\alpha)^{-(1+\varepsilon)}]^{(1+\alpha)/[\varepsilon-\alpha(1-\varepsilon)]} \tag{26}$$

and

$$x^* = [\sigma\alpha^{2\varepsilon}\beta^{\varepsilon-1}\varepsilon^{-\varepsilon}(1+\alpha)^{-(1+\varepsilon)}]^{1/[\varepsilon-\alpha(1-\varepsilon)]}. \tag{27}$$

Now it will be recalled that (17) and (18) are merely the first-order conditions for each firm's profit maximizing exercise. In Appendix 1 we shall note that for (25)–(27) to represent a market equilibrium we shall need to suppose that $\varepsilon > \alpha(1-\varepsilon)$. Otherwise an equilibrium does not exist. Assume then that $\varepsilon > \alpha(1-\varepsilon)$. (This, as we noted earlier, is trivially true if market demand is inelastic (i.e. $\varepsilon > 1$).) It is then immediate from (27) that the greater is the size of the market (i.e. the greater is σ), the greater is R & D expenditure per firm and, therefore, the greater is (unit) cost reduction. And so is industry output in equilibrium the greater.[12] Likewise, the costlier is R & D technology (i.e. the greater is β), the smaller is industry output. This is precisely what intuition suggests. However, note that the costlier is R & D technology the *smaller* is equilibrium R & D expenditure per firm (and hence industry-wide R & D expenditure) if demand is *elastic*; but it is *greater* if demand is *inelastic*. It is this last which is not intuitively immediate.

[12] The late Jacob Schmookler, in a series of writings, stressed the importance of the growth in demand for a product in stimulating R & D activity designed towards cost reduction and quality improvement. See, for example Schmookler (1962).

It will be recalled that equations (25)–(27) have been arrived at on the supposition that firms in equilibrium earn negligible profits. It is then clear that if $\varepsilon(1+\alpha)/\alpha$ is an integer, a free-entry symmetric equilibrium exists, where firms in equilibrium earn precisely zero profits and where the number of firms in equilibrium is given by (25).[13] Now, while the number of firms must be an integer, $\varepsilon(1+\alpha)/\alpha$ will not be, except by fluke. However, if ε/α is 'large', the largest integer less than $\varepsilon(1+\alpha)/\alpha$ is 'large'. Then condition (25) suggests that if we set $n^* = [\varepsilon(1+\alpha)/\alpha]$ (i.e. the largest integer less than $\varepsilon(1+\alpha)\,\alpha$), then such a number of firms can sustain an equilibrium, in the sense that if each chooses the pair $(x^*, Q^*/n^*)$ which satisfies conditions (26) and (27), each will have maximized its profits given the choice of others, and its maximized profit level will be so low that condition (19) will also be satisfied, thus deterring further entry into the industry. In Appendix 1, we shall note that this is in fact the case. By construction we shall note that a free-entry symmetric equilibrium exists if ε/α is 'large', and that by choosing either α to be sufficiently small or ε to be sufficiently large we can force the equilibrium level of profit per firm to be as small as we care to make, so as to allow the zero profit condition (21) to be as good an approximation as we want.[14] However, it should be noted that the two limiting values of α and ε lead to different characteristics of industry equilibrium. To see this use equation (24) in equation (17) to obtain

$$p(Q^*)/c(x^*) = 1 + \alpha(x^*). \tag{28}$$

Assume that α and ε are both constants. *Notice now that* $\varepsilon/n^* \to 0$ *as* $\alpha \to 0$, *and from* (28) *we conclude that* $p(Q^*) \to c(x^*) = \beta$ *as* $\alpha \to 0$. *In the limit, as* $\alpha \to 0$, *the present model reduces to the conventional model of a perfectly competitive industry.* However, $\varepsilon/n^* \to \alpha/(1+\alpha)$ as $\varepsilon \to \infty$ and in particular, equation (28) implies that *if industry demand is highly inelastic market equilibrium sustains a great many firms. Nevertheless the ratio of market price to marginal cost of production can be much greater than unity.*

Earlier we noted that it was natural to regard n^{-1} as the index of

[13] Since we have already supposed that $\varepsilon > \alpha(1-\varepsilon)$, it follows that $\varepsilon(1+\alpha)/\alpha > 1$.

[14] For equation (17) to make sense n^* must exceed $\varepsilon(Q^*)$. But if ε and α are both constants, then if either α is 'small' or ε is 'large', $n^* = [\varepsilon(1+\alpha)/\alpha] > \varepsilon$. Here, and in what follows, bold square brackets round a number will denote the largest integer not exceeding the number.

industrial concentration for the model at hand. Indeed, unguided intuition might suggest that if the equilibrium number of firms is large the industry resembles the conventional competitive model. The foregoing result suggests that this is wrong. In fact several authors (e.g. Kalecki, 1954) have used instead the ratio of product price to 'prime cost' (i.e. $p(Q)/c(x)$ here) as a measure of the *degree of monopoly* in an industry. Now, a glance at equation (28) tells us that an industry could at the same time be characterized by a low degree of concentration (large n^*) and a high degree of monopoly (large $p(Q^*)/c(x^*)$). This would be so if both ε and α are 'large', so that $n^* \equiv [\varepsilon(1+\alpha)/\alpha] \simeq \varepsilon$, and therefore, n^* is 'large'. Indeed, presently we shall note that for the model at hand the degree of monopoly is a much better index of market imperfection than the degree of concentration.

Now, in a cross-section study of industries differing from one another in terms of the elasticity of the unit cost function, we would note that those facing a larger elasticity are characterized by a greater degree of monopoly. If these industries face the same demand elasticity, equation (17) tells us that those characterized by a greater degree of monopoly contain a smaller number of firms. But then equation (22) tells us that these in turn are associated with a higher index of research intensity, Z^*. The question arises whether R & D expenditure per firm is higher. This in general is hard to tell. However, suppose α and ε are both constant, so that equilibrium is characterized by (25)–(27). It should now be noted from (27) that if α is 'small' and demand is inelastic (i.e. $\varepsilon > 1$), $\partial x^*/\partial\alpha > 0$, so that the greater is α the greater is R & D expenditure per firm in oligopoly equilibrium. But this in turn means that cost reduction is greater in such industries *Somewhat paradoxically, then, we would observe greater cost reduction in those industries that are characterized by a higher degree of monopoly power.*

It remains for us to compare the performance of the free entry oligopoly equilibrium with that of the socially managed industry. Continue to assume that $p(Q)$ and $c(x)$ satisfy (7) and (9) respectively. We then note from (11) and (26) that $Q_s > Q^*$. Market equilibrium output is less than the socially optimal output, a result which is not immediately obvious since one may have thought that the pressure of competition (free entry) would drive the market price down to a level below what is socially optimal, by forcing each firm to invest more in R & D than is desirable for society. The question then arises whether cost reduction is greater or less in the oligopoly market than in the socially optimal one. On comparing (10) and (27) one notes that $x^* \gtrless x_s$ as $(n^*)^{-\varepsilon} \gtrless (1+\alpha)$. It follows that $x^* < x_s$, and hence that there is insufficient cost reduction in the oligopoly industry. But industry-wide R & D expenditure in the market economy is n^*x^* and the question arises how this compares with x_s. On using (10), (25) and (27) it is now easy to confirm that $n^*x^* \gtrless x_s$ as $(n^*)^{\alpha(\varepsilon-1)} \gtrless (1+\alpha)$. This implies that if ε is 'large' (i.e. demand is highly inelastic), then $n^*x^* > x_s$ and, therefore, that total R & D expenditure in the market economy exceeds the socially optimal level. *Thus the market economy may be characterized both by excessive expenditure on R & D* (n^*x^*) *and too low a rate of technical progress* (x^*) *as compared to the socially managed one.* The point of course is that the market encourages too much duplication here. To see this sharply we may note from (10) that $x_s \to (\alpha\beta)^{1/(1+\alpha)}$ as $\varepsilon \to \infty$. However, from equation (27) it is immediate that $x^* \to 0$ as $\varepsilon \to \infty$, but $n^*x^* \to \infty$. *Thus welfare loss due to competition is unbounded as* $\varepsilon \to \infty$, *even though each firm serves an infinitesimal fraction of a finite demand as* $\varepsilon \to \infty$.

Matters are quite different though for the other limit economy. On comparing equations (10) and (27) it is immediate that $x^* \to 0$ and $x_s \to 0$ as $\alpha \to 0$. Note as well that as $\alpha \to 0$ we have $n^*x^* \to 0$, even though $n^* \to \infty$. Therefore, in the limit, as $\alpha \to 0$, welfare loss due to the industry being privately managed is nil. As we noted earlier, the industry in this case is the conventional competitive one, characterized by a lack of distortion. Welfare loss due to competition in this limit economy is nil.

(3) Oligopoly with Barriers to Entry

It has been our purpose so far to explore the implications of an endogenous market structure on the amount of innovative activity. We have captured this in our model via the free-entry condition (13). Entry sustains effective competition. This, as we noted in the introduction, implies that the pace of innovative activity must be traced neither to the degree of concentration, nor to the degree of monopoly in the industry in question, but to more basic ingredients such as demand conditions, R & D technology, the nature of the capital market, etc. Nevertheless, it is the case that several authors have claimed a slowing down in the intensity of innovations in advanced capitalist economies, and have traced it to an increasingly monopolistic character of capitalism.[15]

Now, we have already noted on several occasions that the degree of monopoly, $p(Q)/c(x)$, is not an explanatory variable. Nor, if there is free entry, is the number of active firms an explanatory variable. Indeed, we have noted that with free entry into the industry it can readily happen that industries characterized by a greater degree of monopoly are *more* innovative, *not less*. It is then worthwhile inquiring into the relationship between the degree of monopoly and the reduction in the unit cost of production in an environment where there are *barriers to entry*. We can then see whether allowing new firms to enter would result in greater cost reduction in equilibrium. Thus let the number of firms be exogenously given, say n. Formally, $[(Q_1^*, x_1^*), \ldots, (Q_i^*, x_i^*), \ldots, (Q_n^*, x_n^*)]$ is an equilibrium if for $i = 1, \ldots, n$

$$\left.\begin{aligned} &\left[p\left(\sum_{j \neq i} Q_j^* + Q_i^*\right) - c(x_i^*)\right] Q_i^* - x_i^* \\ &\geq \left[p\left(\sum_{j \neq i} Q_j^* + Q_i\right) - c(x_i)\right] Q_i - x_i \quad \text{for all} \;\; x_i, Q_i \geq 0. \end{aligned}\right\} \tag{29}$$

Since we are interested only in symmetric equilibria, the foregoing definition of an equilibrium implies that conditions (17) and (18) must be satisfied, which we rewrite here as

$$p(Q^*)\,[1 - \varepsilon\,(Q^*)/n] = c(x^*) \tag{30}$$

and

$$-\,c'(x^*)\,Q^*/n = 1. \tag{31}$$

Since n is given, there are only two unknowns, Q^* and x^*, to be determined from (30) and (31). Suppose, to get explicit solutions, that $p(Q)$ and $c(x)$ satisfy (7) and (9) respectively. From (30) it is clear that since n is exogenously given in the present analysis, we must

15 'Another (reason for the slowing down of the growth of advanced capitalist economies) is the hampering of application of new inventions which results from the increasingly monopolistic character of capitalism' (Kalecki, 1954, p. 159).

assume $n > \varepsilon$ (otherwise (30) and (31) will not possess a solution). It must also be supposed that $n \leq \varepsilon(1 + \alpha)/\alpha$, since otherwise the solution of equation (30) and (31) will result in firms making negative profits and so they would not represent equilibrium conditions. Finally, we shall need to suppose that $\varepsilon > \alpha(1 - \varepsilon)$, a condition we required earlier (for details see Appendix 1). Routine calculations now enable one to solve equations (30) and (31), and they yield

$$x^* = [\sigma(\alpha/n)^{\varepsilon} \beta^{\varepsilon - 1}(1 - \varepsilon/n)]^{1/[\varepsilon - \alpha(1 - \varepsilon)]} \tag{32}$$

and

$$Q^* = (n/\alpha\beta)\, [\sigma(\alpha/n)^{\varepsilon} \beta^{\varepsilon - 1}(1 - \varepsilon/n)]^{(1 + \alpha)/[\varepsilon - \alpha(1 - \varepsilon)]} \tag{33}$$

It will be noticed immediately from equation (33) that in the admissible range $(\varepsilon, \varepsilon(1 + \alpha)/\alpha]$, Q^* is an increasing function of n. *Industry output therefore increases with the number of firms.* Consequently product price decreases. This is the advantage of greater competition. Moreover, from equation (30) it is clear that the degree of monopoly declines as the number of firms in the industry increases. The question that we began with is whether an increase in the number of firms results in greater innovation (i.e. greater cost reduction). From equation (32) it is immediate that the answer is 'no'. *If the number of firms is increased, each firm in equilibrium spends less on R & D, and so unit cost of production in equilibrium is higher.* However, it is easy to confirm from equation (32) that total R & D expenditure, nx^*, increases with the number of firms. The point is that while the industry spends more on R & D as a consequence of increased competition, each firm spends less. The extra expenditure is essentially wasted in duplication. In fact a comparison of equations (10) and (32) shows that $x^* < x_s$. We conclude that for the model at hand (unit) cost reduction is insufficient in a market economy whether or not there are barriers to entry; and consequently, market price for the product is higher than is socially desirable.

This is brought out most forcefully if we consider a monopolist protected by entry barriers. In this case there is, of course, no duplication in R & D. Nevertheless, as we have seen, the monopolist engages in less R & D activity than is socially desirable. This remains true even if the government in a socially managed industry is forced to raise its revenue for R & D expenditure through benefit taxation.

However, the *speed* with which firms carry out their R & D work and, consequently, the *rapidity* with which technological innovations take place in a market economy would appear to be greater if there is free entry into R & D activity, than if active firms were protected by entry barriers into the research sector. In Sec. 4 we shall study the implication of free entry into the research sector on the speed with which R & D is undertaken. For a more complete discussion of the issues see Dasgupta and Stiglitz (1980).

3. NON-CONCAVITIES IN THE VALUE OF PROCESS INNOVATION AND THE DEGREE OF RISK-TAKING

It has already been noted that the indirect social utility function $V(c)$ in equation (3) is a declining convex function (see Fig. 4). We revert to the basic model of Sec. 1 and suppose that c is the unit cost of production associated with the existing best-practice technique. Our aim is to explore the implications of the convexity of $V(c)$ on the choice among risky research projects. To begin with, suppose there are two research strategies to choose from, one of which reduces the cost of production to c^* with certainty, whilst the other, if successful, reduces it to $\tilde{c}$ (with $\tilde{c} < c^* < c$). If unsuccessful, the cost of production remains at c. But suppose the *expected* cost reduction associated with the risky research projects is $c - c^*$. If society's welfare criteria are derived with a view to maximizing expected social utility then if the costs of the two research projects are the same, it would prefer the risky project to the riskless one. This is depicted in Fig. 4.[16] Let us now generalize this example.

Suppose that research projects are indexed by $\alpha(\bar{\alpha} \geq \alpha \geq 0)$. Project-$\alpha$ has probability $h(\alpha)$ of success. If successful, the unit cost of production reduces to $c(\alpha)$. If unsuccessful, the cost of production remains at c. The projects are so labelled that we suppose, without loss of generality, that $c'(\alpha) < 0$. For simplicity, continue to assume that this family of research projects has the same mean outcome; i.e.

$$\left.\begin{array}{l} E\,[c(\alpha)] = c^* = h(\alpha)\,c(\alpha) + [1 - h(\alpha)]\,c, \\ \bar{\alpha} \geq \alpha \geq 0 \quad \text{and} \quad h(0) = 1. \end{array}\right\} \tag{34}$$

[16] If R & D cost is too high society would, presumably, not wish to engage in any research at all, and continue to rely on the c-technology.

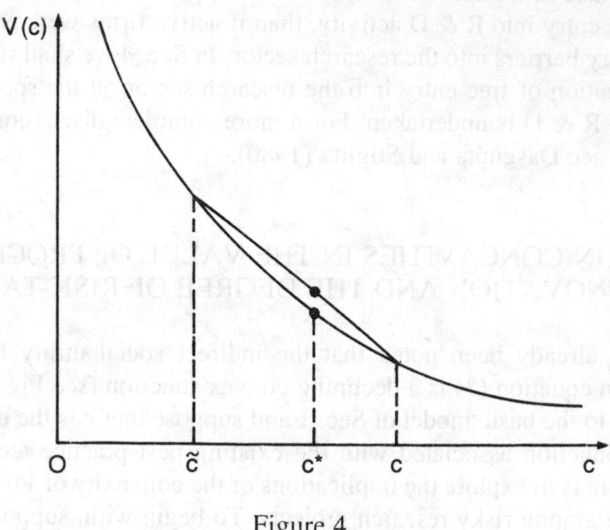

Figure 4

(34) implies that $c(0) = c^*$ and hence $\alpha = 0$ is the riskless project. If we differentiate (34) we obtain

$$c'(\alpha)h(\alpha) = [c - c(\alpha)]\, h'(\alpha). \tag{35}$$

Consequently $h'(\alpha) < 0$. Therefore a higher value of α is associated with a more risky project.

R & D expenditure associated with project-α is $R(\alpha)$. Quite obviously $R(\alpha) > 0$, $\alpha \geq 0$. If $R'(\alpha) \leq 0$, nothing of interest remains to be said. Since $\bar{\alpha}$ is the riskiest project available (the highest value of α in the given family of available research projects) the planner ought to choose $\bar{\alpha}$ (or undertake no research at all). Consequently we consider the other special case; where $R'(\alpha) > 0$. For obvious reasons, suppose in addition that $R''(\alpha) > 0$.

In what follows, we take it that $R(0)$ is 'small', so that the optimum involves some R & D activity. Now if the planner were to choose project-α, expected net social benefits, $E(\alpha)$, would be

$$E(\alpha) \equiv h(\alpha)V\,[c(\alpha)] + [1 - h(\alpha)]V(c) - R(\alpha). \tag{36}$$

Notice that unless we impose further structure on the functions $h(\cdot)$ and $V(\cdot)$, one cannot ensure that $E(\cdot)$ is concave. If it is not, then in general the government will need to conduct global cost-benefit analysis of the 'random' research projects.

Having indicated the problem let us simplify and suppose that (36) is strictly concave. Assuming optimal α lies strictly between 0 and $\bar{\alpha}$ we note that on using condition (35), the necessary and sufficient condition for optimality is:

$$-h(\alpha)\,c'(\alpha)\left(-V'[c(\alpha)]-\frac{\{V[c(\alpha)]-V(c)\}}{[c-c(\alpha)]}\right)=R'(\alpha). \tag{37}$$

The social benefit-cost criterion (37) has an unusual simplicity about it. $-h(\alpha)\,c'(\alpha)$ is the expected marginal reduction in production cost —when a marginally more risky research project is chosen. What the LHS of condition (37) says is that the marginal benefit of stepping up R & D expenditure is $-h(\alpha)\,c'(\alpha)$ times the difference between the *marginal* social benefit from cost reduction $\{-V'[c(\alpha)]\}$ and the *average* social benefit from cost reduction, $\{V[c(\alpha)]-V(c)\}/[c-c(\alpha)]$.

To look at the matter another way, we know in advance that

$$-V'[c(\alpha)]>\{V[c(\alpha)]-V(c)\}/[c-c(\alpha)]$$

(since $V(c)$ is convex and declining). What (37) says is that at an optimum the difference between marginal and average returns ought to be $-R'(\alpha)/h(\alpha)\,c'(\alpha)$.

We have established that a social planner will wish to engage in risky research projects. But then so will a pure monopolist. To see this suppose that marginal revenue from sales is a declining function of sales. Then it is simple to confirm that the monopolist's maximized profit from sales is a convex and declining function of his unit cost of production. Consequently, if the monopolist is concerned with maximizing expected profits, an argument identical to the one we have presented above comes into play. The monopolist too favours risk.

The natural question to ask is whether the monopolist is inclined to engage in the optimum degree of risk and, if not, whether one can establish a bias in his behaviour towards risk. In Appendix 2, we demonstrate that if the family of research projects is restricted to the class we have discussed above, the monopolist undertakes insufficient risk in his R & D effort and invests too little in research and development. But then clearly this would be true even if the family of available research projects were characterized by a slight lowering of expected cost reduction, $(c - c^*)$, with increasing risk (i.e. increase in α). In this case one would observe greater cost reduction *on average* if the industry is controlled by a private monopolist, than if it were socially controlled. The point about this observation is that while cost reduction is a 'good thing' the monopolist, paradoxically, would on average be reducing costs too much, even though his R & D expenditure would be less than that which is socially desirable.

These pure economic environments are the easiest to analyse. With free entry the analysis appears to be unusually complex. But in an oligopolistic environment the market power of a producer increases as his cost advantage over his rivals increases. There is then an a-priori presumption that competition may encourage excessive risk-taking on the part of producers engaged in process innovation. We have been unable to settle the issue when there is free entry into an industry.

4. MARKET STRUCTURE AND THE SPEED OF RESEARCH

We are here concerned with the speed of research, and we continue to illustrate matters in the context of process innovation. Revert to the basic model of Sec. 1 and suppose c to be the unit cost of production associated with the existing best practice technique. As in Secs 1 and 2, we simplify and hypothesize highly goal orientated research. Research now is taken to consist of solving a sequence of problems that will enable the commodity to be produced at a unit cost $c^*(c^* < c)$. There is no uncertainty.[17] If a research unit invests x at $t = 0$ it solves the entire set of problems at date $T(x)$, where $T'(x) < 0$ and $T''(x) > 0$ with $T(x) \to 0$ as $x \to \infty$ and $T(x) \to \infty$ at $x \to 0$ (see Fig. 5).[18]

Consider first competitive conditions. We suppose that currently the market price of the commodity is c. It is understood that the first firm to make the invention is awarded a patent of fixed duration. If there are several winners they share the patent. We need not specify

[17] Models incorporating uncertainty in the date of invention have been discussed in Stiglitz (1970), Dasgupta, Heal and Majumdar (1977), Kamien and Schwartz (1978), Loury (1977) and Dasgupta and Stiglitz (1978).

[18] That is, all potential research units are of identical ability. This assumption is made solely for expositional case, and can be relaxed in the obvious manner.

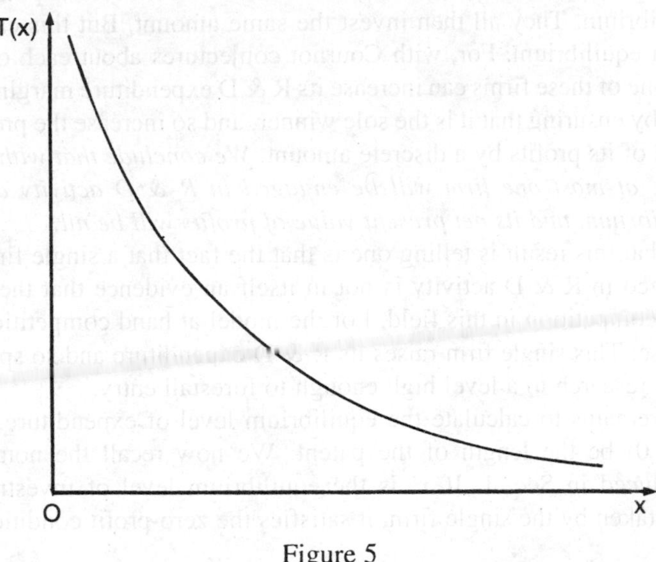

Figure 5

whether in this latter case the winners propose to collude by forming a cartel, or whether they play a Cournot game, as in Sec. 2. All that we need to postulate is that each winner enjoys a positive flow of profits while the patent lasts. It follows that firms may well have an incentive to engage in R & D activity. We take it that each firm knows the R & D strategy of the other firms.

Firms are assumed to be able to borrow freely to finance their R & D activity at a competitive rate of interest $r\,(>0)$. Since by hypothesis $T'(x) < 0$, each firm engaged in R & D will establish only one research unit. In order to explore game equilibria with free entry we shall, as earlier, suppose that firms entertain Cournot conjectures regarding those that are engaged in R & D activity. However, we shall wish to capture the fact that firms engaged in R & D fear the threat of entry by potential entrants. Therefore, it will be supposed that active firms entertain Stackelberg conjectures regarding potential entrants; i.e. they work on the reaction functions of potential entrants. This latter assumption implies that under free entry into R & D activity an equilibrium is characterized by each firm receiving zero present-value of profits, and the former implies that only future winners are engaged in R & D.

Now suppose that more than one firm is active at a potential equilibrium. They all then invest the same amount. But this cannot be an equilibrium. For, with Cournot conjectures about each other, any one of these firms can increase its R & D expenditure marginally, thereby ensuring that it is the sole winner, and so increase the present value of its profits by a discrete amount. *We conclude that with free entry, at most one firm will be engaged in R & D activity at an equilibrium, and its net present value of profits will be nil.*

What this result is telling one is that the fact that a single firm is engaged in R & D activity is not in itself an evidence that there is little competition in this field. For the model at hand competition is intense. This single firm raises its R & D expenditure and so speeds up its research to a level high enough to forestall entry.

It remains to calculate the equilibrium level of expenditure. Let $T^*(>0)$ be the length of the patent. We now recall the notation introduced in Sec. 1. If x^* is the equilibrium level of investment undertaken by the single firm, it satisfies the zero-profit condition

$$(\pi_c/r)\,(1-e^{-rT^*})e^{-rT(x)} = \bullet x\,. \tag{38}$$

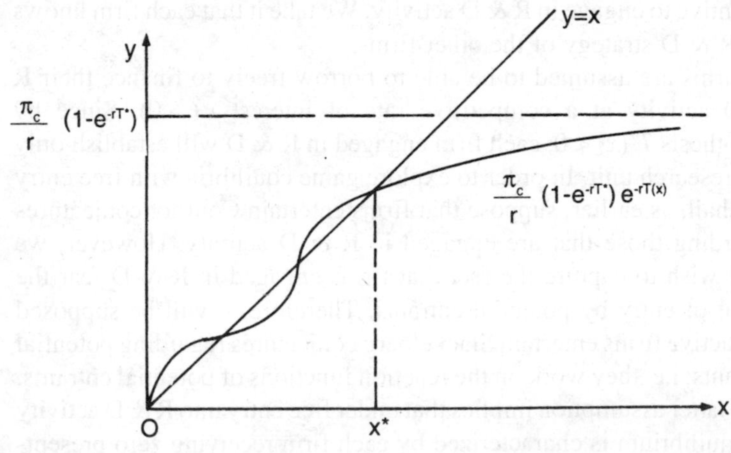

Figure 6

The date of invention is $T(x^*)$. One notes first that $x = 0$ is a solution of equation (38). One notes as well that the LHS of equation (38) is not necessarily a concave function of x. In Fig. 6 we have drawn both the LHS and the RHS of equation (38). As the figure makes clear, the largest solution of (38) is the equilibrium level of R & D expenditure, x^*. An equilibrium therefore exists and it is unique. A glance at Fig. 6 also shows that in a cross-section study of industries with the same R & D technology those characterized by greater demand (i.e. greater π_c) will sustain a greater speed of research.[19]

We now compare the competitive outcome with the socially optimal speed of research. We take it that r is regarded as appropriate to use for discounting social benefits and costs. The social planner is then concerned with choosing x so as to maximize

$$\left[\frac{\pi_s}{r} e^{-rT(x)} - x\right] \tag{39}$$

Notice again that (39) is not in general a concave function of x. However, given the assumptions that we have made about $T(x)$ it is immediate that (39) has a maximum. Let x_s be the optimum R & D expenditure. Then provided it is positive it satisfies the cost-benefit rule

$$-T'(x)\,\pi_s e^{-rT(x)} = 1. \tag{40}$$

It will be recalled that $\pi_s > \pi_c$ (inequality (2)). But a glance at (38) and (40) tells us that one can easily have $x^* > x_s$. When this is so the single firm engaged in R & D activity is forced to incur excessive R & D expenditure because of the *threat* of competition. Market forces encourage too high a speed of research.

The central result of this section, that under free entry, a Cournot–Nash equilibrium for the model considered here sustains at most one firm, survives if we introduce uncertainty in the special form where all firms are obliged to follow the *same* steps in solving the problems

[19] To obtain a feel for orders of magnitude it may be noted that in large corporations R & D projects are often expected to be completed in four to five years and that many such projects involve not undue risk, in many cases the estimated probability of success exceeding 0.8 see Mansfield (1967). Notable examples of risky R & D projects would appear to be in the pharmaceutical industry (see Schwartzman, 1977). For a theoretical exploration of the relationship between market structure, risk-taking in R & D, and the speed of research, see Dasgupta and Stiglitz (1977; 1980).

that are necessary to solve in order to make the c^*-technology viable (i.e. if all research units face the same decision tree). This means that given the pace of R & D activity of the remaining firms a given firm can guarantee that it is the first to invent by choosing a sufficiently high pace of research, even though it is still unable to say at which date the sequence of tasks will be completed by its research unit. With this form of uncertainty it is immediate that at most one firm will incur R & D expenditure at an equilibrium.

It will be granted that the foregoing postulates undue interdependence of research strategies amongst firms. In the sequel to this paper (Dasgupta and Stiglitz, 1978) we move to the opposite extreme and suppose complete independence. In such a case it is clear enough in advance that an equilibrium may well sustain several firms competing in R & D; for no firm can guarantee itself to be the winner.

The point then is this. A key element in the determination of the number of firms competing in R & D activity at an equilibrium is the degree of correlation in the probabilities of success. Typically one would expect the number to be small when correlation is great. But the number of firms engaged in R & D is not an appropriate index for measuring the degree of competition. As we have seen, competition may result in a single firm being so engaged; and engaged in excessive expenditure, leading to excessive speed in research effort.

5. CONCLUDING REMARKS

There is now a fairly large empirical literature investigating various aspects of R & D activity and relating them to the structure of industries in which such activity is undertaken. It is therefore particularly surprising to note the paucity of theoretical explorations in this area. Moreover, so far as we are aware the majority of such explorations have been directed at the behaviour of a single firm engaged in R & D in the midst of an exogenously given environment. In order to make contact with some of the empirical findings and to obtain a less incomplete understanding of these matters it is necessary to move beyond the analysis of a single firm and to consider a set of interacting firms and, if one is interested in the long run as well, to postulate an endogenous market structure. What results is a game environment, and in this paper we have attempted to come to grips with a few of the traditional issues in the theory of industrial organization in the context of a set of simple constructions. In investigating R & D activity in a market economy we have throughout made use of the concept of a game equilibrium. It is, of course, well known that both the existence and characteristics of such equilibria depend on what types of action agents are postulated to choose and on the conjectures that are entertained by agents regarding the responses by other agents to their choice. In this paper we have supposed that firms choose quantities (viz. output and R & D expenditure levels). As regards conjectures the simplest by far to analyse are Cournot ones, namely that other agents do not respond to the given agent's choice. We have, for the most part, supposed such conjectures. However, while plausible in certain circumstances (e.g. in the model of Sec. 2), such conjectures are not plausible in many others. For example, the reader can readily check that an equilibrium does not exist in the model of Sec. 4, if all firms entertain Cournot conjectures about *all* other firms. We have consequently resorted to a set of hybrid conjectures on the part of firms in the analysis of Sec. 4; conjectures that are a-priori, not implausible. There is a clear need, though, of a study of the characteristics of oligopoly equilibria under more sophisticated conjectures on the part of firms and to see how these characteristics vary as conjectures are varied.[20]

One of the most oft discussed issues in the industrial organization literature has been the relationship between the size of firms and the pace of R & D activity. We have discussed some aspects of this issue in our introduction and in Sec. 2. Now if firms are forced to finance their R & D expenditure from internal funds there is a clear presumption that industrial concentration is positively correlated with R & D activity. The model of Sec. 2, being timeless, is consistent with the internal finance hypothesis. However, in Sec. 4, we supposed a perfect capital market with a view to demonstrating that one does not need to resort to the internal finance hypothesis if one wants to argue that only a limited number of firms will typically be engaged in competing R & D activities. Nor in fact, as we have shown, does one need to postulate non-classical goals on the part of firms in order to make contact with some of the empirical findings. We have

[20] For an important analysis of oligopoly equilibrium with barriers to entry, where the focus of attention is on alternative specifications of the conjectures entertained by firms, see Marschak and Selton (1974).

throughout formalized the market economy as one in which firms are engaged in games with complete information. In such contexts it hardly makes sense to postulate anything other than profits as a firm's goals. Matters are different if incomplete information is postulated for firms; and a particularly interesting avenue that has recently been explored (see e.g. Winter, 1971; and Nelson, Winter and Schuette, 1976) consists in supposing in addition that agents have only limited ability to solve complicated maximization problems. Endowed only with 'bounded rationality', firms are postulated to follow some 'satisficing' course of action, and to search locally for improvements if existing courses of action cease to produce satisfactory results.

Quite apart from any details that may be found interesting, the central conclusions of our analysis would appear to be:

(1) Even when one regards industrial structure to be endognous, theoretical considerations are consistent with the empirical finding that when the degree of concentration in industries is small, industry-wide R & D effort is positively correlated with concentration (Sec. 2).

(2) High degrees of concentration are by themselves not an evidence of lack of effective competition (Sec. 2).

(3) When the degree of concentration in industries with free entry is small, R & D effort per firm (and therefore cost reduction) is often positively correlated with concentration. Moreover, the degree of concentration is positively correlated with the degree of monopoly (Sec. 2).

(4) Both optimal R & D expenditure and R & D expenditure per firm in a market economy increase with the size of the market. They decrease with increasing costs associated with R & D technology if demand is elastic and increase with increasing costs if demand is inelastic (Sec. 2).

(5) If there are barriers to entry an increase in the number of firms would result in a decrease in R & D expenditure per firm in a market economy, although industry output would increase, and therefore, the degree of monopoly would decrease (Sec. 2).

(6) There is some presumption that cost-reducing in an industry in a market economy, even when there is free entry, is less than the socially optimal level (Sec. 2). However,

(7) If demand is highly inelastic, *total* R & D expenditure in an industry with free entry exceeds the socially optimal level (Sec. 2). (6) and (7) imply.

(8) There may be excessive duplication of research effort in a market economy in the sense that industry-wide R & D expenditure exceeds the socially optimal level even though cost reduction is lower. In particular, an industry may be characterized by a very low degree of concentration (i.e. a large number of firms) and at the same time engage in a great deal of social waste.

(9) In the case of process innovation a good case can be made for encouraging investment in risky research projects, even if society is risk-averse (Sec. 3).

(10) A pure monopolist (i.e. one protected by entry barriers) appears to have insufficient incentive (a) to undertake R & D expenditure (Sec. 2) and (b) to engage in risky research ventures (Sec. 3 and Appendix 2).

(11) Since the market power of a firm increases as its cost advantage over its rivals increases there is a presumption that competitive markets encourage firms to engage in overly risky research projects (Sec. 3).

(12) If the first firm to succeed is awarded most of the reward for invention, then to the extent the risks that firms undertake are positively correlated, pressure of competition will ensure that only a few firms engage in R & D activity; in extreme cases at most one firm will be engaged in research (Sec. 4).

(13) But the observation that only a few firms are engaged in R & D is not in itself an evidence that a market economy sustains too little R & D activity (Sec. 4). In particular,

(14) Pressure of competition may result in excessive speed in research (Sec. 4), and in general,

(15) There is no presumption that a market economy has a tendency to generate insufficient information.

APPENDIX 1

We shall by construction locate conditions under which a free-entry symmetric equilibrium exists for the model of Sec. 2, when $p(Q)$ and

$c(x)$ satisfy (7) and (9) in the text. In doing this we reverse the order followed in the text and suppose first that there are barriers to entry, so that n is exogenously given.

Consider the solution (32) and (33) of the two first-order conditions (30) and (31). For it to be real-valued one must suppose that $n > \varepsilon$. Let us do so. It will have been noted that the pair $(x^*, Q^*/n)$ in (32) and (33) is the unique solution of the (interior) first-order conditions for the representative profit maximizing firm when it assumes that each of the remaining firms chooses Q^*/n as its output level. We must now locate conditions under which the representative firm earns non-negative profits when it chooses $(x^*, Q^*/n)$.

Let $\pi(x^*, Q^*/n)$ denote the level of its profit. Then $\pi(x^*, Q^*/n) = [p(Q^*) - c(x^*)]\, Q^*/n - x^*$. For this to be non-negative it is necessary and sufficient that

$$[p(Q^*) - c(x^*)]\, Q^*/nx^* \geq 1. \qquad \text{(A1)}$$

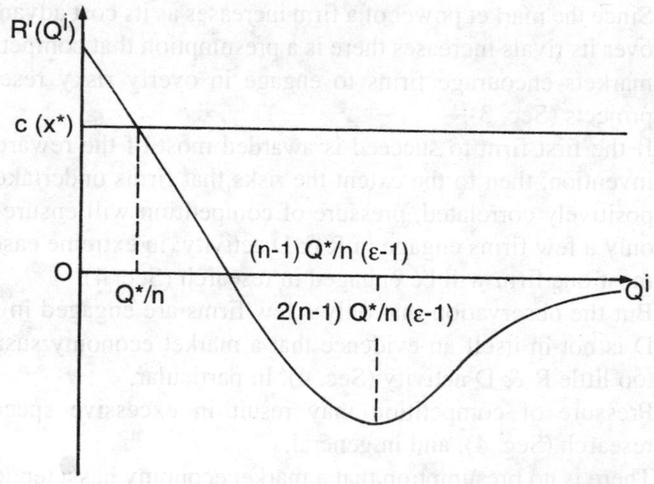

Figure 7 Marginal revenue schedule, $R'(Q_i)$, of firm i, when gross revenue,

$$R(Q_i) = \sigma[Q_i + (n-1)Q^*/n]^{-\varepsilon} Q_i,$$

where Q^* is equilibrium industry output, $\varepsilon > 1$ and $n > \varepsilon$. x^* is equilibrium R & D expenditure per firm.

If we now appeal to the functional forms (7) and (9) and use (32) and (33), routine calculations yield

$$[p\,(Q^*) - c\,(x^*)]\; Q^*/nx^* = \varepsilon/\alpha(x - \varepsilon). \qquad \text{(A2)}$$

It will be noted that for $n > \varepsilon$, the RHS of (A2) is a decreasing function of n and is equal to unity at $n = \varepsilon\,(1 + \alpha)/\alpha$. Combining (A1) and (A2) we therefore conclude that

$$\pi(x^*, Q^*/n) \geq 0 \quad \text{if } \varepsilon < n \leq \varepsilon(I + \alpha)/\alpha. \qquad \text{(A3)}$$

(A3) therefore instructs us to suppose that $\varepsilon < n \leq \varepsilon\,(1 + \alpha)/\alpha$. Let us do so.

It remains to find conditions under which the profit function, $\{p\,[\,(n-1)Q^*/n + Q_i] - c(x_i)\,\}\,Q_i - x_i$, for firm i is concave in the neighbourhood of the point $x_i = x^*$, $Q_i = Q^*/n$. In fact it can be readily checked that if $p\,(Q)$ and $c\,(x)$ have the functional forms (7) and (9) and x^* and Q^*/n are given by (32) and (33), the profit function of the representative firm satisfies the second-order conditions at x^* and Q^*/n if $\varepsilon > \alpha\,(1 - \varepsilon)$ (i.e. if $\varepsilon(1 + \alpha)/\alpha > 1$). Thus, $(x^*, Q^*/n)$ is the global profit maximizing choice for the representative firm if each of the other firms chooses $(x^*, Q^*/n)$ (see Fig. 7). We have therefore proved:

Theorem 1. If $p(Q)$ and $c(x)$ satisfy (7) and (9) and if n is a positive integer, then a symmetric Cournot equilibrium amongst n firms exists if

$$\text{(i) } \varepsilon < n \leq \varepsilon(1 + \alpha)/\alpha, \quad \text{and (ii) } \varepsilon(1 + \alpha)/\alpha > 1$$

Now clearly $\varepsilon(1 + \alpha)/\alpha > 1$ if $\varepsilon > 1$. What we have therefore shown is that if $\varepsilon < n \leq \varepsilon(1 + \alpha)/\alpha$, then a symmetric Cournot equilibrium with n firms exists even if market demand is throughout *inelastic*.

We turn now to locating conditions under which a *free-entry* symmetric Cournot equilibrium exists. Suppose there are n firms in the industry, and suppose for the moment barriers to entry. Then let $(x^*, Q^*/n)$ be the chosen course of action for the representative firm at a symmetric Cournot equilibrium. The market price for the product is $p(Q^*)$. Now define by $\hat{\alpha}$ the solution of the equation

$$p(Q^*) = c(x). \qquad \text{(A4)}$$

$\hat{x}$ is like an entry cost. It is clear that $\exists m > 0$, independent of n, such that *if* $\pi(x^*, Q^*/n) \leq m\hat{x}$, then no additional firm will find it profitable to enter the market even if there were no barriers to entry. Thus, in fact if n has such a value that $\pi(x^*, Q^*/n) \leq m\hat{x}$, condition (19) in the text is satisfied. We now proceed to locate conditions under which $\pi(x^*, Q^*/n) \leq m\hat{x}$. If $p(Q)$ and $c(x)$ satisfy (7) and (9) and if the value of Q^* given in equation (33) is used in (A4), routine calculations show that

$$\hat{x} = (\beta/\sigma)^{1/\alpha}(n/\alpha\beta)^{\varepsilon/\alpha}[\sigma(\alpha/n)^{\varepsilon}\beta^{\varepsilon-1}(1-\varepsilon/n)]^{\varepsilon(1+\alpha)/\alpha[\varepsilon-\alpha(1-\varepsilon)]}. \tag{A5}$$

Moreover,

$$\begin{aligned}\pi(x^*, Q^*/n) &= [p(Q^*) - c(x^*)]Q^*/n - x^* \\ &= (n-\varepsilon)^{-1}[\sigma(\alpha/n)^{\varepsilon}\beta^{\varepsilon-1}(1-\varepsilon/n)]^{1/[\varepsilon-\alpha(1-\varepsilon)]}[\varepsilon(1+\alpha)/\alpha - n].\end{aligned} \tag{A6}$$

Using (A5) and (A6) one notes that

$$\pi(x^*, Q^*/n) \leq \hat{x} \text{ if and only if } \varepsilon(1+\alpha)/\alpha - n \leq mn(1-\varepsilon/n)^{(1+\alpha)/\alpha} \tag{A7}$$

As we are concerned with locating circumstances under which a free-entry symmetric Cournot equilibrium *exists*, we are entitled to choose n. In what follows we shall always choose n to be the largest positive integer not exceeding $\varepsilon(1+\alpha)/\alpha$. Call this n^*. Then $n^* = [\varepsilon(1+\alpha)/\alpha]$. On appealing to Theorem 1, we may now note:

Theorem 2.[21] If $p(Q)$ and $c(x)$ satisfy (7) and (9) respectively, a free-entry symmetric Cournot equilibrium exists if (i) $\varepsilon(1+\alpha)/\alpha > 1$, (ii) $n^* = [\varepsilon(1+\alpha)/\alpha] > \varepsilon$, and (iii) $\varepsilon(1+\alpha)/\alpha - n^* \leq mn^*(1-\varepsilon/n^*)^{(1+\alpha)/\alpha}$.

The foregoing theorem makes explicit the relationship between the parameters of the economy that are sufficient to guarantee the existence of a free-entry symmetric Cournot equilibrium. It should be noted in particular that the conditions in Theorem 2 are satisfied if for any given value of ε, α is chosen small enough and also, for

21 Novshek (1977) has independently proved a result similar to this in a somewhat different context. We are grateful to Morton Kamien for drawing our attention to Novshek's work.

any given value of α, if ε is chosen large enough. That is, an equilibrium exists if ε/α is sufficiently large. This confirms the claims made in the text.

It remains to find conditions under which the use of the zero-profit condition (21) is a good approximation. In fact we have already located such conditions. What we are looking for are conditions under which $\pi(x^*, Q^*/n^*)/x^*$ is 'small'. (A2) then tells us that for the specification given by (7) and (9) in the text this is the same as finding conditions under which $\varepsilon/\alpha(n^* - \varepsilon) - 1$ is negligible. Since by construction $n^* = [\varepsilon(1 + \alpha)/\alpha]$, one can locate ranges for the pair (α, ε) for which the zero profit condition is a good approximation. In particular, one notes that it is a good approximation if ε/α is 'large'. In this case, n^* is, of course 'large'.

APPENDIX 2

In this appendix we compare the degree of risk-taking on the part of the pure monopolist with the socially optimum degree of risk-bearing. Towards this suppose the family of research projects is characterized by (34) and suppose $R(\alpha) > 0$ for $\alpha \geq 0$, $R'(\alpha) > 0$ and $R''(\alpha) > 0$. Let the market demand function be generated by the social utility function (6). Thus the demand function is

$$p(Q) = \sigma Q^{-\varepsilon} \quad (1 > \varepsilon > 0). \tag{A8}$$

Let $V_m(c)$ denote the monopolist's maximum profit from sales when c is the unit cost of production. It is simple to confirm that

$$V_m(c) = \varepsilon\sigma^{1/\varepsilon}(1-\varepsilon)^{(1-\varepsilon)/\varepsilon}\, c^{-(1-\varepsilon)/\varepsilon}. \tag{A9}$$

If the monopolist selects project-α his net expected profit is

$$h(\alpha)\, V_m[c(\alpha)] + [1 - h(\alpha)]\, V_m(c) - R(\alpha), \tag{A10}$$

where $V_m(c)$ is given by (A9). Write

$$A \equiv \varepsilon^{1/\varepsilon}(1-\varepsilon)^{(1-\varepsilon)/\varepsilon},$$
$$g(\alpha) \equiv \{h(\alpha)\, c(\alpha)^{-(1-\varepsilon)/\varepsilon} + [1 - h(\alpha)]\, c^{-(1-\varepsilon)/\varepsilon}\}$$

Then (A10) can be expressed as

$$Ag(\alpha) - R(\alpha). \tag{A11}$$

We now suppose for analytical simplicity that the family of research projects is such that $g(\alpha)$ is concave in α. Then provided the (expected) profit maximizing R & D project lies strictly between $\alpha = 0$ and $\alpha = \bar{\alpha}$, the monopolist will choose that α which is the solution of

$$Ag'(\alpha) = R'(\alpha). \tag{A12}$$

Let α_m be the (unique) solution of (A12).

We turn now to the social planner. He is concerned with social benefit (36). Since social utility has the form (6), $V(c)$ satisfies (8). Write $B \equiv \varepsilon\sigma^{1/\varepsilon}(1-\varepsilon)^{-1}$. Then (36) can be expressed as

$$Bg(\alpha) - R(\alpha). \tag{A13}$$

Since by hypothesis (A13) is strictly concave in α the planner will also wish to engage in an elementary research project. Let α_s $(0 < \alpha_s < \bar{\alpha})$ be the socially optimal research project. Then α_s must be the solution of

$$Bg'(\alpha) = R'(\alpha). \tag{A14}$$

But $B > A$. On Comparing (A12) and (A14) it follows that $\alpha_s > \alpha_m$. This establishes the claim made in the text.

REFERENCES

ARROW, K.J. (1962), 'Economic Welfare and the Allocation of Resources for Invention', in R. Nelson (ed.), *The Rate and Direction of Inventive Activity: Economic and Social Factors*, NBER, Princeton University Press.

BARZEL, Y. (1968), 'Optimal Timing of Innovation', *Review of Economics and Statistics*, 348–55.

DASGUPTA, P., G.M. HEAL and M. MAJUMDAR (1977), 'Resource Depletion and Research and Development', in M. Intrilligator (ed.), *Frontiers of Quantitative Economics*, IIIB, Amsterdam: North Holland.

—— and J.E. STIGLITZ (1977), 'Market Structure and Research and Development', London School of Economics (mimeo.).

—— (1980), 'Uncertainty, Market Structure, and the Speed of Research', *Bell Journal of Economics*, 11, 1–28.

EVENSON, R. and Y. KISLEV (1976), 'Stochastic Model of Applied Research', *Journal of Political Economy*, 84(2), 265–81.

KALECKI, M. (1954), *Theory of Economic Dynamics*, London: George Allen and Unwin.

KAMIEN, M. and N. SCHWARTZ (1972), 'Timing of Innovations under Rivalry', *Econometrica*, 40, 1, 43–60.

—— (1975), 'Market Structure and Innovation: A Survey', *Journal of Economic Literature*, 13, 1, 1–37.

—— (1978), 'Optimal Exhaustible Resource Depletion with Endogenous Technical Change', *Review of Economic Studies*, 45, 179–96.

LEVIN, R.C. (1978), 'Technical Change, Barriers to Entry and Market Structure', *Economica*, 45, 180, 347–62.

LOURY, G. (1977), 'Market Structure and Innovation', Center for Mathematical Studies in Economics and Management Science, Discussion Paper No. 256, Northwestern University.

MANSFIELD, E. (1967), *Econometric Studies of Industrial Research and Technological Innovation*, New York: W.W. Norton & Co.

MARSCHAK, T. and R. SELTON (1974), *General Equilibrium with Price-Making Firms*, Berlin: Springer-Verlag.

NELSON, R.R., M.J. PECK and E.D. KALACHEK (1967), *Technology, Economic Growth and Public Policy*, Washington, DC: Brookings Institution.

—— and S. WINTER (1977), 'Forces Generating and Limiting Concentration under Schumpeterian Competition', *Bell Journal of Economics*, 9(2), 524–48.

—— and H.L. SCHUETTE (1976), 'Technical Change in an Evolutionary Model', *Quarterly Journal of Economics*, 90, 1, 90–118.

NOVSHEK, W. (1977), 'Nash–Cournot Equilibrium with Entry' (mimeo.), Princeton University.

SCHERER, F.M. (1970), *Industrial Market Structure and Economic Performance*, Chicago: Rand McNally.

SCHMOOKLER, J. (1962), 'Economic Sources of Inventive Activity', *Journal of Economic History*, 22.

SCHUMPETER, J. (1947), *Capitalism, Socialism and Democracy* (Second Edition), London: Allen and Unwin.

SCHWARTZMAN, D. (1977), *Innovation in the Pharmaceutical Industry*, Baltimore: John Hopkins University Press.

STIGLITZ, J.E. (1970), 'Perfect and Imperfect Capital Markets' (mimeo.), Paper presented to the Winter meeting of the Econometric Society, Yale University.

WINTER, S. (1971), 'Satisficing, Selection, and the Innovating Remnant', *Quarterly Journal of Economics*, 85, 237–61.

Optimal Patent Length and Breadth[*]

RICHARD GILBERT AND CARL SHAPIRO

1. INTRODUCTION

The primary purpose of the patent system is to reward innovators. Unfortunately, because these rewards are based on the creation of market power, they necessitate some welfare loss. Much of the debate about patent policy had focused on this tradeoff between the dynamic benefits associated with innovation and the static costs of patent monopoly power. This debate has been cast in terms of the optimal lifetime for patents.[1]

Patent policy can be decomposed into two parts: first, a choice of how *much* to reward each patent; and second, how to *structure* each given reward. While the question of how much to reward patentees necessarily requires some estimate of the elasticity of supply of inventions, the efficient way in which to structure a reward of given size does not. It is this latter question that we address here. In particular, we examine the socially optimal mix between patent *length* and patent *breadth*, for a given size of the patentee's prize. In posing this question we begin with a very general definition of patent breadth: we simply identify the *breadth* of a patent with the flow rate of profit available to the patentee while the patent is in force.

Our work suggests that the conventional analysis of optimal patent length, based on the tradeoff between the incentives for innovation and the extent of static monopoly deadweight loss, has been misplaced, or at least takes too limited a view of the instruments that make up

[*] We thank William Baxter, John Vickers, Robert Willig, and a referee for valuable comments. C. Shapiro acknowledges the financial support of the National Science Foundation and the John M. Olin Foundation.

[1] See, for example, Nordhaus (1969) and (1972) and Scherer (1972).

'patent policy'. When patent policy is viewed to be a choice of patent breadth as well as patent length, we find that the optimal length may easily be infinite. The appropriate margin on which patent policy should operate may not be patent length, but rather patent breadth.

We pose the following policy question: What is the optimal mix between patent length and breadth as instruments to reward innovation? Our reduced-form analysis in Sec. 2, addresses this problem quite generally. There we provide a general condition for the optimal length of the patent grant to be infinite.

Our subsequent analysis in Sec. 3 is in the context of a homogeneous product, where we interpret breadth as the ability of the patentee to raise price. In independent work, Klemperer (1990) considers the patent breadth problem in a model of spatial product differentiation. A larger patent breadth in his model corresponds to a larger region of the product space that is included in the patent grant. Thus the focus of Klemperer's analysis is on the optimal *scope* of patent protection, while we emphasize the extent to which a patentee may exploit the patent monopoly for a given coverage of the patent grant.

We show that in a homogeneous-good market, our general condition from Sec. 2 is typically met, so the socially optimal way to reward innovation involves patents of infinite length. This is in contrast to results in the traditional literature on the optimal patent life, which assumes that the degree of patent protection is fixed. A special case of our result appears in Tandon (1982). He shows, in an example using linear demand and constant marginal costs, that optimal patent lifetimes are infinite when patent policy consists of a patent lifetime and a royalty rate for compulsory licensing. Klemperer (1990) also provides an example of customer tastes for which a very narrow, but infinitely long, patent grant is optimal.

Why are infinitely-lived patents optimal? Increasing the breadth of the patent typically is increasingly costly, in terms of deadweight loss, as the patentee's market power grows. When increasing the length of the patent, by contrast, there is a constant tradeoff between the additional reward to the patentee and the increment to deadweight loss, at least if the underlying environment is stationary. So, in many circumstances, the socially cost-effective way to achieve a given reward to innovators is to have infinitely-lived patents with the minimum market power necessary to attain the required reward level.

2. THE GENERAL RESULT

We study the socially cost-effective way in which to achieve any given reward, V, for an innovation. This cost-effectiveness problem is a necessary piece of optimal patent policy.

There are two instruments available to achieve the desired reward: the length of the patent and its breadth. The length is simply the lifetime of the patent grant, which we denote by T. Patent breadth is less straightforward, since 'breadth' can mean many different things. We discuss different interpretations of patent breadth below. But any definition of breadth involves the idea that a broader patent allows the innovator to earn a higher flow rate of profits during the lifetime of the patent. So we begin with a reduced-form specification in which we simply identify breadth with the flow rate of profits, π, available to the patentee while the patent is in force.

Optimal patent policy consists of choosing T and π to maximize social welfare, W, which equals the sum of consumer surplus and profits, subject to achieving the given reward V for the patentee. The key tradeoff is that between social welfare and profits, $W(\pi)$ on a flow basis. The assumption that $W'(\pi) < 0$ reflects the idea that broader patents confer greater market power and associated deadweight loss. Once the patent has expired, flow profits decline to $\bar{\pi}$ and flow social welfare rises to $\bar{W} = W(\bar{\pi})$.

Suppose that the underlying environment is stationary and predictable.[2] Discounted social welfare is given by

$$\Omega(T, \pi) = \int_0^T W(\pi)e^{-rt}\,dt + \int_T^\infty \bar{W}e^{-rt}\,dt,$$

and the present value of the patentee's profits are

$$V(T, \pi) = \int_0^T \pi e^{-rt}\,dt + \int_T^\infty \bar{\pi}e^{-rt}\,dt.$$

The optimal mix between length and breadth involves maximizing $\Omega(T, \pi)$ subject to $V(T, \pi) \geq V$. Our main result is found in the following proposition.

Proposition 1. Suppose that $W''(\pi) < 0$ at all π, i.e. patent breadth

[2] The importance of these assumptions, and the consequences of relaxing them, are discussed in the conclusion.

is increasingly costly in terms of deadweight loss. Then optimal patent policy calls for infinitely-lived patents.

Proof. Define $\phi(T)$ as the flow of profits required in order to achieve a total reward to the patentee of V if the lifetime of the patent is T. By definition,

$$V \equiv \int_0^T \phi(T)e^{-rt}\,dt + \int_T^\infty \bar{\pi}e^{-rt}\,dt = \phi(T)\,\frac{1-e^{-rT}}{r} + \bar{\pi}\,\frac{e^{-rT}}{r}. \qquad (1)$$

Differentiating (1) with respect to T gives

$$o = (\phi(T) - \bar{\pi})e^{-rT} + \phi'(T)\,\frac{1-e^{-rT}}{r}. \qquad (2)$$

Now consider the total welfare that is achieved if the patent lifetime is set at T and the breadth of the patent at $\phi(T)$. Total welfare is $\Omega(T, \phi(T))$. Differentiating with respect to T we have

$$\frac{d\Omega}{dT} = \frac{\partial\Omega}{\partial T} + \frac{\partial\Omega}{\partial\pi}\,\phi'.$$

Since $\partial\Omega/\partial T = (W(\pi) - \bar{W})e^{-rT}$ and $\partial\Omega/\partial\pi = W'(\pi)\,(1-e^{-rT})/r$,

we have $$\frac{d\Omega}{dT} = (W(\phi(T)) - \bar{W})e^{-rT} + W'(\phi(T))\,\frac{1-e^{-rT}}{r}\,\phi'(T).$$

Substituting from (2) for $\phi'(T)$ gives

$$\frac{d\Omega}{dT} = (W(\phi(T)) - \bar{W})e^{-rT} - (\phi(T) - \bar{\pi})\,W'(\phi(T))e^{-rT}.$$

If $W''(\pi) < 0$ on $[\bar{\pi}, \phi(T)]$, then

$$-W'(\phi(T)) > \frac{\bar{W} - W(\phi(T))}{\phi(T) - \bar{\pi}}.$$

Hence $(d\Omega/dT) > 0$ as required. Increasing T always raises welfare, so an infinitely-lived patent is optimal. *Q.E.D.*

The key condition for Proposition 1 is that increasing the patentee's rewards on a flow basis is increasingly costly in terms of social welfare, i.e. $W''(\pi) < 0$. We next explore conditions under which this condition is met, looking more closely at the meaning of the patent breadth variable.

3. OPTIMAL PATENT AND ANTITRUST POLICY

Both patent and antitrust policies can constrain the price set by a patentee. Policies that determine the scope of patent protection affect pricing by defining the products that can substitute for a patented good. Greater protection from infringement—greater patent scope in the sense of Klemperer (1990)—permits a higher optimal price. Other policies affect the ability to exploit the patent grant for any given scope of the grant. For example, attempts by the patentee to set price above some level may require practices such as exclusive territories, price-restricted licenses, tying arrangements, or other vertical restraints, that may call forth antitrust suits, either from private parties or the government. In addition, the patentee may be subject to compulsory licensing at 'reasonable fees' which again imposes a price ceiling. Alternatively, patent protection may determine the costs of imitation and thus the price that the patentee can charge without facing such imitation. In all of these cases patent breadth translates into a maximum price the patentee can charge, or equivalently, a minimum quantity that he must sell. We analyse optimal policy here for this particular interpretation of patent breadth: the ability of the patentee to raise the price for the single product that embodies the innovation.

Our approach in this section should be distinguished from that in Klemperer's (1990) spatial model. In his model, increasing the scope of the patent grant makes non-infringing substitute products less attractive to consumers. With the definition used in this section, patent breadth has no effect on the set of substitute products that are offered to consumers; breadth only affects the price that the patentee can charge. In Klemperer's model, substitution away from the patented product can actually be *reduced* by widening the scope of the patent grant. Klemperer assumes that within the scope of the patent grant, the patentholder offers product varieties to serve every customer's tastes. Therefore, no customer whose most-preferred variety is within the scope of the patent grant need suffer a disutility (in product characteristics) from purchase of the patented good. If the patent grant is very wide in scope, nearly all customers would prefer to buy the patented product (despite a high price) rather than substitute a lower-priced unpatented good with less desirable characteristics. If, in addition, the amount of the product that consumers purchase is not very sensitive to the price, there may be little deadweight loss associated with patents that are very wide in scope.

Thus, in Klemperer's model, patents that are wide in scope and short in duration can be preferred to patents that are narrow in scope and long in duration. In our model, by contrast, the extent of substitution away from the patented product, and the deadweight loss associated with that substitution, always rises with the breadth of the patent. It should be noted that when pricing control is included as a policy instrument along with the scope of patent protection in Klemperer's spatial model, the optimal policy calls for a wide scope of patent protection along with price controls to achieve no more than the desired reward for innovation.

Consider then a process or product innovation for which the (inverse) demand is given by $p(x)$. Welfare is $w(x) = B(x) - C(x)$, where $B(x) \equiv \int_0^x p(z)dz$ is the total benefit function and $C(x)$ is the patentee's cost function. Profits are $\varphi(x) = xp(x) - C(x)$. Call x_m the monopoly output and x^* the welfare-maximizing output. In the relevant range, $x_m < x < x^*$, we make the weak assumptions that $\varphi'(x) < 0$ and $w'(x) > 0$. Define $g(\pi)$ as the inverse function of $\varphi(x)$, i.e. $\varphi(g(\pi)) \equiv \pi$. Then $W(\pi) = w(g(\pi))$.

Proposition 2. If profits and welfare are both concave in output, then welfare is concave in the patentee's profits, so the optimal patent lifetime is infinite.

Proof. Taking derivatives of $W(\pi)$ twice, we have

$$W''(\pi) = w'g'' + w''(g')^2. \tag{3}$$

Since $w' > 0$ and $w'' < 0$, $W''(\pi) < 0$ if $g'' < 0$. But $g'(\pi) = 1/\varphi'(g(\pi))$, so

$$g''(\pi) = -\frac{\varphi''(g(\pi))\, g'(\pi)}{\varphi'(g(\pi))^2}.$$

With $\varphi'' < 0$, and since $g' < 0$ in the relevant range, we indeed have $g'' < 0$. Q.E.D.

Remark. The conditions of Proposition 2 are met if the demand and marginal revenue curves slope down and the marginal cost curve slopes up. Even weaker conditions, however, will suffice to establish the concavity of welfare in the patentee's profits. Suppose that marginal costs do not decrease with output, $c'' \geq 0$. Define $\varepsilon \equiv -p(x)/xp'(x)$ as the elasticity of demand and let θ be the elasticity of ε with respect to price. Then direct calculations demonstrate that $W''(\pi) < 0$ if $\theta > -(1-m)/m$ where $m \equiv (p-c')/p$ is the markup. If the elasticity of demand is constant or increasing in price, this condition is surely met.

Even if the weak conditions of Proposition 2 or the preceding remark are not met, we still know that infinite lifetimes are optimal for 'small' patents.

Proposition 3. For small values of the patentee's reward, V, the optimal policy involves an infinitely-lived patent.

Proof. First we show that for prices sufficiently close to marginal cost, welfare is concave in the patentee's profits. Since welfare is maximized when price equals marginal costs, i.e. when $x = x^*$, we know that $w'(x^*) = 0$ and $w''(x^*) < 0$. For prices close to marginal cost, w' is close to zero and w'' is still negative. Therefore, from equation (3), $W'' < 0$ at such prices.

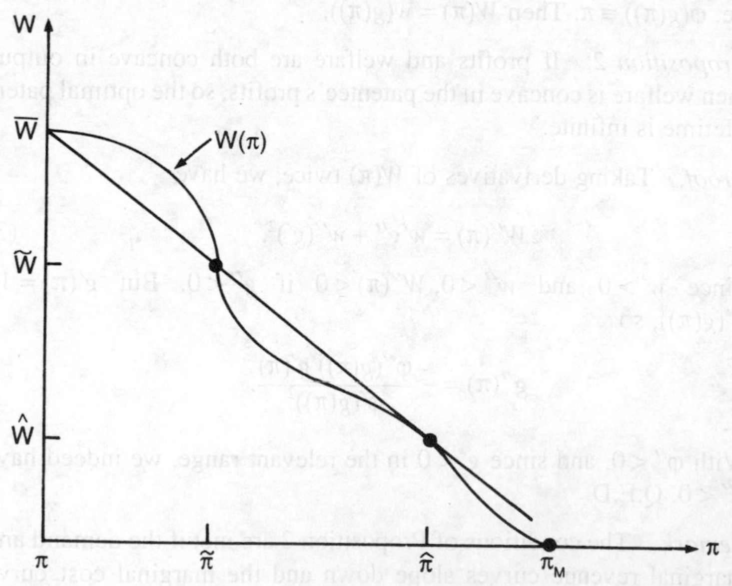

Figure 1 $(\hat{\pi}, \hat{W})$ is not Optimal

Consider any candidate optimum policy with a finite lifetime, $(\hat{\pi}, \hat{T})$. If $W''(\pi) < 0$ on the interval $[\bar{\pi}, \hat{\pi}]$, then we know from the proof of Proposition 1 that a slight decrease in π, with the necessary increase in T to leave V unchanged, will increase welfare. If $(\hat{\pi}, \hat{T})$ is to be an optimum, we must therefore have $W''(\pi) > 0$ for at least some π on the interval $[\bar{\pi}, \hat{\pi}]$. Differentiation of Ω as in Proposition 1 reveals, however, that for $(\hat{\pi}, \hat{T})$ to be a local optimum requires $W''(\hat{\pi}) < 0$. If $(\hat{\pi}, \hat{W})$ is as drawn in Fig. 1, any small change in T away from $\hat{T}$ will lower welfare.

For small values of V, however, we can always find a *non-marginal* change that raises welfare. Refer to Fig. 1. From the properties we have established in the previous two paragraphs, there must exist a $\tilde{\pi} < \hat{\pi}$ with the following two properties: (a) the ratio of flow deadweight loss to flow profits is the same at $\tilde{\pi}$ as at $\hat{\pi}$; and (b) $W(\pi)$ is concave on the interval $(\bar{\pi}, \tilde{\pi})$.

Now consider the alternative policy of allowing a flow of profits $\tilde{\pi}$ over a long enough time period to give a total reward of V. For V small enough, this is always possible, since the flow rate of profits need only be rV. Since this new policy has the same ratio of deadweight loss to 'excess profits' $(\pi - \bar{\pi})$ as does the candidate optimum, and the total excess profits are the same, the total deadweight loss must also be equal. In other words, the new policy is just as good as the candidate optimum. But the new policy can be improved upon with a marginal change to reduce flow profits and increase patent length, since $W''(\pi) < 0$ on the interval $[\bar{\pi}, \tilde{\pi}]$. We can conclude that the original candidate optimum was not in fact optimal. *Q.E.D.*

The optimal policy for small values of V calls for $T = \infty$ and $\pi = rV$. With price close to marginal cost, the deadweight loss is proportional to $(p - c')^2$, so the ratio of deadweight loss to patentee profits approaches zero as V does so. This is a local version of our general theme, that the social costs of patent prizes are minimized by keeping prices as close as possible to marginal cost, i.e. with narrow but lengthy patents.

Propositions 2 and 3 suggest to us that when we consider several instruments of optimal patent policy, i.e. the scope of protection from imitation as well as the length of the patent grant, then optimal policy may well call for infinitely-lived patents. In this sense, previous emphasis on the optimal length of patents seems misplaced. If one takes a broader view of patent policy, either to include the antitrust treatment of intellectual property or protection from imitation, the policy margin or patent length is not a useful one on which to operate.

The optimality of infinitely-lived patents carries over to a patentee offering a range of products relying on the same patent. In this case the optimal policy involves infinitely-lived patents along with Ramsey pricing, since Ramsey pricing is the (static) solution to the problem of achieving a given profit level at least social cost. In the case of products with independent demands, the constant of proportionality between the markup of each good and its elasticity of demand is an increasing function of the overall required profit level, V.

4. CONCLUSIONS

This short article reports a simple but general result in the design of optimal patent policy. If one interprets patent policy broadly enough to include at least one policy instrument that affects the flow of profits from the sale of the patented product, then optimal policy calls for infinitely-lived patents whenever patent breadth is increasingly costly in terms of deadweight loss. We have shown this typically to be the case for the conventional deadweight loss stemming from monopoly pricing of a single patented product. Klemperer (1990) demonstrates that broad, short-lived patents can be optimal if wider patents discourage substitution away from the patented product by making the non-infringing alternatives less attractive to buyers.

Given the overall level of rewards to innovators, our analysis suggests that appropriate treatment of intellectual property calls for longer patent lives combined with more careful antitrust treatment of patent practices, such as the provisions of licensing contracts. Of course, if the current level of rewards to innovators is viewed to be inadequate, then it may be appropriate to give stronger protection from infringement even as patent lifetimes are extended. Our point is that longer patent lifetimes are optimal, whatever one believes about the overall level of rewards to innovators, so long as patent breadth is increasingly costly in terms of deadweight loss.

On the other hand, we must express a warning about the policy-relevance of our finding here. One limitation is clear from the fact that Klemperer obtains a very different result, namely the optimality of very short, very broad patents, if substitution to alternative products is the main source of deadweight loss, rather than substitution out of the product class altogether.

Another limitation in our analysis is due to our assumption that the underlying environment is predictable. Suppose instead that there is uncertainty about future demand and cost conditions. Such uncertainty would have no effect on our results if the firm is risk neutral. If the firm is risk averse, however, efficient risk sharing then calls for broader, shorter patents than in the risk-neutral case. So long as the uncertainty about profits is larger for profits earned in the more distant future, the efficient way to provide the innovator with a given level of expected utility will involve declining (expected) profits over time. If the available policy instrument is patent lifetime, a finite lifetime will be optimal.

The most important limitation of our analysis stems from our assumption that the underlying environment is stationary. We made this assumption to focus attention on a single innovation. In practice, however, inventions build on each other, and a long patent grant may have deleterious effects on the incentives of other firms to engage in related research, for fear that they will be at the mercy of the original patentee.[3] What would have happened in telecommunications, for example, if the telephone were still patented?[4]

In particular, there appears to be a danger that an overly-long patent would retard subsequent innovation by establishing monopoly rights to an entire line of research. If this is the case, the tradeoff between deadweight loss and profits at the margin would no longer be constant as the patent lifetime increases. Rather, there might be increasing social costs in comparison to patentee profits as the patent grant is

[3] Apart from the possibility that the effective market power associated with a given patent may grow over time with the patent's importance, simply the costs incurred by a future would-be inventor to determine whether an invention infringes any existing patents are likely to increase markedly with the statutory patent lifetime. The costs of searching previous patent records, and the uncertainties imposed on inventors, could be large indeed if an inventor were exposed to the risk of being found to infringe a hundred-year old patent.

[4] It would appear that the efficacy of licensing arrangements will be important in evaluating long-lived patents in the context of ongoing technological progress. Note also that defining infringement and enforcing the patent may become more costly over time. This too would be a force favouring finite patent lifetimes.

extended in time. Further modelling of markets with a sequence of related innovations will be required to characterize optimal patent policy in such settings.

REFERENCES

KLEMPERER, P. (1990), 'How Broad should the Scope of Patent Protection Be?', *The RAND Journal of Economics*, 21, 113–30.

NORDHAUS, W. (1969), *Invention, Growth and Welfare: A Theoretical Treatment of Technological Change*, Cambridge, MA: MIT Press.

—— (1972), 'The Optimum Life of a Patent: Reply', *American Economic Review*, 62, 428–31.

SCHERER, F.M. (1972), 'Nordhaus' Theory of Optimal Patent Life: A Geometric Reinterpretation', *American Economic Review*, 62, 422–7.

TANDON, P. (1982), 'Optimal Patents with Compulsory Licensing', *Journal of Political Economy*, 90, 470–86.

INDUSTRIAL ORGANIZATION AND DEVELOPING ECONOMIES

Fragmented Duopoly: Theory and Applications to Backward Agriculture*

KAUSHIK BASU AND CLIVE BELL

1. INTRODUCTION

In certain trades trust is a precondition for exchange or transaction to occur. This would be true where information asymmetries are strong. In buying used cars most of us would prefer to make a purchase from friends and acquaintances (or at least from some of them!). It is well known that in informal credit markets, where formal legal institutions are weak, a person would lend money only to those whom he can trust or over whom he has some control. Thus a landlord may agree to lend money only to his labourers and a merchant may agree to lend only to his regular customers. This has led to a view that credit markets are 'fragmented'.[1] However, when it has come to actually modelling such a case the usual recourse has been to treat it as a case of several monopoly islands. Strictly speaking, however, the market just described is neither a monopoly nor a duopoly since the set of potential borrowers of the landlord would, typically, have some intersection with the set of potential borrowers of the merchant but the two sets would not be identical. What we have is a case in between a monopoly and oligopoly. It is this 'in between' case that is formally characterized and explored in this paper.

* This paper has benefited from the comments of participants in a seminar at the Indian Statistical Institute, New Delhi, and Nirvikar Singh. We are also indebted to two anonymous referees for insightful and constructive criticism of an earlier draft. The usual disclaimers apply.

[1] See Bhaduri (1983); Basu (1983); Bardhan (1984); Platteau and Abraham (1987).

Let us assume that there are n sellers of a certain commodity. Let S_i be the set of potential customers of seller i. To consumers outside S_i, i will never sell goods, irrespective of the price. Consider now two special cases. First, if it is true that

$$S_1 = S_2 = \ldots = S_n,$$

then we have a case of standard oligopoly with n firms. All firms are competing over the same set of customers.

If, on the other hand, $(S_1, S_2, \ldots, S_n)$ happens to be a partition over the set of all potential customers in the economy, then we have a case of n standard monopolies. Each seller has his own exclusive pool of customers.[2]

There is no reason why we have to restrict attention to these two polar cases. We may well have cases where for some i, j, the sets S_i and S_j have some common members but it is not the case that S_i is the same set for all i. We shall describe a market structure where this happens (along with the two polar cases just described) as a *fragmented oligopoly*.

Though we motivated the idea of fragmented oligopoly by talking about the role of trust and control in certain transactions,[3] we believe that this market structure could be usefully applied in many different areas. It clearly has relevance to models of industrial location. Indeed, certain features of location contribute to the fragmentation of rural credit markets when the pattern of settlement is nucleated, as in the case of South Asia's villages, rather than continuous, as in Hotelling's (1929) classic work. It is known, for example, that not all villages have resident moneylenders (Reserve Bank of India, 1954) and that commission agents and traders often have 'territories' made up of several contiguous villages from which most of their clients in moneylending and trade are drawn.[4] Drawing upon these examples, suppose that there are three villages, A, B and C, in a row. Moneylender 1 lives in village A; and moneylender 2 lives in C. If we suppose that the inhabitants of A would go only to their 'resident' moneylender

[2] Such a model is developed in Basu (1987) where the rural credit market is modelled as a collection of independent credit islands.

[3] Trust plays an important role not only in backward markets but in a whole range of interactions in any economy: See Dasgupta (1986).

[4] This was revealed in conversations between commission agents and Bell in the course of fieldwork in Andhra Pradesh and Punjab, India.

and likewise for C, and that those of B would go to whoever charges less, then we have a case of fragmented duopoly. If N_x is a set of people in village X, then this is a special case of the above formal definition with $n = 2$ and $S_1 = N_A \cup N_B$ and $S_2 = N_C \cup N_B$. Thus, though the model that we construct does not belong to the class of location models based on Hotelling's (see, for example, D'-Aspremont, Gabszewicz and Thisse (1979) and Bonanno (1987)) and the properties that we investigate are distinct from the ones that a model of location would focus on, the abstract structure could be used as a basis for a model of locational duopoly.

Another view of our model is that of an oligopoly with switching costs (e.g. von Weizsäcker, 1984; Klemperer, 1987a, b; and Bulow, Geanakoplos and Klemperer, 1985). Indeed our model may be viewed as an application of switching cost theory, with prohibitive switching costs once the 'domains' or 'territories' of firms have been established, to the study of backward markets and agrarian relations. Though our initial model, in abstraction, is a kind of switching-cost model, we develop it in some detail as our aim is to address issues in development and to persuade development economists of the relevance of such models of industrial organization to agrarian theory.

Models of fragmented oligopoly could also find application in activities where because of asymmetric information each seller has a predetermined clientele that trusts him. International trade with prior political fragmentation is another area of possible application of this theory. Though this paper is an abstract analysis of fragmented duopoly and depends little on what actual motivation is used, our interest in the subject arose from an attempt to give a rigorous characterization of the idea of 'market fragmentation' which is so central to development economics and particularly the theory of agrarian structure. It is for this reason that much of the paper dwells on problems of backward agriculture.

When firms possess captive segments of the market, it is natural to ask whether they can practice price discrimination between segments. This is indeed an open question. It is arguable that in fragmented agrarian markets, which are our central concern in this paper, arbitrage is not easy and so price discrimination ought to be treated as feasible. One must, however, remember that in personalized rural markets of the kind described in Bardhan (1984), the possibility of price discrimination may be thwarted by social norms. In different societies, different kinds of discrimination are treated by the people as 'unjust'. The origins of these norms lie in distant history but are often powerful enough to make certain kinds of discriminatory pricing unfeasible. That is, the cost in terms of political dissension is too high from the seller's point of view. It is for this reason that we have in this paper devoted somewhat more attention to the non-discrimination model. We do, however, deal with the case of segment-specific price discrimination in separate sections.

The Cournot–Nash equilibria of a fragmented duopoly in which sellers cannot practise price discrimination are analysed in Sec. 2. Section 3 briefly describes the case where a seller can price-discriminate between market segments. In Sec. 4 a two-period model is constructed in which in the first period the players fight to establish their domains, that is, the S_1's and the S_2's. In the second period they treat S_1 and S_2 as given and play a quantity-setting game. The subgame perfect equilibria of such a two-period game, with and without price discrimination, are examined. The case with price discrimination is taken up in Sec. 5, and the possibility of rent-dissipation in this setting in Sec. 6.

2. THE NASH EQUILIBRIUM OF A FRAGMENTED DUOPOLY WITHOUT PRICE DISCRIMINATION

There are n identical consumers and each consumer's demand function for the commodity in question is given by

$$q = q(p), \tag{1}$$

where p is price and q is quantity demanded. We assume q is a continuous function and $q'(p) < 0$. The inverse demand function is written as follows:

$$p = p(q). \tag{2}$$

There are two sellers (or firms), 1 and 2. The n consumers are partitioned into three sets, N_1, N_2 and N_3, consisting of, respectively, n_1, n_2 and n_3 persons. Thus $n_1 + n_2 + n_3 = n$. The members of N_1 would buy goods from only firm 1. Members of N_2 would buy from only 2. The third group would buy from whoever offers better terms. These three groups will be referred to as the three *segments* of the market.

N_i is firm i's *captive segment*, for $i = 1, 2$; and N_3 will be referred to as the *contested segment*.[5]

Both firms have the same cost function: A cost of c units has to be incurred to produce each unit of the good. An immediate consequence of this assumption is that were the firm able to charge the monopoly price, p^m, in its captive segment of the market, p^m would depend only on the shape of the individual's demand function and c. That is, p^m is then independent of the pattern of market segmentation. This is taken up further in Secs 3 and 5.

Consider now firm i's problem. It has to decide how much to supply to its captive segment, x_i, and how much to apply to the contested segment, q_i. To begin with, it will be assumed that a firm cannot discriminate between consumers in terms of the price charged. The consequence of relaxing this assumption is discussed in Sec. 3.

Suppose each firm has chosen a strategy. That is, we are given (x_1, q_1, x_2, q_2). Clearly the price of the good in the contested segment will be

$$p = p(q_1 + q_2)/n_3.$$

If $q_i > 0$, then the fact that a firm must charge the same price to all customers means that i must charge a price of $p((q_1 + q_2)/n_3)$ even in its captive segment. As price depends on the other firm's choice of q_j, the firm's choice of x_i may not be consistent with demand in the captive segment of its market. Thus i's total profit will be

$$\left[p\left(\frac{q_1+q_2}{n_3}\right)-c\right]\left\{q_i+\min\left[x_i, n_i q\left(p\left(\frac{q_1+q_2}{n_3}\right)\right)\right]\right\}. \quad (3)$$

Note that $n_i q(p((q_1 + q_2)/n_3))$ is the demand for the good in the captive segment when price is $p((q_1 + q_2)/n_3)$; and the shorter side of the market determines the volume of sales when supply is not equal to demand.

It is easy to see, however, that, given q_1 and q_2 (> 0), firm i's choice of x_i can be deduced therefrom. Hence, we may define the profit of

[5] This ought not to be confused with the concept of 'contestable' markets in the literature.

each firm in terms of only q_1 and q_2. Using π_i to denote firm i's profit, we have:[6]

$$\pi_i(q_1, q_2) = \begin{cases} \max_{x_i} \left[p\left(\frac{x_i}{n_i}\right) - c \right] x_i & \text{if } q_i = 0 \\ \left[p\left(\frac{q_1 + q_2}{n_3}\right) - c \right] \left[q_i + \frac{n_i}{n_3}(q_1 + q_2) \right] & \text{if } q_i > 0. \end{cases} \tag{4}$$

The interpretation of this profit function is as follows. Given (q_1, q_2), firm i supplies to its captive segment a profit-maximizing amount of goods. That is, given q_1, and q_2, price is determined by $p((q_1 + q_2)/n_3)$; so that if $q_i > 0$, then in its captive segment, firm i supplies exactly the amount that is demanded, which is equal to $(n_i/n_3)(q_1 + q_2)$. If $q_i = 0$, then the fact that a firm has to charge the same price to all its buyers places no restriction on the price it can charge in the captive segment. In such a case it can charge the monopoly price, p^m, and make monopoly profits. These features are captured in (4).

Let us define the *Nash equilibrium* of the *game* as a (q_1^*, q_2^*) such that $\pi_1(q_1^*, q_2^*) \geq \pi_1(q_1, q_2^*)$, for all q_1 and $\pi_2(q_1^*, q_2^*) \geq \pi_2(q_1^*, q_2)$, for all q_2.

It is useful to have a visual representation of the reaction functions. This would enable us to compare a fragmented duopoly with a traditional duopoly. In Fig. 1, firm 1's reaction functions lie in the NE- and NW-quadrants. If q_2 is zero, firm 1 acts as a monopolist on both its captive segment and the contested segment. In that case, let *OC* be the amount it supplies on its captive segment and *OA* be the amount it supplies on the contested segment. As q_2 rises, firm 1's sales on the contested and captive segments are represented by the lines *AB* and *CD*. It will be shown later that *AB* will be steeper than the 45° line and *CD* will be a rising curve, as shown. As q_2 rises, supply in firm 1's captive segments deviates more and more from the monopoly output *OC*. This happens because a firm has to charge the same price to all customers. As q_2 keeps rising, a point will be reached where firm 1 would prefer to drop out of the contested market and

[6] We assume throughout that $\max_{x_i} [p(x_i/n_i) - c]x_i > 0$, for $i = 1$ or 2. This ensures that production is profitable.

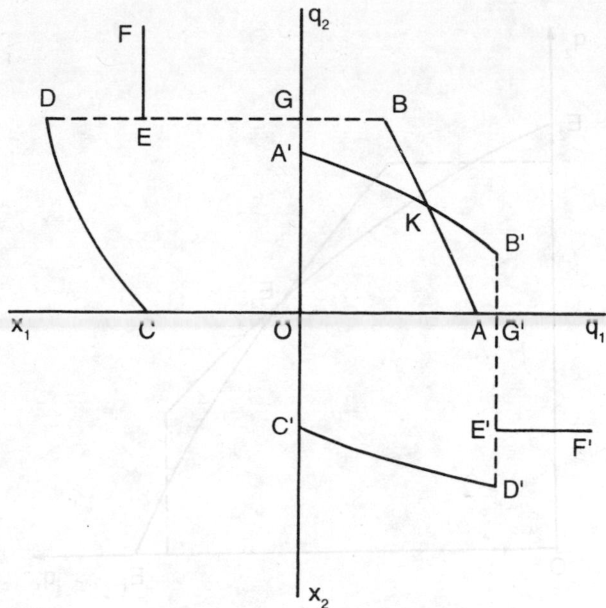

Figure 1 Reaction Functions and Equilibrium in a Fragmented Duopoly

sell the monopoly output to its captive segment. This happens when $q_2 = OG$. For all $q_2 > OG$, firm 1 sells $GE = OC$ units on its captive segment and zero in the contested market.

We have here drawn a case which gives a 'stable' Nash equilibrium (in the sense of Friedman, 1977). It is later shown that this must always be the case. In Fig. 1 we also depict firm 2's reaction functions. These are denoted by the same letters with primes on them. The above discussion makes it clear that for analyzing the Nash equilibria of a fragmented duopoly we could concentrate exclusively on the NE-quadrant because the reactions in the captive segments (i.e. the NW- and SE-quadrants) could be derived mechanically from the happenings in the NE-quadrant.

In the case depicted in Fig. 1 there is only one Nash equilibrium. But since the reaction functions have breaks it appears as if we can have corner equilibria as in models with fixed costs (e.g. Spence, 1979; Dixit, 1979, 1980; Basu and Singh, 1990) as illustrated in Fig. 2. If E_1 had occurred, then firm 1 would be selling OE_1 on the contested

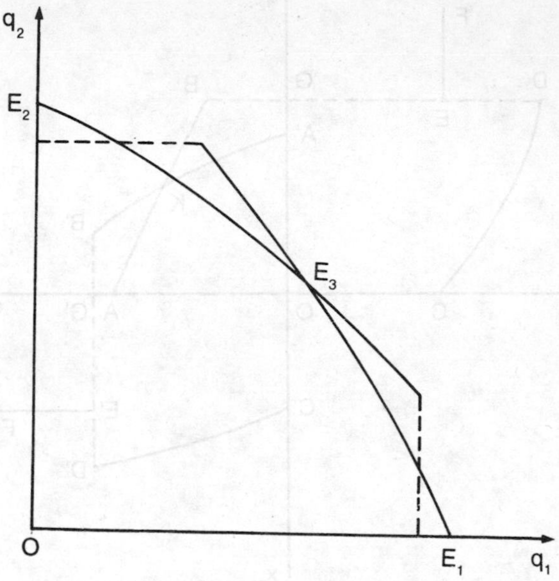

Figure 2 Multiple Equilibria

segment, whereas firm 2 would be selling only to its captive segment. It can, however, be shown that such equilibria can never arise in this model and in order to have such corner equilibria it may be necessary to introduce some fixed costs (Mishra, 1991). It seems to us that in practice, markets do often get partitioned into zones within which each firm acts like a monopolist.[7] However, as things stand, equilibrium is always unique and occurs with both firms supplying to the contested segment.

Let us now take note of a property of the reaction functions which has important implications for our model. Let the function $R_i(q_j)$ denote firm i's optimal (in terms of (4)) choice of q_i given that the other firm has chosen q_j. In case there is more than one q_i which satisfies this condition, we shall assume that R_i specifies the smallest of these q_i's. Thus in Fig. 1, if $q_2 = OG$, then $R_1(q_2) = 0$.

[7] Recall that in this model both monopolists will charge the same price, since customers are identical. If, however, we allow for heterogeneity among customers, then the prices may be different.

Suppose q_2 is such that $R_1(q_2) > 0$. Hence in maximizing π_1 we could (in eq. (4)) concentrate on the case where $q_1 > 0$. That is,

$$\pi_1(q_1, q_2) = \left[p\left(\frac{q_1 + q_2}{n_3}\right) - c \right] \left[q_1 + \frac{n_1}{n_3}(q_1 + q_2) \right].$$

Maximizing π_1 with respect to q_1 gives us the following first-order condition.

$$\frac{\partial \pi_1}{\partial q_1} = (p - c)\left(1 + \frac{n_1}{n_3}\right) + \frac{p'}{n_3} \cdot \left[\left(1 + \frac{n_1}{n_3}\right) q_1 + \frac{n_1}{n_3} q_2\right] = 0. \tag{5}$$

This yields the following theorem.

Theorem 1.

If $R_1(q_2) > 0$, *then* $\partial R_1/\partial q_2 > -1$.

If $R_2(q_1) > 0$, *then* $\partial R_2/\partial q_1 > -1$.

Proof. See Appendix.

Theorem 1 asserts that as long as both firms are operating on the contested segment, a decrease in q_2 by one unit causes an increase in $R_1(q_2)$ by less than one unit; symmetrically, the same applies to firm 2's reaction function.

Using Theorem 1 we can quickly establish some corollaries. Observe that our Nash equilibrium must be stable in the sense that the reaction functions intersect in the 'correct' direction. This is because Theorem 1 implies that in the NE-quadrant of Fig. 1, firm 1's reaction function must be steeper (in magnitude) than firm 2's reaction function.

Corollary 1. As long as firm 1 operates on the contested market, a fall in q_2 *would cause firm 1's supply on its own captive segment to fall.*

Corollary 1 tells us that the slope of the *CD* curve will be in the direction shown. To see this, check that, by Theorem 1, as q_2 falls $q_2 + R_1(q_2)$ must fall. Hence price in the contested segment rises. Since the firm charges all its customers the same price, the price charged by firm 1 in the captive segment rises. Hence, the amount sold on the captive segment must fall.

It is easily shown that if the entire industry (i.e. all the captive and contested segments) was served by a monopolist, output would be less than or equal to that in a fragmented duopoly. It follows that price in a fragmented duopoly would be less than or equal to monopoly price.

First, observe that since all consumers are identical, the volume of output in the industry would be the same whether it was served by one monopolist or t monopolists. If firm 1 is a monopolist supplying $n_1 + n_3$ customers and firm 2 a monopolist supplying n_2 customers, firm 1 would supply CA units and 2 would supply OC' units (in Fig. 1). Hence a single monopolist selling to all n consumers would supply $CA + OC'$ units. Let $(x_1^*, q_1^*, x_2^*, q_2^*)$ be the equilibrium of a fragmented duopoly. If $q_1^* = 0$ or $q_2^* = 0$, then clearly $x_1^* + q_1^* + x_2^* + q_2^* = CA + OC'$. If $(q_1^*, q_2^*) > 0$, i.e. the industry is at a point like K, then Theorem 1 implies $q_1^* + q_2^* > OA$. Since OA is the monopoly output with n_3 buyers, price in the fragmented duopoly equilibrium is less than monopoly price; and output is greater than monopoly output. The above claim, along with Corollary 2 below, tells us that, in some sense, a fragmented duopoly lies where we expect it to lie—somewhere *between* a standard duopoly and a monopoly.

Let us now turn to the properties of the Nash equilibrium and do some comparative statics. If with n_2 and n remaining constant n_1 increases, what happens to firm 1's share in the contested market? In other words, how does the size of one's captive segment affect one's share in the contested segment? The next theorem asserts that this relationship is a negative one. There is here an interesting analogy with Fudenberg and Tirole's (1986, pp. 23–4) analysis in which an incumbent firm, planning to deter entry, prefers not to have a large captive segment.

Theorem 2. If n_1 increases with n and n_2 constant, then a Nash equilibrium, (q_1, q_2), where $(q_1, q_2) > 0$, changes such that 1's relative market share in the contested segment falls (i.e. q_1/q_2 falls).

Since we are looking at a case where in the Nash equilibrium $(q_1, q_2) > 0$, (q_1, q_2) must satisfy (5) and, by symmetry, the following:

$$(p-c)\left(1+\frac{n_2}{n_3}\right)+\frac{p'}{n_3}\cdot\left[\left(1+\frac{n_2}{n_3}\right)q_2+\frac{n_2}{n_3}q_1\right]=0. \qquad (6)$$

Equations (5) and (6) imply

$$\frac{n_1 + n_3}{n_2 + n_3} = \frac{(n_1 + n_3)q_1 + n_1 q_2}{(n_2 + n_3)q_2 + n_2 q_1}.$$

Cross-multiplying and substituting $n - n_1 - n_2$ for n_3, we get

$$\frac{q_1}{q_2} = \frac{n - n_1}{n - n_2}. \tag{7}$$

The theorem is immediate.

Just before stating the theorem we claimed that we were going to look, into the effect of n_1 on the market share. Clearly, this can be interpreted in several ways. What Theorem 2 examined was the effect of n_1 on q_1/q_2 with n_2 and n held constant. What, it may be asked, will be the effect of raising n_1 on q_1/q_2 if n_2 and n_3 are held constant? To answer this, note that (7) implies $q_1/q_2 = (n_2 + n_3)/(n_1 + n_3)$. Hence, firm 1's market share falls if n_1 increases and n is also increased by the same amount.

Equation (7) tells us more than Theorem 2. Market shares in the contested segment in a Nash equilibrium are independent of c and approach equality as n increases with n_1 and n_2 constant.

Theorem 3. The equilibrium price does not vary with changes in n_1 and n_2 as long as $n_1 + n_2$ and n remain unchanged, excepting in the special case where the change in n_1 and n_2 causes a firm to enter or withdraw from the contested market.

This is a somewhat surprising result. It asserts that in the determination of the industry's price and output, what matters is how much of the market is contested and how much captive. Excepting the special case mentioned in the theorem, the exact break-up of the total captive segment into firm 1's and 2's segments is inconsequential.

To prove this, consider first an 'interior solution', i.e. $(q_1, q_2) > 0$. Rewriting (5) and (6) and using (7), we get

$$\frac{p'q_1}{p - c} = -(n - (n_1 + n_2))\,\frac{(n - n_1)}{n}, \tag{8}$$

$$\frac{p'q_2}{p - c} = -(n - (n_1 + n_2))\,\frac{(n - n_2)}{n}. \tag{9}$$

Writing z for $(q_1 + q_2)/(n - (n_1 + n_2))$, from (8) and (9) we get

$$z = \frac{p(z) - c}{-p'(z)} \cdot \frac{2n - (n_1 + n_2)}{n} \tag{10}$$

Equation (10) implies that z will be unchanged as long as $n, n_1 + n_2$ and c remain unchanged. Since price depends on z, price remains unchanged as long as $n, n_1 + n_2$ and c remain unchanged.

If we have a corner solution, the monopoly price will prevail no matter how the segmentation occurs.

It is interesting to observe that (10) implies that we cannot predict the direction of changes in price induced by changes in n or $n_1 + n_2$, unless we impose restrictions on p''. It is easily checked using (10) that a rise in $(n_1 + n_2)$ will cause z to fall, and hence price to rise, if $p'' \leq 0$. In other words, as the contested segment becomes smaller, $p'' \leq 0$ is a strongly sufficient condition for the equilibrium price to rise towards the monopoly price. As a standard duopoly is characterized by $n_1 = n_2 = 0$, we also have.

Corollary 2. If $p'' \leq 0$, industry output (price) in a fragmented duopoly will be less (greater) than that in a standard duopoly.

It is possible to use this model to do more comparative statics exercises and deduce other properties, but that is not the aim here. Instead we apply the theory of fragmented duopoly to a problem in backward agriculture and, in that context, explore how the captive segments of the market are established in a two-period setting. But before doing so, we make a brief digression to show how our model may be adapted to allow segment-specific price discrimination.

3. FRAGMENTED DUOPOLY WITH PRICE DISCRIMINATION

Let us assume, as before, that seller i chooses q_i and x_i but that he is free to set the price in his captive market, wherever he wishes.

Given profit-maximizing behaviour and given q_1, q_2, x_i, firm i will set a price of $p(x_i/n_i)$ in its captive market, and in the contested market price will be given by $p((q_1 + q_2)/n_3)$. If we continue to assume a constant marginal cost, then all the segments get completely dismembered and equilibrium can be worked out separately for each. The monopoly price, p^m, will be charged in each of the captive segments, while the standard duopoly price will hold in the contested segment.

The problem is much more interesting if we suppose that firm i's total cost function, $c_i(\cdot)$, is increasing and convex. Firm i's profit, $\hat{\pi}_i$, is given as follows:

$$\hat{\pi}_i(q_1, q_2, x_i) = p\left(\frac{x_i}{n_i}\right)\cdot x_i + p\left(\frac{q_1+q_2}{n_3}\right)q_i - c_i(q_i + x_i), \quad i = 1, 2.$$

Firm i maximizes this by choosing q_i and x_i. Its first-order conditions are:

$$\frac{x_i}{n_i}p'\left(\frac{x_i}{n_i}\right)+\left(\frac{x_i}{n_i}\right)=c_i'(q_i+n_i) \tag{11}$$

and

$$\frac{q_i}{n_3}p'\left(\frac{q_1+q_2}{n_3}\right)+\left(\frac{q_1+q_2}{n_3}\right)=c_i'(q_i+n_i) \tag{12}$$

The *Nash equilibrium* of a *price-discriminating fragmented duopoly* is given by the (x_1, q_1, x_2, q_2) derived from solving the four equations described by (11) and (12) and by setting i equal to 1 and 2.

Comparative-statics results may be derived in much the same way as in the previous section. For example, assuming that the marginal revenue curve is downward sloping (i.e. the left-hand term in (11) falls as x_i rises and the left-hand term in (12) falls as q_i rises), Corollary 1 can be derived even for the price-discrimination model. Moreover, following Bulow, Geanakoplos and Klemperer (1985), this model can be used to illustrate some surprising results, like how a subsidy in the captive segment of a seller can actually result in the seller being worse off in equilibrium. With these remarks we turn to the analysis of agrarian relations and the determination of the size of the captive and contested segments. We return to the subject of price discrimination in Sec. 5.

4. SUB-GAME PERFECTION IN A TWO-PERIOD MODEL OF AGRARIAN RELATIONS

Since n_1 and n_2 influence the outcome of the one-period fragmented duopoly described in Secs 2 and 3, it is but natural that firms will try to influence, n_1 and n_2 to the extent that they can. For the sake of illustration consider a rural economy with n labourers and two landlords. In period 1 each landlord i decides on the number, n_i, of labourers he will employ on his land.[8] In period 2 the landlords supply credit to them and to the contested segment of the market for loans. This periodization reflects more the priorities of decision than the actual sequence of time. Moreover, in reality period 2 will be further split up involving a first subperiod when the loan is received by the labourers and a second subperiod when the wage is received and the principal and interest is repaid. We, however, ignore this further temporal partitioning of period 2.

We shall assume—and this is not unrealistic—that each landlord has the power to forbid his employees from taking credit from the other landlord. Further, this is in a setting where everybody knows everybody and the landlords consider it safe to give credit to any labourer from this set of villages. Thus the n_1 and n_2 chosen in period 1 become parameters in the second period in the fragmented credit market. Moreover n_1 and n_2 have the same significance as the n_1 and n_2 in Secs 2 and 3 above since landlord i can lend to $n_i + n_3$ labourers where $n_3 = n - n_1 - n_2$.

It is immediately clear that in this model landlord i may hire employees not just to work as labourers but keeping in mind that a larger n_i alters the kind of leverage he has in the credit market. Hence this theory provides a rationale for interlinkage, albeit of a very different kind from the ones found in the literature (e.g. Braverman and Srinivasan, 1981; Braverman and Stiglitz, 1982; Basu, 1983; Mitra, 1983; Bell, 1988).

The natural solution criterion to use in such a two-period model is that of sub-game perfection. We shall first give an abstract characterization of this and then scrutinize a special case.

Let landlord i's production function be

$$X_i = X_i(n_i), \quad X_i' \geq 0, \quad X_i'' \leq 0.$$

To keep the model simple, we assume that labourers have access to other employment opportunities at an exogenous wage, w. In period 2 each landlord earns profits from production and interest from the

[8] We shall assume that the parameters of the model are such that firm 1's chosen n_1 and firm 2's chosen n_2 never sum to greater than n.

credit market depending on what Nash equilibrium emerges from a fragmented duopoly characterized by n_1 and n_2.

In order to state this more formally note that if in a fragmented duopoly n and c are fixed, the fragmented duopoly is entirely defined by (n_1, n_2).

Let us now define a *Nash equilibrium correspondence, N*, as follows. For every pair of non-negative integers n_1 and n_2 such that $n_1 + n_2 \leq n$,

$$N(n_1, n_2) \equiv \{(q_1, q_2) \mid (q_1, q_2) \text{ is a Nash equilibrium in a fragmented duopoly defined by } (n_1, n_2)\}.$$

A specification of which Nash equilibrium will occur in period 2 for each game (n_1, n_2) is a *selection, f*, from the Nash equilibrium correspondence N. That is, $f(n_1, n_2)$ is an element of $N(n_1, n_2)$, for all (n_1, n_2).

Given that c represents the opportunity cost of giving credit and p is the price of credit, we could use π_i as defined in Sec. 2 to be i's profit function in period 2.

For every selection, f, from the correspondence N, we can define each player's profit in the two-period game (assuming zero discounting) as

$$\Omega_i(n_1, n_2, f) = X_i(n_i) - wn_i + \pi_i(f(n_1, n_2)), \quad i = 1, 2, \tag{13}$$

where the absence of price discrimination in the credit market implies that all labourers will pay the same price and hence that both landlords will pay their labourers the exogenous wage w.

The triple (n_1^*, n_2^*, f^*) is a (subgame-) perfect equilibrium if and only if

$$\Omega_1(n_1^*, n_2^*, f^*) \geq \Omega_1(n_1, n_2^*, f^*) \text{ for all } n_1, \quad \text{and}$$

$$\Omega_2(n_1^*, n_2^*, f^*) \geq \Omega_2(n_1^*, n_2, f^*) \text{ for all } n_2.$$

Distorting terminology slightly, we may refer to (n_1^*, n_2^*) as a 'perfect equilibrium' if there exists an f^* such that (n_1^*, n_2^*, f^*) is a perfect equilibrium.

In this setting, labourers are fully rational and make their choices after evaluating the consequences of joining one or other of the captive segments of the market, as opposed to dealing in the contested segment. However, we assume that n is large and labourers do not collude, so that each takes the pattern of segmentation (n_1, n_2) as exogenously given. As noted above, the assumption of a constant marginal cost of funds, c, for both landlords implies that the monopoly price, p^{m}, is independent of the size of each captive market. Hence, if the labourer conjectures that the market will contain no contested segmented (i.e. $n_1 + n_2 = n$), he will face a price p^{m} from both landlords; and since the wage is exogenously given, he will therefore be indifferent between them. If, on the other hand, there is a contested segment, then in the absence of price discrimination, the same price will rule everywhere; and again he will be indifferent as to which segment he joins. That is to say, an interlinked wage and credit contract with either landlord will yield a labourer the same utility as an unbundled deal. Thus, although labourers are not strategic in the sense that the actual choice of n_i is effectively in the hands of the landlords alone, they are fully rational. In brief we model labourers in the same way as consumers are modelled in oligopoly theory.

We analyse the perfect equilibria of the two-period game in the special case where the demand schedule of an individual consumer is linear over the relevant range of outcomes:

$$p = a - bq. \tag{14}$$

We assume that n is so large and the marginal product of labour, i.e. $X'_i(n_i)$, falls so fast that landlords 1 and 2 will never choose n_1 and n_2 for which there is a Nash equilibrium where one firm abandons the contested segment totally. Hence, we could focus on the unique 'interior' Nash equilibrium that occurs for each relevant (n_1, n_2). Let $f(n_1, n_2)$ refer to such a Nash equilibrium

Using (5), (6) and (14), we get

$$\pi_i(f(n_1, n_2)) = \frac{(a-c)^2}{b} \cdot \frac{(n-n_j)n^2}{(3n-n_1-n_2)^2}, \quad i = 1, 2. \tag{15}$$

Hence, using $\bar{\Omega}_i(n_1, n_2)$ to denote $\Omega_i(n_1, n_2, f)$, we have

$$\bar{\Omega}_i(n_1, n_2) = [X_i(n_i) - wn_i] + \left[\frac{(a-c)^2}{b} \cdot \frac{(n-n_j)n^2}{(3n-n_1-n_2)^2}\right], \quad i = 1, 2 \tag{16}$$

Clearly, if n_1^* and n_2^* are such that n_1^* maximizes $\bar{\Omega}_1(n_1, n_2^*)$ and n_2^* maximizes $\bar{\Omega}_2(n_1^*, n_2)$, then (n_1^*, n_2^*) is a perfect equilibrium.

The first interesting feature of the perfect equilibrium to note is that in equilibrium each landlord will be employing labour up to a point where the wage rate exceeds the marginal product of labour. Let $\hat{n}_i$ be such that

$$X_i'(\hat{n}_i) = w.$$

It is easy to see that for all n_2, and all $n_1 < \hat{n}_1$, $\bar{\Omega}_1(\hat{n}_1, n_2) > \bar{\Omega}(n_1, n_2)$. At $n_1 = \hat{n}_1$ a further increase in n_1 causes $\bar{\Omega}_1$ to rise since, at this point, the first expression within brackets in (16) is stationary and the second expression is rising. Hence, landlords always employ in excess of what pure marginal productivity and wage considerations would lead them to do. This result is quite in keeping with Klemperer's (1987b) finding of heightened competition in the 'first' period. It could also be thought of as providing a rationale for the idea that landlords have a penchant for maintaining an excessive number of dependent labourers (see, e.g. Bhaduri, 1983). In addition, this model gives some new insight into the phenomenon of disguised unemployment and surplus labour, since it is possible for marginal product to be not only less that w, but even zero (if X_i' vanishes for finite n_i).

From the first-order conditions of maximizing $\bar{\Omega}_1(n_1, n_2)$ with respect to n_1 and $\bar{\Omega}_2(n_1, n_2)$ with respect to n_2 and denoting the equilibrium values with a star, we have

$$X_1'(n_1^*) + \frac{2(a-c)^2\, n^2(n-n_2^*)}{b(3n-n_1^*-n_2^*)^3} = w$$

and

$$X_2'(n_2^*) + \frac{2(a-c)^2\, n^2(n-n_1^*)}{b(3n-n_1^*-n_2^*)^3} = w$$

These, in turn, imply

$$\frac{X_1'(n_1^*) - w}{X_2'(n_2^*) - w} = \frac{n-n_2^*}{n-n_1^*}. \tag{17}$$

Hence, if $n_2^* > n_1^*$, then $X_1'(n_1^*) > X_2'(n_2^*)$, since from the reasoning above we know that $X_i'(n_i^*) - w < 0, i = 1,2$. It is important to appreciate that this is true though the production functions of the two landlords need not be the same. If we use the extent of divergence of $X_i'(n_i^*)$ from w as an index of production inefficiency, then what we have established is that larger farms (in terms of numbers of workers employed) are the ones exhibiting greater production inefficiency. Also, larger farms have larger shares of the contested segment of the credit market,[9] and hence are larger overall.

5. EQUILIBRIUM IN AGRARIAN MARKETS WITH PRICE DISCRIMINATION

If landlords can practise price discrimination, the labourer who accepts an interlinked contract by going into a captive segment of the credit market knows that he will be charged the monopoly price, p^m, which exceeds that in the contested segment, p^o, should one exist.[10] Thus, in order to make an interlinked contract attractive to labourers, landlords will have to offer a wage premium, δ say, in compensation for the higher rate of interest. Landlords are therefore constrained by the utility equivalence condition.

$$\upsilon(p^m, w + \delta) = \upsilon(p^o, w), \tag{18}$$

where $\upsilon(\cdot)$ is the indirect utility of a labourer.

In this case, (13) becomes

$$\Omega_i(n_1, n_2, f) = [X_i(n_i) - (w + \delta)n_i] + \pi_i(f(n_1, n_2)) \tag{13}$$

with the reminder that f now pertains to the Nash equilibrium as in Sec. 3 (i.e. with price discrimination allowed).

$$\pi_i(f(n_1, n_2)) = n_i p^m \cdot q(p^m) + p\left(\frac{q_1 + q_2}{n_3}\right) \cdot q_i - c(n_i q(p^m) + q_i), \tag{19}$$

where $(q_1, q_2) = f(n_1, n_2)$.

With a linear demand function,

[9] From (5) and (6), we get $(q_1/q_2) = (n - n_1^*)/(n - n_2^*)$. Substituting into (15) yields the required result.

[10] This argument uses subgame perfection which rules out the possibility of landlords committing themselves to some price different from p^m.

$$p^{\mathrm{m}} = (a+c)/2 \quad \text{and} \quad q^{\mathrm{m}} = (a-c)/2b.$$

In a standard duopoly, with $n_3 = n - n_1 - n_2$ given exogenously,

$$p^{\mathrm{o}} = (a+2c)/3 \quad \text{and} \quad q^{\mathrm{o}} = (q_1^{\mathrm{o}} + q_2^{\mathrm{o}})/n_3 = 2(a-c)/3b,$$

and by symmetry,

$$q_1^{\mathrm{o}} = q_2^{\mathrm{o}} = n_3\, q^{\mathrm{o}}/2.$$

Substituting for $(p^{\mathrm{m}}, q^{\mathrm{m}}, p^{\mathrm{o}}, q_1^{\mathrm{o}}, q_2^{\mathrm{o}})$ in (19), some manipulation yields

$$\pi_i(f(n_1, n_2)) = \frac{(a-c)^2}{b} \cdot \left(\frac{5n_i - 4n_j}{36} + \frac{n}{9} \right) \quad i = 1, 2, \quad i \neq j, \qquad (20)$$

which, unlike (15), is linear in (n_1, n_2).

The next step is to obtain the wage premium δ from (18). While the value of δ depends on $\upsilon(\cdot)$, it follows at once from the fact that $(p^{\mathrm{m}}, p^{\mathrm{o}}, w)$ are all independent of (n_1, n_2) that δ must be likewise. Hence, substituting for $\pi_i(\cdot)$ from (20) in (13′), we have

$$\bar{\Omega}_i(n_1, n_2) = [X_i(n_i) - (w+\delta)n_i] + \frac{(a-c)^2}{b} \cdot \left(\frac{5n_i - 4n_j}{36} + \frac{n}{9} \right), \quad i = 1, 2. \qquad (21)$$

As in Sec. 4, in equilibrium each landlord will be employing labour up to a point where the wage rate (including the premium δ in this case) exceeds the marginal product of labour. For when $[X_i(n_i) - (w+\delta)n_i]$ is stationary, π_i is increasing in n_i. Denoting the values of (n_1, n_2) in equilibrium with a star, we have, from (21),

$$X_i'(n_i^*) = (w+\delta) - \frac{5}{36}\frac{(a-c)^2}{b}, \quad i = 1, 2. \qquad (22)$$

Hence, unlike the case without price discrimination, the marginal product of labour is identical on the farms of both landlords.

This result is not very surprising in the light of the fact that the assumption of constant marginal costs makes all the parameters of an individual's wage and credit contracts independent of the pattern of market segmentation, if landlords can practice price discrimination. As we saw in Sec. 3, the cost functions (in this case, for lending) must be increasing and convex for interesting situations to arise from the one-period game with (n_1, n_2) fixed. It is certainly plausible that the cost of lending, for example, is increasing and convex with the size of the captive market, since the landlord must prevent each of his captive clients from borrowing from the other landlord in period 2 and recover monopoly interest charges from them subsequently.

6. RENT DISSIPATION

There remains the question of whether competition for captive segments of the market in period 1 will more than dissipate the rents from lock-in in period 2 (Klemperer, 1987a). Suppose, therefore, that interlinking was banned. In a standard duopoly with $n_1 = n_2 = 0$ and $n_3 = n$, the profit of each landlord from moneylending is, under the above assumptions about costs and demand,

$$\pi_i^o = n(a-c)^2/9b. \tag{23}$$

In this case, the total profit of landlord i in equilibrium is

$$\Omega_i^o = [X_i(\hat{n}_i) - w\hat{n}_i] + n(a-c)^2/9b, \tag{24}$$

where $X_i'(\hat{n}_i) = w$. Subtracting (24) from (21), we obtain

$$\bar{\Omega}_i(n_1^*, n_2^*) - \Omega_i^o = [X_i(n_i^*) - wn_i^*] - [X_i(\hat{n}_i) - w\hat{n}_i] - \delta n_i^* + \frac{(a-c)^2}{b}\left(\frac{5n_i^* - 4n_j^*}{36}\right), \quad i = 1, 2. \tag{25}$$

Since $\hat{n}_i$ maximizes $[X_i(n_i) - wn_i]$,

$$\xi_i \equiv [X_i(n_i^*) - wn_i^*] - [X_i(\hat{n}_i) - w\hat{n}_i] < 0$$

and the (algebraic) sum of the first three terms on the right-hand side of (25) is negative.

Now suppose that one landlord (1, say) has more land than the other; so that, by virtue of (22) and an assumption that land and labour are complementary, $n_1^* > n_2^*$. Now, if the difference in holdings is such that $n_2^* \leq 4n_1^*/5$, it follows at once that the landlord who has the smaller holding would be better off if interlinking were banned.

In order to examine whether the combined rents from lock in of both landlords are more than fully dissipated by heightened competition for captive segments in period 1, we sum over i in (25) and obtain

$$\sum_{i} [\bar{\Omega}_i(n_1^* + n_2^*) - \Omega_i^o(n_1, n_2)] = (\xi_1 + \xi_2) - (n_1^* + n_2^*)\,[\delta - (a-c)^2/36b]. \tag{26}$$

Since $\xi_i < 0$, a strongly sufficient condition for the said rents to be more than dissipated is

$$\delta > (a-c)^2/36b. \tag{27}$$

Now the loss in an individual's net consumer surplus that results from being charged the monopoly price as opposed to the duopoly price is

$$(p^{\mathrm{m}} - p^{\mathrm{o}})\,(q^{\mathrm{m}} + q^{\mathrm{o}})/2 = 7(a-c)^2/72b > (a-c)^2/36b.$$

Hence, as δ is the compensating variation with respect to the increase in price from p^{o} to p^{m}, (27) will indeed hold if consumption in each period is a non-inferior good for a labourer. We have therefore shown that rents from second period lock-in can be more than dissipated in our model, a possibility which appears in other models in the related literature.

By way of comparison, we now examine whether this result will hold if landlords cannot practice price discrimination. Summing (18) over i and subtracting $(\Omega_1^{\mathrm{o}} + \Omega_2^{\mathrm{o}})$, we obtain, in this case,

$$\sum_{i} [\bar{\Omega}_i(n_1^*, n_2^*) - \Omega_i^{\mathrm{o}}(n_1, n_2)] = (\xi_1 + \xi_2) + \frac{(a-c)^2 n}{b}\left[\frac{n(n+n_3^*)}{(2n+n_3^*)^2} - \frac{1}{9}\right] \tag{28}$$

Since $9n(n+n_3^*) > (2n+n_3^*)^2$, strong claims about whether rents are more than fully dissipated cannot be made without knowledge of the shape of $X_i(n_i)$ over the domain $(\hat{n}_i, n_i^*)$, all of which determine the magnitude of ξ_i. We leave this as an open question.

7. CONCLUSION

This paper started by analysing a market structure in which each firm has a *predetermined* set of potential customers. These sets may overlap but they need not coincide totally with one another. Such a structure could emerge in a location-model of oligopoly, but it emerges more naturally in trades where the problem of asymmetric information and moral hazard is high. Such markets were referred to as fragmented oligopolies, and the basic properties of a fragmented duopoly were analysed formally. The next step was to make each firm's set of potential customers endogenous by embedding a fragmented duopoly in a two-period model and then examine its perfect equilibrium. This was done in the context of labour and credit markets in backward agrarian economies. There emerged a rationale for interlinking, albeit of a sort quite different from that advanced in the extant literature on that subject.

Fragmented oligopolies, it was argued, are relevant in a wide variety of situations. The particular model constructed in this paper was meant to be illustrative. By considering alternative strategy sets for firms and different solution concepts, a range of different models of fragmented oligopoly can be constructed. There is, in brief, room for much further exploration.

APPENDIX: PROOF OF THEOREM 1

Given the symmetric nature of the two parts of Theorem 1, it is clearly sufficient to prove either.

From the second-order condition we have

$$\frac{\partial^2 \pi_1}{\partial q_1^2} = 2\frac{p'}{n_3} \cdot \left(1 + \frac{n_1}{n_3}\right) + \frac{p''}{n_3^2} \cdot \left[\left(1 + \frac{n_1}{n_3}\right) q_1 + \frac{n_1}{n_3} q_2\right] < 0. \qquad \text{(A.1)}$$

Taking total differentials in (5), we get

$$p' \cdot \left(\frac{dq_1}{n_3} + \frac{dq_2}{n_3}\right)\left(1 + \frac{n_1}{n_3}\right) + \frac{p''}{n_3} \cdot \left(\frac{dq_1}{n_3} + \frac{dq_2}{n_3}\right)\left[\left(1 + \frac{n_1}{n_3}\right) q_1 + \frac{n_1}{n_3} q_2\right]$$

$$+ \frac{p'}{n_3} \cdot \left[\left(1 + \frac{n_1}{n_3}\right) dq_1 + \frac{n_1}{n_3} dq_2\right] = 0$$

Rearranging terms this may be rewritten as

$$\frac{dq_1}{dq_2} = -\frac{2\frac{p'}{n_3}\cdot\left(1+\frac{n_1}{n_3}\right)+\frac{p''}{n_3^2}\cdot\left[\left(1+\frac{n_1}{n_3}\right)q_1+\frac{n_1}{n_3}q_2\right]-\frac{p'}{n_3}}{2\frac{p'}{n_3}\cdot\left(1+\frac{n_1}{n_3}\right)+\frac{p''}{n_3^2}\cdot\left[\left(1+\frac{n_1}{n_3}\right)q_1+\frac{n_1}{n_3}q_2\right]}. \tag{A.2}$$

Given (A.1) and $p' < 0$, it follows that $(dq_1/dq_2) > -1$. Since (5) implicitly defines the reaction function $R_1(\cdot)$, we have proved Theorem 1.

REFERENCES

BARDHAN, P.K. (1984), *Land, Labour and Rural Poverty*, New York: Columbia University Press.

BASU, K. (1983), 'The Emergence of Isolation and Interlinkage in Rural Markets', *Oxford Economic Papers*, 35, 262–80.

—— (1987), 'Disneyland Monopoly, Interlinkage and Usurious Interest Rates', *Journal of Public Economics*, 34, 1–18.

BASU, K. and N. SINGH (1990), 'Entry-deterrence in Stackelberg Perfect Equilibria', *International Economic Review*, 31, 61–71.

BELL, C. (1988), 'Credit Markets and Interlinked Transactions', in H.B. Chenery and T.N. Srinivasan (eds), *Handbook of Development Economics*, Amsterdam: North-Holland.

BHADURI, A. (1983), *The Economic Structure of Backward Agriculture*, London: Academic Press.

BONANNO, G. (1987), 'Location Choice, Product Proliferation and Entry-deterrence', *Review of Economic Studies*, 54, 37–45.

BRAVERMAN, A. and T.N. SRINIVASAN (1981), 'Credit and Sharecropping in Agrarian Societies', *Journal of Development Economics*, 9, 289–312.

BRAVERMAN, A. and J.E. STIGLITZ (1982), 'Sharecropping and the Interlinking of Agrarian Markets', *American Economic Review*, 72, 695–715.

BULOW, J.I., J.D. GEANAKOPLOS and P.D. KLEMPERER (1985), 'Multimarket Oligopoly: Strategic Substitutes and Complements', *Journal of Political Economy*, 93, 488–511.

DASGUPTA, P. (1986), 'Trust as a Commodity', Economic Theory Discussion Paper No. 101, Cambridge: Cambridge University.

D'ASPREMONT, C., J.J. GABSZEWICZ and J.F. THISSE (1979), 'On Hotelling's "Stability in Competition"', *Econometrica*, 1145–50.

DIXIT, A. (1979), 'A Model of Duopoly Suggesting a Theory of Entry Barriers', *Bell Journal of Economics*, 10, 20–32.

—— (1980), 'The Role of Investment in Entry-deterrence', *Economic Journal*, 90, 95–106.

FRIEDMAN, J. (1977), *Oligopoly and the Theory of Games*, Amsterdam: North-Holland.

FUDENBERG, D. and J. TIROLE (1986), *Dynamic Models of Oligopoly*, London: Harwood Academic Publishers.

GEERTZ, C. (1978), 'The Bazaar Economy: Information and Search in Peasant Marketing', *American Economic Review*, 68, 28–32.

HOTELLING, H. (1929), 'Stability in Competition', *Economic Journal*, 39, 41–57.

KLEMPERER, P.D. (1987a), 'The Competitiveness of Markets with Switching Costs', *Rand Journal of Economics*, 18, 138–50.

—— (1987b), 'Markets with Consumer Switching Costs', *Quarterly Journal of Economics*, 102, 375–94.

MISHRA, A. (1991), 'Clientelization and Fragmentation in Backward Agriculture: A Model Based on Forward Induction (mimeo.), Delhi School of Economics, New Delhi.

MITRA, P. (1983), 'A Theory of Interlined Rural Transactions', *Journal of Public Economics*, 20, 169–91.

PLATTEAU, J.P. and A. ABRAHAM (1987), 'An Inquiry into Quasi-credit Systems in Traditional Fisherman Communities: The Role of Reciprocal Credit and Mixed Contracts', *Journal of Development Studies*, 23, 461–90.

RESERVE BANK OF INDIA (1954), *All India Rural Credit Survey*, Vol. 1, Part 2 (Credit Agencies), Bombay: RBI.

SPENCE, A.M. (1977), 'Entry, Capacity, Investment and Oligopolistic Pricing', *Bell Journal of Economics*, 8, 534–44.

VON WEIZSÄCKER, C.C. (1984), 'The Costs of Substitution', *Econometrica*, 52, 1085–1116.

Trade and Foreign Investment Policies under Imperfect Competition: Lessons for Developing Countries*

SANTIAGO LEVY AND SEAN NOLAN

1. INTRODUCTION

Graduate students undertaking the study of the theory of commercial policy during the late 1970s encountered some algebra, much geometry, and a number of Fundamental Truths. These truths included the views that interventionist trade policies were almost invariable inappropriate (unless justified by the venerable optimum tariff/export tax argument), that reasonable arguments for such intervention were 'third' or 'fourth best' arguments to be ignored under most circumstances, and that the widespread deviations from laissez-faire in reality could be explained by foolish policy making and/or effective 'rent seeking' by the politically well connected. These truths provided the intellectual core of the argument that an 'outward looking' trade policy is an essential component of an effective development strategy. They also provided support for the view that multilateral lending agencies could promote societal (as distinct from interest group) welfare in borrower countries by making trade liberalization a precondition for access to new funds.

Graduate students undertaking the study of the theory of commercial policy a decade later encounter more algebra, less geometry, and little in the way of unqualified truths. The 1980s has seen the

* We would like to thank two anonymous referees, John Harris, Jeffrey Lewis, James Markusen, Michael Roemer, Raul Saez, Fernando Solis, Aaron Tornell, Lou Wells, and Larry Westphal for helpful comments. The usual disclaimers apply.

emergence of a substantial and rapidly growing body of literature on the role of trade policy in market structures characterized by *imperfect competition*; a literature which has produced new policy insights which are at odds with the Fundamental Truths.[1] The key message of this literature is that, when domestic firms compete with foreign firms in a market structure which allows for economic profits, the domestic government can boost aggregate welfare by intervening to shift the competitive outcome in favour of domestic firms; and that trade policy measures (tariffs, export taxes/subsidies, countervailing duties, export performance requirements, etc.) can be appropriate devices for producing such a shift.[2] The case for free trade in this literature is *political* rather than *economic*, relying on the argument that rent-seeking-influenced intervention is likely to produce an outcome inferior to non-intervention even if the optimal intervention package would be better than free trade (Krugman, 1987a).

The new literature on trade policies under imperfect competition has been motivated in large part by policy debates in the industrialized countries, most notably the question as to how the United States (and Europe) should respond to the rising industrial might of allegedly interventionist Japan. The pervasiveness of imperfectly competitive market structures in the industrial sectors of most developing economies suggests that the new literature should also contain important lessons for policy makers in developing countries.[3] Identifying precisely what these lessons are, however, is not straightforward. For one thing, the literature has made use of a large variety of models, each with special features and assumptions; in consequence, it is difficult to distinguish between those results that are robust (and hence of general interest) and those results that are conditional upon particular assumptions (and hence of less general relevance). Furthermore, it has been common practice to construct models which are *symmetric*, in the sense that the home and the foreign countries are

[1] For recent reviews of this literature, see Krugman (1986) and Helpman and Krugman (1989).

[2] For selected analysis of the role of trade policies in improving social welfare, see Markusen and Venables (1988) on tariffs, Brander and Spencer (1985) on export subsidies, Dixit (1988b) on countervailing duties, and Rodrik (1987) on export performance requirements.

[3] See Rodrik (1988) for a discussion of the empirical significance of imperfect competition in developing countries.

modelled as fundamentally similar economies (e.g., having similar cost levels, engaging in two-way intra-industry trade, etc.); while symmetry may be a useful assumption to employ in modelling exercises, it is an important restriction which seems particularly inappropriate for analyzing trade policy issues in a developing country context. Finally, the literature has paid little or no attention to the issue of direct foreign investment (DFI). This is a surprising omission in light of the well-established linkage between protectionist trade policies and DFI in the imperfectly competitive market structures which are at the centre of attention in the 'new' trade policy literature.

This paper has three goals. First, we seek to provide an exposition of the positive and normative analysis of trade policy under imperfect competition which is easily accessible to readers unfamiliar with the minutiae of oligopoly theory. The model we use is simple yet sufficiently general to accommodate various situations as special cases. Second, we seek to provide a unified analysis of trade and DFI, thereby taking explicit account of the fact that trade policy intervention can induce (and can be explicitly deployed to induce) DFI; this integrated treatment enables us to present a richer and more realistic discussion of the alternatives open to policy makers in Less Developed Countries (LDCs). Third, we seek to provide a preliminary assessment of the lessons of this analysis for policy formulation in developing countries—an assessment which, given the limited amount of empirical work on 'new' trade policy currently available, is based largely on our interpretation of the economic intuition underlying the formal results of the analysis.

The structure of the paper is as follows. Section 2 describes the core model and establishes two propositions which underpin most of the results derived in the paper. Section 3 examines the effects of international trade, and provides a preliminary analysis of the welfare impact of tariffs. Section 4 discusses the effects of inward DFI on the domestic economy. Section 5 analyses the problem confronting policy makers: what are the characteristics of the welfare maximizing policy package in an oligopolistic industry where direct foreign investment may occur? Finally, Sec. 6 contains our assessment of the policy implications of our analysis.

Before proceeding further, some general comments are in order. First, the paper is concerned with the effects of trade and foreign investment in a static (i.e. single period) context, in which market structure, cost conditions, entry barriers, etc. are given. Our motivation for focusing on the *static welfare analysis* of trade and investment policies is methodological in nature: it is useful to get the static analysis clarified before proceeding to the multi-period models that can be used to address entry and investment decisions in a meaningful way. Second, the focus of our attention is on industries in which domestic firms sell on domestic markets but do not export; introducing an export market into the model described in Sec. 2 is not difficult, but is omitted here for reasons of space. Third, we assume throughout that wage rates and other factor prices reflect social opportunity costs; the policy issues associated with factor market distortions are well understood and need no further treatment here (Corden, 1974). Finally, we work throughout in a partial equilibrium framework, as is common practice in the literature; the additional considerations introduced by economy-wide resource constraints are touched upon briefly in Sec. 6.

2. A FRAMEWORK FOR ANALYSIS

The market structure we seek to analyse is one in which the domestic market for some product is served by a small number of domestic firms and a small number of foreign firms; the number of firms is sufficiently small that some form of oligopolistic competition ensues. Barriers to entry in the market are such that no new firms can enter the industry within the time period under consideration.[4] Prices in the domestic market are not rigidly linked to prices in foreign markets; firms have sufficient control over their distribution systems to enable them to 'price to market' (i.e. to set different prices in the domestic and foreign markets). Foreign firms may supply the domestic market from production plants abroad or from local production facilities, but do not serve export markets from local plants.[5]

We now describe a formal model with these characteristics, employing convenient functional forms and simplifying technical assumptions where appropriate. The robustness of the ensuing

[4] See Horstmann and Markusen (1990) for a discussion of the policy issues introduced when market structure is endogenously determined.

[5] Direct foreign investments motivated by the desire to export from the host country raises issues different from those considered here.

analysis to changes in these simplifying assumptions is discussed in a separate appendix; in general we find the results to be highly robust, and hence of general relevance.[6]

2.1. The model

2.1.1. *Demand*

Domestic consumers consume three goods, x, y and z. Goods x and y are close but imperfect substitutes for one another. Good z is the 'all other goods' category that appears in microeconomic textbooks; we set its price to unity and use it as numeraire. Preferences of the representative consumer are represented by a quasi-linear utility function of the form

$$\tilde{U}(x, y, z) = U(x, y) + z. \tag{1}$$

For convenience, we assume that $U(x, y)$, takes the functional form:

$$U(x, y) = ax - (b/2)x^2 + ay - (b/2)y^2 - kxy, \ a, b, k > 0; b \geq k. \tag{2}$$

Utility maximization yields inverse demand functions for x and y of the form[7]

$$p_x = a - bx - ky, \tag{3a}$$

$$p_y = a - by - kx. \tag{3b}$$

This demand system has some useful properties. First, the income elasticities of demand for both x and y are zero; hence, the traditional measure of consumer surplus ('the area above the price and below the demand curve') is an exact measure of the gain to consumers from purchasing a product at a given price. Second, the aggregate surplus accruing to consumers from consuming x and y at prices p_x and p_y can be written as

$$CS = U(x, y) - p_x x - p_y y; \tag{4}$$

changes in (4) provide an exact measure of the change in consumer welfare resulting from changes in p_x or p_y. Finally, the parameter k provides an indicator of the degree of substitutability between x and

6 This appendix is available from the authors upon request.

7 Part 1 of the appendix provides further details.

y; a higher value for k (given a and b) denotes a closer degree of substitutability between the two products.[8]

2.1.2. *Supply*

Good x is produced by a single domestic firm; good y is produced by a single foreign firm. Each firm produces under conditions of constant average and marginal costs, c_x (c_y) denoting the marginal cost of the domestic (foreign) firm.[9] The two firms seek to maximize their own profits and do not collude with one another; in selecting its profit-maximizing output level, each firm treats the output level of its competitor as given. The outcome of this form of competition is the Cournot–Nash equilibrium.

The domestic firm's profit function can be written as

$$\Pi_x(x, y) = p_x x - c_x x. \tag{5}$$

The firm's profit-maximizing output level, given the output of its competitor, is obtained by setting $\partial\Pi_x/\partial x$ equal to zero:

$$\partial\Pi_x/\partial x = (p_x - c_x) + x\partial p_x/\partial x = 0. \tag{6}$$

Using (3a), this simplifies to

$$x = (a - ky - c_x)/2b. \tag{7a}$$

In a similar manner, the profit-maximizing output level for the foreign firm, given the output of x, can be shown to be

$$y = (a - kx - c_y)/2b. \tag{7b}$$

Equations (7a) and (7b) are often referred to as the reaction functions (or 'best response' functions): they show the optimal level of output for each firm conditional upon the output level of its competitor.

We rewrite (6) in a manner which highlights a key feature of equilibrium under imperfect competition. Nothing that $\partial p_x/\partial x = -b$, we obtain

[8] Note that $k \leq b$; with $k = b$, the two goods are perfect substitutes and the demand system reduces to $p_x = p_y = a - 2b(x + y)$.

[9] In this section we develop a framework to analyse competition between the domestic and the foreign firm, regardless of the geographical location of the foreign firm. In Sec. 3 the foreign firm will be located abroad (yielding trade); in Sec. 4 the foreign firm may locate at home (yielding DFI).

$$(p_x - c_x) = bx. \tag{8}$$

Hence, profit maximizing behaviour by the domestic firm entails producing at a point at which price exceeds marginal cost, implying in turn that the level of output produced is less than the socially optimal output level.

2.1.3. *Equilibrium*

In equilibrium each firm is maximizing its profits given the output level of its competitor. Hence, the equilibrium output combination is the (x, y) combination which satisfies both (7a) and (7b):

$$x = [2b(a - c_x) - k(a - c_y)]/H \tag{9a}$$

where $H = 4b^2 - k^2 > 0$.

$$y = [2b(a - c_y) - k(a - c_x)]/H \tag{9b}$$

Using (3a) and (3b), the associated equilibrium prices are:

$$p_x = [(2b^2 - bk)a + (2b^2 - k^2)c_x + bkc_y]/H, \tag{9c}$$

$$p_y = [(2b^2 - bk)a + (2b^2 - k^2)c_y + bkc_x]/H, \tag{9d}$$

We have yet to impose constraints on parameter values to ensure that this equilibrium involves non-negative output levels. From (9a) and (9b), a necessary condition for the existence of the duopoly equilibrium is that $a \geq c_x$ and $a \geq c_y$: a firm's costs cannot exceed the maximum price that consumers are willing to pay for its product. Furthermore, c_y cannot be 'too high' relative to c_x (for then the foreign firm would not be able to compete), nor can it be 'too low' (for then the domestic firm would not be able to compete). Letting c_y^{max} (c_y^{min}) denote this upper (lower) bound on c_y, manipulation of (9a) and (9b) yields:

$$c_y^{max} = a(1 - k/2b) + (k/2b)c_x, \tag{10a}$$

$$c_y^{min} = a(1 - 2b/k) + (2b/k)c_x, \tag{10b}$$

Hence, the duopoly equilibrium exists provided that c_y, lies between c_y^{min} and c_y^{max}. With $c_y \leq c_y^{min}$, the domestic firm is unable to compete, and the foreign firm is the sole supplier to the market; with

$c_y \geq c_y^{\max}$, the foreign firm cannot compete, and the domestic firm is the monopoly supplier.[10]

We now examine the response of prices and outputs to changes in firms' cost levels; these results are central to our analysis. From (9) we obtain:

$$\begin{aligned} \partial y/\partial c_y &= -2b/H < 0, & \partial x/\partial c_y &= k/H > 0, \\ \partial p_y/\partial c_y &= (2b^2 - k^2)/H < 1, & \partial p_x/\partial c_y &= bk/H < 1. \end{aligned} \tag{11}$$

Given the symmetric structure of the model, a small increase in c_x gives rise to similar own-price and cross-price effects, and to similar own-output and cross-output effects. Note that a unit increase in a firm's costs results in a less than unit increase in its price, implying that cost increases are only partially passed through into price increases. Note also that an increase in the costs of one firm enables its competitors to increase both its sales level and its price.

2.1.4. *Government*

The government imposes specific taxes on x and y, denoted by τ_x and τ_y. Tax rates may be either positive or negative, with $\tau_i < 0$ implying that good i is subsidized. The assumption that taxes are specific rather than ad valorem simplifies the exposition; nothing of substance depends on this assumption. It proves convenient at this juncture to think of these taxes as sales taxes, though later we use the τ_i notation to denote tariffs and production taxes and subsidies, where appropriate.

Given the presence of a specific tax of $\tau_i (i = x, y)$, the effective unit cost to firm i of supplying the market is $c_i^e = c_i + \tau_i$. A reworking of the preceding analysis shows that equilibrium prices and outputs remain as described by (9), provided one replaces the c_is with their tax-inclusive counterparts, c_i^e. Note that a unit increase in τ_i results in a unit increase in c_i^e; hence, the effects of small changes in τ_i are as described by (11).

2.1.5. *Social welfare*

Aggregate social welfare, SW, is the sum of: (i) consumer surplus, (ii) domestic firm profits and, (iii) net government tax revenue; we thus write

10 We assume that the goods are sufficiently close substitutes (i.e. k/b is sufficiently large) to ensure that $c_y^{\min} > 0$.

$$SW = CS + (p_x - c_x - \tau_x)x + (\tau_x x + \tau_y y). \quad (12)$$

This specification of aggregate social welfare sidesteps the issue of income distribution by weighting each of the components of welfare equally; the incorporation of distributional considerations into the analysis (via an alternative weighting system) is left for the interested reader.

Given the definition of consumer surplus in (4), we can rewrite (12) as

$$SW = U(x, y) - c_x x - (p_y - \tau_y)y. \quad (13)$$

This provides a simple interpretation of social welfare as the utility gain from consuming x and y less the social cost of acquiring the two goods. Note the distinction between the social cost of acquiring good x (the production cost) and the social cost of acquiring good y (the price net of tax): *this asymmetry lies at the heart of many of the results derived below.*

2.2 Two fundamental propositions

We now develop two key properties of the model, which underpin most of the results derived in later sections of the paper. The first step is to introduce the concept of *private welfare, PW*, defined to be the aggregate surplus of domestic consumers and the domestic firm.[11] Setting $\tau_x = \tau_y = 0$ for convenience, we can write

$$PW = [U(x, y) - p_x x - p_y y] + (p_x - c_x)x = U(x, y) - p_y y - c_x x. \quad (14)$$

Much of the analysis of trade and foreign investment policies involves analyzing situations where the cost to the foreign firm of supplying the domestic market is altered, either through taxes and tariffs, or through foreign investment. To facilitate such analysis, we now examine the relationship between PW and the foreign firm's cost level. From (14), the effect on PW of a small change in c_y is given by

$$\begin{aligned} \mathrm{d}PW/\mathrm{d}c_y = {} & (\partial U/\partial x)(\partial x/\partial c_y) + (\partial U/\partial y)(\partial y/\partial c_y) \\ & - p_y(\partial y/\partial c_y) - y(\partial p_y/\partial c_y) - c_x(\partial x/\partial c_y). \end{aligned} \quad (15)$$

[11] The concept of private welfare is used solely for analytical convenience: at no point do we take maximizing PW to be a separate welfare goal from maximizing SW.

Utility maximization ensures that $\partial U/\partial x = \lambda p_x$ and $\partial U/\partial y = \lambda p_y$, where λ is the marginal utility of income; the functional form of the utility function in ensures that $\lambda = 1$ (see Appendix, Part 1). Hence (15) reduces to

$$\mathrm{d}PW/\mathrm{d}c_y = (p_x - c_x)(\partial x/\partial c_y) - y(\partial p_y/\partial c_y). \tag{16}$$

Further differentiation yields the result that $\mathrm{d}^2PW/(\mathrm{d}c_y)^2 > 0$, implying that $PW(c_y)$ is convex for $c_y \in (c_y^{\min}, c_y^{\max})$. Simplification of (16), using (8), (9) and (11), yields the result that $\mathrm{d}PW/\mathrm{d}c_y = 0$ when $c_y = c_y^{\mathrm{c}}$, where

$$c_y^{\mathrm{c}} = (k/b)c_x + (1 - k/b)a. \tag{17}$$

From (10), $c_y^{\min} < c_y^{\mathrm{c}} < c_y^{\max}$: in conjunction with convexity, this implies that $PW(c_y)$ is U-shaped in the range $(c_y^{\min}, c_y^{\max})$.

To establish the form of $PW(c_y)$ outside this range, note that increases in c_y above $c_y^{\max}$ leave PW unchanged because the foreign firm cannot compete under such cost conditions. By contrast, reductions in c_y below $c_y^{\min}$ result in an increase in PW: under these circumstances, the foreign firm is a monopolist, and a fall in cost leads it to lower its price, thereby benefiting domestic consumers. Since $PW(c_y^{\min})$ can be shown to exceed $PW(c_y^{\max})$,[12] we conclude

Proposition 1. The relationship between private welfare and the foreign firm's cost level takes the U-shaped form described in Figure 1.

Understanding this proposition is crucial to understanding most of the results derived below. To see the intuition underlying this U-shaped relationship, consider the two terms in (16) above. The first term represents what we label the *domestic firm output effect*:[13] an increase in c_y results in higher domestic firm sales, which is welfare augmenting because x is a good whose marginal benefit to consumers (p_x) exceeds the marginal cost of producing it (c_x).[14] The second term

[12] A formal proof of this proposition is contained in the Appendix, Part 2; an intuitive explanation is provided in Sec. 3 below.

[13] We use the term 'domestic firm output effect' rather than the more conventional 'production efficiency effect' because in our model domestic production can be carried out by domestic or foreign firms. Hence, welfare and efficiency is not merely a matter of how much is produced domestically, but also of who is producing it.

[14] Note that this domestic firm output effect cannot arise under perfect competition, where price equals marginal costs (i.e. $p_x = c_x$).

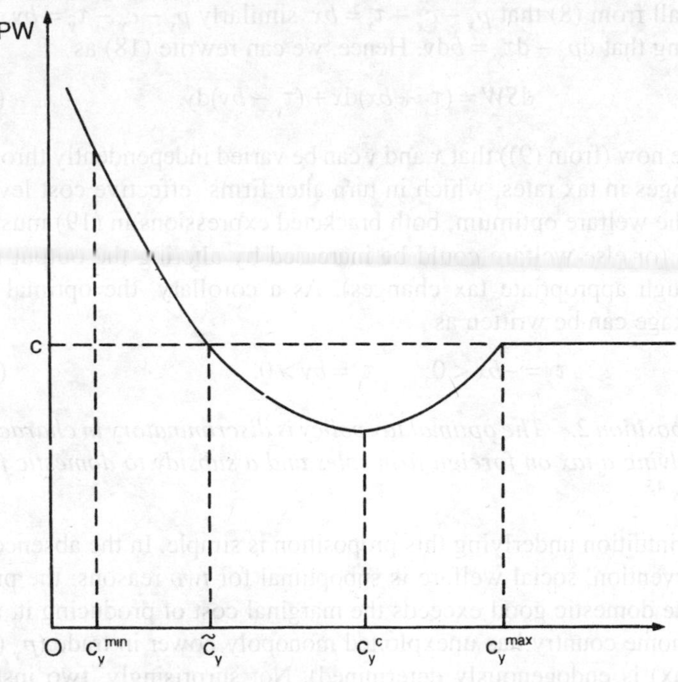

Figure 1

represents the *terms of trade effect* of an increase in c_y: an increase in c_y results in an increase in p_y, which reduces the welfare of domestic consumers of y. From (11), higher values of c_y are associated with higher values of p_x and lower values of y. Hence, a low value for c_y is associated with a strong terms of trade effect (because consumption of y is large) and a weak domestic firm output effect (because $(p_x - c_x)$ is small); the net effect of an increase in c_y is to lower PW. By contrast, a high value for c_y is associated with a weak terms of trade effect (because y is small) and a strong domestic firm output effect (because $(p_x - c_x)$ is large); the net effect of an increase in c_y is to increase PW.

We turn now to examine the role of taxes and subsidies in enabling the government to maximize social welfare. Totally differentiating (13) and simplifying the resulting expression yields

$$dSW = (p_x - c_x)dx + \tau_y dy - y(dp_y - d\tau_y). \tag{18}$$

Recall from (8) that $p_x - c_x - \tau_x = bx$: similarly $p_y - c_y - \tau_y = by$, implying that $dp_y - d\tau_y = bdy$. Hence, we can rewrite (18) as

$$dSW = (\tau_x + bx)dx + (\tau_y - by)dy. \tag{19}$$

Note now (from (9)) that x and y can be varied independently through changes in tax rates, which in turn alter firms' effective cost levels. At the welfare optimum, both bracketed expressions in (19) must be zero (or else welfare could be increased by altering the output mix through appropriate tax changes). As a corollary, the optimal tax package can be written as

$$\tau_x = -bx < 0; \qquad \tau_y = by > 0. \tag{20}$$

Proposition 2. The optimal tax policy is discriminatory in character, involving a tax on foreign firm sales and a subsidy to domestic firm sales.[15]

The intuition underlying this proposition is simple. In the absence of intervention, social welfare is suboptimal for *two* reasons: the price of the domestic good exceeds the marginal cost of producing it, and the home country has unexploited monopoly power in trade (p_y (net of tax) is endogenously determined). Not surprisingly, two instruments are required to achieve an optimum, with each instrument going directly to the source of each distortion: the subsidy increases domestic sales, while the tax improves the terms of trade in a manner familiar from the traditional optimal tariff argument.

The analysis summarized in Proposition 2 assumes that the government has the resources and administrative capability to deploy production subsidies, a questionable assumption in the context of many LDCs. Analysis of the case where the government can only tax sales reveals that the optimal policy package is again discriminatory in character, with $\tau_x = 0$ and $\tau_y > 0$; in addition, the optimal tax on the foreign firm is larger than the optimal tax levied in the case where the domestic firm can be subsidized directly.[16]

15 Proposition 2 is not novel; see Cheng (1988) for a discussion of optimal tax policy under circumstances of imperfect competition.

16 A proof is contained in part 3 of the Appendix.

3. THE EFFECTS OF INTERNATIONAL TRADE

The model described above provides a tractable framework within which to examine the policy issues associated with trade and direct foreign investment. In this section, we focus on trade-related issues, leaving consideration of foreign investment until Sec. 4; for now, we assume that the foreign firm can only supply the domestic market from production facilities abroad.

We begin by exploring the effect of imports on social welfare in the domestic economy. Following the conventions of trade theory, we analyse this issue by comparing the welfare level attained under autarchy (i.e. no imports) with the welfare level attained under free trade. Figure 1 provides a simple method for undertaking such a comparison. In the absence of taxes, social welfare and private welfare are identical, implying that the social welfare level attained at any given c_y can be read off from the *PW* schedule in Fig. 1. Under autarky, the domestic firm is in a monopoly position, and the level of social welfare, SW^A, is given by the distance *OC* in Fig. 1.[17] Under free trade, the social welfare level attained, SW^T, is given by $PW(c_y)$, where c_y must be less than c_y^{max} if there is to be any trade. From Fig. 1, it follows immediately that SW^T exceeds SW^A if c_y is less than $\tilde{c}_y$; as a corollary, SW^T is less than SW^A for all values of c_y between $\tilde{c}_y$ and c_y^{max}. Hence, we conclude that:

Theorem 1. The welfare effect of moving from autarky to free trade is uncertain, with welfare falling for a range of cost levels.

This conclusion provides a sharp contrast with the case of perfect competition, where free trade is always superior to autarky.

A second result of interest can be derived from Fig. 1. Recall that the domestic firm cannot compete under free trade if $c_y < c_y^{min}$. Note from Fig. 1 that the level of private welfare attained under such cost conditions exceeds $PW(c_y^{min})$, which in turn exceeds *OC*, the autarky welfare level. Hence, SW^T must exceed SW^A if c_y is less than c_y^{min}, implying that:

Corollary 1. The welfare effect of moving from autarky to trade must be favourable if it results in the shut-down of the domestic firm.

[17] The superscript T over any variable denotes its value under free trade, while the superscript A denotes its value under autarky.

Thus, the replacement of a domestic monopoly by a foreign monopoly is welfare-enhancing; in contrast, the increased degree of competition involved in moving from domestic monopoly to a duopoly can be immiserizing!

To clarify the intuition underlying these results, we distinguish between the case where the domestic firm survives under free ($x^T > 0$) and the case where the domestic firm is driven from the market ($x^T = 0$). In the former case, the entry of the foreign firm into the domestic market results in an increase in the number of firms, and thus has a *pro-competitive effect.* At first glance, this suggests that trade must be welfare-enhancing, because increased competition (i.e. the entry of a new firm) is typically thought to have a favourable impact on welfare. To see the fallacy of this argument, note that entry is welfare enhancing in a closed economy context if the gains to consumers and the new entrant exceed the losses of the incumbent firms; an outcome which seems likely, but it is not guaranteed. For the entry of a *foreign* firm to be welfare enhancing, however, it is necessary that the gains to consumers exceed the losses of domestic firms: a condition which is clearly more stringent. Intuitively, the gain from the entry of a foreign firm can be decomposed into two elements: (1) the net gain that would result if the new entrant were domestically owned (which is likely to be positive), less (ii) the profits which accrue to the entrant (which are positive); *any presumption that the former effect dominates the latter is flawed*, as the shape of the *PW* schedule in Fig. 1 makes clear.

Additional insights into the ambiguous effect of trade on welfare can be obtained by considering the case where x and y are perfect substitutes (i.e. $k = b$). In this case, welfare levels under autarky and free trade are:

$$SW^A = U(x^A) - c_x x^A, \tag{21}$$

$$SW^T = U(x^T + y^T) - c_x x^T - p_y y^T. \tag{22}$$

Note that $x^T > 0$ only if $p^T > c_x$. Letting $\Delta SW = (SW^T - SW^A)$ denote the net gain from trade, we can write

$$\Delta SW = \{[U(x^T + y^T) - c_x(x^T + y^T)] - [U(x^A) - c_x x^A]\} - [(p^T - c_x)y^T]. \tag{23}$$

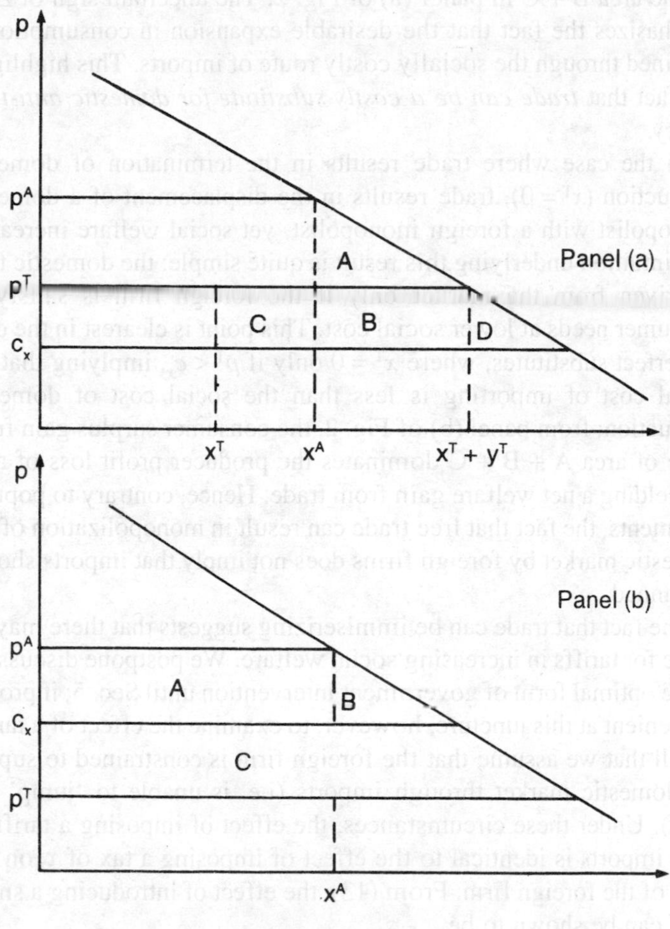

Figure 2

The first term in $\{\cdot\}$ brackets represents the gain in welfare that would occur if the trade-induced expansion in total sales had resulted from domestic output expansion; it is unambiguously positive, and can be represented by the area A + B in panel (a) of Fig. 2. The second term in $[\cdot]$ brackets is the loss to the domestic economy associated with the fact that trade has resulted in a shift in domestic consumption from goods whose *social* cost is c_x to goods whose *social* cost is $p^T > c_x$; this unfavourable *consumption diversion effect* is represented by the area B + C in panel (a) of Fig. 2. The uncertain sign of ΔSW emphasizes the fact that the desirable expansion in consumption is obtained through the socially costly route of imports. This highlights the fact that *trade can be a costly substitute for domestic anti-trust policy.*

In the case where trade results in the termination of domestic production ($x^{\mathrm{T}} = 0$), trade results in the displacement of a domestic monopolist with a foreign monopolist, yet social welfare increases. The intuition underlying this result is quite simple: the domestic firm is driven from the market only if the foreign firm is satisfying consumer needs at lower social cost. This point is clearest in the case of perfect substitutes, where $x^{\mathrm{T}} = 0$ only if $p^{\mathrm{T}} < c_x$, implying that the social cost of importing is less than the social cost of domestic production; from panel (b) of Fig. 2, the consumer surplus gain from trade of area A + B + C dominates the producer profit loss of area A, yielding a net welfare gain from trade. Hence, contrary to popular arguments, the fact that free trade can result in monopolization of the domestic market by foreign firms does not imply that imports should be banned.

The fact that trade can be immiserizing suggests that there may be a role for tariffs in increasing social welfare. We postpone discussion of the optimal form of government intervention until Sec. 5; it proves convenient at this juncture, however, to examine the effect of a tariff. Recall that we assume that the foreign firm is constrained to supply the domestic market through imports (i.e. is unable to 'jump' the tariff). Under these circumstances, the effect of imposing a tariff of τ_i on imports is identical to the effect of imposing a tax of τ_i on the sales of the foreign firm. From (13), the effect of introducing a small tariff can be shown to be

$$\mathrm{d}SW/\mathrm{d}\tau_y \big|_{\tau y=0} = y(1 - \partial p_y/\partial \tau_y) + (p_x - c_x)\, \partial x/\partial \tau_y. \tag{24}$$

The introduction of a small tariff thus has two effects: a *terms of trade effect*, measuring the change in the social cost of acquiring the initial level of imports, and a *domestic firm output effect*, measuring the change in social welfare resulting from the change in the output of domestic firms. From (11), both of these effects are positive, with the terms of trade improving because of less than complete pass-through of the tariff into the consumer price, and the increase in domestic output being welfare-enhancing because price (i.e. marginal social benefit) exceeds marginal cost. Hence:

Theorem 2. A small tariff unambiguously increases social welfare.[18]

Further increases in the level of the tariff have a less clearcut effect on welfare, because the right-hand side of (24) now has an additional term $[\tau_y (dy/d\tau_y)]$ which is negative and becomes more so as τ_y is increased. Using (11) it is easy to show that $d^2 SW/d\tau_y^2 < 0$, implying that $SW(\tau_y)$ is concave within the range of non-prohibitive tariff levels. Hence, the relationship between SW and τ_y is inverse-U-shaped: as τ_y is increased from 0, welfare increases until it reaches a maximum, and then falls as the tariff rate is further increased.

4. THE EFFECTS OF FOREIGN INVESTMENT

We now examine the welfare effects of inward DFI.[19] We identify its effects by comparing an initial situation where DFI is prohibited with the situation that obtains when this prohibition is lifted; the analogy with the autarky/free trade comparison in trade analysis is exact.

To extend our model to examine DFI, we allow the foreign firm to choose between two alternative methods of supplying the domestic market with good y: importing or producing locally. Let c_y denote the c.i.f. cost per unit of y imported, with c_y^* denoting the unit cost of producing y locally; these costs may differ because of inter-country differences in factor prices, productivity levels, etc., or because of transport costs. We assume that the only tax instrument being employed is a specific import tariff of τ_y; adding production and sales taxes is uncomplicated, but provides no further insight.

In deciding how to supply the domestic market, the foreign firm behaves in a cost-minimizing fashion, opting to produce locally (instead of importing) if c_y^* is less than the tariff-inclusive cost of importing $(c_y + \tau_y)$. It proves useful to distinguish between situations where local production is the preferred choice because of the presence of the tariff, and situations where local production would be preferred

[18] This theorem is not novel; see Brander and Spencer (1984) for an early discussion of the effects of tariffs under imperfect competition.

[19] The analysis in this section relies heavily on Nolan (1990).

even under free trade; the decision to produce locally is said to be *cost-induced* if $c_y^* < c_y$, and to be *tariff-induced* if c_y^* exceeds c_y, but is less than $c_y + \tau_y$.

Consider now the situation where local production by the foreign firm is prohibited, and assume that this ban is binding (i.e. $c_y^* < c_y + \tau_y$). Removal of the ban on DFI enables the foreign firm to lower the effective cost it incurs in supplying the domestic market by establishing local production facilities. From (11), this cost reduction strengthens the foreign firm's competitive position vis-à-vis the domestic firm and results in: (i) declines in p_x and p_y, (ii) an increase in consumption of y, and (iii) a decline in consumption of x. The price declines benefit domestic consumers, but the domestic firm's profits fall (because of declining margins and sales volume) and the government loses whatever tariff revenue it had previously collected.

To identify the effect of DFI on social welfare, let SW^0 denote the welfare level prevailing in the initial (pre-DFI) situation, with SW^1 denoting the post-DFI welfare level.[20] SW^0 is the sum of private welfare and government revenue in the initial situation, $PW^0 + \tau_y y^0$; since no tariff revenues are collected in the post-DFI situation, SW^1 is simply PW^1. The change in social welfare resulting from DFI, ΔSW, can be written as:

$$\begin{aligned} \Delta SW \equiv SW^1 - SW^0 &= PW^1 - [PW^0 + \tau_y y^0] \\ &= [PW^1 - PW^0] - \tau_y y^0. \end{aligned} \tag{25}$$

Since $\tau_y y^0 \geq 0$, ΔSW is negative unless PW^1 exceeds PW^0. Note, however, that PW^0 is the private welfare level attained when the foreign firm's effective unit cost is $c_y + \tau_y$, while PW^1 is the private welfare level attained when the corresponding cost is c_y^*. Since $c_y^* < c_y + \tau_y$, it follows immediately from Fig. 1 that PW^1 can exceed PW^0 only if $c_y^* < c_y^c$, implying in turn that:

Theorem 3. A necessary but not sufficient condition for DFI to be welfare-enhancing is that the foreign firm's local production cost, c_y^*, be less than some critical value, c_y^c.

Intuitively, the welfare effect of DFI can be viewed as consisting of

20 Note that the pre-DFI situation can involve trade; SW^0 should not be equated with the autarky welfare level.

two components: the *cost reduction effect* (the welfare change resulting from the decline in the foreign firm's effective cost, $PW^1 - PW^0$), and the *production relocation effect* (the welfare change resulting from the relocation or production by the foreign firm, $-\tau_y y^0$). Since the loss of tariff revenues ensures that the relocation effect is non-positive, welfare can increase only if the improved cost position of the foreign firm translates into an increase in private welfare.[21] From Fig. 1, a decline in the effective cost of the foreign firm cost need not result in an increase in private welfare; and indeed cannot do so unless the new cost level is less than c_y^c.

Two important corollaries follow from Theorem 3. First, since the result holds for any $\tau_y \geq 0$, we concluded that:

Corollary 2. Under free trade, the welfare effect of DFI is ambiguous, with welfare declining unless the foreign firm's local production costs are sufficiently low.

This point merits emphasis because it has often been asserted that, in the absence of a tariff, the pro-competitive effect of inward DFI must be welfare enhancing (e.g. Cardoso and Dornbusch, 1989, Sec. 3). The flaw, in this argument is that the favourable effect of sharper competition in the domestic market is purchased at a cost—the shifting of consumption from goods whose price exceeds social costs to goods whose price equals social cost—which can more than offset the gains from increased competition.

The second corollary is established by recalling from (17) that c_y^c is equal to $\alpha c_x + (1 - \alpha)a$, where $\alpha = k/b$ measures the degree of substitutability between x and y. With perfect substitutability (i.e. $k = b$), c_y^c equals c_x, implying that DFI can enhance welfare only if the foreign firm can produce locally at lower cost than the domestic firm. With less than perfect substitutability, this necessary condition for a welfare gain is less severe, since c_y^c increases as $k \rightarrow 0$. We conclude that:

Corollary 3. Inward DFI is immiserizing unless the foreign firm either: (1) operates at lower cost than the domestic firm when both produce locally, or (ii) supplies a significantly differentiated product.

[21] In a more complex model allowing for profits taxation, worker rents, and other external effects, the production relocation effect could well be positive, implying a much richer set of feasible welfare outcomes.

This conclusion provides a crude but simple criterion which policy makers can apply when assessing proposed investment projects: reject a project unless the foreign company is 'contributing' either a superior technology (i.e. lower cost than the domestic firm) or a substantially different product.

To obtain further insights, we rewrite SW^0 as the sum of: (i) the welfare level that would prevail were the tariff set at zero, SW^T, and (ii) the increment to welfare attributable to the presence of the tariff, $G(\tau_y)$, which may be positive or negative.[22] Note now that SW^T is equal to $PW(c_y)$, since no tariff revenues are collected under free trade; and that SW^I equals $PW(c_y^*)$, since no tariffs are collected when the foreign firm produces locally. Hence, (25) can be rewritten as:

$$\Delta SW \equiv SW^I - SW^0 = SW^I - [SW^T + G(\tau_y)]$$
$$= [PW(c_y^*) - PW(c_y)] - G(\tau_y) . \quad (26)$$

We are now in a position to identify the welfare effects of DFI under a variety of circumstances. Consider first the case where DFI is *tariff-induced* ($c_y < c_y^*$), and assume that $c_y^* < c_y^c$ (for otherwise ΔSW must be negative). From Fig. 1, $c_y < c_y^* < c_y^c$ implies that $PW(c_y) > PW(c_y^*)$. Using (26) we obtain:

Theorem 4. Tariff-induced DFI is immiserizing unless the tariff being jumped was itself welfare-reducing.

The intuition behind this result is simple: tariff-induced DFI involves a switch from a *socially* cheaper to a *socially* more expensive supply source. This unfavourable diversion of 'trade' from outside to inside the tariff wall is immiserizing unless the tariff being jumped was itself a costly distortion.

As a corollary to Theorem 4, note that tariff-induced DFI can be welfare-enhancing if the tariff in place is immiserizing ($G(\tau_y) < 0$). This, however, does not provide grounds for allowing DFI under such circumstances. Lowering the tariff to the level at which the foreign firm is indifferent between local production and importing ($\tau_y = c_y^* - c_y$) eliminates the incentive for the foreign firm to 'jump' the tariff; it also yields a no-DFI outcome which is Paretor-superior to the DFI outcome, in the sense that private welfare is the same in

[22] Recall from Theorem 2 that a tariff can be welfare-enhancing.

both situations, while the government obtains revenue only in the no-DFI outcome.[23] Hence, lowering the tariff is a better policy choice than allowing DFI, yielding the conclusion that:

Corollary 4. Tariff-induced DFI should never be permitted unless tariff rates are (irrationally!) cast in stone.

Consider now the case where DFI is *cost-induced* ($c_y^* < c_y$). The interesting insight in this situation is that DFI can reduce welfare even if the conditions of Theorem 3 are satisfied. To see this, note from (26) that ΔSW can be negative either: (i) because $[PW(c_y^*) - PW(c_y)]$ is negative or, (ii) $G(\tau_y)$ is positive. $PW(c_y^*)$ can be less than $PW(c_y)$ if c_y^* is close to (but less than) c_y^c *and* c_y lies sufficiently to the right of c_y^c (see Fig. 1). $G(\tau_y)$ is positive when the initial tariff is welfare-enhancing: the evasion of such a tariff by a cost-induced investment reduces welfare if $[PW(c_y^*) - PW(c_y)]$ is less than $G(\tau_y)$. Hence, we obtain:

Theorem 5. Cost-induced DFI can be welfare-reducing even if the firm is 'contributing' a better technology and/or differentiated product.

We conclude this section by noting the main policy insights generated by the analysis. First, even under free trade DFI can lower social welfare if the firm is 'contributing' neither a lower cost technology nor a substantially different product; thus, arguments for facilitating DFI only on the grounds of 'promoting competition' are flawed. Second, tariff-induced DFI is welfare-reducing under most circumstances, and should only be permitted if tariff rates are very high (so that jumping the tariff is good) and immutable, an unlikely state of affairs. Third, even 'good' DFI projects (cost-motivated projects which meet the superior technology/distinctive product criteria) can be welfare-reducing if, for example, they result in the avoidance of a welfare-enhancing tariff. Whether this implies that policy makers should restrict 'good' investment projects and/or employ alternative taxation instruments requires an analysis of the *optimal* policy package, a task to which we now turn.

[23] With a tariff of $(x_y^* - c_y)$, the foreign firm's effective cost is not affected by where it locates: therefore, prices and sales levels (and hence private welfare) are also unaffected by its location choice.

5. THE OPTIMAL POLICY PACKAGE

The preceding discussion has established that free trade can be immiserizing, and that direct foreign investment can lower aggregate welfare. This section explores the policy implications of these insights, by examining the forms of policy intervention needed to maximize aggregate welfare. In practice, government intervention is frequently motivated by goals other than welfare maximization; we focus on this policy goal partly because it is the established practice in the trade policy literature, and partly because it provides a useful benchmark case.

The point to note at the outset is that the optimal form of intervention is dependent on the range of policy instruments assumed to be available to the government. In this paper, we shall follow trade-theoretic convention and confine our attention to the case where the government can only: (i) tax (or subsidize) sales, domestic production, and imports, and (ii) license (refuse to license) DFI.[24] In addition, we explore the implications of imposing the following restrictions on the set of policy choices: (i) ruling out the use of subsidies, and (ii) requiring that the government avoid discriminating directly between *firms*. We refer to the first situation as the *revenue-constrained government* case; its practical relevance is obvious. The second situation is referred to as the *limited discriminatory capability* case; it is also of practical importance, as countries frequently choose to treat locally-owned firms and local subsidiaries of foreign firms in an even-handed fashion.

We begin by considering the policy design problem when direct foreign investment is not feasible. Recalling Proposition 2, we can state:

Theorem 6. When DFI is not feasible, the optimal policy package involves taxing foreign firm sales and subsidizing domestic firm sales.

The proof and intuition underlying the result are provided in Sec. 2, and need no further discussion. Note that this optimal tax/subsidy policy can be implemented in a number of ways: letting τ' and s' denote the optimal tax and subsidy rates, respectively, the government

[24] Extending the analysis to allow for the use of profits taxation, content requirements, ownership requirements, etc. lies beyond the scope of the paper, although the model developed above can be usefully employed to explore many of these issues.

could impose: (i) a tariff of τ' and a domestic production subsidy of s', or (ii) discriminatory sales taxes, set at τ' for the foreign firm and $-s'$ for the domestic firm, or (iii) a general sales tax of τ' and a domestic production subsidy of $\tau' + s'$.

Two comments on Theorem 6 are in order here. First, when revenue constraints (or limited administrative capabilities) preclude the use of subsidies, the optimal policy mix involves taxing only the sales of the foreign firm, at a rate higher than that employed when subsidies can be deployed. Second, the requirement that government intervention not directly discriminate between different firms does not preclude the implementation of the optimal tax/subsidy policy: policy options (i) and (iii) above do not involve treating individual firms differently, but instead discriminate between outputs originating in different countries.

We turn now to examine the optimal policy package when direct foreign investment is a feasible option for the foreign firm. In this case the problem of identifying optimal policies is substantially complicated, as tariffs may induce DFI (which, as shown, may not be desirable) or, alternatively, DFI might allow foreign firms to avoid welfare-enhancing tariffs. At the same time, when DFI is allowed, there is *an additional source of gain* from government policy: the possibility of forcing the foreign firm to produce in the lowest-cost location which, in turn, generates a greater profit base from which rents can be extracted by an appropriate tax instrument.

To analyse this issue, we develop one further diagrammatic tool. Let $\bar{c}_y$ denote the cost to the foreign firm of supplying the domestic market exclusive of taxes and subsidies; $\bar{c}_y$ equals c_y when the firm chooses to import, and equals c_y^* when it produces locally. Recall from Proposition 2 that the welfare-maximizing policy associated with a given value of $\bar{c}_y$ involves taxing sales by the foreign firm and subsidizing sales by the domestic firm; let $SW'(\bar{c}_y)$ denote the welfare level attained when this optimizing tax/subsidy scheme is deployed. Assume now that welfare is maximized for the prevailing level of $\bar{c}_y$, and let $\bar{c}_y$ decline by ε. Note that increasing the tax on foreign firm sales by ε would restore private welfare to its initial level, while providing the government with more revenues than it received initially. Since aggregate welfare would now be higher than its initial level, it follows a fortiori that the maximum welfare level attainable after the cost decline must exceed the initial welfare maximum; hence,

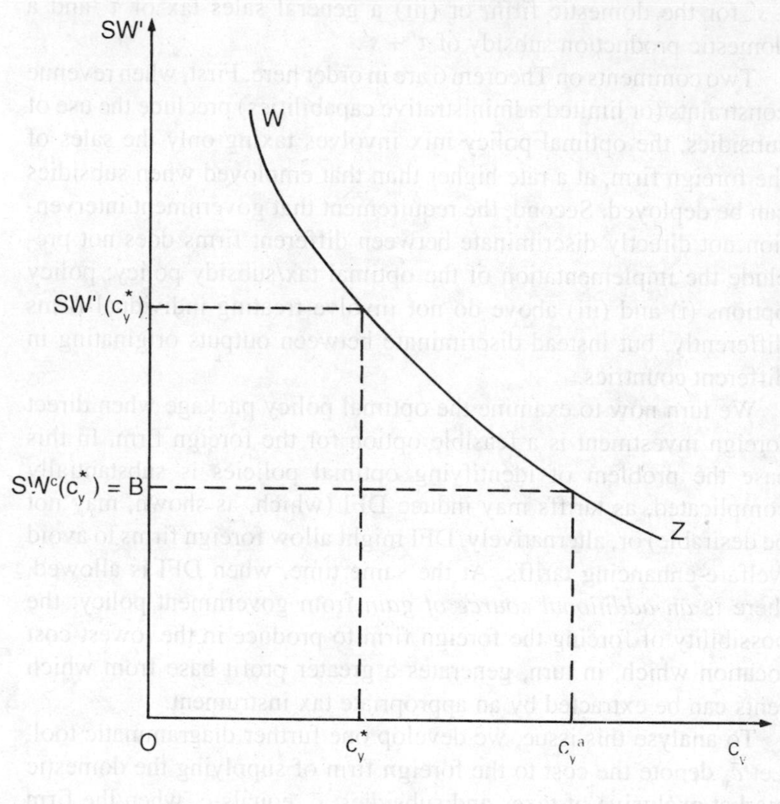

Figure 3

$SW'(\bar{c}_y)$ is a *strictly decreasing function* of $\bar{c}_y$, as represented by the WZ schedule in Fig. 3.

Consider now the situation where the government is not revenue-constrained and has full discriminatory capability. The maximum welfare level attainable when the foreign firm chooses to import is $SW'(c_y)$; the maximum welfare level attainable when it chooses to produce locally is $SW'(c_y^*)$. The highest attainable welfare level is the larger of these two values; since $SW'(\,)$ is a decreasing function of $\bar{c}_y$, this is the value of $SW'(\,)$ associated with the smaller of c_y and c_y^*. As a corollary, attainment of this welfare optimum requires that:

(i) the foreign firm supplies the domestic market from the low-cost location, and (ii) the government deploys the optimal tax and subsidy levels corresponding to the lower cost level.

What specific instruments should be deployed to ensure the attainment of the welfare optimum? First, note that cost minimization leads the foreign firm to choose the low-cost method of supplying the market *if its location choice is not distorted by the policy regime*; there is no need to 'push' the firm towards the socially desirable location choice. Second, note that a tariff is a poor device for taxing foreign firm sales: it acts as a tax measure only if the firm chooses to import, and pushes the domestic firm to produce in the high-cost location when $c_y < c_y^* < c_y + \tau_y$. Third, note that a direct sales tax is an effective device for taxing the sales of the foreign firm (since it cannot be evaded) without affecting its choice of location. Finally, note that the required degree of subsidization of the domestic firm can be attained either through a firm-specific sales subsidy or a firm-specific production subsidy. We conclude, therefore, that the optimal policy package takes the form of: (i) a direct tax on sales by the foreign firm, (ii) no tariffs or investment restrictions, and (iii) a subsidy on sales by the domestic firm.

The discussion to date has focused attention on the case where the government is not revenue-constrained. Reworking the argument developed here for the no-subsidy case will convince the reader that a revenue-constrained government with full discriminatory capability would choose a discriminatory sales tax as its only intervention measure. We conclude that:

Theorem 7. A government with full discriminatory capability should not limit trade or foreign investment; it should implement a discriminatory tax/subsidy system which favours domestically-owned firms at the expense of foreign-owned firms.

Two comments are in order. First, when DFI is a feasible outcome, socially desirable discrimination between domestic and foreign firms has to be explicitly firm-based (treating products differently on the basis of who produces them) rather than location-based (treating products differently on the basis of where they are produced). Second, while discrimination between domestic and foreign firms is desirable, the form which discrimination should takes does not involve trade barriers or investment restrictions.

Consider now the policy design problem when the government cannot engage in explicit firm-based discrimination.[25] Note that the maximum welfare level attainable when the foreign firm produces abroad is still $SW'(c_y)$; the discriminatory tax/subsidy treatment needed to attain this welfare level can be attained through location-based discrimination (tariffs and domestic production subsidies). In contrast, the maximum welfare level attainable when the foreign firm produces locally is strictly less than $SW'(c_y^*)$; when the foreign firm produces locally, the government cannot engage in discriminatory treatment, and the gains from discrimination must be foregone. Hence, having the foreign firm produce abroad provides an advantage (the ability to engage in discriminatory taxation) that is not available when it produces locally.

To clarify the implications of this insight for policy formulation, let $SW^c(c_y^*)$ denote the maximum welfare level attainable when the foreign firm produces locally; it is represented by the distance OB in Fig. 3, and is less than $SW'(c_y^*)$ by an amount equal to the gains from discrimination. Let c_y^a denote the value of $\bar{c}_y$ at which $SW'(\bar{c}_y) = SW^c(c_y^*)$; since WZ is downward-sloping, c_y^a lies to the right of c_y^*. From Fig. 3, note that

$$SW'(c_y) > SW^c(c_y^*) \text{ iff } c_y < c_y^a. \tag{27}$$

As a corollary, the welfare optimum involves the foreign firm producing abroad (locally) if c_y is less than (exceeds) c_y^a. Note that there are a range of values for c_y, namely, $c_y \in (c_y^*, c_y^a)$ in which the welfare optimum involves the foreign firm producing abroad *even though it could produce locally at lower cost*: the gains from discrimination that can be realized when the foreign firm produces abroad more than offset any gains realized from having the foreign firm produce in the lower-cost location.

We can now describe the characteristics of a no-discrimination optimal policy package. When $c_y < c_y^a$, the optimal policy involves allowing the firm to produce locally, and engaging in non-discriminatory sales taxation; since $c_y > c_y^*$, the firm will voluntarily

25 The factors limiting the ability of governments to engage in firm-based discrimination include: (i) limited administrative capability, and (ii) the desire to maintain a 'favourable investment climate' by treating local subsidiaries of foreign firms and domestic firms in an even-handed fashion.

choose to produce locally, and any tariff would be redundant. When $c_y > c_y^a$, the welfare optimum involves the foreign firm producing abroad, and the implementation of a discriminatory tax/subsidy scheme. Given that firm-based discrimination is ruled out by assumption, the implementation of discriminatory taxation involves the use of a tariff (to tax foreign firm sales) and a production subsidy (to subsidize domestic firm sales). Since there are strong incentives for the foreign firm to 'jump' this tariff, the tariff/subsidy scheme must be accompanied by a ban on DFI.

To summarize, the optimal policy package takes one of two forms: (i) free trade, unrestricted investment, and non-discriminatory tax when $c_y > c_y^a$ and (ii) a tariff, a production subsidy, and ban on DFI when $c_y < c_y^a$. A reworking of the argument will convince the reader that the presence of a no-subsidy constraint would alter these qualitative results only to the extent that it would eliminate the production subsidy. Recalling that c_y^a exceeds c_y^* by a non-trivial amount, we conclude that:

Theorem 8. A government with limited discriminatory capability should levy a tariff on imports and restrict inward DFI; foreign investment proposals should be approved only if local production costs of the foreign firm are substantially less than the costs it incurs when it produces abroad.

The contrast with Theorem 7, where the government has full discriminatory capability, is quite striking! The difference between the two sets of policy recommendations is best understood in terms of the familiar distinction between 'first-best' and 'second-best' policies. In the market structure described by our model, there are gains to be obtained from discriminatory treatment of domestic and foreign firms *and* gains to be obtained from ensuring that foreign firms produce in the lowest cost location. When the government has the ability to discriminate explicitly between firms, the first-best case, both of these gains can be realized through an explicitly discriminatory tax/subsidy scheme. When the government cannot directly discriminate between firms, the second-best case, the gains from discrimination can be realized only through trade and investment restrictions, the use of which may entail the 'by-product distortion' of having the foreign firm produce in the high cost location (as occurs when $c_y^* < c_y < c_y^a$). We conclude, therefore, that:

Corollary 5. The case for restricting trade and direct foreign investment is 'second-best' in nature, arising only if government cannot discriminate explicitly between domestic-owned and foreign-owned firms.

It should not (but may) be necessary to note that describing a policy as 'second-best' does not imply that it has little practical relevance. It is our opinion that the case where the government has limited discriminatory capability is of practical relevance for many developing countries.

A remark on robustness

The analysis to date has been conducted within the framework of a simple model of imperfect competition. In a separate appendix,[26] we have provided an analysis of the robustness of our results to changes in the many simplifying assumptions employed above. The main results are as follows. First, linearity of demand is convenient but not necessary; the results go through provided the demand system is, loosely speaking, well behaved. Second, increasing marginal costs present no problems, while strongly decreasing marginal costs, as usual, create difficulties for the existence of equilibrium. Third, introducing fixed costs creates discontinuities which require care in evaluating the effects of small changes near the discontinuous points. More interestingly, they enrich the analysis by generating situations where socially desirable entry is not privately profitable.[27] Fourth, modifying the analysis to allow for non-Cournot behaviour by firms is straightforward, and yields no qualitatively new insights. Fifth, allowing for more than two firms is also uncomplicated; the magnitude of optimal intervention is smaller with more firms, but the qualitative results are unchanged. Sixth, competitive foreign supply in the absence of market segmentation can be incorporated as a particular case of the model. In general, these extensions create nuances and alter the magnitudes of optimal taxes and subsidies, but do not invalidate the central propositions of our analysis. We therefore claim that the preceding analysis is quite robust.

[26] As noted previously, this appendix is available from the authors upon request; it is not included here for reasons of space.

[27] This raises the issue of role for government policy in stimulating entry into an industry; for a discussion of some of the issues involved, see Horstmann and Markusen (1990).

6. ASSESSMENT

In the 180-odd years since the first readers of Ricardo's *The Principles of Political Economy and Taxation* learned how England and Portugal could gain from trading with one another, the theory of international trade policy has been inextricably linked to general equilibrium theory and hence, indirectly, to the theory of perfectly competitive market structures. It has only been in the last decade that trade theorists have made serious efforts to move outside the often-assumed but rarely-observed world of perfect competition; these efforts have resulted in a body of work loosely referred to as 'new trade theory'. In the preceding sections, we have provided an exposition of what we believe are the insights of the theory of greatest relevance to LDCs.[28] We turn now to discuss the implications of these insights for policy formulation in developing countries.[29] We first summarize the main results, contrasting them sharply with the conventional results obtained under perfect competition. Then we discuss the implications of these results for policy design in LDCs, taking account of the (limited) available empirical work on these issues. Finally, we provide our view of the overall importance of this approach and some directions for further research.

Lesson 1. Competition from foreign firms need not always be beneficial. Contrary to the commonly held view, the pro-competitive effects of freer trade or foreign investment need not always increase welfare. We have shown that the increased competition associated with the entry of foreign firms into the domestic market can reduce welfare. The point to note is that the proposition 'entry of new firm is good' is not equivalent to the proposition 'entry of new *foreign* firm is good', because the gains to the entrant in the latter case are not a component of domestic welfare.

Lesson 2. Imports can be excessive under laissez-faire. A key result

[28] One issue often associated with the new trade theory but omitted in our presentation is the Brander–Spencer (1985) case for export subsidies. It is now generally recognized [cf. Helpman and Krugman (1989, Ch. 5)] that this 'strategic' argument for export subsidies is of questionable importance even for the large industrial economies.

[29] For alternative interpretations, see Srinivasan (1988), Helpman (1989), and Corden (1990).

of competitive trade theory is the proposition that, under laissez-faire, the volume of imports is 'just right'.[30] In contrast, policy makers at times hold the belief that, left to themselves, consumers import 'too much', and the imports should therefore be restricted. The analysis developed here gives precision to this intuition; we have shown that imports can be excessive under imperfect competition *without* having to resort to arguments based on factor market distortions or 'irrational' preferences for foreign-produced goods. Under imperfect competition the prices consumers face do not reflect social opportunity costs: the price of domestic goods is too high, and the price of imports is too low.[31] At these distorted prices, it follows that imports are too large and domestic consumption is too small.

Lesson 3. Foreign investment can be harmful, even under free trade. It has long been accepted that tariff induced DFI can be welfare reducing, if only because tariffs distort the firm's location choice. The analysis in Sec. 4 indicates that DFI can be harmful even under free trade, and is welfare enhancing only if the foreign firm provides either a superior technology or a substantially different product. The intuition underlying this argument is that a strengthening of the competitive position of a *foreign* firm in the domestic market can be welfare reducing, because the gains to domestic consumers may be more than offset by the loss to domestic producers.

Lesson 4. Policies that discriminate in favour of domestically-owned firms can be beneficial. One corollary of the position that imports under laissez-faire, are 'just right' is that policies which discriminate between domestic and foreign owned firms (e.g. tariffs, discriminatory sales taxes or procurement practices in government agencies, etc.) are welfare reducing. Our analysis indicates that, under imperfect competition, the *optimal* policy involves some degree of discrimination in favour of domestic firms. The logic underlying this position follows directly from Lesson 1: if laissez-faire leads to excessive consumption of foreign products, the optimum policy presumably

[30] Competitive trade theory recognizes that imports are excessive when the country has the ability to influence its terms of trade, but this argument is not thought to be very relevant for LDCs [cf. (Srinivasan, 1988)].

[31] The price of imports is too low unless the home country is unable to influence the price at which it imports, i.e. is 'small' in the import market; see the discussion in Part 8 of the Appendix.

involves measures designed to shift consumption towards goods produced by domestic firms and away from goods produced by foreign firms.

The preceding discussion has highlighted what we believe are the most important results that emerge from analysing trade and investment policies within the framework of imperfect competition. We turn to consider the policy implications of this analysis. In discussing policy, it is important to maintain a distinction between the *form* which intervention should take and the *magnitude* of the intervention measures; we discuss these issues in sequence.

Section 5 provided a discussion of the form which policy intervention should take under imperfect competition.[32] The main conclusion was that the first-best policy package involved *firm-based* rather than *location-based* discrimination: subsidies to domestic firms, taxes on the sales of foreign firms (independent of their production location), and a laissez-faire attitude to trade and investment. The presence of government revenue constraints did not alter the character of this package: subsidies to domestic firms disappeared and the optimal tax on foreign firm sales increased, but there were no grounds for influencing the foreign firm's location choice. It was only when the government could not explicitly discriminate between foreign and domestic firms that a case emerged for employing tariffs and investment restrictions as a *second-best* device for engaging in discrimination.

As a practical matter, it is our assessment that developing country governments are typically not in a position to finance production subsidies, or to engage in explicit firm-based discrimination. In consequence, the second-best package of deploying tariffs and undertaking careful screening of DFI proposals seems to be the most reasonable form of intervention. It should be noted, however, that effective investment screening is not an easy task: even if one can establish and staff a competent and corruption-free Foreign Investment Licensing Board, the problem remains that investment proposal evaluation depends heavily on information supplied by would-be investors whose incentives to provide accurate information are

[32] Recall, however, that the set of policy tools assumed to be available to policy makers in our analysis was limited; expanding the analysis to allow for other instruments is a task for further research.

obviously limited. Without effective investment screening, the danger of deploying tariffs as a discriminatory device is that they can give rise to tariff-induced DFI, the adverse welfare effects of which were clearly spelled out in Sec. 4 above. Given the difficulties involved in effective screening of DFI, we conclude that tariff rates should be kept at relatively low levels, if only to prevent the high-cost tariff-induced DFI which is a commonly observed feature in many developing countries.

Reference to the need for 'low' tariffs leads naturally to the issue of the orders of magnitude of the optimal tax/subsidies required to achieve the welfare optimum. Empirical analysis of optimal intervention under imperfect competition is a relatively recent research activity, and only a few papers directly address the question of optimal tax and subsidy rates.[33] However, these studies are united on one key conclusion; *the optimal tax and subsidy rates are not large*, particularly if viewed from the perspective of the nominal tariff rates observed in many developing countries.

Given the importance of this point, we briefly mention some of the main empirical results. Dixit (1988) provides an analysis of optimal intervention policy for the US auto industry: he finds that even in the extreme case where the government is unable to subsidize domestic producers *and* the opportunity cost of labour is only one half the market wage, the optimum tariff is of the order of 20 per cent. Note that this tariff is obtained for a country where there is a strong terms of trade argument for tariffs! A more relevant study for LDCs is Saez (1988), who analyses the refrigerator industry in Chile under the assumption that the price of imports is exogenously given. Saez finds the optimal second-best tariff rate to be of the order of 6 per cent; when account is taken of divergences between the private and the social cost of labour, the optimal tariff increases to about 8 per cent. Other related empirical work (e.g. Laussel et al., 1988) suggests second-best tariffs that are of a similar order of magnitude.

In assessing the implications of these tariff estimates for policy formulation, it is important to note that the studies in question employ partial equilibrium methodology, where it is typically assumed that resources can be attracted into the target industry at fixed prices, thereby leaving cost conditions in other industries unchanged. In a

[33] For a general review of this literature, see Richardson (1989).

general equilibrium framework, these resource movements are effected through factor price changes which have *adverse* effects on other sectors, some of which may themselves be characterized by imperfectly competitive market structures; as a result, socially desirable output increases in one sector may be obtained at the expense of socially undesirable output decreases in another sector.[34] These general equilibrium effects do not negate the argument for intervention, but the magnitudes of the optimal taxes and subsidies are likely to be smaller once they are factored into the analysis.

The empirical results obtained to date are far from conclusive and certainly further work along these lines is required. However, taken in conjunction with (i) the general equilibrium considerations mentioned above, (ii) the difficulties of effectively screening inward direct foreign investment, and (iii) the limited opportunities for developing countries to extract large terms of trade gains through tariff protection, they lead us to conclude that:

Lesson 5. Given the available empirical evidence, imperfect competition in the industrial sector of developing countries does not justify nominal tariff rates in excess of 15 per cent. This is an important lesson for at least two reasons. One, it provides an essential qualification to the earlier arguments for interventionist policies: while discrimination in favour of domestic firms is desirable, the optimal degree of discrimination is limited when contrasted with the intervention practised in many developing countries under import-substitution policies.[35] Two, it provides a quick rule of thumb for evaluating the welfare effect of trade liberalization in industries characterized by imperfect competition: tariff reductions that leave the nominal tariff rate at (or close to) 15 per cent are likely to be welfare-enhancing. As a corollary, it is only when liberalization involves reductions in already low tariff rates that the possibility of welfare losses arises. Since most trade liberalization efforts in developing countries involve reductions (but not the elimination) of high tariffs, we conclude that:

[34] This point is emphasized by Dixit and Grossman (1986).

[35] This point has been well made by Rodrik (1988), who notes that 'if one conclusion can be drawn from (his) analysis, it is the following: the levels of protection observed in the manufacturing sectors of most developing countries vastly exceed any that could be justified by the presence of imperfect competition.

Lesson 6. Imperfect competition in the industrial sector of developing countries is not an argument against trade liberalization measures of the type typically under consideration.

7. CONCLUDING REMARKS

This paper has concerned itself with the tasks of (i) examining the effects of trade and foreign investment under oligopolistic competition, and (ii) identifying the appropriate intervention strategy in such industries. As the preceding analysis has made clear, much can be gained from the 'struggle to escape' from the perfectly competitive paradigm that has dominated trade policy analysis since Ricardo. Models of trade under imperfect competition provide a clear-cut rationale for discriminating between domestic and foreign firms, a position which many policy-makers find intuitive but which conventional competitive models cannot rationalize. At the same time, we note that the case for taxing imports and limiting direct foreign investment is second-best in nature, and that the limited empirical evidence suggests that optimal second-best tariffs are not that large. From this angle, it would appear that our policy prescriptions are not radically different from those derived from competitive theory. Why are our policy prescriptions so 'orthodox'?

A re-reading of the classic arguments for interventionist industrial policies in developing countries provides what we think may be the answer.[36] These arguments stress the inadequate incentives for *investment* in developing countries, and emphasize the failures of markets to organize and coordinate investment decisions. In contrast, the elaborate welfare analysis constructed in the 1960s and 1970s in response to these arguments was almost exclusively *static*, with efficiency in the allocation of existing resources at centre-stage. The analysis developed above moved outside the conventional framework *only* in the sense that we have allowed for small numbers of firms; it still is an exercise in static welfare analysis, albeit about welfare rectangles rather than triangles. As a result, we have yet to address

[36] Among the 'classics', we would include Hirschman (1958), Myrdal (1957), Rosenstein-Rodan (1943), and Scitovsky (1954); see Little (1982) for a critical discussion of these contributions, and Stiglitz (1989) for a more contemporary discussion of market failures in LDCs

the interventionist arguments in a framework where they can be appropriately assessed.

The challenge for future research, therefore, is to move beyond the one-period time frame to an intertemporal analysis where investment decisions are the centre of attention. Some of the 'new trade theory' models with an intertemporal dimension (e.g. Spencer and Brander, 1983; Krugman, 1984) indicate that interesting insights can be obtained from such research; the more recent work of Murphy et al. (1989a, b) also provides important insights. Our belief is that such research probably will provide further arguments for interventionist industrial policies, but that *trade* policy measures will play a secondary role in any optimal intervention package. Whether this view is sound judgment, or the manifestation of a failed struggle to escape from established modes of thought remains to be seen!

REFERENCES

BRANDER, J. and B. SPENCER (1984), 'Tariff Protection and Imperfect Competition', in H. KIERZKOWSKI (ed.), *Monopolistic Competition and International Trade*, Oxford: Blackwell.

—— (1985), 'Export Subsidies and International Market Share Rivalry', *Journal of International Economics*, 18, 83–100.

CARDOSO, E. and R. DORNBUSCH (1989), Foreign Private Capital Flows, in H. Chenery and T.N. Srinivasan (eds), *Handbook of Development Economics*, Amsterdam: North-Holland.

CHENG, L.K. (1988), Assisting Domestic Industries Under International Oligopoly, *American Economic Review*, 78, 4, 746–58.

CORDEN, W.M. (1974), *Trade Policy and Economic Welfare*, Oxford: Oxford University Press.

—— (1990), 'Strategic trade policy: How New? How Sensible? PRE Working Papers', Series No. 396, Washington, DC: The World Bank.

DIXIT, A. (1988), 'Optimal Trade and Industrial Policies for the U.S. Automobile Industry', in R. Feenstra (ed.), *Empirical Methods for International Trade*, Cambridge, MA: MIT Press.

DIXIT, A. and G. GROSSMAN (1986), 'Targeted Export Promotion with Several Oligopolistic Industries', *Journal of International Economics*, 21, 233–49.

EATON, J. and G. GROSSMAN (1986), 'Optimal Trade and Industrial Policy under Oligopoly', *Quarterly Journal of Economics*, 101, 383–406.

HELPMAN, E. (1989), 'The Non-competitive Theory of International Trade and Trade Policy', Proceedings of the World Bank Annual Conference on Development Economics, Washington, DC: The World Bank.

HELPMAN, E. and P. KRUGMAN (1989), *Trade Policy and Market Structure*, Cambridge, MA: MIT Press.

HIRSCHMAN, A. (1958), *The Strategy of Economic Development*, New Haven, CT: Yale University Press.

HORSTMANN, I. and J. MARKUSEN (1992), 'Endogenous Market Structures in International Trade', *Journal of International Economics*, 32, pp. 109–29.

KRUGMAN, P. (1984), 'Import Protection as Export Promotion', in H. Kierzkowski (ed.), *Monopolistic Competition and International Trade*, Oxford: Oxford University Press.

—— (ed.) (1986), *Strategic Trade Policy and the New International Economics*, Cambridge, MA: MIT Press.

—— (1987a), 'Is Free Trade Passe'?, *Journal of Economic Perspectives*, 2, Fall, 131–44.

—— (1987b), 'Increasing Returns and the Theory of International Trade', in T. BEWLEY (ed.), *Advances in Economic Theory*, Cambridge: Cambridge University Press.

LAUSSEL, D., C. MONTET and A. PEGUI-FEISSOLLE (1988), 'Optimal Trade Policy under Oligopoly: A Calibrated Model of the Europe–Japan Rivalry in the EEC Car Market', *European Economic Review*, 32, 1548–65.

LITTLE, I.M.D. (1982), *Economic Development: Theory, Policy and International Relations*, New York: Basic Books.

MARKUSEN, J. (1981), 'Trade and the Gains from Trade with Imperfect Competition', *Journal of International Economics*, 11, 531–51.

MARKUSEN, J. and A. VENABLES (1988), 'Trade Policy with Increasing Returns and Imperfect Competition: Contradictory Results with Competing Assumptions', *Journal of International Economics*, 24, 299–316.

MURPHY, K.M., A. SHLEIFER and R.W. VISHNY (1989a), 'Industrialization and the Big Push', *Journal of Political Economy*, 97, 5, 1003–6.

—— (1989b), 'Income Distributions, Market Size, and Industrialization, *Quarterly Journal of Economics*, 104, 537–64.

MYRDAL, G. (1957), *Economic Theory and Underdeveloped Regions*, London: Duckworth.

NOLAN, S. (1990), 'Import Substituting Direct Foreign Investment and Host Country Economic Welfare' (mimeo.), Cambridge, MA: Harvard Institute for International Development.

RICHARDSON, J.D. (1989), 'Empirical Research on Trade Liberalization with Imperfect Competition: A Survey', NBER Working Paper Series No. 2883, Cambridge, MA: NBER.

RODRIK, D. (1987), 'The Economics of Export Performance Requirements, *Quarterly Journal of Economics*, 102, 633–50.

—— (1988), 'Imperfect Competition, Scale Economies, and Trade Policy in Developing Countries', in R.E. Baldwin (ed.), *Trade Policy Issues and Empirical Analysis*, Chicago: The University of Chicago Press, London.

ROSENSTEIN-RODAN, P. (1943), 'Problems of Industrialization of Eastern and South Eastern Europe', *Economic Journal*.

SAEZ, R. (1988), 'Trade Policy under Imperfect Competition: A Simulation Exercise for Chile', Boston University, Center for Latin American Development Studies, Discussion Paper Series No. 83.

SCITOVSKY, T. (1954), 'Two Concepts of External Economies', *Journal of Political Economy*.

SPENCER, B. and J. BRANDER (1983), 'International R & D Rivalry and Industrial Strategy', *Review of Economic Studies*, 707–22.

SRINIVASAN, T.N. (1988), 'Recent Theories of Imperfect Competition and International Trade: Any Implications for Development Strategy?' (mimeo.), Department of Economics, Yale University, CT.

STIGLITZ, J. (1989), 'Economic Organization, Information and Development', in H. Chenery and T.N. Srinivasan (eds), *Handbook of Development Economics*, Ch. 5, Amsterdam: North-Holland.

GOVERNMENT INTERVENTION

Behaviour of the Firm under Regulatory Constraint*

HARVEY AVERCH AND LELAND L. JOHNSON

In judging the level of prices charged by firms for services subject to public control, government regulatory agencies commonly employ a 'fair rate of return' criterion: After the firm substracts its operating expense from gross revenues, the remaining net revenue should be just sufficient to compensate the firm for its investment in plant and equipment. If the rate of return, computed as the ratio of net revenue to the value of plant and equipment (the rate base), is judged to be excessive, pressure is brought to bear on the firm to reduce prices. If the rate is considered to be too low, the firm is permitted to increase prices.

The purpose here is (a) to develop a theory of the monopoly firm seeking to maximize profit but subject to such a constraint on its rate of return, and (b) to apply the model to one particular regulated industry—the domestic telephone and telegraph industry. We conclude in the theoretical analysis that a 'regulatory bias' operates in the following manner: (1) The firm does not equate marginal rates of factor substitution to the ratio of factor costs; therefore the firm operates inefficiently in the sense that (social) cost is not minimized at the output it selects. (2) The firm has an incentive to expand into other regulated markets, even if it operates at a (long-run) loss in

* The authors, research economists at The RAND Corporation, are indebted to Kenneth Arrow who suggested a mathematical framework when the ideas in this paper were in an early state of development. Any views expressed in this paper are those of the authors. They should not be interpreted as reflecting the views of The RAND Corporation or the official opinion or policy of any of its governmental or private research sponsors. An earlier version of this paper was presented at the Econometric Society meetings on December 28, 1961 in New York.

these markets; therefore, it may drive out other firms, or discourage their entry into these other markets, even though the competing firms may be lower-cost producers. Applying the theoretical analysis to the telephone and telegraph industry, we find that the model does raise issues relevant to evaluating market behaviour.

1. THE SINGLE-MARKET MODEL

First we shall consider a geometrical and a mathematical framework showing the effect of the regulatory constraint on the cost curves of the firm employing two factors. The essential characteristic to be demonstrated is: if the rate of return allowed by the regulatory agency is greater than the cost of capital but is less than the rate of return that would be enjoyed by the firm were it free to maximize profit without regulatory constraint, then the firm will substitute capital for the other factor of production and operate at an output where cost is not minimized.

Figure 1 denotes the firm's production where capital x_1 is plotted on the horizontal axis and labour x_2 on the vertical axis. The market

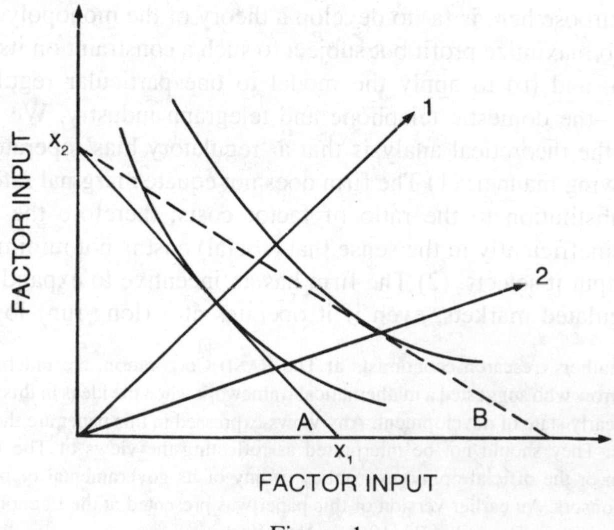

Figure 1

or 'social' cost of capital and labour generates the iso-cost curve A and the *unregulated* firm would move along expansion path 1 where market cost is minimized for any given output. With regulation, however, the cost of capital to the firm—the 'private' cost—is no longer equal to market cost. For each additional unit of capital input, the firm is permitted to earn a profit (equal to the difference between the market cost of capital and rate of return allowed by the regulatory agency) that it otherwise would have to forego. Therefore, private cost is less than market cost by an amount equal to this difference. The effect of regulation is analogous to that of changing the relative prices of capital x_1 and labour x_2: iso-cost curve B becomes relevant and the firm moves along expansion path 2—a path along which market cost is not minimized for any given output. The firm finds path 2 advantageous simply because it is along that path that the firm is able to maximize total profit given the constraint on its rate of return.

Treating the problem mathematically, we now consider a monopoly producing a single homogeneous product using two inputs. Define

$$z = z(x_1, x_2), \quad x_1 \geq 0, \quad x_2 \geq 0$$

$$\frac{\partial z}{\partial x_1} > 0, \qquad \frac{\partial z}{\partial x_2} > 0, \tag{1}$$

$$z(0, x_2) = z(x_1, 0) = 0$$

as the firm's production function. That is, marginal products are positive, and production requires both inputs.

We write the inverse demand function as

$$p = p(z). \tag{2}$$

Profit is defined by

$$\pi = pz - r_1 x_1 - r_2 x_2 \tag{3}$$

where the r_i $(i = 1, 2)$ are factor costs presumed constant for all levels of factor input.

Let x_1 denote the physical quantity of plant and equipment in the rate base, c_1 the acquisition cost per unit of plant and equipment in the rate base, u_1 the value of depreciation of plant and equipment during a time period in question, and U_1 the cumulative value of depreciation. Let x_2 denote the quantity of labour input and r_2 the labour wage rate. The regulatory constraint is:

$$\frac{pz - r_2 x_2 - u_1}{c_1 x_1 - U_1} \leq s_1 \tag{4}$$

where the profit net of labour cost and capital depreciation constitutes a percentage of the rate base (net of depreciation) no greater than a specified maximum s_1.

For simplicity, we assume that depreciation (u_1 and U_1) is zero and we define capital so that its acquisition cost or value c_1 is equal to 1, i.e. the value of the rate base is equal to the physical quantity of capital.[1] The 'cost of capital' r_1 (to be distinguished from the acquisition cost of plant and equipment measured by c_1) is the interest cost involved in holding plant and equipment. The allowable rate of return s_1 is the rate of return allowed by the regulatory agency on plant and equipment in order to compensate the firm for the cost of capital—the interest cost—involved in holding plant and equipment. Therefore, the constraint may be rewritten as

$$\frac{pz - r_2 x_2}{x_1} \leq s_1 \tag{5}$$

or

$$pz - s_1 x_1 - r_2 x_2 \leq 0. \tag{6}$$

For $s_1 < r_1$, the allowable rate of return is less than the actual cost of capital, and the firm withdraws from the market. For, from (6), if $x_1 > 0$,

$$pz - r_1 x_1 - r_2 x_2 = pz - s_1 x_1 + (s_1 - r_1)x_1 - r_2 x_2 \leq (s_1 - r_1)x_1 < 0.$$

If $x_1 = 0$, $\pi = - r_2 x_2$ from (3), and the firm can further reduce its loss by setting $x_2 = 0$. Then $\pi = 0$. Therefore, $s_1 \geq r_1$; the allowable rate of return must at least cover the actual cost of capital.

[1] Alternatively, one could construct a dynamic rather than a static model and consider positive values for depreciation; but to do so would complicate the results without contributing much additional insight into the behaviour of the firm.

The problem then is to maximize (3) subject to (6).[2] Define the Lagrangian expression:

$$L(x_1, x_2, \lambda) = pz - r_1x_1 - r_2x_2 - \lambda[pz - s_1x_1 - r_2x_2]. \qquad (7)$$

The Kuhn-Tucker necessary conditions[3] for a maximum at $\bar{x}_1, \bar{x}_2, \bar{\lambda}$ are

$$r_1 \geq (1-\lambda)\left[p + z\frac{dp}{dz}\right]\frac{\partial z}{\partial x_1} + \lambda s_1, \qquad x_1 \geq 0 \qquad (8.1)$$

$$r_1 > (1-\lambda)\left[p + z\frac{dp}{dz}\right]\frac{\partial z}{\partial x_1} + \lambda s_1 \quad \text{implies } \bar{x}_1 = 0 \qquad (8.2)$$

$$(1-\lambda)r_2 \geq (1-\lambda)\left[p + z\frac{dp}{dz}\right]\frac{\partial z}{\partial x_2}, \qquad \bar{x}_2 \geq 0 \qquad (8.3)$$

$$(1-\lambda)r_2 > (1-\lambda)\left[p + z\frac{dp}{dz}\right]\frac{\partial z}{\partial x_2} \quad \text{implies } \bar{x}_2 = 0 \qquad (8.4)$$

$$pz - s_1x_1 - r_2x_2 \leq 0, \qquad \tilde{\lambda} \geq 0 \qquad (8.5)$$

$$pz - r_2x_2 < s_1x_1 \qquad \text{implies } \tilde{\lambda} = 0. \qquad (8.6)$$

Assuming $\tilde{\lambda} > 0$, it is clear from (8.1) that $\lambda = 1$ if and only if $r_1 = s_1$. If $\lambda = 1$, $r_1 = s_1$. This does not involve any variables, and it follows that any x_1, x_2 which satisfies (8.5) is a solution.

For $s_1 > r_1$, which is the interesting case, it follows that $0 \leq \lambda < 1$. From (8.6), s_1 may be chosen large enough so that $\lambda = 0$ (i.e. at some high level of allowable rate of return s_1, the value $x_1\ (s_1 - r_1)$ exceeds the level of unconditionally maximized profit, and the constraint is ineffective). If we now let $s_1 \rightarrow r_1$, λ varies continuously, and since

[2] Since (6) is an inequality, we are faced with a non-linear programming problem. However, the similarity of the results to ordinary marginal conditions is obvious.

[3] If the total revenue function, *pz*, is concave in the relevant range of operation, it is clear that the Kuhn-Tucker conditions in this case are also sufficient. Given a concave *pz*, it is possible to define the dynamic gradient process corresponding to the static Kuhn-Tucker conditions showing the firm's input variation over time. But we do not do this here since we are primarily interested in equilibrium and the optimal inputs under regulation.

$\lambda \neq 1$, we have $0 < \lambda < 1$. For the unregulated monopoly, the marginal conditions are:

$$r_i = \left[p + z\frac{dp}{dz}\right]\frac{\partial z}{\partial x_i}, \qquad (i = 1, 2). \tag{9}$$

Under conditions of effective regulatory constraint ($\lambda > 0$) equations (8.3) and (9) disclose that, as in the case of unregulated monopoly, the input of x_2 is such that its marginal cost r_2 is equal to its marginal value product. In contrast, equations (8.1) and (9) disclose that the input of x_1 is such that its marginal cost r_1 is greater than its marginal value product,[4] i.e. its use is expanded beyond the point at which its marginal cost would be equal to its marginal value product.

From equations (8.1) and (8.3) when the equalities hold, the marginal rate of substitution of factor 1 for factor 2 is:

$$\frac{-dx_2}{dx_1} = \frac{r_1}{r_2} - \frac{\lambda}{(1-\lambda)}\frac{(s_1 - r_1)}{r_2}. \tag{10}$$

Since

$$\frac{\lambda}{(1-\lambda)}\frac{(s_1 - r_1)}{r_2} > 0, \quad \lambda > 0, \quad s_1 > r_1,$$

then

$$\frac{-dx_2}{dx_1} < \frac{r_1}{r_2}. \tag{11}$$

The firm adjusts to the constraint, then, by substituting capital for the cooperating factor and by expanding total output. Comparative equilibrium outputs are shown in Fig. 2. If the regulated firm were constrained to move along the socially efficient expansion path 1 in Fig. 1, it would operate at OC in Fig. 2. Here price is slightly above

[4] Clearly

$$\frac{r_1 - \lambda s_1}{1-\lambda} = r_1 - \frac{\lambda}{1-\lambda}(s_1 - r_1) \geq \left[p + z\frac{dp}{dz}\right]\frac{\partial z}{\partial x_1}.$$

Since $0 < \lambda < 1$, $s_1 > r_1$, it follows immediately that:

$$r_1 > \left[p + z\frac{dp}{dz}\right]\frac{\partial z}{\partial x_1}.$$

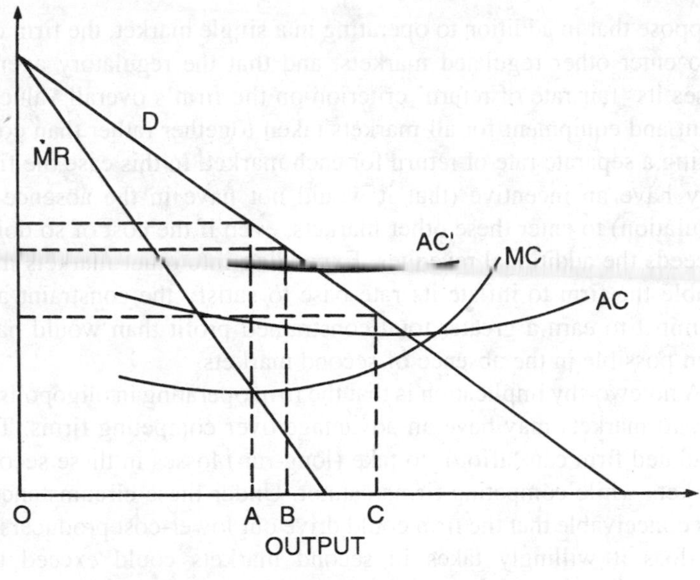

Figure 2

average cost AC to reflect the fact that $s_1 > r_1$ (profit is not entirely eliminated). Since the regulated firm moves along path 2, the social cost curve rises from AC to AC', and the regulatory constraint is satisfied at the lower output OB. The effect of regulation is to force the firm to expand output from the unregulated position OA, but output does not expand to C because a portion of what would otherwise be profit is absorbed by cost. The extent to which regulation affects output depends upon the nature of the production function. If it involves fixed proportions, i.e. min $((x_1/a), (x_2/b))$, the regulated firm is constrained to the efficient expansion path and it moves all the way to OC. If the production function is linear and if the iso-output curves have a slope equal to $-(r_1/r_2)$, the firm could substitute x_1 for x_2 and, with no change in marginal rate of substitution, hold output constant. In this case it could remain at OA, the unregulated monopoly output, under the condition that at output OA

$$pz - s_1x_1 - r_2x_2 \leq 0, \qquad x_2 = 0.$$

2. THE MULTIMARKET CASE

Suppose that in addition to operating in a single market, the firm can also enter other regulated markets, and that the regulatory agency bases its 'fair rate of return' criterion on the firm's overall value of plant and equipment for all markets taken together rather than computing a separate rate of return for each market. In this case the firm may have an incentive (that it would not have in the absence of regulation) to enter these other markets, even if the cost of so doing exceeds the additional revenues. Expanding into other markets may enable the firm to inflate its rate base to satisfy the constraint and permit it to earn a greater total constrained profit than would have been possible in the absence of second markets.

A noteworthy implication is that the firm operating in oligopolistic second markets may have an advantage over competing firms. The regulated firm can 'afford' to take (long-run) losses in these second markets while competing firms cannot. Under these circumstances, it is conceivable that the firm could drive out lower-cost producers—the loss it willingly takes in second markets could exceed the difference between its costs and the lower costs of other firms. It may succeed, therefore, in either driving lower cost firms out of these markets or of discouraging their entry into them. This is unlike the textbook case of 'predatory price-cutting' where the regulated monopolist may temporarily cut prices in outside competitive markets to drive out rivals and subsequently raise prices to monopoly levels. The monopolist would ordinarily engage in such a practice only if he had the expectation that in the long run he would make a positive profit in these additional markets; but here even in the case of a long-run loss the regulated firm may find operations in such markets to be advantageous as long as the firm is permitted to include its capital input in these markets in its rate base.

Moving to a mathematical treatment, let us consider an extreme example where operating in a second market permits the firm to act as an unconstrained monopoly in the first market, i.e. operating in the second market permits satisfaction of the regulatory constraint such that the firm can operate in the first market at output OA in Fig. 2. We shall assume that for any combination of factors along the socially optimal expansion path in market 2 the firm is just able to break even in that market. That is, for any equilibrium x_{12}, x_{22}

$$p_2 z_2 - r_1 x_{12} - r_2 x_{22} = 0. \tag{12}$$

The constraint for n markets is written:

$$\sum_{i=1}^{n} p_i z_i - s_1 \sum_{i=1}^{n} x_{1i} - r_2 \sum_{i=1}^{n} x_{2i} \leq 0. \tag{13}$$

Denoting output and factor inputs in market 1 as $\bar{z}_{11}$ and $\bar{x}_{11}, \bar{x}_{21}$ respectively at the output at which profits is unconditionally maximized in market 1, we have

$$p_1 \bar{z}_1 - s_1 \bar{x}_{11} - r_2 \bar{x}_{21} = m,\ m > 0 \tag{14}$$

where m is the value of 'excess' profit in market 1 that would violate the constraint (13) if the firm operated only in market 1. However, by moving along its expansion path in market 2 the firm can choose a level of capital input such that

$$p_2 \bar{z}_2 - s_1 \bar{x}_{12} - r_2 \bar{x}_{22} = -m. \tag{15}$$

Adding (14) and (15) we see that the firm can now satisfy constraint (13) without foregoing any profit in market 1. While the unregulated firm would be indifferent about operating in market 2, the regulated firm in this example finds market 2 attractive because it can add capital to the rate base at 'no loss'; i.e. for any capital input in market 2 the output generates revenues just equal to factor cost. Since in market 2 the actual cost of capital is below the allowed rate of return, the firm can apply the difference in satisfying the constraint in market 1 and thereby enjoy additional profit equal to $s_1 - r_1$ for each unit of capital in market 2.

This analysis suggests that even if the firm suffers a loss in market 2 (measured in terms of social costs r_1 and r_2) it may still operate there provided the value of $x_{12}(s_1 - r_1)$ exceeds this level of loss. If it suffers a loss it would no longer operate in market 1 at the profit-maximizing output *OA* in Fig. 1; seeking to equate the marginal value product of capital in both markets, it would move toward *OB*.

In the literature on public utility economics, concern is frequently expressed that the firm will attempt to inflate its rate base to increase its profit. However, the problem is generally viewed as one of proper valuation of rate base, i.e. the firm would always have an incentive to have its property stated at a value higher than its cost. The problem has given rise to a great deal of controversy about proper valuation, especially concerning original versus reproduction cost, and depreciation policy.[5] In the present study the problem of rate-base inflation is not viewed as one of valuation but rather as one of *acquisition*—quite apart from the problem of placing a valuation upon the rate base, the firm has an incentive to acquire additional capital if the allowable rate of return exceeds the cost of capital.

3. THE TELEPHONE AND TELEGRAPH INDUSTRY

Turning to the domestic telephone and telegraph industry, we find that the market structure and the regulatory setting are consistent with those described in the model. And the implications drawn from the model, concerning relative factor inputs and incentives to operate in some markets even at a loss, raise issues relevant to assessing market behaviour of firms in the industry.

For our purposes, the notable feature of the industry's market structure is that the degree of competition does vary from one subsector to another. Common carriers have monopoly positions with regard to public message telephone and telegraph services, while they compete with each other in supplying private line services to customers who, in addition, are free to construct private wire facilities for their own use as an alternative to purchasing from the common carriers.

The principal supplier of public message telephone service is the Bell Telephone System. Besides the parent corporation, American Telephone and Telegraph Company, the Bell system includes 22 subsidiary 'associate' companies of which 20 are primarily or wholly owned by AT&T. Each of the associated carriers provides local exchange and toll service within the state or group of (contiguous) states that comprises its 'operating territory'.[6] The Bell system holds

[5] For examples of the manner in which the problems have previously been treated see Clark (1939, Chs 19, 20), Troxel (1947, Chs 12, 17) and Wilcox (1955, pp. 515–16).

[6] AT&T, through its Long Lines Department, provides interstate line and radio facilities to connect the separate operating territories of the associated companies; in addition, in some cases Long Lines participates in providing interstate service internally within the territories of the multistate associated companies.

about 98 per cent of all facilities employed in long-distance message toll telephone service in the United States, and about 85 per cent of all facilities employed in local telephone service. The remaining 15 per cent of local exchange facilities are in the hands of about 3200 'independent' telephone firms, most of which are very small. These carriers connect with the Bell system, under service- and revenue-sharing agreements, and provide an integrated nationwide network. Competition does not exist among firms in the public message telephone business. Although many firms are in the industry, each has its own exclusive local marketing area.[7]

In the telegraph field, in contrast to telephone, public message telegraph service is offered only by the Western Union Telegraph Company. This is a much smaller subsector in terms of revenues than public message telephone service. In 1959 Western Union revenues for the former were about $170 million, while Bell and independent connecting carrier revenues for the latter were $7 billion.

Bell and Western Union compete in common markets in providing other services. Until recently Bell (together with independent connecting carriers) was sole supplier of private-line telephone service. However, in 1961 Bell and Western Union negotiated facilities contracts[8] that enable Western Union to offer private-line telephone service in competition with Bell. Western Union and Bell both provide telegraph exchange service and private-line telegraph service—Bell's teletypewriter or TWX service is similar to Western Union's Telex, and Bell's teletype private-wire service is similar to Western Union's leased circuit teleprinter offering. In addition, a new competitive element has recently been introduced: as an alternative to purchasing private-line telephone and telegraph services from the common carriers, firms outside the communications industry may now operate their own microwave facilities to provide communication among their geographically separated plants.[9]

[7] A good description of the industry and its present-day market structure is contained in 'National Association of Railroad and Utilities Commissioners' (1951, pp. 4–34).

[8] These contracts permit Western Union to lease Bell communications facilities in order to enter markets that it could not feasibly serve if confined to its own facilities.

[9] While railroads and public utilities, the so called 'right-of-way' companies, have historically been permitted by law to employ privately owned radio communications facilities for their internal needs, it was not until 1960 that the way was cleared (by a final decision of the Federal Communications Commission in Docket 11866) for other firms to provide their own communications facilities.

Intrastate services of the common carriers are regulated by individual state regulatory commissions; interstate operations are regulated by the Federal Communications Commission (FCC). These agencies use a 'fair rate of return' criterion in regulating prices within their respective jurisdictions. The services of each common carrier are generally lumped together in computing the rate of return to be regulated. For example, in regulating Bell's service the FCC routinely considers together all revenues, plant investment, and operating costs of Bell's interstate services in computing a rate of return to serve as the basis or decisions about price adjustments.[10] Likewise, most state agencies compute an overall rate of return for each carrier for all of its intrastate operations within the state in question.

Since the interesting implications of the model rest on the assumption that the allowable rate of return exceeds the actual cost of capital, the question arises as to whether revenues of the industry do exceed factor costs. While it is impossible to treat this question exhaustively here, there is some reason to believe that revenues are generally in excess of costs. We have been told by representatives in both the industry and in regulatory agencies that justification exists for allowing a return in excess of cost to give firms an incentive to develop and adopt cost-saving techniques. If the firm is left only indifferent as among a wide range of activities it has no positive incentive to minimize costs for any given activity. Consequently, regulatory agencies do not typically view with disfavour rates of return which are (within broad limits) somewhat in excess of rates they would judge to reflect cost. Positive profit is sometimes generated by the 'regulatory lag' phenomenon: as the firm adopts new cost-saving technology or as its business volume rises for output subject to decreasing costs, its rate of return rises. However, the regulatory agency does not react immediately to force prices down. Rather, a lag of years may be involved. An example of this can be drawn from the interstate telephone operations of the Bell System. In its overall interstate operations Bell experienced a decline in its rate of return from 7.5 per cent to 5.2 per cent from 1950 to 1953. Reasoning that a rate in the neighbourhood of 5 per cent was too low, it filed revised tariff schedules increasing interstate message toll rates by about 8 per

[10] It is true that special studies of the separate services are occasionally made by the FCC in order to determine individual rates of return. Evidence from one such study will be presented below.

cent—an increase expected to bring the rate of return up to about 6.5 per cent. The FCC, agreeing that earnings under the old tariff were inadequate, allowed the new tariff to go into effect. There is a strong implication in the FCC staff memoranda written at the time that a fair rate of return was considered to be in the neighbourhood of 6 per cent.[11] After the increase went into effect in 1953, the rate of return rose to 6.6 per cent in 1954, 7.7 per cent in 1955, reached a peak of 8.5 per cent in early 1956, and continued in excess of 7 per cent during 1957 and 1958. Despite an interstate toll rate reduction in 1959, the rate of return amounted to almost 8 per cent in 1959 and 1960. the fact that the rate of return remained above a 6 per cent level during most of the decade meant that for a number of years revenues in interstate operations exceeded the FCC Staff estimate of cost.[12]

One implication drawn from the model is that the firm increases its ratio of capital input to cooperating factor input in a manner that increases social costs at the equilibrium output. Do the common carriers in this industry overinvest in this fashion? Unfortunately, empirical evidence is not available to us on the issue of bias in favour of investment in plant and equipment. However, one point should be made: the regulatory agencies exert little direct control over investment decisions that would force the firm to follow the socially optimal expansion path. The FCC, for example, follows a 'used and useful' criterion in judging whether a given item is to be included in the rate base of plant and equipment. If the item is being employed in operations, and if it is useful (judged partially on subjective grounds),

[11] A clear, concise account of the manner in which the FCC regulates interstate telephone and telegraph services is contained in *Consent Decree Program of the Department of Justice* (1958, pp. 3427–45).

[12] The rise in Bell's rate of return is partly attributable to Bell's striking success in developing and adopting new cost-saving technology. The average book cost per circuit mile of Long Lines plant declined from roughly $230 in 1925 to $30 in 1960. The strong long-run incentives apparent in Bell's activities to cut costs may be construed as prima-facie evidence that it enjoys positive profits. Of course, one could argue that another factor is present—entrepreneurship—whose cost would more or less offset the positive profit; i.e. in the economic sense (in contrast to the accounting sense) revenue may just cover cost and the firm still has incentive to minimize cost. But here we are concerned with the *marginal* cost of capital to the firm compared to the *marginal* return to capital allowed by the regulatory agency. If the latter exceeds the former, the 'regulatory bias' emerges regardless of whether total cost includes a fixed charge attributable to an additional factor.

it is included. While common carriers are required routinely to provide a formidable list of reports concerning current operations, the relatively small staffs of the regulatory agencies available for research and investigative tasks, the lack of satisfactory criteria upon which to make judgments, and the heterogeneity of both factor inputs and service outputs would make extremely difficult if not impossible the task of detecting such bias.

The second implication drawn from the model is that due to the nature of regulation the firm has an incentive to operate in some markets even at a loss. Again, there is no clear-cut evidence which shows whether common carriers in this industry do, in fact, operate at a loss in some markets. However, evidence is available disclosing that (1) fears of 'unfair' competition based on operations at 'non-compensating' prices play a prominent role as a source of conflict between the carriers themselves and between the carriers and the FCC; and (2) in attempting to establish a commercial communications satellite system, the federal government has enacted a law containing provisions that (to serve 'public ends') appear to exploit the willingness of common carriers to operate in markets at a loss. We shall now discuss some of this evidence.

The FCC undertook a study in 1956 of interstate private-line services offered by the common carriers in order to determine the relationship between price and cost for these services on a more precise basis than is possible by considering only the overall rate of return for each carrier on all its interstate services. In the course of the study Bell submitted data (based on 1955 operations) showing that its telephone grade services were earning at a rate of 11.7 per cent, and its teletypewriter (telegraph) grade services at 2.6 per cent.[13] On the basis of this evidence, the FCC ordered interim price reductions in telephone grade services (in which Bell at the time was sole supplier) and permitted an increase for both Bell and Western Union for telegraph services (in which the two carriers do compete). The FCC expected the price adjustments to reduce substantially the spread between Bell's rates of return on telephone and telegraph grade services and to increase Western Union's rate of return on telegraph services.

[13] The initial decision of the FCC staff in this study (not adopted by the Commission at this writing) is contained in *Initial Decision* (1961).

During the study Western Union criticized Bell's behaviour that allegedly resulted in Bell's relatively low rate of return on the telegraph services competitive with Western Union's own offerings. In the words of the FCC staff (*Initial Decision* 1961, p. 54):

Western Union refers to evidence of record indicating that during the twenty-year period preceding this investigation, all principal private line telegraph rate adjustments were initiated by AT&T and, with one exception, all were rate reductions. Western Union alleges that AT&T has received a non-compensatory return on its private line telegraph service while enjoying a substantial return from services not competitive with Western Union . . . According to Western Union, it follows that AT&T has engaged in unfair competition by maintaining unreasonably low rates for a competitive service and shifting the resulting financial burden to other services.[14]

Western Union's allegations, if true, would indicate that in conformity with the model, Bell is operating in private-line telegraph at a loss. However, it is impossible, for two reasons, to determine from the evidence in the FCC study whether this is in fact the case. First, the evidence in the record is simply not sufficient to determine what earnings level is 'proper', i.e. what earnings level would just cover the cost of capital.[15] Second, the rates of return quoted above are based on 'fully allocated cost' as opposed to marginal cost. In our model, the firm operates at a loss in a market only if the additional revenues it receives by operating in that market are below the additional costs it incurs. And whether operations in that market impose a 'financial burden' (to use Western Union's words) on the other services depends on whether additional revenues do cover the additional costs.[16] But fully allocated costs are something else again. These include the costs of facilities used solely for the service in

[14] For AT&T's reply see *Reply Brief of the Bell System Companies*, 1961, pp. 14–18.

[15] The FCC staff concluded that AT&T's proper earnings levels is 7¼ per cent and for Western Union 9 per cent. This conclusion was contested by Bell in its reply brief: 'These [FCC staff] findings are made despite the fact that there is not a word of testimony in the record concerning the overall costs of capital to either carrier, much less the costs of capital for their private-line services' (*Reply Brief of the Bell System Companies*, p. 4). See also *Exceptions of Bell System Companies to the Initial Decision Released July 14, 1961 (1961)*.

[16] A good statement of this point is contained in *Brief of the Bell System Respondents in Support of Lawfulness of Revised Telpak Tariff under Section 202 (a) of the Communications Act (1961)*.

question and, in addition, they include an allocation of the 'common' costs incurred by the carrier. For example, the telephone instrument itself is necessary in providing both intrastate and interstate message toll service as well as local exchange service; a transcontinental microwave system carries both public message toll and private-line traffic. In computing a rate of return for each of these services, it is necessary to allocate the costs of facilities having multiple uses. In general, the FCC allocates these costs in accordance with relative time of use. If a given facility is employed by service A 50 per cent of the time and by service B 50 per cent of the time, the cost of the facility is split equally between A and B. For our purposes, however, the crucial question is whether the cost of the facility could have been cut in half if either service A or service B had not been offered.[17] Is allocation on the basis of relative time in use an accurate reflection of marginal costs generated by each service? We may presume an affirmative answer only if the industry is subject to constant costs. However, the available evidence is not sufficient to determine whether the industry is, in general, subject to constant costs in the relevant range of output. If, on the contrary, it is subject either to decreasing or to increasing costs, use of the conventional cost allocation procedures would tend either to overstate or to understate marginal costs for particular services. Because of these possibilities, the rates of return commonly quoted for a particular communications service cannot be used as a reliable guide in determining whether a loss, in the relevant sense, is being incurred in providing that service and whether a financial burden is thereby being imposed upon the other services.

Competition between Bell and Western Union will probably continue to be a lively issue in future FCC investigations. In February 1962, the FCC was reported to have had 'under consideration for some time an overall study of telephone vs. telegraph competition'; in the same month the American Communications Association (a union representing Western Union employees) 'formally petitioned for an investigation into the extent and effect of participation by the American Telephone and Telegraph Co. in domestic and international telegraph communications'.[18]

[17] For purposes of this simple illustration, we are assuming a zero elasticity of demand substitution between A and B.

[18] *Telecommunications Reports* (26 Feb. 1962, p. 1).

Our model suggests that apprehension about the nature of competition in the industry is justified since a common carrier, regulated as described above, would (under certain conditions) have an incentive to operate at a loss in competitive markets and to shift the financial burden to its other services. In this sense, it would have an 'unfair' advantage over other firms which do not have other markets sufficiently profitable to bear the loss of competing with it.[19] Unfortunately, however, the FCC and other regulatory bodies are so wedded to the fully allocated cost criteria rather than to marginal cost criteria in judging the 'fairness' of competition, that evidence drawn from future hearings and investigations will probably not throw much light on the question whether common carriers in some markets do, in fact, operate at a loss measured in the relevant economic sense.

Finally, the model appears useful in treating economic implications of the Communications Satellite Act passed by Congress in August 1962, after long and bitter debate (Communications Satellite Act of 1962, Sec. 304a). The Act specifies establishment of a new, private corporation regulated as a separate entity by the FCC to develop and operate the satellite system. The corporation is to be financed in two ways: (1) It may issue capital stock, carrying voting rights and eligible for dividends, to be sold 'in a manner to encourage the widest distribution to the American public' (ibid.). Purchase of this stock is also permitted by 'authorized' communications common carriers[20] subject to the constraint that the aggregate of shares held by these carriers together not exceed 50 per cent of the total shares issued and outstanding. This stock is *not* eligible for inclusion in the carrier's rate base. For convenience in subsequent analysis we shall refer to these securities as 'type I securities'. (2) The Corporation may issue 'non-voting securities, bonds, debentures and other certificates of indebtedness as it may determine'. Communications common carriers are permitted to hold these securities without specified limit, and these securities *are* eligible for inclusion in the rate base of the carrier 'to the extent allowed by the Commission [FCC]' (ibid., Sec. 304b). For convenience we shall refer to these as 'type II securities'.

[19] That is, the unconditionally maximized profits of the other regulated firms may be sufficiently low so that imposition of the regulatory constraint does not induce them to operate at a loss in competitive markets.

[20] Authorized common carriers presumably would include AT&T, Western Union and eight US overseas radio and cable telegraph companies.

The model suggests that, given the provisions of the Act, communications common carriers would have a special incentive to invest in type II securities and that their financial support might constitute a partial subsidy for the satellite corporation. By holding type II securities the common carrier incurs an interest cost (r_1) and collects whatever interest or dividends are forthcoming on type II securities (r_1'). Were the carrier unregulated or were the securities not eligible for inclusion in its rate base it would purchase securities only under the condition that $r_1' \geq r_1$. Since, however, the investment in type II securities can be included in the overall rate base of the carrier, the carrier has an incentive (again under certain conditions) to invest more than would otherwise be the case.

Consider the example where the carrier receives a zero return on its investment in type II securities, i.e. $r_1' = 0$ at all levels of investment; therefore, the carrier suffers a loss of r_1 for each dollar of investment. If, however, the allowable rate of return (s_1) is greater than the interest cost (r_1) the regulatory constraint on the carrier's other services is relaxed, permitting prices and profits to be raised in the other sectors. For each dollar in type II securities, the carrier's overall profit would *rise* by the value ($s_1 - r_1$): The loss involved in the investment in type II securities would be more than offset by the increased profits elsewhere resulting from inflation of the rate base and relaxation of the regulatory constraint. The carrier, then, may have an incentive to hold type II securities even if a direct loss is involved.

Two closely related implications arise from this analysis: First, the costs to the satellite corporation of obtaining money capital will fall if it can sell type II securities to common carriers at a return that is below their own interest cost (and if their own rate of interest is no higher than that which the satellite corporation would otherwise have to pay). To the extent that these funds provided at reduced cost to the satellite corporation permit a shift downward in its cost curves, the communications toll rates it charges to users of satellite services would also fall below the level that would have been established had the satellite corporation been forced to resort to conventional financing.[21]

[21] These users include both US and foreign international common carriers who would employ the satellite relays primarily for transoceanic communications links in combination with or as a substitute for submarine cable and radio. To the extent that

Interestingly, a reduction in satellite communications toll rates by reducing financing costs to the satellite corporation, shifting the burden to other services, was intended by the sponsors of the bill that led to the Satellite Act. Senator Kerr, when introducing the bill to the Senate in February 1962, stated (Congressional Record, 1962, p. 1670):

> [This bill strives for] . . . a privately owned corporation in which the existing American companies engaged in the international communications business would be able to invest, with their investments treated the same as the acquisition of new equipment and thus includable in their rate bases. This important feature permitting the rate of return for all communication services to be spread over a broad base would insure lower charges for communication satellite services.

Second, inclusion of type II securities in the carrier's rate base may permit the satellite corporation to operate even if its total revenues do not cover total market costs. In this case type I securities issues may be small, since little if any dividends would be earned, and the bulk of financial support might come from common carriers holding type II securities at a return below the market rate of interest.[22] Again, the losses in satellite operations would be covered by revenues from telephone and telegraph services provided by the carriers.

4. CONCLUSIONS

The preceding analysis discloses that a misallocation of economic resources may result from the use by regulatory agencies of the rate-of-return constraint for price control. The firm has an incentive to substitute between factors in an uneconomic fashion that is difficult for the regulatory agency to detect. Moreover, if a large element of common costs exists for the firm's outputs in the various markets, the widely used 'fully allocated' cost basis for rate-of-return computation is likely to prove unsatisfactory in determining whether the

users of the satellite system are the same carriers which invest in type II securities, their subsidy to the satellite corporation would be more or less offset by the reduction in toll rates they pay to the satellite corporation. However the Act specifies no particular relationship between the amount of type II securities they respectively hold and their relative use of the satellite system.

22 In this case type I securities would be attractive primarily because of the voting rights they confer.

firm is operating at a loss in any given market, or whether its activities in some markets tend to restrict competition in an undesirable manner. At the same time, regulatory practices that provide an incentive for the firm to operate in some markets even at a loss may constitute a convenient mechanism through which certain activities of the firm judged to be in the 'public interest' can be subsidized.

Our analysis suggests lines of further inquiry: We have considered only the telephone and telegraph industry, but the issues raised by the model may be relevant to evaluating market behaviour in other industries as well. It is notable that Means (1962) has advocated that certain large non-regulated firms judged to be 'collective enterprises' be encouraged, by tax incentive, to engage in 'target pricing' where they aim for a profit equal to a fair rate of return on investment. By following this approach to pricing, which is similar to that employed in public utilities, the danger exists (which he does not recognize) that these firms would be exposed to the same pressures discussed above of inflating their rate bases by substituting capital for labour and by expanding into unprofitable new lines in order to satisfy the authorities that they were using 'proper' target pricing. It might prove worthwhile to examine the effect of target pricing in steel and other industries discussed by Means in the light of the preceding analysis. Furthermore, it might be interesting to explore alternative forms of government control that, by avoiding the return-on-investment criterion for price regulation, do not generate the bias disclosed here.

REFERENCES

American Telephone and Telegraph Co. (1961), *Brief of Bell System Respondents in Support of Lawfulness of Revised Telpak Tariff under Section 202 (a) of the Communications Act*, regarding FCC Docket No. 14251.

—— (1961), *Exceptions of Bell System Companies to the Initial Decision Released July 14, 1961*, regarding FCC Docket Nos 11645, 11646, 12194.

—— (1960), *Proposed Findings and Conclusions of the Bell System Companies*, regarding FCC Docket Nos 11645, 11646.

—— (1961), *Reply Brief of the Bell System Companies*, regarding FCC Docket Nos 11645, 11646, 12194.

CLARK, J.M. (1939), *Social Control of Business*, Second Edition, New York: McGraw-Hill.

FEDERAL COMMUNICATIONS COMMISSION (1961), *Initial Decision* (adopted July 6, 1961), regarding Docket Nos 11645, 11646, 12194.

MEANS, G.C. (1962), *Pricing Power and the Public Interest*, New York: Harper.

NATIONAL ASSOCIATION OF RAILROAD AND UTILITIES COMMISSIONERS (1951), *Message Toll Telephone Rates and Disparities*, Washington.

Telecommunications Reports (Washington).

TROXEL, EMERY (1947), *Economics of Public Utilities*, New York: Rinehart & Co.

US CONGRESS, *Congressional Record* (Senate) (1962), 7 Feb. 1962, 87th Cong., 2nd sess, Washington.

—— (1958), *Consent Decree Program of the Department of Justice*. Hearings before the Anti-Trust Subcommittee of the House Committee on the Judiciary, 85th Cong., 2nd sess. Washington 1958. Pt. 2, American Telephone and Telegraph Co. (3 vols)

US PUBLIC LAW 87–624, Communications Satellite Act of 1962, 87th Cong. 31 Aug. 1962.

WILCOX, CLAIR (1955), *Public Policies toward Business*, Chicago: R.D. Irwin.

Regulating a Monopolist with Unknown Costs

David P. Baron* and Roger B. Myerson

1. INTRODUCTION

In their classic papers Dupuit (1944) and Hotelling (1938) considered pricing policies for a bridge that had a fixed cost of construction and zero marginal cost. They demonstrated that the pricing policy that maximizes consumer well-being is to set price equal to marginal cost and to provide a subsidy to the supplier equal to the fixed cost, so that a firm would be willing to provide the bridge. This first-best solution is based on a number of informational assumptions. First, the demand function is assumed to be known to both the regulator and to the firm. While the assumption of complete information may be too strong, the assumption that information about demand is as available to the regulator as it is to the firm does not seem unnatural. A second informational assumption is that the regulator has complete information about the cost of the firm or at least has the same information about cost as does the firm. This assumption is unlikely to be met in reality, since the firm would be expected to have better information about costs than would the regulator. As Weitzman has stated,

> An essential feature of the regulatory environment I am trying to describe is uncertainty about the exact specification of each firm's cost function. In most cases even the managers and engineers most closely associated with production will be unable to precisely specify beforehand the cheapest way to generate various hypothetical output levels. Because they are yet removed from the production process, the regulators are likely to be vaguer still about a firm's cost function (1978, p. 684).

* The first author's work has been supported by a grant from the National Science Foundation, Grant No. SOC 77–07251.

As this observation suggests, it is natural to expect that a firm would have better information regarding its costs than would a regulator. The purpose of this paper is to develop an optimal regulatory policy for the case in which the regulator does not know the costs of the firm.

One strategy that a regulator could use in the absence of full information about costs is to give the firm the title to the total social surplus and to delegate the pricing decision to the firm. In pursuing its own interests, which would then be to maximize the total social surplus, the firm would adopt the same marginal cost pricing strategy that the regulator would have imposed if the regulator had known the costs of the firm. This approach has been proposed by Loeb and Magat (1979) but leaves the equity issue unresolved, since the firm receives all the social surplus and consumers receive none. To resolve the equity issue. Loeb and Magat propose that the right to the monopoly franchise be auctioned among competing firms as a means of transferring surplus from producers to consumers. However, if there are no other producers capable of supplying the product efficiently, an auction will not be effective. Thus, in this paper we will not assume that an efficient auction could be conducted. In the absence of the auction possibility, it is clear that consumers would be better off by allowing the firm to operate as a monopolist rather than transferring the total surplus to the firm, since in that case consumers would at least receive some benefit from the firm's output. Another approach that might be considered to transfer surplus from producers to consumers would be to levy a lump-sum tax against the firm. When the regulator does not know the cost, however, it runs the risk that if the tax is set too high the firm may decline to supply the good.

The approach taken in this paper to regulation under asymmetric information is based on the work of Myerson (1979, 1981) and involves the design of a regulatory policy that recognizes that the firm may have an incentive to misreport its cost in order to obtain a more favourable price. An incentive-compatible regulatory policy in which the firm has no incentive to misreport its cost can, however, be shown to be at least as good as any non-incentive-compatible regulatory policy, so the regulator need only consider incentive-compatible policies. That is, since the regulator does not know the firm's costs, the regulator must set the firm's price and subsidy as a function of some cost report from the firm, and the regulatory policy must satisfy the constraint that the firm should have an incentive to report truthfully the information desired by the regulator. Because of this constraint, the regulatory policy can be optimal only in a constrained sense, and a welfare loss results from the informational asymmetry.

The optimal regulatory policy necessarily depends on the regulator's prior information about the firm's costs. If it is optimal for the firm to produce, the optimal pricing rule will be shown to depend only on the regulator's information about costs. As with the first-best solution, the optimal regulatory policy under asymmetric information is such that production is warranted only if the social benefit resulting from the optimal pricing rule is at least as great as the 'adjusted' fixed cost. In order to implement a regulatory policy, it is necessary to provide the firm with a fair rate of return, and in Dupuit's and Hotelling's complete-information case with a constant marginal cost and a fixed cost, a subsidy equal to the fixed cost is used to induce the firm to produce. In the regulatory policy considered here, a subsidy is used both to reward the firm sufficiently so that it will produce and to induce the firm to reveal its costs.

In Sec. 2 we define the basic model used to describe the regulator's problem, and in Sec. 3 we analyse that problem and derive the optimal regulatory policy. In Sec. 4 the general properties of this optimal policy are discussed. The special cases of known fixed costs and of known marginal costs are discussed in Secs 5 and 6.

2. BASIC STRUCTURES

To model the problem of regulating a natural monopoly when its cost structure is not known to the regulator, we could let the monopolistic firm have costs determined by some function $C(q, \theta)$, where q is the quantity produced and θ is a cost parameter that is unknown to the regulator. To keep the problem mathematically tractable, however, we shall assume that the firm's cost function is bilinear in q and θ of the form

$$C(q, \theta) = (c_0 + c_1\theta)q + (k_0 + k_1\theta) \quad \text{if } q > 0, \quad \text{and } C(0, \theta) = 0. \qquad (1)$$

where c_0, c_1, k_0, k_1 are known constants satisfying $c_1 \geq 0$ and $k_1 \geq 0$.

For mathematical simplicity, we assume that the range of possible θ is bounded within some known interval from θ_0 to θ_1 ($\theta_0 < \theta_1$).

To interpret this cost function, observe that $k_0 + k_1\theta$ represents a fixed cost incurred to produce any positive output, and $c_0 + c_1\theta$ represents the marginal cost of producing each unit after the first. For example, this formulation is general enough to include, as special cases, the case of unknown marginal costs ($C(q, \theta) = k_0 + \theta q$) and of unknown fixed costs ($C(q, \theta) = \theta + c_0 q$), which will be discussed in Secs 5 and 6, respectively.

We assume that the firm knows the true value of its cost parameter θ, but that θ is not known to the regulator. Furthermore, the regulator is not assumed to be able to audit the cost actually incurred by the firm, so that the regulatory policy cannot be based on the true cost of the firm. Thus, if the regulator asks for a cost report from the firm, we must anticipate that the firm would misreport its cost function whenever this was to its advantage.

The regulator's problem is to decide how the firm's regulated price and subsidy should be determined, as functions of some cost report from the firm. The following observation is central to the analysis of the regulator's problem:

Proposition (The Revelation Principle): *Without any loss of generality, the regulator may be restricted to regulatory policies which require the firm to report its cost parameter θ and which give the firm no incentive to lie.*

In different contexts this revelation principle has been discussed in several other recent papers (see Dasgupta, Hammond, and Maskin, 1979; Gibbard, 1973; Harris and Townsend, 1981; and Myerson, 1979. To see why it is true, suppose that the regulator chose some general regulatory policy, not of the form described in the proposition. For each possible value of θ, let $\Psi(\theta)$ be the cost report that the firm would submit if its true cost parameter were θ. That is, $\Psi(\theta)$ maximizes the firm's expected profit, when it is confronted with this regulatory policy and its true cost parameter is θ. Now consider the following new regulatory policy: ask the firm to report its cost parameter θ; then compute $\Psi(\theta)$; and then enforce the regulations that would have been enforced in the original regulatory policy if $\Psi(\theta)$ had been reported there. It is easy to see that the firm never has any incentive to lie to the regulator in the new policy. (Otherwise it would have had some incentive to lie to itself in the originally given policy.) Thus, the new policy is of the form described in the proposition, and it always gives the same outcomes as the original policy.

Following the Bayesian approach, we assume that the regulator has some subjective prior probability distribution for the unknown parameter θ prior to receiving any cost report from the firm. We let $f(\cdot)$ be the density function for this probability distribution, and we assume that $f(\theta)$ is a continuous function of θ with $f(\theta) > 0$ over the interval $[\theta_0, \theta_1]$ and with $F(\theta)$ denoting the cumulative distribution function for θ.

The demand function is assumed to be known by both the firm and the regulator. We let $P(\cdot)$ denote the inverse demand function, so that $P(q)$ is the price at which the consumers demand the output q.

Ignoring income effects, the total value $V(q)$ to consumers of an output quantity q is the area under the demand curve, given by

$$V(q) = \int_0^q P(\tilde{q})d\tilde{q}. \tag{2}$$

The consumers' surplus is then $V(q) - qP(q)$.

We assume that the regulator has consumer and producer surplus objectives and has three basic regulatory instruments available to achieve its objective: (i) the regulator can decide whether to allow the firm to do business at all; (ii) if the firm is in business, then its price or quantity of output may be regulated; and (iii) the firm may be given a subsidy or charged a tax. Now, using the revelation principle, we may consider only regulatory policies under which the firm's cost report will reveal its cost parameter θ, so the regulatory instruments can be chosen as functions of θ. Thus, we shall describe a regulatory policy by four outcome functions (r, p, q, s), to be interpreted as follows. For any $\hat{\theta}$ in $[\theta_0, \theta_1]$, if the firm reports that its cost parameter is $\hat{\theta}$, then $r(\hat{\theta})$ is the probability that the regulator will permit the firm to do business at all.[1] Since $r(\hat{\theta})$ is a probability, it must satisfy

$$0 \le r(\hat{\theta}) \le 1. \tag{3}$$

[1] A regulatory policy that has a positive probability that there will be no output may seem unrealistic, but in the optimal regulatory policy $r(\theta)$ will equal one unless the consumer surplus is less than an 'adjusted' fixed cost, in which case $r(\theta) = 0$.

If the firm does go into business after reporting $\hat{\theta}$, then $p(\hat{\theta})$ will be its regulated price, and $q(\hat{\theta})$ will be the corresponding quantity of output, satisfying[2]

$$p(\hat{\theta}) = P(q(\hat{\theta})). \tag{4}$$

Finally, $s(\hat{\theta})$ will be the expected subsidy paid to the firm if it reports cost parameter $\hat{\theta}$. For example, if the firm would get a subsidy $s^*(\hat{\theta})$ if it were allowed to go into business, but would get no subsidy if it were not allowed to go into business, then the expected subsidy is $s(\hat{\theta}) = r(\hat{\theta})s^*(\hat{\theta})$. If $s(\hat{\theta})$ is negative, then it represents a tax on the firm.

The firm is assumed to be risk neutral. Thus, given a regulatory policy (r, p, q, s), if the firm's cost parameter is θ, and if the firm reports θ honestly, its expected profit $\pi(\theta)$ is

$$\pi(\theta) = [p(\theta)q(\theta) - (c_0 + c_1\theta)q(\theta) - k_0 - k_1\theta]r(\theta) + s(\theta). \tag{5}$$

If the firm were to misrepresent its cost and report $\hat{\theta}$, when θ is its true cost parameter, its expected profit would be

$$\pi^*(\hat{\theta}, \theta) = [p(\hat{\theta})q(\hat{\theta}) - (c_0 + c_1\theta)q(\hat{\theta}) - k_0 - k_1\theta]r(\hat{\theta}) + s(\hat{\theta}). \tag{6}$$

Thus, to guarantee that the firm has no incentive to misrepresent its cost, we must have

$$\pi(\theta) = \underset{\hat{\theta}}{\text{maximum}}\ \pi^*(\hat{\theta}, \theta) \tag{7}$$

for all θ in $[\theta_0, \theta_1]$.

We assume that the regulator cannot force the firm to operate if it expects a negative profit. So the regulatory policy must also satisfy the individual rationality condition.

$$\pi(\theta) \geq 0 \tag{8}$$

for all θ in $[\theta_0, \theta_1]$.

[2] It is easy to show that if the firm is risk neutral, then randomized pricing policies cannot be optimal. On the other hand, if there were uncertainty about the demand curve, then the regulator would have to choose between regulating price and letting quantity be random, or regulating quantity and letting price be random. Weitzman (1974) has studied this issue in a similar context. If consumers are homogeneous, then non-linear pricing policies like those of Spence (1977) are not relevant.

We say that a regulatory policy (r, p, q, s) is *feasible* if it satisfies the four constraints (3), (4), (7), and (8) for all θ in $[\theta_0, \theta_1]$. Thus, when the regulator uses a feasible regulatory policy, the firm will be willing to submit honest cost reports and to operate whenever permitted. The regulator's problem is to find a feasible regulatory policy that maximizes social welfare, which will be specified next.

If consumers are risk neutral and have additively separable utility for money and the firm's product, the net expected gain for the consumers from a regulatory policy (r, p, q, s) would be[3]

$$\int_{\theta_0}^{\theta_1} ([V(q(\theta)) - p(\theta)q(\theta)]r(\theta) - s(\theta))f(\theta)d\theta.$$

That is, the consumers' expected gain is the expected consumers' surplus from the marketplace minus the firm's expected subsidy, which must be paid by the consumers through their taxes. The regulator's expectation of the firm's profit (before θ is known) is

$$\int_{\theta_0}^{\theta_1} \pi(\theta)f(\theta)d\theta.$$

We assume that the regulator maximizes a weighted sum of the expected gains to consumers plus the expected profit for the firm. Specifically, we assume that there is some number α, satisfying $0 \leq \alpha \leq 1$, such that the regulator's objective is to maximize

$$\int_{\theta_0}^{\theta_1} ([V(q(\theta)) - p(\theta)q(\theta)]r(\theta) - s(\theta))f(\theta)d\theta + \alpha\int_{\theta_0}^{\theta_1} \pi(\theta)f(\theta)d\theta \quad (9)$$

3. DERIVATION OF THE OPTIMAL POLICY

We first state and prove two lemmas that provide a more useful characterization of the regulator's problem than the definitions given in the preceding section.

Lemma 1: *A regulatory policy is feasible if and only if it satisfies the following conditions for all* θ *in* $[\theta_0, \theta_1]$*:*

[3] See Schmalensee (1972) for an analysis of the expected consumer surplus as a measure of welfare.

$$0 \le r(\theta) \le 1, \tag{3}$$

$$p(\theta) = P(q(\theta)), \tag{4}$$

$$\pi(\theta) = \pi(\theta_1) + \int_{\theta}^{\theta_1} r(\tilde{\theta})(c_1 q(\tilde{\theta}) + k_1) d\tilde{\theta}, \tag{10}$$

$$\pi(\theta_1) \ge 0, \text{ and} \tag{11}$$

$$r(\theta)(c_1 q(\theta) + k_1) \ge r(\hat{\theta})(c_1 q(\hat{\theta}) + k_1) \quad \text{for all } \hat{\theta} \ge \theta. \tag{12}$$

Proof: First we show that feasibility (defined by conditions (3), (4), (7), (8)) implies the conditions in the lemma. Since (3) and (4) are simply repeated from the definition and (11) is implied by (8), we only need to show (10) and (12).

From (7) for any θ and $\hat{\theta}$

$$\pi(\theta) \ge \pi^*(\hat{\theta}, \theta) = \pi(\hat{\theta}) + r(\hat{\theta})(c_1 q(\hat{\theta}) + k_1)(\hat{\theta} - \theta). \tag{13}$$

using the definitions (5) and (6). Thus

$$r(\hat{\theta})(c_1 q(\hat{\theta}) + k_1)(\hat{\theta} - \theta) \le \pi(\theta) - \pi(\hat{\theta}) \le r(\theta)(c_1 q(\theta) + k_1)(\hat{\theta} - \theta) \tag{14}$$

where the second inequality follows from the analogue of (13) with the roles of θ and $\hat{\theta}$ reversed. Then (12) follows from (14), when $\hat{\theta} > \theta$.

Since $r(\theta)(c_1 q(\theta) + k_1)$ is a non-increasing function of θ, it must be continuous almost everywhere in $[\theta_0, \theta_1]$. Thus, if we divide (14) by $(\theta - \hat{\theta})$ and take the limit as $\hat{\theta} \to \theta$, we obtain

$$\pi'(\theta) = -\, r(\theta)(c_1(\theta) + k_1)$$

for almost all θ. Integrating implies that (10) must hold for any feasible regulatory policy.

Conversely, we must show that conditions (7) and (8) are implied by the conditions in the lemma. Condition (8) follows easily from (10) and (11), since $c_1 \ge 0$ and $k_1 \ge 0$ by assumption. To prove (7), observe that (10) implies

$$\begin{aligned}\pi^*(\hat{\theta}, \theta) &= \pi(\hat{\theta}) + r(\hat{\theta})(c_1\, q(\hat{\theta}) + k_1)(\hat{\theta} - \theta) \\ &= \pi(\theta) - \int_{\theta}^{\hat{\theta}} [r(\tilde{\theta})(c_1 q(\tilde{\theta}) + k_1) - r(\hat{\theta})(c_1 q(\hat{\theta}) + k_1)] d\tilde{\theta}\end{aligned}$$

If $\hat{\theta} > \theta$, then the integrand is non-negative (since $\tilde{\theta} < \hat{\theta}$) by (12), so $\pi^*(\hat{\theta}, \theta) \leq \pi(\theta)$. If $\hat{\theta} < \theta$, then the integrand is non-positive, but then the integral is non-negative (since the direction of integration is backwards), so that $\pi^*(\hat{\theta}, \theta) \leq \pi(\theta)$ still holds, as (7) requires. *Q.E.D.*

Lemma 2: *For any feasible regulatory policy, the social welfare function (9) is equal to*

$$\int_{\theta_0}^{\theta_1} [V(q(\theta)) - (c_0 + c_1 z_\alpha(\theta))q(\theta) - k_0 - k_1 z_\alpha(\theta)]r(\theta)f(\theta)d\theta \qquad (15)$$
$$- (1 - \alpha)\pi(\theta_1)$$

where

$$z_\alpha(\theta) = \theta + (1 - \alpha)\,\frac{F(\theta)}{f(\theta)}. \qquad (16)$$

Proof: From the definition of $\pi(\theta)$ in (5), we obtain

$$p(\theta)q(\theta)r(\theta) + s(\theta) = \pi(\theta) + ((c_0 + c_1\theta)q(\theta) + k_0 + k_1\theta)r(\theta). \qquad (17)$$

Also, using (10) from Lemma 1,

$$\int_{\theta_0}^{\theta_1} \pi(\theta)\, f(\theta)d\theta = \int_{\theta_0}^{\theta_1} \left(\int_{\theta}^{\theta_1} r(\tilde{\theta})(c_1 q(\tilde{\theta}) + k_1)d\tilde{\theta} + \pi(\theta_1) \right) f(\theta)d\theta \qquad (18)$$

$$= \int_{\theta_0}^{\theta_1} r(\tilde{\theta})(c_1 q(\tilde{\theta}) + k_1) \int_{\theta_0}^{\tilde{\theta}} f(\theta)d\theta\, d\tilde{\theta} + \pi(\theta_1)$$

$$= \int_{\theta_0}^{\theta_1} r(\theta)(c_1 q(\theta) + k_1)\, F(\theta)d\theta + \pi(\theta_1).$$

Substituting (17) and (18) into (9) yields

$$\int_{\theta_0}^{\theta_1} ([V(q(\theta)) - p(\theta)q(\theta)]r(\theta) - s(\theta) + \alpha\pi(\theta))f(\theta)d\theta$$

$$= \int_{\theta_0}^{\theta_1} ([V(q(\theta)) - (c_0 + c_1\theta)q(\theta) - k_0 - k_1\theta]r(\theta)$$
$$- (1 - \alpha)\pi(\theta))f(\theta)d\theta$$

$$= \int_{\theta_0}^{\theta_1} [V(q(\theta)) - (c_0 + c_1\theta)q(\theta) - k_0 - k_1\theta]r(\theta)f(\theta)d(\theta)$$

$$- (1 - \alpha)\int_{\theta_0}^{\theta_1} F(\theta)(c_1 q(\theta) + k_1)\, r(\theta)\, d\theta - (1 - \alpha)\pi(\theta_1).$$

Formula (15) then follows by straightforward simplification. *Q.E.D.*

Lemma 2 gives a strong suggestion as to what the optimal policy should be. The integrand in (15) is maximized for each θ by choosing $q(\theta)$ to maximize $V(q(\theta)) - (c_0 + c_1 z_\alpha(\theta))q(\theta)$, and by letting $r(\theta)$ equal one or zero depending on whether the bracketed expression is positive or negative. Then the subsidy can be chosen so that π satisfies conditions (10) and (11). But this solution will not be feasible unless the monotonicity condition (12) is also satisfied, and this condition implies that $z_\alpha(\theta)$ must be non-decreasing in θ. Unfortunately, for some densities $f(\cdot)$, (16) need not yield a monotone $z_\alpha(\cdot)$ function. With some carefully chosen definitions, therefore, we now construct another function which is closely related to $z_\alpha(\cdot)$, but which is always monotone non-decreasing.

Given $z_\alpha(\cdot)$ as in (16), let

$$h_\alpha(\phi) = z_\alpha(F^{-1}(\phi)) \tag{19}$$

for any ϕ between 0 and 1. (Notice that the cumulative distribution function $F(\theta)$ is strictly increasing, so that it is indeed invertible.) Let

$$H_\alpha(\phi) = \int_0^\phi h_\alpha(\tilde{\phi})\, d\tilde{\phi} \tag{20}$$

Next, using the notation of Rockafellar [9, p. 36], let

$$\bar{H}_\alpha(\phi) = \text{conv } H_\alpha(\phi). \tag{21}$$

That is, $\bar{H}_\alpha(\cdot)$ is the highest convex function on the interval [0, 1] satisfying $\bar{H}_\alpha(\phi) \le H_\alpha(\phi)$ for all $\phi \in [0, 1]$. Since $\bar{H}_\alpha$ is convex, it is differentiable almost everywhere. Then let

$$\bar{h}_\alpha(\phi) = \bar{H}'_\alpha(\phi) \tag{22}$$

whenever this derivative is defined, and extend $\bar{h}_\alpha(\phi)$ by right-continuity to all $0 \le \phi \le 1$. Finally, let

$$\bar{z}_\alpha(\theta) = \bar{h}_\alpha(F(\theta)). \tag{23}$$

The following lemma summarizes the properties of this $\bar{z}_\alpha(\cdot)$ function that are needed to derive the optimal policy.

Lemma 3: *There exists a continuous function* G_α: $[\theta_0, \theta_1] \to \mathbb{R}$ *such that* $G_\alpha(\theta) \geq 0$ *for all* θ, $\bar{z}_\alpha(\theta)$ *is locally constant whenever* $G_\alpha(\theta) > 0$, *and*

$$\int_{\theta_0}^{\theta_1} A(\theta)z_\alpha(\theta)f(\theta)d\theta = \int_{\theta_0}^{\theta_1} A(\theta)\bar{z}_\alpha(\theta)f(\theta)d\theta - \int_{\theta=\theta_0}^{\theta_1} G_\alpha(\theta)dA(\theta). \quad (24)$$

for any monotone function $A(\cdot)$. *Furthermore,* $\bar{z}_\alpha(\theta)$ *is a non-decreasing function of* θ, *and if* $z_\alpha(\theta)$ *is a non-decreasing function of* θ *then* $\bar{z}_\alpha(\theta) = z_\alpha(\theta)$ *for all* θ.

Proof: The function G_α in the lemma is

$$G_\alpha(\theta) = H_\alpha(F(\theta)) - \bar{H}_\alpha(F(\theta)).$$

G_α is continuous, since H_α and $\bar{H}_\alpha$ are continuous functions. By construction of $\bar{H}_\alpha$, $H_\alpha \geq \bar{H}_\alpha$, and $\bar{H}_\alpha$ is flat (so that $\bar{H}_\alpha = \bar{h}_\alpha$ is locally constant) whenever $H_\alpha > \bar{H}_\alpha$. To derive equation (24), use integration by parts to get

$$\int_{\theta_0}^{\theta_1} A(\theta)(z_\alpha(\theta) - \bar{z}_\alpha(\theta))f(\theta)d\theta$$

$$= \int_{\theta=\theta_0}^{\theta_1} A(\theta)\, d[H_\alpha(F(\theta)) - \bar{H}_\alpha(F(\theta))] = \int_{\theta=\theta_0}^{\theta_1} A(\theta)\, dG_\alpha(\theta)$$

$$= G_\alpha(\theta_1)A(\theta_1) - G_\alpha(\theta_0)A(\theta_0) - \int_{\theta=\theta_0}^{\theta_1} G_\alpha(\theta)dA(\theta).$$

Then observe that $\bar{H}_\alpha(0) = H_\alpha(0)$ and $\bar{H}_\alpha(1) = H_\alpha(1)$, so that $G_\alpha(\theta_0) = G_\alpha(\theta_1) = 0$, because the convex hull of a continuous function always equals the function at the endpoints of the domain in $\mathbb{R}$. $\bar{z}_\alpha(\theta)$ is non-decreasing because $\bar{h}_\alpha$ is the non-decreasing derivative of a convex function. If $z_\alpha(\theta)$ were non-decreasing, then H_α would be convex, so that $\bar{H}_\alpha = H_\alpha$ and $\bar{h}_\alpha = h_\alpha$ and $\bar{z}_\alpha = z_\alpha$. *Q.E.D.*

We can now state the optimal regulatory policy. Let $\bar{p}(\theta)$ and $\bar{q}(\theta)$ be defined by

$$\bar{p}(\theta) = c_0 + c_1\bar{z}_\alpha(\theta), \quad (25)$$

$$P(\bar{q}(\theta)) = \bar{p}(\theta). \quad (26)$$

Let $\bar{r}(\theta)$ satisfy

$$\bar{r}(\theta) = \begin{cases} 1 & \text{if } V(\bar{q}(\theta)) - \bar{p}(\theta)\bar{q}(\theta) \geq k_0 + k_1\bar{z}_\alpha(\theta), \\ 0 & \text{if } V(\bar{q}(\theta)) - \bar{p}(\theta)\bar{q}(\theta) < k_0 + k_1\bar{z}_\alpha(\theta), \end{cases} \tag{27}$$

and let

$$\bar{s}(\theta) = [(c_0 + c_1\theta)\bar{q}(\theta) + k_0 + k_1\theta - \bar{p}(\theta)\bar{q}(\theta)]\bar{r}(\theta) \tag{28}$$

$$+ \int_\theta^{\theta_1} \bar{r}(\tilde{\theta})\,(c_1\bar{q}(\tilde{\theta}) + k_1)d\tilde{\theta}.$$

The following theorem establishes the optimality of this policy.

Theorem: *The regulatory policy* $(\bar{r}, \bar{p}, \bar{q}, \bar{s})$ *given in* (25)–(28) *is feasible and maximizes the social welfare function* (9) *among all feasible regulatory policies.*

Proof: First we check that the regulatory policy is feasible, using Lemma 1. Conditions (3) and (4) are obviously satisfied. To check conditions (10) and (11), we substitute (28) into (5) to obtain

$$\pi(\theta) = \int_\theta^{\theta_1} \bar{r}(\theta)\,(c_1 q(\tilde{\theta}) + k_1)\, d\tilde{\theta} \qquad \text{and} \qquad \pi(\theta_1) = 0.$$

Since $\bar{z}_\alpha(\theta)$ is non-decreasing, $\bar{p}(\theta)$ is non-decreasing, and so $\bar{q}(\theta)$ is non-increasing in θ. Notice that

$$\frac{\partial}{\partial q}[V(q) - P(q)q] = -P'(q)q > 0,$$

since $V'(q) = P(q)$. (Recall (2)). Thus, the consumers' surplus $V(\bar{q}(\theta)) - \bar{p}(\theta)\,\bar{q}(\theta)$ is non-increasing in θ, since $\bar{q}(\theta)$ is non-increasing, and so $\bar{r}(\theta)$ is also non-increasing in θ. Thus (12) is satisfied.

Now we show that the regulatory policy is optimal. When we substitute equation (24) into formula (15), using $A(\theta) = -r(\theta)(c_1 q(\theta) + k_1)$, we find that the regulator's social welfare function (9) is equal to

$$\int_{\theta_0}^{\theta_1} [V(q(\theta)) - (c_0 + c_1\bar{z}_\alpha(\theta))q(\theta) - k_0 - k_1\bar{z}_\alpha(\theta)]r(\theta)f(\theta)d\theta \tag{29}$$

$$-\int_{\theta=\theta_0}^{\theta_1} G_\alpha(\theta)\, d[-r(\theta)(c_1 q(\theta) + k_1)] - (1-\alpha)\pi(\theta_1),$$

for any feasible regulatory policy. Since $G_\alpha(\theta) \geq 0$ and $[-r(\theta)(c_1q(\theta) + k_1)]$ is non-decreasing, the second integral in (29) must be non-negative for any feasible policy; but this integral equals zero (its optimal value) for the policy $(\bar{r}, \bar{p}, \bar{q}, \bar{s})$, because $\bar{z}_\alpha(\theta)$, $\bar{q}(\theta)$, and $\bar{r}(\theta)$ are locally constant whenever $G_\alpha(\theta) > 0$. In the third term in (29), $(1 - \alpha)\pi(\theta_1) \geq 0$ for any feasible policy (since $\alpha \leq 1$), but this term equals zero (again, its optimal value) at the policy $(\bar{r}, \bar{p}, \bar{q}, \bar{s})$. Finally, to optimize the first integral in (29), we want to choose each $q(\theta)$ so that

$$0 = V'(q(\theta)) - (c_0 + c_1\bar{z}_\alpha(\theta))$$

and we want to choose each $r(\theta)$ so that

$$r(\theta) = \begin{cases} 1 & \text{if } V(q(\theta)) - (c_0 + c_1\bar{z}_\alpha(\theta))q(\theta) \geq k_0 + k_1\bar{z}_\alpha(\theta), \\ 0 & \text{if } V(q(\theta)) - (c_0 + c_1\bar{z}_\alpha(\theta))q(\theta) < k_0 + k_1\bar{z}_\alpha(\theta), \end{cases}$$

But these equations are equivalent to (25)–(27), since $V'(q(\theta)) = P(q(\theta))$, so $(\bar{r}, \bar{p}, \bar{q}, \bar{s})$ maximizes the first integral in (29) among all feasible policies. So $(\bar{r}, \bar{p}, \bar{q}, \bar{s})$ maximizes (29), which is equivalent to maximizing (9). *Q.E.D.*

4. ANALYSIS OF THE OPTIMAL SOLUTION

If the regulator had complete information about the firm's costs, the optimal policy would be to set price equal marginal cost and to subsidize the firm by an amount equal to its fixed cost, unless this subsidy exceeded the consumers' surplus in which case the firm would not produce. That is, if θ were known to the regulator, the complete-information solution would be

$$p(\theta) = c_0 + c_1\theta, \qquad q(\theta) = P^{-1}(p(\theta)), \tag{30}$$

$$r(\theta) = \begin{cases} 1 & \text{if } V(q(\theta)) - p(\theta)q(\theta) \geq k_0 + k_1(\theta), \\ 0 & \text{if } V(q(\theta)) - p(\theta)q(\theta) < k_0 + k_1(\theta), \end{cases} \tag{31}$$

$$s(\theta) = (k_0 + k_1\theta)r(\theta). \tag{32}$$

Of course, this policy is not feasible for the regulator when θ is unknown, because it does not satisfy the incentive-compatibility constraint (7). The firm would have positive incentives to misrepresent its costs by reporting costs higher than the true θ. However, it is instructive to compare our optimal policy (25)–(28) to this complete-information solution (30)–(32). The optimal $\bar{p}(\theta)$, $\bar{q}(\theta)$ and $\bar{r}(\theta)$ are chosen as if the regulator were applying the complete-information solution to $\bar{z}_\alpha(\theta)$ rather than to θ. Since $\bar{z}_\alpha(\theta)$ is greater than θ, this transformation from θ to $\bar{z}_\alpha(\theta)$ may be viewed as an accommodation to the firm's incentive to overstate its costs in the complete-information solution. There is no obvious relationship between the optimal subsidy $\bar{s}(\theta)$ in (28) and the complete-information subsidy in (32), because $\bar{s}(\theta)$ is determined by the need to prevent the firm from misrepresenting its costs, whereas the subsidy in (32) was only designed to cover the firm's fixed costs.

Another parallel between the optimal regulatory policy under uncertainty and the complete-information solution is that both $\bar{p}(\theta)$ in (25) and $p(\theta)$ in (30) are determined independently of the demand curve. That is, in both cases the optimal regulatory price depends only on the regulator's information about the firm's costs.

Since the optimal regulated price $\bar{p}(\theta)$ is generally strictly higher than the firm's marginal costs $(c_0 + c_1\theta)$, and since $\bar{p}(\theta)$ does not depend on the demand curve, the optimal regulated price $\bar{p}(\theta)$ may in some cases be higher than the unregulated monopoly price $p_M(\theta)$ determined by the usual $MR = MC$ condition. To see that this can indeed happen, suppose $k_0 = k_1 = 0$ (so fixed costs are zero) and consider a marginal cost $c_0 + c_1\theta$ and the corresponding price $\bar{p}(\theta)$. Since $\bar{p}(\theta)$ is independent of the demand function, a demand function can be chosen that intersects the price axis between marginal cost and the regulated price $\bar{p}(\theta)$. Clearly, the monopoly price must be lower than $\bar{p}(\theta)$ in this example, since demand is zero at $\bar{p}(\theta)$.

From an ex post point of view, it may seem inefficient and paradoxical for the regulator to ever force the firm to charge a price higher than the unregulated monopoly price. To understand why this may be optimal, observe that the regulator wants to encourage the firm to admit that it has low costs, whenever this is true, so that a low price can be set to generate a large consumers' surplus. But to prevent the firm from misrepresenting its costs when it has low costs, the regulator either must reward the firm with subsidies for announcing low costs or must somehow punish the firm for announcing high costs. Such punishments may take the form of forcing the firm to charge a price above the monopoly price when its costs are high or of not permitting the firm to produce ($\bar{r}(\theta) = 0$). From this point of view supermonopoly prices may be seen as a less extreme punishment than complete shut-down, since they still generate some consumers' surplus.

In general, all the regulator's instruments $(\bar{r}, \bar{p}, \bar{q}, \bar{s})$ are used together to guide the firm to honestly report its cost parameter while generating the highest possible social welfare. The optimal regulatory price $\bar{p}(\theta)$ is a non-decreasing function of θ, while the quantity produced $\bar{q}(\theta)$ is non-increasing in θ. From (27), the function $\bar{r}(\theta)$ is non-increasing in θ, with $\bar{r}(\theta) = 1$ for all θ below the critical value θ^* at which

$$V(\bar{q}(\theta^*)) - \bar{p}(\theta^*)\bar{q}(\theta^*) = k_0 + k_1\bar{z}_\alpha(\theta^*),$$

and with $\bar{r}(\theta) = 0$ (denoting shut-down) for all θ above θ^*. Differentiating (28) in the interval where $\bar{r}(\theta) = 1$, yields

$$\bar{s}'(\theta) = \bar{q}'(\theta) \cdot ([c_0 + c_1\theta] - [P(\bar{q}(\theta)) + \bar{q}(\theta)P'(\bar{q}(\theta))]). \tag{33}$$

Since $\bar{q}'(\theta) \leq 0$, and since the second factor in (33) is just marginal cost minus marginal revenue at $\bar{q}(\theta)$, $\bar{s}(\theta)$ is decreasing in θ when the regulated price $\bar{p}(\theta)$ is below the monopoly price $p_M(\theta)$, and $\bar{s}(\theta)$ is increasing in θ when $\bar{p}(\theta) > p_M(\theta)$. To understand these results, observe that the difference between $\bar{p}(\theta)$ and $p_M(\theta)$ tends to give the firm some incentive to misrepresent its costs in order to obtain a price closer to the monopoly price. The subsidy $\bar{s}(\theta)$ then must vary with θ so as to offset this incentive.

However, whether the subsidy is increasing or decreasing θ, the firm's expected profit is always decreasing in θ when $\bar{r}(\theta) = 1$, since by (10)

$$\pi'(\theta) = -\bar{r}(\theta)(c_1\bar{q}(\theta) + k_1).$$

Consequently, if the firm has a low cost parameter, it will be allowed to earn a greater profit than if it had a high cost parameter in order to provide a reward for reporting its lower costs. The profit $\pi(\theta_1)$ of a firm with the highest possible cost is zero, since there is no need to reward such a firm.

Let us now see how our optimal solution varies with α, the weight given in the social welfare function to the firm's profits. First we must establish the following basic mathematical result, a corollary of Lemma 3.

Corollary: *For any* θ *in* $[\theta_0, \theta_1]$, $\bar{z}_\alpha(\theta)$ *is a non-increasing function of* α.

Proof: Pick any α and β such that $0 \leq \alpha < \beta \leq 1$. Let $\Delta(\theta) = \bar{z}_\beta(\theta) - \bar{z}_\alpha(\theta)$ and let $\Delta^+(\theta) = \max[0, \Delta(\theta)]$. From Lemma 3, we obtain

$$\int_{\theta_0}^{\theta_1} \Delta^+(\theta)(z_\beta(\theta) - z_\alpha(\theta))d\theta$$

$$= \int_{\theta_0}^{\theta_1} \Delta^+(\theta)\Delta(\theta)d\theta + \int_{\theta=\theta_0}^{\theta_1} G_\alpha(\theta) - G_\beta(\theta))\, d[\Delta^+(\theta)]$$

The integrand $\Delta^+(\theta)\Delta(\theta)$ is obviously non-negative for all θ. Whenever $\Delta^+(\theta)$ is increasing in θ, $\bar{z}_\beta(\theta)$ must be increasing in θ, and so $G_\beta(\theta) = 0$. Similarly, whenever $\Delta^+(\theta)$ is decreasing in θ, $\bar{z}_\alpha(\theta)$ must be increasing, and so $G_\alpha(\theta) = 0$. Thus $\int(G_\alpha - G_\beta)d\Delta^+ \geq 0$, and so $\int(\Delta^+)(z_\beta - z_\alpha)d\theta \geq 0$. But $\Delta^+(\theta) \geq 0$ and

$$z_\beta(\theta) - z_\alpha(\theta) = (\alpha - \beta)F(\theta)/f(\theta) < 0$$

for all $\theta > \theta_0$, so $\Delta^+(\theta) = 0$ for all θ, which implies $\bar{z}_\alpha(\theta) \geq \bar{z}_\beta(\theta)$.

Q.E.D.

To get a more intuitive understanding of this result, observe that, in the special case when $z_\alpha(\theta)$ is increasing in θ, we have $\bar{z}_\alpha(\theta) = z_\alpha(\theta)$. Then, $z_\alpha(\theta) = \theta + (1 - \alpha)F(\theta)/f(\theta)$ is seen to be decreasing in α.

The optimal regulated price $\bar{p}(\theta) = c_0 + c_1\, \bar{z}_\alpha(\theta)$ is thus a decreasing function of α, while $\bar{q}(\theta)$ is an increasing function of α. This feature of the optimal solution may seem counterintuitive, but it is due to the incentive problem created by the asymmetry of information. To interpret the welfare implication, substitute (1) and (5) into the social welfare function (9) to obtain

$$\int_{\theta_0}^{\theta_1} [(V(q(\theta)) - C(q(\theta), \theta))r(\theta) - (1 - \alpha)\pi(\theta)]f(\theta)d\theta$$

The term $(V(q(\theta)) - C(q(\theta),\theta))r(\theta)$ is the gross surplus, and $(1 - \alpha)\pi(\theta)$ may be interpreted as the welfare omission resulting from a weight smaller than one given to the firm's interests. As α approaches one, the welfare omission goes to zero, and the optimal regulated price decreases towards the marginal cost, which in the limit maximizes the gross surplus.

The range of cost parameters for which the firm is allowed to produce increases with α; that is, $\bar{r}(\theta)$ is a non-decreasing function of α, for any θ. To see this, recall the definition of $\bar{r}(\theta)$ in (27), and observe that

$$\frac{\partial}{\partial\alpha}(V(\bar{q}(\theta)) - P(\bar{q}(\theta))\bar{q}(\theta)) = -P'(\bar{q}(\theta))\bar{q}(\theta)\frac{\partial\bar{q}(\theta)}{\partial\alpha} \geq 0,$$

while $(\partial/\partial\alpha)(k_0 + k_1\bar{z}_\alpha(\theta)) \leq 0$. Thus θ^* is an increasing function of α, where

$$\theta^* = \max\{\theta \mid \bar{r}(\theta) = 1\}.$$

The profit of the firm may be written as

$$\pi(\theta) = \int_\theta^{\theta^*} (c_1\bar{q}(\tilde{\theta}) + k_1)d\tilde{\theta}$$

Since $\bar{q}$ and θ^* are both increasing in α, $\pi(\theta)$ is an increasing function of α, for any fixed θ. Thus, although the consumers are paying lower prices as α increases, the firm's total revenue must be increasing in α. For any θ, either the firm's subsidy $\bar{s}(\theta)$ must be increasing in α, or the price reduction must be associated with an increase in operating profit $\bar{p}(\theta)\bar{q}(\theta) - C(\bar{q}(\theta), \theta)$. The latter condition happens only in those cases when $\bar{p}(\theta)$ is higher than the unregulated monopoly price $p_M(\theta)$, so we should expect that $\bar{s}(\theta)$ is usually (but not always) increasing in α.

The net expected gain to consumers,

$$\int_{\theta_0}^{\theta_1} [(V(\bar{q}(\theta)) - \bar{p}(\theta)\bar{q}(\theta))\bar{r}(\theta) - \bar{s}(\theta)]\, f(\theta)d\theta$$

is a decreasing function of α, because the regulator is decreasing the relative weight given to this term in his objective function as α increases.

To give an overall measure of how the optimal regulated prices vary with α, we can compute the expected price $E\bar{p}(\theta)$:

$$E\bar{p}(\theta) = c_0 + c_1 \int_{\theta_0}^{\theta_1} \bar{z}_\alpha(\theta) f(\theta) d\theta$$

$$= c_0 + c_1 \int_{\theta_0}^{\theta_1} z_\alpha(\theta) f(\theta) d\theta$$

$$= c_0 + c_1 \left[\int_{\theta_0}^{\theta_1} \theta f(\theta) d\theta + (1 - \alpha) \int_{\theta_0}^{\theta_1} F(\theta) d\theta \right]$$

$$= c_0 + c_1 (\alpha E\theta + (1 - \alpha)\theta_1),$$

where $E\theta$ is the expected value of the cost parameter. (In the above derivation, the second equality follows from Lemma 3 with $A(\theta) = 1$; the last equality follows from integration by parts.) When the firm's interests are given no weight ($\alpha = 0$), the expected price is equal to the highest possible marginal cost, $c_0 + c_1\theta_1$. When the firm's interests are given equal weight with the consumer's interests ($\alpha = 1$), the expected price equals expected marginal cost. Between these extremes, the expected price decreases linearly in α.

For the case of $\alpha = 1$, we get $z_1(\theta) = \theta$, which is increasing, so by Lemma 3,

$$\bar{z}_1(\theta) = z_1(\theta) = \theta.$$

Thus, price is always equal to marginal cost $c_0 + c_1\theta$ when $\alpha = 1$, and our optimal solution coincides with the solution proposed by Loeb and Magat (1979).

5. THE CASE OF KNOWN FIXED COSTS: AN EXAMPLE

To illustrate our optimal solution, let us consider an example with known fixed costs. Let $k_1 = c_0 = 0$ and $c_1 = 1$, so that $C(q, \theta) = k_0 + \theta q$ and θ represents the unknown marginal cost. Suppose that θ is uniformly distributed on $[\theta_0, \theta_1]$, so $f(\theta) = 1/(\theta_1 - \theta_0)$. The optimal price function is then

$$\bar{p}(\theta) = \theta + (1 - \alpha)(\theta - \theta_0)$$

$$= (2 - \alpha)\theta - (1 - \alpha)\theta_0, \quad \text{for } \theta \in [\theta_0, \theta_1],$$

which is increasing in θ and has range $[\theta_0, \theta_1 + (1-\alpha)(\theta_1 - \theta_0)]$. Let us assume a linear demand function of the form

$$q = P^{-1}(p) = a - bp, \quad \text{where} \quad b > 0 \quad \text{and} \quad a > 2b\theta_1.$$

Then the quantity $\bar{q}(\theta)$ that the firm will sell if its marginal cost is θ is given by

$$\bar{q}(\theta) = a - b[(2-\alpha)\theta - (1-\alpha)\theta_0].$$

This function may be interpreted as an adjusted (inverse) demand function expressed as a function of the marginal cost instead of the price.

The demand function and the adjusted demand function are represented in Fig. 1. Let us assume that the fixed cost k_0 satisfies

$$V(\bar{q}(\theta_1)) - \bar{p}(\theta_1)\bar{q}(\theta_1) \geq k_0,$$

so that the firm will produce for any $\theta \in [\theta_0, \theta_1]$. The profit of the firm is

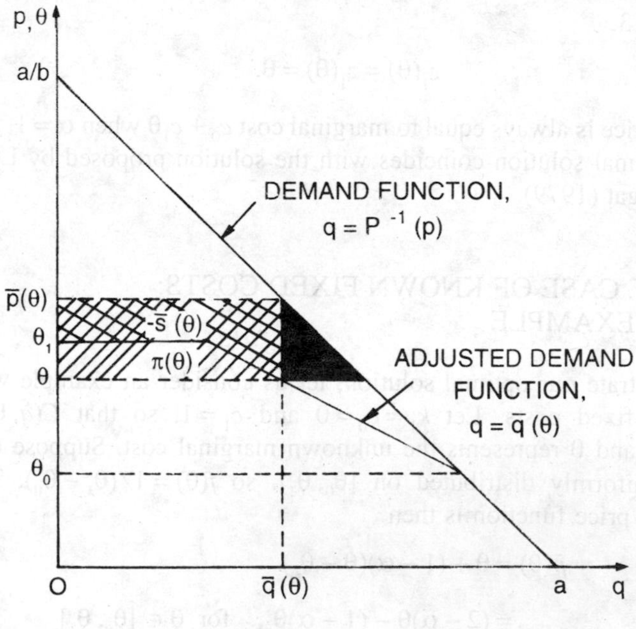

Figure 1

$$\bar{\pi}(\theta) = \int_{\theta}^{\theta_1} \bar{q}(\tilde{\theta})d\tilde{\theta}$$

which is positive for $\theta < \theta_1$ and is represented by the slashed area below the adjusted demand function and above the horizontal line at θ in Fig. 1. Thus, the firm's profit from the optimal regulatory policy is equal to what the consumers' surplus would be if demand were shifted to the adjusted demand function and if price were set at marginal cost. That is, from the firm's perspective, the optimal regulatory policy looks like the policy of Loeb and Magat (1979) (in which the subsidy equals the consumers' surplus) except that the demand curve has been effectively shifted by the regulator.

The subsidy $\bar{s}(\theta)$ paid by consumers to the firm is from (28):

$$\bar{s}(\theta) = \int_{\theta}^{\theta_1} \bar{q}(\tilde{\theta})d\tilde{\theta} - ((\bar{p}(\theta) - \theta)\bar{q}(\theta) - k_0)$$

where the last term is the operating profit of the firm. If $k_0 = 0$, the subsidy for the example is negative and $-\bar{s}(\theta)$ is represented by the cross-hatched area in Fig. 1. The net gain to consumers $(V(\bar{q}(\theta)) - \bar{p}(\theta)\bar{q}(\theta) - \bar{s}(\theta))$ is thus the upper triangle above $\bar{p}(\theta)$ plus the tax $(-\bar{s}(\theta))$ levied on the firm. The welfare loss that results, because of the need to screen the possible marginal costs that the firm might have, is the solid triangle represented by the difference between the price $\bar{p}(\theta)$ and the marginal cost θ.

As the weight α accorded the firm's interests in the social welfare function is increased, the price $\bar{p}(\theta)$ decreases and equals θ at $\alpha = 1$. The adjusted demand function rotates upward as α is increased and coincides with the demand function for $\theta \in [\theta_0, \theta_1]$ when $\alpha = 1$. The subsidy paid by consumers to the firm is then

$$\bar{s}(\theta) = \int_{\theta}^{\theta_1} (a - b\tilde{\theta})d\tilde{\theta}$$

so the firm is paid the entire surplus represented by the prices between θ and θ_1 when $\alpha = 1$. The welfare loss $L(\theta)$ in our example is

$$L(\theta) = \int_{\theta}^{\bar{p}(\theta)} [P^{-1}(p) - \bar{q}(\theta)]dp = \frac{1}{2}b((1 - \alpha)(\theta - \theta_0))^2$$

Thus, as α is increased, the welfare loss is reduced, but also the net consumer surplus is reduced because of the greater subsidy paid to the firm. For $\alpha = 1$ the welfare loss is eliminated, and the solution given here is essentially the solution proposed by Loeb and Magat (1979) in which consumers surrender all of the surplus corresponding to the possible marginal costs that the firm might have.

6. THE CASE OF KNOWN MARGINAL COST

Consider now the case in which the regulator knows the marginal cost but does not know the fixed cost. Let $c_1 = k_0 = 0$ and $k_1 = 1$, so that $C(q, \theta) = \theta + c_0 q$ and θ is the unknown fixed cost. Then

$$\bar{p}(\theta) = c_0, \quad \text{and}$$

$$\bar{r}(\theta) = \begin{cases} 1 & \text{if } V_0 \geq \bar{z}_\alpha(\theta), \\ 0 & \text{if } V_0 < \bar{z}_\alpha(\theta), \end{cases}$$

where

$$V_0 = V(P^{-1}(c_0)) - c_0\, P^{-1}(c_0).$$

The term $V_0 = V(P^{-1}(c_0)) - c_0 P^{-1}(c_0)$ is the consumer surplus resulting from a price equal to marginal cost. Since $\bar{z}_\alpha(\theta)$ is non-decreasing in θ, there exists a θ^* such that

$$\bar{r}(\theta) = \begin{cases} 1 & \text{if } \theta \leq \theta^*, \\ 0 & \text{if } \theta > \theta^*, \end{cases}$$

where[4]

$$\theta^* = \bar{z}_\alpha^{-1}(V_0).$$

The subsidy paid to the firm is

$$\bar{s}(\theta) = \begin{cases} \theta + (\theta^* - \theta) = \theta^* & \text{if } \theta \leq \theta^*, \\ 0 & \text{if } \theta > \theta^*, \end{cases}$$

and the profit of the firm is

$$\pi(\theta) = \begin{cases} (\theta^* - \theta) & \text{if } \theta \leq \theta^*, \\ 0 & \text{if } \theta > \theta^*, \end{cases}$$

[4] If $V_0 > \bar{z}_\alpha(\theta_1)$, then let $\theta^* = \theta_1$. If $V_0 < \bar{z}_\alpha(\theta_0)$, then $\theta^* = \theta_0$.

Notice that θ^* is non-decreasing in α by the Corollary in Sec. 4.

This regulatory policy may be interpreted as an auction in which the regulator offers to pay θ^* to the firm if it will produce and sell its output at the marginal cost c_0. The offer will be accepted if the firm has a cost parameter at least as low as θ^* and will otherwise be rejected. A welfare loss can result because the firm is not allowed to produce if it has a cost parameter θ between θ^* and V_0 even though the consumer surplus exceeds the fixed cost. The welfare loss resulting in our optimal policy is zero if $\theta \geq V_0$ because even in the complete-information solution the firm would not have produced. If $\theta < \theta^*$, the welfare loss is the difference between the subsidy $\bar{s}(\theta)$ and the complete-information subsidy θ less the proportion α of profit included in the welfare function. The difference ΔS in the subsidy is

$$\Delta S = (\theta^* - \theta) = \pi(\theta),$$

which is the profit of the firm under the optimal policy, and the welfare loss is thus $(1 - \alpha)\pi(\theta)$. If the cost parameter satisfies $\theta^* < \theta < V_0$, so that the firm does not produce under our policy while it would under the complete-information solution, the welfare loss is the consumer surplus V_0 less the subsidy θ that would be paid in the complete information solution. The welfare loss $L(\theta)$ is thus

$$L(\theta) = \begin{cases} (1-\alpha)(\theta^* - \theta) & \text{if } \theta \leq \theta^*, \\ V_0 - \theta & \text{if } \theta^* < \theta < V_0, \\ 0 & \text{if } \theta \geq V_0. \end{cases}$$

The expected welfare loss is then obtained by taking the expectation of $L(\theta)$.

7. GENERAL TWO-PARAMETER UNCERTAINTY

In this paper, we have assumed the regulator to be uncertain about both the marginal cost and fixed cost of the firm, provided that these two unknowns vary collinearly. (Recall (1).) More generally, one may try to compute optimal regulatory policies for cost functions of the form

$$C(q; c, k) = \begin{cases} c \cdot q + k & \text{if } q > 0, \\ 0, & \text{if } q = 0, \end{cases}$$

where c and k are random cost parameters (known by the firm) having some general probability distribution on $\mathbf{R}_+^2$. Although we have not been able to extend the optimal solution explicitly to this general two-parameter case, we expect that most of the qualitative results discussed here should still be valid. However, at least two of our more technical results do not extend to the general case. We can show examples in which the optimal regulatory policy does involve proper randomization with respect to shutting down the firm, so that r is strictly between 0 and 1 for some values of the cost parameters. Also, the result that the optimal regulated price is independent of the demand curve does not extend to the general two-parameter case.

For example, suppose that the two cost parameters (c, k) could be $(1, 0)$ (low costs), or $(1, 4)$ (high fixed cost), or $(3, 0)$ (high marginal cost), all with equal probability 1/3. Let demand be $P(q) = 7 - 3q$. For $\alpha = 0$, the optimal regulatory policy is[5]

$$\bar{p}(1, 0) = 1, \quad \bar{q}(1, 0) = 2, \quad \bar{r}(1, 0) = 1, \quad \bar{s}(1, 0) = 2,$$

$$\bar{p}(1, 4) = 1, \quad \bar{q}(1, 4) = 2, \quad \bar{r}(1, 4) = .5, \quad \bar{s}(1, 4) = 2,$$

$$\bar{p}(3, 0) = 4, \quad \bar{q}(3, 0) = 1, \quad \bar{r}(3, 0) = 1, \quad \bar{s}(3, 0) = -1.$$

Notice that, with high fixed costs, the regulator must randomize over whether to let the firm go into business. However, if we raise the demand curve to $P(q) = 8 - 3q$, then the optimal regulatory policy changes to

$$\bar{p}(1, 0) = 1, \quad \bar{q}(1, 0) = 2.33, \quad \bar{r}(1, 0) = 1, \quad \bar{s}(1, 0) = 4,$$

$$\bar{p}(1, 4) = 1, \quad \bar{q}(1, 4) = 2.33, \quad \bar{r}(1, 4) = 1, \quad \bar{s}(1, 4) = 4,$$

$$\bar{p}(3, 0) = 3, \quad \bar{q}(3, 0) = 1.67, \quad \bar{r}(3, 0) = 1, \quad \bar{s}(3, 0) = 0.$$

Notice that the regulated price for a firm with high marginal cost changes from 4 to 3 as the demand curve shifts. With the higher demand, it becomes more worthwhile to keep the $(1, 4)$-type in business, even though this requires a higher subsidy to the $(1, 0)$-type.

[5] These solutions can be verified by standard Lagrangean techniques. The key step is to linearize the incentive-compatibility and individual-rationality constraints by writing them in terms of $q^0 = r \cdot q$. $s^0 = s + p \cdot q \cdot r$, and r.

Then, with a higher subsidy to the (1, 0)-type, it is no longer necessary to raise the price for the (3, 0)-type to screen it from the (1, 0)-type.

Essentially the two-parameter problem is more complicated because there are incentive constraints in two directions to worry about. For example, a low-cost firm (1, 0) must not be able to gain by reporting high fixed cost (1, 4), and it must also not be able to gain by reporting high marginal cost (3, 0). Of these two constraints, both are binding in our example with the lower demand curve, but only the first of the two constraints is binding with the higher demand curve. The greater difficulty in solving the general case of two-parameter cost functions arises because of this ambiguity as to which of these directional incentive-compatibility constraints may be binding in the regulator's optimization problem.

REFERENCES

DASGUPTA, P.S., P.J. HAMMOND and E.S. MASKIN (1979), 'The Implementation of Social Choice Rules: Some Results on Incentive Compatibility', *Review of Economic Studies*, 46, 185–216.

DUPUIT J. (1952), 'On the Measurement of the Utility of Public Works', *International Economics Papers*, 2, 83–110 (translated by R.H. Barback from 'de la Mesure de l'Utilité des Travaux Publics', *Annales des Ponts et Chaussées*, 2nd Series, 8, 1844).

GIBBARD, A. (1973), 'Manipulation of Voting Schemes: A General Result', *Econometrica*, 41, 587–602.

HARRIS, M. and R.M. TOWNSEND (1981), 'Resource Allocation Under Asymmetric Information', *Econometrica*, 49, 33–64.

HOTELLING, H. (1938), 'The General Welfare in Relation to Problems of Taxation and of Railway and Utility Rates', *Econometria*, 6, 242–69.

LOEB, M. and W.A. MAGAT (1979), 'A Decentralized Method for Utility Regulation', *Journal of Law and Economics*, 22, 399–404.

MYERSON, R.B. (1979), 'Incentive Compatibility and the Bargaining Problem', *Econometrica*, 47, 61–74.

—— (1981), 'Optimal Auction Design', *Mathematics of Operations Research*, 6, 58–73.

ROCKAFELLAR, R.T. (1970), *Convex Analysis*. Princeton: Princeton University Press.

SCHMALENSEE, R. (1972), 'Option Demand and Consumer's Surplus:

Valuing Price Changes Under Uncertainty', *American Economic Review*, 62, 813–24.

SPENCE, M. (1977), 'Nonlinear Prices and Welfare', *Journal of Public Economics*, 8, 1–18.

WEITZMAN, M.L. (1978), 'Optimal Rewards for Economic Regulation', *American Economic Review*, 68, 683–91.

—— (1974), 'Prices vs. Quantities', *Review of Economic Studies*, 41, 477–91.

The Interdependence between Ownership Status and Market Structure: The Case of Privatization

CHAIM FERSHTMAN*

INTRODUCTION

Recently different governments have adopted the policy of transferring government-owned enterprises to private ownership. This policy is known in the economic jargon as 'privatization'. Bearing in mind that such a policy is not easily reversible, it is not surprising that privatization policy has become a major political issue, with dedicated supporters and opposition. Although the main economic justification for privatization is the efficiency argument, there is a need for detailed theoretical and empirical analyses regarding the behaviour of nationalized firms and the implications of privatization on the market equilibrium.[1]

An important aspect of privatization is the relationship between the ownership status and the decision-making process in the firm. However, when we wish to consider the effect of privatization on the firm's behaviour and performance, we cannot ignore the market structure in which the firm operates. The implications of privatization can be different in a monopolistic market from in an oligopolistic market (see also Delbono and De Fraja, 1987). In this paper I wish

* I would like to thank Dieter Bos and an anonymous referee for many valuable comments. Financial assistance from the Foerder Institute of Economic Research is gratefully acknowledged.

[1] For previous works see Davies (1971), Meyer (1975), Pescatrice and Trapani (1980), Marchand, Pestieau and Tulkens (1984), Rees (1984, 1988), Kay and Thompson (1986), Bos and Peters (1989) and Vickers and Yarrow (1988).

to highlight some of the implications of privatization policy on the strategic interaction in oligopolistic markets, and the interdependence between the firms' ownership status and the market structure in which they operate. I believe that such an investigation is an essential stage in understanding the implications of privatization on market performance. The convention that nationalization reduces profits is examined and it is demonstrated that in a duopolistic market we should expect the opposite result. The equilibrium in the market can be such that a partly nationalized firm realizes higher profits than its private, profit-maximizing competitor.

Even when a nationalized firm is the single firm in an industry and enjoys a complete monopolistic power, before enhancing any privatization policy one should examine whether the reason that the nationalized firm has survived as a natural monopoly is its ownership status. It is demonstrated that the existence of a firm as a natural monopoly is not independent of its ownership structure. In addition, it is shown that the feasibility to deter entry depends also on the incumbent's ownership structure. These are surprising results, since they indicate that firms' ownership status can determine the market structure in which they operate.

The paper is organized as follows. Sec. 1 presents a simple Cournot-type duopolistic competition when one of the firms is partly nationalized while its competitor is private. In Sec. 2 we examine the role that nationalization can play in entry deterrence. Using Dixit (1980) and Eaton and Lipsey's (1981) framework, we consider the implications of privatization on the attractiveness of entry, the possibility to deter entry, and the relationship between the incumbent degree of nationalization and its position as a natural monopoly. Production inefficiency and price competition in a differentiated-goods duopoly are briefly discussed in Sec. 3.

1. A MODEL OF DUOPOLISTIC INDUSTRY WITH ONE PRIVATE FIRM AND ONE PARTLY NATIONALIZED FIRM

The traditional economic literature adopts the profit maximization hypothesis in the analysis of the behaviour of private firms. It is clear, however, that once the firm is nationalized, it might have objectives other than profit maximization (see for example Niskanen, 1975; Bos, Tillmann and Zimmermann, 1984; Delbono and De Fraja, 1987; and Rees, 1988).

Consider a duopolistic industry in which the first firm is partly nationalized while the second firm is privately owned. Let θ_1 be the proportion of the government's control of the first firm. The inverse demand function is assumed to be linear such that the market price is given by $p = a - b(q_1 + q_2)$. We assume for convenience, that both firms have identical linear cost functions $C_i(q_i) = q_1$ and that there is no cost inefficiency associated with nationalization.

Given the above assumptions, the ith firm's profit function is given by $\pi_i(q_1, q_2) = \{a - b(q_1 + q_2) - c\}q_i$, which yields the profit maximization reaction function:

$$\hat{q}_i(q_j) = (a - bq_j - c)/2b, \quad j \neq i. \tag{1}$$

The social welfare function, which is a sum of producer and consumer surplus is a function of q_1 and q_2 and is given by

$$W(q_1, q_2) = (1/2)\,[a + \{a - b(q_1 + q_2)\}](q_1 + q_2) - c(q_1 + q_2). \tag{2}$$

Given q_j, the social welfare function is maximized at

$$\tilde{q}_i(q_j) = (a - bq_j - c)/b, \quad j \neq i, \tag{3}$$

which is the reaction function of a social welfare-maximizing firm.

A complete analysis of the behaviour of a partly nationalized firm must consider the conflict situation between the directors representing private owners' interest and the directors representing the government's interest. If decisions are made by voting using the majority rule, the firms behave either as profit-maximizing or as welfare-maximizing. In this paper we assume that the conflict between the two interest groups is resolved by a compromise. In particular, we let the partly nationalized firm's choice of output be a compromise between $\hat{q}$ and $\tilde{q}$ such that its reaction function is[2]

[2] For a detailed discussion on the objective function of a partly nationalized firm, see Bos and Peters (1989). I would like to thank Dieter Bos for pointing out that maximizing an objective function that consists of profits and social welfare is not equivalent to our above assumption regarding the firm's output choice. However, the implication of maximizing $U_\theta(\pi, W)$ is that the firm chooses an output that is a combination of $\tilde{q}$ and $\hat{q}$.

$$\psi_1(\theta_1, q_2) = \theta_1\, q_1(q_2) + (1-\theta_1)\hat{q}_1(q_2) = (a - bq_2 - c)(1+\theta_1)/2b. \quad (4)$$

Proposition 1. In a duopolistic market with one partly nationalized firm and the private firm,

(a) the equilibrium price declines as θ_1 increases;

(b) when $0 < \theta_1 < 0.6$, i.e. when the government owns less than 60 per cent of firm 1, the equilibrium profits of the partly nationalized firm are above the regular Cournot equilibrium profits;

(c) the profits of the partly nationalized firm are maximized at $\theta_1 = 1/3$;

(d) in the above duopolistic market, as long as $0 < \theta_1 < 1$, the partly nationalized firm has higher profits than its private competitor. Moreover, the private firm's profits are below the regular Cournot profits.

Proof. Solving the two reaction functions (1) and (4) yields the following equilibrium:

$$q_1^* = (1+\theta_1)(a-c)/(3-\theta_1)b, \quad (5a)$$

$$q_2^* = (1-\theta_1)(a-c)/(3-\theta_1)b, \quad (5b)$$

and the equilibrium price is

$$p^* = \{(1-\theta_1)a + 2c\}/(3-\theta_1). \quad (6)$$

(a) Differentiating (6) with respect to θ_1 yields

$$\partial p^*/\partial\theta_1 = \{(1-\theta_1)a + 2c - a(3-\theta_1)\}(3-\theta_1)^2 < 0. \quad (7)$$

(b) The Cournot equilibrium profit is $\pi_1^c = (a-c)^2/9b$. Using (5a) and (6) yields that, in our model, the first firm's profit is

$$\pi_1^* = (a-c)^2(1-\theta_1^2)/(3-\theta_1)^2\, b. \quad (8)$$

Comparing π_1^c with π_1^* indicates that, for $\theta_1 < 0.6$, $\pi_1^* > \pi_1^c$.

(c) Maximizing (8) with respect to θ_1 yields that $\arg\max_{\theta_1} \pi_1^* = 1/3$.

(d) Using (5b) and (6) yields

$$\pi_2^* = (1-\theta_1)^2(a-c)^2/b(3-\theta_1)^2. \quad (9)$$

Comparing π_1^* and π_2^*, it is evident that

$$\pi_2^* - \pi_1^* = 2(a-c)^2\, \theta_1(\theta_1 - 1)/b(3-\theta_1)^2, \qquad (10)$$

which implies that for $\theta_1 = 0$ and $\theta_1 = 1$, $\pi_2^* = \pi_1^*$, but for every $0 < \theta_1 < 1$, $\pi_2^* < \pi_1^*$. Using (10), one can also conclude that $\pi_2^* < \pi_2^c$.

Q.E.D.

Proposition 1 implies that in a duopolistic market the partly nationalized firm, regardless of its degree of nationalization, earns higher profits than its private competitor. Since we assume that both firms are identical with respect to their cost functions, it is clear that the difference in profits is due to the strategic interaction between the two firms rather than to any production efficiency or inefficiency associated with the privatization process.

The analysis in this section is carried out under restrictive assumptions of linear demand and cost functions and a simplified description of the decision-making process in a partly nationalized firm. However, it is important to note that, as long as the reaction functions are downward sloping (strategic substitutes) and the objective function of the partly nationalized firm has some element of social welfare maximization, results similar to ours can be obtained.

The partial nationalization serves as a credible commitment to increase output beyond the profit-maximizing level. Thus, as the degree of nationalization increases, the firm's reaction function shifts rightward. Standard analysis indicates that such a shift results in higher profits for the partly nationalized firm. Clearly, the level of nationalization that maximizes profits is the one that pushes the reaction function far enough so that the Stackelberg point becomes the new Nash equilibrium.

From (5a) and (5b), note that $q_1^*/(q_1^* + q_2^*)$ is an increasing function of θ_1. Thus, partial nationalization increases the market share of the nationalized firm. If firms have unequal production cost such that the nationalized firm is *a priori* less efficient, nationalization may promote inefficiency if it increases the share of the output produced by the inefficient firm. Clearly, the overall contribution to welfare of nationalization consists of the direct effect of greater output and the loss arising from production inefficiency. Using the linear case discussed previously and analysing the unequal cost case yields the following.

Proposition 2. Nationalization of an inefficient firm in duopolistic markets may result in lower social welfare.

Proof. The proof is straightforward and similar to the proof of Proposition 1. After calculating the equilibrium quantities, we can use equation (2) to calculate the social welfare with and without nationalization. Assuming enough cost inequality will finish the proof. Q.E.D.

2. NATIONALIZATION AND ENTRY DETERRENCE

In the previous section it was demonstrated that the firms' ownership structures affect the market equilibrium. Since the first step in analysing the entry deterrence problem is to analyse the post-entry game, a potential entrant, in its entry decision, should take into account the ownership status of the incumbent firms, thus establishing the interdependence between the ownership status and the market structure in which firms operate.

The main issue in such an analysis is whether the ownership structure of the incumbent firm is some form of an entry barrier. Consider, for example, a firm that has the opportunity of entering into two different markets. In both these markets there is a single incumbent firm and identical demand functions. Further, assume that the potential entrant and the two incumbents have identical cost functions. The only difference between the two markets, however, is that in the first market the incumbent is private while in the second it is partly (or totally) nationalized. In analysing the relative attractiveness of the two markets, one should discuss all the differences between private and nationalized firms and their effects on entry deterrence. For example, the partly nationalized firm might enjoy the support and backing of government agencies. This support can be very helpful in particular when government's contracts provide an important share of the market demand, or when the advantage of having the government's financial backing plays an important role in the market competition. On the other hand, assuming that nationalized firms are less efficient, and if cost advantage plays an important role in the market competition, the potential entrant might prefer to compete against a nationalized firm rather than against a private firm.

In Sec. 1 we demonstrated that, when a profit-maximizing firm faces a partly nationalized competitor, its profits are below the regular Cournot equilibrium profits (see Proposition 1). Thus, a profit-maximizing potential entrant prefers to enter a market in which its competitor, i.e. the incumbent firm, is private.

The analysis in this section is based on Dixit (1980) and Eaton and Lipsey (1981). In these models it was assumed that firm's cost function is given by

$$TC_i(q_i, k_i) = \begin{cases} f_i + w_i q_i + r_i k_i, & q_i < k_i \\ f_i + (w_i + r_i) q_i, & \text{otherwise,} \end{cases} \tag{11}$$

where q_i is the quantity produced by firm i, k_i is the ith firm's capacity, f_i is the fixed cost, w_i is the variable cost per unit, and r_i is the cost of having one unit of capacity. Capacity costs are assumed to be sunk, such that when $q_i < k_i$ the firm still has to pay $r_i\, k_i$.

The problem is modelled as a two-stage game. In the first stage the incumbent firm, denoted henceforth as firm 1, chooses a capacity level k_1. In the second stage the second firm has to decide whether or not to enter. If entry occurs there is a Cournot-type competition, the equilibrium of which both firms can calculate.

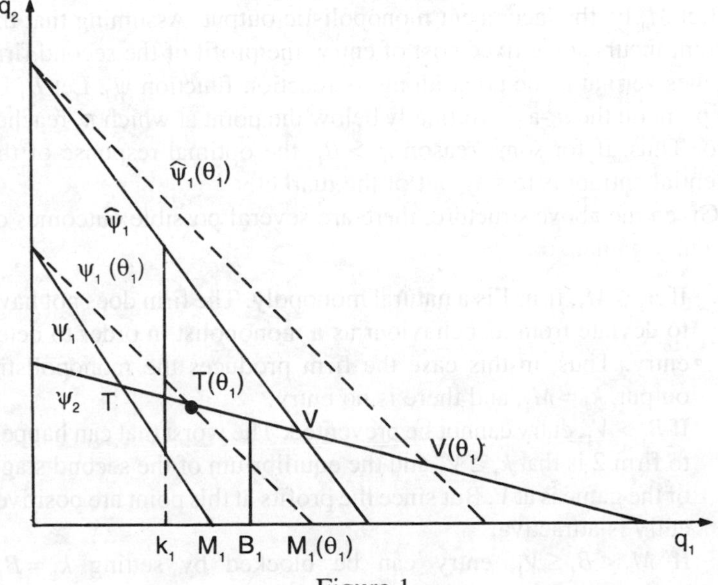

Figure 1

The interaction between the two firms is better illustrated by a reaction function analysis (see Fig. 1). Firm 1, by making strategic decisions with respect to k_1, can alter its second-period reaction function and hence the equilibrium of the duopolistic game. Consider first the case in which firm 1, the incumbent, is completely private. Let ψ_1 be the 'full cost reaction function' of the first firm, i.e. the reaction function when the marginal costs are $w_1 + r_1$, and let $\hat{\psi}_1$ be its 'variable cost reaction function', i.e. its reaction function when the marginal cost is only w_1. Since the choice of k_1 is made in period 1, the reaction function of firm 1 in period 2 depends on its choice of capacity k_1, and, as is illustrated in Fig. 1, the incumbent's reaction function in the second period is identical to $\hat{\psi}_1$ until q_1 reaches the full capacity level of k_1, then the reaction function goes down to ψ_1. Since the potential entrant has not yet any capacity, its reaction function in the second period is its full cost reaction function denoted in the figure as ψ_2. The above description indicates that, if the two firms are in the market, the Nash equilibrium is on ψ_2 between $T = (T_1, T_2)$ and $V = (V_1, V_2)$, depending on the choice of k_1. When $k_1 \leq T_1$, the equilibrium in the second stage is at T. When $k_1 \geq V_1$ the equilibrium is at V, and when $T_1 < k_1 < V$, the equilibrium point is on ψ_2 between T and V.

Let M_1 be the incumbent monopolistic output. Assuming that the entrant incurs some fixed cost of entry, the profit of the second firm reaches zero at some point along its reaction function ψ_2. Let B_1 be the point on the q_1-axis vertically below the point at which π_2 reaches zero. Thus, if for some reason $q_1 > B_1$, the optimal response of the potential entrant is to stay out of the market.

Given the above structure, there are several possible outcomes of the entry game:

(a) If $B_1 \leq M_1$, firm 1 is a natural monopoly. The firm does not have to deviate from its behaviour as a monopolist in order to deter entry. Thus, in this case the firm produces the monopolistic output, $k_1 = M_1$, and there is no entry.

(b) If $B_1 > V_1$, entry cannot be prevented. The worst that can happen to firm 2 is that $k_1 \geq V_1$ and the equilibrium of the second stage of the game is at V. But since the profits at this point are positive, entry is attractive.

(c) If $M_1 < B_1 \leq V_1$, entry can be blocked by setting $k_1 = B_1$.

However, in this case entry deterrence may not be the best strategy for firm 1, since its profit as an artificial monopoly may be below its profits in the duopolistic market.

In order to discuss the implications of ownership status on the strategic interaction between the incumbent and the potential entrant, let us consider now the case in which the potential entrant is private while the incumbent is partly nationalized.

Proposition 3. The ownership status of the incumbent firm affects its incentives and ability to deter entry. In particular, (a) it is possible that a firm is not a natural monopoly while being private but that alteration of its ownership structure so that it becomes partly nationalized can transform the firm to a natural monopoly; (b) when $B_1 > V_1$ entry cannot be deterred by a private firm, but it is possible that when the incumbent firm becomes partly nationalized entry deterrence becomes feasible.

Proof. The proof is based on the reaction function analysis presented in Fig. 1. An increase in θ_1 alters the firm's objective function and induces a rightward shift of its reaction function. Thus, for a given $\theta_1 > 0$, the 'full cost reaction function' is $\psi_1(\theta_1)$ while the 'variable cost reaction function' is $\hat{\psi}_1(\theta_1)$. It is clear now from Dixit's analysis that the equilibrium in the post-entry game lies on ψ_2 between $T(\theta_1)$ and $V(\theta_1)$. We denote as $M_1(\theta_1)$ the monopolistic output of a partly nationalized firm. Our previous analysis yields that $M'_1(\theta_1) > 0$. As was defined above, natural monopoly occurs when $B_1 \leq M_1(\theta)$. Thus, when $M_1 < B_1 < M_1(\theta_1)$, as is depicted in Fig. 1, a private firm is not a natural monopoly while a partly nationalized firm, with θ_1 large enough so that $B_1 < M_1(\theta_1)$, is a natural monopoly.

$V_1 < B_1 < V_1(\theta_1)$ implies that a private firm cannot deter entry since $V_1 < B_1$, but that, if θ_1 is large enough and $B_1 < V_1(\theta_1)$, the partly nationalized firm has the power to prevent entry. Since $V'_1(\theta_1) > 0$, the reverse situation is not plausible. Q.E.D.

Proposition 3 implies that the firm's ownership status affects the market structure in which the firms operate. For example, an industry remains monopolistic while being partly nationalized and then once it is privatized a new firm might find it attractive to enter the industry transforming it to a duopoly. Clearly, in such cases the possible change in market structure affects the price that the government can get for its share of the firm as private buyers realize that future profits might decline as a result of the anticipated competition in the market.

In analysing the effect of privatization, the main focus in the literature has been the efficiency gain as it is widely believed that private firms operate more efficiently. Even if we accept this view, the total evaluation of privatization policy should consider also its implication on market structure. In particular, it follows from Proposition 3 that it is possible to have welfare gain from privatization if such a policy leads to a more competitive market structure. This competition might be more beneficial to the economy than having a firm that maximizes a combination of profits and welfare.

The above analysis was carried out under the assumption that the potential entrant is private while the incumbent is partly nationalized. Clearly, we can carry out a similar analysis when we let the incumbent be private while the potential entrant is partly nationalized. Such an analysis will no doubt indicate that the possibility of entry deterrence, and the existence of natural monopoly, may depend on the ownership structure of the potential entrant.

3. SOME REMARKS ON COST INEFFICIENCY AND PRICE COMPETITION

In the previous two sections we assumed that the degree of nationalization affects only the firm's objective function. We have modelled the firm as a rational decision-maker that is doing its best to achieve its goals. This point of view translates itself to the assumption that both the private and the partly nationalized firms have identical cost functions. However, casual observation and empirical works indicate that nationalized firms are technically inefficient. (For more details see Bos, 1988; Bos and Peters, 1989; Perelman and Pestieau, 1988; and Rees, 1988). But an increase in profits after privatization does not necessarily imply that the firm produces inefficiently while being nationalized. Clearly, as was stated previously, changing the ownership structure of the firm affects its objective function. Nationalized firms can produce efficiently and yet observe lower profits simply because they are not profit-maximizers. Even if we accept the view that nationalized firms produce inefficiently, one needs a specific model that incorporates management's effort as one of the inputs needed for production, and such a model can be used in analysing the relationship between managerial effort and the incentives facing the management. For use of agency theory to explain public firms' inefficiency, see Rees (1988).

Letting production cost depend on the degree of nationalization, and bearing in mind our results for the equal-costs case, we can use continuity arguments to conclude that it is possible that in a duopolistic market a partly nationalized firm is inefficient in production but still realizes higher profits than its private, cost efficient, profit-maximizing rival.

The underlying assumption in our analysis so far has been that the product is homogeneous and that firms compete through quantities. Such assumptions imply that the firms' reaction functions are downward-sloping. It is already recognized in the literature that, once we change the strategic variable and consider price competition, the results might be reversed. (See, for example, Brander and Spencer, 1985; Bulow, Geanakoplos and Klemperer, 1985; Eaton and Grossman, 1986; Bonanno and Vickers, 1988; Freshtman and Judd, 1987; Fudenberg and Tirole, 1984; Shapiro, 1989; and Vickers, 1985.)

Consider a differentiated-goods duopoly in which firms compete through prices. Let the first firm be partly nationalized. Standard analysis indicates the following.

Proposition 4. In a differentiated-goods duopolistic market the equilibrium prices decline as θ_1 increases. For every $\theta_1 > 0$, the profit of the partly nationalized firm is *below* the regular Bertrand equilibrium profits.

Comparing Propositions 1 and 4 indicates that the effect of privatization on the firms' performance in an oligopolistic market depends on the nature of the competition in the market as well as on the degree of privatization. When price is the strategic variable, nationalization leads to lower profits while in quantity competition an increase in the degree of nationalization may lead to higher profits.

4. CONCLUDING REMARKS

The analysis of markets in the traditional microeconomic theory has been based on the assumption that firms are profit-maximizers and that the production cost function is independent of the firm's ownership structure. When we discuss the implications of nationalization of firms we have to re-examine these two basic assumptions and to replace them with a model that describes the relationship between the firm's behaviour and performance and its degree of nationalization. In this paper we concentrate only on one aspect of this relationship, namely, the relationship between the degree of nationalization and its performance in oligopolistic markets. We have shown that privatization can lead to lower profits if the firm operates in a duopolistic market. This result holds if nationalization is associated with some degree of production inefficiency. There is, however, one important remark that should be emphasized. In this paper we do not discuss the decision-making process in firms that are partly nationalized. We simply assume that partly nationalized firms put some emphasis on social welfare so that they are not profit-maximizers, and that there is some production inefficiency that is associated with nationalization. Thus there is certainly a need for further investigation of these two aspects of nationalization: (1) a model that specifies the decision-making process in a nationalized firm and in particular the bargaining between the representatives of the different owners; (2) a model that describes the relationship between the degree of nationalization, the managerial incentives, and their effect on the firm's production efficiency.

REFERENCES

BONANNO, G. and J. VICKERS (1988), 'Vertical Separation', *Journal of Industrial Economics*, 36, 257–66.

BOS, D. (1988), 'Recent Theories of Public Enterprise Economics', *European Economic Review*, 32, 409–14.

—— and W. PETERS (1989), 'A Normative Approach to Privatization', *Journal of Public Economics*.

——, G. TILLMANN and H.G. ZIMMERMANN (1984), 'Bureaucratic Public Enterprises', *Zeitschrift fur Nationalokonomie*, Sup. 4, 127–76.

BRANDER, J. and B. SPENCER (1985), 'Export Subsidies and International Market Share Rivalry', *Journal of International Economics*, 18, 83–100.

BULOW, J.I., J.D. GEANAKOPLOS and P.D. KLEMPERER (1985), 'Multimarket

Oligopoly: Strategic Substitutes and Complements', *Journal of Political Economy*, 93, 388–511.

DAVIES, D.D. (1971), 'The Efficiency of Public Versus Private firms in a Competitive Environment: The Case of Australia's Two Airlines', *Journal of Law and Economics*, 14, 149–66.

DELBONO, F. and G. DE FRAJA (1987), 'Alternative Behaviour of a Public Firm in Oligopoly' (mimeo.), Lincare College, Oxford.

DIXIT, A.K. (1980), 'Investment and Entry Deterrence', *Economic Journal*, 90, 95–100.

EATON, J. and G.M. GROSSMAN (1986), 'Optimal Trade and Industrial Policy under Oligopoly', *Quarterly Journal of Economics*, 101, 383–406.

EATON, B.C. and R.G. LIPSEY (1981), 'Capital, Commitment, and Entry Equilibrium', *Bell Journal of Economics*, 12, 593–604.

FERSHTMAN, C. and K. JUDD (1987), 'Equilibrium Incentives in Oligopoly', *American Economic Review*, 77, 927–40.

FUDENBERG, D. and J. TIROLE (1984), 'The Fat Cat Effect, the Puppy Dog Ploy and the Lean and Hungry Look', *American Economic Review, Papers and Proceedings*, 74, 361–8.

KAY, J.A. and D.J. THOMPSON (1986), 'Privatization: A Policy in Search of a Rationale', *Economic Journal*, 96, 18–32.

MARCHAND, M., P. PESTIEAU and H. TULKENS (1984), 'The Performance of Public Enterprises: Normative, Positive and Empirical issues', in M. Marchand, P. Pestieau and H. Tulkens (eds), *The Performance of Public Enterprises*, Amsterdam: North-Holland.

MEYER, R.A. (1975), 'Publicly Owned Versus Privately Owned Utilities: A Policy Choice', *Review of Economics and Statistics*, 42, 391–9.

NISKANEN, W.A. (1975), 'Bureaucrats and Politicians', *Journal of Law and Economics*, 18, 617–93.

PERELMAN, S. and P. PESTIEAU (1988), 'Technical Performance in Public Enterprises—A Comparative Study of Railways and Public Services', *European Economic Review*, 32, 432–41.

PESCATRICE, D.R. and J.M. TRAPANI (1980), 'The Performance and Objectives of Public and Private Utilities in the United States', *Journal of Public Economics*, 13, 259–76.

REES, R. (1984), 'The Public Enterprise Game', *Economic Journal*, 94, 109–23.

—— (1988), 'Inefficiency, Public Enterprise and Privatization', *European Economic Review*, 32, 422–31.

SHAPIRO, C. (1989), 'Theories of Oligopoly Behaviour', in Richard

Schmalesnsee and Robert D. Willig (eds), *Handbook of Industrial Organization*', Amsterdam: North-Holland.
VICKERS, J. (1985), 'Delegation and the Theory of the Firm', *Economic Journal*, 95, Conference Supplement, 138–47.
—— and G. YARROW (1988), *Privatization: An Economic Analysis*, Cambridge: MIT Press.

Alternative Strategies of a Public Enterprise in Oligopoly*

GIOVANNI DE FRAJA AND FLAVIO DELBONO

1. INTRODUCTION

In 1966 Merrill and Schneider claimed that

> one easily gets the impression from the existing body of economic literature that the productive facilities of a concentrated industry can be owned and controlled in only three ways: complete private ownership and control, complete government ownership and control, and private ownership restricted by close government supervision in the form of regulation (as of public utilities) and anti-trust laws (p. 400).

They then explored the case in which the government affects the running of a concentrated industry from 'inside', through a public firm which interacts with private firms. While this form of 'mixed oligopoly' could be observed quite often especially in Western European economies, it had not received a great deal of attention in the specialized literature. We believe that more than twenty years later their judgment still holds true (a few recent references on models of mixed oligopolies are Harris and Wiens 1980; Beato and Mas-Colell, 1982; Bos, 1986; Ch. 11; Cremer, Marchand and Thisse, 1987 and Sertel, 1987).

In this paper, following the suggestions of Merrill and Schneider (1966), we wish to study a situation in which private and public firms

* This paper is a revised version of De Fraja and Delbono 1986, presented at the 1986 European Economic Association Congress, Vienna, and at the 1986 European Meeting of the Econometric Society, Budapest. We are extremely grateful to Giacomo Bonanno, Kate Fishwick, Claude Henry, John Vickers, two anonymous referees of this journal, and the audience at the meetings for constructive comments on previous drafts.

compete both using only market instruments. When we talk about public and private firms, we think of firms which pursue different objectives. The pudding of a private firm is not baked with any social welfare ingredient, whereas social welfare should ultimately be the very *raison d'etre* of a public firm.

Apart from theoretical reasons, this subject also deserves attention for empirical reasons: one can observe a large variety of markets in which private and public firms produce similar commodities and compete on equal terms. The book by Parris, Pestieau and Saynor (1987) contains a complete and up-to-date collection of data illustrating the relative importance of private and public producers in various markets in some European countries.[1]

The plan of the paper is the following. In Sec. 2 we set out the main features of the oligopolistic market we consider, and briefly discuss some related literature. In Sec. 3 we illustrate the model, and compare four alternative behaviours of the public authority: the 'extreme' cases (nationalization, and profit maximization) and those in which the public enterprise maximizes welfare with and without Stackelberg leadership. Section 4 contains our main results. Among them, we show that, under reasonable circumstances, the welfare is higher in a pure oligopoly than when the public firm strives to maximize welfare. Another interesting result is that when the public firm has the leadership it is always optimal to price above marginal cost. Section 5 contains concluding remarks.

2. THE SETTING

We study the problem within the following simplified framework. We consider an industry in which $(n+1)$ firms produce a homogeneous commodity. We adopt a static, partial equilibrium analysis; we assume complete knowledge on the part of all agents,[2] and we

[1] In another work in preparation we try to apply the model proposed in this paper to the insurance market in Italy. Another interesting example is the Italian television broadcasting market, where the national network (RAI) competes with several profit minded companies.

[2] As Harris and Wiens (1980, p. 127) have argued, the assumption that the public authority knows all other firms' technology seems more defendable when a public firm is one of the producers.

rule out any principal-agent complication (public managers do have the same objective as the public authority, for instance because their actions are perfectly monitored).

In the market we are modelling there are n private firms and a public firm which compete in quantities.[3] All firms have the same technology, imposing a positive fixed cost, increasing marginal costs and no capacity constraint. This assumption justifies the presence of a finite and 'small' number of firms, and leaves some non-trivial scope for public intervention. In fact, if the marginal cost were constant the problem faced by the public firm would have the simple solution of pricing at the marginal cost and supplying the difference between demand and private firms' output.[4]

Firms have different goals; the private ones try to maximize their profits, the public firm, instead, wishes to maximize social welfare, given by the sum of producers' and consumers' surplus (equation (3) below).

We rule out the presence of potential entrants. Our approach is in the spirit of the literature on the subject and aims at generalizing it. Merrill and Schneider (1966) allow the output price to be different across firms, and assume that the government wants to maximize the aggregate output. Their approach is short run, there are capacity constraints, and firms have constant marginal costs. They show that the government 'cannot keep the industry working at capacity output unless it owns all of the capacity in the industry', (pp. 409–10). This conclusion has a similar flavour to ours, as we show that the full efficiency can be reached only through nationalization of the whole industry (case M in Sec. 4).

An interesting model is Beato and Mas-Colell's (1984). They study a two-firm market, without fixed costs, and look for the conditions under which the marginal cost price rule is the best simple rule for a welfare maximizing firm. With regard to this point, we show that, if private and public firms play a Cournot game, the public firm does price at marginal cost. This is not the case when it is a Stackelberg leader.

[3] A similar problem is investigated by Rees (1976, Sec. 7.1), where the public firm produces a good 'which is a close substitute to that produced by a single monopoly' (p. 130).

[4] Setting the price is also the simple optimal solution when marginal costs are constant and different across firms. For a discussion of this case, see our 1987 paper (p. 4). An excellent account of pricing rules of public firms is Bos, 1986.

In another paper (De Fraja and Delbono, 1987), with a more general framework, we establish the existence of an equilibrium when the public firm is the Stackelberg leader, and we show that when the public firm is a Cournot player, the Cournot–Nash equilibria are generically Pareto-inefficient. In this paper we confine our attention to the characterization of the equilibria in a simpler context.

3. THE MODEL

There are $n+1$ firms which have the same technology, and, except in case E below, different payoff functions. The zeroth firm is the public one, the remaining n firms are private and seek to maximize their profits. The output level of firm i is q_i, $i = 0, 1, \ldots, n$. While aware that a non-symmetric outcome may arise, we only consider identical production for the n private firms, i.e. $q_i = q$, $i = 1, 2, \ldots, n$. There are circumstances in which this assumption needs to be relaxed, as we show in next section.

The inverse demand function is given by:

$$p = D(q_0, q) = a - Q \qquad a > 0 \tag{1}$$

where p is the price, q_0 is public firm's output, q is the output of one of the private firms, and $Q = q_0 + nq$ is the output. The cost function is:

$$c(q) = c + kq^2/2 \qquad k > 0. \tag{2}$$

We specify the social welfare function as the sum of consumers' and producers' surplus:

$$\begin{aligned} W = W(q_0, q) &= \int_0^Q (a - t)\, dt - nc(q) - c(q_0) \\ &= [a^2 - p^2 - 2(n+1)c - kq_0^2 - nkq^2]/2. \end{aligned} \tag{3}$$

We want to calculate q_0, q, p, Q, π_0 (the public firm's profit), π (the private firm's profit), and W, in four regimes, which differ in the behaviour of the public firm.

These regimes are described and labelled as follows.

S, for *Stackelberg*: the public firm acts as a Stackelberg leader, and maximizes the social welfare. The public authority calculates q and p as functions of q_0; then constructs the function $T(q_0) = W(q_0, q(q_0))$; eventually it maximizes T with respect to q_0.

N, for *Nash*: we look for a Nash equilibrium of the $(n+1)$-player game; a Nash equilibrium is therefore obtained as solution of the following $(n+1)$ simultaneous equations:

$$\partial W/\partial q_0 = 0; \quad \partial \pi_i/\partial q_i = 0, \quad i = 1, 2, \ldots, n$$

where π_i is the profit of the ith firm. In the symmetric outcome $q_i = q_1$, $i = 2, 3, \ldots, n$.

Now we define the 'extreme' cases.

E, for *entrepreneur* (or, if the reader prefers, egoist): this is the case of pure oligopoly, equivalent to that in which the public firm maximizes its own profit, as any private firm; again we restrict our attention to the symmetric Nash equilibria. This is of course like an oligopolistic market without any public intervention; the equilibrium is found by solving the $(n+1)$ equations:

$$\partial \pi_i/\partial q_i = 0, \quad i = 0, 1, \ldots, n.$$

M, for *public monopoly*: the public authority 'nationalizes' the whole sector, and maximizes its welfare function. In the case of nationalization, the public authority can give the public managers two different kind of instructions, the effects of which, given our simple model, turn out to be the same. First, deciding the optimum number of 'firms', indicated as n^*, and each of their output levels. Second, again deciding the optimum number of firms, and imposing on them as the objective of maximizing welfare.[5]

4. RESULTS

Table 1 collects the expressions of the magnitudes we are interested in the four cases. We give now our main results, obtained through

[5] In the first case it sets the gradient of the welfare function to zero and $(n+1)$ linear equations in q_i, $i = 0, \ldots, n$, are obtained, the only solution of which is the symmetric one, which is also the first order condition for a welfare maximizing firm, in a game where all other firms want to maximize welfare too. Of course, the optimal number is chosen by calculating the welfare with different values of n.

Table 1

Values of the relevant magnitudes in the four cases

	S	N	E	M
q_0	$\frac{at}{t+k\beta^2}$	$\frac{a(k+1)}{t}$	$\frac{a}{1+\beta}$	$n^* = a\sqrt{\frac{k}{2c}} - (k+1)$
q	$\frac{ak\beta}{t+k\beta^2}$	$\frac{ak}{t}$	$\frac{a}{1+\beta}$	$\sqrt{\frac{2c}{k}}$
Q	$\frac{a(nk\beta+t)}{t+k\beta^2}$	$\frac{a(1+k+kn)}{t}$	$\frac{a(n+1)}{1+\beta}$	$a-\sqrt{2ck}$
p	$\frac{ak(1+k)\beta}{t+k\beta^2}$	$\frac{ak(k+1)}{t}$	$\frac{a(1+k)}{1+\beta}$	$\sqrt{2ck}$
π_0	$\frac{a^2 k[\beta^2(1+k)^2-n^2]}{2(t+k\beta^2)^2} - c$	$\frac{a^2(k+1)^2}{2t^2} - c$	$\frac{a^2}{(1+\beta)^2}\left(1+\frac{k}{2}\right) - c$	0
π	$\frac{a^2 k^2 \beta^2}{(t+k\beta^2)^2}\left(1+\frac{k}{2}\right) - c$	$\frac{a^2 k^2}{t^2}\left(1+\frac{k}{2}\right) - c$	$\frac{a^2}{(1+\beta)^2}\left(1+\frac{k}{2}\right) - c$	
W	$\frac{t+kn(1+\beta)}{2(t+k\beta^2)}a^2 - (n+1)c$	$\frac{(1+k)^3+nk(nk+2+4k+k^2)}{2t^2}a^2 - (n+1)c$	$\frac{(3+k)+(4+k)n+n^2}{2(1+\beta)^2}a^2 - (n+1)c$	$\frac{1}{2}\left(a-\sqrt{2ck}\right)^2$

$t = (1+k)^2 + nk$ $\beta = 1+k+n$

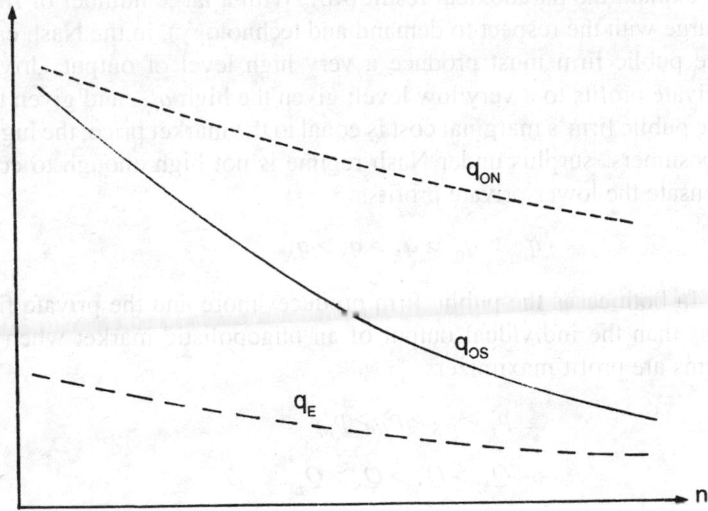

Figure 1 The public firm's optimal output as a function of n under three regimes, q_{0N}: the public firm is a Nash player and maximizes welfare; q_{0S}: it is a Stackelberg leader and maximizes welfare; q_E: it is a Nash player and maximizes profit.

easy and lengthy rearrangements of the first order conditions described in the previous section.[6]

$$W_M > W_S > \max \{W_N, W_E\} \tag{4a}$$

there exists $m \in R_+$, such that $W_E < W_N$ if $n < m$ and vice versa. (4b)

As the intuition might suggest, W_M is greater than the welfare in all other cases, and W is greater in S than in cases E and N. Result (4b), on the contrary, is fairly surprising; it can be inferred that if the public firm cannot have the move advantage, then, if the market is competitive enough, it is socially better for the public firm to try to maximize its own profit instead of pursuing a social goal (but see below for an important exception). Figure 1 illustrates the public firm's optimal output as a function of n, under the three regimes, and it can be used

[6] Some of the results of this section are derived also in De Fraja and Delbono 1987, with other functional forms for the demand and the technology.

to explain the paradoxical result (4b). With a large number of firms (large with the respect to demand and technology), in the Nash case, the public firm must produce a very high level of output, driving private profits to a very low level; given the high q_{0N}, and given that the public firm's marginal cost is equal to the market price, the higher consumers' surplus under Nash regime is not high enough to compensate the lower private profits.

$$q_{0N} > q_{0S} > q_E > q_S > q_N . \tag{5}$$

In both cases the public firm produces more and the private firm less than the individual output of an oligopolistic market when all firms are profit maximizers.

$$p_E > p_S > p_N > p_M \tag{6}$$

$$Q_M > Q_N > Q_S > Q_E \tag{7}$$

$$\pi_E > \pi_S > \pi_N \tag{8a}$$

$$\pi_{0S} > \pi_S ; \quad \pi_{0N} > \pi_N . \tag{8b}$$

As the consumers' surplus is a decreasing function of the price, consumers are better off with the Nash regime, and worse off with the regime labelled *E*. For private firms it is the other way round. This point can be used to provide an explanation for the result (4b): while in general the higher the level of output, the better off the consumers, efficiency requires that this total output should be divided among firms as equally as possible, given the shape of the cost functions. While under the Nash regime there is a greater output (7), and therefore a higher consumers' surplus, the inequality in firms' production is maximum under this regime (5), and therefore the average cost of a unit of the good sold is higher. When there are many firms, an oligopolistic market is close to a competitive one, and the negative effect of the inequality due to the presence of the public firm outweighs the positive effect of the increase in total output.[7]

Indicating with C_0' and C' the marginal cost of the public firm and private firms respectively, we have:

$$p_S > C_{0S}' > C_S' \tag{9a}$$

[7] We owe this observation to a referee.

$$p_N = C'_{0N} > C'_N \tag{9b}$$

$$p_E > C'_E \tag{9c}$$

$$p_M = C'_M \tag{9d}$$

Nobody ever produces at a marginal cost higher than the market price. We notice that, in the nationalized industry, full efficiency is reached.[8] (9c) is well known. (9b) simply says that in case N the public firm does price at the marginal cost.

Notice that if the public firm is Stackelberg leader, pricing at the marginal cost *is not optimal* (9a). An explanation for this fact can be found by observing that, thanks to the Stackelberg leadership, the public firm is able to 'move' some of its production to the private producers, (in fact it is also $q_S > q_N$).

As far as the public firm's profit is concerned, the ordering of the three cases is not independent of the parameters. Some numerical examples show that in some circumstances the public firm gets a higher profit in the Nash regime than when it strives to maximize its own profit.[9] This is more likely to occur in a more competitive market (n large). Coupled with the consideration regarding the ordering of welfares, this result seems rather paradoxical. Moreover, the switching points between welfare and public firm's profit in the two cases do not coincide. There are circumstances in which the attempt to maximize social welfare is a really disastrous policy: not only social welfare, but also the public firm's profit, are lower in this case than when the public authority strives to maximize profit (for instance, with $k = 4$ and $n = 6$, $\pi_{0N} < \pi_E$ and $W_N < W_E$).

Let us examine now the case where the public authority nationalizes the whole industry. As it appears from Table 1, each firm produces the quantity that minimizes the average cost; the optimal number of firms is the one which satisfies the whole demand. It is also worth stressing that in this case the optimal policy for the public authority can be implemented simply by imposing on the productive

[8] (9d) shows that the case we have labelled M corresponds to the Walrasian regime in Beato and Mas-Colell, 1984.

[9] This result parallels the conclusion of Vickers 1984, where a firm obtains a lower profit when its payoff function is the profit than when it is an average of profit and sales.

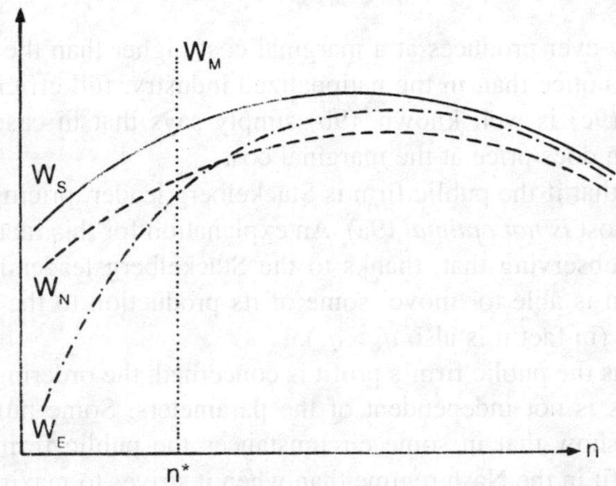

Figure 2 Social welfare as a function of n under the four regimes. W_N: the public firm is a Nash player and maximizes welfare; W_S: it is a Stackelberg leader and maximizes welfare; W_E: it is a Nash player and maximizes profit; W_M: nationalized industry.

units a price equal to the minimum cost. One also notices that the optimal number of firms is lower when the industry is nationalized than in the other cases (see Fig. 2).

This fact may be interpreted by saying that when there are profit maximizing firms, the public authority faces a tradeoff: a higher number of firms, while reducing the distance between price and marginal cost of the various firms, due to greater competition, has a negative effect on welfare due to the presence of the fixed costs.

So far we have examined only equilibria in which all private firms produce the same amount of output. This assumption must be relaxed at least when they would produce a positive output making a negative profit and fixed costs are not sunk: it is easily seen that, if $c > 0$, when n is large enough, there does not exist a symmetric (among private firms) Cournot–Nash equilibrium. When the parameters are such that private profits, as given by Table 1, are negative, we construct the following Cournot–Nash equilibrium output vector:[10]

$$q_{0N} = a(1+k)/[(1+k)^2 + m_N k]$$

$$q_{iN} = ak/[(1+k)^2 + m_N k] \quad \text{for} \quad i = 1, 2, \ldots, m$$

$$q_{iN} = 0 \quad \text{for} \quad i = m+1, \ldots, n$$

where m_N is the largest integer such that π_N, as given by the formula in Table 1, is greater than zero; m_S and m_E are analogously defined in cases S and E. From (8a) and noticing that π_N and π_E decrease as n increases, we obtain

$$m_E > m_S > m_N > n^* \tag{10}$$

From (10) it is clear that for certain values of the parameters the comparison among the equilibria of the various regimes, as given in Table 1, is not sensible. Table 1 should therefore be rewritten substituting n with m_S, m_N, or m_E, as appropriate, when the private profit would be negative calculated using n. This argument may change some of our previous conclusions. Suppose the industry is such that $a = 80, k = 0.05, c = 10, n = 20$. In this case we obtain: $W_S = 2976.13$, $W_E = 2975.83$, $\pi_S, \pi_E > 0$. If the public firm displays Nash behaviour only three firms can remain in the market (i.e. $m_N = 3$) and W_N is now 3041.16 (for comparison it can be said that $n^* = 2.95$ and $W_M = 3120.5$).

Informally, suppose the public authority faces an industry described by the parameters above, and it has to decide what to do. If it buys a firm and plays a Cournot–Nash game, seventeen of the private firms will have to leave the market, as the public firm will produce a huge output (see Fig. 1) and only three private firms will be able to make positive profits. On the contrary, if the public firm leaves room for all the existing firms, behaving as a Stackelberg leader, the inefficiency due to the large number of firms producing with high fixed costs yields a lower social welfare than in the former case. Of course this story is highly incomplete: the effects of closing down firms should be considered, and a dynamical analysis should

[10] We ought to consider $n!/[(n-m)!m!]$ equilibria which are all alike except for the identity of the firms.

be carried over. For instance, the above example might change radically if fixed costs are sunk, that is if closing down firms is costly.

To close this section, it is worth stressing that results analogous to those presented here are obtained if more than one public firm is allowed on the stage. As intuition might suggest, the welfare effects are strengthened if the public authority can determine the output levels of two or more production units rather than that of just one of them.

5. CONCLUDING REMARKS

The main conclusions that can be drawn from the simple model we have proposed are the following.

Nationalization is always socially better than Stackelberg leadership, which is in turn socially better (except in particular cases) than Cournot–Nash behaviour. If the Stackelberg leadership is not available to the public firm, which instructions should the public policy makers give the public firm? It depends upon the market structure. When the market is not 'too oligopolistic'—when there is a number of firms close to the optimal one—then the policy makers would do better to tell their managers to try to maximize profits, instead of worrying about social welfare. (4b) shows that, in this case, trying to improve the social welfare leads to a situation worse than if the public firm had acted to maximize profit.

Asked whether they would like a public intervention in their market, private entrepreneurs would answer negatively; but if there is really no way of avoiding competition with a public firm, they would prefer it to behave as a Stackelberg leader. The level of output of a welfare maximizing firm without any move advantage would be so high that very little room would be left for them (see Fig. 1). It may be worth stressing that in the Stackelberg case none of the firms, not even the public one, sells at the marginal cost. We have also shown that circumstances exist in which it may be socially optimal to bankrupt some firms.

REFERENCES

BEATO, P. and A. MAS-COLELL (1984), 'The Marginal Cost Pricing as a Regulation Mechanism in Mixed Markets', in M. Marchand, P. Pestieau and H. Tulkens (eds), *The Performance of Public Enterprises*, Amsterdam: North-Holland.

BOS, D. (1986), *Public Enterprise Economics*, Amsterdam: North-Holland.

CREMER, H., M. MARCHAND, J.F. THISSE (1987), 'The Public Firm as an Instrument for Regulating an Oligopolistic Market', Discussion Paper No. 8710, C.O.R.E., Louvain.

DE FRAJA, G. and F. DELBONO (1986), 'Alternative Behaviour of a Public Firm in Oligopoly', Working Paper No. 8, Associazione Borsisti L. Jona, Turin.

—— (1987), 'Oligopoly, Public Firm, and Welfare Maximization: A Game-Theoretic Analysis', *Giornale degli Economisti e Annali di Economia.*

HARRIS, R.G. and E.G. WIENS (1980), 'Government Enterprise: An Instrument for the Internal Regulation of Industry', *Canadian Journal of Economics*, 13, 125–32.

MERRILL, W.C. and N. SCHNEIDER (1966), 'Government Firms in Oligopoly Industries: A Short Run Analysis', *Quarterly Journal of Economics*, 80, 400–12.

PARRIS, H., P. PESTIEAU and P. SAYNOR (1987), *Public Enterprise in Western Europe*, London: Croom Helm.

REES, R. (1984), 'The Public Enterprise Game', *Economic Journal, Conference Papers*, 94, 109–23.

SERTEL, M. (1987), 'Regulation by Participation' (mimeo.).

VICKERS, J. (1984), 'Delegation and the Theory of the Firm', *Economic Journal, Conference Papers*, 94, 138–47.

Annotated Bibliography*

ARTICLES

1. THEORY OF THE FIRM

AOKI, M (1982), 'Equilibrium Growth of the Hierarchical Firm : Shareholder-employee Cooperative Game Approach', *American Economic Review*, 72, 1097–1110. A cooperative game model of the firm is used to analyse the issue of conflicts of interest between employees and shareholders of a firm.

—— (1986), 'Horizontal versus Vertical Information Structure of the Firm', *American Economic Review*, 76, 971–83. A comparative study of the efficiency of two information structures—hierarchical and vertical—of the firm in coordinating operational decisions among technologically interrelated divisions.

COASE, R. H. (1937), 'The Nature of the Firm', *Economica*. This pioneering work traces the choice between firms and markets to transaction-cost differentials.

FERSHTMAN, C. and K.L. JUDD (1984), 'Equilibrium Incentives in Oligopoly', *American Economic Review*, 77, 927–40. Shows that in strategic contexts, owners of firms trying to maximize profits might provide managerial incentives that are not fully linked to profits. (Similar results are also obtained by Sklivas and Vickers).

GROSSMAN, S. and O. HART (1980), 'Takeover Bids, the Free-rider Problem, and the Theory of the Corporation', *Bell Journal of Economics*, 11, 42–64. Considers the optimal amount of dilution of property rights of minority shareholders via exclusionary devices which prevent them from sharing the increase in value due to improvements by a rider, which are used to overcome the free-rider problem that would otherwise hinder the efficiency of functioning of the market for corporate control.

GROSSMAN, S. and O. HART (1986), 'The Costs and Benefits of Ownership:

* Pradheepa Neelakantan's assistance in preparing this annotated bibliography is gratefully acknowledged.

A Theory of Vertical and Lateral Integration', *Journal of Political Economy*, 94, 691–719. Clarifying the definition of ownership as the possession of 'residual rights of control' i.e. the right to make decisions when contingencies unspecified in incomplete contracts arise, the authors examine the conditions under which integration would be beneficial.

GROUT, P.A. (1984), 'Investment and Wages in the Absence of Binding Contract: A Nash Bargaining Approach', *Econometrica*, 52, 449–60. Shows that if the union facing a firm has any 'bargaining power', then the investment by the firm is lower in the absence of binding contracts than if contracts are binding.

HART, OLIVER and JEAN TIROLE (1990), 'Vertical Integration and Market Foreclosure', Brookings Papers on Economic Activity, Special Issue, 205–76. Shows how vertical integration changes the nature of competition in upstream and downstream markets by identifying conditions under which market foreclosure will be a consequence or a purpose or both of such integration.

HOLMSTROM, B. (1982), 'Moral Hazard in Teams', *Bell Journal of Economics*, 13, 324–40. This article studies moral hazard with many agents. It analyzes the appropriate incentive schemes to tackle the free-rider problem in teams.

KLEIN, B., R.A. CRAWFORD and A.A. ALCHIAN, (1978), 'Vertical Integration, Appropriable Rents, and the Competitive Contracting Process,' *Journal of Law and Economics*, 21, 297–326. Suggests that the possibility of post contractual opportunistic behaviour might provide a rationale for the existence of particular institutions and the form of governmental intervention or contractual provisions as alternatives to vertical integration in a wide variety of cases.

MARRIS R. and D.C. MUELLER (1980), 'The Corporation, Competition, and the Invisible Hand', *Journal of Economic Literature*, 18, 32–63. The authors compare the normative properties and the positive predictions of the prevailing neoclassical theory of the firm with the recent literature in industrial organization and argue that the latter is more consistent with empirical evidence than the neoclassical model.

RIORDAN, M. and OLIVER WILLIAMSON (1985), 'Asset Specificity and Economic Organization', *International Journal of Industrial Organization*, 3, 365–8. This article discusses the issue of choice among feasible organizational modes. It shows that internal organization is favoured over market procurement as asset specificity increases.

SAH, R.K. and J. STIGLITZ (1986), 'The Architecture of Economic Systems: Hierarchies and Polyarchies', *American Economic Review*, 76, 716–27. Individual's judgements entail errors; they sometimes reject good projects and accept bad projects (ideas). This paper shows that the architecture of an economic system affects the errors made by the system, as well as how those errors are aggregated.

SKLIVAS, S. D. (1987), 'The Strategic Choice of Managerial Incentives', *Rand Journal of Economics*, 18 (See FERSHTMAN and JUDD).

TIROLE, J. (1986), 'Hierarchies and Bureaucracies: On the Role of Collusion in Organizations', *Journal of Law, Economics and Organization*, 2, 181–214. In a three-tier hierarchy (principal/supervisor/agent), the principal might have to offer a coalition proof contract to forestall collusion between the supervisor and the agent.

VICKERS, J. (1985), 'Delegation and the Theory of the Firm', *Economic Journal*, Supplement, 95, 138–47 (See FERSHTMAN and JUDD).

2. OLIGOPOLY MODELS

BERGSTROM, T. and H. VARIAN (1985), 'Two Remarks on Cournot Equilibria', *Economics Letters*, 19, 5–8. Extends the result that output and price in a Cournot industry are independent of marginal costs in a conjectural variations model. Also shows that industry output in a symmetric Cournot equilibrium maximizes social welfare with more weight given to the consumer welfare term than to the profit term.

BRESNAHAN, T.F. (1981), 'Duopoly Models with Consistent Conjectures', *American Economic Review*, 71, 934–45. Imposes the condition that each firm's conjectures about the way other firms react to it will be correct in the neighbourhood of the equilibrium to obtain the 'consistent conjectures equilibrium'.

BULOW, J., J. GEANAKOPOLOS and P. KLEMPERER (1985), 'Multi-market Oligopoly: Strategic Substitutes and Complements', *Journal of Political Economy*, 93, 488–511. Defines strategic substitutes and complements and shows that a firm's actions in one market can change competitors' strategies in a second market by affecting its own marginal costs in the latter.

DAVIDSON, C. and R. DENECKERE (1986), 'Long Run Competition in Capacity, Short Run Competition in Price, and the Cournot Model', *Rand Journal of Economics*, 17, 404–15. The authors investigate the nature of equilibrium in markets in which firms choose the scale of operation before they make pricing decisions and demonstrate that the equilibrium tends to be more competitive than the Cournot model would predict.

DIXIT, A. K. (1982), 'Recent Developments in Oligopoly Theory', *American Economic Review*, 72, 12–17. This article focuses on (i) research into strategic behaviour yielding credible threats of entry deterrence and (ii) specification of conditions under which all such threats are empty, i.e. into issues such as contestability.

—— (1987), 'Strategic Behaviour in Contests', *American Economic Review*, 77, 891–7. This paper considers the effect of precommitment in contests where the rivals expend effort to win a prize.

KLEMPERER, P. and M. MEYER (1985), 'Price Competition versus Quantity Competition: The Role of Uncertainty', *Rand Journal of Economics*, 17, 618–38. It is shown that exogenous uncertainty about market demands give firms strict preferences between setting price and quantity.

KREPS, D.M. and J.A. SCHEINKMAN (1983), 'Quantity Precommitment and Bertrand Competition Yield Cournot Outcomes', *Bell Journal of Economics*, 14, 326–37. A two-stage oligopoly game is considered in which there is simultaneous production in the first stage and price competition in the second stage. Under mild assumptions the unique equilibrium outcome is the Cournot outcome.

MASKIN, E. and J. TIROLE (1988a), 'A Theory of Dynamic Oligopoly I: Overview and Quantity Competition with Large Fixed Costs', *Econometrica*, 56, 549–69.

—— (1988b), 'A Theory of Dynamic Oligopoly II: Price Competition, Kinked Demand Curves, and Edgeworth Cycles', *Econometrica*, 56, 571–99.

—— (1987), 'A theory of Dynamic Oligopoly III: Cournot Competition', *European Economic Review*, 31, 947–68. The authors study the Markov Perfect Equilibrium (MPE) of an alternative- move infinite-horizon duopoly model where the timing is meant to capture the presence of short-run commitments. The model is applied to a natural monopoly in paper I and to price competition in paper II. The third paper considers competition in the absence of fixed costs (Cournot competition).

SEN, A. (1991), 'Cournot Oligopoly with Bargaining', *Economics Letters*, 36, 133–36. The generalized Nash bargaining solution is used to model output decisions of rival firms in a Cournot oligopoly.

Expressions for price cost margins and the objective function that a Cournot equilibrium implicitly maximizes, are obtained.

SINGH, N. and X. VIVES (1984), 'Price and Quantity Competition in a Differentiated Duopoly', *Rand Journal of Economics*, 15, 546–54. This article shows that if firms can only make two types of binding contracts (Price or Quantity contracts) with consumers, it is a dominant strategy for each firm to choose the quantity (price) contract, provided the goods are substitutes (complements).

VIVES, X. (1985), 'On the Efficiency of Cournot and Bertrand Competition with Product Differentiation', *Journal of Economic Theory*, 36(1), 166–75. In a differentiated products setting with *n* varieties, it is shown that under certain conditions, prices and profits are larger and quantities smaller in Cournot than in Bertrand competition and as *n* grows both equilibria converge to the efficient outcome at a rate of 1/*n*.

3. PRICE DISCRIMINATION

BERGSTROM, T. and J.K. MACKIE-MASON (1991), 'Some Simple Analytics of Peak-load Pricing', *Rand Journal of Economics*, 22, 241–9. The authors show that for a utility constrained to operate with a fixed rate of return on capital, the introduction of peak load pricing can plausibly reduce the price of the service both in the peak and off peak times.

COASE, R.H. (1972), 'Durability and Monopoly', *Journal of Law and Economics*, 32, 203–26. In this seminal paper, Coase has conjectured that the producer of an infinitely durable good loses all his monopoly power when the period between his price adjustments converges to zero.

FELDSTEIN, M. (1972), 'Equity and Efficiency in Public Sector Pricing—the Optimal Two-part Tariff', *Quarterly Journal of Economics*, 86, 175–87. This paper has developed a framework for combining considerations of equity and efficiency in optimal public sector pricing.

KAHN, C. (1986), 'The Durable-goods Monopoly and Consistency with Increasing Costs', *Econometrica*, 54, 275–94. Derives the equilibrium behaviour of a monopoly producer of a durable good in a continuous time framework.

MUSSA M. and S. ROSEN (1978), 'Monopoly and Product Quality', *Journal of Economic Theory*, 18, 301–17. Examines how a monopolist may use quality differences to discriminate among consumers.

Schmalensee, R. (1981), 'Monopolistic Two-part Pricing Arrangements', *Bell Journal of Economics*, 12, 445–66. This article is concerned with two-part tariffs and the pricing of a fixed input and a variable input, to maximize profits.

Stokey, N. (1979), 'Intertemporal Price Discrimination', *Quarterly Journal of Economics*, 93, 355–71. Provides a formal analysis of the durable goods monopoly problem in continuous time and confirms Coase's intuition.

—— (1981), 'Rational Expectations and Durable Goods Pricing', *Bell Journal of Economics*, 12, 112–28. In a continuous time model of intertemporal price discrimination under the assumption of no production costs, for a large class of consumer utility functions the firm's profit maximization strategy is to forego the opportunity to price discriminate. If there are positive costs of production the seller finds it profitable to sell the good to different consumers at different prices at different dates.

Varian, H. (1985), 'Price Discrimination and Social Welfare', *American Economic Review*, 75, 870–5. Confirms Schmalensee's (1981) result that output increase is a necessary condition for price discrimination to increase social welfare in the case of increasing marginal costs also. A sufficient condition for welfare to increase under profit maximizing price discrimination is given.

4. PRODUCT DIFFERENTIATION

Bonanno, G. (1987), 'Location Choice, Product Proliferation and Entry Deterrence', *Review of Economic Studies*, 54, 37–45. Shows that in some circumstances entry prevention may be more a case of production specification, i.e. making particular location decisions in product space, rather than product proliferation.

Brander, J.A. and J. Eaton (1984), 'Product Line Rivalry', *American Economic Review*, 74, 323–34. This paper examines product line selection by firms with its focus on demand rather than on cost conditions.

Eaton, B.C. and R.G. Lipsey (1975), 'The Principle of Minimum Differentiation Reconsidered: Some New Developments in the Theory of Spatial Competition', *Review of Economic Studies*, 42, 27–49. Considers the question of how robust is the tendency toward minimum differentiation in the face of changes in the specification of the model.

ECONOMIDES, N. (1984), 'The Principle of Minimum Differentiation Revisited', *European Economic Review*, 24, 345–68. In a differentiated duopoly model where firms set prices, the Bertrand paradox re-emerges if products are only slightly differentiated. This paper shows that the problem disappears either if customers have reservation prices or if competition occurs in terms of two rather than only one attribute dimension.

GABSZEWICZ J.J. and J. THISSE (1986), 'On the Nature of Competition with Differentiated Products', *Economic Journal*, 96, 160–72. Shows that more stability is to be expected under vertical than under horizontal product differentiation.

HART, O.D. (1985), 'Monopolistic Competition in the Spirit of Chamberlin: Special Results', *Economic Journal*, 95, 889–908. Examines whether there is too little or too much variety when there is monopolistic competition. The analysis leads to the conclusion that the answer is ambiguous.

—— (1985), 'Monopolistic Competition in the Spirit of Chamberlin: A General Model', *Review of Economic Studies*, 52, 529–46. The existence of a monopolistically competitive equilibrium is established. In the limit, firms are negligible and yet face downward sloping demand curves.

HAY, D. (1976), 'Sequential Entry and Entry-deterring Strategies in Spatial Competition', *Oxford Economic Papers*, 28, 240–57. The purpose of this paper is to examine the location choice of firms if they enter (i) sequentially and (ii) if there is immobility of capital goods making relocation difficult.

HOTELLING, H. (1929), 'Stability in Competition', *Economic Journal*, 29, 41–57. Classic treatment of the location problem.

LANCASTER, K.J. (1966), 'A New Approach to Demand Theory', *Journal of Political Economy*, 74, 132–57. Proposes a framework starting from the premise that what gives consumers utility are not goods themselves, but the characteristics embodied in those goods. A good should then be analyzed as a bundle of characteristics.

PERLOFF, J.M. and S.C. SALOP (1985), 'Equilibrium with Product Differentiation', *Review of Economic Studies*, 52, 107–20. A model of product differentiation which combines elements of both spatial and representative consumer formulations is used to examine properties of single and multiple price equilibria.

PHILIPS, L. and J.-F. THISSE (1982), 'Spatial Competition and the Theory of Differentiated Markets', *Journal of Industrial Economics*, 31,

1–9. A survey, introducing a special issue of *Journal of Industrial Economics* with the same title that includes a number of papers on the subject.

SHAKED, A. and J. SUTTON (1982), 'Relaxing Price Competition through Product Differentiation', *Review of Economic Studies*, 49, 3–13. A three stage game is considered in which firms choose whether or not to enter, quality of the product and price. When there is a small cost of entry, the unique perfect equlibrium is one in which exactly two firms enter, produce distinct goods and earn positive profits at equilibrium.

SPENCE, A.M. (1976), 'Product Selection, Fixed Costs, and Monopolistic Competition', *Review of Economic Studies*, 43, 217–35. Investigates the effects of fixed costs and monopolistic competition on the selection of products and product characteristics in a set of interacting markets.

—— (1976), 'Product Differentiation and Welfare', *The Economic Review*, 66, 407–14. Points out that there would be a loss in welfare due to non-marginal cost pricing of existing products. There is also a welfare loss which results from product selection by firms. Equilibrium variety may be above or below optimum.

RAUBITSCHEK, R. (1987), 'A Model of Product Proliferation with Multi-product Firms', *Journal of Industrial Economics*, 269–80. Uses a two stage model to examine product proliferation.

5. ENTRY AND EXIT

AGHION, P. and P. BOLTON (1987), 'Contracts as a Barrier to Entry', *American Economic Review*, 77, 388–401. Incumbents and buyers by signing an exclusive dealing contract form a coalition which acts like a non-discriminating monopolist with respect to the entrant and the penalty clause (which becomes effective on breach of contract) enables them to extract the entrant's surplus.

BULOW, J., J. GEANAKOPOLOS and P. KLEMPERER (1985), 'Holding Excess Capacity to Deter Entry', *The Economic Journal*, 95, 178–82. By relaxing the restrictive assumption that each firm's marginal revenue is always decreasing in the others' output, the author's confirm Spence's (1977) original intuition that firms might in some circumstances rationally hold idle capacity to deter entry.

CAVES, R. and R. PORTER (1977), 'From Entry Barriers to Mobility Barriers', *Quarterly Journal of Economics*, 91, 241–67. Attempts to generalize the theory of barriers to entry, into a theory of barriers to mobility (among subgroups of an industry), which accounts for the behaviour of entrant as well as incumbent firms.

CUBBIN, J. (1981), 'Advertising and the Theory of Entry Barriers', *Economica*, 48, 289–98. It shows that an entry barrier effect of advertising can exist as long as the entrant's prospective demand curve is made less favourable by the mere fact of the established firm's present advertising.

DIXIT, A. (1979), 'A Model of Duopoly Suggesting a Theory of Entry Barriers', *Bell Journal of Economics*, 10, 20–32. This paper does not take entry prevention as a prior constraint and it allows existing firms to choose their best strategy in mind keeping the reactions of prospective entrants. It is shown that a greater absolute advantage in demand (or cost) for established firms makes entry harder, but lower cross-price effects with potential entrants' products makes entry easier.

EATON, B. and R. LIPSEY (1981), 'Exit Barriers are Entry Barriers: The Durability of Capital as a Barrier to Entry', *Bell Journal of Economics*, 11, 721–9. An incumbent monopolist's threat that in the event of entry, he will stay in the market 'long enough' that the entrant's present value of profit at time of entry will be non-positive will be credible, only if his capital is sufficiently durable. Hence, the durability of capital may serve as the monopolist's barrier to exit.

EATON B. and R. WARE (1987), 'A Theory of Market Structure with Sequential Entry', *Rand Journal of Economics*, 18, 1–16. This article sets out a theory of market structure with sequential entry. Only demand and cost conditions and the structure of the entry game are specified exogenously; the number of firms, the size distribution and the market price are determined as the equilibrium to this entry game.

FUDENBERG, D. and J. TIROLE (1983), 'Capital as a Commitment: Strategic Investment to Deter Mobility', *Journal of Economic Theory*, 31, 227–50. Analyses how an early entrant in a market can exploit its head start by strategic investment.

—— (1984), 'The Fat-Cat Effect, the Puppy-Dog Ploy, and the Lean and Hungry Look', *American Economic Review Papers and Proceedings*, 74, 361–6. Describes four types of behavioural strategies that the incumbent may use to deter or accommodate entry.

—— (1986), 'A Theory of Exit in Duopoly', *Econometrica*, 54, 943–60. The only strategic variable in the model in this paper is the timing of exit and hence the game analysed here is a 'war of attrition game'.

GASKINS, D. (1971), 'Dynamic Limit Pricing: Optimal Pricing under Threat of Entry', *Journal of Economic Theory*, 2, 306–22. Examines how the dominant firm in an industry takes into account the gradual but continuous entry of competitors in determining its optimal pricing behaviour.

GELMAN, J. and S. SALOP (1983), 'Judo Economics: Capacity Limitation and Coupon Competition', *Bell Journal of Economics*, 14, 315–25. The fringe competitor partially offsets its demand disadvantage by engaging in capacity limitation and discount pricing, thus credibly reducing the threat posed to the dominant firm. The rational incumbent is thus induced to accomodate the entrant.

GHEMAWAT, P. and B. NALEBUFF (1985), 'Exit', *Rand Journal of Economics*, 15, 184–93. In a declining industry, there is a unique perfect equilibrium for firms with asymmetric market shares and identical unit costs in which survivability is inversely related to size. The largest firm is the first to leave and the smallest firm is the last.

KREPS, D. and R. WILSON (1982), 'Reputation and Imperfect Information', *Journal of Economic Theory*, 27, 253–79. In repeated interactions, players may seek to gain a reputation in the early stages of the game for being 'tough'. The authors re-examine Selten's chain store paradox and show that the addition of a 'small' amount of imperfect or incomplete information about the players' payoffs is sufficient to give rise to the 'reputation effect'.

MATTHEWS, S. and L. MIRMAN (1983), 'Equilibrium Limit Pricing: The Effects of Private Information and Stochastic Demand', *Econometrica*, 51, 981–95. A potential entrant uses prices to make inferences about industry conditions. Conditions are obtained for entry threats to result in limit pricing, lower entry probabilities and lower expected profits for potential entrants.

MILGROM, P. and J. ROBERTS (1982), 'Predation, Reputation and Entry Deterrence', *Journal of Economic Theory*, 27, 280–312. Shows that if a firm is threatened by several potential entrants, then predation against early entrants may be rational because it would help the firm to gain a reputation for 'toughness'.

SEN, A. (1993), 'Entry and Managerial Incentives', *International Journal of Industrial Organization*, 123–37. Considers the structure of managerial incentives in the face of entry and shows that such incentives can be used to deter entry if there is a fixed cost of entry.

SCHMALENSEE, R. (1974), 'Brand Loyalty and Barriers to Entry', *Southern Economic Journal*, 40, 579–91. Shows how advertising, through its ability to create loyalty to the products of existing firms, can erect barriers to entry.

—— (1983), 'Advertising and Entry Deterrence', *Journal of Political Economy*, 90, 636–53. The incumbent monopolist never finds it optimal to advertise more if entry is possible. This is in contrast to other investments (say in productive capacity) for entry deterrence.

SPENCE, A. M. (1981), 'The Learning Curve and Competition', *Bell Journal of Economics*, 12, 49–70. This article develops a model of competitive interaction and industry evolution in the presence of a learning curve, which is a function relating the unit costs of the individual firm to accumulated volume.

SPULBER, D. F. (1981), 'Capacity, Output and Sequential Entry', *American Economic Review*, 75, 897–9. Presents a dynamic model of entry and derives necessary and sufficient conditions under which the incumbent firm will maintain a constant level of output (the Sylos postulate) or hold excess capacity (the Excess Capacity hypothesis) to deter entry.

Williamson O. E. (1968), 'Wage Rates as Barriers to Entry: The Pennington Case in Perspective', *Quarterly Journal of Economics*, 85, 85–116. This paper shows that for wage premiums even to be seriously contemplated as entry barriers the differences in technology between large and small scale firms (i.e. labour/capital ratio) must be larger for the small scale operators.

6. CARTELS AND COLLUSION

ABREU, D. (1986), 'Extreme Equilibrium of Oligopolistic Supergames', *Journal of Economic Theory*, 39, 191–225. An analysis of optimal punishments and constrained Pareto optimal paths of symmetric oligopolistic supergames. A remarkably simple two dimensional stick and carrot characterization of optimal symmetric punishment is obtained.

BASU, K. (1992), 'Collusion in Finitely-repeated Oligopolies', *International Journal of Industrial Organization*, 10, 595–609. The supergame constructed in this paper is one in which the stage game is itself an extensive form game in which firms can observe each others' initial production and respond by producing more before the product is sold on the market. With this structure a discriminating trigger strategy can be devised which generates collusive behaviour among fully rational firms with finite lives.

BENOIT, J.P. and V. KRISHNA (1985), 'Finitely Repeated Games', *Econometrica*, 53, 905–22. Attempts a systematic study of subgame perfect equilibria of finitely repeated games with incomplete information. A folk theorem, viz. under weak conditions, any feasible individually rational payoff of the one-shot game can be approximated by the average payoff in a perfect equilibrium of a repeated game with a sufficiently long horizon, is proved.

BERNHEIM, B.D. and M.D. WHINSTON (1985), 'Common Marketing Agency as a Device for Facilitating Collusion', *Rand Journal of Economics*, 16, 269–81. The authors present a model of agency delegation where firms non-cooperatively select agents, announce output prices and choose compensation schemes. There exists an equilibrium in which each firm sets a collusive output price and employs a commission scheme to compensate the (same) agent.

FRIEDMAN, J.W. (1971), 'A Non-cooperative Equilibrium for Supergames,' *Review of Economic Studies*, 38, 1–12. Proves that any payoffs better for all the players than a Nash equilibrium of the constituent game are the outcome of a *perfect* equilibrium of the repeated game, if players are sufficiently patient.

GAL-OR, E. (1985), 'Information Sharing in Oligopoly', *Econometrica*, 53, 329–43. The author considers an oligopolistic market where firms face an uncertain demand for their product. It is demonstrated that no information sharing is the unique Nash equilibrium regardless of the degree of correlation among the private signals of the state of demand.

KREPS, D.M., P. MILGROM, J. ROBERTS and R. WILSON (1982), 'Rational Cooperation in the Finitely-repeated Prisoners' Dilemma', *Journal of Economic Theory*, 27, 245–52. Shows that in finitely-repeated games, incomplete information about one or both players' options, motivations or behaviour can explain cooperation between players.

LI, L. (1985), 'Cournot Oligopoly with Information Sharing', *Rand Journal of Economics*, 16, 521–37. Investigates the equilibrium behaviour of firms in the exchange of their private information about their uncertain environment. Firms never reveal private information if there is uncertainty about the intercept of the demand function. But private information is perfectly revealed if there is uncertainty about the marginal cost of production.

MACLEOD, W.B. (1985), 'A Theory of Conscious Parallelism', *European*

Economic Review, 27, 25–44. The rationality of conscious parallelism (i.e. the matching of price changes) is studied within the context of a dynamic oligopoly model.

PERRY, M.K. and R.H. PORTER (1985), 'Oligopoly and the Incentives for Horizontal Merger', *American Economic Review*, 75, 219–27. Considers the incentives of firms to merge and studies industry asymmetries caused by the merger of subsets of firms.

ROTEMBERG, JULIO J. and G. SALONER (1986), 'A Supergame Theoretic Model of Price Wars During Booms', *American Economic Review*, 76, 390–407. This paper explores the response of oligopolies to fluctuations in the demand for their product and makes the point that oligopolies find implicit collusion more difficult when demand is relatively high. The reason is that rewards from undercutting are high when demand is high and deferred punishments may not deter anticollusive behaviour if demand tends to return to normal levels when the punishment is administered.

STIGLER, G.J. (1964), 'A Theory of Oligopoly', *Journal of Political Economy*, 72, 44–61. Stigler suggests that the greatest obstacle to collusion in the absence of entry would be 'secret price cutting'. It is difficult to enforce collusion, since it is difficult to detect price undercutting by member firms.

7. INNOVATIONS

ARROW, K.J. (1962), 'Economic Welfare and the Allocation of Resources for Invention', in NBER, *The Rate and Direction of Economic Activity*, Princeton, N.J.: Princeton University Press (see introduction).

DASGUPTA, P. and J. STIGLITZ (1980), 'Uncertainty, Market Structure and the Speed of Research', *Bell Journal of Economics*, 11, 1–28. This paper studies the nature and consequences of competition in R&D and its effect on product market competition.

D'ASPREMONT, C and JACQUEMIN, A. (1988), 'Cooperative and Noncooperative R&D in Duopoly with Spillovers', *American Economic Review*, 78, 1133–7. This article shows that if there are large spillover effects in R&D undertaken by firms, cooperation in R&D (though not in production) increases both R&D expenditure and quantities of production when compared with the non-cooperative solution.

LEE T. and L. WILDE (1980), 'Market Structure and Innovation: A Reformulation', *Quarterly Journal of Economics*, 94, 429–36. This paper investigates the relationship between market structure and innovative activity and concludes that under certain conditions as the number of firms in the industry increases, the equilibrium investment in R&D increases.

LOURY, G.C. (1979), 'Market Structure and Innovation', *Quarterly Journal of Economics*, 93, 395–410. An equilibrium model of investment in R&D under rivalry is presented. It is seen that more competition reduces individual firm investment incentives in equilibrium yet leads under certain conditions to an increased probability that the innovation will be introduced by any future date.

NOVOS, I.E. and M. WALDMAN (1984), 'The Effects of Increased Copyright Protection: An Analytical Approach', *Journal of Political Economy*, 92, 236–46. The authors show that when the costs of obtaining a potentially non-excludable good from the secondary market are also taken into account, contrary to previous economic analyses social welfare loss due to underutilization is increased.

REINGANUM, JENNIFER E. (1985), 'Innovation and Industry Evolution', *Quarterly Journal of Economics*, C, 81–100. This paper considers a market where one firm is the current incumbent and other firms are challengers and a sequence of innovations so that the successful firm can reap monopoly profits only until the next better innovation is developed. A fully optimising behavioural model is used to derive the equivalent of the Schumpeterian process of 'creative destruction'.

RIORDAN, M.H. (1992), 'Regulation and Pre-emptive Technology Adoption', *Rand Journal of Economics*, 23, 234–49. Illustrates how price and entry regulations influence timing of technology adoption by altering profit flows.

WRIGHT, B.D. (1983), 'The Economics of Invention Incentives: Patents, Prizes and Research Contracts', *American Economic Review*, 73, 691–707. This paper considers the choice between the three main types of research incentives for a given market structure, viz, patents, prizes and direct contracting for research services.

8. GOVERNMENT INTERVENTION

BAUMOL, W.J. and D.E. BRADFORD (1970), 'Optimal Departures from Marginal Cost Pricing', *American Economic Review*, 60, 265–83.

Draws attention to the proposition that prices which deviate in a systematic manner from marginal cost will be required for an optimal allocation of resources even in the absence of externalities, to correct for distortions arising from taxes levied by the government to compensate for the deficit resulting from a marginal cost pricing or for any other purpose.

BAUMOL, W.J. and A.K. KLEVORICK (1970), 'Input Choices and Rate-of-Return Regulation: An Overview of the Discussion', *Bell Journal of Economics*, 1, 162–90. This paper seeks to disprove the following proposition of the Averch–Johnson model: The profit maximizing firm under regulatory constraint will use a capital output ratio and produce an output greater than that it would in the absence of regulation. Models of regulatory lag are presented and their implications for policy are discussed.

BECKER, G.S. (1983), 'A Theory of Competition among Pressure Groups for Political Influence', *Quarterly Journal of Economics*, 98, 371–400. Presents a theory of competition among pressure groups for political influence. This analysis unifies the view that governments correct market failures with the view that they favour the politically powerful.

DAUGHETY, A. (1984), 'Regulation and Industrial Organization', *Journal of Political Economy*, 92, 932–53. This paper examines the effects on (individual) firm behaviour and inter-firm rivalry, of industry wide price regulation by the state.

DEMSETZ, H. (1968), 'Why Regulate Utilities?' *Journal of Law and Economics*, 11, 55–65. Demsetz argues that a governmental entity could constrain a monopolist utility to competitive levels of price and output without need for commission regulation by auctioning a franchise contract to manage the natural monopoly.

FAULHABER, G.R. (1975), 'Cross-subsidization: Pricing in Public Enterprises', *American Economic Review*, 65, 966–77. In this paper the authors have defined and analyzed the issues of cross subsidization in enterprises with economies of production.

LAFFONT, J.-J. and J. TIROLE (1986), 'Using Cost Observation to Regulate Firms', *Journal of Political Economy*, 94, 614–41. Considers the problem of regulating a firm on the basis of announced costs. The optimal incentive contract is found to be linear in cost overruns.

—— (1991), 'Privatization and Incentives', *Journal of Law, Economics and Organization* (special issue) 7, 84–105. This paper compares the incentives of a public enterprise with those of a private regulated firm.

LOEB, M. and W.A. MAGAT (1979), 'A Decentralized Method for Utility Regulation', *Journal of Law and Economics*, 22, 399–404. The authors propose a system in which the utility chooses its own price and the regulatory agency subsidizes the utility on a per unit basis equal to the consumer surplus at the selected price. The proposed system eliminates the need for any cost data from the utility and for any regulatory action if there are cost saving advances in technology or inflationary pressures and the regulatory lag is avoided.

PELTZMAN, S. (1976), 'Towards a More General Theory of Regulation', *Journal of Law and Economics*, 19, 211–40. A rational regulator would tend to maximize political returns. This same force which makes regulators seek a broad-based coalition operates on the price structure and is responsible for the pervasive tendency of regulation to engage in cross subsidization.

POSNER, R. (1974), 'Theories of Economic Regulation', *Bell Journal of Economics*, 5, 335–58. This article compares the various theories advanced to explain the observed pattern of government regulation of the economy which include the public interest theory, the interest group or the capture theory and Stigler's economic theory.

RAMSEY, F.P. (1927), 'A Contribution to the Theory of Taxation', *Economic Journal*, 37, 47–61. Classic treatment of the second-best pricing problem.

RIORDAN, M.H. (1984), 'On Delegating Price Authority to a Regulated Firm', *Rand Journal of Economics*, 15, 108–15. This article models a regulated environment in which the regulated firm possesses better information about demand conditions than does the regulator.

RIORDAN, M.H. and D.E.M. SAPPINGTON (1987), 'Awarding Monopoly Franchises', *American Economic Review*, 77, 305–32. This article addresses the question of how to award a monopoly franchise so as to maximize expected consumers' welfare when potential producers initially possess imperfect private information about production costs.

SCARPA, C. (1994), 'Regulation as a Bargaining Process: Negotiation Over Price and Cost-reducing Investments', *Oxford Economic Papers*, 46, 357–65. Develops the idea that industry regulation can be treated as a bargaining between a firm and the public authority.

SPULBER, D.F. and D. BESANKO (1992), 'Delegation, Commitment and the

Regulatory Mandate', *Journal of Law, Economics, and Organization*, 8, 126–54. This paper provides a theoretical framework to examine the strategic dimension of delegated authority which analyses power sharing between the congress, president and agency administrators.

9. INDUSTRIAL ORGANIZATION AND DEVELOPING ECONOMIES

ANANT, T.C.A., K. BASU and B. MUKHERJEE (1995), 'A Model of Monopoly with Strategic Government Intervention', *Journal of Public Economics*, forthcoming. Argues that instead of casting the government in the role of a Stackelberg leader *vis-à-vis* private firms, it is more realistic to cast it in a more symmetric strategic position. Shows that the firm may commit itself to a cost function that is everywhere more inefficient than another feasible cost function.

BALDWIN, R.E. (1992), 'Are Economists' Traditional Trade Policy Views Still Valid?', *Journal of Economic Literature*, 30, 804–29. Recent literature on trade theory examines trade policy under imperfectly competitive market conditions and concludes that there is a unilateral economic motive for interventionist trade policy in certain cases. But there must be appreciation of the differences between analysing the effects of oligopoly in highly simplified theoretical models and trying to implement this policy in the real world of imperfect information, rent seeking and economic nationalism.

BASU, K., S. BHATTACHARYA and A. MISHRA (1992), 'Notes on Bribery and the Control of Corruption', *Journal of Public Economics*, 48, 349–59. An auditor or a policeman bargaining over a bribe with a person he has arrested has to take into account the fact that he, in turn, may be caught taking this bribe and be involved in a similar bargain. The paper tries to model this recursion problem.

BRANDER, J.A. and B.J. SPENCER (1985), 'Export Subsidies and International Market Share and Rivalry', Journal of International Economics, 18, 83–100. The terms of trade move against a country that subsidizes its industries, but its welfare can increase because, with imperfect competition, price exceeds the marginal cost of exports. International non-cooperative equilibrium involves such subsidies by producing nations even though they are jointly suboptimal.

DIXIT, A.K. (1984), 'International Trade Policies for Oligopolistic

Industries', *Economic Journal*, 94, 1–16. Surveys recent work in international trade with imperfectly competitive economies.

DIXIT, A.K. (1988), 'Antidumping and Countervailing Duties under Oligopoly', *European Economic Review*, 32, 55–68. This paper constructs a conjectural variations model of international oligopoly in which the home country's optimal policy responses to the foreign government's subsidies and foreign firms' dumping can be calculated. Some theoretical support is found for partial countervailing duties, but not for any antidumping duties.

DUTTA, B., S. GANGOPADHYAY, D. RAY and K. SENGUPTA (1993), 'Profitability and Concentration: Entry Deterrence in a Model of Location', in B. Dutta et al. (eds) *Theoretical Issues in Development Economics*, Bombay: Oxford University Press. Examines the conditions under which location choices that can be feasibly used to deter entry are also optimal choices.

KABIRAJ, T. and S. MARJIT (1993), 'International Technology Transfer under Potential Threat of Entry: A Cournot–Nash Framework', *Journal of Development Economics*, 42, 75–88. Analyses the possibility of technology transfer from a technologically advanced foreign firm to the domestic firm of a less-developed country when the product market is characterized by Cournot–Nash competition.

MARKUSEN, J.R. and A.J. VENABLES (1988), 'Trade Policy with Increasing Returns and Imperfect Competition: Contradictory Results from Competing Assumptions', *Journal of International Economics*, 24, 299–316. This paper sets out a single model within which policy under different market structures can be examined. It is concluded that the effects of policy are greater when markets are segmented than when they are integrated.

MISHRA, A. (1994), 'Clientelization and Fragmentation in Backward Agriculture: Forward Induction and Entry Deterrence', *Journal of Development Economics*, 45, 271–85. Extending Basu and Bell's analysis, the paper shows that a firm, by forming captive segments in a market, can deter its rivals from competing with it.

MOOKHERJEE, D. and I. PNG (1995), 'Corruptible Law Enforcers: How should they be Compensated?' *Economic Journal*, 105, 145–59. Examines whether corruption is an efficient way of motivating an agent whenever enforcement authority is delegated.

OSMANI, S.R. (1991), 'Wage Determination in Rural Labour Markets: The Theory of Implicit Cooperation', *Journal of Development Economics*, 34, 3–23. Using the framework of repeated non-cooperative games, the paper argues that the process of determination of daily wage rate in rural labour markets is best seen as an act of 'implicit cooperation' among workers.

BOOKS AND MONOGRAPHS

1. GAME THEORY

AUMANN, R.J. and S. HART (1992), *Handbook of Game Theory, Volumes I and II*, Amsterdam: North-Holland.

FRIEDMAN, J. (1977), *Oligopoly and the Theory of Games*, Amsterdam: North-Holland.

FUDENBERG, D. and JEAN TIROLE (1993), *Game Theory*, Cambridge MA.: MIT Press.

KREPS, D.M. (1990), *Game Theory and Economic Modelling*, Oxford: Clarendon Press.

RASMUSEN, E. (1989), *Games and Information*, Oxford: Basil Blackwell.

2. INDUSTRIAL ORGANIZATION

BAIN, J. (1966), *Barriers to New Competition*, Cambridge: Harvard University Press.

Basu, K. (1993), *Lectures in Industrial Organization Theory*, Oxford: Blackwell Publishers.

BAUMOL, W.J., J.C. PANZAR and R.D. WILLIG (1982), *Contestable Markets and the Theory of Industry Structure*, New York: Harcourt, Brace, Jovanovich.

BERLE, A.A. and G.C. MEANS (1932), *The Modern Corporation and Private Property*, New York: Macmillan.

CARLTON, D.W. and J.F. PERLOFF (1990), *Modern Industrial Organization*, Harper Collins Publishers.

CHAMBERLIN, E.H. (1933), *The Theory of Monopolistic Competition*, Cambridge, Harvard University Press.

CLARKSON, K.W. and R.L. MILLER (1982), *Industrial Organization*, New York: McGraw-Hill.

DAUGHETY, A.F. (ed.) (1988), *Cournot Oligopoly*, Cambridge: Cambridge University Press.

HAY, D.A. and D.J. MORRIS (1991), *Industrial Economics and Organization*, Oxford: Oxford University Press.

JACQUEMIN, A. (1991), *The New Industrial Organization*, Cambridge, MA.: MIT Press.

MILGROM, P. and J. ROBERTS (1992), *Economics, Organization and Management*, New Jersey: Prentice Hall.

Phlips, L. (1983), *The Economics of Price Discrimination*, Cambridge: Cambridge University Press.

REID, G. (1987), *Theories of Industrial Organization*, Oxford: Basil Blackwell.

ROBINSON, J. (1933), *The Economics of Imperfect Competition*, London: Macmillan.

SCHERER, F.M. and D. ROSS (1990), *Industrial Market Structure and Economic Performance*, Boston: Houghton Mifflin Company.

SCHMALENSEE R. and R. WILLIG (eds) (1989), *Handbook of Industrial Organization*, Vols I & II, Amsterdam: North-Holland.

SHARKEY, W.W. (1982), *The Theory of Natural Monopoly*, Cambridge: Cambridge University Press.

TIROLE, J. (1988), *The Theory of Industrial Organization*, Cambridge MA.: MIT Press.

WATERSON, M. (1984), *Economic Theory of the Industry*, Cambridge: Cambridge University Press.

WILLIAMSON, O.E. (ed.) (1990), *Industrial Organization*, England: Edward Elgar.

3. GOVERNMENT INTERVENTION

BAILEY, E.E. (1973), *Economic Theory of Regulatory Constraint*, Lexington, Mass.: D.C. Heath.

EVANS, DAVID S. (ed.) (1982), *Breaking up Bell*, New York: Elsevier Science Publishing Co.

FROMM, G. (ed.) (1981), *Studies in Public Regulation*, Cambridge, MA.: MIT Press.

JONES, L.P. (1982), *Public Enterprise in Less Developed Countries*, Cambridge: Cambridge University Press.

KAHN, A.E. (1975), *The Economics of Regulation*, New York: John Wiley and Sons.

KRUGMAN, P.R., (ed.) (1986), *Strategic Trade Policy and the New International Economics*, Cambridge, MA.: MIT Press.

LAFFONT, J.-J. and J. TIROLE (1993), *A Theory of Incentives in Procurement and Regulation*, Cambridge, MA.: MIT Press.

MACAVOY, P.W., W.T. STANBERG, G. YARROW and R.T. ZECKHAUSER (eds)

(1989), *Privatization and State-owned Enterprises*, Boston: Kluwer Academic Publishers.

SPULBER, D. F. (1989), *Regulation and Markets*, Cambridge MA.: MIT Press.

VICKERS, J. and G. YARROW (1988), *Privatization—An Economic Analysis*, Cambridge, MA.: MIT Press.

WEISS, L.W. and M.W. KLASS (1981), *Case Studies in Regulation: Revolution and Reform*, Boston: Little Brown.

4. OTHERS

AXELROD, R. (1984) *The Evolution of Cooperation*, New York: Basic Books,.

CHANDLER, A. (1966), *Strategy and Structure*, New York: Doubleday & Co.

DIXIT, A.K. and B.J. NALEBUFF (1991), *Thinking Strategically*, New York: W.W. Norton.

DOERINGER, P. and M. PIORE (1971), *Internal Labor Markets and Manpower Analysis*, Lexington, Mass.: Heath.

HELPMAN, E and P.R. KRUGMAN (1985), *Market Structure and Foreign Trade: Increasing Returns, Imperfect Competition, and the International Economy*, Cambridge, MA.: MIT Press.

Williamson, O. E. (1985), *The Economic Institutions of Capitalism: Firms, Markets, Relational Contracting*, New York: Free Press.

Name Index

Subject Index